THE GLOBAL COVENANT

The Global Covenant

Human Conduct in a World of States

ROBERT JACKSON

OXFORD
UNIVERSITY PRESS

*This book has been printed digitally and produced in a standard specification
in order to ensure its continuing availability*

OXFORD
UNIVERSITY PRESS

Great Clarendon Street, Oxford OX2 6DP

Oxford University Press is a department of the University of Oxford.
It furthers the University's objective of excellence in research, scholarship,
and education by publishing worldwide in

Oxford New York

Auckland Cape Town Dar es Salaam Hong Kong Karachi
Kuala Lumpur Madrid Melbourne Mexico City Nairobi
New Delhi Shanghai Taipei Toronto
With offices in
Argentina Austria Brazil Chile Czech Republic France Greece
Guatemala Hungary Italy Japan South Korea Poland Portugal
Singapore Switzerland Thailand Turkey Ukraine Vietnam

Oxford is a registered trade mark of Oxford University Press
in the UK and in certain other countries

Published in the United States
by Oxford University Press Inc., New York

Oxford is a registered trade mark of Oxford University Press
in the UK and in certain other countries

Published in the United States
by Oxford University Press Inc., New York

ISBN 0-19-926201-2

For Jennifer

Preface

This book addresses some vital normative questions that arise when human beings around the world organize their political lives and conduct their political relations on the basis of a society of independent states. The study investigates modern international society by paying particular attention to the norms of state sovereignty and the ethics of statecraft and with particular reference to the post-1945 and post-1989 periods. It presents a comprehensive analysis of the most important international issues of our time, including peace and security, war and intervention, human rights, failed states, territories and boundaries, and democracy. It draws on a family of closely related disciplines of classical international scholarship: diplomatic and military history, international legal studies, and international political theory. It addresses fundamental methodological questions and presents the elements of a human sciences approach to the study of world politics.

I have three principal aims in mind which are pursued in the three parts of the book: first, to rejuvenate the classical scholarship associated with the 'English School' which posits the foundation idea of international society as a defining feature of the modern political world; second, to extend that mode of analysis to the investigation of important normative issues of contemporary world politics; and third, to evaluate the pluralist and anti-paternalist body of international norms disclosed by that investigation and to assess its future prospects. I refer to that normative arrangement of world politics by the expression 'the global covenant'.

The study can be read as an extended essay on international freedom. Modern international society is a very important sphere of human freedom: it affords people the political latitude to live together within their own independent country, according to their own domestic ideas and beliefs, under a government made up of people drawn from their own ranks: international freedom based on state sovereignty. We should understand international freedom as a specific historical expression of classical liberalism: negative liberty for territorial groups: a doctrine which began its historical journey to the four corners of the world in the seventeenth century but only completed it in the second half of the twentieth century. After the Second World War the political leaders of the world reconstituted and enlarged modern international society. Membership in that world-wide association was arranged for people living in every corner of the globe. For the first time in history politics everywhere was now based on local state sovereignty. Western empires and colonies were a thing of the past. The quasi-empire known as the Soviet Union also was dismantled. In short, political freedom based on locally sovereign states was finally established on a truly global scale. That historical achievement has not yet received the attention it deserves from international relations scholars.

I have sought answers to six primary questions in attempting to add to our knowledge of modern international society: What sort of normative arrangement is it? What are its historical origins? How should we theorize it? What is its *modus operandi*: how does it operate in practice? Can it be justified? What are its future prospects? In seeking answers the book puts normative questions at the top of the scholarly agenda of world politics where I believe they properly belong, it supplies a revised classical international society perspective for studying those questions, and it uses that approach to try to illuminate some noteworthy normative episodes and problems of contemporary world politics. It understands the society of states as a historical arrangement of norms and institutions which is periodically reconstituted in response to changing ideas and circumstances. It views international law as a basic element of the evolving society of states. It notices that foreign policy, diplomacy, war, intervention, trade, aid, and other activities of statespeople are subject to a special political ethics—the ethics of statecraft—which also evolves over time.

The idea for this book was prompted by a parochial attitude that I became more aware of after the publication of another book under the title *Quasi-States: Sovereignty, International Relations and the Third World*. Some reviewers read that book as a study of international law or international history but not international politics which they saw as a separate discipline. They evidently thought of these subjects as existing in watertight academic compartments. They did not fully comprehend the background approach of that earlier study which was based on classical international scholarship which combines history, jurisprudence, and political theory—that is, it adopted a holistic and interdisciplinary approach to its subject. I came to feel that I might be able to make a contribution to international studies if I could set out, systematically, that classical approach. I also thought such a study was urgently required to come to academic grips with the momentous changes in world politics wrought by the end of the cold war. This book is the result of that effort. It operates on the assumption that international scholarship cannot be chopped up and forced into separate academic compartments. If we want to understand the global society of states we have to know something about all these subjects and how they relate to each other.

That parochial attitude usually reflected a positivist approach to international studies as a quasi-scientific subject. Most positivist international relations scholars seem unaware of the classical tradition of international scholarship and its humanist approach. Perhaps that reflects the fact that there has not been a major theoretical study of international society since the publication of Hedley Bull's *The Anarchical Society* in 1977. The posthumous publication of Martin Wight's *International Theory: The Three Traditions* in 1991 was based on lectures given at the London School of Economics in the 1950s. Neither of these seminal works could respond to events surrounding the end of the cold war and the start of a new era in world politics. Nor could they respond to the move away from positivism in international studies which gathered speed in the 1990s. Unfortunately neither Wight nor Bull probed at any great depth the philosophy or methodology underlying classical international society scholarship. I thought the time was ripe for a major work that attempted to do just that. Several early chapters are devoted specifically to the methodological foundations of the classical humanist approach and all the other chapters build on that analysis.

I also felt that my study should make an effort to teach the classical approach to a new generation of international relations scholars as well as carry it out in the analysis. With that important consideration in mind I have written the book in a didactic and pedagogical style, using ordinary English as far as possible and keeping technical terminology to a bare minimum. Each chapter is organized with a view to developing the argument in a logical and clear manner. An attempt has been made throughout the study to employ illustrations, examples, and case studies—historical and contemporary, Western and non-Western—to illuminate general points. I have targeted an audience consisting of university academics and their students, undergraduates as well as graduates. It is my hope that this book will make a contribution to classical international society scholarship and also make it more widely known, especially in the USA.

The argument takes the form of connected essays that approach the subject of modern international society from different directions in the aim of shedding as much light on it as possible in a book-length study. Part I surveys the theory and history of international society and spells out the elements of the classical humanist approach. It begins by noticing that international relations is a distinctive sphere of human relations which calls for a human sciences approach and it introduces the craft discipline involved in such an approach. It reformulates some of the core ideas of the political theory of international society and the situational ethics of independent statecraft with a view to showing that foreign policy, diplomacy, war, etc., are human activities through and through and, as such, are subject to standards of human conduct. It brings the discussion in this part of the book to a close by surveying the pluralist architecture of international society from a broader historical and theoretical perspective.

Part II looks at various normative practices and problems of post-1945 and post-1989 world politics, including the expanding notion of security in a pluralist world, practices involved in justifying conventional war, some difficulties in fitting a doctrine of humanitarian intervention into the *jus ad bellum* of the post-1945 international society, predicaments of state sovereignty and great power responsibility raised by the existence of 'failed states', the evolving theory and practice of international boundaries, and some problems of employing democracy as a foundation norm of a global international community. The thrust of the analysis is to disclose the extent to which some of the most controversial and difficult issues of world politics during that period involved fundamental value questions.

Part III addresses two concluding issues: the justification of the global covenant overall and its prospects as a normative framework of world politics for the twenty-first century. The penultimate chapter rehearses some important criticisms of the modern world of sovereign states and it responds to several proposed scenarios for going beyond that world. The final chapter anticipates a continuing evolution of international society and it presents an argument that defends the global covenant as the best available normative arrangement for conducting international relations in the present and foreseeable circumstances of world politics. In making that argument I have in mind a famous claim about democracy attributed to Winston Churchill: it is the worst form of government except for all the rest.

The research upon which the book is based was made possible by two grants from the Social Sciences and Humanities Research Council of Canada. I am grateful to the Council for their continuing support of my work. Some of the arguments in the second part of the book were influenced by conversations with several officials of the OSCE and NATO who must remain anonymous. I would like to thank them for taking the time to respond to my enquiries concerning the directions of post-cold-war international society.

A preliminary version of the manuscript was written during 1993–4 when I was Visiting Senior Research Fellow at Jesus College, Oxford. I would like to thank the Principal, Peter North, and the Fellows for inviting me to spend my sabbatical leave in their congenial academic company. During that year early renditions of the argument were presented piecemeal at the London School of Economics and Political Science, Cambridge University, Bristol University, the University of Kent, and the University of Wales at Aberystwyth. I particularly wish to thank James Mayall, Peter Wilson, Spyros Economides, Ian Clark, Nick Rengger, John Groom, Chris Brown, Steve Smith, and Ken Booth for inviting me to try out some of my initial ideas at the seminars and conferences they organized. In autumn 1994 I presented some thoughts on the ethics of statecraft at Harvard, and on state sovereignty at Stanford. I would like to thank Robert Keohane and Stephen Krasner for arranging these seminars.

Later versions of the argument were presented between 1997 and 1999 at the Department of Political Science, Aarhus University, at the Twenty-fifth Anniversary Conference of the Leonard Davis Institute for International Relations, the Hebrew University, Jerusalem, at a workshop on the island of Santorini organized by the Institute of International Relations of Panteion University, Athens, at a Carnegie Council workshop on responsibilities of the great powers at Boston University, at a conference on failed states at Purdue University, and at the Alistair Buchan club, St Antony's College, Oxford. I would like to register my thanks to Georg Sørensen, Sasson Sofer, Dimitri

Constas, Cathal Nolan, Joel Rosenthal, Michael Stohl, Adam Roberts, Andrew Hurrell, and Anne Deighton for inviting me to these stimulating academic venues.

Prototype statements of some of the argument have appeared elsewhere and I would like to acknowledge the publications and the scholars who made that possible: *The Third World Security Dilemma* (edited by Brian Job), *Beyond Westphalia: National Sovereignty and International Intervention* (edited by Gene Lyons and Michael Mastanduno), *Ideas and Foreign Policy* (edited by Judith Goldstein and Robert O. Keohane), *International Political Theory Today* (edited by Ken Booth, and Steve Smith), *The Ethics of Statecraft* (edited by Cathal Nolan), *International Theory: Positivism and Beyond* (edited by Steve Smith, Ken Booth and Marysia Zalewski), *The Globalization of World Politics* (edited by John Baylis and Steve Smith), *Canada Among Nations 1995* (edited by Max Cameron and Maureen Molot), *The International System in a Grotian Moment* (edited by J. Ellis and O. Okafor), *International Society and the Development of International Relations Theory* (edited by B. A. Roberson). Fragments of Chapters 7 and 13 appeared in *Political Studies*; early ancestors of Chapters 9 and 10 were published in *Review of International Studies* and *International Journal*. Some of the argument in Chapter 3 was influenced by my co-authored text with Georg Sørensen: *Introduction to International Relations* (OUP, 1999).

Several former or current graduate students of the University of British Columbia contributed to this study and to my continuing education on the subject of international relations. Some of the normative arguments on war and security grew out of initial conversations with Terry Kersch whose own work on the morality of the national interest has been a source of illumination. Don Kossuth and Will Bain read early drafts of some chapters and provided perceptive comments which proved extremely useful in making revisions. I owe Terry, Don, and Will a very considerable intellectual debt. I am particularly grateful to Will for engaging me in a challenging conversation on the subject of this book over a period of several years which helped shape the final version of its argument.

I would like to thank four colleagues who were willing to read the penultimate version of the manuscript on short notice. Sasson Sofer interrupted his sabbatical leave in the Arizona desert to examine it from the point of view of the history and sociology of diplomacy. In addition to reading the book from a liberal angle Mark Zacher also submitted in unfailing good humour to my frequently vocalized angst during our time of troubles at UBC in 1994–6. Kal Holsti supplied some characteristically wise and insightful criticisms of the argument from a realist vantage point and provided invaluable advice on moving toward final publication. Georg Sørensen scrutinized it from the perspective of modern sovereign statehood; he also provided the encouragement that I needed to bring the book to a final closure. I am also grateful to the anonymous readers of Oxford University Press who persuaded me that I should make one final, thorough revision of the manuscript.

Georg Sørensen made arrangements for me to spend three pleasant months during the spring and summer of 1999 in the company of his international relations colleagues in the department of Political Science, University of Aarhus, working on a joint project on globalization funded by the Danish Social Science Research Council. During that period I was able to carry out final revisions. I would like to thank the chair of the department, Peter Nannestad, for making arrangements for me to work in a quietly efficient university environment free from the normal interruptions of academic life.

This project was started in 1992 and as the years passed it became a metaphorical albatross draped around my neck. I am particularly grateful to Tim Barton of the Clarendon Press for expressing an interest in publishing the book which had the positive effect of encouraging me to roll up my sleeves and complete the manuscript. I also want to thank his colleague, Dominic Byatt, for taking the beast off my hands and ending its suffering by putting it into press.

My wife Margaret provided the love, humour, and household administration that was absolutely essential for me to struggle with this project for seven years. I also thank my son-in-law, Steven Preece, who fortified me with characteristically stimulating conversation and excellent drink during frequent visits to Oxford in connection with research that went into it.

My greatest debt is to my daughter, Jennifer Jackson Preece, who read both an earlier version and a later version of the manuscript and provided many criticisms and suggestions which helped clarify the argument and sharpen its presentation. Her own work on national minorities and ethnic cleansing had a strong influence on several chapters. She came up with the subtitle which she jotted down on an Air Canada napkin while we were conversing over drinks high above the north Pacific on our way from Vancouver to Seoul. She also supplied cheerful scolding and cunning flattery on more than a few occasions when I was convinced that the mountain was too high for my limited mountaineering skills and equipment. I dedicate this book to her with the enchantment that flows from a realization that my child has become my academic colleague and intellectual confidante.

R.J.

Summertown
September, 1999

Contents

II. Practices and Problems of Contemporary International Society

III. Value and Future of International Society

Contents

1

The Normative Dialogue of International Society

This introductory chapter opens with two conversations, one imaginary and one historical, which illustrate that value questions are at centre stage in world politics. It then recapitulates the political conversation of humankind by focusing on the discourses of diplomacy and international law. It goes on to outline the basic norms of international society: procedural norms of international law which are part of a larger ethics of political principle, and prudential norms of statecraft which are part of a larger ethics of political virtue. The chapter ends by stating a central thesis of the book: namely that a normative dialogue of world politics is possible to the extent that it is divorced from the values of particular civilizations—such as that of the West or that of East Asia or that of the Muslim world.

Two Conversations of World Politics

Let us begin with a brief imaginary conversation between a senior career diplomat in the United States Department of State, and a respected public television journalist. The interview takes place several years after the end of the cold war. It concerns the US foreign policy response to a military intervention by Russia the previous day in a small Islamic state located in Central Asia which was formerly part of the Soviet Union but is now a member of the United Nations. That new state is the site of a bitter civil war that poses a threat to its Russian minority population.

Journalist: What is the latest news on the Russian intervention?
Diplomat: Our ambassador indicates that their army have occupied the capital. They are currently patrolling the city which is calm. Our own people are safe. The Islamic government have fled the city and they appear to be operating from a mountainous region in the south of the country. Their ambassador has called upon us for assistance. They have requested a meeting of the UN Security Council as soon as possible.
Journalist: What is our policy?
Diplomat: We are using our good offices to help bring the parties into a dialogue which hopefully will lay the basis for a peaceful settlement of their dispute.

Journalist: Are you in contact with the Russians?

Diplomat: We are seeking further clarification from Moscow. We have reminded them of their obligations under the UN charter which forbids military intervention unless it is in self-defence or an enforcement action by the Security Council against threats to peace or acts of aggression. Otherwise it would have to be invited by the Islamic government. From what we know that is not the case here. Moscow appears to have acted on their own.

Journalist: Have the Russians given their reply yet?

Diplomat: They claim that the Islamic government have lost control of the situation. They are concerned about protecting fellow Russians who live there and may be in danger. Moscow have also said that they are operating within their sphere of influence and that their military intentions are exclusively to prevent the spread of the conflict and to limit human suffering of non-combatants by bringing the conflict to an end as soon as possible. They say that they have no intention of occupying the country or taking it over and that they intend to withdraw their military forces once they are satisfied that the Islamic government can maintain law and order and guarantee the safety of the Russian minority.

Journalist: Are you satisfied with that?

Diplomat: No, not entirely. We are pleased that they are concerned to prevent human suffering and we certainly do not want the conflict to spread to other countries in the region. Their concern about the resident Russian population in the country is understandable. But we are not satisfied that they have a legal right to intervene as defined by the UN charter. The Russian minority are citizens of that new country. They decided to remain there when the newly independent state was formed after the disintegration of the Soviet Union. We do not accept and indeed we reject any claim that Moscow has a sphere of influence—either in that part of the world or anywhere else—within which they are entitled to operate at their own discretion. International law does not recognize spheres of influence. We have asked for further clarification on that point.

Journalist: What answer will satisfy you?

Diplomat: That they acknowledge their obligations under the UN charter and that they give us assurances that they intend to abide by its requirements. If they give such assurances we would of course expect them to conduct their foreign and military policies accordingly.

Journalist: You are asking them to withdraw then?

Diplomat: We are asking them to satisfy the international community that they have a valid right to be there. If they cannot do that, we expect them to withdraw.

Journalist: What if they fail to provide such assurances?

Diplomat: Well, that is a hypothetical question. I don't want to get into that.

I can only say that we expect them to live up to their international obligations. That is what we expect of all members of the United Nations.

Journalist: Wouldn't it be unwise to try to hold them to that? What if we place our relations with Russia in jeopardy? Aren't you worried about provoking the Russians into a hostile attitude towards the United States and possibly risking another cold war? Should the legal niceties of the UN charter be allowed to stand in the way of our relations with Moscow?

Diplomat: We want to maintain good relations with the Russian government and we are making every effort to reassure them that we understand their difficult situation. We have offered to send a special ambassador to speak to all parties involved in the conflict with the aim of finding a peaceful basis for resolving the dispute. If that is unacceptable to any of the parties, as an alternative we have suggested that the Organization for Security and Cooperation in Europe become involved to help find a solution to the conflict which respects international law. Russia is a member of that organization. However, I must make one thing absolutely clear: the United States cannot turn a blind eye to this intervention simply because Russia is a great power with whom we have very important relations. That would create a terrible precedent: it would send the signal that powerful states are free to engage in military intervention against weak states in violation of the UN charter as long as it is in their own sphere of influence. That would undermine the new world order that we have been committed to building up since the end of the cold war.

Journalist: Hasn't the United States intervened in small neighbouring states in its own backyard? In Grenada, for example, or more recently in Haiti? Didn't we justify our intervention in Grenada by saying that we were protecting American citizens who were being threatened?

Diplomat: I do not accept that our intervention in Grenada is comparable to the Russian intervention yesterday. That action was taken during the cold war and was dictated by the hard realities of that period. But the world situation has changed dramatically since then. Our new world order can only be realized if all states, large and small, respect the UN charter and avoid taking such matters into their own hands. Our recent military involvement in Haiti was authorized by the Security Council and was aimed solely at restoring the democratically elected government of that country.

Journalist: I understand that the Islamic government and other governments in the region have asked for US military assistance. Are there any plans to get involved militarily?

Diplomat: We are not anticipating any direct military involvement. We are in communication with the Islamic authorities in the country who are still the internationally recognized government. We are in contact with other governments in the region. And we are consulting with our allies and friends.

Journalist: What actions will you be taking?

Diplomat: We are trying to arrange an emergency meeting of the Security Council for later this evening or early tomorrow. The Secretary of State will be meeting with the Russian ambassador shortly and we shall be making our position very clear to him. We subscribe to the UN charter. That has been our position and we have stated it on many occasions. That was our position during the Gulf War. That is still our position. We hope to persuade Moscow that it should also be their position, because it is the only legitimate basis of international relations. We believe that a return to the cold war would not be in the best interests of the United States or Russia or anybody else.

Journalist: But you know how unstable Russia is at the moment. Aren't you providing the ultra-nationalists and neo-communists in that country with political ammunition that could upset American–Russian relations? Wouldn't it be unwise to put our relations with Moscow at risk over this issue?

Diplomat: We are fully aware of that danger. We believe, however, that the risk would be even greater if we turned a blind eye to their intervention. The Russian government have said they are committed to the UN charter. We are seeking confirmation of that commitment. As I indicated, we have offered to provide our good offices in seeking a peaceful resolution of the conflict. We are hopeful that they will accept our offer so that this episode can be brought to a peaceful resolution as soon as possible.

Journalist: What is the United States government prepared to do in the event that the Russians do not withdraw their military forces? Would the United States be prepared to counter the Russian intervention if they do not withdraw? Would the Congress accept that? Are the American people prepared to accept that?

Diplomat: Again, that is hypothetical. You are getting far ahead of events.

Journalist: It's a real possibility, isn't it?

Diplomat: We are confident it will not come to that. I'm afraid I must cut this short. The Secretary of State will be meeting with the Russian ambassador within the next hour. A press conference is scheduled for ten o'clock tomorrow morning at the White House. The President will be making a full statement at that time.

Journalist: Will the President be answering questions afterwards?

Diplomat: As far as I know, yes.

Even though this interview is fictitious I think any observer of world politics will be reminded of international episodes that have taken place. It is the sort of dialogue that we expect to find in world politics nowadays. We have watched interviews like it on television, listened to them on radio, and read about them in newspapers and newsmagazines. Anyone who keeps half an eye on world affairs could follow the conversation without any difficulty. The mass media communicate reports of such events to millions of people around the world on a daily basis. CNN and the BBC make a good living from broadcasting such events to their world-wide audiences. As the conversation indicates, ethical questions are not divorced from foreign policy. On the contrary, they are entangled in it.

The foregoing dialogue is made possible by moral and legal ideas and a corresponding normative vocabulary with which both the imaginary journalist and the imaginary diplomat are intimately familiar. They recognize the values at stake and they know how to talk about them: they know the practical language of international ethics. It is their professional business to ask value-laden questions, answer them, and engage in discourse in connection with them. They do so on behalf of others, in this case the United States government who are a major participant in the event and the American news media who are interested commentators. From their different perspectives they are both aware that there are other parties and bystanders who have a legitimate interest or concern: at a minimum the American public and its political representatives as well as foreign governments. The Islamic government and the Russian government, and other governments, both Western and non-Western, obviously are important and legitimate players in the episode and must be taken into account by US foreign policy.

Normative discourse in international relations, as in any other sphere of human relations, operates by reference to certain assumptions and expectations concerning justified and unjustified conduct. The imaginary State Department official is expressing concern about upholding the norm of non-intervention which is a fundamental injunction of the UN charter. He is fully aware, also, that the state engaging in armed military intervention, Russia, is an important power with whom the United States has a vital interest in maintaining good relations. The journalist is trying to probe what US foreign policy will be in the event that the procedural norm of non-intervention comes into conflict with the prudential goals of American national security. The Russians say they want to prevent the spread of the conflict, which implies a concern to limit war and preserve international order. Other values are also at stake in the crisis. There is the value of human rights which has a potent rhetorical appeal in contemporary world politics: states wish to be seen as protecting human rights. The Russians want to be identified with a humanitarian action. They also say they are acting to protect fellow Russians living in that country with regard to whom they feel they have a responsibility. The protection of minorities is a legitimate concern of international relations.[1] In addition, they claim they are operating within their sphere of influence: that is something that has no place in contemporary international law but may be recognized tacitly in diplomatic relations. So the Russians may be appealing to American self-interest in their own sphere, the Western hemisphere. There is an implied quid pro quo.

---

[1] Jennifer Jackson Preece, *National Minorities and the European Nation-States System* (Oxford: Clarendon Press, 1998).

There is an assumption in the dialogue that all these values are of great importance, and that the challenge faced by US foreign policy is to find a way to uphold all of them and to avoid sacrificing any of them. The conversation indicates that may not be an easy thing to do under the circumstances. The journalist is quick to notice the parallel with the US interventionist actions in their own backyard, and raises the issue of a double standard. If the US government has done the same thing in the not very distant past how can they now occupy the high moral ground? That question points to the expectation that foreign policies should not be fashioned expediently to suit the needs of the moment. In other words, foreign policies should be based on consistent rather than selective moral principles. However, the state department official is at some pains to emphasize the importance of circumstances in such activities, noting that they have changed fundamentally since the end of the cold war. That suggests that situational contexts are valid and indeed important normative considerations in judging the morality of foreign policy.

Statespeople cannot avoid normative questions: they come with the territory. Being in positions of responsibility and wielding substantial and sometimes awesome power, political leaders, military leaders, and other people who engage in international relations on behalf of states cannot escape from such questions— even if they steer them aside or refuse to answer them. At almost every turn they are confronted by normative controversies to which they must respond in one way or another. Failing to respond or refusing to respond carries with it all the usual problems that result from ignoring or treating with contempt the enquiries of others who have a legitimate concern about one's policies or activities. Responding ordinarily means justifying policies and the actions that result from those policies. To ask for a justification is to call for a reasonable answer that invokes something more than mere opportunism or expediency: a normative response to the question. That usually involves pointing to some generally accepted basis of justification.

As indicated, international ethics and world politics are not separate spheres; they are different aspects of the same sphere. Stateleaders can of course ignore international norms or heap scorn upon them, as Hitler did in the 1930s and as other dictators have done before and since. But they cannot escape from them as long as they are in effect and most members of international society demand that they be generally respected. The practical activity of international politics cannot be undertaken outside of moral and legal referents which constitute the normative framework of such activity. World politics is constitutively normative: it incorporates its own distinctive ethics which have been worked out over time by statespeople. They have constructed it and they are bound by it until they change it. That inescapable quality of international ethics is evident even during times of war, when international law and morality are especially vulnerable.

The following account of a famous conversation with Stalin at the 1943 Tehran Conference is given by Churchill in his wartime memoirs:

The German General Staff, he [Stalin] said, must be liquidated. The whole force of Hitler's mighty armies depended upon about fifty thousand officers and technicians. If these were rounded up and shot at the end of the war, German military strength would be extirpated. On this I thought it right to say: 'The British Parliament and public will never tolerate mass executions . . . The Soviets must be under no delusion on this point.' Stalin however, perhaps only in mischief, pursued the subject. 'Fifty thousand,' he said, 'must be shot.' I was deeply angered. 'I would rather,' I said, 'be taken out into the garden here and now and be shot myself than sully my own and my country's honor by such infamy.[2]

Churchill went on to say that Stalin and his Foreign Minister Molotov told him afterwards 'that they were only playing, and that nothing of a serious character had entered their heads.' Churchill also said that he was 'not . . . fully convinced that . . . there was no serious intent'.[3]

Hans Morgenthau quotes Churchill's statement as a self-evident indication that ethics are at the heart of world politics—even great power politics during the depths of the most destructive war in history.[4] However, it is necessary to address a common criticism that ethical claims made by statespeople are merely window dressing on ulterior or selfish motives. It does not matter for our purposes whether Churchill's statement is an accurate representation of the conversation.[5] It still reveals a fundamental normative attitude which Churchill evidently felt obliged to publicize in his memoirs. I think it is reasonable to suppose that Churchill has a self-serving motive to present his wartime statecraft in the most favourable light. But that ordinary human weakness does not undercut what he is saying. Churchill knows that his account of the conversation will register with his readers because Stalin's proposition, whether he is joking or not, is morally outrageous: it is a proposal to commit a monstrous war crime. It is criminal because it involves nothing less than murder, indeed mass murder. The laws and ethics of war embody a fundamental normative distinction between authorized killing of enemy soldiers during the heat of battle and cold-blooded murder of prisoners of war. Churchill clearly believes that his readers fully grasp that moral distinction.

Statespeople do not operate on the assumption that their actions are value neutral and thus exempt from normative justification or condemnation. If foreign policy were purely instrumental Churchill's memoir would not be intelligible: Stalin's reported remarks would not be capable of provoking moral outrage

---

[2] Winston S. Churchill, *Closing the Ring; The Second World War* (Boston, Mass.: Houghton Mifflin, 1951), 373–4.

[3] Ibid. 374.

[4] Hans J. Morgenthau, 'Human Rights and Foreign Policy', in Kenneth W. Thompson (ed.), *Moral Dimensions of American Foreign Policy* (New Brunswick, NJ: Transaction Publishers, 1994), 341–2. The episode is also discussed in H. Butterfield and M. Wight (eds.), *Diplomatic Investigations* (London: Allen & Unwin, 1966), 125–8.

[5] The conversation occurred at a dinner hosted by Stalin. President Roosevelt and his advisers were there along with Churchill's and Stalin's advisers and interpreters.

because they could easily be construed as a plausible exercise of compelling power with no moral implications. We are left wondering if that is basically how Stalin perceived foreign policy: the survival of the strong and the destruction of the weak. If foreign policy were exclusively instrumental the real episodes depicted by the fictional conversation between the US State Department official and the public television journalist also would not have taken place. Indeed, such episodes could not take place because normative concerns and considerations would not exist. Yet such episodes do take place and there is an established and familiar normative language for conducting such international conversations.

A prevailing inclination of international relations scholarship during the second half of the twentieth century was to represent politics and ethics as mutually exclusive spheres. The defining moment in the formation of that academic mind-set is probably E. H. Carr's famous antithesis between 'reality' and 'utopia' which he also portrays as a conflict between politics and ethics.[6] According to Carr, on one side is power or the 'world of nature', and on the other side is morality or the 'world of value' which is portrayed as a kind of dream world which has little if any contact with reality.[7] At the end of his book Carr retreats from this position to a degree: 'If, however, it is utopian to ignore the element of power, it is an unreal kind of realism which ignores the element of morality in any world order.'[8] That is a move in the direction of the position taken in this study which is that morality is an inherent and inescapable element of international relations—as it is of any sphere of human relations.

The 'realist' thinking represented by Carr's antithesis is misleading because it poses a false dichotomy which Carr seemed to recognize at the end of his book. In relations between human beings, including international relations, there is no choice between the instrumental and the normative, between power and morality: one cannot contemplate the use of power, or actually use power, without justifying it in some way. Politics and ethics are not separate spheres, with politics representing the real world and ethics representing an ideal world. Politics and ethics are coupled, and they are both part of the real world. It is not that they are necessarily equal partners in world affairs, because that surely is not always the case. It is rather that they must both be present, because one individual or group cannot contemplate or exercise power against another individual or group without being expected to justify it: that is, without recognizing them as human beings. People are not automated or mechanical things. People are human beings who make choices, and whose policies and actions must be justified to other people. Statespeople are human beings too.

There is a dialectic between power and norms that is virtually a defining feature of human society. That does not of course mean that power cannot be exercised in human affairs with complete disregard or disdain for accepted norms.

[6] E. H. Carr, *The Twenty Years' Crisis, 1919–1939* (New York: Harper & Row, 1964), ch. 2.
[7] Ibid. 20–1.   [8] Ibid. 235.

Power has often been abused or exploited, and it is a safe prediction that such malpractice will continue as long as men and women inhabit the earth—or wherever their technology takes them. It only means that actions which violate certain norms ordinarily would be viewed as morally objectionable if they cannot be otherwise justified. That is because most people expect those with power, particularly the military and economic power of the state, to act responsibly. That means they must justify their exercise of power. Statespeople expect that of each other.

As indicated, politics—and particularly international politics—is a distinctive human activity with a characteristic ethics all its own. Just as there are medical ethics, legal ethics, business ethics, environmental ethics, and distinctive ethical requirements in many other spheres of human endeavour, so also is there international ethics which—in the kind of political world that we live in—concerns the uses and abuses of the power of sovereign states in their relations. It aims centrally at regulating the foreign policies and international activities of statespeople. The heart of international ethics is the ethics which applies to those people: the ethics of statecraft. The activity of statecraft is obviously a normative activity and not merely an instrumental activity. Foreign policy-makers are assumed to operate in full awareness that their actions are subject to normative appraisal by other statespeople and by still other interested or concerned parties. They are not assumed to be operating in a moral void. Hans J. Morgenthau has written: 'Let me say . . . in criticism of those who deny that moral principles are applicable to international politics, that all human actions in some way are subject to moral judgement. We cannot act but morally because we are men.'[9] That is the voice of a classical realist. Natural law theorists and Kantian theorists say much the same.[10]

Morgenthau's point has merit and we shall encounter that view of international ethics in later chapters. But there is a more immediate and I believe more reliable historical reason why moral principles are involved in world politics: because they have been put there by the men and women who engage in the activity of statecraft. They have been put there because statespeople are for the most part prepared to recognize each other and respect each other despite geographical, political, racial, ideological, national, cultural, or civilizational differences between them. That is of course because they are involved with each other: they are in contact with each other and must therefore find a reliable way of doing business. As a rule, people will do business only if they have confidence in their prospective business partners. Confidence is based on a reasonable expectation of reciprocity. What is true of business in tha
true of politics, including international politics. The norm

[9] Morgenthau, 'Human Rights and Foreign Policy,' 341.
[10] These normative traditions are explored in Terry Nardin and D
Traditions of International Ethics (Cambridge: Cambridge University Press,

international society is here disclosed as consisting of norms of mutual recognition, mutual regard, and reciprocity—among others.

The Political Conversation of Humankind

Once people from different parts of the world recognize each other politically they are also, *ipso facto*, communicating politically because recognition is a sign of acknowledgement. Signs and signals are acts of communication. World politics, like any other politics, is to a very significant extent a realm of discourse and dialogue. As Michael Oakeshott once put it: 'politics has always been three-quarters talk'.[11] He was not debunking or dismissing political rhetoric, as some commentators are apt to do. On the contrary, he was recognizing discourse as the essential property of political activity.

One of the most significant developments in the history of international politics was adoption of the originally European discourses of diplomacy and international law by political authorities around the world—whether that was done reluctantly (e.g. by Japan and the Ottoman Empire in the nineteenth century who thereby renounced their self-defined status as beyond the states system and superior to it) or enthusiastically (e.g. by Asian and African anti-colonial nationalists in the twentieth century who thereby escaped from European imperialism and gained independence).[12] Before the twentieth century there was no express political dialogue on a global scale, no political conversation of humankind that embraced all civilizations and cultures. The institution of such a conversation was a specific achievement of modern statecraft connected with the expansion of the society of states. The remarkable achievement of instituting a global political discourse obviously was a lengthy and complicated historical development which occurred in fits and starts with many halting steps forward and many sidesteps and steps backward. The historical details are beyond the scope of this inquiry. But a few summary comments on that history and the central ideas involved are necessary if we seek to understand how world politics has come to have its present normative shape and *modus operandi*. I enlarge upon them in Chapter 7.

The discourses of diplomacy and international law are characteristic of an international society in that they both presuppose and disclose acknowledgement and recognition of foreign political authorities. Those discourses were among the earliest expression of a global human society and they are still arguably the most significant expression. Until they were instituted, political authorities around the

---

[11] M. Oakeshott, *Rationalism in Politics and Other Essays*, new and expanded edn (Indianapolis: Liberty Press, 1991), 206.

[12] See Hedley Bull and Adam Watson (eds.), *The Expansion of International Society* (Oxford: rendon Press, 1984).

world had no explicit and reliable means by which to judge each other's policies and actions and communicate that normative assessment. That is to say: they had no common codes of conduct divorced from domestic norms or their own particular cultures or civilizations; they had no international norms apart from the implicit normative injunctions and minimalist intercommunication afforded by their common humanity; they shared no political discourse. The world before then was politically inarticulate if it was not mute. The globalization of international society made possible for the first time a political conversation of humankind that overcame the limited intercommunication if not the silence of the past. The significance of that historical development is not always sufficiently appreciated by international relations scholars.

The construction of a global society of sovereign states, rather like the building of a medieval cathedral or a great mosque, took place over a long period of time. The historical starting-point, at least symbolically, is the Peace of Westphalia (1648) and the sixteenth and seventeenth centuries more generally, at which time the basic norms of the society of states were worked out in European political, diplomatic, and military practice.[13] But that European international society was not thought up and started from scratch at that time. It was fashioned from pre-existing institutions and practices, such as resident diplomacy and international conferences which had a history dating back to medieval times, the laws of war which had practical roots in European feudalism and intellectual roots in Christian moral teachings, and the *jus gentium*—'what was common to the laws of all peoples'—which dated back to the Roman Empire.[14] The norms of modern international society have of course changed their specific content over the centuries. They have waxed and waned. They have been attacked and defended, violated and upheld. But even though they have on several occasions been trampled upon they have always been restored afterwards, usually in a new embodiment which attempted to respond to the problem which brought about the previous international crisis. That is what the great international congresses and conferences attempted to do: Utrecht in 1712, Vienna in 1815, Paris in 1919, and San Francisco in 1945.[15] And that is what the 1990 Charter of Paris which marked a formal end to the cold war also endeavoured to do. That evolutionary continuity is testimony to the historical staying power of those same international norms.

Europeans could readily recognize each other and institute normative relationships because they shared a common civilization even if they divided over religion or politics. Arguably that made it possible for them to jointly construct the first modern international society after their medieval religious unity had been shattered by the Renaissance, the Reformation, and its aftermath of

---

[13] See Martin Wight, *Systems of States*, ed. Hedley Bull (Leicester: Leicester University Press, 1977), esp. chs. 4 and 5.

[14] F. H. Hinsley, *Sovereignty* (London: Watts, 1966), 163.

[15] See A. Osiander, *The States System of Europe, 1640–1990* (Oxford: Clarendon Press, 1994).

widespread European war, particularly the Thirty Years War (1618–1648). Writing in the eighteenth century Voltaire considered Europe to be 'a sort of great commonwealth partitioned into several states'. About the same time Vattel said 'Europe forms a political system in which the Nations inhabiting this part of the world are bound together by their relations and various interests into a single body.'[16] Similar ideas were expressed by other publicists of the day and there is little doubt but that modern international society is rooted in the political culture of the European peoples. Yet it eventually extended far beyond Europe and even beyond the West. It came to embrace everybody on earth. How we might understand the remarkable globalization of what was originally not only a Western but a specifically West European institution is an issue that is raised and answered in a preliminary way at the end of the chapter. It is amplified throughout the remainder of the book.

It would not be very wide of the mark if we dated the start of the movement towards a *global* society of states to the first acts of inclusion of non-Western political systems within what had up to that time been a strictly Western international society from which people of non-Western civilization, and of religions other than Christianity, were deliberately excluded as full and equal members. Those first acts of inclusion in which non-Western political authorities become recognized and equal members of the society of states occurred in the second half of the nineteenth century. It is important to emphasize that non-European political authorities entered into international society: they acceded to it and became part of it, and in the course of doing so they greatly expanded and significantly changed an evolving institution. In short, they globalized and further humanized what up to that time had been a restrictive and ethnocentric European-cum-Western order.

Martin Wight sees the beginning of universalization in the Ottoman Empire's accession to the Treaty of Paris (1856) which settled the Crimean War and admitted that Muslim state to international society which was then still termed 'the public law and concert of Europe'.[17] But the Ottoman Empire (Turkey), even if it did not share the Christian religion, was half-European in both ethnic and cultural terms. And it could of course be argued, very plausibly, that the Treaty of Paris only formalized what for several centuries had been a continuous diplomatic dialogue between various European states and what diplomats used to refer to as 'the sublime porte'. The same club of European states, now with the active participation of the USA, still engaged in major acts of non-Western exclusion and subordination. At the Berlin Conference of 1884–5 almost the entire African continent was subjected to partition and colonization by half a dozen or so European imperial powers: an act that received the general assent of international society at the time. In addition to commercial and

---

[16] Both quotations are from Adam Watson, *The Evolution of International Society* (London and New York: Routledge, 1992), 206–7.
[17] Wight, *Systems of States*, 117.

political considerations an important justification was the avowed paternalist aim of 'instructing the natives and bringing home to them the blessings of civilization'.[18]

The extension of international society beyond Europe and America was first generally recognized by the Hague Conferences of 1899 and 1907, at which most of the states of the Americas and several non-Western states were represented, including most notably Japan. A further expansion of international society was brought about through changes of international law and diplomacy involved in founding the League of Nations (1919) and the United Nations (1945). The construction of a fully global society of locally sovereign states was only completed in the period after 1945. Many states became independent with the active encouragement of the UN and with a view to joining that organization immediately afterward. The UN General Assembly became a vocal site of anti-colonial opposition which undermined the international legitimacy of colonies and culminated in the Assembly's celebrated 1960 Declaration on the Granting of Independence to Colonial Countries and Peoples (Resolution 1514). That broke the back of moral and legal resistance to decolonization: after 1960 it was no longer possible to justify the possession of colonies if their inhabitants wanted to be independent. Ever since that time it has been about as difficult to justify colonialism as it is to justify slavery or racism.[19] After the cold war the Soviet Union was dismantled. Every one of its component 'republics' became independent and joined Russia as members of international society.

The global covenant is the first attempt in world history to construct a society of states that operates with a doctrine of recognition and non-intervention that bridges different civilizations and cultures around the world. Prior to the twentieth century the covenant between sovereign states was not yet universal. In that regard the global covenant differs fundamentally from the Concert of Europe, the Ottoman Empire, the medieval *respublica Christiana*, the Roman Empire, the states system of the ancient Greeks, the Chinese Empire, and other noteworthy historical arrangements between political systems which were hierarchical or exclusionary. In those previous systems there were 'barbarians' or 'savages' or 'infidels' or 'pagans' who remained outside the political order. And many people who were inside were subordinated by it: for example, colonial subjects and wards of imperial states. After the Second World War that completely changed in what amounted to nothing less than an international reformation of decolonization, self-determination, and political independence that spread throughout what came to be known as the Third World. Today everybody is an insider of international society. No colonies of any importance remain in existence. And all member states have rights of juridically equal sovereignty

[18] General Act of the Conference of Berlin (1885), Art. VI.

[19] For further discussion of this point see Robert H. Jackson, 'The Weight of Ideas in Decolonization,' in J. Goldstein and R. O. Keohane (eds.), *Ideas and Foreign Policy* (Ithaca, NY: Cornell University Press, 1993), 111–38.

no matter how unequal they may be in other respects. In short, the global covenant is horizontal rather than hierarchical, inclusive rather than exclusive, and is based expressly on the pluralist ethics of equal state sovereignty, self-determination, and non-intervention.

International society as it has evolved since 1945 arguably is the first attempt in history to arrange world politics on an institutional basis which respects the political independence and sovereign equality of people throughout the entire world and not merely in the West or more developed parts of the world. The post-1945 society of states constitutes and conducts what is the first bona-fide normative discourse that communicates with and accommodates all the world's cultures and civilizations: human political diversity on a global scale. For the first time in modern history, indeed for the first time ever, virtually every man and woman on earth is a member of a locally independent country that is generally recognized by international society.

For the past half century there has been a political conversation of humankind conducted by means of international society. All independent governments can dialogue with each other through the system of diplomacy, and they can make normative sense of each other's conduct and normative judgements about it by making reference to international law. They can communicate within international organizations to which they now have a sovereign right to belong. Justification and condemnation of the foreign policies and international activities of national governments throughout the world is coherently feasible because it can be based on the norms of the international society to which all such governments subject themselves as sovereign states. The discourses of diplomacy and international law get around the big obstacles of cultural and civilizational difference that previously jammed if they did not silence global dialogue. Today those discourses can be employed just as effectively in Beijing, New Delhi, or Nairobi, as in Washington, London, or Paris. When UN representatives from about 190 countries annually assemble in New York they share a familiar political discourse for interacting with each other. The same can be said of other international organizations and of bilateral relations between individual states—regardless of their geographical location, their domestic political norms, or the civilization or culture to which they at the same time still belong. That historical development of a global political discourse is an explicit achievement of statespeople.

The numerous specific motives that inclined Western states to recognize non-Western states and predisposed the latter to reciprocate are far beyond the scope of this study. Suffice to say that it was rooted in the practical normative difficulties of permanently denying that human beings of different cultural or civilizational backgrounds are worthy and reliable communicants once regular contact has been made with them. If people from the different quarters of the planet are going to deal with each other politically on a regular basis they are going to have to find some mutually intelligible and mutually acceptable, or adequate, terms upon which they can conduct their relations. Those terms must go beyond existing cultures and civilizations. International relations cannot be constructed on muddle or confusion or misunderstanding or deep mistrust: that is a recipe for chaos. And formally unequal relations, such as imperialism, are ultimately intolerable and unsustainable because they do not recognize the equal dignity and thus the full humanity of both parties.

Fundamental to the global covenant is recognition of 'the other'. There probably is an underlying ability of human beings everywhere to recognize each other as fellow human beings—however remote their kinship and however large their cultural differences might actually be. This normative way of thinking is usually referred to as 'natural law'.[20] Today we can get beyond natural law, however, because we now live in an institutionalized political world that consists of laws, rules, practices, usages, organizations and other arrangements of international relations which have been put in place by statespeople according to their ideas of how they might coexist, communicate, and co-operate for certain purposes while yet remaining distinctive and apart and thus retaining their separate political identities and their local political monopolies as masters in their own house. That practical international construct is of course not a static and unchanging body of norms. It exists in time and it changes over time: it is specifically historical. It came into existence, it has evolved, and it continues to evolve. This book accordingly views the global covenant as an unfolding human institution and thus as a fundamentally historical subject whose future destiny is unknown.

Here I part company with those scholars, some of them natural law theorists and some of them classical realists, who base their theories on a postulated unchanging *human nature*. That is a shaky foundation for international ethics because in a human world of obvious and profound social diversity it comes closer to an assertion, or article of faith, than an empirical assessment. The global covenant is not exposed to the main limitation of natural law ethics: reasonable doubt about the claim that certain moral tenets are inherently or 'naturally' known by all human beings, by virtue of their common reason and regardless of their particular cultural characteristics or historical circumstances. Just a glance at human civilizations and cultures in different parts of the world at different times discloses how varied and variable human nature actually is in practice. On almost any empirical view, human nature usually turns out to be human natures. Nor is it exposed to the main limitation of the sort of realist theory which presupposes a permanent 'Machiavellian' human nature: that is, statespeople locked in a never-ending struggle for security and survival. The

---

[20] This is the doctrine that morality is common to and recognizable by all men an all places and at all times despite their particular differences of ethnicity, culture, lar ization, etc. See Joseph Boyle, 'Natural Law and International Ethics,' in Nardin *Traditions of International Ethics*, pp. 112–35.

long-standing amicable and co-operative relations between many states places heavy doubt on that proposition.

To sum up thus far. International ethics is a historical subject: a study not of what human beings are supposed to be but, rather, of what human beings manage to be and manage to do together. One of the most noteworthy things that humans manage to be is very different from one time or place to the next. Yet in spite of their noteworthy differences—whether those differences stem from geographical location, custom, religion, nationality, language, ethnicity, ideology, or form of government—they also manage to co-exist, communicate, and even co-operate for certain purposes. They can create a political dialogue that can bridge their differences, at least up to a point, without having to suppress them or obliterate them.

Basic Norms of the Global Covenant: Procedural

The expression 'the global covenant' is thus intended to emphasize that contemporary international relations is far more than a narrowly defined Machiavellian world of 'power politics' but is also far from an expansively defined Kantian 'community of mankind'. It is an intermediate world between these extremes: a world of dialogue between separate but recognized political others. The global covenant constitutes the only standards of political conduct which apply around the world and are acknowledged as such. It connects human beings everywhere through their membership in a sovereign state and regardless of any particular characteristics they disclose regarding their domestic way of life.

As I hope the previous discussion makes clear, we cannot fully comprehend world politics without mastering its normative discourse. That conversation or dialogue is basically conducted via two different vocabularies: the vocabulary of international procedure which is part of a larger ethics of principle, and the vocabulary of international prudence which is part of a larger ethics of virtue. The first vocabulary centres upon the morality of state sovereignty, as disclosed, for example, by international law. The second vocabulary focuses on the ethics of statecraft and the claims of the national interest. Both vocabularies are evident in the conversation that opened this chapter. The remarks which follow are only an abridged account of the procedural and prudential norms of the global covenant as we have come to know them during the second half of the twentieth century. Subsequent chapters expand on these remarks.

The basic procedural norms of the global covenant are specified by the Organization of Security and Cooperation in Europe (OSCE) in the 'Helsinki Decalogue' to which signatories of the Helsinki Final Act (1975) committed themselves. They are listed by the OSCE in the following order: (1) sovereign equality, respect for the rights inherent in sovereignty; (2) refraining from the threat or use of force; (3) inviolability of frontiers; (4) territorial integrity of states; (5) peaceful settlement of disputes; (6) non-intervention in internal affairs; (7) respect for human rights; (8) equal rights and self-determination of peoples; (9) co-operation among states; (10) fulfilment in good faith of obligations under international law.[21] These norms, especially the most important ones, are procedural in that they lay down ways and means of conducting international relations that *restrict* activities. They are typical liberal-constitutional norms of a political world based on the principle of independent states, of international freedom.

These procedural norms are by no means confined to the states of Europe and North America that belong to the OSCE. On the contrary, they are at the heart of the global covenant and are prominent in the UN charter from which they were derived. Their order of presentation indicates the procedural hierarchy of international society that states are willing to commit to. It is evident that the six most important norms all pertain to the sanctity and preservation of equal state sovereignty and the regulation of armed force and peaceful settlement of disputes between states. Human rights became prominent in international discourse in the second half of the twentieth century but they have not achieved the same standing as the procedural norms of state sovereignty. The global covenant also incorporates additional significant norms, including peacekeeping, peace enforcement, international aid, and environmentalism, among others. Although they can only be mentioned in passing at this point, these latter norms may give an indication of where to look to discern the directions that international society might take as we move into the twenty-first century. But as yet these latter norms do not have the same standing as the basic procedural norms listed above. One could of course refer to many other procedures, such as those which pertain to the use of force in armed conflict as contained in the Geneva Conventions and other bodies of international law: *jus in bello*. I shall be making reference to some of them in the chapters which follow. But the foregoing were the main procedural references for justifying international relations at the onset of the twenty-first century.[22]

The cornerstones of this procedural arrangement are the doctrines of state sovereignty and non-intervention which express the underlying normative

---

[21] *OSCE Handbook*, 3rd edn. (Vienna: OSCE, 1999), 10.

[22] At the time of writing there was much discussion and debate about UN reform as indicated, for example, by the Report of the Commission on Global Governance chaired jointly by Ingvar Carlsson and Shridath Ramphal. But the commission's recommendations for adapting 'old norms' such as sovereignty and self-determination, reconceptualizing the principles of security, reforming the United Nations, and so on, remain for the most part conjectures and speculations. Whether the proposed new norms and structures will be adopted remains to be seen. If they were it would mark a significant normative change in which the claims of state sovereignty would be reduced. See *Our Global Neighborhood: The Report of the Commission on Global Governance* (New York: OUP, 1995), 68. For further analysis of these proposals see Ch. 14.

pluralism of modern international society. The most important procedural norm—*grundnorm*—of the global covenant is clearly expressed by Article 2 of the UN charter. Article 2(4) lays down the fundamental principle of state sovereignty: 'All members shall refrain in their international relations from the threat or use of force against the *territorial integrity* or *political independence* of any state.' That underlines the importance of the norm of *uti possidetis juris* according to which existing international boundaries are the pre-emptive basis for determining territorial jurisdictions in the absence of mutual agreement to do otherwise. Article 2(7) proclaims the companion principle of non-intervention: 'Nothing contained in the present Charter shall authorize the United Nations to intervene in matters which are essentially within the domestic jurisdiction of any state.'

The security and survival of states, and the society of states, is strongly evident in the basic procedures that apply to international peace and security. Chapter VI lays down articles for the 'pacific settlement of disputes' between states. Chapter VII gives the Security Council authority to employ armed force to defend international peace and security if it is threatened by any aggressor state. A central normative feature of the present international society is acquisition by the Security Council of many of the state's traditional rights to employ armed force across international boundaries otherwise than in self-defence. According to Article 24, member states 'confer on the Security Council primary responsibility for the maintenance of international peace and security, and agree that in carrying out its duties under this responsibility the Security Council acts in their behalf'. And they likewise pledge 'to accept and carry out the decisions of the Security Council' (Article 25). Chapter VII of the charter contains the articles which specify the responsibilities of the Council 'with respect to threats to the peace, breaches of the peace, and acts of aggression'. The only right of war that remains in the hands of independent states is the 'inherent right' of self-defence (Article 51): 'Nothing in the present Charter shall impair the inherent right of individual or collective self-defense if an armed attack occurs against a Member of the United Nations, until the Security Council has taken measures necessary to maintain international peace and security.' That is an affirmation of the moral and legal sanctity of states as the building blocks of modern international society. These procedures define the *jus ad bellum* of post-1945 international society: the basic rules governing the resort to armed force in the relations of sovereign states.

A basic underlying principle on which the UN charter rests is that international responsibility must be commensurate with national power: it is on the great powers that the charter places the main responsibility for the maintenance of international peace and security. The five permanent nuclear-armed members of the Security Council each possess a veto which reflects a recognition of the reality that if great powers cannot agree on an action it probably should not be taken because it might provoke a conflict between them which could be dangerous if not disastrous. Majority voting has been suggested to replace the veto.

That would transform the Council from an international organization based on individual great powers into a system of international government but without the capacity to enforce majority decisions against a recalcitrant but powerful—possibly a nuclear-armed—minority. But that is unlikely to happen anytime soon owing to the unwillingness of great powers or most states, for that matter, to give up their prerogatives of independence which such a change would involve at least to some degree.

The foregoing procedural dimension of the global covenant is as interesting for the norms that are absent as it is for those that are present. There are several important norms of classical international society, noticeably present in the seventeenth, eighteenth and nineteenth centuries, that were either restricted or abolished in the twentieth century under the auspices of the League of Nations and the United Nations. Most noticeable is the absence of an expansive set of discretionary sovereign state rights regarding the international use of armed force: the right of war and intervention, the right of conquest, and the right of colonization. International society changed fundamentally as a result of the abolition of these historic states' rights. For example, the abolition of colonialism made possible the construction of a global society of states. It is surprising how little attention these important normative changes have received from international relations scholars.

At their most literally juridical the procedural norms of the global covenant are embodied in the charter of the United Nations, the Helsinki Final Act of the OSCE, the Charter of the Organization of African Unity, and other treaties, protocols, accords, conventions, declarations, resolutions, and formal undertakings between sovereign states. We might conclude that the global covenant consists of these international organizations and especially the UN. That would be an erroneous conclusion. The global covenant is not by any means identical with the UN. It grew out of historical practices and institutions that predated the UN by several centuries. It is properly conceived as the pluralist and anti-paternalist ethics that underpins the UN: it is the underlying moral and legal standards by reference to which relations between independent states can be conducted and judged. That fundamental normative reality of international human relations, rather than the UN, is the subject this book is concerned to investigate.

Basic Norms of the Global Covenant: Prudential

None of the foregoing basic procedural norms of the global coven— absolute. No rules of international law are absolute. Nothing in sphere is absolute. There are no 'categorical imperatives' in int in practice. The ethics of statecraft is inherently circumspectual. in the international sphere, even more than other political spher or situation, within which activities take place is extremely important: foreign policy must always operate within what Edmund Burke termed 'the empire of circumstances'.[23]

All the foregoing basic procedural norms are qualified in one way or another and most qualifications disclose the contingent character of international ethics. That applies even to equal sovereignty and non-intervention. The norm of equal sovereignty is obviously qualified by the existence of great powers. In former Yugoslavia, for example, the Security Council imposed an arms embargo to reduce the threat to regional peace and security, the effect of which was to deny Bosnia-Herzegovina's 'inherent' right of self-defence. Even the norm of non-intervention is curbed in explicit ways: it does not prevent the Security Council from authorizing international intervention; and of course it does not stand in the way of states soliciting the intervention of other states in their domestic jurisdiction.

Procedures are only effective if they are generally observed. But even if they are observed by most statespeople most of the time procedures will never eliminate the problem of choice in world politics, or displace the need for statespeople with intellectual ability and moral stamina who are called upon to make those choices in a responsible or at least defensible way. There is always an element of discretion in the application or observation of procedures. No international society could dispense with foresight, judgement, circumspection, sense of responsibility, and other political virtues on the part of the men and women who conduct the foreign policies of independent countries. The world of the global covenant is a sphere of power and freedom and thus a world in which there are not only opportunities but also risks and dangers. It is a significantly prudential world. Prudence is a normative concept when it concerns others besides ourselves: it is a political virtue to take care not to harm others. In politics, international politics especially, prudence arguably is the cardinal virtue because power is so great.

One may be tempted to understand the ethical problem of international relations as fundamentally that of subjecting the uses of power to the requirements of normative procedure. That view can lead to the conclusion that, when procedural norms are bent by the dictates of power, it is a failure of ethics and proof that, at base, international relations is a sphere of hypocrisy and power politics. That conclusion would be misleading, however, because when power is employed in human relations it has to be justified, and most of the controversy surrounding the use of power is whether or not it can be vindicated. Those justifications could of course be in conflict with each other. We therefore have to allow for the possibility that a violation of normative procedure could be justified by other moral considerations, such as those of prudence, in which case one norm is taking precedence over another. That would not be hypocrisy at all.

<hr>

[23] Quoted by A. Watson, *Diplomacy: The Dialogue between States* (London: Methuen, 1982), p. 15.

The normative approach of this study can perhaps be summarized as follows: on the one hand international ethics consists in the obligation of every state-leader to obey international law. This ethical requirement is the same for all states regardless of any further particulars about them: whether they are large or small, rich or poor, powerful or weak; whether they are located in the northern or the southern hemisphere; whether their citizens are Christians or Muslims or followers of any other religion; whether their domestic constitutions are democratic or non-democratic, and so forth. Procedural international ethics is thus a general ethics which focuses on rules and largely ignores particular circumstances.

On the other hand, the practical ethics of world politics cannot ignore the fact that states differ enormously in their particular characteristics and capacities and allowance must be made for those differences. States have many distinctive features which are morally relevant and with which they must come to grips in their relations and transactions. The territory, population, size, military strength, economic development, culture, and social structure of every state is different. A great power has fundamental global capabilities and responsibilities that minor or medium powers do not have. Every state has its own governmental organization which defines and structures its highest political offices in its own distinctive way. Each state has at any one time a particular collection of political leaders who occupy those offices. Every national leader looks out upon the world from a particular vantage point—a territorial site—which may be similar to that of other leaders but is never identical. The view from London is not the same as that from Washington—even if it is similar on many issues. Every state has its own history and is thus moving through historical time in its own orbit—even if that orbit is part of a larger world history.

Every state has its own national interests which flow out of that particular situation and which may coincide with those of other states but need not. The national interest is not some kind of impersonal mechanism or process which automatically asserts itself in the relations of states—as positivist international relations theory implies. It is a moral idea governing the conduct of statespeople: the idea that the nation and its population are a treasure which they have the responsibility to safeguard in the conduct of their foreign policies. Defending the national interest discloses prudence, patriotism, public-spiritedness, and other civic virtues, which are the virtues of republicanism and are perhaps most clearly evident in the political discourse of the United States.

The ethics of statecraft is, above all else, a situational ethics the core of which is the norm of prudence. Political activity, like any other social activ   ·¹ʷays affected by the situation which is basically made up of other peo material circumstances. Statespeople are called upon to make de times hard choices, and frame policies in response to issues as fronted by them—which is to say that they are called upon to decisions and policies of other statespeople with whom they h;

must have political relations. Hard choices are decisions that cannot be avoided, and involve not merely economic or political costs but also moral liabilities. The key to understanding the situational ethics of statecraft is the correct appreciation of circumstances which are at base confining considerations, rather than accommodating ones, that limit what one is able to do. They are actualities which must be taken into account in making or carrying out a decision. Not only would it be foolish to ignore the circumstances, it would be irresponsible. In that respect, circumstances are a moral idea.

The situational ethics of statecraft could be summed up as the intellectual and moral disciplines—the political virtues—that stateleaders should be able to call upon to make responsible choices in confining circumstances. Responsible choices are not to be confused with perfect choices. Human decisions, especially political decisions, cannot be expected to be perfect. They can only be expected to be justified. Responsible choices are the best choices in the circumstances, or at least the most defensible choices. The political virtues are disclosed when statespeople strive to make responsible choices—no matter what the outcome, which is always bound to be less than completely good. The political virtues, and particularly the virtue of prudence, provide a pertinent basis for judging the conduct of politicians in addition to that furnished by procedural norms. Both standards of conduct, and not merely one or the other, are necessary for understanding and appraising the foreign policies and international activities of statespeople and their agents and representatives.

Unity in Diversity

The procedural and prudential norms of the global covenant are a response to the fact and implied value of political diversity on a global scale. They disclose the endeavour to recognize and respect the reality of different local experiments in political living in different parts of the world. They represent the quest for unity in diversity.

The society of states solution to the search for unity is very different from the historically far more usual approach, namely the search for unity in conformity with the dictates and demands of an imperial state. Because the global covenant can accommodate human diversity on a world-wide scale—not without considerable awkwardness—it has proved to be an acceptable or at least a tolerable basis on which national leaders can conduct relations with each other from their different locations on the planet. In principle those leaders represent humanity in its full heterogeneity: all the races, ethnic groups, nationalities, languages, civilizations, cultures, religions, ideologies, forms of government, geographical particularities, historical memories, and the rest. The normative basis upon which they conduct their relations obviously has to be somehow divorced from that world-wide local particularism while at the same time respecting it.

The global covenant enables stateleaders to relate to each other, to co-exist with each other, and to cooperate with each other without sacrificing their political independence and the domestic values and life-ways upheld by it.

Thus, as indicated, the global covenant is a response to the pluralistic reality of the variously constructed and differently lived human condition around the world: its fundamental underlying ethos is pluralism. It is positive evidence that human beings across the planet can not only recognize each other as locally sovereign fellow human beings, and deal with each other on that basis, but that they have entered into a historical pact with each other which contains specific standards of conduct to which they all submit by the act of mutual recognition and reciprocity as sovereign states.[24] Furthermore, and this is the most remarkable feature, that international arrangement exists despite the absence of a common underlying culture or civilization comparable to the one that supported the European society of states in times past.

Hedley Bull has commented on this important point in an essay on Martin Wight's notion of international society:

Wight raises but does not answer the question whether the cultural unity that is a necessary presupposition of states-systems consists simply in a common morality and code, leading to agreement about the basic rules of coexistence among states, or whether it requires common assumptions of a deeper kind—religious or ideological . . . The central question about the global states-system of our own times is perhaps whether . . . any sense of cultural unity can still be said to exist. This is a question which Wight does not, unfortunately, discuss systematically . . .[25]

Bull is referring to the following statement by Wight: 'How can we describe this cultural community? Does it consist essentially in a common morality and a common code, leading to agreed rules about warfare, hostages, diplomatic immunity, the right of asylum and so on? Does it require common assumptions of a deeper kind, religious or ideological?'[26] Elsewhere Bull argues that 'all historical international societies have had as one of their foundations a common culture' the core of which is 'diplomatic culture—the common stock of ideas and values possessed by the official representatives of states'.[27] Bull ended his best known work, *The Anarchical Society*, with a speculation that the cosmopolitan culture upon which the normative dialogue of world politics depended 'may need to absorb non-Western elements to a much greater degree if it is to . . . provide a foundation for a universal international society'.[28]

---

[24] Here, as elsewhere, I am influenced by the pluralist political theory of Isaiah Berlin, *The Crooked Timber of Humanity* (New York: Vintage Books, 1992).

[25] Hedley Bull, Introduction to Wight, *Systems of States,* 18.   [26] Ibid. 34.

[27] Hedley Bull, *The Anarchical Society: A Study of Order in World Politics,* 2nd ed (London: Macmillan, 1995), 304. For an assessment of Bull on this point see James der Derian, 'Hedley Bull and the Idea of Diplomatic Culture,' in R. Fawn and J. Larkin (eds.), *International Society after the Cold War* (London: Macmillan, 1996), 84–100.

[28] Bull, *Anarchical Society*, 305.

The answer advanced in this book is that the normative dialogue of world politics consists essentially of a common code of conduct which statespeople are called upon to observe in their foreign policies and international activities. Statespeople are expected to conduct political business across international boundaries. They are driven to do that not least because of reason of state: it is necessary. They find themselves having to deal with political representatives and agents of foreign states—not only those that belong to their own civilization but many others that belong to different civilizations, some of them very different from their own. They are thus required, in order to do political business with such statespeople, to rise above their own particular civilizations or cultures. They are assisted in dealing with such people by the availability of international law which, although European in origin, has been adopted around the world. They also manage to do that because they have recourse to diplomatic practices, originally European but now universal, which affirm the core value of equal recognition of the agents and representatives of all sovereign states. What statespeople also seem to possess is a common ability to recognize the limits imposed by the circumstances under which they must operate in their conduct of foreign policy. Statespeople can reasonably be expected to act with circumspection and prudence, and they can justifiably be criticized for failing to do that. The political virtues (prudence, judgement, etc.) can serve as a universal standard for assessing the international conduct of such people. Prudence is not a European or Western virtue; it is a virtue of men and women everywhere.[29]

The rapid global expansion of international law and diplomatic practice in the twentieth century is an indication of the ease with which and extent to which the society of states can accommodate the numerous and various political systems of a large and highly diverse planetary population. But that does not require that statespeople must necessarily share deeper assumptions regarding social morality or political culture that are characteristic of particular civilizations, such as that of the West, or that of East Asia, or that of the Muslim world. On the contrary, the existence and success of their international statecraft requires that all such particular norms be set aside in favour of the global covenant. Civilization used to be a barrier to the political conversation of humankind. That is no longer so. The global covenant has made it possible for political people the world over to rise above their own civilizational parochialism in dealing with each other.

Thus, although the global covenant is historically rooted in a particular civilization, that of post-medieval Europe, it is no longer associated exclusively with Western civilization as it still was as recently as 1945. It now serves as a bridge

---

[29] See the discussion in Ch. 15.

[30] It has been suggested, in connection with Bull's writing on the subject, that 'diplomatic culture is about bringing alien peoples into the dominant international discourse of the day'. See Der Derian, 'Hedley Bull and Diplomatic Culture', 85.

between the diverse cultures and civilizations of the contemporary world. It provides a channel for normative discourse and dialogue between the approximately 190 independent states that are rooted in those different cultures and civilizations.[30] Discerning that normative arrangement of contemporary world politics, scrutinizing its *raison d'être* and *modus operandi*, and making it intelligible in academic terms, is the project of this book. In short, my aim is to take up the theory of international society at the point at which Martin Wight and Hedley Bull left it, to revise it, and to employ it to investigate some important normative controversies which beset world politics after the cold war.

I

Theory and History
of International Society

2

International Human Relations

This chapter introduces the mode of reasoning employed throughout the book: that international relations is entirely a sphere of human relations, nothing more and nothing less. No part of it exists beyond human relations. The chapter briefly contrasts that humanist conception with a positivist social science conception of international relations as self-existing structures and self-propelling systems.[1] It then proceeds to rehearse, in one epigrammatic statement, seven main features and facets of international relations as a distinctive and fundamentally important human activity. They are spelt out in the chapters which follow.

Prologue

The subtitle of the book is intended to make the point that international relations is a human activity, and like any other human activity, it is carried on very significantly by reference to a normative framework of a distinctive kind. I shall argue that world politics cannot be divorced from moral questions because it involves human beings in their role as stateleaders and citizens and in various other international roles; it also affects other people who are not directly or indirectly involved in the activities of particular states. 'International ethics' or 'the ethics of statecraft' or 'the morality of the states system' are expressions that only make sense if people are involved: they are the only creatures to whom morality in the usual meaning applies or can apply.

We cannot speak intelligibly of states or states systems as if they were entities that exist apart from people—like planets travelling through space along gravitational paths determined by the physical forces of nature. World politics is not a natural world; it is a world created and inhabited by people. States, like houses, are human constructs: they are built on a piece of land to provide a home for certain people who become the resident population. The society of states is also a human arrangement: it is organized and operated wholly by people, the

---

[1] For an example of a structural analysis of international relations, see K. Waltz, *Theory of International Politics* (Chicago: McGraw-Hill, 1979), 95.

most important of whom are representatives and agents of sovereign states; it consists primarily of the standards of conduct statespeople have agreed between themselves or have come to accept for judging each others' foreign policies and international activities. Statebuilding and statecraft are human activities. The relations of states are nothing more and nothing less than the relations of statespeople, including their agents and representatives.

There is no part of international relations that lies outside of human activity, either above it as in the conception of social forces that function independent of human volition, or below it as in the conception of the genetic templates that mould animal behaviour. There is of course a sociological sphere, including the unintended consequences of human activities, that is a very significant feature of international relations as of other forms of human relations. For example, there are foreign exchange markets that register almost countless individual decisions but are controlled by no single person or firm or government or any other agent or agency.[2] Free markets are, in a manner of speaking, self-regulated. But that means that many decision-makers are involved, no decision-maker is in command, and all decision-makers are reacting to each other. It does not mean that markets exist and function independent of the people involved.

Everything in international relations is touched and shaped by a human action somewhere or sometime. The correct term for our academic field should be international human relations. Our subject, properly conceived, is a study of the various distinctive activities that human beings in that sphere of human conduct manage to engage in: what they are faced with, who they must contend with, how they respond to others and how others respond to them, what they get up to in their relations, and so forth. They must contend with foreign countries, particularly their governments. They are faced with making decisions in regard to those foreign people and without losing sight of their own people. They get up to all sorts of foreign-policy activities acting either alone or jointly, in competition or co-operation, with the representatives and agents of other states.

Many of those decisions, policies, and activities if not indeed most of them have an indelible normative aspect. It has been said that 'morality is the art of mutual accommodation'.[3] That was said of individual morality but it applies even more forcefully to international morality. 'Accommodation' is a human relation and not a mechanical function: it is based on mutual recognition; it involves give-and-take, reciprocity. Central to accommodation is communication and thus discourse. International relations fundamentally involves a conversation or dialogue which seeks information, clarification, and the avoidance of misunderstandings, miscalculations, and discord between statespeople; it also seeks

---

[2] Karl Popper speaks in this vein of sociological laws. See his *The Open Society and its Enemies*, i. *The Spell of Plato* (Princeton: Princeton University Press, 1971), ch. 5.

[3] Michael Oakeshott, *Rationalism in Politics and Other Essays*, new and expanded edn. (Indianapolis: Liberty Press, 1991), 297.

and sometimes achieves agreements, collaboration, and concord between them. Modern international society is based on principles and practices of mutual accommodation—not at its extremities but at its foundations.

Seven Faces of International Human Activity

When I therefore use the expressions 'international society' or 'society of states' I am positing international relations as a distinctive human engagement with various features or facets that differentiate it from other kinds of human activity. They can be summarized as follows. First, international relations is always and entirely a form of human relations; foreign policy is a human activity. Second, international relations are undertaken by statespeople—agents and representatives of states—whose exchanges and interactions, disputes and agreements, and various other dealings and arrangements carry the stamp of sovereign authority and power. Third, a very significant part of international relations is discourse and dialogue between those people concerning what policies or activities, ours as well as theirs, are expedient or justified in the circumstances. Fourth, because it is a human activity, international relations inescapably involves moral issues which are at the centre of the subject—and not on the periphery as some might believe. Fifth, modern international society is basically a normative framework by reference to which foreign policy, diplomacy, the threat or use of armed force, and other international activities are to be judged. Sixth, modern international society is a specifically historical institution: it has only existed for a certain period of time; it will not go on existing indefinitely. Seventh, international relations involves a special kind of political ethics that centrally concerns the foreign activities of statespeople: the ethics of statecraft is at the heart of international ethics. These points can be enlarged upon.

1. International Relations as a Human Activity

An underlying assumption of this study is that international politics is a human activity in its entirety: international relations, properly conceived and understood, is a branch of human relations. The expressions 'human activity' and 'human relations' are used to emphasize that international relations do not occur automatically or mechanically or functionally. There is no part of international relations that lies beyond human conduct. There is no international 'system' or 'structure' that exists and functions outside human decision, responsibility and control. There are no 'social forces' in the sense of hidden causes that manipulate world politics in spite of the interests or concerns or wishes or desires or hopes or fears of the people involved. There may be a physical reality but there is no political reality independent of human thought and action.

This requires qualification. There are of course countless coincidences of human activity which are a feature of our daily lives. Machiavelli draws our attention to the important role of chance and luck—*fortuna*—in human affairs.[4] He believed that people were more or less in control of about half their activities and the other half was in the hands of *fortuna*. Things happen in our relations with others which we cannot anticipate or plan for with any precision; people or events may surprise us. That is a noteworthy feature of international relations historically. In this sphere of human relations, as in any other human sphere, things which are unforeseen or unexpected can and do happen with little or no warning: for example, the Japanese attack on Pearl Harbor, the end of the cold war, and the disintegration of the Soviet Union. There are also sociological laws which are captured by the notions of unintended consequences of individual actions, for example, in economic markets.[5] But unintended consequences cannot occur without the involvement of people who set them in train. Commodity prices are said to be set by supply and demand. But that is merely a shorthand way of saying that they are arranged in almost countless deals between buyers and sellers: they are human arrangements. Everything about international relations is touched by a human mind and a human hand at some point. Nothing is left untouched either directly or indirectly. Even the highest technology is subject to human design, direction, and responsibility. Automatically programmed missiles and other automated military technology are no exception. The words 'programmed' and 'automated' make it clear that human minds and human hands are involved or implicated.

An important flaw of the international society tradition, and also some classical realist arguments, relates to this point. They posit the state as an actor and in so doing they can leave the impression, which most international society scholars would not wish to leave, that states somehow operate independently of people. They speak of international society as a 'society of states', not of people, but that shorthand expression should not mislead us into thinking that the society of states is something separate from people or that people are not involved in that society. All societies involve people. States are not things or objects or entities in themselves. States cannot speak or listen or therefore communicate on their own. They cannot act on their own. They cannot exist on their own. States are political associations that are constituted and sustained by people in every respect.

This point probably requires elaboration because it is so easy to slip into the habit of thinking of states as things on their own: for example, the well-known realist image of states as billiard balls. But the state does not move on its own. It is not an actor on its own. It does not have an intelligence or conscience or

---

[4] N. Machiavelli, *The Prince*, ed. G. Bull (Harmondsworth: Penguin Books, 1961), ch. 25.

[5] F. A. Hayek argues that 'there exist orderly structures which are the product of the action of many men but are not the result of human design': *Law, Legislation and Liberty, i. Rules and Order* (Chicago: University of Chicago Press, 1973), 37.

will or capacity of its own. The state is not a mechanical entity propelled by forces beyond the control of men and women. It is not a functional or quasi-biological entity. The state is a human construct. It is entirely a product of human imagination, reason, will, and effort. It is essentially an idea that people have come up with to organize and conduct their common or public life. It is a good idea in the opinion of many people and it certainly is a very popular idea historically. It is an idea that has been put into effect as a political institution that prescribes certain standards of human conduct with the aim of shaping human activity in certain ways. The society of states is also and equally a human construct. There is no 'system' or 'structure' of states *as such*. It is not something 'out there' that is independent of human beings. There are no states and there is no states system separate from statespeople and other people involved in these institutions and their activities. There is nothing about the states system that is inevitable or given in the nature of things.

R. G. Collingwood makes this fundamental point in terms of a categorical distinction between history and nature which are incommensurate ideas that should never be confused or conflated: 'the activity by which man builds his own constantly changing historical world is a free activity. There are no forces other than this activity which control it or modify it or compel it to behave in this way or in that, to build one kind of world rather than another.' He hastens to add that this does not mean that man is 'free to do what he pleases' for he or she is always constrained by the human situation which consists of other men and women.[6] Complete freedom and complete restraint are rarely if ever encountered in human conduct. In other words, international relations is an historical world and there is no part of it that is natural or supernatural, controlled by non-human forces. The sociological belief that there are 'social forces' in human affairs that operate over the heads of people bears a remarkable resemblance to the theological belief that there is a god that arranges and controls human destiny.

By 'human activity' I refer to actions that are taken, either directly or indirectly, in regard to people: human activity is activity between and among people: it is *inter homines*.[7] Human activity can be distinguished by the way people relate to each other as compared to the way they relate to non-humans. We cannot relate to other people the way we relate to animals. We can and do eat cows and pigs. We can and do keep dogs and cats as pets. People have sometimes kept other people as slaves: but that is a controversial practice because it expressly denies the freedom and dignity of other human beings. Slavery is a widespread and recurrent practice historically and it is still practised in some places in Africa and the Middle East. But human activity cannot be fully human unless it affirms the values of human freedom and dignity.

A significant feature of human affirmation is communication and dialogue—which is an activity that we can only engage in with other humans and involves

---

[6] R. G. Collingwood, *The Idea of History* (London: OUP, 1975), 315, 316.
[7] M. Oakeshott, *On Human Conduct* (Oxford: Clarendon Press, 1975).

openness to them and exchange with them. To dialogue or communicate with
somebody is to regard him or her as a communicant or conversationalist or inter-
locutor: somebody to whom we can make something known and can hear from
either directly or through an interpreter or intermediary. The act of communicating discloses a prior act of recognizing: it is our recognition of others and
their recognition of us. This point provides a springboard to international
human activity. Statespeople recognize each other and communicate with each
other, usually via intermediaries, and those activities are at the heart of international relations. A great deal of international activity has to do with communicating. That is noticeably the case with diplomacy which is aptly characterized
as 'the dialogue of states'.[8]

People engage in various kinds of relations with other people out of necessity
and also out of choice: people cannot live without each other but they usually
like to choose whom they live with. This is of course a big and complicated subject. Suffice to say that international human activity is undertaken at will and is
thus volitional even when it is imperative or necessary, even when the requirement for a quick foreign-policy decision is urgent and the latitude for choice is
narrow. That may be the case when the threat or use of armed force is involved,
during wars and other armed conflicts. It is very rare for anybody involved in
international relations to have a completely free hand: even leaders of the greatest powers are limited by the circumstances (human as well as non-human) in
which they find themselves. Perfect international autonomy, which is sometimes
contained in the concept of the superpower, may be an ideal or a hope or a fear
but it is not a reality. Nobody involved in international relations, including the
President of the United States, is even remotely like an all-powerful god. The
belief that there are singular determining powers in world politics—by reference
to which international events, especially bad ones, are explained—properly
belongs to the categories of superstition or myth.

2. *International Relations as Relations of Statespeople*

The international human relations to be focused on in the following chapters
involve those special people who act on behalf of sovereign states, particularly,
although not exclusively, the great powers. I shall refer to such people by the
neologism 'statespeople'. I use the plural form intentionally because it captures
the reality of world politics which is fundamentally pluralistic: a world of states.
Statespeople are, shall we say, the organizers and managers who attend to the
ordering and operating of the states system—which also means they can bring
about disorder and even chaos, either intentionally or inadvertently. They are
not the only people involved in international relations, far from it, but they
clearly are the most important people involved. To ignore them would be to dis-

---

[8] A. Watson, *Diplomacy: The Dialogue between States* (London: Methuen, 1982).

regard the leading actors on the stage of world politics: the world politicians. International relations are therefore to be defined as foreign policies and activities that are undertaken by agents and representatives of states which give rise to exchanges, interactions, agreements, disagreements, collaboration, discord, and various other dealings and arrangements between their countries, many of which carry the stamp of their sovereign authority and power. Foreign policies are activities that have foreign statespeople and their countries in view.

Statespeople are far more involved with their own domestic societies than they are with international society. In modern democracies national elections are usually won or lost on issues of domestic policy, not on issues of foreign policy. Human activity is more elaborate and intensive within state jurisdictions than between them. That is because states are the places where people make their homes and where they live out their lives and where they acquire their identities and their understandings of what life involves, what is important, how they should live, whom they should live with, etc. Today the population of the entire planet lives in particular, named territorial spaces that are constitutionally independent of each other: e.g., the USA, Germany, Russia, China, Japan, India, Egypt, South Africa, Mexico, Brazil, Australia, etc. They are the platforms of authority and power upon which statespeople stand.

Independent states are separate zones of human activity within which domestic norms are meant to apply in judging human conduct. For that purpose, every state has its own laws, rules, institutions, traditions, customs, etc. We could only reasonably judge the domestic conduct of the President of the United States by reference to the US constitution which defines the authority and powers of the office. We could not reasonably judge it by reference to the British constitution or the Japanese basic law. That obviously would be absurd. But states rarely, if ever, exist in complete isolation from each other. On the contrary, they exist side by side and statespeople must deal with that bordering and encountering reality. Statespeople are closer or more distant neighbours to each other. We can reasonably expect them to be peaceful and law-abiding neighbours even if they cannot always be good neighbours. International relations consists very largely of those neighbourhood dealings. International ethics and the ethics of statecraft in particular are reserved for judging the relations of independent statespeople in terms of the standards of conduct they acknowledge for dealing with each other. And we can reasonably judge the conduct of all statespeople without exception by those international standards.

If the world's human population was not organized into separate states—that is, if people were instead organized on some other political basis—international ethics as we have known it for the past several centuries would be unknown. If the people of the world were politically organized on the basis of a single global community, perhaps a federal arrangement of some kind, the ethics of world politics would reflect that different institutional fact. The political world would be one state rather than many states. World politics would thus involve domestic ethics rather than international ethics. But that is not the case and it is unlikely to become the case any time soon. The world is still organized on a basis of sovereign states. That fundamentally affects the normative judgements that we can make about international relations.

None of that is altered by market transactions, commerce, trade, finance, communications, transportation, tourism, travel, drug traffic, electronic mail, or other activities and relations that intersect or overfly international boundaries and involve people in different countries around the world. This is of course a controversial point. Some scholars think that these transnational activities are transforming the world in such a fundamental way that it is undermining or eroding the distinction between the domestic and the international and specifically the sovereignty of states: the 'globalization' thesis.[9] I address that argument in later chapters.

Here I merely wish to make the following point. Transnational activities are a striking feature of our era which signal some of the ways and directions in which human relations on the planet are changing at the present time. These changes are important. They are technological, economic or social circumstances that statespeople must deal with. They may adversely affect state institutions and may even undermine them or weaken them in certain ways. But they do not constitute or involve moral or legal claims that challenge the authority of state sovereignty. They do not constitute a global political institution that is a rival or alternative to the society of states. At the present time there is no rival or alternative to the society of states for organizing and conducting political life on a global scale. Advocates of the globalization thesis usually fail to draw this fundamental distinction—probably because they are basing their argument on economics and sociology rather than politics and law. In not drawing it they make a big category mistake: they conflate or confuse socio-economic patterns of behaviour with moral-legal standards of conduct.

We begin to arrive at a preliminary notion of international society: it is a practical normative answer to the anarchical condition of world politics. International society is an institutional response to the fact that the earth's population is divided among separate territory-based political communities which are deemed to express the will of local populations to an independent political existence and to conduct their domestic affairs according to their own norms and values. Because those political communities exist side by side and even cheek by jowl, their leaders are obliged to arrange a normative framework of some kind for conducting their relations—if they wish to deal with each other in an orderly way as fellow human beings. The main alternative to a society of independent states is to treat foreign people as non-humans or as inferior humans: for example, a political hierarchy of independent and dependent political communities. That

---

[9] D. J. Elkins, *Beyond Sovereignty: Territory and Political Economy in the Twenty-First Century* (Toronto: University of Toronto Press, 1995).

was of course tried by Europeans in their outward imperial expansion in earlier centuries. They attempted to draw a normative distinction between themselves and peoples of other continents, civilizations, and cultures. Those 'others' were at one time treated virtually as non-people. Later they were treated as inferior people and then as colonized people. But the dehumanization or subordination or colonization of foreigners proved to be a failure. It was not viable over the longer term because it could not be fully justified in human terms. Eventually it was abandoned. That led to the global expansion of international society based on locally-sovereign states. That is where we are today. We should, I think, be mindful of the enormous moral achievement that is represented by the building of a global international society based on state sovereignty.

3. Discourse and Dialogue of Statespeople

A very significant part of international human relations, and arguably the most significant part, is discourse and dialogue concerning what policies or activities, ours as well as theirs, are desirable or advisable or appropriate or acceptable or tolerable or prudent or politic or judicious or justified in the circumstances. That discourse of statespeople is in certain basic respects the 'politics' of international politics and is traditionally conducted by means of the institution we know as diplomacy. Politics is fundamentally a communication activity in which politicians present different arguments or opinions regarding an issue that interests or concerns them and with a view to arriving at an agreement or arrangement or accommodation that they can live with—at least for the time being.[10] In politics talk is not trivial; on the contrary, it is fundamental. Written or verbal discourse is the main vehicle of political activity. Without discourse there could be no politics in the ordinary meaning of the word. Without international discourse there could be no international relations.

Diplomatic dialogue also discloses the 'international' of international politics: that is, an activity that involves agents or representatives of different states who are interested in or concerned about the same issue and who have every right to voice their interests and concerns to the other statespeople, and to be heard by those statespeople, even if no agreement or concurrence of views results from their exchange. International discourse is expressed in many ways: speeches, public announcements, secret communications, correspondence, declarations, resolutions, press conferences, white papers, trial balloons. It is carried on bilaterally and multilaterally, secretly and openly, continually and intermittently, directly and indirectly, etc. It is carried on in many different venues: state visits, international conferences, international organizations, third-party capitals, convenient secret locations—and other sites too numerous to mention even in

---

[10] M. Oakeshott, *Rationalism in Politics and Other Essays*, new and expanded edn. (Indianapolis: Liberty Press, 1991), 206.

passing. These are only a few of the almost endless means and ways that states-people find to communicate with each other on matters of common interest or concern. That activity is at the centre of international relations.

4. International Relations Involve Moral Issues

Human activity and human relations entail moral issues—questions of good and bad, right and wrong—which can only be raised by the activities of human beings in relation to each other. Moral issues cannot be raised by natural events such as earthquakes and floods. But such issues can of course be raised by human responses or failures to respond to earthquakes, floods, and other natural disasters that people can be caught in. Thus once human beings are involved in relations they are also *ipso facto* involved in morality and ethics (I use these terms interchangeably). And because human activity is initiated by humans—not determined for them by some external force, such as God or nature—and involves decisions and policies that affect people, it also involves morality. The core of morality is the notion that we cannot justifiably relate to other people as if they were things or tools or objects to be used or dealt with in whatever way we determine or desire. It is a fundamental moral principle that people must be treated as human beings. That means that their freedom and dignity must be respected. When we speak of human conduct and misconduct we are recognizing that moral principle.

The circumstances in which policies, decisions and actions are contemplated and taken are also morally relevant considerations in judging human conduct. Circumstances are enabling or limiting conditions that affect what anyone in a particular situation can accomplish. Circumstances are usually a mitigating factor in determining responsibility. International activities are particularly subject to circumstances. Foreign policy is in some fundamental respects an activity confined within limiting circumstances. That is because the situation is affected and usually complicated by the presence of several or even many independent statespeople who may be interested or involved in the same episode. Their presence ordinarily cannot be ignored. That usually circumscribes the decisions anyone involved in foreign affairs can reasonably take, and it hinders or inhibits the policies they can carry out.

It is usually easier and more effective to act locally than at a distance: we can get a better handle on a local situation. It is also more compelling to act locally: in practice our responsibilities to those in our immediate vicinity—family, friends, colleagues, fellow citizens—are greater than our responsibilities to more distant others beyond our borders. That means that international standards of human conduct are lower and looser than domestic standards. The moral life of domestic society is more vital and more deeply felt than that of international society because we are more regularly and more profoundly affected by people nearby. Distant people, particularly people in foreign countries, do not usually have the same effect on us. As a rule, our own government is far more involved in our lives, far more important to us, than foreign governments are. Most people live locally. The state is their largest locale. Their country is where their life is arranged and lived for the most part. Very few people have several states as their locale (dual citizenship or foreign residency rights). A common but reliable indicator of that fact is the far greater quantity of domestic news as compared to foreign news in the news media of most countries. People want news about their own country which, in a manner of speaking, is news about themselves. When we go abroad and read the foreign newspapers we usually find little news about our own country. Those newspapers are responding to their local readers and not to visitors. The former far outnumber the latter.

In other words, the anarchical condition of international relations has profound moral implications: it is the fundamental institutional condition of world politics that limits the judgements we can make about foreign policy and other international activities. The domestic and the international are significantly different spheres of political life. Each sphere has different standards of conduct. That means that international ethics should not be confused with domestic ethics. As a rule, the first standard is less demanding and less exacting than the second standard.

5. *International Society as a Normative Framework*

As already indicated, international society is a moral and legal framework by reference to which foreign policy, diplomacy, the threat or use of armed force, and other international political activities are to be judged. International society, like domestic society, has normative codes which define crimes and other forms of misconduct. The most explicit code of conduct in world affairs is the law of nations, international law. Other international codes are the practices of diplomacy and the procedures of international organizations. As indicated, however, the codes of international society are usually less demanding and less exacting than those of domestic societies. International law enforcement is weaker and looser.

Classical international society scholars do not say that normative ideas are the only ideas that frame the conduct of international relations. They note that instrumental notions, ideas of accidents and contingencies, and other important notions are involved in any rational attempt to understand the way that statespeople think and act toward each other. International activities can obviously be instrumental as well as non-instrumental. The political relations of statespeople are certainly instrumental, that is, they are dictated and guided by concern about goals. Some of Machiavelli's advice to statespeople, although by no means all of it, is clearly instrumental: he is telling them how best to survive and succeed in an uncertain and sometimes dangerous world of intellectually imperfect and morally flawed people.[11] Instrumental conduct is to be expected in any kind of human activity and certainly in political activity of an international sort.

But the political relations of statespeople are not wholly instrumental by any means; they have a normative dimension. Classical international society scholars believe that non-instrumental and specifically moral ideas are at the heart of human activity in the international sphere no less than the domestic sphere or other spheres of human life. That is again because international relations are specifically human relations: people cannot live together and deal with each other over the longer term without acknowledging and observing shared norms which recognize and respect their common humanity. It is the same for states-people. Without ignoring and much less denying the importance of the instru-mental dimension of international activity, which should be obvious to anybody who takes an interest in world affairs, it is the normative dimension that I am particularly concerned to investigate. For it is that dimension which comes to grips with what it means to be human and to engage in human relations with people outside one's own community, with neighbours, with foreigners, and sometimes with distant others whose civilization or culture is almost beyond understanding. The global covenant is a normative bridge between even very different and distant civilizations and cultures.

6. *International Society is Historical*

Modern international society is a specifically historical institution that is intim-ately connected with the Westphalian era of world politics of the past three or four centuries. Political institutions are historical by definition: they are time-bound arrangements of human affairs. Somebody came up with the idea for them at some point in time. The idea caught on, was put into effect, and was supported and sustained over time by the people involved. That happened in the case of the Westphalian society of states. It was a response of Europeans to the decline of the medieval Christian empire that caught on in the seventeenth and eighteenth centuries. It subsequently was expanded to encompass the entire world. It thus arose at a certain time, it has lasted for a significant period of time which is virtually coterminous with the modern era, and it can reasonably be expected to persist for some time to come. Like all successful political institu-tions, international society evolves over time in response to changing ideas and circumstances. But it can also be expected to be changed beyond all recognition, or even abandoned altogether and replaced with a different political arrange-ment, at some time in the future. It is a typical political institution in these and other respects.

Some scholars think that a fundamental movement away from global inter-national society toward a different arrangement of world politics is presently

---

[11] N. Machiavelli, *The Prince*, tr. by George Bull (Harmondsworth: Penguin Books, 1961).

under way.[12] I shall argue that those people are mistaken. The turning of the second millennium is no more likely to usher in a post-Westphalian or post-modern era than that of the first millennium marked the advent of the second coming of Christ whose arrival back on earth was erroneously forecast by certain Christian theologians and priests, some of the leading intellectuals of the time. It is far more likely that the new era will present new challenges to the Westphalian order. Before we make any confident predictions about a fundamental international transformation involving the end of state sovereignty, we should be mindful of the historical fact that the society of states has responded successfully to many challenges over the past three or four centuries, not least of which are the scientific revolution, the enlightenment, the rise of nationalism, and the industrial revolution.

7. Statecraft invokes a Special Ethics

International ethics must be firmly distinguished from private morality and other moral spheres. That distinction is fundamental to any solid normative understanding of world politics. Behind it is the recognition that different kinds of human activity are subject, at least up to a point, to different standards of conduct which relate to the activity in question. Concrete human activities and the practical ethics which apply to them are interrelated. Human life is far too extensive and differentiated and complex to allow for just one morality. We recognize that by the expressions 'medical ethics', 'environmental ethics', 'business ethics', 'legal ethics', 'private morality', 'public morality', 'political ethics', 'military ethics', 'international ethics', and so on. These ethical systems may overlap, and most of them probably do overlap, but they are not interchangeable. That means, for example, that we cannot judge the actions of public officials by the standards of private morality without confusing two different moralities. We cannot judge teachers or social workers by the same standards that we use to judge parents. Nor can we judge foreign policy by the standards of domestic policy. We cannot judge the President of the United States by the same standards that we use to judge the President of General Motors. We must apply standards that are commensurate with the activity. That would seem to be a matter of experience, observation, and common sense.

International ethics centrally concerns the foreign activities and relations of statespeople: the ethics of statecraft are at the heart of international ethics. Statecraft, just like any other craft, involves certain characteristic norms and values which define and validate the activities that are associated with it and carried on in its name. Diplomacy involves norms of recognition, respect, conciliation, honour, integrity, reliability. War involves norms of restraint, courage,

---

[12] See Richard Falk, 'A New Paradigm for International Legal Studies: Prospects and Proposals,' in R. Falk, F. Kratochwil, and S. H. Mendlovitz (eds.), *International Law: A Contemporary Perspective* (Boulder, Colo., and London: Westview, 1985), 651–702.

honour, non-combatant immunity, humane treatment of prisoners. We could not intelligently and responsibly assess the moral weight of those activities if we judged them by reference to business ethics or private morality or medical ethics or any other extraneous standards of conduct. Nor could we intelligently and responsibly judge them by the standards of our own preferred ideologies: that would impose our own values on the people we study. That might make us feel good, even superior, but it cannot shed any academic light on the subject. We can only judge international activities by the standards of the practitioners, statespeople. That is how we can reasonably hold them to account. We can of course evaluate their standards of conduct and we must do that if we hope to carry out a comprehensive and balanced normative analysis. But we can only appraise the standards intelligently and responsibly from the perspective of the international human activities to which they are meant to apply.

It is important to be clear about the character of international ethics and the basic values it serves. It is fundamentally pluralist and anti-paternalist. By 'pluralist' I mean that international ethics affirms the moral value of independent political communities, sovereign states. And it affirms the moral value of the society of such states. By 'anti-paternalist' I mean that it repudiates the principle that some states are responsible for other states to the point where the former may intervene in the sovereignty of the latter with good intentions but without their consent or without any other generally recognized international grounds for such action such as the right of self-defence or the value of international peace and security. Paternalism and independence are antithetical ideas.[13]

The political world of humankind is inclined to be pluralistic. Modern world politics is decentralized: there are many centres located around the world. The greater part of the political life of the earth's population is carried on locally: the population and territory of the world is partitioned into diverse local political systems. Arguably that is dictated by the geographical size of the earth which is still very large even if people are discovering ways to move around it far more rapidly and easily than in the past. World government is a project whose enormity would boggle the mind of most people who think about it. Even single governments for each continent boggles the mind—except, perhaps, in the case of Europe but even there it is unlikely to encompass the whole of Europe. Locally based political life is also dictated, and even more so, by the earth's large human population, the vast majority of whom are inclined to arrange their lives jointly with people who live in the same locality. Most people want to live together with people like themselves. They want to live together in separate political groups that make it possible for them to express their own ideas, values, and beliefs: to

[13] J. S. Mill, 'A Few Words on Non-Intervention,' in J. S. Mill, *Essays on Politics and Culture*, ed. G. Himmelfarb, (New York: Anchor Books, 1963); also see I. Kant, 'On the Relationship of Theory to Practice in Political Right,' repr. in H. Reiss (ed.), *Kant's Political Writings* (Cambridge: Cambridge University Press, 1977), 74.

be free to do their own thing in their own way in their own country. That, too, would seem to be obvious from experience, observation, and common sense. In short, all people share a common humanity, but most people are inclined to live in families, countries, and other restricted population groups. They are thus inclined to live apart from others.

That widespread human proclivity creates a fundamental political problem: the mutual accommodation and orderly coexistence of those assorted political groups that share the finite territory of the planet and cannot usually retreat into splendid isolation. How can their relations be arranged and managed so that they can live side by side in an orderly and peaceful way and enjoy an opportunity to flourish domestically in their own distinctive ways? The international society of locally sovereign states based on the principles of equal sovereignty, territorial integrity, and non-intervention can be understood as a practical institutional response to that problem. Understood in that way, international society is an arrangement to uphold human equality and human freedom around the world. State sovereignty is one of the very few clusters of important political values— probably it is the only one at the present time—around which the political world can rally and unite: not democracy, not human rights, not the environment, but sovereignty. The division of the world's geography and population into a number of different locally sovereign states is an obvious fact, but its deeper human meaning, significance, and value is often lost to view. To probe and hopefully shed some light on that deeper subject is a fundamental aim of this book.

3

Recovering the Classical Approach

This chapter rejuvenates the classical international society approach by enlarging upon the argument that international relations is a human activity. It begins by reviewing three approaches to international relations scholarship: positivism, post-positivism, and humanism. It argues that only the third approach can correctly comprehend the human character of world politics. Pursuing that point in the remainder of the chapter, it calls attention to fourteen classical texts for studying international human conduct. It proceeds to interrogate two leading positivist theories of international relations with the aim of disclosing the shortcomings of excluding norms and values from the inquiry. It goes on to examine and reject a standard criticism of moral claims in political life: the so-called window-dressing critique. The final section prepares the way for a commentary on the craft discipline of humanist inquiry in the next chapter.

Retrieving the Human Sciences

The behavioural revolution of the 1950s and 1960s brought about almost a complete take-over of the discipline of political science, especially in the USA, by positivist attitudes and methods of research.[1] Traditional normative inquiry was abandoned to the care of the political theorists. With the missionary zeal of recent converts, the American behaviouralists recruited and educated a new generation of political scientists who had little knowledge of their classical predecessors and even less interest in knowing anything about them. All previous political science was obsolete and should not be taken too seriously. It was like Aristotle's biology: it belonged in a curiosity shop. That is more or less what the behaviouralists taught their students, and that is what their students who later came to dominate political science, especially in the USA, were evidently prepared to believe. That was emphasized by Kenneth Waltz in a guarded criticism of Martin Wight and Hedley Bull: 'they did theory in a sense not recognized as theory by philosophers of science'.[2] In other words, their theories were not 'scientific' theories in the positivist meaning of the term.

[1] See e.g. H. Eulau, *The Behavioral Persuasion in Politics* (New York: Random House, 1963).
[2] F. Halliday and J. Rosenberg, 'Interview with Ken Waltz,' *Review of International Studies*, 24 (July 1998), 385.

1. Positivism

Among other things, positivism is an attitude which postulates the unity of the natural sciences and the social sciences via a common philosophy and methodology. Positivist social scientists endeavour to operate with basically the same scientific standards as natural scientists. Of particular concern here, however, is the positivist view of human beings and their relations: the positivist philosophy of the human condition. The philosophers make explicit what the social scientists usually only imply about human behaviour.

For positivists the human world is taken to be part of the natural world, and as such it can only be known to us via our sense perception of it. Sensations—touch, taste, smell, sound, sight—are the bedrock of human behaviour and human relations. There is no human world beyond that which is perceived by our senses. To believe otherwise is to surrender to superstition: (for example, religion). Human behaviour is a series of more or less transient sensual experiences: some of them pleasurable and thus attractive like drinking wine or having sex, others painful and repulsive like touching a hot iron or catching the scent of a skunk, and still others and perhaps most somewhere between these poles. The study of human sense perception is, for positivists, the key to unlocking the mysteries of human behaviour.

At the base of positivism is the assumption that human relations consist in the assertion of selves or egos. Selves are bundles of desires which are registered either by individuals alone or jointly with others, either in collaboration or in competition. People are considered to behave in such a way as to serve themselves and gratify themselves, from the offerings of food or sex or money or power that life makes available to those who can find a way of obtaining them. Human life is a long-term project of personal gratification carried on sometimes alone but perhaps more often in conjunction with others who have the same basic desires and can see the same advantage in combining or competing to obtain the objects that satisfy them. Other people are implicated in most of our desires. Human desires and the ways in which they drive human behaviour, at base, are what positivist social scientists make it their business to track down and explain in their studies. That overt human behaviour is their basic data.

This would seem to be a caricature of the human condition. I believe it is a caricature, but I am prepared to accept that it is half the truth. I can see part of myself and part of other selves in this image. Yet one of the foremost positivist philosophers of the twentieth century, A. J. Ayer, believed it was the whole truth more or less.[3] Not only that, he evidently lived his life by constantly seeking personal satisfaction from others with whom he had instrumental relations; he entered into those relations to gratify his own desires. His life has been characterized as 'the hollow man's story' and is seen to mirror his positivist

---

[3] A. J. Ayer, *Language, Truth and Logic* (London: Penguin, 1960).

philosophy of human behaviour.[4] The positivist conception of human beings conceives of them as ciphers of pleasure and pain. In effect, the behaviour of every man and woman is modeled on that of A.J. Ayer: social science positivism is the story of hollow men and women:

Experience goes the way it goes, that is all: sensations are the fundamental reality, the bedrock on which everything else precariously rests . . . this fits perfectly Ayer's own attitude to life: the Ayerian self is but a fleeting succession of experiences, some nice, some not so nice, while the selves of others exist primarily as tools to make sense of his own subjectivity . . . the assertion of ego . . . is at the heart of the positivism in which he was so willingly trapped.[5]

Because positivists are committed to the development of a science of human behaviour they require a conception of human beings and their relations which can make that possible. Most conceptions of the human world that are more or less true to the subject, such as those of the classical human sciences, do not allow that development because they draw on an image of human relations that includes both the assertion of selves and the recognition of others: that is, they contain an essential normative element. That is ruled out by positivist social science because it invokes questions of right and wrong, good and bad, in human relations. Such questions are not derived from sense perception. They lie beyond our senses. They cannot be answered or even raised by a positivist approach.

The positivists see humans more or less as materialists who are engrossed in their own sensual experiences and deal with each other in egoist terms: here is a conception that makes something approaching a social science of human behaviour possible. One example of such a conception is that of human activities as dictated by calculations of pleasure and pain, gains and losses, costs and benefits, with a view to achieving goals that supply human satisfaction. That is the instrumental view of human behaviour advanced by some utilitarians who see human beings as more or less efficient calculators of costs and benefits, and more or less preoccupied processors of goods and services that satisfy their wants and desires. That is a mechanical view of human relations: people process information for the purpose of achieving goals which satisfy their cravings: the human person is a sort of information processor, a calculator or computer.[6]

Something along this line of thinking has been imported into international relations by conceiving of states as giant egoists: they are seen to process information, to calculate costs and benefits, to formulate and carry out policies with a view to obtaining goods and services to satisfy the wants and desires of their

---

[4] C. McGinn, 'The Hollow Man's Story', *The Times Literary Supplement* (25 June 1999), 3–4. Also see Ayer, *Language, Truth and Logic*.

[5] McGinn, 'Hollow Man's Story', 4.

[6] An influential study of that sort is H. A. Simon, *Administrative Behavior* (New York: Free Press, 1965).

people. The national interest is seen to be the aggregate of wants and desires of the national population: the state is A. J. Ayer writ large. The state system is 190 A. J. Ayers, each one of them striving to indulge themselves—if necessary, and probably unavoidably, at the expense of each other. World politics is based on self-existent, self-centred, self-asserting, and self-seeking states. This can lead to an image of interstate relations as a set of billiard balls which collide from time to time as states single-mindedly pursue their interests. The positivism of Ayer was recently dismissed as 'old-fashioned' and 'unnecessary' by a defender of positivist international relations theory.[7] But Ayer's model of human beings is lurking behind positivist accounts of political behaviour, including international relations—even if it is never addressed openly in the analysis.

Social science positivists operate with 'models' or 'frameworks for analysis' which are intended to lead to 'explanations' of human behaviour.[8] Theories are generalizations about data: they are always theories about some phenomenon. Positivists adopt what might be called an indoor/outdoor orientation to research: the phenomenon they are researching is 'out there', which implies that the researcher is 'in here'. The researcher is looking upon the people under research as external entities or objects of some kind to be explained, the way that a wildlife biologist would explain the behaviour of wolves in mating season. International relations are seen in the same external way: as a system or structure of behaviour that calls for explanations elicited from models or conceptual frameworks applied in research.

The positivist researcher is engaged in the systematic gathering of 'data' and the establishment of 'data banks' to be used for testing hypotheses and building up verifiable propositions ('empirical theories') about the phenomenon being investigated.[9] Data are usually statistical data, although not always. Social science data are not facts or evidence of ordinary human experience which accumulate over time: they are not synthetic. They do not register events or occurrences or incidents or experiences or circumstances or affairs or relations of people in the course of living their lives and getting on with whatever activities they are involved in, the doings and goings on of ordinary human activity. Social science data are generated in the course of research by applying data-collecting methodologies: data are analytic. They are produced by researchers for purposes of research. They are laundered or massaged in such a way as to be amenable to the testing of the data with the aim of achieving a scientific explanation of them. The positivist social scientist is not seeking to enhance or deepen his or her pre-existing, common-sense understanding of the human world that has been acquired from living in it and paying attention to the way human activity is carried on. That kind of experiential understanding—and the

---

[7] M. Nicholson, *Causes and Consequences in International Relations* (London: Pinter, 1996), 18.
[8] See the useful discussion ibid. 22–5.
[9] See J. Singer, *Resort to Arms: International and Civil Wars 1816–1980* (Beverly Hills, Calif.: Sage, 1993).

historical knowledge derived from it—is held to be unreliable and unscientific because it is subjective.

The positivist approach is conducive to an instrumental outlook. It views human behaviour as goal-oriented and goal-seeking. In international relations positivists often operate with a conception of foreign policy as an activity of promoting and pursuing the national interest understood as that which will satisfy the wants and gratify the desires of the nation. Positivism in international relations lends itself to an instrumental foreign-policy analysis. The role of political scientists, in commenting on foreign policy, is akin to the well-known 'if' role of the scientific or economic adviser: if you choose that goal these are the advantages and problems, the benefits and costs, that could be expected. That instrumental approach leaves unexplored large areas of human life, including international political life, that have to do with questions of values and norms. Should a particular goal be chosen in the first place? Can the decision be justified? Other people can of course be treated as mere tools for gratifying ourselves, but that raises an obvious and fundamental question: should they be treated that way? Classical ethics and common sense both hold that they ought not to be treated in that way because they are not tools; they are people, and they ought to be treated as such. As a philosophy and methodology for studying human beings and their relations, positivism suffers from a fatal flaw: it cannot supply answers to normative questions; it cannot even ask such questions. At best, it can only ask instrumental questions: if I do that, then what is likely to happen?

The instrumental approach is half right. But it is only half the story of human relations. I was once on a flight to Sweden to give a lecture on international society after the cold war. I fell into a conversation with the Swedish passenger seated besides me. I told her I was going to the university of Uppsala. I said I was not sure how to get my lecture going with an opening flourish that would connect with my Scandinavian audience. I asked her if there was anything she could tell me about the Swedish psyche. She said that was an easy question to answer. On one shoulder every Swede carries the ghost of old Odin, the Viking god of power and battle, lover of wine and women, who tells him or her to enjoy life to the full.[10] On the other shoulder every Swede carries the ghost of Martin Luther who preaches duty, responsibility, humility, concern for others. I said to her: doesn't that put you in a bit of a dilemma? Oh no, she said, because every Swede has a head between his or her two shoulders and is able to decide when to listen to Odin, and when to listen to Luther.

Positivists have difficulty coming to grips with the notion of norms and values in human affairs: they have a clear image of old Odin, but they have a fuzzy image of Martin Luther—if they see him at all. They cannot clearly see human relations as involving normative issues. At best, they see it as involving choices

---

[10] See E. Roesdahl, *The Vikings* (Harmondsworth: Penguin Books, 1998), 149–50.

concerning how to satisfy wants and desires: cost-benefit choices, maximizing choices, satisfying choices, comfortable choices. But such choices do not present normative issues. They only present problems of estimation and calculation in the efficient pursuit of goals which fuel our wants and desires.

When normative subjects are addressed they are usually reconceptualized into positivist terms. Sometimes values are translated into goals understood as objects of human desire and activity. Humans are conceptualized as goal-oriented and goal-directed actors. As indicated, that fits into the instrumental conception of policy analysis. Political scientists become policy advisers. Their knowledge is directed toward achieving expedient behaviour; it is instrumental. Sometimes norms are handled as economists would handle them: i.e., as preferences.[11] But preferences are not the same as norms. What we would prefer to do is not the same as what we ought to do. Preferences indicate latitude and choice; norms indicate restraint and constriction of choice. Preferences disclose a world of wants and desires; norms disclose a world of responsibilities which morally or legally limit what one can justifiably do in the situation. Sometimes positivists try to come to grips with norms by reconceptualizing them as something causal: that is, a norm is conceived to be an independent variable that has an impact on a dependent variable. Values and norms are considered to be important because they are seen to trigger or track behaviour. They can thus be employed to explain behaviour in cause and effect terms.[12]

Some other positivist conceptions of values and norms are considered in the next chapter; suffice to say that they tend to distort the subject. That is because norms and values, properly understood, do not lend themselves to any analysis which seeks to employ the philosophy and methodology of natural science. A norm is not an element of the physical or natural world. It is not something 'out there' that can be perceived by our senses. It cannot be unlocked by a study of sense perceptions. It is not a causal force or independent variable. Nor is it merely an effect of human interaction, an outcome. A norm is not an instrument. A value is not simply a goal that calls for instrumentally rational (that is, goal-seeking) behaviour. And it is impossible to translate a norm, in the usual moral or legal sense of the term, into a preference, without destroying the original idea.

The normative world of human relations is made by people; it is not given in the nature of things. It is artificial rather than natural and consists, significantly, of the thoughts and ideas of the people involved regarding how they ought to live their lives in proximity with each other. A norm in the classical meaning of the term is a legal or moral obligation or requirement or expectation, a standard of human conduct. Norms are pointed to by people involved in relations with each other who are seeking to justify their conduct or that of their friends or

---

[11] See David Easton, *The Political System*, 2nd edn. (New York: Knopf, 1971), 221.
[12] See J. Goldstein and R. Keohane (eds.), *Ideas and Foreign Policy* (Ithaca, NY: Cornell, 1992), 11–12.

allies; people also point to norms to criticize or condemn the conduct of other people. Norms carry weight in the sense that to disregard them or deny them would require a justification of roughly comparable or equal importance. When I go to court with a complaint that my legal rights have been violated by my employer I am making a normative claim. When diplomats representing Yugoslavia went to the UN Security Council in 1999 with a complaint that NATO violated the sovereignty of their country by dropping bombs on its territory they were making a normative claim. Norms are considerations of a moral or legal kind that cannot be overlooked or dismissed—if one hopes to justify whatever policy or activity one is contemplating or engaging in.

We could say that norms are the grammar or syntax of human relations. They are the practices and usages, the forms and modalities, according to which human activity in any sphere is assessed as to its correctness: its rightness or wrongness, its goodness or badness. The basic problem with positivism emerges at this point: it fails to discern, or it turns a blind eye to, this social arrangement by reference to which human activity is evaluated. In international relations that shortcoming is clearly evident in the positivists' usual neglect of international law and diplomatic practices, which are important elements of the grammar of international discourse. It is also evident in their neglect of the prudential ethics of statecraft. Positivists seem to operate with an assumption that international relations can be explained satisfactorily without studying the norms by reference to which the international practitioners assess each other's foreign policies and international activities. Statecraft is conceived to be a wholly instrumental activity. The problem of positivism, in that important respect, is something like the problem that would result if we tried to grasp the point of a football game, tried to make sense of the activity on the field, by looking at the overt behaviour of the people running around without knowing anything about the procedural and prudential rules of the game. I once tried to figure out the game of cricket that way. The reader can imagine how far I got. I was driven to ask the person seated next to me to clarify what was going on.

Positivists declare for a value-neutral political science. That could mean that the social scientist does not allow his values to influence his analysis. In practice, however, it usually means merely that value-premises are not stated or defended. Value-neutrality is problematic in so far as it can involve the masking of values in the name of social science and thus the failure to examine them. It is not so much that positivist studies of world politics are value-neutral but that values are hidden beneath the surface of their texts. Value-neutrality could also mean that social scientists exclude values from their studies in the belief that they are not suitable subjects of scientific analysis. That is also problematic because it excludes half the human world from the analysis, arguably the most important half.

Social science positivism is a blind alley. Value-neutrality or value-exclusion is an unempirical and ultimately an unsustainable research orientation because norms and values are embodied by human relations. People cannot escape from them in living and dealing with each other. Their lives are shaped and conditioned by normative obligations, requirements, and expectations. Statespeople cannot escape either. People are value-embodied creatures: they are value-conscious and value-oriented. People take up or construct norms and subject themselves to them. That happens when people observe customs and traditions or enact laws which they go on to observe and even venerate: for example, the American constitution and Bill of Rights. That is what it means to be human in the modern era and in previous eras too. Statespeople are no different than other people in that regard. Thus it is not only that norms and values enter into our activity as researchers and scholars, which is undoubtedly the case. Norms and values are an intrinsic part of our subject. They cannot be removed from the subject by the researcher, by framing an hypothesis or generating a theory that excludes them. The inescapable normative reality of human relations, including international relations, does not lend itself to study by methodologies modelled on those of the natural sciences. The study of norms and values in world politics—or in any other sphere of human relations—calls for a non-positivist approach.

2. Post-Positivism

The intellectual limitations of social science positivism for gaining insight into international relations as a sphere of human relations, and for theorizing those relations, led to a reaction in the 1980s and 1990s: what has been termed 'post-positivism'.[13] An increasing number of international relations scholars were attracted by other approaches, and particularly by critical theory, postmodernism, and constructivism.[14] These post-positivist approaches can only be discussed in passing.

According to critical theorists, the international system is a specific construction of hegemonic powers. Not only do those powerful states rule the world, but they have made it in their own image: the states system serves their interests and values. They manipulate the system, and all the people caught up in it, for their own advantage. Knowledge of such a system cannot be neutral. Scholars cannot stand outside the human world and study it objectively. They can only stand inside it because they are part of it. But that means their knowledge will be slanted and distorted by their position or perspective within it, whether it is, for example, the perspective of those who live in the powerful states and are privileged by it or the opposite perspective of those who live in the powerless states and are handicapped and hobbled by it. Political science, including the study of international politics, is contaminated by an inclination (conscious or

---

[13] S. Smith, K. Booth, and M. Zalewski (eds.), *International Theory: Positivism and Beyond* (Cambridge: Cambridge University Press, 1996).

[14] I am indebted to Georg Sørensen for his comments on this section.

unconscious) toward certain values, interests, groups, parties, classes, nations. Robert Cox expresses that view in a frequently quoted remark: 'Theory is always for someone and for some purpose'.[15] Critical theorists, somehow managing to divorce themselves from their typical middle-class status in developed Western countries which should incline them to the first perspective, see it from the latter perspective. How they manage to do that is not clear. Their theory is anti-hegemonic and emancipatory. They want to undermine the states system by exposing it and discrediting it, with a view to seeing it replaced by another system that is more attuned to human equality and human needs.

Postmodernists see the human world, including the international world, as historically arbitrary: it is lacking in rationality; it has no rhyme nor reason. It is like the world of the California hippies of the 1960s; it consists of 'happenings', incomprehensible human events. Many postmodernists are anti-foundational. They reject the search for rational explanations of human behaviour as fruitless and self-deluding. In effect, they see the entire human world as populated by hippies and composed of happenings. There is no objective reality upon which scientific theory can be erected; everything involving human beings is subjective and elusive. Human behaviour eludes any attempt to pin it down scientifically. Social science is not neutral; rather, it is historical, it is cultural, it is political, and therefore biased. Every theory postulates what counts as 'facts'. There is no impartial standpoint to decide between rival empirical claims. Narratives, by which they mean scholarly texts, are always constructed by a scholar and they are thus always contaminated by his or her standpoint and prejudices. Narratives can be deconstructed, that is, taken apart to disclose their arbitrary elements and biased intentions. How postmodernists manage to find the rational analysis to do that is not clear.

We can reasonably ask postmodernists why we should accept their analysis if all theory is arbitrary. Why should their deconstruction be any more reliable than the original construction? In the same sceptical vein, if theory is always an expression of political interests (rather than academic curiosity), as critical theorists claim, political science is neither science nor scholarship: it is politics. That means that critical theory is politics too. That may of course be true. But if it is true why should the emancipatory theory of the critical theorists be accepted? If every account of the social world is arbitrary and biased, then critical theory and postmodernism cannot be spared: their critiques can be turned upon themselves.

Richard Ashley says there is no 'positionality'—that is, there are no stable platforms or certitudes—upon which social speech, writing, and action can be based.[16] But is that not a position? Ironically, what makes postmodernism intelligible is its conformity to some basic conventions of academic inquiry which are

---

[15] R. Cox, 'Social Forces, States and World Orders', *Millennium*, 10 (1981), 126–55.
[16] R. Ashley, 'The Achievements of Post-Structuralism', in Smith *et al.*, *International Theory: Positivism and Beyond*, 240–53.

at the foundations of knowledge. Some postmodern writings may be awkwardly composed and larded with obscure jargon. But they nevertheless conform to the conventions of grammar in whatever language they are written. Postmodernists live their lives as we live our lives within the social framework of interpersonal standards of time, space, direction, distance, which are marked and measured by calendars, clocks, maps, compasses. There are similar standards operating throughout the entire world of human relations, including international relations. Postmodernists—including Richard Ashley—cannot escape from the rational constructs of human life in their own lives.

A more worrying problem is the tendency for postmodernism to degenerate into nihilism. Narratives are taken apart with nothing to take their place. Criticism is made merely for the sake of criticism. Cynicism and even fatalism may take hold. Ultimately, postmodernists can become estranged from the social and political world they seek to understand. A world exclusively of contingency and chance, such as Ashley portrays—rather than one of contemplation and action as well as contingency and chance, such as Machiavelli discerns—leaves human beings prisoners of their fate rather than intelligent and responsible builders of their world.[17] Such a postmodernist world is devoid of rational meaning. Values and beliefs are meaningless. Nihilism cannot provide any rational foundations of knowledge of human relations because it rejects the possibility of human reason and the freedom and responsibility that go with it.

There is a third way in post-positivist international relations scholarship that tries to avoid the political bias of critical theory and the anti-rationalism of postmodernism: what is termed 'constructivism'. Constructivists accept that there is no external, objective reality as such when it comes to human relations. Their key idea is that the social world, including the international world, is a human construction. It is not something 'out there', as behaviouralists and positivists believe. Rather, it is an inter-subjective domain: it is meaningful to the people who made it and live in it and who must therefore be able to understand it. Contemporary constructivists often leave the impression that they believe they have come up with a revolutionary way of studying human relations. But constructivism is an old methodology that can be traced back at least to the eighteenth-century writings of Giambattista Vico.[18] For Vico, the natural world is made by God, but the historical world is made by human beings.[19] It is of course that latter world that we are seeking to understand. It is the fact that we made it that makes it intellectually accessible to us. So we have an insight into

---

[17] Ibid. 240–53.

[18] L. Pompa, *Vico: Selected Writings* (Cambridge: Cambridge University Press, 1982). According to Collingwood, this is the doctrine that 'the condition of being able to know anything truly, to understand it as opposed to merely perceiving it, is that the knower himself should have made it . . . the fabric of human society is created by man . . . and every detail of this fabric is . . . eminently knowable to the human mind'. See R. G. Collingwood, *The Idea of History* (London: OUP. 1975), 64–5.

[19] Pompa, *Vico*, 26.

the world of human relations that we do not possess with regard to the natural world.

Alexander Wendt captures the mood of constructivism in the study of international relations: 'anarchy is what states make of it'.[20] There is no objective international world apart from the practices and institutions that states arrange among themselves. In making that statement he argues that anarchy is not some kind of external given, or natural reality, which dictates a positivist logic of analysis. 'Self-help and power politics are institutions, not essential features of anarchy'.[21] Here Wendt is disagreeing fundamentally with the central thesis of a leading positivist theorist of international relations, Kenneth Waltz. The anarchical condition between sovereign states is not a given in the same way that the geographical environment between them is given in the nature of things. Rather, it is something they have constructed between themselves. States construct the international anarchy that defines their relations.

There are some important implications that follow from the constructivist argument. If 'anarchy is what states make of it' the existing international system is a historical creation. And if states—i.e., statespeople—change their conceptions of who they are, what their interests are, what their concerns are, then the situation will change accordingly because the situation is nothing more or less than what they think up, decide and do. States could decide, for example, to reduce their sovereignty or even to give up their sovereignty. If that happened there would no longer be an international anarchy as we know it. Instead, there would be a brave new, non-anarchical world. Moreover, if world politics is a social or historical construction it will be impossible to predict what international relations will be like in the future, especially the more distant future. By that time we might have constructed something entirely different that cannot be foreseen or predicted. That historical flux of international human activity means that a predictive social science of international relations cannot be achieved.

But that is not a conclusion that many constructivists are satisfied with. They see themselves as involved in building a scientific discipline of international relations in the positivist sense: a set of propositions that can in principle be refuted, making it possible for the advancement of their science. They do not see themselves as accepting the more modest goals of a humanistic science of international relations. So constructivists usually want to remain within the positivist social science project while rejecting the notion of an external, objective reality. What they accept is an inter-subjective reality: the claim that between human agents, including those agents who act on behalf of states, there can be mutual understanding, shared ideas, jointly held practices, and common rules that acquire a social standing that is independent of any of those agents.

[20] A. Wendt, 'Anarchy is what States Make of it', *International Organization*, 46 (1992), 394–419.
[21] Ibid. 395.

Constructivists believe that a positivist social science of international relations can be built upon an analysis of that inter-subjective reality. In emphasizing inter-subjectivity rather than objectivity their approach is not positivist, but in emphasizing scientific explanation rather than historical understanding it is positivist.

The methodological problem with constructivism emerges at this point: it has a split personality.[22] Constructivists seek to reconcile two categorically different conceptions of human relations, humans as creators of a world they build for themselves and humans as creatures of the world in which they find themselves. These conceptions are not reconcilable. To try to reconcile them is like trying to reconcile the belief that the world is round with the belief that it is flat. If we want to become acquainted with the world of international relations in scholarly terms that capture with accuracy and some insight its human character and *modus operandi*, we shall have to give up on the positivist social science project and return to the classical humanist approach.

3. Humanism

The historical and institutional human sciences should be firmly distinguished from the positivist and post-positivist social sciences. Positivists abandoned the classical humanist approach in the name of science understood as an objective empirical inquiry: natural science. Critical theorists and postmodernists refused to return to the classical approach in the name of either political emancipation or anti-rationalism: relativism. Constructivists are uncomfortable because the human sciences do not claim to be science in the positivist sense of the term. The metaphysical problem facing the post-positivists emerges at this point: they are the unacknowledged children of the positivists. Their thought is formed and distorted by their rebellion against their parents.

As indicated, a major aim of this study is to renovate and refurbish the classical humanist approach in the area of international studies to bring it fully up to date to address some of the most important normative questions of contemporary world politics. The discussion here is merely by way of a brief introduction. It will be amplified and expounded upon throughout the rest of the book. In many quarters of political science, particularly the USA, the classical approach is either forgotten or is known only in a cursory way. Unfortunately, political scientists—and no doubt scholars of most other subjects—tend to forget as much and as rapidly as they learn, and they forget what is important as well as what is not important. American political scientists, and many others, suffer from a kind of amnesia regarding the history of their discipline before the behavioural revolution. They have largely forgotten their classical tradition.

[22] For a rejection of this claim see A. Wendt, 'On Constitution and Causation in International Relations', *Review of International Studies*, (Dec. 1998), 101–17.

The classical approach is important because it contains the accumulated insights and reflections of many generations of commentators on the subject of human relations. It is a body of knowledge with a long history. In international relations it dates back to the writings of the ancient Greek historian Thucydides which were composed some 2,400 years ago. But it is also as contemporary as the writings of Martin Wight and Hedley Bull which were composed in the mid- and late-twentieth century. I shall be concerned mainly with the classical humanist approach as carried on by recent scholarship.

What, then, is the classical humanist approach? It is the mode of scholarship that prevailed in political science prior to the behavioural revolution and was largely based on historical analysis, legal–institutional scholarship, and political thought. Traditional political science was part of 'civil science', the core of which was the 'humanist school of jurisprudence' which examined the norms of human societies from a historical and comparative perspective.[23] Civil science was centrally preoccupied with discerning and understanding human conduct, its character, and its *modus operandi*, in various spheres of political life, especially that of law and the state.[24] The civil scientists fashioned and operated with concepts which captured the normative core of social roles (*status, dignitas*, etc.), of social relations (*contractus, obligatio*, etc.), of social groupings or associations (*civitas, societas, universitas*, etc.), and of relations of authority and power (*jurisdictio, dominium, potestas, imperium*, etc.).[25] The Latin terminology is not important; the ideas are. The ideas seek to grasp basic distinctions in human conduct. But the Latin is useful for capturing and carrying those ideas. Two of these ideas have a large role in this study: *societas* and *universitas*. They are defined in the next section.

The humanists were comprehensive or holistic in their approach to the study of human relations. They did not see themselves as narrow specialists. They did not understand the human sciences as technical subjects. They understood them as non-technical subjects. Political science was conceived as based on a combination of classical political theory, history, and law. Political theory was regarded as basic to all theoretical understanding of political subjects. That was because it was recognized that political theory was embedded in its subject: the rules and institutions of the sovereign state gave intimations of its political theory. Classical political theory was not a model or conceptual framework or hypothesis *about* political life. It was a disclosure *of* political life. Anyone who set out to contribute to classical political science would be expected to have a good grounding in political theory which was drawn from observations and reflections

---

[23] See Donald R. Kelley, *The Human Measure: Social Thought in the Western Legal Tradition* (Cambridge, Mass.: Harvard, 1990), 113–18.

[24] See Robert H. Jackson, 'Civil Science: Comparative Jurisprudence and Third World Governance', *Governance*, 1/4 (Oct. 1988), 380–414.

[25] Kelley, *Human Measure*, 118. An American classic of the genre is C. H. McIlwain, *The Growth of Political Thought in the West* (New York: Macmillan, 1932).

on political life by a long lineage of political theorists. Political theory was not a cloistered discipline—the way it became in the late twentieth century when many political theorists were preoccupied with scholastic debates on abstract topics far removed from ordinary political experience. Classical political theory was a generalist subject: it looked out upon the political world: it tried to comprehend the ways and workings of historical political worlds and their thought in academic terms.[26] The same could be said of the classical humanists' approach to the study of history and law.

The human sciences endeavored to interpret the living world of human relations with the aim of giving an academic account of it. Donald Kelley conveys the gist of the approach: 'Central to all these concepts, of course, was the theory of law, including the practice of "interpretation", which transformed law into "civil science"'.[27] Interpretation is also at the heart of the classical international society tradition: discerning significant international activities, such as diplomacy or war, diagnosing those activities to see what they are all about, construing their point or in other words clarifying their meaning and purpose, and spelling out that analysis in precise and well-suited language with a view to giving an academic account of it. The human sciences seek to render human life intelligible in academic terms. An important element of interpretation is translation: translating the ordinary idiom of human activity into academic language without losing any of the original meaning. In short, humanist scholars endeavor to make sense of human activity in different spheres of life; to theorize that activity; to comprehend its general character and *modus operandi*; and to delineate it with accuracy and clarity. Here, then, is a sophisticated approach to the study of international relations from which we stand to learn a great deal. I expand on these remarks in the next chapter.

As indicated, the classical humanist approach is pre-positivist rather than post-positivist: it does not reject science in the meaning of the human sciences; it only rejects the positivist conception of science modelled on the natural sciences. It seeks to give a scholarly interpretation of human activity—the affairs, the course or run of things, the current of events—in the international sphere of human relations. That is not something that can be modelled or explained: it cannot be pinned down by a scientific hypothesis or theory; it does not lend itself to 'models' or 'frameworks for analysis'. Human activity can only be discerned, construed, interpreted, and hopefully understood in a way that satisfies our curiosity about it. Classical international relations theories are academic accounts of the goings on, doings, dealings, and proceedings of statespeople and other people involved in world affairs. Theorizing involves reflecting on that political activity in the aim of drawing a larger picture of it. The classical approach does not employ 'data' or 'data banks'; it operates with evidence or facts thrown up or left behind by the activities of statespeople. The record of

[26] McIlwain, *Growth of Political Thought.*   [27] Kelley, *Human Measure*, 118.

what they say or do is what we are seeking to come to grips with in academic terms. Statespeople leave a trail of their activities, much of it a paper trail: speeches, policy statements, legislation, treaties, resolutions, agreements, etc. It is that synthetic evidence spawned by human activity that the classical approach tries to locate and to interpret in academic terms.

The human sciences seek to make academic sense of human activity by trying to get inside its mentality without surrendering to the beliefs, values and prejudices of the people under study. They hold that normative inquiry can be descriptive as well as prescriptive and that academic interpretation of norms can be carried out with a fair measure of detachment—that is, scholarly integrity. 'Detachment' is not value neutrality. Nor is it scientific objectivity. Rather, it means being aware of our moral and political premises, being frank about them, and holding them firmly in check.[28] This study is not free of value judgements. But it is more concerned with making academic sense of the basic norms of world politics than it is with judging them or defending them or criticizing them. That task is left by and large to the final two chapters. The main international norms and values that I shall be scrutinizing and ultimately defending are the mainstays of a pluralist and anti-paternalist society of independent states: sovereignty, self-determination, territorial integrity, non-intervention. They are at the institutional heart of international relations historically, and they call for a normative inquiry of a kind that the classical approach seeks to provide.

In short, the classical approach is not divorced from the world of human affairs; it is wedded to it. The humanist scholar can make sense of the world of human affairs because he or she is part of it. The fact that the scholar is living in the world is what makes the world intelligible. Humanist scholarship always builds on ordinary experience. The best of classical humanist scholarship is wise in the ways of the world: it is worldly.

Classics for Studying International Society

Every academic book is, in a manner of speaking, an intellectual autobiography. An intimation of the ideas contained in this study first began to take shape in my mind when I was a doctoral student at the University of California at Berkeley in the 1960s. That was a time when behaviouralism and other versions of social science positivism were invading and conquering American political science. Even though it was never completely defeated on the academic field of battle and it continued to wage a rearguard campaign, classical political science went into a decline in North America from which it has not yet recovered. I was never persuaded by positivism because it seemed to overlook or ignore or fail to

---

[28] That view is held by some political behaviouralists. See Easton, *Political System*, 225.

comprehend or misconstrue the most important questions: value questions, normative questions. I was determined to stay with the pre-positivist approach of historical, institutional and philosophical analysis which seemed to offer a broader and deeper understanding of politics as a human activity *par excellence*.

I started to read some classics of the human sciences and came across a brilliant study by one of the master social historians of the nineteenth century which captured political life in what for me was and still is a remarkably insightful and intellectually satisfying way. In his magisterial work *The Civilization of the Renaissance in Italy* Jacob Burckhardt wrote of 'the state as a work of art' and he wrote of foreign policy and even war as works of art too.[29] He meant that these human activities were the products of 'reflection and calculation' which were part of 'a great intellectual process' involving art, architecture, science, religion, private life, and much else besides. He was of course referring to the transformation of medieval Europe into modern Europe via the Renaissance, the beating heart of which was located in northern and central Italy in the fifteenth century. That revolutionary change, together with the equally important Protestant Reformation which followed closely on its heels, are at the root of the Westphalian turn towards modern international politics. When I look back I realize that I have spent much of my academic life trying to grasp the deeper significance of Burckhardt's insights.

Garrett Mattingly's unrivalled study of *Renaissance Diplomacy* picks up some of the threads of Burckhardt's arguments and provides a fascinating account of the revolutionary transition from medieval to modern in that special sphere of political life that lies beyond the domestic jurisdiction of the state and specifically involves foreign policy, diplomacy, and the law of nations. The final sentences of Mattingly's book can serve as an opening to my own:

> In the same century in which they lost their last chance to unify their society around the traditions of Latin Christendom, Europeans began their unique mission . . . they began to unite in one society the peoples of the globe. The next significant effort to achieve the rule of law among nations could not confine itself to the heirs of a single tradition. It would have to embrace mankind.[30]

The influence of Mattingly will be evident in many of the chapters which follow.

While most American political scientists were marrying and moving in with positivist social science many of their British contemporaries remained faithful to the classical approach. That orientation to international relations scholarship was not only kept alive but was broadened and deepened by the writings of Martin Wight, Hedley Bull, and John Vincent.[31] My introduction to Martin

---

[29] Jacob Burckhardt, *The Civilization of the Renaissance in Italy* (New York: Harper & Row, 1958).

[30] G. Mattingly, *Renaissance Diplomacy* (New York: Dover, 1988), 256.

[31] Martin Wight, *Power Politics*, 2nd edn., ed. Hedley Bull and Carsten Holbraad (Harmondsworth: Penguin Books, 1986); Martin Wight, *Systems of States*, ed. Hedley Bull (London:

Wight was the second edition of his book *Power Politics*, which I discovered quite by accident in a university bookshop in 1979. I then came across *Diplomatic Investigations*, which is a collection of essays on international society edited by Herbert Butterfield and Martin Wight that includes Wight's masterful essay 'Western Values in International Relations'.[32] That essay is a major source for this study. I later read Wight's *Systems of States* which contains many of the core historical and theoretical ideas of the classical international society approach. One should also mention Martin Wight's posthumous *International Theory: The Three Traditions*, based on lectures he delivered at the London School of Economics and Political Science in the 1950s. In 1985 I met John Vincent at a British International Studies Association Conference and shortly afterwards began to read his work, most notably *Nonintervention and International Order* and *Human Rights and International Relations*.[33]

But the book that did most to establish the high academic credentials of the English school is without doubt Hedley Bull's *The Anarchical Society* which was published in 1977. I heard about it from a colleague not long afterwards. It quickly and correctly established itself as the basic text of the classical international society approach. It presents most of the important arguments of that approach and it manages to do it with greater clarity of argument, precision of writing, and depth of analysis than any other major work of the tradition. It has been the definitive statement of the tradition since it was published.

Martin Wight, Hedley Bull, and John Vincent share to a remarkable degree a common intellectual perspective and sensibility in trying to grasp the human dimensions and problems of international relations. That is not surprising in so far as Bull was at one time a junior colleague of Wight at the London School of Economics and Political Science, and Vincent was at another time a graduate student of Bull at the Australian National University. That gives their work exceptional unity of theme and purpose. All three authors discern similar voices in the political conversation of humankind and they weave them into parallel and mutually reinforcing accounts of international relations. A voice in this context is a distinctive and coherent expression of certain values and beliefs concerning world politics: a normative perspective. Taken together, they disclose a strong family resemblance, what is often referred to as a school of international theory: the 'English School'. Wight explored the voices of realism, rationalism, and revolutionism and their historical dialogue. Bull examined the interaction of order and justice as fundamental values of world politics. Vincent explored the

Leicester University Press, 1977); Martin Wight, *International Theory: The Three Traditions* (Leicester and London: Leicester University Press for the RIIA, 1991). Hedley Bull, *The Anarchical Society*, 2nd edn. (London: Macmillan, 1995). Also see Tim Dunne, *Inventing International Society: A History of the English School* (London: Macmillan, 1998).

[32] H. Butterfield and M. Wight (eds.), *Diplomatic Investigations* (London: Allen & Unwin, 1966).

[33] R. J. Vincent, *Non-intervention and International Order* (Princeton: Princeton University Press, 1974); R. J. Vincent, *Human Rights and International Relations* (Cambridge: Cambridge University Press, 1986).

interplay between pluralist norms and solidarist norms in modern international society. Wight, Bull, and Vincent consider international studies to be a non-technical, humanist inquiry into a distinctive set of questions, the most important of which are normative at their core. Is there an international society? What is the institutional embodiment of that society? What are the core values upheld by a society of states? What is the main justification of state sovereignty? Is there a community of humankind? How can human rights fit into a world of sovereign states? Is there a morality of the global commons? Responses to these questions, and others like them, are presented in the chapters below.

This book also reflects other intellectual influences which stem from having spent many years teaching political theory and international ethics. In the 1970s I came across the 'civil philosophy' of Michael Oakeshott as set out in his books *Rationalism in Politics* and *On Human Conduct*.[34] Oakeshott referred to his approach as a civil theory: a theory of civility, civil association, and the civil condition in human conduct. In trying to discern the human character of international society I found Oakeshott's distinction between *societas* and *universitas* particularly useful: human relations characterized by coexistence of independent selves who conduct themselves by freely observing common standards of conduct ('morality as the art of mutual accommodation') versus human relations characterized by collective enterprise between mutually dependent partners, or collaborators, in the pursuit of a conjoint purpose ('the morality of the common good').[35] Oakeshott also made it plain that the 'green world' of practice came before the 'grey world' of theory: that is, the professor is hostage to the politician, rather than his or her master.[36] Both of these distinctions will be evident throughout this book.

Two other influential political theorists are R. G. Collingwood and Isaiah Berlin. Collingwood's *The Idea of History* helped me to understand the subject-matter of history as thought and ideas, an entirely human world of the past.[37] His *The New Leviathan* clarified the pivotal role of civility in human relations on a world-wide scale: civility was a normative basis upon which to carry on international human activity.[38] Finally, there is a book, only one of many by the same author, whose composition attracts the eye of the reader—to borrow a phrase from Martin Wight—'like Roman masonry in a London suburb': Isaiah Berlin's *The Crooked Timber of Humanity*. Berlin's writings probe more deeply than those of any other commentator that I have read the meaning and significance of normative pluralism in modern political life.[39]

In carrying out this study I have also been influenced by famous political and legal theorists of the past—for example, Machiavelli, Grotius, Hobbes, Kant—

---

[34] M. Oakeshott, *Rationalism in Politics*, (Indianapolis: Liberty Press, 1991); M. Oakeshott, *On Human Conduct* (Oxford: Clarendon Press, 1975).

[35] Oakeshott, *Rationalism in Politics*, 297.   [36] Ibid. 184–218.

[37] Collingwood, *Idea of History*.

[38] R. G. Collingwood, *The New Leviathan* (New York: Crowell, 1971).

[39] Isaiah Berlin, *The Crooked Timber of Humanity* (New York: Vintage Books, 1992).

whose ideas and arguments are at the heart of the classical tradition. It should be emphasized, however, that this study is not a review of academic theories of international ethics. Much less is it a treatise on moral philosophy. I am entirely content to leave that to the moral philosophers. But this book draws on political theory and moral philosophy in the same way that classical political science draws on them, and the way that Martin Wight or Hedley Bull drew upon those disciplines: as bodies of knowledge for understanding diplomacy, war, intervention, and other important international human activities.

These publications fundamentally altered my understanding not only of international relations but of politics more generally. I have been particularly inspired by Hedley Bull's magisterial study and in writing my book I have pointedly tried to go beyond his. I have tried to do that in three ways. First, I directly and explicitly investigate international relations as a branch of human relations to counter the positivist view of the subject outlined above. I have also been moved to do that because the human foundations of international relations are only implicit in the work of Bull. To clarify and illuminate those foundations I have resorted to the political theory of human conduct presented in the above-noted works of Michael Oakeshott, R. G. Collingwood, and Isaiah Berlin. My study attempts to bring the international society scholars and the political theorists of human conduct together in one extended academic family. Second, I have specifically focused on the ethics of statecraft, which is not explored systematically by Bull. I have tried to do that by linking the ethics of statecraft to the morality of international society. Third, I have investigated those subjects in the living context of important international episodes that have occurred since the fall of the Berlin Wall in 1989, which Bull did not live to witness. The point here is to emphasize that norms and values are part and parcel of very important international events. I have tried to make a contribution to our understanding of the post-cold-war world. In proceeding in this way it is my hope that this work can transport the classical approach well into the twenty-first century.

Bringing Values back into View

As indicated, a strong inclination of mainstream international relations scholarship during the cold war, especially in the USA, was the marginalization of normative inquiry. Positivism was in the saddle in political science. International ethics for several decades was a sideshow in the overall scholarly enterprise. Ironically, and very interestingly, some outstanding positivist studies of international relations during that era nevertheless contain underlying normative assumptions and concerns. In other words, even though positivist theorists of international relations usually do not expressly engage in normative inquiry as such, their arguments often carry important implications of a normative kind. There is a normative iceberg lurking just beneath the surface. Positivist social science theories, however, provide no way of getting beneath the surface and exploring those underlying foundations of the subject. That is evident from a brief analysis of the arguments of two leading international relations theorists of the positivist era: Kenneth Waltz and Thomas Schelling.

Waltz's *Theory of International Politics* professes to be a 'theory' not in the classical political theory sense of moral and legal theory—but in the philosophy of science meaning of the word: scientific explanation.[40] In his book he presents a structural analysis which purports to be purely explanatory and to exclude normative issues. But even a cursory review indicates that normative concepts and categories are intrinsic to his argument, not at its extremities but at its foundations. That argument rests upon a fundamental postulate which structures Waltz's entire analysis: 'International systems are decentralized and anarchic'.[41] International anarchy consists in the interactions of like units, namely sovereign states. In Waltz's words: 'To say that a state is sovereign means that it decides for itself how it will cope with its internal and external problems.'[42] Thus state sovereignty means being in a position to decide, a condition which is usually signified by the term independence: sovereign states are postulated as being independent of other sovereign states. But what is independence? Waltz says that each state is formally 'the equal of all the others. None is entitled to command; none is required to obey'.[43] I believe that is an accurate characterization of state sovereignty.

But to argue in that way is to acknowledge that the relations of states are based, in the most fundamental or constitutive sense, on a procedural norm. Just beneath the surface of Waltz's text, and occasionally on the surface too, there is a recognition of the moral and legal framework of international politics. For to say that independence is an 'entitlement' is to take notice of a norm which is acknowledged: in this case the norm of 'equal' state sovereignty. For Waltz, all states are equal only in a formal-legal sense; they are unequal, often profoundly so, in a substantive sense. That, too, is an accurate portrait of international reality. But it means that a norm of state equality exists which all states without exception, and despite their frequently profound substantive inequalities, are expected to observe in their relations with each other. At this point we are into a normative inquiry, and correctly so, because these are fundamental procedural features of international relations as a norm-based human activity.

Formal-legal equality of states is a constitutive norm of contemporary international society: it is something that all statespeople are bound to acknowledge and respect. That is different from the substantive inequality of states, which is an inherent reality that statespeople would be wise to take into account if they

[40] Kenneth Waltz, *Theory of International Politics* (New York: McGraw-Hill, 1979), 1.
[41] Ibid. 88.   [42] Ibid. 96.   [43] Ibid. 88.

hope to succeed in their relations with each other but is not something that they are bound to recognize and respect. Much the same can be said of the independence of states which is not the same as the relative freedom of great powers and the relative constraints on small powers. Independence is not the same as autonomy, which is a substantive condition or relation. Independence is a formal or constitutional condition of the states system. Both the norm of equality and the norm of independence are clearly and explicitly recognized *as norms* in international practice. Both are written into contemporary international law. Waltz's conception is entirely consistent with that. He presupposes the constitution of contemporary world politics.

The distinctive awkwardness of his international relations theory emerges at this point: it is presented as a positivist social scientific account of international politics; but it cannot avoid employing what are inherently normative concepts and categories and cannot avoid making what are implicitly normative assumptions and indeed resting its entire case on normative foundations. Thus, although Waltz makes no explicit reference to ethics, his subtext is profoundly normative. But wanting to couch his theory in philosophy of science terms he is unwilling, or unable, to address fundamental normative questions raised by his major premiss that states are formally equal and independent political bodies: for example, the recognition of states, national security as a value, the crime of aggression, the right of self-defence, the moral doctrine of non-intervention, the ethical standing of human rights, and related core normative topics that characterize international relations as a human activity. The normative assumptions, implications, and consequences of world politics organized on the basis of state sovereignty are not investigated. His positivist social science theory provides no assistance in addressing such questions because it cannot conceive of international relations as a branch of human relations with distinctive normative problems and its own ethics.

Thomas Schelling's *The Strategy of Conflict* also presupposes values and carries moral implications.[44] Schelling comes closer than Waltz to conceiving of international relations as a branch of human relations: his analysis clearly is that of a human activity and not a structural process, as in the case of Waltz. But international human activity is explicitly treated by Schelling as exclusively instrumental in character. Strategy is assumed to be reducible to instrumental maxims derived from game theoretic reasoning.

A central concept that Schelling employs is that of a 'threat': his analysis concerns how statespeople can deal rationally with the threat and dangers of nuclear war. But the concept of threat has a definite normative drift, namely the value at stake.[45] What is that value? If it is a personal threat, the value at stake is the security and well-being of the person at risk. Personal security is a generally recognized

[44] Thomas C. Schelling, *The Strategy of Conflict* (Cambridge, Mass.: Harvard University Press, 1980).

[45] Ibid. 123–31.

value of fundamental importance; for Hobbes it is a basic 'right of nature'.[46] If it is an international threat, the value at stake is the security of the state or nation at risk. National security is also a generally recognized value of fundamental importance. But the value in this case is not narrowly self-regarding and self-interested, as when we worry only about our own personal safety. On the contrary, it is other-regarding, publicly interested, and indeed public-spirited for it involves the security and well-being of many other people besides ourselves: usually large populations organized as nation-states and consisting almost entirely of people unknown to us. To defend their security is an 'inherent right' of sovereign states, according to the UN charter. In short, national security is a fundamental political value.

Schelling is fully aware that rational behaviour is motivated not only by a conscious calculation of advantages but also by 'an explicit and internally consistent value system'.[47] But the character of values and the role of value systems are not explicitly investigated by Schelling beyond making it clear that behaviour is related to values, such as the national interest for example. The *modus operandi* of the specific values involved in nuclear strategy—peace, security, survival, and so forth—is not uncovered by Schelling's analysis. Values are taken as given and treated instrumentally; their normative aspects and implications are not investigated.

For Schelling the activity of statecraft is exclusively and technically instrumental and thus free from moral choice. He identifies and dissects with sharp insight various mechanisms, stratagems and moves which, if followed by the principal actors, could generate collaboration and avoid disaster in a conflict-ridden world of nuclear-armed superpowers. In the stratagem of drawing nuclear rivals into collaboration so as to reduce the risks and dangers of nuclear war there are intimations of normative questions: as indicated, risk and danger are value-laden concerns. However, Schelling's analysis does not probe the ethics of statecraft which are involved in such a laudable endeavour; it merely presupposes them without comment. The normative aspects of foreign policy, and in this case the justifications of intelligent strategy in a dangerous world of nuclear armed superpowers, are intimated by his argument but largely hidden beneath the surface of his text.

To bring them to the surface we can ask a couple of questions. Why should foreign policy-makers behave in the sophisticated way that Schelling recommends? What is the point of knowing and mastering the collaborative stratagems he sets forth? The only reason, it seems to me, is because foreign policy-makers are assumed to be enlightened human beings, and not monsters, who carry heavy responsibilities for safeguarding fundamental human values: for example, the security and well-being of the nations on whose behalf they are

---

[46] Thomas Hobbes, *Leviathan*, ed. Michael Oakeshott (Oxford: Blackwell, 1946), 85.

[47] Schelling, *Strategy of Conflict*, 4.

working, and that of innocent third parties who could also be at risk. But these responsibilities are nowhere discussed explicitly and thus the reader could think, and most readers perhaps do think, that the subject about which they are reading is a technical-instrumental subject, a scientific subject, and not a human and ethical subject, which at base it is. What Schelling does not furnish is the underlying ethics of statecraft which would make his analysis of strategy ultimately intelligible in terms of fundamental human values, such as the values of security and peace which in a nuclear age are simultaneously personal, national, and international concerns. If he had done that we would appreciate the moral significance of the human activity of nuclear strategy.

Behind the many mechanisms, stratagems, and moves that Schelling unveils in his unrivalled and profoundly insightful analysis of the non-zero-sum game of international conflict is an unacknowledged political ethic: namely that nation-states, in his case the USA, are public repositories of a way of life that is cherished by millions of inhabitants and worthy of the greatest concern and care in the conduct of foreign policy. In other words, although Schelling is furnishing a scientific analysis based on game theoretic reasoning, whether he realizes it or not his profoundly important book is intimating a sophisticated ethics of statecraft which rests on prudence as a cardinal political virtue but takes the instrumental and technical aspects of prudential statecraft in a nuclear age further than any previous writer on the subject. But unfortunately that fundamental subject is not investigated by Schelling.

As indicated in Chapter 1 and spelt out at greater length in later chapters, prudence and other political virtues are inherently normative categories: standards of conduct for preserving and promoting what is of value and indeed of extreme importance not only to ourselves but to others who will be affected by what we do or fail to do. Prudence is a pivotal ethical requirement in the responsible exercise of power and particularly great power, as most classical realist and just-war theorists make plain. What Schelling is taking for granted is nothing more or less than the heart of traditional international ethics which invisibly underpins his entire analysis. It is unfortunate that his book—like that of Kenneth Waltz and other positivist social science analyses of international relations—provides hardly more than a tantalizing glimpse of that vital underlying subject.

It is unfortunate in two ways. First, no matter how brilliant their analyses might be in other respects, they cannot come to grips with the moral dimension of international relations which practitioners wrestle with. They cannot supply answers to the following questions. What is at stake? What is the fundamental human point of the structures and stratagems they analyse? They do not ask such questions let alone answer them. Indeed, they leave the impression that asking them would be unhelpful to the research enterprise and would be a sign of intellectual weakness. I believe the reverse proposition is more accurate: by avoiding such questions their analyses fail to probe the normative core of the subjects they are theorizing. They cannot therefore provide a rounded empirical understanding of a subject which is constitutively normative in practice. That is a heavy price to pay for scientific respectability. Second, by conveying their argument in the language of positivist social science they create the impression that their analyses are value-free, when in actuality they rest on unstated and, presumably, unexamined normative premises. In other words, their analyses are laden with values but they are not made explicit and they cannot readily be scrutinized with a view to assessing their importance. That should be recognized for what it is: an unnecessary and thus regrettable deficiency.

Here, then, are arguably the two best books on positivist international relations theory of the past forty years, written by two outstanding American scholars. For what they attempt, they are remarkable achievements. The problem is they do not come to grips with the fully human dimension of the subject they are dealing with. They leave out the core of the subject. Neither of them even begins to analyse, let alone to examine at length, the normative dimension of international relations. If Waltz and Schelling had included an explicit analysis of their normative premises and the values at stake they would have sacrificed the strictly positivist conception of their projects. But they would have gained a greater depth of analysis more in tune with the normative realities of human activity in the international sphere. Their theories would have been deeper and truer to international human experience. These same criticisms can be applied to positivist international relations theory generally. There are almost countless positivist analyses of international relations that have been published in the past half century that suffer from the same fundamental shortcomings.

To sum up: we must get beyond social science positivism because it limits unduly the questions we can ask about international relations and thus the answers we come up with and the theories we construct. Its cumulative overall effect is the impoverishment of our discipline.

The Window-Dressing Critique

The claim that international politics is a human activity that involves norms and values is often countered by what is known as the window-dressing critique. This is usually presented as a riposte to which there supposedly is no effective response. According to that objection, the normative sphere is merely rhetorical camouflage to cover up, or dress up, or render palatable by clever civilized rhetoric, the hard and sometimes brutal realities of power and narrow self-interest in world politics. Thus, when statespeople claim to be acting out of concern for international peace or human rights or world prosperity or the global environment or any other important value it is only to mask their real intent and deceive others. In short, norms are a convenient and commonplace way of obscuring selfish or ulterior motives and actions in international relations. This is a favourite refrain of those who hold a deeply suspicious view of international political activity, whether hard-bitten journalists who are cynical about the possibility of international ethics, or politically motivated ideologues who are seeking to discredit states and statespeople, or bitterly disappointed former idealists whose fondest hopes for humankind have been crushed by such people.

This critique has a curious implication: namely that the ethics of statecraft fails to recognize and make provision for selfish motives and other human deficiencies and shortcomings. The reality is exactly the opposite. The classical ethics of world politics—for example, classical realism or the just-war tradition—is fully attuned not only to the possibility but the historical actuality of such behaviour. Both traditions postulate the moral imperfection of humans and try to respond to it. They presuppose the possibility that statespeople are morally flawed like everybody else. That is what the ethics of statecraft is centrally concerned with. And that is why the classical approach operates with the moral notion of virtue and vice which can get at the responsible and irresponsible conduct of such people. This book can be read as an extended reply to the window-dressing critique and to cynicism about the reality and importance of international norms. But it is necessary at this point to make at least a preliminary specific response.

The window-dressing critique can be made at the level of both theory and practice. At the level of practice, the critics are saying that statespeople employ normative discourse and make normative claims in the attempt to deceive others who would perhaps object or stand in the way were their true intentions known. Normative discourse is actually an instrument of deception. Norms and values, as masks, are in the same logical category as manipulation. At the level of theory, the critics are saying that international relations scholars, such as myself, who take norms and values seriously and seek to give a scholarly account of them, are not only naïve—are themselves victims of the deception—but are also failing to get at the truth about international relations: that is, that it is devoid of morality. Normative inquiry into world politics is in the same logical category as lack of knowledge.

These are severe indictments. But they do not terminate the debate because there are some rather obvious replies to them both in theory and in practice. As regards practice, if normative discourse is so transparent, why do practitioners go to the trouble of making normative claims at all? If scholars—who are, so to speak, seated in the stadium some distance away from the field of play—can readily enough see through these deceptions by the players on the field and can penetrate the real intentions behind them, then presumably statespeople—who are those players in the middle of the action—can also see through them. Otherwise how would they manage to be in the tough game of international politics? But if the players perceived normative claims as merely window-dressing, presumably they would not make them for they would have no reason to do so.

Such claims would have no practical effect because everybody would recognize what was being attempted, everybody would see through them, and making them would thus be a pointless and indeed useless thing to do. There would be no moral pretensions. There would be no hypocrisy. And there would be no practical normative language of international politics either. There would be no use for it. World political discourse would be wholly instrumental.

Yet there is an elaborate normative discourse whose vocabulary is well-entrenched in foreign policy, diplomacy, international law, international organization, trade, finance, aid, and other historical and contemporary activities and practices of international relations. The endeavors by states at moral justification are recurrent, vigorous, and virtually universal. Even war and intervention—which are often portrayed as paradigmatic instrumental activities—are expressed and carried on by means of not only instrumental language but normative language also. It would be impossible to discuss either war or intervention in purely instrumental terms because profound values are at stake: peace, freedom, security, survival. And once such values are raised about our activities we have entered into a normative world.

Hedley Bull has made the point that it is impossible to understand war or to engage in war in a purely instrumental way: 'In any actual hostilities to which we can give the name "war", norms or rules, whether legal or otherwise, invariably play a part'.[48] The dreadful human activity of war raises some of the most profound problems of moral and legal justification. During the Gulf War (1990–1) Iraq went to a lot of trouble in trying to justify its invasion of Kuwait and the USA and other countries went to a lot of trouble in trying to justify their military response to it.[49] On any view of war as a human transaction it would be not only surprising but shocking if Iraq and the USA made no attempt to justify their actions in moral and legal terms. So the practical world of international politics does seem to take norms very seriously indeed. That some parts of the academic world do not is the puzzling thing.

As regards theory, what are the grounds for debunking academic open-mindedness concerning normative claims and counterclaims in international relations? One typical answer is the following: history provides ample and indeed abundant instances of deceptive conduct in international relations, such as lying and spying, which we must realistically take into account in our theories. That is undoubtedly so: lying is a fact of human behaviour. But lying is not only a fact: it is behaviour which must be justified one way or the other, or it must be condemned, or it must be condoned. Lying is based on a norm. It does not and cannot exist on its own. Lying is behaviour which has been negatively appraised

---

[48] Bull, *Anarchical Society*, 179.

[49] See the elaborate moral and legal arguments made by states and international organizations involved in the conflict recorded in E. Lauterpacht (ed.), *The Kuwait Crisis: Basic Documents* (Cambridge: Grotius Publications, 1991), and M. Weller (ed.), *Iraq and Kuwait: The Hostilities and their Aftermath* (Cambridge: Grotius Publications, 1993).

by reference to the standard of conduct of telling the truth. Much the same can be said of spying and other kinds of deceptive conduct. Lying and spying are prototypic international activities which no international relations theory worthy of the name could ignore but must endeavour to understand. The usual interpretation is to note that the national interest, or national security, or some other moral consideration of overriding importance justifies such behaviour. But that is a normative analysis.

Other criticisms which parallel the window-dressing critique can only be mentioned in passing. One is the claim that national leaders may genuinely believe they are acting in accordance with normative considerations and requirements, but the ground upon which they base their belief is erroneous and they are actually labouring under a kind of 'false-consciousness'.[50] Politicians, like everybody else except those special people who make such analyses, are manipulated by their belief systems which, in turn, are reflections of the power structures in which they are entrapped. That view of international relations is often associated with Marxist analysis, particularly critical theory. This book can be read as an extended rejoinder to views of politicians as, *by definition*, either cynical or deluded in their moral concerns. Some politicians may of course be cynics, and some may be naïve, but that is not because they are politicians. It is because they are human beings and, as such, are subject to the usual human shortcomings and human failings. The same can be said of some academics and, indeed, of certain members of any group one would care to name.

Another criticism is the assertion that state leaders provide justifications only because they are attentive to domestic public opinion and always have their eye on the next election. Ordinarily it would not be reasonable to expect democratic politicians to ignore domestic public opinion. They are constitutionally bound to their national publics. The democratic constitutions to which they are subject require them to listen to public opinion. They could only be expected to ignore public opinion if a fundamental value were at stake, such as national security, in which case political leaders would be expected to educate public opinion and in extreme circumstances possibly even to deceive the public, and not bow to it. Rather than view the obvious responsiveness of democratic politicians to public opinion as morally dubious behaviour, it would be better to understand it as an integral part of political ethics in democracies.

To sum up: something fundamental to international politics is involved in taking norms seriously, which is to say that something equally fundamental is lost if norms are overlooked, ignored, obscured, dismissed, or debunked by our analysis. That something is the core of the subject: its human dimension and the basic norms and values which are always at stake in human relations. If normative analysis is excluded from international relations scholarship, for what-

---

[50] The origins of this kind of analysis is K. Mannheim, *Ideology and Utopia* (London: Routledge, 1946).

ever reason, the result will be at best an incomplete or partial understanding of the subject and at worst a misleading caricature of it.

The Classical Approach and Social Science

As indicated, the classical approach conceives of international relations as a branch of human relations with its own distinctive normative issues. It sees those issues as an inherent feature of the subject which must be included in our academic inquiries if we are seeking to capture the subject in its entirety and its correct proportions. We cannot exclude such issues if we wish to be empirical in our understanding of the subject.[51]

As far as social science positivism is concerned, the classical approach sees it as resting on a category mistake.[52] A 'category mistake' is a mistake of assigning something to the wrong logical type, as when the notion of a human 'mind' is understood in the same physical terms of cause and effect that might be employed to understand the notion of a human 'body'—i.e., 'brain'. This fundamental distinction is captured by Michael Oakeshott in a delightful way by referring to the difference between a wink and a blink:

the movement of a human eyelid is a categorially [sic] ambiguous identity; it may be a wink or it may be a blink, a wink which is an exhibition of intelligence, a subscription to a 'practice' and has a reason, and a blink which is a component of a 'process' to be understood in terms of a 'law' or a 'cause'.

So when I detect the movement of an eyelid in a human face looking at me it is my hope that it is a wink, for a wink is an act of communication and it could be the beginning of an interesting story or even a delightful relationship. A blink is merely something that even my dog is capable of doing. It probably is fascinating only to eye surgeons or physiologists or anatomists.

According to the classical approach—to repeat an important point—the theorist of human affairs is a human being who can never divorce himself or herself completely from human relations: he or she is always *inside* the subject and seeks to *understand* it and *interpret* it by gaining insight into the mentality of the people involved and the circumstances in which they find themselves.[53] Being part of the subject—being human—is in fact the principal source of insight into human relations, including that branch we refer to as international relations, that anyone can have. We are able to get inside the subject of human relations to a

---

[51] The positivist distinction between empirical and normative in political science is misplaced: all human activity, including political activity, involves norms and values. That is what it means to be human.

[52] See G. Ryle, *The Concept of Mind* (Harmondsworth: Penguin Books, 1963), 20–4.

[53] Martin Hollis and Steve Smith, *Explaining and Understanding International Relations* (Clarendon: Oxford University Press, 1991).

depth and to an extent that we could never achieve in the study of packs of wolves.[54]

That means that the ideas people have about their relations are crucially important to understand. That applies as much to international relations as to any other sphere of human relations. It also means that interests, concerns, intentions, ambitions, calculations, miscalculations, desires, beliefs, hopes, fears, confidence, caution, doubt, uncertainty, confusion, and related dispositions and inclinations must be at the centre of normative inquiry into world politics because they are part and parcel of human activity in that sphere. As it happens, these are among the most significant and enduring features of international relations which go a long way toward characterizing the subject. We can fully grasp those features in our accounts of the subject. We can get into the subject via our human understanding. But our academic accounts cannot be objectively true in the positivist scientific meaning. We cannot pin human activity down to that extent. International relations scholarship can only be—as Hedley Bull once put it—'a scientifically imperfect procedure' which has at best a 'tentative and inclusive status'.[55] The target of Bull's criticism was the positivist social science theories of international relations of the latter half of the twentieth century which laid a claim to hard scientific knowledge that they did not and could not live up to. Any scholar who aspires to achieve a positivist social science of international relations is unrealistic if not utopian. Kenneth Waltz and Thomas Schelling are utopians in that sense.

The positivist project is unrealistic not merely because humans are complex and their behaviour is extremely difficult to capture in the scientific terms of confirming or refuting hypotheses. If it were only a question of complexity a science of human behaviour would remain a possibility. It would only require an adequate methodology and technology. Some social scientists seem to believe, rather naïvely, that computers will eventually make that possible. But it is more and indeed far more than a question of methodology. Human behaviour cannot be predicted scientifically because humans have minds, and because they can make up their minds and change their minds concerning the basic question of how they wish to live. They can be quite unpredictable in doing that. They have fertile imaginations. They keep on coming up with new ideas which they take seriously and employ to rearrange their individual and joint lives. There is a bedrock sense in which the study of human relations, including international relations, must in the final analysis be a study of minds. That means that political science must be a study of the ideas—political ideas—that human beings have come up with for conceiving and conducting their relations with each other over time and space. That also means the knowledge it arrives at can only be tentative and provisional.

[54] See Collingwood, *Idea of History*, 64–5.

[55] H. Bull, 'International Theory: The Case for a Classical Approach', in K. Knorr and J. N. Rosenau (eds.), *Contending Approaches to International Politics* (Princeton: Princeton University Press, 1969), 20.

The human mind cannot be understood by scientific analysis for it is not a thing, out there, that can be analysed as such. It can only be understood by human insight and communication: by an encounter of minds. In that sense we can speak of international relations as both a practical human experience and an academic subject. For the purposes of this study international relations is a subject as well as a discipline. As indicated, it is a humanist subject: a civil science rather than a natural science. It is a study of instrumental and noninstrumental considerations involved in human relations and activities (*nomos*); it is not a study of things or other natural occurrences (*physis*).[56] R. G. Collingwood puts this point well: 'the historian is not interested in the fact that men eat and sleep and make love and thus satisfy their natural appetites; but he is interested in the social customs which they create by their thought as a framework within which these appetites find satisfaction in ways sanctioned by convention and morality'.[57] In other words, although people have compulsions that derive from their animal nature (blinks), it is how they build and conduct their common and joint lives via the ideas they come up with that is far more interesting and important (winks).

People clearly need one another for they cannot survive and flourish in isolation from each other: in that sense human relations are a natural necessity of human existence. Aristotle thought that man 'is by nature a political animal' and that it was most natural for people to live in a state (*polis*) which was the institution that best provided for human flourishing, for the good life.[58] A *polis* for Aristotle is a political system that is free to make alliances with foreign powers on its own initiative; it is sovereign. That implies that interstate relations are natural and best too. But the political foundations of human relations are not a given to the extent that this may imply. Ancient Greeks may flourish in a *polis* or independent state but neither they nor anybody else is destined to live in such a political system. There are many different political arrangements, besides the ancient Greek *polis* or the modern state, that humans have come up with to pursue the good life—just as there are many different conceptions of such a life.

Human relations are not determined by human nature or God or anything else. They are a cultural and historical artefact. They are contrived by human beings and are thus improvised and changed from time to time and from place to place. Because they can change their minds and come up with new ideas about how they wish to live humans can also change the content and direction of their common and joint lives. People can decide up to a point who they shall be involved with and how they shall live together. They can abandon their parents or children, divorce their wives or husbands, and leave their country. They can change the institution of marriage. They can reform their constitution. They can even change their most cherished values: for example, Europeans over the

---

[56] See Kelley, *Human Measure*, esp. chs. 2 and 15.   [57] Collingwood, *Idea of History*, 216.
[58] Aristotle, *The Politics*, tr. Sinclair (Harmondsworth: Penguin Books, 1962), book 1, ch. 2.

course of several centuries came to value political freedom and equality more than Christian redemption and salvation. That value shift marked the big change from medieval to modern. Over distance and over time humans create not only a remarkable diversity of cultures and civilizations but also passages of history and historical change. And because it is based on new ideas, or novel combinations of old ideas, the course of human history cannot be predicted with anything resembling scientific accuracy. Where humans will be a thousand years from now is impossible to say. Where they were a thousand years ago is different from where they are today. Most of that has to do with the fact that many different generations of people are involved in a thousand years of human history and none of them is fatally bound to the ideas or beliefs or knowledge or routines or customs or habits of their predecessors.

Human beings live in time and over time. Their lives have a past, a present, and—hopefully—a future. International relations, like all other branches of human relations, is an historical activity and thus a changing subject.[59] Very little in human relations is fixed; very much is in flux. That does not mean that there are not human faculties and dispositions that disclose themselves over vast temporal and spatial distances: intelligence, stupidity, knowledge, ignorance, affection, love, hatred, co-operation, discord, trust, suspicion, respect, contempt, are but a few. These are more or less permanent features of human activity and human relations. Nor does it mean that the societies that men and women produce by their actions cannot stand virtually still for long periods, as, for example, medieval Europe. But any political mould can be broken: that is because humans can be discontent as well as content with the world in which they live; they can imagine a different and better life; they can adopt new values and abandon old ones; they can come up with innovative ideas and techniques about how to live together or apart, they can look back to the past, they can borrow from their neighbours, and they can endeavour, with greater or lesser success, to put those innovations or recollections or borrowings into effect at certain times or places. They might even be able to escape from earth someday. About all they cannot do is escape from their humanity. But they can still conceive of their humanity and display their humanity in very different ways.

In short, people are free within the constraints of human nature and whatever circumstances they find themselves in to decide whether or not to retain, modify, or abandon current practices, institutions, laws, rules, policies, or any other social arrangements they come up with. That imaginative and innovative and imitative faculty of men and women, and also their well-known fickleness, produces changing political worlds and thus a continually unfolding, recurrently surprising, and never fully predictable human history. Thus, even though human nature at least in this respect remains more or less the same, because human beings have minds and operate with ideas which they can and do change,

---

[59] Collingwood, *Idea of History*.

sometimes abruptly and without warning, there can be no fully reliable scientific guide to human behaviour.

That has important implications for the study of international relations. It means, for example, that there could be intersocietal relations without the idea—or the institutions which express the idea—of sovereign statehood as we have known it for the past three or four centuries. There have been such situations in the past. The Christian empire of medieval Europe (*respublica Christiana*) is one instance. The aboriginal societies of pre-colonial America and pre-colonial Africa are other instances. The Chinese imperial civilization is yet another instance.[60] In the future the international society that we have known for the past several centuries could disappear—if political life around the globe took on a decidedly different form and *modus operandi* in which independent political communities—i.e., sovereign states—become far less important. This is merely to repeat the main point that human relations are socially constituted and can thus have different shapes and substances at different times and places. That applies to the international sphere of human relations. That means that, just as each generation of statespeople by their actions helps to produce the international history of their own time with its distinctive possibilities and problems, so, too, will each generation of international relations scholars have something fresh to say about those activities.

The classical humanist approach rests on a fundamental conviction: that there is much to be learnt from the long history of observation and reflection on international relations and from the many theorists who have contributed to that tradition. Of course there will always be some theorists—but only a select few—who stand head and shoulders above the crowd: their theories speak to us from across the centuries. Thus we return time and again to Machiavelli or Grotius or Kant for insights into the problems of international relations not only in their time but also in our time. Yet even the greatest theorists can never have the final word on international relations or, indeed, on any other sphere of human relations. Contemporary theorists working in the classical tradition are not imprisoned by the thought of past thinkers. They are intellectually free to engage in their own independent thinking and to make their own theoretical contributions, drawing where they can on the insights of earlier thinkers. There is always something more to be said about human relations. That is because humans are restless creatures: they are continually seeking after something—often something different or even something new and unprecedented. And it is the business of scholars of human relations to discern whatever people are up to and to give a scholarly account of their activity. That is evident in the flourishing international relations scholarship of our own time, a few studies of which will in the future perhaps be regarded as classics.

---

[60] Other historical variations are reviewed in Adam Watson, *The Evolution of International Society* (London and New York: Routledge, 1992).

International studies is not a progressive scientific discipline in which new discoveries allow us to discard old theories at no cost to our knowledge. Martin Wight once observed that 'the political, diplomatic, legal and military writers who might loosely be termed "classical" have not been superseded as a result of recent developments in sociology and psychology'.[61] We could say the same about recent developments in economics or computer science. Each generation of thinkers must struggle anew with the problem of understanding human relations in the international sphere, learning what they can from past generations, paying close attention to the workings of the world in which they live, noticing how it is changing if it is changing at all, and from that inquiry trying to add something to our inherited stock of knowledge. That is not meant to imply that our knowledge of international relations is fixed and static; on the contrary, it is dynamic and evolving. Classical international relations scholarship is a body of knowledge that has been built up over time and is continually being augmented as each generation of scholars attempts to respond to each generation of practitioners.

Recovering the classical approach is not a return to the outmoded ideas and theories of the past. Rather, it is bringing our knowledge of those ideas and theories into contact and communication with our attempt to understand the present and the future. It involves acquainting ourselves with sophisticated and articulate ways of seeing and understanding international relations which have stood the test of time. It is not a current fashion that is in danger of disappearing tomorrow. Classical international relations scholars are the custodians of some very important theories of world politics which never become entirely obsolete and remain open to further elaboration and reformulation.[62] Yesterday's normative theories are challenged by today's or tomorrow's experiences and by new theories which attempt to capture those experiences in academic terms. But old theories, certainly the most outstanding, are rarely superseded entirely by new theories. Old theorists still manage to communicate from across the centuries, and we read Thucydides not merely out of antiquarian curiosity.

The classical approach to international relations involves being fully conversant with the best of the theories we inherit from our predecessors, taking them up in our own thinking and writing, making our contribution, and passing them on to anyone who may be interested in the hope that they will do the same and thereby keep the tradition alive. Abandoning those theories is cutting ourselves off from our intellectual roots. Preserving them and trying to improve upon them is our contribution to the larger civilization of which we and the traditions are a part.

---

[61] Quoted by Dunne, *Inventing International Society*, 122.

[62] See e.g. the essays in Terry Nardin and David Mapel (eds.), *Traditions of International Ethics* (Cambridge: Cambridge University Press, 1992).

4

The Classical Approach as a Craft Discipline

The chapter moves the discussion forward by spelling out what the classical approach basically involves as a research enterprise. It characterizes that enterprise as a craft discipline—and not a strictly scientific or technical subject. Along the way it investigates several closely related topics, including some erroneous conceptions of norms in social science, the tension between academic detachment and political engagement, the dialogical modality of international ethics, the ethics of practitioners, and the difference between practice and theory. The final section outlines the stages of research involved in carrying out a classical normative inquiry into world politics.

Normative Inquiry into World Politics

There are five things to notice or keep in mind when it comes to normative inquiry into world politics: (1) Political scientists operate with contradictory conceptions of norms: some conceptions cannot lead to normative inquiry in the meaning of that term in classical political science. (2) There is a fundamental difference between a detached and disinterested orientation to international scholarship and a politically activist orientation. (3) International ethics and political ethics generally have a dialogical modality: it is a world of human communication, of question and answer, of dialogue and discourse. (4) International ethics is created by statespeople: it is their normative equipment. (5) Theory is a hostage to practice and not the other way about, as is often assumed.

1. The Study of Norms

Misunderstanding of normative inquiry is produced by the ambiguous meaning of 'norm' in social science discourse. A good point of departure in any discussion of norms is a fundamental distinction between nature and artifice which is captured by Karl Popper in terms of 'natural laws'— 'i.e., a law that is factual and can be tested to see whether it is verifiable or falsifiable'—and 'normative laws'—'i.e., such rules as forbid or demand certain modes of conduct'.[1] Positivist

---

[1] K. R. Popper, *The Open Society and its Enemies, i. The Spell of Plato* (Princeton: Princeton University Press, 1971), 57. Michael Oakeshott refers to his political theory as 'civil theory'. *On*

social scientists could be characterized as those scholars who seek to *discover* patterns of social behaviour, conceived as an objective external reality, and to *explain* that reality in terms of falsifiable empirical propositions.[2] By contrast, classical humanists could be characterized as those scholars who seek to *discern, clarify, and elucidate* human conduct: human activity is assessed by reference to normative standards of some kind. There can be no positivist explanations of human conduct. That would confuse these basic categories. There can only be history, philosophy, jurisprudence, and related modes of understanding, interpreting, and elucidating its character and *modus operandi*.

One prominent meaning of norm is sociological: a norm is a conceived to be a pattern of behaviour: a norm is how people usually behave. That is a positivist concept of norm. In studying norms positivists are studying behaviour: norms are 'recurring patterns of behaviour.'[3] They are thus predictors of, or guides to, the way people behave. That is not the meaning of norm employed in this study. Here the meaning is moral and legal: as already indicated, a norm is a standard of conduct by which to judge the correctness, rightness or wrongness, the goodness and badness, of human activity. In studying norms in the classical way we are studying conduct and not merely behaviour. In studying behaviour scientifically one could study animal behaviour as well as human behaviour. But it is impossible to study animal conduct in any recognized meaning of the term. Conduct (and misconduct) is exclusively a human activity that is judged by a moral or legal standard of some kind.

Popper's distinction is a categorical distinction: each side is an entirely different mode of knowledge resting on contrasting metaphysical assumptions about the subject-matter. Political scientists, in conceptualizing norms, are sometimes prone to confuse, to mix up, to try to bridge, or to stretch this basic distinction. For example, it has been said that 'Norms may "guide" behaviour, they may "inspire" behaviour, they may "rationalize" or "justify" behaviour, they may express "mutual expectations" about behaviour, or they may be ignored.'[4] Here in one sentence are five different notions, some of them inconsistent and even contradictory notions, of what a norm is said to involve. To combine these different notions is to invite and perhaps commit a category mistake: the mistake, in this case, of considering norms as both causes of behaviour

Human Conduct (Oxford: Clarendon, 1975), 108–84. I have explored the idea of 'civil science' in 'Civil Science: Comparative Jurisprudence and Third World Governance', *Governance*, 1, 4 (Oct. 1988), pp. 380–414.

[2] The positivist approach to international theory is elegantly defended by Michael Nicholson, 'The Continued Significance of Positivism?' in S. Smith, K. Booth and M. Zalewski (eds.), *International Theory: Positivism and Beyond*, (Cambridge: Cambridge University Press, 1996), 128–45.

[3] See S. P. Huntington, 'Political Development and Political Decay,' *World Politics*, 17 (1965), 386–430. Also see Janice E. Thompson, 'Norms in International Relations,' *Group Tensions*, 23 (1993), 67–83.

[4] F. Kratochwil and J. G. Ruggie, 'International Organization: The State of the Art on the Art of the State', *International Organization*, 40 (1986), 767.

and standards of conduct. Some post-positivist analysis, particularly constructivism, is marked by such ambiguous conceptions of norms and normative study.

There is a distinction in positivist social science between empirical theory and
normative theory which indicates that norms could not be candidates for empirical inquiry. That clearly is a mistaken way of thinking. The human world is
significantly composed of norms, of standards of conduct. Those standards have
a historical existence: that is, past as well as present human worlds are constructed, in part, of norms and are even founded upon fundamental standards
of conduct which give those worlds some of their most distinctive characteristics. When historians study the conduct required of Christian kings during the
Middle Ages or that demanded of Roman governors during late antiquity or that
expected of member states of the United Nations today, they are engaged in an
empirical analysis of basic political norms. It would be impossible to make much
sense of Latin Christendom or the Roman Empire or present-day international
society or any other political world, past or present, without grasping the basic
norms that the people of the day use to justify or vindicate their political conduct.

But standards of conduct are not empirical in the same (external) sense that
perceptible objects are empirical. For example, we can see the car approaching
on the other side of the road. But we cannot see the rules of the road that are
supposed to govern the driver of that car. We can see the solid line painted down
the middle of the road. That line is of course a perceptible object. But it is our
understanding of what that line signifies when we see it that makes it an operative element of the driver's world. The line is a normative—that is, procedural—idea or concept. The rules of the road have an 'existence' in that human
understanding sense of the word. Norms exist socially and historically in the
sense that a certain set of people who are engaged in a specified activity are subject to them at that place and time. They exist as ongoing standards of human
conduct. Particular norms exist in the sense that people engaged in an activity—
such as driving a car—could reasonably be expected to have them in mind as
they act. When caught breaking a traffic rule it would not be a valid excuse to
say that we were unaware of the rule: the activity of driving presupposes a
knowledge of the rules. That operative notion of a norm also applies to the particular set of people—statespeople—who 'drive' the approximately 190 ships of
state. They are subject to standards of conduct which are the equivalent of
traffic regulations: international law, diplomatic practice, rules of international
organizations, etc. That latter meaning of 'empirical' as referring to norms that
'exist' at a certain place and time in regard to certain activities is the meaning
employed in the classical approach.

A related misunderstanding is the belief that normative inquiry is exclusively
prescriptive in character. I am here referring to a recommendatory or policy
analysis—rather than an interrogatory or expository analysis—which aims at giving advice or proposing a course of action to be followed: expert advice based

on technical knowledge. That is the normative posture of the consultant or adviser who is a quasi-practitioner or 'expert'. It is the usual outlook of foreign policy analysis. I have not completely refrained from making prescriptive statements in the chapters which follow and I do provide a defence of the pluralist and anti-paternalist ethics of world politics in the final chapter. But this book is not conceived as a prescriptive account or a policy analysis of world politics.

University scholars are not in a good position to offer policy advice because they lack the immediate experience and precise, up-to-date information which are crucial to successful policy-making. They are not where policy is made and they cannot therefore have a very good feel for the situation and its constraints and demands. Louis J. Halle, who spent a number of years in the US State Department during and after the Second World War and went on to become a distinguished professor at the Graduate Institute of International Studies in Geneva, started one of his books with the following comment:

Anyone who has experienced international relations in a foreign office, on the one hand, and has taught in the universities, on the other, knows that they are not the same thing. The difference . . . is fundamental . . . The immediate presumption, especially in an empirical society like our own, is that the difference ought not to exist. International relations as practiced in foreign offices is the real thing, and the real thing is what ought to be taught.[5]

Halle's point is that the practical world of foreign policy and the theoretical world of academic analysis are worlds apart and although 'the one ought not to be without some relevance to the other', to confuse them is fatal—for both parties.[6] Theory and practice are categorically different modes of understanding. This point is expanded below.

A further confusion is the equation of normative inquiry with moralizing in which the professor turns his or her lectern into a pulpit and gives a sermon rather than a lecture. A normative analyst is here represented as somebody who is standing in judgement and rendering judgement. In giving a sermon he or she is also indulging personal values and beliefs. That is the posture of the politically engaged intellectual as contrasted to the politically detached, or agnostic, academic. I cannot claim this book is free of personal bias. I obviously do not claim it is value-free. On the contrary, it is a study of what I consider to be the most important norms and values at stake in world politics at the present time. The project of this book is to locate those values and interrogate them with a view to understanding them in academic terms. What they are is a matter of observation, discernment, and judgement—hopefully a sceptical and detached judgement—on my part. It may be worth repeating a few remarks by Hedley Bull on this issue:

What is important in an academic inquiry into politics is not to exclude value-laden premises, but to subject these premises to investigation and criticism, to treat the rais-

---

[5] Louis J. Halle, *The Society of Man* (London: Chatto & Windus, 1965), 17.   [6] Ibid. 32.

ing of moral and political issues as part of the inquiry. I am no more capable than anyone else of being detached about a subject such as this. But I believe in the value of attempting to be detached or disinterested, and it is clear to me that some approaches to the study of world politics are more detached or disinterested than others.[7]

2. Detachment or Engagement?

The traditional academic study of norms is expository: it involves observation, discernment, interrogation, diagnosis, and explication. These are among the most important stages of classical normative inquiry, the goal of which is theoretical understanding. This book is an expository analysis of contemporary normative controversies in world politics of which many have deep historical roots. My purpose is exactly the same as Hedley Bull's purpose in writing *The Anarchical Society*: 'it is the purely intellectual one of inquiring into the subject and following the argument wherever it might lead.'[8]

Hedley Bull maintains that scholars should be as disinterested as possible in order to carry out scholarship that is properly academic and is not a vehicle of their own personal values or political ideology. He clarifies this important point in a defence of the classical approach:

The tradition of detached and disinterested study of politics is, I believe, a very delicate plant . . . Its survival depends on a form of commitment that is not political, but intellectual and academic: a commitment to inquiry as a distinct human activity, with its own morality and its own hierarchy of priorities, that is necessarily brought into conflict with the prevailing political values in any society.'[9]

I would add that it is not only prevailing values that our inquiries should be sceptical about. It is also reforming values, which perhaps pose even more of a challenge to disinterested academic studies because those values are, as a rule, more appealing to academics. What Bull is referring to is the ethics of scholarship, which is particularly important in political science for the obvious reason that partisanship in our field of study is always an immediate temptation. He sees partisanship as one of the big vices of academic life that scholars ought to do their best to resist. The endeavor to do that is for Bull a difficult academic challenge but it is also an essential responsibility of academic inquiry: it is at the heart of the ethics of scholarship.

Some scholars cannot accept Bull's definition of academic responsibility. They have set themselves the ambitious task of reforming international society theory to make it more relevant to improving human conditions on the planet. That is what critical theorists are endeavoring to do. They are often inclined to

---

[7] H. Bull, *The Anarchical Society*, 2nd edn. (London: Macmillan, 1995), xviii.

[8] Ibid., p. xv.

[9] H. Bull, 'New Directions in the Theory of International Relations', *International Studies* 14 (1975), 280–90.

see the state as Rousseau saw it: an institution that keeps people in chains.[10] They see the society of states in a similar way and they seek to employ their critical knowledge to reform international society.[11] In exposing the injustice of the current states system they are hoping to pave the way, in thought, toward progressive international change. In adopting that activist orientation they are rejecting the classical view of scholarship as based on the academic values of detachment and scepticism. The classical approach is criticized for not facing up to the value implications of its mode of inquiry, for accepting the historical subject it is seeking to understand. In other words, it is seen to underwrite the international *status quo*. Classical international society theorists are understood to be prejudiced in favour of past and present normative arrangements of world politics. They are criticized for not looking forward to the future in terms of the progressive change that might be possible and preferable to existing arrangements. In short, the classical approach hides a political conservatism.

Critical international society theory is an offshoot of neo–Marxist critical theory, as discussed in the previous chapter.[12] Critical theorists of international society are not content with discerning and elucidating international society as a distinctive historical arrangement of political life. They are seeking to change it if that is necessary to bring about a better life for the population of the planet. For such theorists a better life is one that is more conducive to human equality and human liberation across the globe. They are critical of modern international society, as they see it, for tolerating inequality on a global scale: allegedly by acquiescing to the political hegemony of the great powers, by ignoring the economic hegemony of world capitalism, and by upholding a doctrine of sovereignty and non-intervention which serves as a barrier to the emancipation of human beings trapped in countries with despotic governments and destitute economies. Emancipation conjures up an image of liberating slaves and thus it implies that the population of many countries are, in effect, enslaved by the current states system. In defining the role of the academic in these terms critical international society theorists are declaring, in the manner of Karl Marx, that the responsibility of knowledge workers is not merely to understand world politics. Their primary responsibility is to provide knowledge to change the world for the better. That rejection of agnosticism in favour of activism places them in a very different position from that of Martin Wight and Hedley Bull.

The question of the scholar's orientation to his or her subject is a fundamental question. How it is answered will shape the character of the resultant scholarship. Is it the business of academics to change the world for the better as they

[10] J.-J. Rousseau, *The Social Contract*, tr. Maurice Cranston (Harmondsworth: Penguin Books, 1968), 49.

[11] K. Booth, 'Security and Emancipation', *Review of International Studies*, 17 (Oct. 1991), 313–26. Also see K. Booth (ed.), *Statecraft and Security* (Cambridge: Cambridge University Press, 1998).

[12] See A. Linklater, *Beyond Realism and Marxism: Critical Theory and International Relations* (London: Macmillan, 1990).

define that value—keeping in mind that there could be different and even contrary definitions which could pit one academic activist against another and might
politicize academic life? Or is it the business of academics to render the subject
they are studying intelligible in proper academic terms? As indicated, it was the
view of Martin Wight and Hedley Bull that academics have the latter responsibility exclusively. That is a responsibility to understand international society in
the fullest, deepest, and most comprehensive way possible. For Wight that
involved the necessity of hearing not only the Grotian (rationalist) voice but also
the Machiavellian (realist) voice and the Kantian (revolutionist) voice as well. As
indicated previously, a voice is a distinctive and coherent expression of certain
values and beliefs concerning world politics. To listen to only one of these voices
is to close one's mind to the other two and thus to engage in a one-dimensional
and partial analysis. Wight regards modern international society as a discourse
between these three equally legitimate and equally important voices. For Bull it
meant studying justice as well as order in international society both of which he
saw as fundamental values whose place and role in world politics had to be understood as fully as possible. His major legacy is to have provided such an understanding. What is distinctive about Wight and Bull is their open-mindedness and
even-handedness in considering important values: their view is inclusive and
holistic.

The classical international society approach to normative inquiry is a pluralistic approach. By 'pluralistic' I mean that international human conduct, taken
as a whole, discloses divergent and even contradictory ideas, values, and beliefs
which must be recognized by our theories, and assimilated by them, if they are
to be faithful to reality. If scholars of international society seek to carry out an
empirical inquiry they must allow for the tensions and contradictions of human
experience in that sphere of human conduct: contingency as well as rationality,
intentions but also unintended consequences, ours as well as theirs, right and
might, prudence alongside procedure, humanity as well as sovereignty, desire
and duty, virtue and expediency, goals and rules, ideals and practices, and the
rest.[13]

To engage in classical international society scholarship is thus not a question
of selectively favouring either conservative values or revolutionary values. It is
not a question of favouring any value. It is not the role of academics to promote
values. That is the business of politicians and other political activists. Values are
of course the subject of normative inquiry. In the case of international society
there is a family of important values including peace, security, independence,
order, justice, human rights, environmental protection, and other values like
them, which it is the business of scholars to inquire into and try to comprehend
as fully as possible. Normative inquiry in the classical manner is the business of

---

[13] For more see R. Jackson, 'Pluralism in International Political Theory,' *Review of International
Studies*, 18 (July 1992), 271–81.

interrogating values and addressing value questions. That would include at some point, probably at the end of our inquiries, the assessment and justification of certain values if we were convinced that they were, on balance, of greater importance. We might end our inquiry by arriving at a view of the subject that gave moral priority to justice over order, or to human rights over sovereign rights, or more generally to solidarism over pluralism, or we might end by reversing that priority.

But to arrive at such a considered evaluation after a lengthy inquiry is not the same as starting our inquiries with a view to promoting our values. That latter orientation is not an academic orientation. It is a political orientation. If political scientists adopt such an orientation to their inquiries from the beginning they have, in effect, given up on academic study as a disinterested and detached study.[14] The role of the political scientist, as I understand it, is to try to give a plausible and coherent interpretation of the political practitioner's world: to construe that world in applicable academic terms in one's teaching and writing. Once that is achieved one's academic responsibility in that regard is at an end.

3. The Dialogical Modality of International Ethics

Normative questions, and questioning, are central to everyday political life and they are just as central to international politics as they are to domestic politics. Being in positions of responsibility and wielding substantial and sometimes awesome power, national leaders and other people who engage in international relations cannot escape from such questions—even if they fail or refuse to answer them. At almost every turn they are confronted by normative controversies of one kind or another to which they must respond in one way or another. Responding means justifying their policies and the actions and consequences that flow from those policies. Failing to respond or refusing to respond carries with it all the usual problems that result from treating with contempt the enquiries of others who have a legitimate concern about our policies or actions. To ask for a justification is to call for a reasonable answer that invokes something more than narrow self-interest: a normative and not merely an instrumental response to the question. Thus a very important feature of world politics as indeed of all politics is the dialogical interplay involved in justifying policy— in this case foreign policy.

Normative inquiry into world politics seeks to come to grips theoretically with questions such as the following. Which groups of people qualify for recognition as sovereign states? Are the international responsibilities of all states the same or do some states have special responsibilities? Are there any circumstances under which a sovereign state's right of self-defence could be legitimately

---

[14] See the insightful discussion in J. A. Schumpeter, 'The Sociology of the Intellectual,' in J. Sklar (ed.), *Political Theory and Ideology* (New York: Macmillan, 1966), 114–22.

infringed? Is international society responsible for providing personal security or is that an exclusively domestic responsibility of sovereign states? Is international society responsible for the governance of independent countries whose governments have for all intents and purposes ceased to exist? Must 'ethnic cleansing' always be condemned? Can the goal of spreading democracy around the world—in the perhaps reasonable hope of securing greater peace in the future—justify military intervention and occupation of a country in the present? Can we reasonably expect national leaders to put their own soldiers in danger to protect human rights in foreign countries? Is there any moral basis for justifying the use of force to change international boundaries or partition states? In short, these are some of the most difficult but also the most urgent questions that could be asked about contemporary world politics.

It is important to emphasize that these questions cannot be answered in the abstract and without regard to historical situations if we hope to be relevant. They are not purely philosophical questions. They do not address transcendental issues. They are historically situated. They arise in the evolving historical context of the modern sovereign state. Most of them are questions about the morality of the society of states and the ethics of statecraft that have arisen in recent decades and particularly since the end of the cold war. We cannot even attempt to answer these questions with academic conviction unless we are informed about the historical context.

When this book was being written these questions, and many others like them, were being asked repeatedly, insistently, and even with a sense of urgency. They were at the centre of international attention and concern. Many of them are addressed in the following chapters. Some of them have been raised time and again throughout the long history of international relations: for example, questions of war, peace, security, independence. But some of them are breaking new ground: for example, questions of humanitarian intervention. They were posed in reference to concrete events such as the Gulf War, the situation in the former Soviet Union, the wars in former Yugoslavia, the humanitarian crises in Somalia and Rwanda, the intervention in Haiti, and comparable episodes elsewhere: they are historically situated. Each one is a reminder that fundamental questions concerning world politics are questions about important values. None of the foregoing questions could be intelligibly posed, and much less responded to, if world politics were a purely instrumental activity as Schelling portrays it, or a structural process as Waltz makes it out to be.

4. An Ethics of Practitioners

Even though international ethics is as wide-ranging as the subject of world politics itself, at its core it concerns the moral choices of a very select category of people. It is the distinctive ethics of the men and women who wield the power of states: it is a construct of statespeople. It is the normative equipment required for carrying out their responsibilities. The answers to international normative questions, such as those listed above, are provided in the first instance and most significantly by the practitioners involved. An important task in the academic study of international ethics is to interrogate those answers with the aim of spelling out, clarifying, and scrutinizing the framework of justification disclosed by them. Most of this book is devoted to that academic task.

State sovereignty has long been and still is a towering feature on the landscape of world politics. The partitioning of the world into sovereign states, whatever we may think of it, affects profoundly the shape and substance of the practical ethics of world politics. The sovereign state is universally present on the planet and everywhere it defines not only the citizenship of people—i.e., their basic rights and obligations—but very often also their political identity and allegiance, perception of friend and foe, conception of security, source of welfare, and much else besides. There is no longer a territorial sphere beyond international society that is occupied by parallel civilizations.[15] The world is still divided among different civilizations but no civilization today is geographically outside the states system in the way that the Islamic world or the civilization of China in times past were outside the Christian world where the states system was originally located. Today everybody around the world is inside a particular sovereign state, is a citizen or subject, and is thus also inside the society of states. That global political fact has profound normative implications and consequences.

Statespeople, like everybody else, operate in a flow of human activity. Nobody knows that experience in any intimacy except themselves and their immediate advisers and confidants. The stream of human activity that they are involved in is one of the most important currents of history; perhaps it is the most important. The main current of modern international history is the record of their activities. Statespeople are historical actors: their activities are a contribution to the making of international history in their own time of office. The main platforms from which they operate are the ruling offices of particular sovereign states, the states on whose behalf they conduct foreign policy and engage in foreign relations. There is a common humanity, of course, which is acknowledged by the cosmopolitan discourse of human rights and humanitarian assistance. There are countless non-governmental organizations of one kind or another which engage in activities that cut across the boundaries of states. There is a vast international market-place that encircles the planet. There is all that and more besides. But the territory and population of the world is still partitioned into sovereign states which are the primary right and duty bearing units of world

---

[15] This ancient image of a world divided by incommunicable civilizations has been revived by S. P. Huntington, *The Clash of Civilizations and the Remaking of World Order* (New York: Simon & Schuster, 1996). Huntington grossly underestimates the international society basis of world politics and the extent to which the political world today is globalized on that basis. Huntington's argument is criticized in Ch. 14.

politics whose leaders are the principal international agents who carry the heaviest responsibilities for managing world affairs. They are the leading actors around which the political drama unfolds: they constitute the dramatis personae of history.

International ethics is shaped fundamentally by the heavy weight of state power, both military power and economic power, in the hands of statespeople: in no other sphere of human relations is organized power as consequential. Today the largest concentrations of power on earth are in the control of a few states: the five permanent nuclear armed members of the UN Security Council (P-5) and the seven leading economic powers of the developed countries (G-7). Very significant state power is of course distributed far more widely. Indeed, organized power, both destructive power and constructive power, is greater than it has ever been. Some national leaders have it within their power to destroy life on the planet as we know it. And some also have the power to improve planetary living conditions and to protect the planetary environment. Their military and economic power has profound normative implications and consequences— including the moral issue of how it can be justified. At base, therefore, international ethics is an ethics of responsibility because some very powerful players are involved who can do a lot of good and also a lot of harm. Indeed, their actions taken together affect virtually everyone on the planet, both for the better and for the worse.

This raises an important question: how can academics assess those actions in correct normative terms? International ethics is not an applied ethics: it is not thought up by moral philosophers or political theorists and then applied to politicians or other political actors. International ethics does not originate in the offices of university professors. There is no relevant moral standpoint outside international politics, such as John Rawl's 'veil of ignorance', from which to judge impartially the conduct of international actors—not if we aim to capture the situational realities of moral choice in that demanding sphere of human relations.[16] That would impose a standard of conduct on the subject that was not its own. University professors cannot determine the moral standards of politicians. Even the most brilliant philosophers have no role as moral instructors to politicians. The reason for that is not hard to find: philosophers are not in the same role and situation as politicians. Even at the best of times philosophers are unlikely to possess anything more than limited concrete knowledge of the situations in which politicians must operate on a daily basis. In other words, philosophers are poorly placed to know the details of the politician's situation, a knowledge of which is essential for intelligent and responsible political action.

[16] On the 'veil of ignorance' which is supposed to set up a fair procedure for determining social justice, see John Rawls, *A Theory of Justice* (Cambridge, Mass.: Harvard University Press, 1971), 136–42. This theory has been applied to international relations by Charles R. Beitz, *Political Theory and International Relations* (Princeton: Princeton University Press, 1979).

Just like ethics in any other sphere of human activity, international ethics develops within the activity itself—in this case the activity of world politics—and is adapted to the characteristics and limits of human conduct in that sphere. International ethics is not *external* to the human activities and practices of world politics: it is not something brought in from outside. International ethics is *internal* to world politics: it is the moral standards worked out over time by the practitioners involved; it is the normative world within which they are obliged to operate; it is embodied in the practice of statecraft. To understand the practical ethics of world politics the scholar must be willing to enter imaginatively and with discernment, although not uncritically, into the situation of the people who make foreign policy and conduct the relations of states, the most important of whom are national leaders. Scholars must assess the conduct of statespeople by the standards that are generally accepted by those same statespeople. Otherwise our normative inquiries lose touch with political reality and become irrelevant.

5. Practice and Theory

The argument that international ethics is the handiwork of statespeople becomes clearer from a brief analysis of the distinction between theory and practice. They are different kinds of knowledge and their relationship is not quite what it is often made out to be. It is a common assumption that theory comes before practice: we contemplate and then we act. Academic political theorists are particularly prone to make that assumption. Theorists certainly can and do shape the world indirectly through their theories, both when they are right and when they are wrong: the theories of Machiavelli and Marx moulded the future to a significant extent. But theoretical knowledge usually cannot be converted directly into practical know-how because some indefinable insight rooted in particular talents and derived from relevant experience is also involved. Political science graduates are not guaranteed solely by their academic credentials to become successful politicians. That clearly is absurd, for they would still have to acquire practical political know-how which can only be derived from experience in a political role, such as serving an apprenticeship in the office of a political party or political official.

By political theory I do not refer to scholastic debates among political theorists and moral philosophers about a theorist and his or her theory.[17] As indicated previously, by political theory I mean theoretical understanding of the existential political world, either contemporary or historical. That is political theory in the classical meaning. Such political theory is parasitic on political

---

[17] Unfortunately academic political theories nowadays are often unworldly, inward-looking, and incestuous. Many political theorists are content with taking up the arguments of other political theorists in a seemingly endless round of introverted scholastic disputation that is largely devoid of any curiosity about political experience and political history, about the world outside the academy. The recurrent debates surrounding John Rawls's theory of justice are a case in point.

practice: it is empirical in the classical meaning of seeking to give an account of the world of human experience. We need a historical event or episode—a human activity, occurrence, or coincidence—before we can theorize it. Thucydides' 'realist' international theory depends, for its existence, on the Peloponnesian War fought between Athens and Sparta from 431 BC to 404 BC, which provoked him to write it.[18] Theory is the knowledge of the observer and is generally characteristic of academic subjects. Theorizing in the human sciences is discerning and interpreting intellectually whatever part or aspect of the world of human relations the theorist happens to be curious about. Theoretical knowledge of human activity involves recognition of some historical episode as intellectually important, investigation of it, and reflection on it with the aim of giving an account which satisfies at least some of our curiosity about it. Classical theorists are trying to understand something and to convey that understanding—either verbally or in writing—to others who are interested in obtaining such knowledge. Theorizing ultimately is putting curiosity to rest.

Practice is entirely different. It involves knowing how to do something—for example, how to play chess, how to speak Russian, how to conduct a political campaign, how to command an armoured brigade, how to present a legal argument in a court of law, how to negotiate a peaceful settlement of an international dispute, and an endless number of other practical activities that human beings manage to engage in.[19] Practical knowledge is possessed by those who are able to engage effectively in an activity. Political practice is an engagement: engaging a problem or situation which involves other people who are also engaging the same thing but not necessarily from the same angle or with the same interests or concerns in mind. Engaging in a practice is acting on something, usually by either trying to preserve it or to change it but in any event trying to come to grips with it. Practical knowledge of human affairs ultimately is knowing how to put the human world into a better alignment with our interests and concerns.

Theoretical knowledge, as academically solid as it may be, is not a substitute for practical know-how. For example, we know that the duke of Wellington led the Allied Powers to a decisive victory over the Grand Army of Napoleon at the Battle of Waterloo on 18 June, 1815 and we have a pretty good idea that Wellington did this by making the most of his opportunities and the military means at his disposal before and during the battle. Maybe he also was lucky on that day. Yet, as much as we may discover and learn about that remarkable military achievement from our historical researches and reflections, we would not expect that, owing solely to our academic knowledge of the event, we could have pulled it off ourselves. That would call for talents and experience which scholarly knowledge alone cannot supply. But it would not prevent us from

[18] Thucydides, *History of the Peloponnesian War*, tr. by Rex Warner (Harmondsworth: Penguin Books, 1972).

[19] For a definitive analysis of this distinction see G. Ryle, *The Concept of Mind* (Harmondsworth: Penguin Books, 1963), ch. 2.

recognizing the force and significance of Wellington's achievement and communicating our understanding to others. We might even be better equipped to
give a complete account of the Battle of Waterloo than Wellington or Napoleon
themselves could give. The historian has a broader view of the past than those
who were present at the time. But one cannot take a theory and use it to enter
into the world of practice. Theorists cannot communicate with practitioners in
the language of theory—at least not if they wish to be clearly understood; they
can only communicate with other theorists in that language. That is what the
language of theory is for.

Theory is not a key to practice. A philosopher put that point as follows: 'a
soldier does not become a shrewd general merely by endorsing the strategic
principles of Clausewitz; he must also be competent to apply them'.[20] Practical
competency derives from talent and training honed by experience—which is
why young officers who have just graduated at the top of their class at West
Point or Sandhurst and possess the most up-to-date military education do not
start their careers as generals. That is not to doubt that military academies help
prepare men and women for a military career. Presumably there would not be
military academies if they did not have a utilitarian value of that sort. Yet practical know-how, even if it is furthered by such means, is still fundamentally
honed by experience.

Practical manuals are, as a rule, no substitute for talent and experience,
although they are, of course, an excellent aid to them. Cookbooks undoubtedly
have a practical use. However, even an excellent cookbook probably will not
suffice for someone to become a chef unless he or she has talent for cooking.
The cookbook is at best an abridgement or summary of practical knowledge and
cannot begin to communicate everything that is relevant to the activity of cooking.[21] We cannot say or write down everything we know about an art or a craft
that we have mastered. Much that we know will remain unarticulated. Most
people will only acquire the culinary art by carefully and repeatedly preparing
different recipes, ideally under the supervision of an experienced chef. Even
then some people may still not be very good cooks. Practice does not always
make perfect. Talent is also required.

Machiavelli's famous book *The Prince* offers what purport to be practical maxims concerning how to achieve political power and hold on to it.[22] However, we
could not become successful politicians by studying Machiavelli's political maxims because, as indicated, we would still have to know how to apply them, and
that know-how comes from gaining experience and not from reading books. The
main value of *The Prince* is as an essay in political theory—one of the most
important such essays ever written. Machiavelli is famous as a theorist of pol-

---

[20] G. Ryle, *The Concept of Mind* (Harmondsworth: Penguin Books, 1963), 32.
[21] M. Oakeshott, *Rationalism in Politics and Other Essays* (new and expanded edn.) (Indianapolis:
Liberty Press, 1991), 184–218.
[22] N. Machiavelli, *The Prince*, ed. G. Bull (Harmondsworth: Penguin Books, 1961).

itics and war, not as a diplomat or soldier. Practical knowledge is knowing how to get on effectively with whatever human activity one is engaged in. It is practical in that it is the crucial element that helps to get the job done. Otherwise it is impractical.

To sum up: practice and theory offer two different kinds of insight into human relations. The first kind of insight is the know-how of the participant who can make things happen or prevent things from happening or can at least influence, if not shape, the subsequent course of the human activity he or she is involved in: the player who can score winning goals; the politician who can conduct successful election campaigns; the soldier who can win battles; the lawyer who can defend clients; the diplomat who can defuse a situation and bring about an agreement. The second kind of insight is the knowledge of the observer, whose role is to construe the course and outcome of those same events by figuring out their point, discerning their deeper meaning, trying to grasp their significance, and generally by giving an academic account of the episode— in the classroom or in an article or book—which at least partly satisfies our aspiration to understand the subject in the most intellectually comprehensive way possible.

International Relations as a Craft Discipline

The classical humanist approach calls upon the scholar to enter with imagination and insight into the roles and situations of statespeople, not with the aim of advising them but, rather, with the hope of understanding their conduct. If we cannot talk to such people directly—which is not an option for most scholars—we can always fall back on the empirical method of historians. We can interrogate the evidence that statespeople leave in their tracks: the record of their policies and actions and the statements by which they attempt to justify them. The history of the public activities of statespeople and other political practitioners leaves a trail of evidence behind, like the tracks of a wild animal in the snow, which the international relations scholar can follow in the hope of capturing intellectually his or her quarry.

What is a craft discipline? It is not a scientific discipline that calls for knowledge of the philosophy of science or requires mastery of the best currently available techniques or methods of research. A craft is not a science or a technique. It is more like an art. Mastering a craft involves deep familiarity with the material that one is working with: its characteristics, limitations, and possibilities. A craftsman or craftswoman knows from experience what can be achieved by carefully working on the material with the proper tools and in the correct way. Craftsmanship is judged by its works. Crafts are the creation of craftsmen and craftswomen who work according to the same standards of excellence. Crafts involve proper ways of doing things based on past experience. Crafts consist in the established practices of the craftspeople. There are certain dispositions and skills, certain virtues, that are conducive to certain crafts and are associated with them. A virtue is disclosed in performance: virtuosity is revealed in an excellent performance. Thus while many musicians can produce music from their instruments only a few musicians are virtuosi. The music they can make is the most excellent that anyone is capable of producing. Their musical virtuosity, their musicality, sets the highest standard that is attainable. But the musical virtues are evident to some degree in anyone who can make music that others want to listen to.

Virtues are centrally involved in the craft of political science even though they do not capture much attention from political scientists, as compared to methodology. Perhaps that is because research methods and techniques can be packaged and taught through textbooks and classroom exercises which are necessary for education on a massive scale such as we have today. But the virtues of classical political science cannot be taught that way. They can only be imparted in a teacher–student relationship that is akin to that of a master and an apprentice of a medieval craft.

Some political scientists are outstanding scholars and we make that judgement by reference to the excellence of their scholarship. An outstanding scholar is somebody who has a deeper and broader understanding of the most important and difficult subjects of his or her discipline. Only a very few political scientists achieve that high level of academic knowledge. That is not merely a question of good methodology. It is far more a question of academic virtue. All political scientists can be fairly judged by the academic virtues involved in the study of human affairs, including, among others, mastery of existing knowledge, insight into the subject, creative imagination, discernment, detachment, judgement, even-handedness, and scepticism. When scholars of human relations write academic letters of reference for their students or colleagues these are the standards by which they assess their scholarship. A craft discipline is mastered by degree and marked by degrees. Each subsequent degree recognizes a deeper and more comprehensive knowledge of the same subject. That is a medieval notion and it is still the way we think about mastering academic disciplines in the human sciences.

The craft discipline of classical international society scholarship involves the following main stages of research. First, it calls for attention to those theorists who have something to say which is not only sound or wise but also perceptive and precise concerning the subject at hand—or rather the human activities related to that subject which they are noticing, scrutinizing, reflecting on, and writing about. We should begin by reading the classical works that provide the foundation of learning upon which we can, hopefully, build. Classical commentators, past and present, who offer some of the most profound commentaries would certainly include Thucydides on political necessity, Augustine on the just war, Machiavelli on power politics, Grotius on natural law and international law, Hobbes on the state and the state of nature, Burke on prudence and civility, Kant on the human community and the rule of law, J. S. Mill and Michael Walzer on freedom and non-intervention, Max Weber on the ethics of responsibility, Arnold Wolfers on statecraft and moral choice, Herbert Butterfield on the tragic element of international conflict, Hans Morgenthau on political wisdom, and Stanley Hoffmann on duties beyond borders.[23] This is only a personal selection from a long list of outstanding commentators on international relations, past and present, many of whom shall appear in the chapters which follow.

Second, as emphasized above, the classical approach involves paying attention to what statespeople and other important international players are doing, and saying, which includes scrutiny of their pronouncements and those of others with whom they are dealing. That requires a sharp and sceptical watchfulness for the justifications employed by international actors: those justifications, which abound in world politics, are the specific empirical subject that we are theorizing. These are usually recorded and reported, and that is what we interrogate when we engage in such an inquiry.

Third, those justifications must be interrogated in the context of the situation in which they are made. By this I mean that the statements of statespeople and other important international players should be scrutinized with a view not only to their explicit content and referents, but also their discernible intentions, and what they assume or take for granted about the conduct of international relations. Discerning this latter, often implicit, ideational context of international justifications is the most important theoretical understanding to be derived from the interrogative process. That is because it discloses the real, or lived, normative world of the people involved and is thus anchored in human experience and human history. An international relations scholar working in the classical tradition would seek to become conversant with evidence of international justifications surrounding a particular controversy, to know what is going on and thus to acquire some sense of the practitioner's situation and what he or she has in mind and is prepared to disclose publicly. Public disclosure is important because it usually gives an indication of how a leader wishes to be seen in order to secure public approval for his or her policy.

Fourth, that interrogation should be carried out with the major normative preoccupations of classical scholarship in mind. What do the UN Security Council resolutions and the US Congressional debates on the Gulf War disclose about war as a normative idea? What do the justifications and condemnations of UN and US operations in Somalia tell us about intervention as a normative idea? How do these episodes inform our normative theories of war and intervention? The classical scholar should be able to report not only what is going on or what

---

[23] Particular works of these authors are cited in various chapters. I could refer to many other contemporary authors who have left a mark on my thinking. But if I did I would not know where to stop. Many of their works are also cited.

happened. He or she should also be able to interpret those goings-on in the light of our inherited body of classical knowledge of the subject. Unfortunately, many international relations scholars who are conversant with the goings-on of world politics, who even justifiably pride themselves on being well-informed about current political events, often do not take that theoretical step. They do not connect their own otherwise excellent research to the larger classical tradition within which they might very well be working. They break off their scholarly hunt at the most critical moment and leave unanswered the most fundamental theoretical questions.

Of course, any theoretical conclusions are always bound to be provisional for they are connected, ultimately, with the historical events and episodes that provoked them in the first place. History rarely stands still and so we must be open to revising or changing our theories. But I take encouragement from the fact that some provisional statements about events that are very localized in space and time have a way of becoming long-standing theorems of international studies. Thucydides' fascinating dialogue on necessity and choice in the Peloponnesian War, by our standards a minor conflict fought in a tiny corner of Europe more than two millennia ago, is the classic case in point.[24] These theorems are always our main points of reference in theorizing new international episodes or problems. They are our academic inheritance. By taking them up as a theoretical point of departure, our own work becomes part of the classical literature of international relations. When we take up the classical approach we are seeking to make a contribution to that literature. We do that by theorizing the international relations of our time in classical terms and thereby pass on the tradition, hopefully enhanced by our own scholarship, to future generations of scholars and students.

Fifth, our theoretical writings should avoid academic jargon beyond the absolute minimum that is necessary for communicating with other scholars. Our academic inquiries should take up the living language of the subject: we ought to be at home with the practical discourse of international relations. That is because international relations—like all human activity—consists fundamentally of language, the principal vehicle for its expression. In studying international human conduct we are in a basic sense studying the practical language by which foreign policy, military affairs, diplomacy, international commerce, are not only expressed but are also carried on. The practical language of the human activity we are studying, in our case the activity of international relations, gives a good indication of the direction our theories of that activity should take.

That language contains many clues about our subject because, as indicated, it is fundamentally relational, it is dialogical. Its vocabulary has been fashioned to facilitate communication, interaction, and exchange between statespeople and other important international players. It facilitates question and answer, address

---

[24] Thucydides, 'The Melian Dialogue', *History of the Peloponnesian War*, 400–8.

and rejoinder, offer and counter-offer, acceptance and refusal, agreement and disagreement, accusation and denial, condemnation and justification, and many other dialectical pairs. International relations, as indeed all human relations, is interactive and transactive: the expressions 'international' or 'transnational' are intended to capture exactly that characteristic. So when we theorize international relations we should always be alert to the on-going dialogue of the political actors who are contemplating actions, initiating actions, or responding to actions which affect each other—and may also be of interest or concern to other people who are not directly involved but are also affected or might be affected. That dialogical activity is at the heart of our subject. By employing the literary device of the dialogue, classical Greek theorists, such as Thucydides, in some ways get closer than modern theorists to capturing the true character and *modus operandi* of international human relations.

If we resort to a more theoretical terminology, as we must in order to connect our writings with the classical tradition, our terms should be a translation of ordinary language that expresses a more general idea but does not lose any of the original meaning. That is how the theoretical vocabulary of the classical approach is fashioned: it is derivative of and based on ordinary language. Thus, the origin or derivation of classical terms of art, such as 'international order', 'international society', 'Westphalia', 'rationalism,' can always be traced to the practical discourse of international relations. Hedley Bull's notion of international order is not far removed from the ordinary language of diplomacy. Martin Wight's notion of 'rationalism' is traceable to the language of international law. Even in terminology, the theorist is always hostage to the practitioner.

Normative inquiry can only be expressed in the language of human conduct; it cannot be expressed in the language of natural science or mathematics or any other extraneous technical vocabulary, because it requires moral vocabulary, the source of which is the ordinary language of human conduct. Our theoretical language should therefore avoid stipulative definitions that have no reference to ordinary language. A stipulated definition is one that is made up by the researcher. Such definitions are arbitrary from the point of view of their subject. They are rejections of the language of experience and practice. They cut us off from the people and activities we are trying to learn more about. They have the unfortunate effect of alienating the world of political science from the world of politics. Such definitions are a currency of positivist and post-positivist political science and they have contributed significantly to the scholasticism of those approaches.

This discussion can be summed up as follows: the classical approach to the study of international relations is first of all acquaintance with the literature on the subject to which we ourselves are seeking to make a contribution. Secondly, it is familiarity with the actors' understandings of their world. In becoming conversant with the sayings and doings of statespeople the classical scholar thereby becomes vicariously conversant with the world of practice. Those sayings and doings are of course registered in almost endless speeches, policy statements, parliamentary debates, resolutions, declarations, announcements, press conferences, interviews, press releases, broadcasts, reports, and various other statements and commentaries. The point of interrogating such evidence is not merely to be informed about what is going on—although that undeniably is important. The point is larger: if we are seeking theoretical knowledge about international relations we need to be informed because we want to theorize from a basis of fact rather than fiction.

Classical international society scholars are seeking to achieve deeper insight into and wider knowledge of a subject that consists entirely of human relations and thus contains and displays all the complexity, uncertainty, ambiguity, and confusion of human thought and action. Classical scholars recognize the limits of knowledge in their discipline even as they strive to reach those limits in their own inquiries. They are under no illusions about that and they know from experience that their ignorance concerning the subject they are studying will always exceed their knowledge of it. To believe, as some social scientists evidently do believe, that there are research methodologies or technical languages that can or could get the correct and complete measure of international human relations is academic vanity and self-delusion.

5

The Political Theory of International *Societas*

This chapter sets out the political theory of international relations understood as a 'society' with its own distinctive standards of conduct. It opens with a discussion of the social character of international relations and international history. It then enquires into the constitutional framework of international relations which has been and still is primarily a *societas* of states. It goes on to consider the place, in such a society, of international organizations, non-governmental organizations, transnational networks, and human rights. It investigates the distinction between an international system and an international society, the prudential and the procedural aspects of international activity, and, lastly, the role of political ideals in international law.

The Social Elements of International Relations

That international relations ought to be understood as a distinctive society is the fundamental premiss of the classical approach.[1] As indicated in an earlier chapter, classical theorists do not see international relations theory as involving 'models' designed by the researcher and 'applied' to explain the subject from outside. They see the theorist as somebody who enters into the subject and interprets it from inside. The theory of international society is thus by and large consistent with what Max Weber refers to as *verstehen* or interpretative sociology which focuses on social action.[2] However, the classical approach cannot stay with Weber's further assertion that 'the interpretive understanding of social action' can be employed 'to arrive at a causal explanation of its course and effects.'[3] Here Weber is disclosing a split personality virtually identical to that of

[1] See, among others, Hedley Bull, *The Anarchical Society*, 2nd edn. (London: Macmillan, 1995) and Martin Wight, *Systems of States*, ed. Hedley Bull (Leicester: Leicester University Press, 1977). Also see Terry Nardin, *Law, Morality and the Relations of States* (Princeton: Princeton University Press, 1983).

[2] Max Weber, *Economy and Society: An Outline of Interpretive Sociology*, ed. by G. Roth and C. Wittich, iii (New York: Bedminster Press, 1968), 1375. Also see Martin Hollis and Steve Smith, *Explaining and Understanding International Relations* (Oxford: Clarendon Press, 1991).

[3] M. Weber, *The Theory of Social and Economic Organization*, ed. by T. Parsons (New York: Free Press, 1964), 88.

contemporary constructivists, as noted previously. But his interpretive account of social action remains one of the best available. So what follows is an instance of Weber as classical sociologist and not as positivist social scientist.

Weber defines 'social action' as any human activity which is 'meaningfully related to the behaviour of other persons'. The social is entirely between humans: it is the world of 'more or less durable relationships of human beings', the world *inter homines.*[4] Anything external to human relations, such as physical forces or biological processes, is not part of the social world properly speaking. Weber gives the following example: 'Social action does not occur when two cyclists . . . collide unintentionally; however, it does occur when they try to avoid the collision or sock one another afterwards or negotiate to settle the matter peacefully.' Weber rests his concept of the social on human intentionality. That is misleading because the accident could result from a lack of attention—negligence—on somebody's part which would be a legitimate cause for complaint. Falling asleep at the wheel is not an excuse that could exonerate a driver of all responsibility if it resulted in an accident.

What Max Weber is rightly emphasizing, however, is a fundamental distinction between a mere physical event—the collision itself—and the social content of the same event—its human involvement and meaning. Social actions may of course involve physical forces which humans have managed to harness in their ceaseless quest for power: for example, the mechanical force of bicycles or B-52 bombers. But social actions are never merely physical events: they are not acts of nature or God. They are produced exclusively and entirely by humans. In Weber's example, the collision itself is a mere physical (external) phenomenon, but the social aspect of the collision is a categorically different human (internal) episode. We cannot make sense of the event as a human episode unless we know what was in the minds of the people involved, such as misunderstanding, recklessness, aggressiveness, carelessness, even absentmindedness, or some other plausible human inclination that could lead to such an event. If it were a collision of cars rather than bicycles and somebody was seriously injured or killed, some such account of the episode would be sought by affected parties, by insurance companies, by the police, and possibly by a court of law.

'Social' implies human relations which are by definition reciprocally intelligible: that is, relations which are an encounter of human intelligence and thus involve recognition, communication, interaction, transaction, and other contacts and exchanges between people. Social action presupposes human orientations and inclinations in anticipation of acting, reacting, interacting, transacting, and so on. That means that predispositional factors such as interests, concerns, intentions, ambitions, calculations, miscalculations, wishes, beliefs, hopes, fears, confidence, doubt, uncertainty, and so forth must also be a focus of analysis. Such orientations undoubtedly enter into the international sphere of human

---

[4] M. Oakeshott, *On Human Conduct* (Oxford: Clarendon Press, 1975), 23.

relations in which they have a geographically very wide and historically very long field of play. Some—interests, fears, uncertainty, and miscalculations—are virtually signposts of international life historically.

It is thus important to emphasize that international relations are not a dependent variable of some external non-human reality which shapes those relations and holds the key to our knowledge of them. There are no background 'social forces' or 'social structures' unconnected with human agency which somehow mysteriously drive or constrain international relations and seem to operate as the secular version of providence in world affairs. The international society approach rejects that positivist social science conception. But it does not doubt that there are of course plenty of human and physical *circumstances* which limit the choices and actions available in international politics. Let us set aside physical circumstances and focus on human circumstances alone. We know from personal experience how far our own situation is shaped by the presence, expectations, intentions, and actions of other people: our lives are entangled in their lives and the consequences of that for all parties involved are profound. That is a fundamental axiom of classical sociology. The same can generally be said of those human organizations we refer to as sovereign states: they also are entangled with each other and affect each other and are of interest and concern to each other. That, too, has important consequences. Making sense of those entanglements and consequences is a basic aim of the classical international society approach.

The involvement of states, or rather statespeople, with each other raises important questions of a distinctive kind which go a long way to characterizing the subject of international relations as a special social sphere. Here are some that immediately spring to mind. Are foreign governments willing to coexist with us or are they unwilling? Are they friendly, indifferent, or hostile? How will they react to what we are trying to do? Do they understand our situation or misunderstand it? What are their future plans and intentions with regard to ourselves? Will they take us into account or will they ignore us and pass us by? Will they recognize and respect our rights and legitimate interests? Can we trust them? Do they trust us? Can they be influenced by us? Will they do what they say or are they misleading us? How can we survive and prosper in these various circumstances? What should our policy be in anticipation of such possibilities? These are historically recurring questions: they are the questions the ancient Melians asked of the Athenians, and the Athenians of the Persians and later of the Romans; and they are the questions that modern Poles ask of the Russians, and the Russians of the Americans.[5] In short, they are typical questions of international politics.

International relations are thus social in the classical Weberian inter-subjective meaning of the word, and profoundly so. The social action basis of international

---

[5] 'The Melian Dialogue', in Thucydides, *History of the Peloponnesian War*, tr. Rex Warner (Harmondsworth: Penguin Books, 1972), 400–8.

relations is evident even in our contemporary era of high technology. Military hardware does not eliminate the social basis of international conflict any more than bicycles or automobiles or aircraft eliminate the social basis of personal human mobility. States can collide via their armies, navies, and air forces but such military collisions are not the product of autonomous forces. On the contrary, they are entirely a result of intelligible and meaningful human decisions and actions. War, for example, is not merely a mechanical clash of force. War, for Hedley Bull, is basically a normative relation: 'a clash between the agents of political groups who are able to recognize one another as such and direct their force at one another only because of the rules that they understand and apply. Above and beyond this, because human beings have moral feelings and make moral choices, they have these feelings and make these choices when they are at war.'[6] War is a human institution and not an autonomous force.

That does not mean that war is always intentional. States could collide accidentally via their armed forces: unplanned or inadvertent firings of armed ballistic missiles are possible and a great deal of thought and effort goes into preventing it from happening. If such an event occurred it might be excusable at least up to a point: nothing in human affairs is fool proof or fail safe; we can speak intelligibly of both mechanical error and human error. One could object that such an event should have been prevented because the danger is so obvious. Thus it could still reveal negligence: for example, lack of an effective system of missile control. The source of the worry about such a conceivable accident, apart from the direct suffering and damage it would cause, is of course the rational fear that it would be construed as an intentional action by the other side and would thus be misunderstood as a hostile act that could lead to a war nobody wanted. In short, even the high-tech world of electronically guided weaponry is a social world through and through.

The social character of international relations is evident across historical time in so far as history is not merely a record of (external) occurrences which happened at some time in the past. The historical past is not an autonomous process. The past did not happen in spite of the people involved at the time. On the contrary, they made it happen. What happened is what they did or failed to do. The historical past, what we know about the past, is the remnants and residue of the activities of the people alive at the time that we have managed to access in our historical inquiries: their affairs, disputes, agreements, clashes. History is the register and record of (internal) human episodes and is thus something meaningful—both to the people involved and to the historian who is looking back at them.[7] The study of history is the postscript examination of the evidentiary trail of a past human experience: perhaps a triumph, perhaps a defeat, perhaps a lost opportunity, perhaps a disaster, perhaps a tragedy, or per-

---

[6] Hedley Bull, 'Recapturing the Just War for Political Theory', *World Politics* 32 (1979), 595–6.
[7] This humanistic conception of history is spelt out at length by R. G. Collingwood, *The Idea of History* (London: Oxford University Press, 1975), esp. part v.

haps—as most often is the case—merely a past event of no great moment. But whether it was a minor event involving a small number of people or a major episode involving entire nations that past happening is indicative of authentically social relations in the Weberian sense of the word: it is the product of the humans involved. That means that it is inherently normative because humans— either as individuals or as groups—cannot do things to each other or with each other that do not sooner or later raise the issues of right and wrong, good and bad. Human relations raise moral questions.

Consider, for example, the extraordinary episode of D-Day, 6 June, 1944. That momentous event during the Second World War was a clash of armed force of epic proportions: an occasion when huge rival military enterprises locked horns in a titanic struggle of air, sea, and land battle. But it was not only a clash of armed force because—like any other employment of force between human beings—it had to be justified in some way, and it was justified. For one party and for most third parties, the allied invasion of Normandy was the first scene, hopefully of the final act, to liberate Europe and rid the world of the scourge of Nazism. For the other party, at least the Nazi elite in Berlin but probably also many of their followers, the invasion was an assault on the Third Reich. Although each side's justification could of course be treated in a morally relativist fashion, in historical fact the Allied justification carried far greater weight than the Nazi justification. Indeed, one of the biggest vulnerabilities of the Nazis was their moral vulnerability. They could not justify their military conquest and occupation of Europe to almost anyone except themselves. My basic point, however, is simply that one could not fully grasp either the Normandy invasion or the Second World War as a whole without comprehending the profoundly important normative issues at stake.

To sum up: the classical approach regards international relations as a meaningful human activity not merely in part but in its entirety; it is a distinctive sphere of human relations; it exists in historical time and changes over time. International relations is thus a story of war and peace; of declaring war, making peace, and rejecting or accepting peace offers; of giving assurances, forming open alliances, and entering into secret pacts; of threatening and appeasing; of negotiating and breaking off negotiations; of diplomatic communications and exchanges; of espionage; of attacking and defending; of intervening, liberating, isolating, terrorizing, 'ethnic cleansing', and hostage taking; of broadcasting propaganda and jamming foreign broadcasts; of trading and investing; of claiming and offering foreign aid; of receiving and repatriating refugees, and of many other distinctive international activities in which humans engage. All those activities raise value questions. If the study of international relations seeks to be empirical it must be able to give an academic account of such questions.

The Constitutional Framework of International Society

It is important to be as clear as possible about the concept of international society so that we know what we are referring to when we employ the term. A good preliminary conception is provided by Alan James.[8] He says it is formal in character; it is a society of states which are 'notional persons' (or corporate personalities) but obviously not real persons; it is a body of rules (protocol, morals, and law) which define 'proper behaviour' for its members; and it is a channel of diplomatic communication between them. The term 'proper behaviour' may be misleading because international society is more than merely a world of propriety: it is fundamentally a world of expected and required conduct; that is, it is a 'constitutional' world in the full meaning of the term.

International society, like any other society, consists of members, but they are a very special category, namely sovereign states. According to Alan James, state sovereignty is 'the very basis of international relations' because it is 'the qualification which states must have before they can join international society'.[9] In international law states are the primary right and duty bearing units: 'the foremost category among the territorially organized subjects of international law'.[10] States are the subjects of international law but that does not mean that states are the creatures of international law. Rather, the opposite is the case: international law has been created by sovereign states; they are its authors. They have made themselves its subjects. States are the leading authorities of international society, their authority is what makes international law authoritative. International society, in that fundamental respect, is a construct of statespeople. States are also the principals from whose constitutions and offices the authority and power of statespeople can be said to derive. It cannot be derived internationally, from external authorities. That latter way of thinking was terminated by the treaties of Westphalia and Utrecht, when *respublica Christiana* was in effect repudiated. It was a rejection of the medieval notion that states were creatures of a larger community of Christians. Statespeople correctly understood are the representatives and agents of states rather than the representatives or agents of a political or religious community of some kind that is above the states.

The conceptual key to international society is the manner in which sovereign states associate and relate: the character and *modus operandi* of their association and relations. It is formal in a significant way: it involves procedural standards of conduct, an essential normative basis of which is international law. However, it is also substantive in an equally significant way as it involves the pragmatic

---

[8] Alan James, 'International society,' *British Journal of International Studies*, 4 (July 1978), 91–106.

[9] Ibid. 104.

[10] G. Schwarzenberger, *A Manual of International Law*, 6th edn. (London: Professional Books, 1976), 44.

encounters of the separate national interests of those same independent states which, although subject to international law, are still free to lay down their own foreign policies. In international life, as in domestic life, freedom is—in Hobbes's famous phrase—'the silence of the law'.[11] International law is silent on many things, and that opens a sphere of discretion for statespeople. But states are not internationally free to do anything they wish because they are still entangled in substantive relations with each other: they have an effect on each other both in what they do and what they fail to do. That carries inevitable normative implications. A comprehensive concept of international society should thus include not only the formal relations of independent states but also their substantive interactions and transactions. This concept will be spelt out in a later section.

There are some common misunderstandings about the character of international society, particularly the contemporary version, which should be addressed first. One might perhaps think that international society is a world government of some kind. That would of course be an utter misconception. The society of states has no authority or power apart from what states commit to its activities and organizations: international society consists of what states are prepared to agree or accept in their relations. The international organizations that states institute to facilitate their relations should not be misunderstood as independent authorities of some kind which exist apart from the states who organize them. The UN, for example, is the creature of its member states; it has no independent authority or power of its own of any significance. It cannot act on its own without regard for its member states. International organizations are more like colonies than independent governing agencies. They are subordinate authorities under the thumb of the independent states that create them.

International society does not have a 'government' in any significant meaning of that word. It might be thought, for example, that the UN Security Council or the UN Secretariat constitute a sort of government of international society. But the Security Council does not possess the authority to act independently of its member states. The Council is a puppet of its members, especially the five permanent members, who pull the strings. Neither the permanent members nor the ordinary members of the Council nor any other members of the UN have provided the Council or any other UN body with the power to be constitutionally independent of themselves. The officials of the UN Secretariat, including the Secretary-General, are international civil servants who are beholden to the UN member states, particularly the great powers. Their sphere of discretionary authority and action is modest. Even when international organizations do possess very substantial power, as in the case of the military power of NATO, it is not held independently of its member states. The Council and Secretary-General of NATO are organs and agents of its member states, particularly its

---

[11] T. Hobbes, *Leviathan*, ed. Michael Oakeshott (Oxford: Blackwell, 1946), 143.

leading members, Germany, France, Britain, and the USA—especially the latter. The most important political organs of international society historically are the organs of diplomacy which nowadays often operate multilaterally via international organizations but are still anchored to sovereign states.

The society of states is not especially significant as an actor *in itself.* When it engages in substantial activities, such as armed enforcement activities under the UN charter, certain of its member states actually do the engaging and enforcing on its behalf, employing whatever means they are prepared to commit to the enterprise. International society possesses no military power or economic resources of any significance. As indicated in previous chapters, international society is basically a normative framework with regard to which the foreign policies and other international actions of states can be evaluated without imposing an external standard they do not commit to. Its norms provide an *internal* basis of evaluation: pertinent cues and expectations which statespeople have regarding acceptable or at least tolerable international conduct. The significance of international society resides in their general willingness to operate by reference to its norms.

The fact that international society consists of associated sovereign states does not mean that it possesses the same attributes that its member states possess. The attributes of sovereign states are summarized in standard definitions of international law and typically include the following (taken from the Montevideo Convention on Rights and Duties of States): a permanent population, a defined territory, a government, and the legal capacity, or right, to enter into relations on a basis of equality with other states.[12] Something very much like that is certainly what classical international society theorists have in mind when they make reference to sovereign states.

International society lacks almost all of the foregoing attributes of sovereign states. It does not have a permanent population or any territory of its own. International society is not a place: it occupies no significant geographical space anywhere on earth. Nobody 'lives' in international society the way millions of people do live in particular countries. The territories of its members are not its own: they fall under the separate and exclusive jurisdiction of those individual member states. International society does not control the planet in the political and legal way that sovereign states do control their own territories. It does not possess external sovereignty; it is not independent. Nor does it possess internal sovereignty. It cannot independently raise taxes: it has no population to tax. Nor can it mobilize armed forces or engage in other substantial activities that sovereign states do engage in as a matter of course. International society is lacking almost entirely in the assets and instrumentalities that sovereign states possess, although in vastly different and unequal measures, virtually by definition.

---

[12] Ian Brownlie, *Principles of Public International Law*, 3rd edn. (Oxford: Clarendon Press, 1979), 74.

One must always keep in mind the distinction between the framework and the actors: international society is the framework, states are the actors. International society is, by and large, a *societas* rather than a *universitas*: it is an association of independent and legally equal member states of varying substance, rather than a substantive and purposive enterprise in its own right; it basically consists of standards of conduct which statespeople are expected to observe in their foreign relations.[13] I shall spell this out in a later section.

The Auxiliary Framework of International Society

States and their relations do not exhaust the concept of international society: other echelons are also involved. International society also consists of international organizations (IGOs), non-governmental organizations (NGOs) and transnational networks, and individual human beings seen as composing a world society. The twentieth century witnessed an unprecedented expansion of both international organization and non-governmental organization world-wide; it also saw a very noteworthy extension of international humanitarian law which was a response to the crimes committed during the terrible wars of the century.

1. International Organizations

The previous discussion of international organization can be summarized. Although they do not constitute a government in the strict meaning of the term, international organizations are none the less significant auxiliaries of international society. They are subordinate authorities: they act on behalf of the states that set them up. They facilitate communication between statespeople and other international players—the political dialogue of international society—with regard to a vast range of subjects and issues. They also facilitate international action with regard to numerous and various substantive issues such as peacekeeping, the adjustment of international monetary relations, the provision of international development assistance, the regulation of international transport, the elimination of disease, especially contagious diseases, the monitoring of refugee movements. Such activities and organizations are important, of course, but they are a secondary embodiment of international society. International society would exist and in the past it has existed in the absence of UN peacekeeping forces, the IMF, the World Bank, the International Air Transport Association, the World Health Organization, the UN High Commission for Refugees, and so on. The primary embodiment, as Alan James rightly emphasizes, is its associated sovereign states. The UN has existed since 1945, the

---

[13] This distinction is investigated by Oakeshott, *On Human Conduct*, 201–24.

International Labor Organization has existed since 1919, and other international organizations have existed for a longer or a shorter time. The Universal Postal Union has existed for more than a century. Some international organizations have come and gone, such as the League of Nations. But the framework within which these organizations exist and with regard to which they are understood—the historical society of states—has existed continuously since the seventeenth century.

It is thus important to remember that the society of states has existed with less international organization, and with different IGOs, than it discloses today. Prior to the twentieth century the connections and communications between states consisted mostly of the organs of diplomacy. That usually involved bilateral dialogue between states; occasionally it also involved multilateral dialogue in conference or congress diplomacy, as at Vienna in 1815 or Berlin in 1878.[14] Today, however, there is an elaborate global framework of IGOs through which diplomatic dialogue is continually conducted.[15] But, as also indicated, all IGOs without exception, including the UN, are creatures of states: they have been designed and set up by states; they are operated by international civil servants beholden to states. They do not exist or operate on their own; to conceive of them in that way would be to commit the category mistake noted earlier. In short, although IGOs are an important element of international society, especially nowadays, they do not possess the political or legal independence and thus the primary stature that sovereign states alone possess. IGOs are better conceived as auxiliary organizations of international society. They constitute a noteworthy organizational means by which the society of states conducts its increasingly multifarious global, regional, and functional business.

2. *Nongovernmental Organizations and Civil Society*

International society also manifests what might be referred to as a 'transnational society' which consists of NGOs that operate around the world.[16] One is here referring to business enterprises and labour organizations, scientific, technical and professional associations, religious societies and humanitarian movements, cultural organizations, environmental groups, sports associations, and other virtually countless private or voluntary organizations which operate across international boundaries and are interested in or concerned with an almost endless number of issues or values. In the final decades of the twentieth century the activities of NGOs expanded rapidly and at the time of writing many NGOs

---

[14] Keith Hamilton and Richard Langhorne, *The Practice of Diplomacy* (London and New York: Routledge, 1995), 90–8.

[15] See Evan Luard, *International Agencies* (London: Macmillan, 1977).

[16] See Joseph Nye and Robert Keohane (eds.), *Transnational Relations and World Politics* (Cambridge, Mass.: Harvard University Press, 1972). Also see the critical discussion of this idea, and related ideas of world politics, in Bull, *Anarchical Society*, ch. 11.

were deeply involved in shaping the international agenda on a diverse range of substantive issues, from ancient ruins in Guatemala to the zebra population of East Africa and just about everything in between. Today NGOs constitute a world-wide network of ever increasing complexity and traffic.

It is often claimed nowadays that international society is being transformed by the mushrooming world of NGOs to such an extent that states are relinquishing or losing their primary social standing in international relations. This argument does correctly draw our attention to transnational networks which are indeed expanding at a rapid rate and do now constitute an important feature of international society. And it is undoubtedly the case that NGOs and sovereign states reciprocally 'benefit from each others' presence'.[17] It is also the case that there are 'networks of knowledge and action' constructed by 'decentered, local actors, that cross' international boundaries with some regularity and frequency and without too much difficulty.[18] But any claim that a 'global civil society', consisting of such actors and networks, is displacing global international society based on sovereign states seriously misconstrues the character of international society. It is hugely misleading to claim that NGOs and sovereign states 'coexist' because that implies an equality between both parties that does not exist. If there were such coexistence we would be living in a radically different world. And to say that global civil society crosses 'the reified boundaries of [sovereign] space as though they were not there' is to hint that sovereign states have lost control of their territories and equally to imply that global civil society is in control. But the fact is, nothing like that is in existence or even on offer. That image of global civil society is almost entirely false.

That is evident both in practice and theory. NGOs and transnationalism presuppose the prior existence of sovereign states and the society of states, including state territorial jurisdictions, international law, international boundaries, in regard to which they are understood. The states system opens a political space of freedom for transnational activity. That has long been the case historically. The states system made it practical for business enterprise to operate with confidence beyond national borders and on a global scale. The interstatal is the necessary background political reality, or context, in which transnational activities are carried on by countless NGOs. Such organizations operate within the framework of states, not the reverse. They operate under the political condition of international peace and order that the states system alone creates and upholds. In the absence of that political condition they would face great operational difficulties.

Moreover, all NGOs—even large multinational business enterprises—are lacking the crucial means, territory and sovereignty, to operate completely on

[17] See M. J. Peterson, 'Transnational Activity, International Society and World Politics', *Millennium*, 21 (Winter 1992), 371–88.

[18] R. Lipschutz, 'Reconstructing World Politics: The Emergence of Global Civil Society', *Millennium*, 21 (Winter 1992), 390.

their own and independent of particular sovereign states. Wherever in the world NGOs operate, a locally sovereign state is their host. No NGO could move around and locate in different parts of the world—at least not openly and easily—without the permission or indulgence or indifference of particular states whose territorial jurisdictions they necessarily must operate from. NGOs do not float in the air. Even if they did, states control the airspace. Even if business enterprises can use their economic clout to open the doors of independent states by influencing their governments, they still do not possess the sovereign keys that unlock them. That is the crucial condition in the entire arrangement: states are sovereign and NGOs are dependent on their sovereignty.

The interstatal is also the underlying assumption against which NGOs and transnationalism are theorized. States and the society of states are not theorized against a background assumption of transnational society. States are understood first and foremost on their own terms. They are the primary referents of international society whatever we may think of that. NGOs are secondary or tertiary referents. They are understood in the context of our idea of a world of sovereign states. Most theories of world politics, including transnational theories, operate with an assumption of sovereign states even if it is only silently present. As indicated earlier, the states are the authorities of international society. NGOs are not authorities at all. They are vehicles that engage in private activities and voice opinions which they direct at state authorities and their international organization subordinates. NGOs are opinionated about the special issues that concern them: international trade and commerce, human rights, international aid, disaster relief, wildlife protection, consumer protection, scientific research, travel and tourism, and an endless number of other issues that certain NGOs consider to be important. NGOs may capture and may shape public opinion in certain states, even international public opinion between states, on issues of concern to them: an excellent example is the role of Greenpeace in shaping international opinion on the environment. NGOs are sometimes opinion leaders. But they are not authorities either nationally or internationally. They exercise authority over nobody except their own members.

There is a common misunderstanding, that flows out of a political sociology understanding of international relations, that the primacy of the sovereign state in world politics is a question of 'influence': 'It is an unacceptable analytical bias to decide, before research starts, that only states have any influence . . . Until the evidence indicates otherwise, we must assume that governments and NGOs interact with each other . . . Who actually determines outcomes will vary from issue to issue.'[19] This entirely misses the point about the exclusive legal standing of states in world affairs: their sovereignty. It is not a matter of academic research whether or not states possess legal primacy. It is a matter of inter-

---

[19] P. Willetts, 'Transnational Actors and International Organizations in Global Politics', in J. Baylis and S. Smith (eds.), *The Globalization of World Politics* (Oxford: Clarendon Press, 1997), 288.

national political practice. And sovereign state primacy is not a sociological question of 'influence'. It is a constitutional premiss—that is, a norm—of international relations organized as a *societas* of states. Just as interest groups inside states recognize state authorities by seeking to influence their domestic laws and policies but do not and cannot claim the legal authority of states, so also do NGOs seek to influence states' foreign policies and international relations but they do not and cannot claim the international legal authority—that is, sovereignty—of states. That does not mean that interest groups are not important; it means that they are not sovereign. The difference is categorical and fundamental. But since so many international relations scholars view world politics through the conceptual lenses of political sociology or political economy it is necessary to spell out this point.

State sovereignty is not a sociological idea or an economic notion as it is sometimes erroneously made out to be. It is sometimes said that states are losing their economic sovereignty to international capital markets. That claim is conceptually confused. The expression 'economic sovereignty' is a conflation of two different concepts that are best kept in separate compartments if we wish to be clear. A better term might be economic autonomy. This is a positivist, stipulated definition of sovereignty. It is not a definition derived from the actual practices and institutions of sovereignty. Sovereignty is a legal notion in actual practice: that is, as that term is used by practitioners. That is not to say that sovereignty and economics are unrelated. Obviously they are related. It is merely to point out that the relation is a contingent relation and not a conceptual relation. Economic autonomy is the *notion* that a country's economy is insulated from foreign economic influence or involvement or control. That may or may not be desirable in any particular case. But it is a matter of policy and not one of definition. Rather than speak of the decline or loss of 'economic sovereignty' it would be more to the point to speak of the difficulties that independent governments face in trying to pursue nationalistic economic policies, especially in our era of transnationalism and globalization.

Robert Keohane views sovereignty as a 'bargaining resource'.[20] He speaks of states 'bargaining away' their sovereignty to the EU as if it is something that is instrumental rather than constitutional.[21] If we think about sovereignty that way there is no question but that the EU involves a voluntary loss of sovereignty on the part of its member states. But that again is a misleading way to think of sovereignty. The EU states that are opting to join the 'Euro' currency zone are deciding to exercise their sovereignty in that way. That is a matter of policy and not of sovereignty. Their sovereignty is being used to authorize certain common rules and activities in co-operation with other EU member states. Sovereignty

---

[20] Keohane, 'Hobbes's Dilemma and Institutional Change in World Politics: Sovereignty in International Society,' in H.-H. Holm and G. Sørensen (ed.), *Whose World Order?* (Boulder, Colo.: Westview, 1995), 177.

[21] Ibid. 177.

is not a resource to exchange. That misconception can probably be laid at the feet of political economists. Sovereignty is a status, a legal standing, and thus a right to engage in relations and to make agreements with other sovereign states on a basis of formal equality.

NGOs can only exist and transnationalism can only operate under conditions of international peace, order, stability, which are among the major substantive concerns and justifications of a society of states. NGOs, like everybody else, are significantly dependent on international order which can only be obtained via the activities of sovereign states and especially the great powers. If the condition of international order can be said to exist, it is because states make it a reality. It does not happen automatically. And under present circumstances that is the only plausible way that it could happen. Neither IGOs nor NGOs nor anybody else can make it happen. International business enterprise relies on the states system. People who move or travel or tour from country to country also rely on the states system. That includes academic critics of the states system who travel to international academic conferences. When we fly around the world in Boeing 747s at 37,000 feet it is the states system that controls the airspace and the airports that make that possible. One of the best established propositions of world politics is that during periods of international disorder, such as war, among the first casualties are commercial, personal, scientific, academic, and other cross-border activities.

The sociologists who employ the expression 'global civil society' seemingly fail to notice the core political meaning of the term 'civil'—or they fail to construe it correctly. Two hundred years ago Kant drew attention to the then misleading use of the term '*social* state' to refer to the conditions associated with the '*civil* state'. He noted that in the 'state of nature' 'there may well be society of some kind, but there is no "civil" society, as an institution securing the mine and thine by public laws'.[22] In other words, civil society is a society under the rule of law; without the rule of law there is no civil society. That applies internationally: international civil society is under the protection and the jurisidiction of the *societas* of sovereign states.

To summarize, there is a very important sense in which sovereign states and the society of states are, both conceptually and substantively, preconditions of transnational society. NGOs are best conceived as subsidiary organizations of international society whose activities depend on the conditions of peace and order created by the society of states. They operate within the political space— the sphere of international freedom of trade, transport, travel—that is kept open by that global political arrangement. Without that freedom they could not operate—at least not openly and easily. NGOs perform a role in international

---

[22] I. Kant, 'Introduction to the Science of Right', in R. M. Hutchins (ed.), *Great Books of the Western World*, xlii. *Kant* (Chicago: Encyclopedia Britannica, 1952), 402.

politics not unlike that of interest groups or lobbies in a domestic political system based on individual and group freedom. Indeed, in many ways they are best conceived as international lobbies that are seeking to influence the foreign policies of states and the practices of the society of states. They recognize states and try to influence them. They are not seeking to overthrow the states system for that would be suicide.

3. Human Rights and World Society

International society theorists refer to 'world society' which they sometimes see as the most fundamental society on earth. They have in mind the universalist idea of every member of the world's population possessing a global status and rights as a human being—human rights—regardless of the country in which he or she happens to live. Sometimes and indeed quite often human rights are seen as superior to sovereign rights: a view typical of cosmopolitan theorists. Hedley Bull at times expresses a similar view: 'the ultimate units of the great society of all mankind are not states (or nations, tribes, empires, classes or parties) but individual human beings.'[23] But that is a philosophical idea rather than an actual practice of international society. Bull is speaking in philosophical terms and not in terms of diplomacy or international law.

In practice individuals are most of the time objects rather than subjects of international law. Until the twentieth century that was clearly the case. Human rights were almost invisible: except for some specific humanitarian concerns in the waging of war. That changed very noticeably in the twentieth century. The United Nations' declarations and conventions of human rights of the second half of the century, and those of other IGOs, indicate that human rights are an international concern of states. But they do not indicate, at least not yet, that human beings are subjects of international law on a basis of parity with states. On most issues and in most places it is still the case that sovereign states have primacy. It is only in certain parts of the world where international organization is more elaborate, as in the Council of Europe and the European Union, that the individual enjoys a significant international legal standing. That is because in that region of the world, unlike most other regions, the international and the domestic are increasingly interwoven: 'The more closely international law approximates to national law, the more the individual has a chance to become a direct bearer of legal rights and duties.'[24] In Europe domestic law increasingly affirms and upholds the civil and political rights of its population. It is that idea—the sanctity of the individual—that is infiltrating the international community of

---

[23] Bull, *Anarchical Society*, 22. See Nicholas J. Wheeler, 'Pluralist or Solidarist Conceptions of International Society: Bull and Vincent on Humanitarian Intervention', *Millennium*, 21 (Winter 1992), 463–88.
[24] Schwarzenberger and Brown, *A Manual of International Law*, 65.

Europe. The states of Europe are internationalizing their domestic human rights practices. International society in Europe is taking upon itself responsibilities for defending human rights. Elsewhere that is much less the case and in many places around the world it is not the case at all. In short, pluralism is accommodating human rights, but in doing so pluralism is not giving way to solidarism.

The solidarist conception of a world society confronts many practical difficulties and obstacles, most of which are deep-seated: in what existential sense can all the people on earth actually form a 'society'? The 'community of humankind' is an abstraction and not an actuality. The actuality is a world population of about six billion who have no collective existence as a community. In other words, the community of humankind is a moral vision but not yet a political reality. How can those six billion people associate for political purposes? To date, the only globally inclusive 'world society' to which virtually every human belongs, if only indirectly, is the society of states via his or her citizenship in a particular state. As indicated previously, the legal status of human beings in international law, as expressed by the law of human rights, is something that has been acknowledged and erected by sovereign states. Thus, human rights and by implication 'world society' do have a positive historical existence but only as constructions of the society of states. Today many scholars and some practitioners are anticipating the dawning of a new political world with normative signposts that point to the ascendancy of world society. Some believe that such a world is already in existence. But at the start of the twenty-first century there is no conclusive evidence that that is so. Most of the evidence presented in later chapters indicates, without too much ambiguity, that we are still living in a political world in which states continue to be the primary normative units and referents.

This discussion can be summed up as follows: states are the principal components of international society, and IGOs and NGOs are auxiliary and subsidiary echelons. Their existence is dependent on the states which form them (IGOs) or make space for them (NGOs). Real flesh-and-blood people, men and women and their children, are of course the ultimate normative references for international society: there is a fundamental moral sense in which they are primary and everything else is secondary or tertiary. Humans are ends and not means. To think otherwise is to be in possession of a monstrous idea. States are not ends. States are organizations that are formed and sustained by people for the benefit of those same people and maybe also for the common good of the world at large. In international legal and political practice, however, states and their citizens usually come before the world as such and its human population as such. In so far as the population of the world can express itself politically, it is only via the society of states. That is the way the institution of world politics has been arranged historically. World society and world politics is the work of statespeople. Whatever normative standing humans enjoy in world politics is largely owing to states—it is specifically due to the spread of liberal democracy based on individual rights. This point is pursued in later chapters.

International System and International Society

How should we conceive of international society as an activity and not merely a framework? How should international activity be theorized?[25] Hedley Bull in effect responds to these questions by drawing an important distinction between 'system' and 'society' in international relations.[26] The former obtains 'where states are in regular contact with one another, and where in addition there is interaction between them sufficient to make the behaviour of each a necessary element in the calculations of the other'. That is the classical realist image of international relations as a political arena of self-regarding state actors. The latter, by contrast, only exists 'when a group of states, conscious of certain common interests and common values, form a society in the sense that they conceive themselves to be bound by a common set of rules in their relations with one another, and share in the working of common institutions'. That is the rationalist image of international relations as a normative framework whose principals, sovereign states, have a regard for other states as well as themselves and act accordingly.

Hedley Bull's distinction between system and society is useful and certainly much use of it has been made by classical international relations scholars. But it is also unfortunate because the notion of system can leave the erroneous impression that some international relations are mechanical or functional, which they cannot be if they express and register the activities of statespeople. 'Regular contact' and 'interaction' between the agents or representative of states clearly are social relations, for how else can human beings be in contact and interact with each other? Humans are not things. The reference is to human interaction and not to a physical relation. Hedley Bull is a classical political scientist and not a positivist social scientist: an international 'system' by his definition is a social (historical) relation and not a natural (mechanical or functional) phenomenon. Bull's distinction contributes to the positivist misunderstanding because 'system' is a term that invites the billiard-ball image of international relations as a mechanical 'clash of forces'.[27] The main focus is on the balls moving and colliding on the table (external objects, movements, and forces), and any explanation of their motions and collisions has something to do with the *nature* or

---

[25] In writing this section I have been influenced by Michael Oakeshott's thought on human relations in general and political activity in particular. See especially Michael Oakeshott, *Rationalism in Politics and Other Essays*, new and expanded edn. (Indianapolis: Liberty Press 1991).

[26] Bull, *Anarchical Society*, 10–13.   [27] Ibid. 13–14.

structure of the system of which they are a part. The main focus is not where it should be: on the rules, stratagems, players, and—most important—what might be going on in the *minds* of statespeople (internal thoughts, ideas, expectations, assumptions, concerns, beliefs, convictions, calculations, and so on) as they *contemplate* their next foreign policy move. In short, Bull's notion of states system can be misunderstood in a way that he would not wish, as a positivist concept.

International society ought to be seen as a continuum of social relations, from mere awareness and very limited and intermittent human contact and communication at one extreme, to extensive and continuous human interaction and dialogue through an elaborate institutional framework at the other extreme. The closer international relations come to the latter pole, the more elaborate will international society be. The current international society is far more elaborate— i.e., worked out in far greater detail in many more areas of mutual interest or concern—than any previous international society in history.

Bull's distinction is better conceived in terms of two types of human activity: instrumental and non-instrumental.[28] The former refers to precepts, maxims, calculations, stratagems, tactics, and other expedient considerations involved in an actor's decisions and endeavours to carry out a course of action or to respond to the anticipated or actual decisions and actions of other actors. Instrumental activity is usually conceived as driven by pure self-interest. That leads to a distinctive kind of international relations based on narrowly conceived prudential considerations. This is the Machiavellian *modus operandi* of international politics. The latter refers to legal and moral obligations and requirements involved in international status and membership. As indicated, Bull speaks of members of international society as being 'bound' by common (non-instrumental) rules. These moral and legal bonds reflect a regard for the rights and legitimate interests of other members of the society of states. Being bound expresses the idea of required and expected conduct befitting a good citizen of the society of states. That conduct typically involves respect for international law and established standards of diplomatic conduct. That leads to a distinctive kind of international relations based on legal and moral obligation. If statespeople refuse to be bound in that way or neglect those obligations they are repudiating their international citizenship. This is the Grotian *modus operandi* of international politics.

Both Machiavellian orientations and Grotian orientations to international relations are authentic social orientations in Max Weber's classical rendering of the term: both are ideas about how to understand a human situation and act upon that understanding. For example, if as a stateleader I believe that something is in the national interest, such as a military alliance or a free trade agreement with another country, I am expressing my reading of the situation and the advantages it has (or might have) for my country. That is an outward instrumental orientation to other international actors but at the same time also an

---

[28] M. Oakeshott, 'The Rule of Law' in *On History and Other Essays* (Oxford: Blackwell, 1983).

inward normative orientation to the national interest. Likewise, if I believe that we are entitled to something, such as respect for our sovereignty and independence, I am again expressing my understanding of the situation and what it requires of the actors involved. That is an outward normative orientation to international action. International relations ordinarily consists of both instrumental activity and normative activity on the part of the statespeople involved.

There is ambiguity in the notion of instrumental activity when it is extended from focusing on the human individual to focusing on the human community including, especially, the nation-state. Instrumental activity between individual human beings is, by definition, self-regarding expedient behaviour and thus it could not be behaviour which takes the rights and legitimate interests of others into account. When I personally am the self in question, a self-regarding relation between myself and another person is purely and exclusively instrumental or expedient: self-interest is my interest alone or that other person's interest alone, both of which might conflict or might coincide in an encounter between us. But when we—you and I together—are the self; as in the case of fellow citizens of a particular state, then a self-regarding relation is no longer purely and exclusively instrumental or expedient. Self-interest is not my interest or your interest exclusively; it is not even the mutual accommodation of our self-interests. Rather, it is our common interest. Self-interest at that point acquires a shared or joined aspect. It is a non-instrumental and specifically moral idea. It is also noteworthy that at that point the state discloses the character of a *universitas* which is often expressed via the notion of the 'national interest': that which is deemed to be for the common good of its citizens.

When the government and citizens of a country are the referent of the self, then self-interest is pursued not for selfish reasons but for the good of the nation, the national interest. Contrary to what is often supposed, the national interest is a fundamental moral obligation of those who are in positions of national responsibility: statespeople.[29] To defend the national interest is a burden that statespeople must bear; they are bound to defend it. If they neglect the national interest they are neglecting one of their fundamental responsibilities. To defend the national interest is to act as a guardian of the state conceived as a political community with its own intrinsically valuable way of life. That communitarian value is the central value of the morality of classical realism. The belief that the national interest is not a moral idea, and that the national interest and morality are antithetical ideas, is one of biggest blind spots and misunderstandings of contemporary studies of international relations. For purposes of this study the national interest is a moral notion that is part and parcel of the ethics of statecraft as discussed at length in the next chapter.

---

[29] These remarks are influenced by T. J. Kersch, 'The Idea of the National Interest: A Conceptual Analysis in the Context of the Gulf War' (Ph.D. thesis, University of British Columbia, 1995).

The fact that international society theory makes provision for prudential statecraft may perhaps explain why theorists who adopt that approach, such as Martin Wight and Hedley Bull, could be seen as classical realists. However, that disregards the theory's external obligation aspect which is just as central to the approach: international society theorists are realists but they are also rationalists. The reason for including both dimensions is not only to avoid the abstraction and distortion that comes from focusing only on the one or the other. It is also to be faithful empirically to the normative practice of states which discloses both dimensions. The classical international society approach strives to comprehend the holistic and pluralistic character of international ethics.

Prudential Association and Procedural Association

Martin Wight points out that 'the principles of prudence and moral obligation . . . have held together the international society of states throughout its history, and still hold it together'.[30] That expresses a basic thesis of the classical approach upon which this book seeks to build. It is both possible and desirable to enlarge upon this fundamental insight by drawing on the closely related theories of Michael Oakeshott and Terry Nardin.[31] Any human association, including international society, can be understood as a *combination* of prudential association and procedural association. Before we look into these contrasting modes of international society it is important to emphasize that they are standards of conduct: that is, norms by reference to which international activity can be assessed. When we play the game of life we are usually acting with some regard, however great or small, for both what is prudent in the circumstances, and what is procedurally required.

These interactive ideas can be employed to understand the character and *modus operandi* of the building blocks of international society: sovereign states. The state can be conceived as a prudential association under the direction of statespeople in their role as 'managers' of the state's *apparatus of power* (which ordinarily consists of personnel, finances, technology, equipment, land, buildings, and various other means and resources). That is the classical realist image of the state; in its pure form it is the idea of a *Maachtstaat*, a state founded on

---

[30] H. Butterfield and M. Wight (eds.), *Diplomatic Investigations* (London: Allen & Unwin, 1966), 13.

[31] Oakeshott refers to a fundamental distinction between 'enterprise association' based on instrumental relations between humans, and 'civil association' based on non-instrumental relations. See Oakeshott, *On Human Conduct*. For a more incisive statement of his argument see 'Rule of Law', 119–64. Nardin draws a parallel distinction between 'purposive association' and 'practical association': *Law, Morality and the Relations of States* (Princeton: Princeton University Press, 1983), esp. ch. 1.

power in the service of the national interest.[32] However, the state can also be conceived as an obligatory association under the authority of statespeople in their role as incumbents of the state's *offices of authority* (which ordinarily consist of presidential or prime ministerial offices, a cabinet, a legislature, courts, and so forth as defined by a constitution of some kind). Statespeople are expected to frame their policies and conduct their activities within the procedural limits set by the offices they occupy. That is the classical rationalist image of the state; in its pure form it is the idea of a *Rechtstaat*: a state founded on constitutionalism and the rule of law.[33] I am not saying this is the way states are. It is the way they are usually required to be. It is certainly the way most important states are required to be. These are contrasting ways of construing and appraising the conduct of statespeople who could be said to possess dual personae: they are at one and the same time both managers of the state's instrumental assets and resources, and upholders of the state's constitution and laws. We commonly judge the conduct of statespeople by reference to both prudential criteria and procedural criteria which may come into conflict from time to time.

These two ideas carry over into corresponding conceptions of international society which involves both power politics and the rule of law. When the state is conceived exclusively as a power apparatus the relations of such states take on a corresponding character of prudential association. That is a realist image of statespeople relating to each other and dealing with each other with their self-regarding national interests in mind and by operating with prudential ethics: that is, cautionary considerations intended to avoid trouble, inconvenience, drawbacks, danger, harm. Sometimes international relations is an encounter and even a collision of national interests, and sometimes it is a joining or a combining of national interests. When we speak of 'alliances', 'coalitions', 'common markets', and similar instrumental arrangements between sovereign states, we are employing expressions which emphasize the notion of states as joint power agencies that collaborate internationally in terms of their respective national interests. That obviously is a fundamentally important historical feature of international relations and a basic image of classical international relations scholarship.

When, on the other hand, the state is conceived exclusively as an office of authority or body of laws, the relations of such states take on a corresponding character of procedural association. That is a rationalist image of statespeople recognizing each other and dealing with each other by observing common practices and by making and respecting mutual agreements. When we speak of 'domestic jurisdiction', 'diplomatic immunities', 'treaty obligations', and similar

[32] See C. Navari, 'The State as a Contested Concept in International Relations', in Navari (ed.), *The Condition of States* (Birmingham: Open University Press, 1991), 3–11. In the early modern era of the states system the interest in question was more narrowly understood as that of the state or even that of the ruler and his or her dynasty.

[33] Oakeshott, 'Rule of Law', 155. Also see Navari, 'State as a Contested Concept', 11–15.

non-instrumental relations between states we are employing expressions which emphasize the notion of states as right and duty bearing units: that is, procedural or legal association between states understood as law-making and law-abiding agents. That, too, is a fundamentally important historical feature of international relations and a basic image of classical international relations scholarship.

Prudential association between states ordinarily is entangled in procedural association between states: the *Maachtstaat* and the *Rechtstaat* usually exist and operate in tandem and not in isolation. For example, military alliances are arranged to provide security for the allied states and thus respond prudentially to their national interests. But military alliances are commonly sealed by treaty obligations which are intended to bind the parties into an association which is far more than a fair-weather friendship: NATO is a familiar, long-standing, and successful case in point. Commercial treaties respond, in a similar vein, to the economic self-interests of states. There is a legal doctrine expressed by the Latin phrase *rebus sic stantibus* which holds that a treaty is binding only as long as there is no fundamental alteration in the circumstances which prevailed when it was agreed. But commercial treaties also rely on basic non-instrumental terms and conditions such as equitable terms of trade, property rights, performance of contracts, stable rules of currency convertibility, and other standard procedures of international commerce which are far more than merely expedient or time-bound for the parties involved. Treaties between states must have an authoritative standing or legitimacy independent of self-interest or circumstance to exist over time as stable and predictable arrangements between states. Treaties are an integral element, indeed a foundation element, of the society of states.

This second aspect of international association, the obligation aspect, is often not accepted at face value. Classical realists are sceptical about international law as a normative standard for judging the conduct for independent states. They do not of course question the existence of international law. What they question is the significance and efficacy of international law. They usually suggest that international law exists in practice only because it is a cover of civility and legality on a mode of international relations which is fundamentally self-regarding and self-seeking in character. In other words, it is a procedural disguise to obscure the truth about international relations which is largely if not entirely self-regarding and prudential in character. That is a version of the window-dressing argument. More charitably, procedural association is seen as a super-structure of international relations which only holds up because it is supported by a foundation of state power and self-interest. The *Maachtstaat* carries the *Rechtstaat* on its broad shoulders. In other words, the national interest of states is of fundamental importance and the rights and legitimate interests of states are secondary. International law is primarily and predominantly an instrumental relationship and only secondarily a normative relationship between states, if it is normative at all.

For example, Michael Oakeshott denies that procedural association—what he terms civil association—exists in international relations. He sees the political world external to the sovereign state as a world exclusively of instrumental conduct. His argument rests on a positivist theory of law as solely the product of a sovereign state as the domestic rule of law. Because there is no international sovereign there can be no authoritative rules and no predictable enforcement of treaty obligations in the international sphere. In short, there can be no international rule of law. According to Oakeshott, 'most of so-called international law is composed of instrumental rules for the accommodation of divergent interests' that is prudential association.[34] That undoubtedly is a widely held view and it is even held by some international lawyers.[35]

This brings to the surface a fundamental proposition which lies behind much of the analysis in this book. Self-interest and other elements of prudential conduct comprise an important and indeed a profound human reality which is strikingly evident in international relations. Human beings are undoubtedly self-interested and it is not stretching a point to say that they must be that way in order to live and thrive. Self-regard and perhaps even self-love is in their best interests. If procedural standards of conduct are too stringent for the situation, or too demanding of the people involved, they will probably be ignored and would in that way lose whatever normative import they might otherwise have. Neither international law nor any other law could be based on self-sacrifice. Classical international society scholars, such as myself, nevertheless argue that international law involves not only prudential considerations but also procedural obligations.

What has been said of international law could also be said of traffic regulations: namely that whatever efficacy they have rests ultimately on driver self-interest. Traffic laws regulate the flow of traffic and prevent accident and injury only because they are a prudential response to the self-interest of drivers: everybody wants to get somewhere and nobody wants to get into an accident along the way. But traffic laws can perform that service only by setting and imposing normative standards of conduct—the rules of the road—which presuppose not only a self-interested and prudent disposition but also a tolerably law-abiding and other-regarding disposition on the part of drivers. Do drivers obey the traffic laws out of fear of an accident or fear of the traffic police? Undoubtedly they do. But arguably they also obey those same regulations out of a recognition of their authoritativeness and a certain regard for others with whom they are sharing the road. The traffic police cannot be everywhere. There are of course places in the world where traffic laws are ignored. Presumably that is because the drivers in those places have no interest in obeying and no fear of disobeying: maybe there

---

[34] Oakeshott, 'Rule of Law', 163.
[35] See the probing criticism of contemporary rationalists in G. Schwarzenberger, 'The Grotius Factor in International Law and Relations', in H. Bull, B. Kingsbury, and A. Roberts (eds.), *Hugo Grotius and International Relations* (Oxford: Clarendon Press, 1990), esp. 312.

are no traffic police or maybe they are corrupt. But those drivers must also have no respect for the law and no sense of duty towards it.

Traffic laws operate on the assumption they will be generally respected. Otherwise why have them? Drivers are assumed to be responsible adults—as indicated by the usual age limit for acquiring driver's licenses. That limit assumes an ability to drive but it also assumes the responsibility to drive safely with regard not only to oneself but also to others. Safe driving obviously serves the self-interests of individual drivers. But it also serves the legitimate interests of everybody else who is sharing the road. Dangerous driving is generally considered to be not only unwise but also wrong. Since others are involved, safe driving is the responsibility of drivers at all times while they are out on the road. Safe driving means obeying the rules of the road—regardless of any benefits or advantages that can be derived from doing that—and demonstrating the courtesy that such an obligation clearly implies.[36]

This analysis can be extended to international relations. Terry Nardin argues—I believe correctly from both a historical and a legal perspective—that international law consists significantly of authoritative, non-instrumental practices (customs, usage, conventions, and so forth) based on the juridical equality of sovereign states. For Nardin, the pre-eminent historical character of international law is that of a normatively binding relationship: procedural association or what he terms practical association. The non-instrumental rules of international society are made authoritative not by the prescriptions of one commanding overarching sovereign but by the common practices and agreements of all sovereigns. States sometimes commit to noninstrumental rules inadvertently out of self-interest. Nardin puts the point very well: 'even the most narrowly self-interested state cannot ignore the fact that any claim formulated as a legal right . . . may if generally accepted come to impose limits on its own conduct'.[37] Thus if as a nationalist leader I claim independence of my country from colonial rule and my claim is successful, as has happened on well over a hundred separate occasions since 1945, I thereby subject my government to the obligatory rules of international law, such as the doctrine of non-intervention, even if I conduct my foreign policy entirely in accordance with the prudential considerations of national interest—or, as in the case of many dictators, my own personal interest. In short, even the most narrowly self-interested stateleader can become ensnared in international legal obligation.

Stateleaders must surely have many different motives for entering into treaties on behalf of their state, and those motives may sometimes be entirely self-serving. But their motives are separate from their obligations. Sovereign states subject themselves to the obligations of customary international law in virtue of being sovereign states. And sovereign states subject themselves to the obligations

---

[36] In practice, of course, drivers are obeying the rules of the road as much out of habit as anything else, but it is the source and the shape of that habit that is at issue here.

[37] Nardin, *Law, Morality and the Relations of States*, 185.

of treaties in virtue of signing them and thus giving them their consent. The fact that states can and do make 'reservations' when they commit to treaties confirms the seriousness with which they regard their treaty obligations.

But what if international obligations are ignored or defied? That raises the age-old question of enforcement. It has to be emphasized that enforcement of obligations in international relations is an uncertain and inconsistent activity even at the best of times. There obviously is no one sovereign in international society; there are many sovereigns. Organized power is not absent but it is divided between sovereign states and that division raises distinctive problems of international law enforcement. Yet even though there is no single overarching power in world politics there nevertheless are several major powers who are in a position to act as quasi-sovereign agents of enforcement. Occasionally great powers perform the role of international law enforcement: for example, the USA, Britain, and France during the Gulf War. The real problem arises when great powers fall out among themselves, as happened in the 1930s and the result-ant Second World War, and again during the cold war. That enforcement deficiency arguably is the single most important limitation of international law as a purely legal order. It is also the single most important reason for regarding international law less as a strictly legal order and more as an ethical order. It makes international society more reliant for its existence as a normative order on the good citizenship of statespeople. And it makes the theory of international society and international law more like a political and moral theory and less like a strictly legal theory. Procedural association in international relations is thus less a question of enforcement and more a question of membership and, indeed, of citizenship.

There can be no denying the problem of international law enforcement in a society of states. But nor can the general observation of international norms in the society of states that exists at the present time be denied. As indicated, at the turn of the twenty-first century, there were about 190 sovereign states in existence. That means that the potential for aggression, forcible intervention, illegal occupation, and other serious acts in violation of international law is con-siderable. The mathematical possibility of international conflicts is far greater than the number of states. Yet the incidence of such actions has been remark-ably low by historical standards since the present international society based on the current post-1945 norms of the global covenant was instituted. That may be owing to many things, including a widespread lack of motivation to be an inter-national outlaw. It may reflect a rational instrumental concern about the un-desirable consequences that may follow. But it may also reflect the general legitimacy of the basic norms of the global covenant which forbid such inter-national actions. It is perhaps worth noting that, before the twentieth century, when such actions were not forbidden, they occurred more frequently.

One important reason for that may be the fact that sovereign states are far more involved with each other today than they ever were in the past: their society is an ongoing, recurrent, continuous, daily reality. It is no longer intermittent and spasmodic as it often was in previous centuries. Many states are in constant and intimate relations with each other: the states of North America and Western Europe being the best example of that close association. In that regard we might say that international society, at least the international society of Western states as reflected in NATO, the OECD, the EU, and other such organizations, is becoming more domesticated and indeed more like domestic society. That feature of contemporary international society, the growing involvement of states with each other, is investigated at greater length in later chapters.

To sum up thus far: these two social modalities, prudential association and procedural association, are present as vital considerations in the conduct of international relations, as subsequent chapters shall indicate. Arguably no human society, including international society, is possible or even conceivable in the absence of both dispositions on the part of the people involved. I am not saying that these two social modalities are always equally present in world politics: that is an empirical question. It is obvious that international relations can be conducted with little regard, if any, for the rule of law and occasionally even without much prudence. Nor am I saying that these modalities exhaust the normative basis of international society, which clearly is not the case. I am only saying that it makes sense to include both of them in our international theories because the practical world of international relations includes both of them as basic references for justifying foreign policies and other international activities. These are two interconnected and mutually communicative ways of engaging in international relations and thus of theorizing those same relations.

Ideals in International Law

The classical notion of international law as usages and practices which invoke an obligation on the part of the practitioners, an anthropological conception of international law, is a relatively old idea that presupposes a pluralist image of international society. The prevalent historical modality of classical international law is that of practice: usage and customs which sovereign states acknowledge in their relations and to which they are generally expected to subscribe. That was law that responded to the concrete situations and requirements of its subjects, sovereign states. It was a way of defining and attempting to regulate their foreign activities and relations. It was called for by statespeople. It was the norms that such people were usually prepared to recognize and observe in their relations. It was practitioners' law. It was in that sense practical. Historically those international legal practices included the laws of war, the right to make treaties, the obligation to obey their terms, the right to send and receive envoys, the immunity of diplomats, recognized title to particular territory, and so forth. These traditional practices of international law have long been evident and they are still evident today—usually dressed in modern clothing and makeup. Here, then, is international law expressed in the classical rationalist discourse of *societas*.

In the twentieth century, however, international law took a new turn and assumed an additional and different persona, at least in certain respects. According to Terry Nardin, international law took on characteristics of purposive association.[38] By 'purposive' he means that it became defined in some areas by its goals or aims rather than its practices and procedures: that is, international law disclosed the characteristics of a *universitas*. International law acquired a new normative discourse, what Dorothy Jones labels a 'declaratory tradition'.[39] The use of the term 'tradition' is ill-chosen because what is referred to is not something long established and valued that is handed down from one generation to the next. Instead, she is drawing our attention to the fact that twentieth century and especially post-1945 international law frequently consists of declared goals and ideals towards which statespeople avow to strive in their foreign policies. These are declarations of intent regarding future conduct rather than acknowledgements of actual practices. According to Jones, 'this sustained effort has created a body of reflections and rules that is closer to moral philosophy than it is to positive law'.[40]

Some of that undoubtedly announces the arrival of the USA as a world power that has inserted its love of progressive change and its future-oriented domestic political discourse of goals and ideals into international relations. The formative moment of the declaratory discourse in international relations was perhaps an April 1917 address to the USA Congress by President Woodrow Wilson, which pronounced a declaration of war on Germany in Kantian terms of the moral purpose of fighting 'for a universal dominion of right by such a concert of free peoples as shall bring peace and safety to all nations and make the world itself at last free'.[41] That ironically has some echoes of the pre-modern European political past. If we substitute 'righteous' for right and 'Christian' for free the statement could have been made by any number of medieval popes bent on crusading for *respublica Christiana*. Making the world safe for democracy, which is once again a popular idea among Western intellectuals and politicians, has solidarist medieval echoes. Although Wilson speaks of 'free peoples' and 'nations', which evokes an image of pluralism, he also speaks of 'the world itself' being 'at last free', which evokes an image of solidarism. He clearly has in mind a world of a certain political kind, namely a world of free democracies. In the circumstances

---

[38] Nardin, *Law, Morality and the Relations of States*, 23.

[39] Dorothy V. Jones, 'The Declaratory Tradition in Modern International Law', in Terry Nardin and David R. Mapel (eds.), *Traditions of International Ethics* (Cambridge: Cambridge University Press, 1992), 42–61.

[40] Ibid. 42.

[41] Quoted by Inis L. Claude, Jr., *Swords into Plowshares*, 2nd edn. (New York: Random House, 1959), 44. Wilson's famous 'Fourteen Points', which listed the war aims of the USA is characteristic of the declaratory modality.

of 1917, and still in the circumstances of today, that is a revolutionary pronouncement and a remarkable one for the leader of a great power. It is remarkable for its lack of regard for the existing world order and the values at stake in that order. It is remarkable because it is progressive in a sphere of human conduct that is usually conservative.[42] This issue is taken up in later chapters.

That progressive idealist outlook has been noticeably evident since the adoption of the UN charter in 1945, in many respects an American document, which begins with a resounding declaration to save future generations from the scourge of war, to reaffirm human rights, to establish conditions of justice, and to promote social progress. It is evident in the Universal Declaration of Human Rights (1948), the UN Conference on Trade and Development (1964), the UN Convention on Human Rights (1966), the Convention for the Protection of the World Cultural and Natural Heritage (1972), the Charter of Economic Rights and Duties of States (1974), the UN Convention on the Elimination of All Forms of Discrimination Against Women (1980), the UN Convention on the Law of the Sea (1982), the UN Conference on Environment and Development (1992), and many other declarations, resolutions, and conferences which spotlight and seek to promote substantive world goals or ideals.[43]

The same basic discourse is also evident in the Report of the Commission on Global Governance which goes further than any other international commission of inquiry in seeking to identify and specify a global morality which includes 'neighborhood ethics', 'a global civic ethic', 'principles of global governance', and a long list of goals and ideals many of which appear on the idealist agenda of world politics.[44] They include 'the right of all people to' 'a secure life', 'an opportunity to earn a fair living', 'participation in governance at all levels', 'equal access to information', and 'equal access to the global commons'. And they include, correspondingly, their 'responsibility to' 'contribute to the common good', 'promote equity, including gender equity', 'protect the interests of future generations', 'preserve humanity's cultural and intellectual heritage', and 'work to eliminate corruption'.[45] So here is a report which conceives of the world as a single moral community, a *universitas* of some kind, and not merely a pluralistic *societas* of states, and which seeks to identify the global goals and ideals that states and individuals on the planet should collectively strive for in the years and decades to come.

What marks off the solidarist approach of declaratory law from the pluralist approach of classical law is thus its expression as proclamations and affirmations

---

[42] M. Wight, 'Why is there No International Theory?' in Butterfield and Wight (eds.), *Diplomatic Investigations*.

[43] This developing aspect of international society is particularly evident in the area of the environment. See Andrew Hurrell and Benedict Kingsbury (eds.), *The International Politics of the Environment* (Oxford: Clarendon Press, 1992).

[44] *Our Global Neighbourhood: The Report of the Commission on Global Governance* (New York: Oxford University Press, 1995).

[45] Ibid. 336–7.

rather than precedents and practices. It is future-oriented and progressive rather than past-oriented and conservative. It announces a sought-after ideal condition of world affairs which member states of the UN and other international organizations see themselves as striving to bring about by both individual and collective efforts, for example, the abolition of war, the establishment of world peace, the eradication of disease, the elimination of poverty, the fostering of humanitarianism, the expansion of democracy, the preservation of the environment, and much else. Hence the use of the word 'shall', according to Jones, 'takes on a different meaning than that of an obligation . . . [and instead] it becomes the strongest possible assertion of the conditions that the states think ought to obtain in their ideal world'.[46] In short, certain attractive images or visions of the future are held up as normative referents in world politics.

Here international law is held to serve political purposes. To proclaim certain ideals—liberty, equality, happiness, fraternity, humanity, justice, to mention only the most famous—is a political act. Politics is in some fundamental respects the pursuit of ideals which are values that are held in esteem, are hoped for, even longed for, and are often actively sought after by those who cherish them. The pursuit of ideals is one of the most distinctive political activities of the modern Western world, which gave it to the rest of the world and brought it into international relations. It has been argued that there is little or no place for the pursuit of ideals in the hard world of international politics. That is the view of Martin Wight in one of his more realist essays.[47] But that view fails to recognize the full scope for the pursuit of ideals in the international sphere and consequently it underestimates their significance and impact—which some of Wight's most important work does fully recognize.[48] There is no doubt but that some international declarations have entered into the international conduct of states and in so doing have significantly affected the character and *modus operandi* of international ethics and international law. Certainly that can be argued in the case of the recurrent human rights declarations which have given a distinctive form and content to international relations since the 1948 Universal Declaration of Human Rights. States clearly do make reference to human rights in judging each other's conduct. Human rights are a standard of conduct in contemporary world politics.

Some political ideals have had a marked historical impact on international law and the conduct of international relations. Two noteworthy examples are anti-slavery and anti-colonialism. The General Act of the Berlin Conference (1885) which authorized the partition of Africa among certain European powers carried forward the anti-slavery movement which was injected into international relations and international law at various congresses in the nineteenth century largely by the efforts of Britain. Colonizing powers were duty bound to 'suppress slavery

---

[46] Jones, 'Declaratory Tradition', 50.   [47] Wight, 'No International Theory?' 23–41.
[48] M. Wight, *International Theory: The Three Traditions* (London: Leicester University Press, 1992).

and especially the slave trade'. The treaty reflected ideas, beliefs, and convictions which were prominent among Europeans in the latter half of the nineteenth century which carried over into the twentieth century.

Colonialism is another case in point and a more significant case because it directly involves the question of territorial jurisdiction, state sovereignty. Here was an international institution that had been accepted and defended for centuries. But it became very controversial in the twentieth century: it was the target of widespread criticism, was not effectively defended in ideological terms, and lost its normative force. It was eventually displaced by an alternative international institution which embodied the normative idea of self-determination and self-government. The change was unambiguous, rapid, and conclusive: within a decade from about the mid-1950s to the mid-1960s the international system was transformed from one which included a large number of legal overseas dependencies of European colonial powers (formal empires) to one in which most colonies had become independent states and the universal end of Western colonialism was inevitable and in sight. The change was global in scope. The ideals of self-determination and self-government not only pre-empted colonial values but also precluded their reform—for example, into international trusteeship or associate statehood.[49] We now live in a territorial world that everywhere consists exclusively of locally independent states which are the basic political units.

The end of the slave trade and decolonization were remarkable episodes of international change with far-reaching consequences. They were revolutionary episodes for the people involved, most of whom acquired rights and freedoms they had previously been denied. But they were a reformation with regard to the society of states: they made that society more congruent with its core value of sovereignty and more globally inclusive; they corrected major normative anomalies in the system. The end of the slave trade corrected the anomaly of both free individuals and unfree individuals within the same political universe which was based, fundamentally, on a notion of freedom, state sovereignty. The sovereign enfranchisement of colonial peoples corrected the anomaly of both sovereign peoples and non-sovereign peoples in the same society of states. The institutionalization of those ideals did not constitute a repudiation of the system.

The political enfranchisement movement within Western states in the nineteenth century brought the heretofore excluded majority of national populations into the status of citizenship but it did not overthrow the system—as Marx and others had wished. In the same way, decolonization brought non-Western peoples into the states system without overthrowing the system or fundamentally altering the system—as contemporary dependency theorists and critical theorists wished. The change was not revolutionary in the way that Westphalia was rev-

---

[49] R. Jackson, 'The Weight of Ideas in Decolonization', in J. Goldstein and R. Keohane (eds.), *Ideas and Foreign Policy* (Ithaca, NY: Cornell University Press, 1993), 111–38.

olutionary and in the way that the Bolshevik takeover of Russia as a preparation for taking over the capitalist world was revolutionary. So these are instances of ideals being incorporated into an evolving and expanding order of international law. They give striking evidence of the historical capacity of international society to reform itself from time to time.

That is not so clearly the case with some elements of the declaratory tradition which give intimations of a significantly different kind of political world. Many declaratory ideals intimate an international society which is predominantly solidarist in its normative framework and *modus operandi*. That is one that is organized on a purposive basis for pursuing goals and values which are common to all states and indeed to everyone on earth: the common good of the world, global *universitas*. The goal is not to reform the *societas* to eliminate practices, such as slavery or colonialism, that contradict its *modus operandi* and violate its core values. The goal is to change international society into a fundamentally different normative arrangement that is based on values that elevate non-state elements above the state, the elimination of individual poverty everywhere in the world, terms of trade that favour underdeveloped countries as a social class, elevation of human rights above sovereign rights, intervention in sovereign states on humanitarian grounds, domestic democracy as a qualification for membership of international society, the protection and preservation of the environment on a global (that is, non-sovereign) basis, the law of the sea that collectivizes the ocean bed as a world jurisdiction under a world authority, the elimination of gender discrimination regardless of religion or culture, and so forth. That many of these goals are worthy and humane no reasonable person could deny. Certainly, on the face of it, any questioning of goals, such as putting an end to poverty or to the destruction of the environment wherever it occurs, would seem to be completely unwarranted. But that many of these same goals might and probably would interfere with the existing *societas* of states no reasonable person could deny either.

The global international society that presently exists is still predominantly pluralist in its normative framework: it does not usually act collectively in regard to common goals. The goals and purposes that command international attention and dictate action are those of particular states or groups or alliances of states. International society is first and foremost a *societas* of those fewer than 200 political systems that have managed to gain independence and recognition as sovereign states. Only in Europe and perhaps more generally in the West are there fairly clear indications of an emergent *universitas*. But it is regional and not universal. The European Union is the best example in that it involves an institutional framework that is geared to common purposes, especially in the economic sphere. It has a rudimentary government that is in some ways independent of the governments of its member states. But the prospect of something like that happening on a global scale in the foreseeable future is remote. What does seem to be happening, as later chapters indicate, is the emergence of an international society of mixed character and uneven depth from one global region to the next: in certain parts of the world, notably in Europe and the West more generally, international society is taking on solidarist characteristics connected with democracy, human rights, etc. These states are coming to share many domestic values and institutions and thus they are coming increasingly to resemble each other. They are committing to these shared values in their international relations. The distinction between domestic and foreign is becoming blurred. But in the rest of the world, and more generally, international society still seems to be not very ambiguously a *societas* of sovereign states. Even in the West most states are still very far from submerging their sovereignty in a greater political community. Overall the international society remains pluralistic in character.

Ideals are a problematical foundation of international ethics in a pluralist society of states which rests, fundamentally, on procedures and practices and confines ideals largely to the domestic politics of states. The pursuit and realization of political ideals requires collective effort and that is far more readily forthcoming within states than it is between states. Without such backing the declaration of ideals rings a bit hollow.

Signing declarations which proclaim praiseworthy goals is not at all the same as subscribing to procedural obligations, for example, treaties. Lumping practices and precedents together with ideals and goals shifts the emphasis away from (binding and realistic) duties and toward (unbinding and idealistic) aspirations. Rather than reinforcing and deepening the traditional moral basis of international society—which is a classical liberal order based on the independence of states—the declaratory approach may have the opposite effect of undermining it by stretching it and diluting it. Since we can hold people to their treaty obligations, at least in the sense of pointing to any of their shortcomings in that regard, we have a solid basis for normative judgement. Violations of the rules of non-intervention would be an instance of that. But since we cannot hold people to their aspirations in that we cannot require them to achieve their goals, we have a far weaker basis for normative judgement.

The declaratory tradition encourages a lower level of moral obligation in world politics by politicizing morality. Ideals do not carry as much weight as obligations. They are not binding on anyone. Instead, they are easy and undemanding, so everybody is eager to sign up. The elimination of world poverty and the protection of the global environment and comparable ideals and goals are laudable on almost any view. That they might eventually be achieved is something that any reasonable person would hope. But they are not standards of conduct that anybody can be bound to right now. What is of importance in human conduct is what one is doing right now, or what one did yesterday, or what one failed to do—not what one might or might not do at some unspecified future time. That problem of the low current purchasing power of ideals as standards of conduct is evident in the contemporary laws of armed conflict.

Geoffrey Best has documented the counterproductive effects of the expansive codification of the post-1945 laws of war which have tried to set higher, more elaborate, and more demanding standards in the conduct of warfare than politicians and soldiers reasonably could be expected to achieve in the circumstances of modern warfare, even with exceptional goodwill on all sides.[50] The standards are ideals to hope for and to strive for but they are not currently obtainable. Aspirations have run far ahead of expectations. In so doing the codes, such as the Geneva Conventions and Protocols, unfortunately become discredited and the laws of war are rendered academic as moral referents.

The historical activism that characterizes the United Nations and other contemporary international organizations has greatly increased the issues brought within their ever expanding orbit of scrutiny and concern. The number of UN General Assembly resolutions is large and it continues to grow annually. UN Security Council resolutions have multiplied rapidly since 1990. Many politicians sign the declarations in full awareness that they are not obliged to achieve or even pursue the ideals they affirm. They evidently sign because it is deemed to be good public relations. The affirmation is all that is required. Affirmations are easy to make and their value as standards of conduct is correspondingly low. They do not bind those who make them: in that sense they do not fulfil Bull's above-noted definition of the bonds involved in international society. Many, if not indeed most, of those resolutions cannot be realized or enforced under present circumstances. That may have the corrosive effect of discrediting the United Nations and other international organizations when their declarations are not fulfilled or even pursued in the actual conduct of member states or other parties to whom they apply.[51] In extreme cases declarations may contribute to cynicism among those who expect international actors to live up to their ideals and are bitter when they fail or refuse. Is there any more efficient way of morally discrediting oneself than by declaring an intention to do something that is deemed to be urgently required and worthwhile and then failing to do it? Taken to extreme, ideals become politicized in the form of propaganda calculated to garner political support. The declaratory tradition, in that regard, invites the politicization of international ethics. That has the effect of confusing ethics with ideology.

---

[50] G. Best, *War and Law since 1945* (Oxford: Clarendon Press, 1993), esp. 403–22.

[51] Nardin, *Law, Morality and the Relations of States*, esp. pp. 97–112. Geoffrey Best has registered a similar criticism of the post-1945 laws of war. See his *War and Law since 1945*, esp. part II.

6

The Situation Ethics of Independent Statecraft

Because sovereign states are the foundation of the international *societas*, the people who are responsible for acting on their behalf are the foremost subjects of international ethics. The ethics of statecraft is the heartland of international ethics. This chapter outlines a classical approach to the subject that interrogates the following connected topics: international ethics as a special ethical sphere, the distinction between standards and circumstances, the relationship of power and responsibility, the situational character of international responsibility, and the political virtues that statespeople are called upon to possess. The thrust of the argument is to bury the erroneous belief that foreign policy and other international activities of statespeople are devoid of normative direction or content. It also rejects the illusory belief that the conduct of statespeople can be judged by applying the theories of moral philosophers. That doctrine might appeal to some scholars but it is misleading: it places the proverbial cart (moral theory; scholars) before the horse (moral practice; politicians). The chapter argues that academics can only judge statespeople by their standards.

States and Statespeople

International ethics must begin, in the classical manner, with the ethics of statecraft because statespeople—leaders of the major powers especially—are the ones who have the greatest ability and opportunity to affect the lives of the largest number of people around the world, particularly, with regard to military power. That alone makes it a fundamentally important subject. I am not suggesting that our normative enquiries can or should stop at that point. There are other important ethical subjects in world politics and some of them are discussed in later chapters. But when we come to discuss them we cannot avoid looking carefully at the principal players on the stage of world politics: statespeople.

Statecraft is a differentiated sphere with its own ethics. That is the ancient Greek way of thinking about ethics and it is still the most discerning way.[1]

[1] G. M. A. Grube (tr.), *Plato: Republic* (Indianapolis: Hackett, 1992), I. sec. 342; Terence Irwin (tr.), *Aristotle: Nicomachean Ethics* (Indianapolis: Hackett, 1985), I. sec. 1098.

Every sphere of human activity involves a distinctive ethics of some kind: defining powers and connected responsibilities by which it is regulated. Different standards of conduct apply to different human activities and we can perhaps think of human activity as divided into 'fields' or 'games'. All games have rules but each game has its own specific rules. Drivers are duty bound to observe traffic signs and signals. Lawyers and teachers are duty bound to observe their respective professional codes of conduct. Scientists are duty bound not to doctor the evidence upon which their research findings are based. Political scientists are duty bound to convey their academic knowledge to their students to the best of their ability and to keep it as uncontaminated by their political beliefs as they possibly can. When people engage in an activity they subject themselves to the normative standards deemed to apply at the time. They remain subject to them until such time as the norms are changed or they depart. It is exactly the same for the people who act on behalf of independent states in world politics.

Most human activities could not exist without norms, formal and informal, which constitute the frame that defines and shapes the activity. That is what a political constitution is. That is what rules of the game are. Games cannot exist without rules of the game and they cannot be played unless the players know the rules and observe them at least most of the time.[2] Otherwise uncertainty, disorder, and possibly even chaos would enter into their activities: if the rules of certain team games were not observed by most of the players, the game would probably deteriorate into a brawl. Much the same can be said about political activities. That is the *raison d'être* of a political constitution. Most people recognize that the activities they are involved in have norms to regulate them and that they ought to observe the norms in their conduct because that is what they are required to do and otherwise their relations could deteriorate. The activity could not exist without their observance of its norms. Standards of conduct are conventional and historical: they are crafted by the people involved in an activity and they are reformed by them from time to time in response to changing ideas and circumstances. They cannot be crafted by people who are not involved, for such outsiders cannot know with any precision what is required. Statespeople and their advisers are the only ones who know what the activity of statecraft requires. Speaking historically, they established a 'constitution' for ordering and regulating their international activities which they revise from time to time. The post-1945 version of that normative framework is what I have dubbed 'the global covenant': it consists exclusively of standards of conduct that statespeople themselves have instituted for judging each other's international activities.

The norms of the global covenant apply to sovereign states which are the primary members of international society, as previously indicated. But sovereign

---

[2] This way of looking at human activity is elaborated in Ray Monk, *Ludwig Wittgenstein: The Duty of Genius* (London: Vintage, 1991), esp. 570 ff.

states are not agents or actors in themselves. They are abstractions, ideas. They are the most essential component ideas of a larger idea about the political organization of humankind: the idea of the society of states. Ideas are not actors. States cannot act on their own. They cannot observe norms. They have no responsibilities. That belongs to statespeople, the agents and representatives of sovereign states who act on their behalf. M. J. Peterson puts the point well:

> States remain the primary members of the community—not merely the entities with the greatest range of capabilities, but also the entities with the widest range of rights, duties, and legal capacity under the rules of international law. However, these states are abstract collective entities unable to accomplish anything except through designated human agents. Those who rule domestically also serve as the state's agents in international affairs—exercising its rights, ensuring fulfillment of its obligations, and committing its resources and reputation in relations with other states and other types of actor on the world scene.[3]

The ethics of statecraft obviously apply specifically to statespeople. The reference is of course to national leaders who are involved in the conduct of foreign policy on behalf of an independent country. Usually they present themselves to the world as duly appointed constitutional officeholders. From a classical international society perspective, however, it does not matter whether the foreign policy of a state is under the direction of a constitutional officeholder (for example George Bush) or a personal dictator (for example, Saddam Hussein). International society does not discriminate between democrats and dictators. Instead, it assumes that every independent state has designated agents who act on its behalf when it comes to dealing with other independent states. There almost always is some leader or leadership group who make decisions on behalf of a sovereign state and who thus carry the responsibilities that go with it. Grave problems arise when there is no governing authority in a sovereign state: Somalia was a case in point in the 1990s. But that is a rare exception.

One might object that the foregoing definition of statespeople is too restrictive and overlooks many other people who are likely to be involved in foreign policy, whether subordinate state officials, citizens, or members of international or transnational organizations. There is of course no question but that all public officials, high or low, are accountable for their actions. If they are not accountable their public offices and the state itself are in question. Privates, no less than generals, are subject to national military regulations and they are also subject to the Geneva Conventions. Clerical staff in foreign ministries are subject to legislation governing official secrets and they can be tried for spying and punished if found guilty. So responsibility is clearly a general feature of public administration. However, the powers and responsibilities of the many functionaries employed by foreign ministries, defence ministries, and other state agencies clearly derive from the senior authorities in charge of them. That hier-

---

[3] M. J. Peterson, *Recognition of Governments* (London: Macmillan, 1997), 1.

archical authority is the very basis of any state for without it no state could exist. Responsibility for making foreign policy or military policy clearly rests with the leading officials of the state, particularly the politicians.

The objection that the definition overlooks citizens is important because citizens are constitutionally part of the state. The responsibilities of citizens in the area of international relations is a tricky subject that we shall encounter in later chapters. Citizens obviously are involved in foreign policy to the extent that they stand behind it and help to sustain it: for example, by supporting a national war effort or by underwriting the national economy. The rise of the national state and even more the democratic state has involved citizenries in the international activities of their country. Democratic governments are usually reluctant to frame foreign policies that go against public opinion; they try to be responsive to public opinion. That means that citizens have some voice in foreign policy. But voice is not the same as responsibility. In so far as elected national leaders occupy political offices which give them discretionary authority to actually determine foreign policy they bear the main responsibility for whatever good or harm results. Leaders of democracies, like leaders of any other independent countries, can take the credit when things go right and they must likewise accept responsibility when things go wrong. They are the players and teams on the field of international relations. Citizens are watching them from the stadium: their role is limited to supporting their team.

One might also object that the definition overlooks those many important people who occupy the offices of IGOs and NGOs involved in interactions or transactions across international boundaries. Such people regularly engage in humanitarian, financial, commercial, technological, scientific, medical, cultural, and other activities that intersect the borders of states. These organizations are very important and much work remains to be done in understanding their normative role, as distinguished from their functional or instrumental role, in international relations. Consider, for example, the heavy responsibilities involved in the development and management of air traffic regulations which seek to ensure that air traffic around the world conforms at all times to the fundamental value of personal and public safety. One need only think of the vast and complicated international air traffic control system which exists for that purpose, and the almost countless individuals, on the ground and in the air, who are responsible for operating it with these values foremost in view. Here, then, is an expanding and important area of international ethics.

Yet, however weighty and personally demanding the managerial and operational responsibilities of such people may be, they are not as heavy, indeed not nearly as heavy, as the responsibilities of statespeople, especially the leaders of the major powers. IGOs are required to operate within a framework of guidelines set by the governments of the member states of those organizations. If there is to be a better and safer system of air traffic control, statespeople are the ones in whose hands the decision to develop and install it ultimately rests. By the same token, NGO leaders may represent important private constituencies and they may be concerned about important issues, such as world poverty or human rights or environmental protection. But they are not responsible to anyone except their private constituencies. They do not carry the burden of official public duty, particularly the military burden, which statespeople and especially the leaders of the great powers must carry. It consequently is with statespeople that international ethics must fundamentally be concerned.

World politics at its core is an exclusive game. The ethics of statecraft is a special ethics that applies to a very select group of people: the leading political practitioners of international relations. There were fewer than 200 sovereign states at the start of the twenty-first century. Probably only a limited number of statespeople are involved in the actual conduct of foreign policy as the principal agents or representatives of any such state. If we assume that, on average, there are likely to be no more than 100 people in each country who actually *make* foreign policy by determining the key decisions, then there are fewer than 20,000 people world-wide who are the primary subjects of international ethics.[4] If we are referring to the major powers, which could be defined as the five permanent members of the UN Security Council who are the foremost military powers and the seven leading economic powers, (some nine countries when overlapping membership is subtracted), we are referring to under 1,000 people. But the number of people involved is not important: who those people happen to be is what is important. And they happen to be the most consequential political people on the planet. They are a small number, but their decisions and actions affect virtually everybody on earth, for better and for worse. A handful of people were directly responsible for the Second World War but virtually the entire population of the planet was eventually affected by that conflict at least to some degree. That is why the ethics of statecraft, in spite of applying directly only to a small number of people, is such an important subject.

Standards and Circumstances

For Hedley Bull the classical international society approach is 'characterized above all by explicit reliance upon the exercise of judgment' on the part of the scholar of world politics.[5] Exercising academic judgement is not the same as standing in judgement: the study of political ethics is not a political activity; the student of international ethics is not a political activist. Nor is it the same as

---

[4] The USA is an exception. Both Houses of Congress are involved in foreign policy, and military policy which is probably a larger number of statespeople than in any other country.
[5] Hedley Bull, 'International Theory: The Case for a Classical Approach', in K. Knorr and J. N. Rosenau (eds.), *Contending Approaches to International Politics* (Princeton: Princeton University Press, 1969), 20.

applying the (external) standards of a particular academic philosophy of ethics to the conduct of statespeople and judging them on that basis. The ethics of statecraft is not an applied ethics. Nor is it a technical activity: there is no science or technique of judgement. Statespeople can only be judged academically— that is, non-politically—by their own (internal) standards of conduct. The job of the scholar is to figure out what those standards are and to interpret and assess their use in practice by the people under study. Scholarly interpretation of political conduct is a form of discernment: the scholar is called upon to employ his or her insight and sensibility to uncover, distinguish between, and appraise the various normative considerations that are in play in foreign policy and other international activities. Scholarly judgement is like aesthetic or artistic judgement. The political scientist who seeks to give a scholarly account of the ethics of statecraft is like the theatre or literary critic who tries to assess the merits of a stage-play or a novel. That is not a question of applied ethics or scientific or technical expertise. It is a question of human insight and understanding.

International ethics often provokes scepticism from hard realist scholars who see only a contradiction in that expression. Yet it also provokes the same sceptical response from committed idealist scholars who see only a rationalization of power in the same expression. These perspectives are actually very near to each other and when they are pushed to the limit they come down to the same negative assessment.[6] For hardened realists the conduct of foreign policy is governed by narrow self-interest and expediency. For committed idealists international relations ought to be governed by universal moral standards, such as human rights or social justice. Advocates of each approach usually end up agreeing that international politics discloses a lot of expediency but not much morality. Hard realism might even be a refuge for some disillusioned idealists. Both of these moral outlooks are often indistinguishable from cynicism: they see statespeople as egotistical, as self-serving, and ultimately as hypocrites who speak the language of morality while single-mindedly pursuing their narrow self-interests and acting entirely out of expediency.

It must go without saying that a study that is undertaken without scepticism about the ethical limits of statecraft should raise serious doubt in our minds: foreign policy is shot through with expediency. It also goes without saying that scholars of international ethics should adopt a critical stance, avoid rationalization, and lay open the conduct of statespeople to appropriate moral standards. The exercise of scholarly discernment involves seeing what the appropriate standards are. At a minimum scholars should avoid extreme positions which usually blinker judgement in these matters. They should steer well clear of the superficial and quick-fix analyses of would-be foreign-policy advisers. They

[6] See Martin Wight, *International Theory: The Three Traditions* (Leicester and London: Leicester University Press for the Royal Institute of International Affairs, 1991), 47.

should also stay well beneath the high-minded condemnations of alienated ideal-ists with outsider mentalities who cannot or will not enter into the situation of ordinary, morally flawed statespeople. The ethics of statecraft is a middle-of-the-road, empirically based inquiry that probes the normative sphere in which ordinary statespeople are obliged to operate.

In scrutinizing the international conduct of statespeople scholars should always keep both standards and circumstances fully and equally in view. The problem with most idealists is that they only see the standards of conduct. The problem with most realists is that they only see the circumstances in which the activities take place. Here we can learn something from American and English courts of law where breaches of the law by the accused are judged not only by applying the appropriate standards but also by interrogating the evid-ence with the aim of determining whether or not circumstances mitigate the accused's involvement in the crime. No reasonable and fair judgement would otherwise be possible. Crimes do not occur in a vacuum: they are situated in time and place among certain people. The same can be said of international ethics. One cannot divorce standards from circumstances and judge international action according to the one or the other without relapsing into the lofty idealist outlook or the narrow realist outlook. If only standards are applied to assess the conduct of a political leader, the analysis will be too empirically undiscriminat-ing and too morally demanding. By the same token, however, if only circum-stances are taken into account, the analysis will be too empirically yielding, and ultimately too complacent. Anyone who wishes to grasp the normative charac-ter of statecraft must chart a middle course between these unsatisfactory extremes.

The ethics of statecraft should be understood as a situational ethics in which both standards and circumstances have an important place. Martin Wight had a good insight into the subject and one of his most important reflections gives an indication of the classical approach we ought to take in attempting to understand it:

Statesmen act under various pressures, and appeal with varying degrees of sincerity to various principles. It is for those who study international relations to judge their actions, which means judging the validity of *their* ethical principles. This is not a process of sci-entific analysis; it is more akin to literary criticism. It involves developing a sensitive awareness of the intractability of *all* political situations, and the moral quandary in which *all* statecraft operates.[7]

This passage is sufficiently important to merit reiteration. If we wish to do justice to the subject of international ethics as a historical practice, Martin Wight is saying that we must interrogate stateleaders' ethical principles in judging their conduct. We cannot impose our principles. And he is saying that we must be

---

[7] Wight, *International Theory*, 258 (emphasis added). I am grateful to Nick Wheeler for draw-ing this passage to my attention.

attuned to the concrete situations in which all statespeople are obliged to operate. We cannot ignore their situations. Wight was an admirer of Edmund
Burke's philosophical statecraft. Burke has written:

I cannot stand forward and give praise or blame to anything which relates to human
actions, and human concerns, on a simple view of the object, as it stands stripped of
every relation, in all the nakedness and solitude of metaphysical abstraction.
Circumstances (which with some gentlemen pass for nothing) give in reality to every
political principle its distinguishing color and discriminating effect.[8]

If we wish to survey the ethics of statecraft—which is renowned for ambivalence
and confusion—we shall have to accept that statespeople will often find themselves in a 'moral quandary' from which there can be no easy escape. We have
witnessed many such moral quandaries since the end of the cold war: Somalia,
Bosnia, Rwanda, Kosovo, East Timor, etc.

Power and Responsibility

In a celebrated essay written in the idiom of classical political science, Max
Weber identifies politics in its deepest normative meaning with a demanding
'ethic of responsibility'. Political activity at the highest levels calls for 'relentlessness in viewing the realities of life, and the ability to face such realities and
to measure up to them . . . [the politician] then acts by following an ethic of
responsibility and somewhere he reaches the point where he says: "Here I stand;
I can do no other." '[9] Even if this sounds overly dramatic and seems to echo
Martin Luther it would be hard to find a better portrayal of the basic ethic
involved in statecraft which is by any standard a morally demanding activity.[10]
    In considering the word 'responsibility' there is an important distinction to
keep in mind: anyone who is in a position of responsibility is accountable *to*
somebody and is also answerable *for* something.[11] Both of those dimensions of
responsibility are defined constitutionally by the sovereign state and the society
of states. At a minimum stateleaders are answerable to their citizens and to the
leaders of other states. Statespeople are answerable for their policies and for failures of policy. They are also answerable for omissions of policy: for not having
a policy to address a pressing problem. I am not saying that statespeople always
act responsibly, because it is obvious that they do not. I am only saying that they

    [8] Edmund Burke, *Reflections on the Revolution in France*, ed. J. G. A. Pocock, (Indianapolis:
Liberty Press, 1987), 7.
    [9] Max Weber, 'Politics as a Vocation', in H. H. Gerth and C. Wright Mills (eds.), *From Max
Weber: Essays in Sociology* (New York: OUP, 1958), 120–8. For an important recent study which
is critical of Weber's thesis see Daniel Warner, *An Ethic of Responsibility in International Relations*
(Boulder, Colo.: Lynne Reinner, 1991), esp. ch. 1.
    [10] Max Weber was a Lutheran.   [11] See the penetrating discussion, ibid. 20–3.

occupy positions of responsibility and, as such, they are responsible to others for their policies and actions. The offices that statespeople occupy are commonly understood as 'positions of responsibility'. Responsibility comes with the power and authority conferred by the positions. National leadership positions are the most important political posts. That is because a stateleader can authorize policies and activities that can significantly affect many other people—other states (and their citizens) as well as the citizens of his or her own state. Sometimes those consequences can be profound, for example, during times of war or economic crisis.

Responsibility is a requirement and expectation of conduct. The political offices leaders occupy normally specify requirements of the office: what its occupation and exercise calls for procedurally. Political offices entail procedural requirements virtually by definition. Incumbents are subject to those requirements as legal conditions for holding office. But responsibility is also an expectation of conduct in the circumstances. The circumstances under which leaders operate usually set the limits of what can be expected. Circumstances are especially important in world politics which is a pluralistic sphere in which the power of any one state, or any combination of states, is definitely limited once we get beyond the very exceptional area of nuclear weapons. The pluralist character of international society shapes and conditions the responsibilities of statespeople. There is no one political authority that is responsible for the condition of the world and accountable to the people of the world. There is no global *universitas*. As indicated in the previous chapter, the UN is not a *universitas*. The political world is still a *societas* of sovereign states. The UN Security Council exists to uphold the *societas* of states. The politics of the world in many important respects must be catered for locally. That is not only the consequence of a society of states; it is the intention. The main point of the balance of power and other basic arrangements and norms of international society is to prevent a global hegemon from arising. That stems from a deeply held and historically informed worry that the negative consequences of a world policeman would greatly outweigh the positive consequences. Some of the biggest and most important wars of modern history have been fought to prevent that from happening.

International pluralism diminishes the responsibility of great powers, and it deliberately seeks to do that. But it does not eliminate it and nor does it seek to eliminate it. The great powers are still responsible for whatever they do or could have done in the circumstances and it is still possible to ask the following question: faced with the fratricide in Somalia or Rwanda or Bosnia-Herzegovina or Kosovo or East Timor what should the USA have done? The question arises because the American leaders were in a position to do something and even if they decided to do nothing they were affecting the situation by their inaction. Washington was answerable for its foreign policy as regards the conflict in Bosnia because as the greatest power of the day the USA could affect the

Bosnian situation in either a positive or a negative way, by inaction as well as by action: it was probably the only state that could get the belligerent parties to enter into a peace agreement. However, the leaders who were primarily answerable for the war in Bosnia-Herzegovina were the leaders of the warring parties involved: the Serbian and Croatian warlords and their foreign manipulators in Belgrade and Zagreb. They brought the conflict about and it could not be brought to an end without their co-operation as well as that of the Bosnian government. That tells us something about the pluralistic and localized character of responsibility in world politics, particularly since the end of the cold war.

'Responsibility' invokes an answer that can put to rest the question 'How do you justify that policy or action?' The question can be asked of anyone on those occasions when he or she is saying or doing something which impacts—or is intended to impact or is likely to impact—on somebody else. That question is particularly pointed if the action seems uncalled for in the circumstances at the time and the impact is detrimental. That is the negative responsibility to forbear from inflicting needless and unjustified hardship or damages or suffering on others. We would not put the question if the consequences were benign. We would, however, also put the question if it addressed a refusal or failure to say something or do something which is called for in the circumstances and could have beneficial results. That is the positive responsibility to come to the assistance of others when the occasion demands and it is possible and wise to do so.

It might be thought that positive responsibilities take priority over negative responsibilities in international relations. In our present-day world of political activism that is very easy to believe. We live at a time when the capacity and desire to take political action is probably greater than it has ever been. Many domestic political cultures became activist in the twentieth century. Western political culture is an activist political culture. But world politics based on the *societas* of states is not fundamentally activist. It is closer to the opposite pole: it is forbearant far more than activist; it is basically *laissez-faire*. Activism in world politics is confined mainly to the sphere of international peace and security and global economics: on those great issues of world affairs the great powers are required to be vigilant and active. But even here activism is usually directed at preventing a political or economic crisis from getting worse. The ethics of statecraft reflect a greater concern about preserving a good that presently exists (preserving peace) than about pursuing a good that does not presently exist (eradicating world poverty). It is conservative more than progressive: it seeks to conserve existing values more than it seeks to create new values. Activism is not fundamental to the ethics of statecraft. Forbearance and toleration are fundamental. International ethics is a harness and a bridal more than spurs and a saddle: it is a classical liberal ethics.

While the ethics of statecraft concern the responsibilities of all statespeople, it gives special attention to the leaders of the great powers because they can cause the greatest harm and do the greatest good in world politics. Great power brings greater responsibility: great powers can justifiably be called upon to maintain or restore international peace and security or to uphold or repair the world economy. Great power also obviously brings greater privilege: great powers can justifiably expect other states to recognize their special status and respond to their legitimate claims and demands. Another way of putting this is to say that great powers have greater ability to act and thus they can be said to have greater responsibilities. Responsibility for global peace and security nowadays falls on the USA. It is the only truly global military power at the present time. Other major military powers are regional rather than global. Responsibility for the world economy is more pluralistic: it resides not only with the USA but also with the European Union (especially Germany), Japan, and a few other leading economic powers or centres. China is poised to join this select group.

We may doubt that post-Soviet Russia has much military responsibility owing to a decline in its power stemming from the disorganization of its armed forces and the chaos of its economy. Certainly, Russia at the start of the twenty-first century was not the great power that the Soviet Union managed to be during the cold war. But we should be mindful of the care that was taken by the USA and other leading Western powers to secure the acquiescence of Russia to the expansion of NATO. And we should notice how Russia was asked to attend meetings of the G-7 even though its economic strength and discipline does not warrant its full membership in that leading body. That courtship is a clear indication that Russia remains a great power, even if its stature is not as high as it was during the cold war. Responsibility is similarly attuned to power in many other international spheres.

We thus have a right to expect every stateleader without exception to observe the UN Charter in the conduct of foreign military policy and to observe the rules of international trade in the conduct of foreign economic policy. But we have no right to expect the leaders of minor military powers to be responsible for world peace or to expect the leaders of poor countries to be responsible for the global economy. That obviously would be absurd. However, we have every right to expect the major military powers and the leading economic powers to bear those responsibilities. These generally are the sort of expectations that we find operating in world politics.

Here we approach a central question in the study of international ethics: what conduct can we reasonably expect from the people who occupy high state offices or similar positions, who have access to the greatest concentrations of military and economic power, and who always exercise some discretion in its employment? We can legitimately expect them to strive to carry out their international responsibilities to the best of their abilities in the circumstances in which they find themselves. We have a right to expect that because we must assume, in operating with a conception of responsibility, that those people are capable of exercising power in a way that would qualify as being 'responsible'. We must assume that national leaders, all of them, are intelligent and conscientious people; that they know what their international responsibilities are; that they will endeavour to act responsibly as far as that is possible in the circumstances. We realize of course that some national leaders will not always act in that manner and a few may never act that way. That is an inescapable reality of politics and politicians. But we must take it for granted that all of them are capable of such action. If we assumed that some leaders were not capable, we would have no basis for judging their conduct.

As it happens, the ethics of the global covenant apply to all stateleaders without exception and these assumptions are made by the practitioners themselves. How can we say that? Because otherwise they could not reasonably expect or demand answers from each other as regards controversial policies and actions. They could not even get into a normative controversy. They could not raise normative questions about each other's foreign policies. Yet we know that statespeople do exactly that all the time. They recognize that they are legitimately subject to normative questioning about their foreign policies from their political counterparts in other countries.

The basic ethos of responsible statecraft can be summarized. In practice, as indicated, we can legitimately expect statespeople to authorize military actions or make economic decisions which disclose care and judgement and give due regard to other states and anybody else who might be affected. We can legitimately expect them not to act recklessly with the security or welfare of their own people. We can also justifiably expect them not to beggar their neighbours or trample on the rights and legitimate interests of other states. We could not expect that if all stateleaders were foolish or vicious or indifferent to moral argument. In that case there would be no compass points for judging international human conduct. There would be no international law. There would be no diplomatic practices. There would be no political virtues. There would be no normative dialogue of world politics. We would be adrift in a disconnected and silent world of moral relativism. That is not how international society operates.

In saying that we can legitimately expect stateleaders to act responsibly, I do not wish to suggest that they all have the same opportunities to be responsible, or even the same responsibilities. Clearly they do not because their power and circumstances are not all the same. As indicated, only a small number of powers have major responsibilities for peace and prosperity across the world. If responsibility is the alter-ego of power in world politics the responsibilities of statespeople cannot everywhere be the same because the military and economic power available to them definitely is not the same. The substantive conditions of states which underpin their power are highly variable across the globe. This brings us back to the fundamental distinction between great powers and other states.

There has always been unequal responsibility between the great powers and everybody else: minor powers can benefit from peace and prosperity but they cannot contribute greatly to it—at least not on an individual basis. World peace is contingent on peace among the great powers: if they are at war, the world will be at war, even if everybody else is at peace—which would be unlikely. Global prosperity is contingent on prosperity among the big developed economies: if they are in depression everybody else will be dragged down with them. The two World Wars and the great depression of the twentieth century are obvious cases in point. The vast majority of states can only affect world peace and global prosperity marginally and locally. So differential responsibilities are particularly evident in world politics because countries differ enormously in the weight of their organized power. That differential power and responsibility dictates that the ethics of statecraft must be particularly concerned, although not exclusively concerned, with the conduct of the great powers. The leaders of those powers have the heaviest burdens of responsibility in world politics.

We arrive at the heart of the matter. The ethics of statecraft is fundamentally about hard choices faced by a select class of men and women (statespeople) who are obliged to operate in a sphere of human relations over which they exercise limited control even at the best of times. Hard choices are decisions that cannot responsibly be avoided, and involve not merely personal or political costs but also moral liabilities. They are normative choices: they are difficult and demanding in the moral and not merely the instrumental sense of the word. Hard choices are not choices between one's responsibilities and one's self-interests. They are choices between conflicting but equally compelling interests or concerns, and even more than that they are choices between different but equally fundamental responsibilities when they come into conflict. They are choices between values. They are choices between greater and lesser goods but also, and probably more often, between greater and lesser evils. They involve sacrifice: not only sacrificing oneself but sacrificing others as well. They consequently have an element of tragedy which is a standing feature of war and some other theatres of international relations.[12] Tragedy involves sacrificing something of value for the sake of another value, and making the sacrifice with a heavy heart but in the conviction that the alternative is worse. Embarking on war is virtually an acceptance of the tragic events which are bound to follow.

Hard choices may also involve 'dirty hands': the moral taint that derives from engaging in actions which have to be taken in the circumstances and which involve an inescapable element of wickedness. Many decisions surrounding the development and testing of nuclear weapons are morally tainted. Any leader whose country is involved in war will also know what that is all about. Anyone who hopes to understand war must try to access that same understanding. That is the darker side of the ethics of statecraft.

But there is a brighter side which is expressed in President Charles De Gaulle's definition of a stateleader 'as somebody who takes risks, including moral

---

[12] See H. Butterfield, 'The Tragic Element in Modern International Conflict,' *History and Human Relations* (London: Collins, 1951), 9–36.

risks'.[13] De Gaulle may have been thinking of his own role in leading the Free French forces in opposition to the Vichy French government which collaborated with the Nazis in the Second World War: a calculated action which divided the French nation. A more recent example of what De Gaulle surely had in mind is the 1993 decision of Israeli Prime Minister Yitzhak Rabin and PLO leader Yassir Arafat to take, after decades of bitter and bloody conflict, the very high risk of signing a peace accord and trusting each other to embark in good faith on a course of reconciliation and coexistence between the Israeli and Palestinian peoples. Both leaders made this decision despite the high likelihood of dividing their respective national constituencies and provoking civil war. Whatever they decided they would bear the responsibility for the consequences, bad as well as good. The 1995 assassination of Rabin is a sober reminder of not only the political hazards but also the personal danger involved in moral risk-taking by national leaders. This extraordinary human episode cannot begin to be captured by a purely instrumental method of analysis, such as regarding it merely as a high stakes game of poker.

Situational Ethics

The ethics of statecraft is a situational ethics. Human conduct is situational by definition. By contemplating or engaging in international activities, such as foreign policy or diplomacy, statespeople always find themselves in a situation which consists of other statespeople and their activities. That situation is largely made by the statespeople involved: it basically consists of their policies and activities and the ideas, beliefs, values, interests, concerns, convictions, understandings, misunderstandings, which inform them. The situation can of course change by changes of mind (or heart) on the part of the people involved. 'If minds change, as they do, this merely means that with the lapse of time a new situation has arisen.'[14] Situations can be neglected but they cannot be avoided: if a statesman or stateswoman neglects the situation, 'the situation will not neglect him [or her]'.[15] That is because other people are inescapably involved and whatever we do or fail to do cannot change that circumstantial reality.

Other people are an unavoidable part of our circumstances, and we are part of their circumstances, and that is our joint fate. International situations can be manœuvred by clever intrigues and subterfuges and threats but not easily, and the results may be different from what was intended. Spying and coercive diplomacy are part of the equipment of statecraft. Conspiracy theories of international relations correctly recognize that situations can be manipulated, but they greatly

[13] Quoted by Stanley Hoffmann, *Duties Beyond Borders* (Syracuse, NY: Syracuse University Press, 1981), 18.
[14] R. G. Collingwood, *The Idea of History* (London: OUP, 1975), 316.   [15] Ibid. 316.

exaggerate the ease with which that can be accomplished. Most situations cannot be controlled with confidence even by great powers. International circumstances are even more difficult to control than domestic circumstances. When other people are involved, things can go wrong, events can turn out differently than anticipated or intended. Situations can of course be responded to and they should be: it is a responsibility of statespeople to face up to their situation and deal with their circumstances in a way that could answer any reasonable criticisms. During the cold war, the leaders of the Soviet Union, China, and the USA were each other's most important circumstance. During the Second World War Hitler, Tojo, Stalin, Roosevelt, and Churchill were each other's most important circumstance. These leaders were obsessed with each other's political and military intentions.[16] They had to be obsessive because they were involved in great life-and-death struggles with each other. Statespeople ignore their circumstances at their peril: that is a virtual axiom of the situational ethics of statecraft.

How should scholars of international relations try to come to grips with the situational ethics of statecraft? Political scientists can second-guess the normative choices of statespeople after the event, knowing how they turned out. But that is not the same as having to make the choices themselves and thus exercising judgement on the spot in full awareness that, whatever is decided, the responsibility is one's own. Scholars should avoid abusing their hindsight by engaging in any kind of gratuitous second-guessing activity comparable to what American football fans refer to as 'Monday morning quarterbacking': phony wisdom about how the game should have been won that sports commentators flaunt after the big Sunday game is over. Collingwood indicates what is involved: the task of the student of human conduct, including the conduct of statespeople, is 'to think himself [or herself] into' the action being observed and reflected upon.[17] Probably the best that scholars of international relations can do in that regard is try to grasp the situations of the statespeople involved: to imagine what it must have been like to be in the shoes of a president or prime minister or foreign minister or military commander or finance minister at the time the choices were confronted and the decision was taken. Exercising scholarly judgement in these matters involves entering vicariously into the international situations of the statespeople under study and attempting to discern the normative issues at stake. In doing that, scholars are doing justice to the people they are studying. That might be a preliminary definition of the ethics of a humanist political science.

How can the scholar get into the shoes of the stateleader? Basically it is no different than the general human capacity to put oneself in somebody else's place before judging his or her actions.[18] It is no different than the literary critic

---

[16] That is evident from Churchill's memoirs. See Winston S. Churchill, *The Second World War* (Boston, Mass.: Houghton Mifflin, 1951).

[17] Collingwood, *Idea of History*, 213.

[18] Ibid. 226. Collingwood's discussion of the role of imagination in historical inquiry is the background to these remarks.

or theatre critic placing himself or herself in the position of the playwright or in the role of the actor in order to judiciously assess the play or its performance. It is no different than the sports writer viewing the game on the field and critically appraising the play of the players and the teams. Observing and analysing the actions of statespeople is essentially the same: we can transport ourselves via our imaginations and background knowledge into their political roles. We can gain background knowledge by reading history and by keeping up with current international events. Having put ourselves metaphorically in their shoes, we are in a position to try to judge the normative import of their actions.

There are, of course, limits set by the fact that we are not literally in their shoes and we cannot know all the particulars of their situation. And it is worth remembering that no human can ever adopt the persona of any other human being in the sense of living their life and having their experiences. All lives are unique at least in that regard. But other humans are not completely inscrutable: we can manage to make sense of each other's actions whether we are trying in a practical way to deal with each other or we are attempting in an academic way to interpret human conduct. We can try to fathom the situations of other people. Even if we cannot know all the details of a stateleader's situation we can and must recognize the import of situations in their conduct of international relations. The academic point of doing that is not to pretend to know more than they know or to give them gratuitous advice. It is to construe their conduct correctly.

A circumstance is by definition a condition ('an accessory condition' according to Webster) that affects what one is able to do at that time and place.[19] Circumstances are actualities which must be taken into account in making or carrying out a decision—if one hopes to be successful. In conventional legal thought, responsibility is always affected by circumstances, and circumstances are always a factor in determining responsibility. Thus, not only would it be foolish to ignore the circumstances, it would be irresponsible. Circumstances are not fixed, but shift and change so that at one time or place an opportunity for action might arise which might not exist at another. That is because the world of human relations, including international relations, is always in flux. Correctly recognizing and seizing the moment of opportunity is a virtue in a stateleader. By ignoring the circumstances in which politicians find themselves, in all likelihood political scientists will only end up by misconstruing their decisions and perhaps misrepresenting them as well. Here is the voice of Edmund Burke who was far closer to the centres of decision-making than most political scientists:

A statesman differs from a professor in a university; the latter has only the general view of society; the former, the statesman, has a number of circumstances to combine with those general ideas, and to take into his consideration . . . A statesman, never losing sight

---

[19] *Webster's Seventh New Collegiate Dictionary* (Springfield, Mass.: G. and C. Merriam, 1967).

of principles, is to be guided by circumstances; and, judging contrary to the exigencies of the moment, he may ruin his country forever.[20]

In approaching and making decisions national leaders could perhaps fail to recognize their circumstances or could misunderstand them; or they could ignore them even if they were aware of them. But they could not escape from them because a circumstance is, by definition, a surrounding and impinging state of affairs that we cannot control and bend to our will but something in which we are entangled none the less. Important decisions involving foreign policy are always affected by the circumstances in which they are taken. Statespeople cannot responsibly avoid the circumstances in which they find themselves. And if students of international ethics want to have a realistic grasp of the subject they ought to appreciate the limits of choice, in that respect, that all decision-makers face.

Consider, for example, President Truman's fateful decision to drop nuclear bombs on Hiroshima and Nagasaki in August 1945. Many have subsequently condemned that decision as immoral—usually on the just-war grounds that it deliberately targeted civilians. But any moral appraisal will only be realistic if it takes into account Truman's responsibilities in the circumstances at the time: the climax of a world war in which the USA was a victim of Japanese aggression at Pearl Harbor and had for several years fought a series of fierce air, land, and sea battles, at great sacrifice in American lives, to drive Japanese forces back across the Pacific. And the Americans did that with no ambitions of territorial conquest of their own. We would have to consider the choices open to Truman at that time. Should he use the bomb in the hope of bringing the war to a speedy and favourable conclusion and knowing that would save the lives of many American soldiers but would also kill and injure an unknown but probably very large number of Japanese civilians? Should he order an invasion of Japan which would almost certainly result in heavy losses to American troops and probably even higher casualties to Japanese civilians, if the destruction and occupation of Germany is anything to go by, something Truman was fully aware of. Should he order a naval blockade of Japan which might eventually starve its inhabitants into submission? Other conceivable options also might have been available to Truman.

President Truman's moral responsibility, as seen from the perspective of situational ethics, was to determine which measures would bring victory and the prospect of future world peace with the least additional suffering. If his decision stands condemned it must not have been the best choice in the circumstances. Perhaps the best choice, if it were available, would have been the awesome but clearly less dangerous demonstration of one bomb in the coastal waters of Japan in the hope of provoking Japanese leaders to capitulate. We should of course

[20] Quoted by Albert R. Coll, 'Normative Prudence as a Tradition of Statecraft', *Ethics and International Affairs*, 5 (1991), 45.

remember that Truman had only two nuclear bombs at his disposal and there was no guarantee they would explode.[21] Even if that stratagem failed to persuade the Japanese leaders to accept the terms of unconditional surrender the one bomb remaining could still be deployed in the hope of ending the war then and there. But the Japanese leaders would now bear the responsibility. Some might argue that, by having attacked Pearl Harbor, the Japanese bore that responsibility anyway. But that observation can be criticized for failing to distinguish between the justification of embarking on a war of self-defence against an aggressor (*jus ad bellum*) and the justification of the manner in which war is waged (*jus in bello*). Of course there may be other important circumstances which affected Truman's decision. If there were other practical possibilities at the time they would also have to be canvassed if the decision taken was to be the most responsible one in the circumstances.

At the end of the day that is always a matter of judgement. There is no science or rational technique that can take the place of judgement. There is only making the best of a difficult situation, acting intelligently with regard to circumstances and conscientiously with regards to standards of conduct. Since circumstances are always particular, by definition, there can be no fixed and permanent ethical principles governing such decisions—any more than there could be a fixed and permanent foreign policy for all circumstances. For if decision-makers are reasonable and informed of the situation in which they find themselves, their policies must change as circumstances change. Machiavelli defended the following proposition in one of his discourses on statecraft: whoever desires continued good fortune must change his conduct with the times.[22] Assuming that decision-makers are responsible agents in the meaning of 'responsibility' employed in this book, there can only be the requirement that due account be taken of all the relevant circumstances and standards before making a decision. That would be a requirement and expectation of responsible statecraft.

We can sum up the argument thus far. Since the decisions and actions of stateleaders are always made in concrete circumstances of time and place, scholars who seek to understand the ethics of statecraft are obliged to adopt some version of situational ethics. This is not the ethics of the ideal choice or the best choice or even the least costly choice. And it is not moral relativism in which common standards of conduct are abandoned. Rather, it is the ethics of the best choice in the circumstances, or perhaps the least damaging choice if in the circumstances prevailing at the time all choices are deplorable and destructive to some degree—which is common in war.[23] That is the decision that we feel

---

[21] I am grateful to John Groom for reminding me of this important fact.

[22] N. Machiavelli, *The Discourses* (Harmondsworth: Penguin Books, 1970), book 3, discourse 9.

[23] This standard has also been identified by Michael Oakeshott as the most appropriate one for appraising human conduct in politics. See his *Rationalism in Politics and Other Essays*, new and expanded edn. (Indianapolis: Liberty Press, 1991), 10.

bound to make, however reluctantly, after canvassing the options available, taking into account as best we can their foreseeable consequences, taking stock of our procedural and prudential responsibilities as we understand them, and being honest with ourselves and forthright with others. Arguably the best hope a responsible leader could have for such a decision is not that its consequences will prove his or her cleverness, but that he or she will be able to live in clear conscience with the consequences, whatever they turn out to be. Arnold Wolfers identifies 'the best moral choice that circumstances permit' as the distinctive ethics of statecraft: 'nonperfectionist ethics'.[24] That is as good a definition of the subject as I have been able to find.

The foregoing discussion is intended to underline an important characteristic of the ethics of statecraft: it resembles politics in some fundamental respects, in its characteristic ambiguities, uncertainties, contingencies, and inconclusiveness. It is a political ethics. The ethics of statecraft is inherently provisional: whatever can be justified can only be justified for the time being. Tomorrow the situation might change: the people involved might change; they might change their minds and their policies. That might affect us. It might change our relations and dictate a revision of our policies—just as President Gorbachev's reform of the Soviet Union dictated a change of American foreign policy. World politics is not a sphere of moral absolutes or moral certainties: in politics there are few if any absolutes and no certainties. In foreign policy that is especially so. World politics is a sphere of human conduct with many ambiguities. Political ideologues or religious fundamentalists or anybody else who is convinced in advance of the permanent and invincible moral superiority of his or her position—i.e., those who hold fast to a heartfelt conviction or an article of faith come hell or high water—are the furthest removed from the moral outlook actually required of people involved in world politics. Ideological or religious crusaders are among the worst enemies of world politics.

For responsible statespeople, certainly for national leaders of the major powers whose international responsibilities are the heaviest, the best choice in the circumstances is something closely akin to the moral equivalent of the political art of the possible: the ethics of imperfection.[25] The responsible statesman or stateswoman must be a politician and not an anti-politician. The responsible statesman or stateswoman might be defined as somebody who can make the best of a bad situation. That worldly but also civilized self-discipline would be an instance of political virtue.

---

[24] Arnold Wolfers, 'Statesmanship and Moral Choice', in *Discord and Collaboration* (Baltimore: The Johns Hopkins University Press, 1965), 51. Stanley Hoffmann adopts a similar approach in *Duties beyond Borders*.

[25] In my view the leading commentator on the subject of human imperfection in politics is Edmund Burke. See, especially, 'Letters on a Regicide Peace', in F. W. Raffety, *The Works of Edmund Burke* (Oxford: OUP, 1928), vol. VI.

Political Virtue in International Relations

Arnold Wolfers's concept of non-perfectionist ethics supplies a strategic opening for studying responsible choices in international relations. But it understates
a crucial consideration: the actors and their conduct. For once we bring circumstances into the picture we must also bring actors equally into that picture:
we are only interested in circumstances for the light they shed on human conduct. We look at the circumstances to understand the conduct but we might just
as well look at the conduct to figure out the circumstances. The one sheds light
on the other. What can we reasonably expect of statesmen and stateswomen in
the circumstances of foreign affairs in which they find themselves? This
undoubtedly is the most difficult question in the ethics of statecraft. We can
only answer it if we have some worldly way of diagnosing and illuminating the
conduct and misconduct of people in such positions. I am convinced that the
best way is by returning to the classical idea of the virtues and specifically political virtue. The virtues probe conduct in itself.

The virtues draw our attention to concrete human conduct in the historical
situations in which it occurs. As such, the virtues should be distinguished from
abstract moral axioms, for instance, the categorical imperative advocated by
Kant or the closely related principles of justice recommended by Rawls or the
criterion of utility proposed by Bentham. Such moral axioms emphasize the universal or general and downplay the particular or situational. In other words, they
are anti-historical. When we assess the conduct of national leaders by reference
to the political virtues we are viewing it in relation to what could reasonably be
expected of a person in that position of responsibility in the circumstances at
the time. As indicated, by the 'political virtues' I refer to the dispositions and
disciplines, intellectual and moral, that are required to make the best choice that
circumstances permit, or the least worse choice if all choices are deplorable to
some degree, which is not uncommon in international politics. One definition of
political virtue is the ability to steady down, to ignore the surrounding clamour,
to forbear from acting according to impulse or temptation or passion or dogma,
and to carefully determine the most responsible course of action in the circumstances. Any political leader who is irresolute or indecisive or corrupt or incau-
tious or fanatical is giving evidence of political vices and not political virtues.
The prudential stateleader has been characterized by Burke in the following
terms: 'to dare to be fearful, when all about you are full of presumption and
confidence, and when those who are bold at the hazard of others would push
your caution and disaffection, is to show a mind prepared for its trial'.[26]

Political virtue obviously involves 'character': the self-respect, strength of
will, open-minded outlook, and other mental dispositions and disciplines that

---

[26] Quoted by L. I. Bredvold and R. G. Ross (eds.), *The Philosophy of Edmund Burke* (Ann Arbor:
University of Michigan Press, 1967), 38.

are necessary to do what is morally required in the circumstances. Character is not personality; the second is a psychological category, but the first is a moral category. When we study somebody's character we are not merely studying his or her psychological propensities to act; we are studying their dispositions and disciplines in endeavouring to recognize and do the right thing in the circumstances. We are studying their ability to harness their personality. We might explain the particular actions of a leader in a particular situation by reference to his or her personality: that is a field day for biographers and historians and journalists which may reveal a lot about personal behaviour. But the ethics of statecraft is not about describing or explaining the personal behaviour of particular leaders; it is about construing their public actions by reference to the standards of conduct which apply to them. A personality is something we all have but character is something we do not always demonstrate. Character is a moral faculty which overcomes the ever present possibility and temptation of personal self-indulgence.

The virtues come into play in human conduct because there is almost always some room for discretion in the choices that people make. They could miscalculate, they could misunderstand the situation, they could do the wrong thing, they could act prematurely or too late. It is that freedom to make mistakes, and then to compound the problem by reciprocating, which gives international relations its roller-coaster dynamics: that was a feature of the cold war which thankfully never got totally out of hand by reaching the stage of using nuclear weapons. The exercise of political virtue in the form of intelligence, prudence, and good judgement, on both sides, always managed to contain the dangers of such moments before events spun entirely out of control. The American and Soviet leaders ultimately used their discretion in a responsible way—even if their occasional stupidity or dogmatism or recklessness or negligence or poor judgement set such hazardous events in motion in the first place. The Cuban missile crisis of 1963 is an example. Discretion has been conceived as an area of human behaviour 'left open by a surrounding belt of restriction': Ronald Dworkin uses the metaphor of 'the hole in a doughnut' to capture the idea.[27] In other words, when we employ the term discretion we always have in mind a background of non-instrumental standards of conduct (laws, regulations, etc.) in relation to which the open space of discretion can be said to exist.

To repeat an important point, responsibility attaches itself to both offices and incumbents of offices. We speak of official responsibilities or duties. For holders of high political office in well-organized states official responsibilities are defined by the constitution and other laws or customs that institute the office or are encompassed by it. The rules that define the office also define the responsibilities of the office: an office is a set of defined responsibilities. In the case of

---

[27] Ronald Dworkin, 'Is Law a System of Rules?' in Ronald Dworkin (ed.), *The Philosophy of Law* (Oxford: OUP, 1979), 52.

the office of President of the United States those responsibilities are set out in the constitution and include the fundamental duty of preserving, protecting, and defending the constitution. To that end the office establishes the incumbent as commander-in-chief and makes available the authority to command the armed forces, to make treaties and appoint ambassadors (with the advice and consent of the Senate), and so forth (Article 2).

The US constitution provides a way of thinking about the discretionary responsibilities of independent statecraft because it is silent on details of presidential responsibility that have emerged over time and have been crafted and honed by presidential incumbents—especially successful presidents—in the conduct of their official duties. Rules of office define the authority and powers of the office: who can occupy the office, how the office shall be occupied, what its jurisdiction is, etc. But rules of office do not and could not say what incumbents of the offices should do with their discretionary authority and power in particular situations. That would be absurd because the details of circumstances and contingencies in particular situations cannot be known in advance. Offices are silent about the policies and actions that incumbents may take within the discretion afforded to them by their office. Procedural responsibility is defined by official rules. But discretionary responsibility cannot be defined that way; it can only be defined by other normative considerations that bear on the conduct of public officials. The most pertinent of all such normative considerations is the virtues that incumbents of political offices can reasonably be expected to bring to their offices and to demonstrate in the exercise of their official authority and powers.

We might think of the political virtues as the norms that fill in the area of discretion in political activity. Thus, for example, under the UN charter member states have a right of non-intervention and thus a corresponding obligation not to intervene—except in lawfully recognized circumstances. The rule of non-intervention is not open to serious doubt as to its legal form or existence. However, it is open to stateleaders to decide when and where and how it shall be enforced. Even if it were possible it might still be unwise to enforce it at all times in every place on earth. If a superpower is engaged in an act of intervention which violates another state's right of non-intervention it may be impossible to do anything about it. Even if something could be done it might still be unwise if it involved an unacceptable risk of major war. In that event discretion might be the better part of valour. The political virtues—in the above examples, the virtues of prudence and judgement—are intended to capture the dispositions and disciplines that decision-makers ought to bring to their discretionary choices. As a normative idea, the virtues draw our attention to concrete human activity, the policies and actions of real people in the historical situations in which they find themselves. When we assess the conduct of national leaders in terms of the political virtues, we are viewing it in relation to what could reasonably be expected of a person in that position of responsibility in the circumstances at the time.

That opens up the subjects of judgement and prudence which are centrally important political virtues in the international sphere. Hobbes provides a useful starting point for capturing their *modus operandi*: judgement is an intellectual faculty which is disclosed by the ability to notice similarities and differences and distinguish between them, by discernment. Exercising discernment in human relations is not always an easy thing to do, and those who are discerning are said 'to have a good judgment'.[28] Hobbes noticed that judgment links up with discretion and is little different from it in practice. However, as already indicated, I think it would be more apt to say that judgement, or lack of judgement, fills in the space left open by discretion.

Thus, exercising political judgement means filling that area of discretion with a decision or policy that is wise and not foolish, that is thought through and not arrived at impulsively, that is timely, that is suited to the task, that shows foresight and not shortsightedness, that accurately anticipates the reactions and repercussions which are most likely to be provoked by it, that correctly estimates its chances of success, that is fully alert to its opportunity costs, and so forth. That sort of mental discipline, which is rooted in experience, Hobbes calls prudence. In practice, judgement flows into prudence and they are difficult to distinguish. Prudence, then, is a special kind of acquired discipline and a particularly important political virtue which derives, in significant measure, from practice, from experience. The specific content of prudence varies from one activity to the next: the prudence necessary for good farming obviously will have a different content than the prudence required for good governing, because the content of these human activities are different, indeed very different. The experience involved in them is different. But there is something that prudence in each sphere has in common: a faculty of foresight and a discipline of caution. Prudence, in that fundamental respect, remains basically the same at all times and places.

Prudence is a human conduct injunction that arises whenever noteworthy power and thus significant hazards are involved or important values are at stake. Thus the farmer must prudently take account of weather forecasts before planting or harvesting. Thus anyone ought to exercise considerable forethought before venturing out on a stormy sea in a small boat: the power equation would make most people bet on the sea unless perhaps the sailor is particularly skilled and experienced in sailing small craft in turbulent waters. A human rather than a natural environment where noteworthy power and hazards are in play is body contact sports, where players are in danger of serious injury and must find the right balance between playing hard and not hurting themselves. Another such sphere is road traffic where both pedestrians and drivers are in danger of accident or injury and must at all times be alert to hazards and surprises. World politics is a similar sphere: it involves noteworthy power and risk, and it calls

---

[28] Thomas Hobbes, *Leviathan* (Oxford: Blackwell, 1946), 43.

for attention, caution, and care. In short, prudence comes into play when the dangers of human activity and the values at stake become noteworthy: being prudent is being alert and knowing very well what is at stake.

Because stateleaders, especially the leaders of the major powers, can affect so many people by their actions or by their failure to act and have at their disposal greater destructive and constructive power than anyone else, a necessary political (and military) virtue is undoubtedly prudence, which has been called 'the center of gravity' around which the entire scheme turns.[29] Burke regarded prudence as a general virtue but in politics as 'the first of virtues'.[30]

International relations offers a particularly wide and long field of play for prudence. Managing the international economy demands prudence on the part of the managers: American, Japanese, and European ministers of finance and central bankers. They have the heavy responsibility to adopt policies that prevent inflation and promote employment not only in their own national economies but across the international economy. But the use of armed force is undoubtedly the international activity in which prudence is most urgently required. Before national leaders decide to embark on war, even if they have a perfect legal right to do it, prudence dictates that they should thoroughly canvass the situation to ensure that no viable alternatives short of war exist which they could avail themselves of. That is a basic moral requirement of the *jus ad bellum*. That is what we can justifiably expect of our political leaders. By the same token, responsible combat calls for careful planning and preparation so that all known exigencies and conceivable contingencies are covered: the terrain, the weather, the deployment of enemy forces, their state of readiness, our state of readiness, their morale, our morale, etc. That is a basic moral requirement of the *jus in bello*. That is what we can justifiably expect of our military leaders. These prudential dicta are fundamental cautions that any responsible political or military leader could be expected to acknowledge and abide by.

Prudence has two main dimensions: self-regarding and other-regarding.[31] The first dimension is the personal or egocentric prudence which looks ahead and proceeds with caution in the anxiety that otherwise something unwelcome or even something terrible might happen to *me*. When the self is simply me personally and nobody else, one can refer to that as instrumental prudence: it is entirely self-regarding. But when the self includes somebody else and becomes *we* and not just me—joint selves or a collective self—as it almost always does in the activities of politics and war, then prudence is no longer entirely self-regarding but has become other-regarding as well. We can speak of that as normative prudence. That is the second, distinctly social dimension of prudence: prudential responsibility; prudential ethics.

---

[29] Ronald Beiner, 'The Moral Vocabulary of Liberalism,' in J. W. Chapman and W. A. Galston (eds.), *Virtue: Nomos XXXIV* (New York: New York University Press, 1992), 153.
[30] Quoted by Bredvold and Ross, *Philosophy of Edmund Burke*, 38.
[31] See Coll, 'Normative Prudence', 33–52.

Prudence can thus involve concern for others, including third parties who we do not wish to harm but who might be harmed by our actions if we are not careful. That could be our children in the back seat or a neighbour crossing the street if we do not slow down. That could be some of our citizens if we fail to proceed cautiously in our foreign policy. That could be our own troops on the ground if we do not lengthen our artillery barrage. That could also be non-combatants caught between our forces and enemy forces. Here prudence is telling us to take full responsibility for our actions by taking into consideration all who might be harmed needlessly. It is still prudence because it involves trying to limit the harm that could result from our activities if we are not careful. Prudence is disclosed by forethought and deliberation before an important decision or action is taken: careful preparation and attention to the situation in its manifest concreteness, and insight into its perceived dangers and potentialities. Thus stupidity, dogmatism, recklessness, lack of foresight, miscalculation, negligence, or poor judgement are among the greatest political and military vices because they needlessly put at risk others who depend upon the decision-maker and the prudential quality of his or her decision.

Prudence and other political virtues are universal requirements of responsible political conduct. The policies and actions of world leaders everywhere and at all times are subject to assessment in these terms. That is because a measure of power, an element of chance and a degree of risk, and a possibility of harm or loss, are always present in world politics. We can be grateful for the prudence disclosed by the American and Soviet leaders who kept nuclear war at bay during the dangerous era of the cold war.[32] The fact that the Russian leaders were communists and dictators and the American leaders were capitalists and democrats has no bearing on the judgement. The same would still hold if the leaders were Chinese or African or Christian or Muslim or male or female. That is because the virtues probe human conduct *in itself*. They have nothing to do with geography or history or culture or civilization or political ideology or social class or ethnicity or gender. They have everything to do with what it means to be a human being and to live a human life. The political virtues are particularly well-attuned to the human character and *modus operandi* of international relations. They neither exaggerate nor understate the ability and opportunity of political leaders to act responsibly.

This discussion is no more than a brief introduction which hardly begins to do justice to one of the oldest and most enduring ethical subjects of political science. But I hope it is sufficient to clarify the central role of political virtue in the ethics of statecraft. In later chapters I employ the concept to analyse the con-

---

[32] They are the ones who can rightly take the credit for that outcome—not those political scientists who seem to suggest that their neo-realist theories were instrumental in that outcome. See J. Mearsheimer, 'Back to the Future: Instability in Europe after the Cold War', in S. Lynn-Jones and S. Miller (eds.), *The Cold War and After: Prospects for Peace* (Cambridge, Mass.: MIT Press, 1993), 141–92.

duct of national leaders during some of the noteworthy normative controversies that arose in world politics after the cold war. In the final chapter I expand on the point that the political virtues, especially prudence, are universal moral considerations that rise above particular cultures and civilizations and transcend moral relativism. For that reason they can serve as foundation stones of international ethics.

7

The Pluralist Architecture of World Politics

This chapter locates the previous discussion in a broader historical and theoretical context with a view to bringing the first part of the book to a close. It opens with a brief recollection of the arrangement of authority during the medieval era in Europe. It proceeds to review some important events surrounding the Peace of Westphalia which is generally regarded as marking, symbolically more than literally, the ending of the solidarist Middle Ages and the beginning of the pluralist era of modern state-centred politics. It goes on to indicate how a *societas* of sovereign states involves a complementary ethics of statecraft and it examines four distinctive political responsibilities of independent statespeople. The final section comprehends modern international society as an institutional arrangement that affirms and seeks to uphold normative pluralism in world politics.

Before Sovereignty

Because it is so easy to take our world of states for granted as a given of political life it may be useful to recollect, if only in brief outline, the European world before sovereignty became a standard of conduct in the relations of monarchies, principalities (ecclesiastical as well as political), republics, confederations—what we refer to as states and the states system. The transformation from medieval to modern involved religious ideas and institutions, specifically Christian ones, not incidentally but fundamentally. The medieval world was arranged and its governance was conducted in terms of Christian ideas and beliefs which were political as well as personal. The formation of the modern European society of sovereign states is, in a very significant way, a religious transformation: the Protestant Reformation. Ultimately, it is a move away from religion, both Protestant and Catholic, in the creation of a secular political world. The important role of religion in our subject is not always recognized by contemporary international relations scholars. If we can understand what that transformation basically involved we should be in a better position to grasp the deeper normative meaning and significance of modern international society.

    Sovereignty can be defined briefly, at the outset, as a single governing authority which is acknowledged to be supreme over all other authorities within a certain territorial jurisdiction and is independent of all foreign authorities. The creation of sovereign authorities was, as Michael Oakeshott puts it, 'a very great change . . . In the middle ages governments were not "sovereign" in this sense and it was never thought proper that they should be.'[1] The assertion of sovereignty by a ruler would be a sin against the Christian God who was the only sovereign of the world and everything in it. It would also be an act of contempt against the Christian authorities who served God on earth, the *respublica Christiana*, which was a dual arrangement: a religious authority (*sacerdotium*) headed by the pope and a political authority (*regnum*) headed by a secular ruler designated as emperor (in the later Middle Ages and early modern era that office was held by the head of the Habsburg dynasty whose seat of power was in Vienna).[2] What was a crime against God's law and against *respublica Christiana* during the Middle Ages became the source of law and the reason of state—what we would term the national interest—during the early modern era. State sovereignty displaced the sovereignty of God and the earthly authorities that served God. Europe was defined as a plurality of *regna*.

A striking impression that the Middle Ages convey to anyone looking back from our vantage point at the dawn of the third millennium is one of bewildering diversity concerning political authority. We live in a plural world consisting of almost 200 states, each one displaying parochial distinctions and differences. But our international society is based on general and uniform rules of equal sovereignty, territorial integrity, non-intervention, etc. The only uniform institution that existed across Western Europe and the most important institution of the Middle Ages was *respublica Christiana*. It holds the key to our understanding of the Middle Ages.

The medieval map of Europe was not a territorial patchwork of different colours representing independent countries under sovereign governments. Instead, it was a complicated and confusing intermingling of lines and colours of varying shades and hues. It was unusual for a king's realm to be consolidated and concentrated at one place. A ruler's territory would often resemble an archipelago: peripheral parts were scattered, like islands, among the territory of other rulers; core parts were perforated and interrupted, like lakes, by the intervening jurisdictions of other authorities. Some rulers held fiefdoms within the territorial domains of other rulers which gave them the status of semi-independent vassals. 'Europe was not divided up into exclusive sovereignties, but was covered by overlapping and constantly shifting lordships.'[3] 'Lordship' involved 'a proprietary right to territory' but it did not imply sovereignty: a duke or a city corporation (for example, London) or a bishop or the head of a religious order

---

[1] Michael Oakeshott, *Morality and Politics in Modern Europe: The Harvard Lectures* (New Haven, Conn.: Yale, 1993), 32–3.

[2] See the probing discussion in C. H. McIlwain, *The Growth of Political Thought in the West* (New York: Macmillan, 1932), 270 ff.

[3] George Clark, *Early Modern Europe* (London: OUP, 1960), 28.

(for example, Cistercians, Benedictines) could exercise lordship which was not restricted to dynastic or even to noble families—although most lordships were the hereditary tenures of such families.[4] Kings and other rulers were the subjects of higher authorities and laws. They were neither supreme nor completely independent. And much of the time local rulers were more or less free from the rule of kings: they were semi-autonomous but they were not fully independent either.

Many old European states were conglomerates whose rulers occupied different offices in their different territories which defined the way they were required to rule those territories—such as the kings of Prussia, who were absolute monarchs in Konigsberg but were imperial vassals of the Holy Roman Emperor in Berlin, or the kings of France who were absolute rulers in Paris but fief-holders of the Habsburgs in Alsace, or the Habsburgs themselves, who were personal autocrats in Vienna and Prague, absolute rulers in Madrid and Lisbon, but were constitutional monarchs in Brussels. In short, the same ruler might have several different political personae around Europe. In the modern era conglomerate states were usually imperial states, such as the British Empire, which consisted of extensive and various overseas territories in several different continents around the world.[5] Decolonization put an end to imperial states in the second half of the twentieth century, just as political modernity had previously brought medieval conglomerate states to an end over a far lengthier period of time.

Respublica Christiana was a unified authority, however ramshackle and shaky, that was devoted to the overarching purpose of Christian redemption and salvation.[6] From the beginning it was centred on the office of the bishop of Rome, who came to be known as the pope (*papa*).[7] (There was a separate Christian empire in Eastern Europe and the Middle East, the Greek-speaking Byzantine Empire, centred at Constantinople—Istanbul—whose patriarch did not recognize the pope as a supreme authority.[8]) Latin Christendom was built, bit by bit, over many centuries after the fall of Rome by the missionary conversion of European 'pagans', typically kings and other rulers, to Christianity. In becoming Christians they subjected not only themselves but also the populations they ruled to the Christian God and to God's representatives and agents on earth, *respublica Christiana*, which was the unifying institution and belief system of Europeans in the western half of the continent.[9] By the twelfth century the pope was recog-

---

[4] M. Keen, *Medieval Europe* (Harmondsworth: Penguin Books, 1991), 262.

[5] M. Wight, *British Colonial Constitutions: 1947* (Oxford: Clarendon Press, 1952), 1–14.

[6] This is a modification of the notion of *universitas* theorized by M. Oakeshott, 'The Rule of Law', in his *On History and Other Essays* (Oxford, Blackwell, 1983); also see M. Oakeshott, *On Human Conduct* (Oxford: Clarendon Press, 1975).

[7] H. Chadwick, 'The Early Christian Community', in J. McManners (ed.), *The Oxford History of Christianity* (Oxford: OUP, 1993), 39–40.

[8] K. Ware, 'Eastern Christendom,' in McManners, *Oxford History of Christianity*, 131–66.

[9] See H. Mayr-Harting, 'The West: The Age of Conversion', in McManners, *Oxford History of Christianity*, 101–31.

nized to possess 'fullness of power' (*plenitudo potestatis*) and in extreme situations 'he could depose a ruler for total incompetence or incorrigible malice'.[10]

If we can stretch a word and speak of 'sovereignty' in medieval Europe, in the first instance the sovereign was the Christian God whose commands were generally acknowledged by Christians as demanding their obedience. In the second instance it was the pope, the bishop of Rome and vicar of Christ, God's representative on earth, who presided over Latin Christendom.[11] The core political idea was the notion that secular authorities no less than spiritual authorities were subjects of a higher authority, God, whose commandments were expressed by the precepts of Christianity. Both secular authorities and religious authorities on earth were Christ's subjects and servants: no significant distinction was drawn between politics and religion. According to Paul of Tarsus, one of the fathers of the Church: 'The state is there to serve God . . . The authorities are there to serve God . . . All government officials are God's officers.'[12] In short, if there was a 'sovereign state' in medieval Europe, it was *respublica Christiana*. Political authority in Europe was solidarist rather than pluralist. Before a plural system of sovereign states could fully emerge, the supreme authority of *respublica Christiana* had to be extinguished or at least rendered superfluous.

One way that could be arranged was via the practice of diplomacy, by which statespeople could dialogue directly with each other and could arrive at independent agreements or treaties. Such agreements could be regarded as a sign of independence. Diplomatic relations between political authorities was nothing new. But it was not until the sixteenth century, and not entirely even then, that diplomacy became confined to the relations of states.[13] Prior to that time, the sending and receiving of political envoys was a far less specialized activity that was carried on by many different kinds of authority, religious and commercial as well as political, local and regional as well as national. Medieval diplomacy was a quasi-domestic dialogue between subjects of the same overall political community; it was conducted within the framework of *respublica Christiana* and it was subject to the papal monarchy, at least in principle if not always in fact. The pope authenticated treaties and judged disputes between kings. Only when communication was entered into with substantial political systems outside Latin Christendom did medieval diplomacy disclose the characteristics of modern diplomacy: for example, in diplomatic relations between the Venetian Republic and the Byzantine Empire. The Republic of Venice, the predominant European trading state of the later Middle Ages, brought many diplomatic practices and institutions to Europe having acquired them from their relations with

---

[10] Michael Donelan, 'Spain and the Indies,' in H. Bull and A. Watson (eds.), *The Expansion of International Society* (Oxford: Clarendon Press, 1984), 80.

[11] J. Canning, *A History of Medieval Political Thought, 300–1450* (London: Routledge, 1996), 84.

[12] As quoted ibid. 19.

[13] See Keith Hamilton and Richard Langhorne, *The Practice of Diplomacy* (London and New York: Routledge, 1995), 22–8.

Byzantium. The Venetians set the standard for other Italian states, and that same standard was later adopted by France, Spain, Austria, England, and eventually by the entire group of European states.

The conviction that the rights, duties, and legitimate interests of states, and the exercise of statecraft, must be guided by a separate political ethics liberated from the Christian Church was first given free and creative rein by the Renaissance Italians. In his magisterial study, Garrett Mattingly observes that 'Diplomacy in the modern style, permanent diplomacy, was one of the creations of the Italian Renaissance . . . The new diplomacy was the functional expression of a new kind of state . . . [*quoting Burckhardt*] "the state as a work of art".'[14] In the late medieval era the city-states of northern and central Italy instituted a states system among themselves that operated very significantly by means of diplomatic dialogue, political intrigue, and war. Their acutely realist kind of political thinking based on what we would term 'power politics' came to be known as *raison d'état* (reason of state) and later as *realpolitik* (reality politics) in which the morality of the state and the ethics of statecraft are sharply distinguished from Christian ethics or common morality and elevated above them.[15] That is nowhere more clearly evident than in Machiavelli's unsentimental theory of statecraft:

the gulf between how one should live and how one does live is so wide that a man who neglects what is actually done for what should be done learns the way to self-destruction rather than self-preservation. The fact is that a man who wants to act virtuously in every way necessarily comes to grief among so many who are not virtuous. Therefore if a prince wants to maintain his rule he must learn how not to be virtuous, and to make use of this or not according to need.[16]

Machiavelli did not reject virtue; he changed the meaning of virtue in political life. In breaking away from *respublica Christiana* and arranging their own international *societas*, the Italians can be said to have fashioned not only diplomacy or even the state (*stato*) but also political modernity itself.

The medieval ecclesiastical-political order began to fall apart during the sixteenth century under the dual shocks of the (initially Italian) Renaissance and the (initially German) Reformation. The political philosophy of Machiavelli and the political theology of Luther gave the clearest voice and, in the case of Luther also the loudest voice, to the shocking idea of political independence expressed in both episodes. The Renaissance idea of independent states soon spread north of the Alps. Other European rulers took their political cue from the Italians and the arts and sciences of the Renaissance, including the political art of independent statecraft, became commonplace throughout Western Europe. Even the papacy itself became a state and indeed a significant power: one among several

[14] G. Mattingly, *Renaissance Diplomacy* (New York: Dover, 1988), 47.
[15] See J. Vincent, 'Realpolitik', in J. Mayall (ed.), *The Community of States* (London: George Allen & Unwin, 1982), 73–85.
[16] Machiavelli, *The Prince*, tr. George Bull (Harmondsworth: Penguin Books, 1961), 91.

rival Italian powers.[17] If the pope was now an Italian statesman, could he still also be the presiding authority of Latin Christendom? Could *respublica Christiana* still exist as an imperial institution in the religious and political life of Europe? The answer to both questions increasingly was 'no'.

The Reformation involved a struggle for religious separatism (by Protestants) against religious orthodoxy (by Catholics) and simultaneously for political authority (by secular rulers) over religious matters, which meant freedom from outside interference. The Protestant theology of Martin Luther disengaged the authority of the state from the overarching religious sanction of *respublica Christiana*.[18] Luther's Reformation theology was political because it petitioned kings and other secular rulers to assert their independence to reform the Church in their country. The petition was eagerly accepted by many rulers in northern Europe, and in that way Luther precipitated a political revolution as well as a religious reformation. Protestantism was found to be politically expedient. Even avowedly anti-Lutherans exploited the political opportunities contained within the idea. One of the clearest instances of disengagement was King Henry VIII of England's divorce not only from Catherine of Aragon, which the pope refused to sanction, but also simultaneously from *respublica Christiana*—as registered in the Act of Supremacy (1534) which abolished papal authority in England and elevated the king to Supreme Head of the Church of England.[19]

The notion of sovereignty is systematically explored at length and in depth for the first time in Jean Bodin's sixteenth-century political treatise *Les Six Livres de la Republique* (1576).[20] This was not a study of *respublica Christiana*. It was a study of the French monarchical state as a free-standing and self-regarding political power. 'It is most expedient for the preservation of the state that the rights of sovereignty should never be granted out to a subject, still less to a foreigner, for to do so is to provide a stepping-stone where the grantee himself becomes the sovereign.'[21] That political counsel was a rejection of the Middle Ages. For political purposes the pope was now a foreigner in France and in other European countries that adopted Bodin's doctrine of independent statecraft.

The conceptual shift in the rationale and justification of government captured in the political theology of Luther and the political theory of Machiavelli and Bodin is at the heart of the revolution from medieval to modern. Political modernity and state sovereignty have gone hand in hand ever since. 'The pluralist moment' is an expression that is intended to capture that fundamental historical change.

[17] J. Burckhardt, *The Civilization of the Renaissance in Italy*, i (New York: Harper & Row, 1958), 120–42.

[18] S. Wolin, *Politics and Vision* (Boston, Mass.: Little, Brown, 1960), 143.

[19] See Norman Davies, *Europe: A History* (London: Pimlico, 1997), 490.

[20] M. J. Tooley (tr.), *Bodin: Six Books of the Commonwealth* (Oxford, Blackwell, n.d.).

[21] Ibid. book 1, ch. 10, p. 49.

The Pluralist Moment

That revolutionary transformation in European history is usually marked by the Peace of Westphalia (1648), and the Thirty Years War that preceded it and provoked it. My intention is not to recapitulate these momentous episodes of European history; it is only to recall that the pluralist ethics of world politics have a history that dates back at least to that time. Between 1618 and 1648 a war raged in the heartland of post-Reformation Europe between two alliances which were at first based on religious distinctions and convictions but soon disclosed political interests and concerns as well: the 'Union' of Protestant German princes and free cities on the one hand, and the 'League' of their Catholic counterparts on the other. The conflict broke out within the Holy Roman Empire, as it is usually called, which was centred on the German-speaking areas of Europe but extended into neighbouring areas (parts of Hungary, Italy, and France, and all of the Netherlands). It was a loose confederation under the imperial leadership of the Catholic Habsburg dynasty; it also had its own parliament in which the various estates and authorities of the Empire were represented.

In 1618 the Habsburg dynasty was the greatest state in Europe, whose territorial jurisdiction extended well beyond the Empire. The Habsburgs were in charge of a vast conglomerate state which consisted of an assortment of diverse territories, some scattered across Europe and some located as far away as North and South America. Their imperial European holdings included Austria, Tyrol, Styria, Carinthia, Carniola, all of Hungary that was not in the control of the Ottoman Turks, Silesia, Moravia, Bohemia, Milan, Naples, Sicily, Sardinia, Burgundy, the Netherlands, and parts of Alsace. They were also kings in Spain and Portugal which lay outside the Empire. Their overseas colonial territories included Chile, Peru, Brazil, and Mexico. It is perhaps not surprising, then, that their motto was *Austriae est imperatura orbi universo* (Austria is universal world empire). Their policy supported the militant Counter-Reformation version of Catholicism which was inspired by the doctrines of St Ignatius and championed by the Jesuits.[22]

Although the conflict began within the Holy Roman Empire, it quickly threatened the more general balance of power in Europe which was already divided, both confessionally and politically, between Protestant and Catholic states—even though most statespeople still loosely thought of themselves in terms of a single overarching idea, the Christian Commonwealth of Europe. Non-German states outside the Empire entered the conflict, beginning with the unsuccessful intervention of the Protestant king of Denmark on the side of the Union in 1624, and expanding with the more sustained and successful intervention of the Protestant king of Sweden on the same side in 1630. The Thirty Years War

[22] C. V. Wedgwood, *The Thirty Years War* (London: Pimlico, 1994), 23–4.

ceased being primarily religious and became overtly political, and pan-European in scope, with the intervention of the Catholic king of France in 1635—not on the side of the League but, rather, in alliance with Protestant Sweden and in opposition to Catholic Spain. Here was one of those historical moments when the change from medieval religious empire to modern international politics was clearly evident. From that time, extensive warfare was waged throughout the heartland of Europe but neither side could gain a decisive military advantage.

After lengthy efforts at peacemaking, in 1644 a dual peace conference was convened at Munster and neighbouring Osnabruck in the north-west German state of Westphalia. The conference was not just between the great powers involved in the conflict: France, Sweden, and the Holy Roman Empire as well as Spain. Rather it was an assembly of representatives of the entire collection of interested or concerned political authorities from the diverse states and statelets of Europe, with the representatives of Catholic states mostly assembling at Munster and those of Protestant states meeting at neighbouring Osnabruck: 135 representatives in all. England, Poland, Muscovy (Russia), and the Ottoman Empire (Turkey) were the only significant European or semi-European states not represented at Munster or Osnabruck.

Finally, late in 1648, dual peace treaties were concluded which had a political dimension and a religious dimension united within the framework of the state. The individual territorial sovereignty of an assortment of about 300 states and statelets of the empire was recognized. These formerly subordinated political entities became independent authorities within their own territories and were henceforth entitled to make treaties with each other and with foreign powers. The Empire was reduced to a hollow shell with no significant power or authority. As regards the religious dimension, Westphalia confirmed the Peace of Augsburg (1555) at which the principle of *cujus regio ejus religio* was formulated, according to which every ruler declared which brand of Christianity, either Catholicism or Protestantism, would be exclusively established within his or her territories. Each particular state became the home of the particular church favoured by the ruler. Although Westphalia made some provisions for religious minorities, in most places people were obliged either to conform to the ruler's declared state religion or to emigrate to another state where the established religion was consistent with their own.[23] If they could mount an effective resistance to the ruler's edicts states fell into. political-religious war and the issue of religion was settled by force. Religion was now the basis of exclusive state authority, of sovereignty.

It is important to understand the Westphalian moment from the perspective of that time and not from the present time—in so far as that is possible. The conceptual and linguistic categories available to the statespeople at Westphalia

---

[23] See Jennifer Jackson Preece, *National Minorities and the European Nation-States System* (Oxford: Clarendon Press, 1998). Also see her 'Minority Rights in Europe: From Westphalia to Helsinki,' *Review of International Studies*, 23 (Jan. 1997), 75–92.

were those of the late medieval era.[24] They understood themselves to be an assembly of Christian rulers and their representatives. They had a notion of being members of one universal community, the basis of which was the Christian religion.[25] They still spoke of 'Christendom' and of their peace congress as the 'senate of the Christian world'. They expressed their agreements in Latin which was still the political language of European statecraft. The peace treaties do not specifically include much evidence for the claim that Westphalia is the crucial turning-point in the emergence of sovereignty. There is no mention of the word 'sovereignty'. Westphalia was an important stage-post, probably the most important, in a lengthy retreat that lasted over several centuries during which time *respublica Christiana* was obliged to surrender more and more authority to the emergent states of Europe.

Westphalia is not a literal moment of political transformation but, rather, the symbol of that change. Westphalia symbolized putting one of the final and most decisive nails in the coffin of the medieval claim that all European states were subject to the spiritual leadership of the pope and the political leadership of the Holy Roman Emperor. After Westphalia that was a hollow claim. As one historian puts it: 'This extraordinary compromise saved the theory of religious unity for each state while destroying it for the Empire.'[26] A modern society of sovereign states had been created out of the political debris of a ruined medieval Christian empire.

When, exactly, the revolution from medieval *universitas* to modern *societas* becomes clearly evident historically is a subject of debate among scholars. Martin Wight sees its tentative beginnings in the conciliar movement within the Church in the fifteenth century.[27] F. H. Hinsley sees its full manifestation only in the Concert of Europe in the 1820s.[28] Most scholars, however, see the seventeenth century and particularly the Peace of Westphalia as the best historical reference point for symbolizing that fundamental turn in European political life. That change was not one moment in time; it was a series of major turning-points in a progressive and eventually irreversible movement away from medieval Christendom. The first major turning-point was the Council of Constance (1414–17) which ended the 'great schism'—when there were several rival popes—and marked the start of a gradual political transition during which the medieval papal monarchy went into decline, and a number of secular monar-

---

[24] 'Well into at least the seventeenth century, the juristic, theological and overtly political works of medieval scholastics continued to be prime sources for the discussion of political thought . . . The writings of . . . Hugo Grotius (1583–1645), amongst very many others, illustrated this trend.' Canning, *A History of Medieval Political Thought*, 186.

[25] See A. Osiander, *The States System of Europe, 1640–1990* (Oxford: Clarendon Press, 1994), 27–8.

[26] Wedgwood, *Thirty Years War*, 42.

[27] M. Wight, *Systems of States* (Leicester: Leicester University Press, 1977), 151. A similar view is taken by Keen, *Medieval Europe*, 314–21.

[28] F. H. Hinsley, 'The Concept of Sovereignty and the Relations between States', in W. J. Stankiewicz (ed.), *In Defense of Sovereignty* (New York: The Free Press, 1964), 285.

chies began to emerge out of the shadow of Latin Christendom.[29] The second major turning-point, arguably the most important and certainly the most symbolic, was the Westphalian peace treaties of 1648 in which the political independence of secular political authorities within the Holy Roman Empire was generally recognized.[30] The third major turning-point, which officially pronounced the death of the *respublica Christiana*, was the Peace of Utrecht (1712–15) which ended the War of the Spanish Succession and resulted in the independence of Holland and Portugal from Habsburg Spain.[31]

The treaties of Westphalia and Utrecht still referred to 'Christendom' but they were among the last to do that. For what had come into historical existence in the mean time was a secular European society of states in which overarching political and religious authority was no longer in existence in any substantive sense. The political-theological arch constituted by *respublica Christiana* had been broken and was lying in pieces on the ground. The solidarism of the Christian empire was supplanted by the anarchical society of sovereign states as the organized form of political authority in the West. 'At Westphalia', according to Martin Wight, 'the states system does not come into existence: it comes of age.'[32]

A *Societas* of Sovereign States

The great political transformation symbolized by Westphalia can be captured conceptually as a reconstitution of European politics from that of a *universitas*, based on the solidarist norms of Latin Christendom, to that of a *societas*, based on the pluralist norms of state sovereignty, on political independence.[33]

The institution of sovereignty sorted out the uncertainty and indeed the confusion around the question of authority that existed in the Middle Ages. The new sovereign state escaped from the medieval system of dispersed authority and successfully established and enforced its own centralized authority. It captured its territory and turned it into state property, and it captured the population of that territory and turned them into subjects and later citizens. Internally, there was no room for semi-independent territory or people or institutions. As indicated, in most cases the Christian churches, Catholic as well as Protestant, fell under state control. Territory was consolidated, unified, and centralized under a sovereign government. The population of the territory now owed final allegiance to the sovereign and had a fundamental duty to obey the laws of the land.

---

[29] See Canning, *History of Medieval Political Thought*, 185.
[30] See the detailed and perceptive discussion in Osiander, *States System of Europe*, ch. 2.
[31] Ibid. ch. 3.   [32] Wight, *Systems of States*, 152.
[33] For a probing analysis of these fundamentally important concepts see Oakeshott, *On Human Conduct*.

Externally, there was no room for any overarching intervening authority comparable to the pope or the emperor. The modern doctrine of non-intervention supplanted the medieval doctrine of intervention as the basic norm of the system—that was and still is the normative heart of Westphalia.

Europe no longer went to war as a single political community in the uniform of *respublica Christiana*, as it had done in the Middle Ages, for example, the Christian crusades to liberate Jerusalem and the rest of the 'Holy Land' from the grip of the Muslim world. There was no overarching European authority to sanction war, which was now the independent right of sovereign states; but there was deemed to be a common interest in peace, the defence of which might require the collective action of such states. It was generally recognized, however, that all states had legitimate interests and statespeople were responsible for advancing and defending their interests and could not ordinarily be expected to sacrifice them—even on the altar of Christianity.

The practical idea of state sovereignty now shaped the relations of the main political groupings of Europe, and those relations were recognizable as bona-fide international relations. European rulers were at liberty to govern their own territories without being subject to the injunctions and interference of *respublica Christiana*; they were free to deal with each other according to their own interests and inclinations and whatever treaties they arranged between themselves or common customs they observed. The law they acknowledged in their relations, in so far as we can speak of it as law, was 'the law of nations' (international law) that had been discerned and spelt out by an emergent tradition of international jurisprudence, the leading exponent of which was Hugo Grotius.[34]

The *societas* of states involved the adoption of characteristically international standards of conduct among which were three fundamental norms. The first norm was *rex est imperator in regno suo* (the king is emperor in his own realm). It declares that sovereign states are not subject to any higher political authority. Every *rex* is independent and equal to every other *rex*. This became a central principle of French public law but it had 'a significance not for France alone and its law but for all *regna* . . . Henry VIII [of England] made a famous statement of it in the Statute of Appeals in 1534.'[35] It was the doctrine of the state as the source of law. The second norm, already noted, was *cujus regio ejus religio*. As indicated, it asserts that outsiders have no right to intervene in a foreign jurisdiction on the grounds of religion, which is no longer considered to be a valid justification for war and armed intervention. Westphalia removed religion from international politics, and by implication it repudiated all sectional ideologies and belief systems as grounds for justifying intervention in the sovereignty of foreign governments.

The third norm was prudential rather than procedural: it affirms the balance of power whose central purpose was to prevent any one state from making a suc-

[34] Hugo Grotius, *De Jure Belli ac Pacis Libri Tres*, tr. F. Kelsey (Oxford: OUP, 1925).
[35] See the penetrating discussion in McIlwain, *Growth of Political Thought*, 268.

cessful bid for hegemony which would, in effect, re-establish an empire over the continent. Adam Watson captures the Westphalian achievement very nicely: it 'was the charter of a Europe permanently organised on an anti-hegemonial principle'.[36] The notion of a countervailing alliance of major powers aimed at preserving the freedom of all member states and maintaining the European society of states as a whole was only worked out by trial and error and fully theorized in the eighteenth and nineteenth centuries. Henry Kissinger has summarized this development:

Europe was thrown into balance-of-power politics when its first choice, the medieval dream of universal empire, collapsed and a host of states of more or less equal strength arose from the ashes of that ancient aspiration. When a group of states so constituted are obliged to deal with one another, there are only two possible outcomes: either one state becomes so strong that it dominates all the others and creates an empire, or no state is ever quite powerful enough to achieve that goal.[37]

With the end of *respublica Christiana*, war in Europe was now clearly an international relation and no longer an ambiguously domestic affair. Since there was no overarching authority and states could affect each other's security, there was deemed to be a common interest in international order, the defence of which might require collective action. And that, in turn, might oblige states who were being threatened by an international menace to take extreme actions which could involve trespassing on the independence of some states for the sake of defending international order. It was generally recognized, however, that all states had legitimate interests which were independent of the common interests of international society; and that statespeople were responsible for advancing and defending those national interests and could not ordinarily be expected to sacrifice them.

Edmund Burke, with his eye on the presumed threat posed to European international freedom by republican and revolutionary France, went so far as to refer to a Europe of sovereign states as 'virtually one great state having the same basis of general law, with some diversity of provincial customs and local establishments'.[38] That idea is sometimes erroneously construed to justify intervention on solidarist grounds. That is not what Burke intended. He did justify intervention in revolutionary France, because the French revolutionaries were alleged by him to have violated the European *societas* of states. Burke saw European international society as based on two fundamental principles: a 'law of neighborhood' (recognition of neighbouring states and respect for their independence) and 'rules of prudence' (the responsibility of statespeople not only to safeguard the national interest but also to preserve international order).[39] The French

---

[36] A. Watson, *The Evolution of International Society* (London and New York: Routledge, 1992), ch. 17.

[37] H. Kissinger, *Diplomacy* (New York: Simon & Schuster, 1994), 20.

[38] E. Burke, *Reflections on the Revolution in France* (Harmondsworth: Penguin Books, 1968).

[39] F. W. Raffety (ed.), *The Works of the Right Honourable Edmund Burke*, vi (Oxford: OUP, 1928), 156–61.

revolutionaries and later also Napoleon violated both principles. Burke was calling for intervention on pluralist grounds. This image and similar images
expressed by other leading European publicists of that time capture the normative essentials of the *societas* of states.

Ever since the seventeenth century, the normative idea of Europe as a *universitas* under a single hierarchical authority has been repudiated, notwithstanding major attempts to reinstate it by armed force: for example, in the later
seventeenth century by French King Louis XIV in the form of universal monarchy, in the late eighteenth and early nineteenth centuries by Napoleon in the
form of universal empire, in the first half of the twentieth century by Lenin and
Stalin in the form of revolutionary communism and by Hitler in the form of the
Third Reich. After 1945 the Soviet Union imposed a communist *universitas* on
Eastern Europe which was enforced by the Red Army until 1989. The history
of attempting to transform Europe into a *universitas* has mostly been a history
of war and revolution. Recently, however, the unity idea has been taken up
again, this time in Western Europe in the democratic form of the European
Union, which has some features of a quasi-*universitas*.

The *societas* of sovereign states is the idea and institution that expresses the
morality of difference, recognition, respect, regard, dialogue, interaction,
exchange, and similar norms that postulate coexistence and reciprocity between
independent political communities. The language of *societas* is the language of
political freedom as opposed to that of *universitas*, which is the language of political hierarchy and religious or ideological orthodoxy based on a political community of some sort. At the fortieth-anniversary celebration of the German
Democratic Republic (East Germany) in 1989 USSR President Mikhail
Gorbachev indicated that Soviet troops would no longer be deployed for internal repression. That precipitated the end of Soviet hierarchy and communist
orthodoxy in Eastern Europe. This new line in Soviet policy was dubbed the
'Sinatra doctrine': everybody could do it their way, in other words, *societas*. It
was in sharp contrast to the pre-existing 'Brezhnev doctrine' of armed interventionism when everybody in the Soviet bloc had to do it Moscow's way, in
other words, *universitas*. The pluralist 'Sinatra doctrine' of non-intervention is
what Westphalia instituted and represents, and it is what the classical tradition
of international relations scholarship is centrally concerned with. It is the core
doctrine of the global covenant.

To date the modern *societas* of sovereign states has proved to be the only generally acceptable and workable basis of world politics. However, the uniting of
the world's population via international society obviously raises normative issues
of a common humanity and a global commons divided among a plurality of sovereign states. That has repeatedly led to anti-pluralist critiques and a desire to
reinstate a *universitas* of some gentler kind based on popular consent rather than
military conquest or political revolution. There is currently an intellectual opposition movement against state sovereignty, at least in some Western academic cir-

cles and particularly among progressive international lawyers.[40] That longing for political and ideological solidarity in world politics is an ironical turn, especially when we remember that *universitas* was originally a medieval political-religious idea, articulated by Christian priests and defended by Christian soldiers, and when we recall that the modern world of sovereign states was instituted as an escape from the ideological orthodoxy and political hierarchy that a *universitas* in political life involves. It is also ironical in light of the successful world-wide revolt against imperialism in the twentieth century which justified the abolition of colonialism in the name of local political freedom: in the name of self-determination and state sovereignty.

Plural Responsibilities of Independent Statecraft

The classical international society tradition does not sufficiently emphasize, or analyse, the linked concepts of *societas* and the pluralist ethics of statecraft, even though these are foundational to its approach. A world of independent states necessarily is a world of plural responsibilities for statespeople. One of the main aims of this book is to make plain this connection and its *modus operandi*.

The practical ethics of statecraft is not a one-dimensional morality. It is multidimensional, pluralistic. Statespeople operate with multiple responsibilities when they engage in the activity of foreign policy. That must be so because they are operating of necessity and not merely of choice in a pluralist world of states. They are answerable to their own citizens. But they are also answerable to other stateleaders. They are responsible for defending the national interest but they also have responsibilities for conditions beyond the borders of their own country—certainly, international order at a minimum. They must find a way to balance their different and sometimes divergent responsibilities. That may seem obvious but the point requires emphasis and expansion because there is a lingering belief that political responsibility stops and starts at national boundaries: that it is a clearly defined domestic sphere. The world of political practice does not draw any such watertight distinction. Responsibility follows power: just as the exercise of state power is both international and domestic, so, too, is political responsibility.

Presidents, prime ministers, and other stateleaders are commonly assumed to have international responsibilities, and they are regularly taken to task whenever they fail to live up to them. If they engage in foreign policies which adversely affect people outside their state they can legitimately be called upon to answer for their actions. If their domestic policies have adverse foreign consequences

---

[40] See Richard Falk, 'A New Paradigm for International Legal Studies: Prospects and Proposals', in R. Falk, F. Kratochwil, and S. H. Mendlovitz (eds.), *International Law: A Contemporary Perspective* (Boulder, Colo., and London: Westview, 1985), 651–702.

they can be called upon to answer for those as well. Statespeople routinely comment, usually in diplomatic language, on the foreign policy of other states—and also on their domestic policies if they are guided by intentions or produce consequences that spill over national borders into other states. Such commentary is not generally considered to be out of bounds. On the contrary, it is an expected part of international political discourse.

Martin Wight distinguishes realism or national responsibility, rationalism or international responsibility, and revolutionism—what I would prefer to label more conventionally as cosmopolitanism—or humanitarian responsibility.[41] There is a fourth dimension that Wight did not separately identify: responsibility for the global commons.

1. National Responsibility

According to this conception the fundamental standard of conduct that statespeople can reasonably be expected to adhere to in their foreign policies is that of national self-interest and specifically national security, the latter being a foundational value of national responsibility. Another such value is national welfare. These normative considerations obviously are characteristic of a world of separate states in which the responsibilities of statespeople are determined by their obligations to the citizens of their own country and by what is considered to be generally in the citizens' best interests, in the national interest. National responsibility is a moral relation between a state and its citizens which dictates that stateleaders always act as far as possible to ensure the well-being of the citizens generally.

It would seem to be obvious that statespeople have national responsibilities, but what is the normative basis for that claim? An important answer can be derived from a familiar theory of political obligation: the state—whether formed by a social contract, by historical evolution, by conquest, or by any other method or episode—is a constitutionally self-contained community that is prior to any international associations it may subsequently form or join. In other words, certain states have been built and are sustained by their populations and it is those people that can reasonably claim priority in defining the responsibilities of the national leaders who are their servants: public servants. According to that domestic-focused way of thinking, international law and international organization are instrumental arrangements which are justified by how well they serve the national interests of states. This is the thinking that inclines many Americans to believe that their domestic laws always trump international law when they come into conflict: for example, the Helms-Burton Act which sought to punish foreign companies—and by implication foreign states—for investing in communist Cuba contrary to American law.

[41] M. Wight, *International Theory: The Three Traditions* (Leicester: Leicester University Press, 1991).

This normative standard for evaluating foreign policies gives rise to Machiavellian precepts such as the following: always put your nation and its citizens first; avoid taking unnecessary risks with their security and welfare; collaborate with other countries when it is advantageous or necessary but avoid needless foreign entanglements; do not subject your population to war unless it is absolutely necessary; avoid putting your own soldiers in harm's way if it is not absolutely necessary; ensure they are well trained and well equipped before they are sent into combat; and so forth. The virtues of national responsibility are the virtues of patriotism and prudence: devotion to one's country and its citizens and scrupulous attention to ensuring that their well-being is safeguarded. Where there is latitude for discretion—which is by far the greater part of foreign policy—the ethics of national responsibility demand that it should be guided by these political virtues.

The idea of national responsibility is deeply rooted in classical realism: stateleaders are responsible primarily to their own people whose national interests they must defend; they are responsible for their well-being, for national security and national welfare. They may also be responsible for international order but only in so far as that is considered to be in the national interest. For classical realists there is little room within a stateleader's responsibilities for the well-being of foreign countries and populations *as such*. That is fundamentally a question of self-interest: will it benefit us? Thus, how one state deals with another state is in the final analysis always a question of expediency. On this view, international relations is an arena of state competition and conflict rather than a society of states. Political responsibility stops at national borders even when interest and power are projected far beyond.

National responsibility is an authentic morality, however, and should not be confused with narrow self-interest. Realism as classically understood is an ethical theory: it conceives of the state as a moral community; it involves defending the national interest, which is a moral idea.[42] The national interest is one of the most important justifications of pluralist world politics, perhaps the most important. It is driven by a moral concern for the flourishing of the national population, for their good life. To defend the national interest is a burden stateleaders must carry. A stateleader could be tempted to ignore the national interest in an overriding preoccupation with his or her political fortunes. He or she might be preoccupied with winning the next election. That is a common failing of democratic leaders. That could work to the detriment of the national interest, which may require that the leader impose some demands for sacrifice on the electorate even at the risk of losing some votes—perhaps higher taxes for the sake of long-term national economic stability, or perhaps compulsory military service for the sake of national defence. As indicated, national responsibility is not the same as

---

[42] See Terry Kersch, 'The Idea of The National Interest: A Conceptual Analysis in the Context of the Gulf War' (Ph.D thesis, University of British Columbia, 1995).

responsiveness to public opinion; sometimes it may require resistance to public opinion, if public opinion cannot recognize and respond to the national interest. Leading and educating public opinion in that regard would be an important leadership responsibility.

2. *International Responsibility*

According to this conception, statespeople have external procedural responsibilities that derive from their state's membership of international society, which brings with it rights and duties as defined today by customary international law, by the UN charter, by other treaties and agreements that independent states enter into, by diplomatic practice, and the like. According to this view, world politics is a constitutional place and not merely an arena of conflicting national interests. States are legally interconnected organizations: they exist in constitutional relation to each other. That constitutive relationship is fundamentally one of political independence in which states recognize each other's legal equality and right of self-government.[43] That means that stateleaders are answerable not only to their citizens but also to each other in the conduct of their policies; they are responsible for upholding international law and the society of states as a whole.

What is the normative basis for claiming that statespeople have a procedural responsibility to international society and its members? The usual answer comes from a theory of international obligation: states have foreign obligations to other states and to international society as a whole, owing to their membership of that society which can be conceived as based on a covenant between states. They have entered into that society and in so doing have acquired specific rights and undertaken specific obligations of that society. In their foreign policies and international activities statespeople can reasonably be expected to adhere to the procedures sanctioned by that society: for example, international law and diplomatic practice.

As in the case of domestic law, international law is silent on many details of responsibility which have to do with acting lawfully in particular international situations. Just as there are virtues that speak to the national responsibilities of statespeople in areas of discretion so, too, are there virtues that speak to their international responsibilities in discretionary areas of international law. They dictate that statespeople should act honourably and with good faith in conducting foreign relations. This normative standard gives rise to Grotian precepts such as the following: recognize that other states have rights and legitimate interests which deserve respect even if they may conflict with the interests of your own state; observe international law; defend it against states that violate it; observe the principle of reciprocity; do not discriminate against states which do

---

[43] See Alan James, *Sovereign Statehood* (London: Allen & Unwin, 1986), ch 1.

not share your domestic values but are good citizens of international society; conduct diplomacy in accordance with established diplomatic practices; and so forth. These precepts are manifestations of the virtues of recognition, regard, restraint, reciprocity, reliability, amicability. These are the classical international virtues—the virtues of diplomacy—that are understood to be conducive to and reflective of good citizenship in the *societas* of states.

The great powers have a special international responsibility that is heavier than that of other states. As indicated previously, a 'great power' is a state whose weight (in military power, in political prestige, in economic wealth) is of such magnitude that it is among a very select group of states whose policies and actions can affect the course of international affairs. They are thus of great interest and concern to everybody else. Historically, as Martin Wight points out, 'the only distinction in normal diplomatic intercourse is that between great powers and other powers'.[44] One of the biggest mistakes anyone could make in assessing the international responsibilities of states is failing to notice or ignoring the moral significance of what is involved in being a great power and how their responsibilities differ from those of other states. That important distinction may be more muted or blurred in our democratic age but the hard reality behind it remains. Power inevitably carries responsibility. Great powers have heavier responsibilities than other states: they are answerable for their conduct regarding the most important international issues which often are the most difficult and with regard to which only great powers can do anything very substantial. There is a special international ethics which has to do with international order and applies exclusively to the great powers.

The great powers are the guardians of international peace and security and if they fail to guard that crucial value—which usually happens historically when they fall out with each other—there will be no such thing because they will imperil it. They are the only ones who can imperil it. The special international procedural responsibilities of the great powers since 1945 have been defined by chapter VII of the UN charter which applies to members of the Security Council, particularly the permanent (great power) members: USA, China, Russia, Britain, France. Their discretionary responsibility involves their judgement as to when and where the norms of international peace and security, as set out in chapter VII, ought to be enforced. That is a political judgement. The norm of international peace and security is not open to doubt as to its legal existence and form. However, it is open to the leaders of the great powers to decide when and where and how it shall be enforced. It might be impossible or unwise to enforce it consistently at all times in every place on earth. Consistency is not a virtue in international relations if it produces clearly undesirable consequences, such as disorder, in which case consistency would have to give way to caution. The core ethics for anybody who wields great power is that of judgement and

---

[44] M. Wight, *Power Politics*, new edn. (Harmondsworth: Penguin Books, 1986), 41.

prudence: full awareness that, whatever one decides to do with one's power, significant consequences are likely to result, either good consequences or bad consequences, not only for oneself but for everybody affected by the decision.

3. Humanitarian Responsibility

According to this conception, statespeople first and foremost are human beings and as such they have a fundamental obligation not only to respect but also, where possible, to defend human rights around the world. It is something that we can reasonably expect them to do. The duty to respect the dignity and freedom of human beings is an obligation that everybody has and from which nobody is exempt. Statespeople are people and therefore they are not exempt. This third traditional approach derives from the ethic of cosmopolitanism in which respect for human beings—whoever they are and wherever they happen to be living—is a fundamental normative consideration in foreign policy.[45]

This criterion of responsible statecraft goes well beyond international responsibility by asserting a moral reference beyond that of foreign countries and their citizens: human beings everywhere and regardless of the country in which they happen to live or be citizens of. The normative hold of that claim derives not only from the fact that statespeople are human beings but also from the fact that they are in a better position than anyone else to help or hinder their fellow humans: not only the people at home but also those in other countries. What is the normative basis for claiming that statespeople are responsible for human rights around the world? The usual answer derives from a universalist conception of human morality: before anyone can be a statesman or stateswoman or a citizen or anything else, he or she is already a human being. That fact is seen to postulate a priori human obligations that everyone must observe, regardless of his or her nationality or civilization or religion or culture or language or class or status or rank or ethnicity or gender. The traditional way of conceiving of one's obligations as a human being is by claiming that there is a natural law, a universal law of reason and of conscience, which statespeople no less than any other people are duty bound to respect. A modern version of that is to claim, as Kant claimed, that there is a fundamental and inescapable duty of mutual recognition and respect that all humans can comprehend and must therefore observe: the so-called categorical imperative which is based on the 'innate right' ('birthright') of human freedom which state jurisdiction and law cannot extinguish.[46]

This normative standard for evaluating foreign policies gives rise to Kantian precepts such as the following: always remember that people of other countries

[45] Martin Wight uses 'Revolutionism' to capture this idea. Many scholars, following Kant, prefer 'Cosmopolitanism'. See Kant's 'Idea for a Universal History with a Cosmopolitan Purpose, in H. Reiss (ed.), *Kant's Political Writings* (Cambridge: Cambridge University Press, 1977), 41–53.

[46] 'The Science of Right', in R. M. Hutchins (ed.), *Great Books of the Western World*, xlii. *Kant* (Chicago: Encyclopedia Britannica, 1952), 401.

or cultures or races are human beings just like yourself; respect human rights; be hospitable and charitable; assist those who are in need of material aid which you can supply at no sacrifice to yourself; in waging war spare non-combatants; and so forth. Procedurally nowadays much of this is captured by international humanitarian law and the laws of war: the Universal Declaration of Human Rights, the Geneva Conventions, etc. The discretionary sphere of humanitarian responsibility is filled in by the virtues of compassion, charity, hospitality, justice, and other moral precepts that recognize the dignity and inviolability of human beings. These are among the most important traditional Christian virtues and it is clear that humanitarian responsibility can readily be understood as the secular version of Christian *caritas*. These normative considerations are characteristic of a world society in which responsibility is defined by one's membership in the human race.

If this humanitarian approach is taken to its logical conclusion states lose their normative standing and are reduced to being merely instrumentalities for protecting human rights and providing for human welfare on a cosmopolitan (world-wide) scale. States are political machinery, utilitarian arrangements. States are no longer political communities in their own right; national societies have no significant moral *status*, and citizenship has no pre-emptive rights and duties attached to it. An exclusively cosmopolitan ethic would have in mind a singular community of all human beings—a *civitas maxima*—without any rival or intervening communities including nation-states. In that vision world politics is a *universitas*.

That visionary political condition was considered to be far-fetched even by Kant, the foremost cosmopolitan theorist of modern times.[47] It continues to be far removed from international political reality, which is still keyed to sovereign states and the *societas* of states. Yet it is important to emphasize, once again, that even though sovereign states remain profoundly significant normative entities in the world as we know it, universal human rights are nowadays enshrined in international law, promoted by IGOs and NGOs and voiced by public opinion. Gross violations of human rights—such as genocide—are a provocation of deeply felt outrage and widely registered condemnation. Concern about human suffering owing to poverty and disease is not confined within the national boundaries of states either. Humanitarian assistance is an established practice of contemporary world politics. To that extent cosmopolitanism captures a real and not merely an ideal facet of contemporary world politics.

4. Responsibility for the Global Commons

The foregoing responsibilities have been evident in international relations for a long time, although to varying degrees and in different historical clothing.

---

[47] See 'Perpetual Peace: A Philosophical Sketch', repr. in Reiss, *Kant's Political Writings*, 93–130.

However, in recent decades a new international norm has come into view which invokes the responsibilities of national leaders for the health of the planet: responsibility for the global commons. That responsibility is most clearly evident in regard to the global environment.[48] That norm is new although the idea upon which it is based, trusteeship, is anything but new. Because human beings now have the power to upset the balance of nature they are increasingly held to have a corresponding responsibility to restore it and preserve it for future generations. Everyone has that conservationist responsibility but it falls most heavily on statespeople who are in a position to regulate activities within their own jurisdictions that are harmful to the environment.

Kant spoke of the natural world of mankind, our natural abode, as a *globus terraqueus* by which he meant that everybody on earth has a natural right to a share of the earth that is prior to the juridical division of the planet into separate sovereign states.[49] That is an early intimation of responsibility for the global commons. In other words, the planet earth is our habitat in a way that is even more fundamental than the way that a particular country is our home. We might be able to make do without our country: for example, we could move to another country if we could persuade their government to let us in. Alternatively we could hunker down if our state collapsed and try to make do with other social arrangements: kinship, friendship, clan organizations, religious organizations, etc. But we cannot make do without the planet upon which we have been destined to live—at least not until we discover another planet suitable for human habitation and figure out how to get there. Until we recreate something akin to Noah's ark, however, we shall continue to bear a responsibility for the health of the earth, a responsibility that increases in proportion to our capacity to poison it. Kant thought of *globus terraqueus* in terms of natural rights: individual members of the human race having natural rights to land which are prior to the legal rights of sovereign states: 'the right of man as a citizen of the world'. That is still basically the idea of the community of humankind. But it can be reconceived in terms of a responsibility for the health of the planet: global trusteeship.

The latter conception leads to an ethic which conceives of statespeople as the chief trustees or stewards of the planet. They are the chief trustees because they have the authority and power to address the problem. This is a solidarist view of the state as a servant of the common good of the earth. According to this ethic, we can reasonably expect stateleaders to act responsibly when it comes to environmental conservation. Conservationist ethics are expressed, increasingly, by a body of domestic as well as international environment law that has been expanding rapidly in recent decades. That is articulating a procedural dimension of international ethics that was undeveloped in times past. As custodians of

---

[48] See Andrew Hurrell and Benedict Kingsbury (eds.), *The International Politics of the Environment* (Oxford: Clarendon Press, 1992).

[49] I. Kant, 'Introduction to the Science of Right', in R. M. Hutchins (ed.), *Great Books of the Western World*, xlii. *Kant* (Chicago: Encyclopedia Britannica, 1952), 456.

the earth, statespeople are not expected to stand by and allow the environment to be destroyed by the heedless or selfish activities of people in their own jurisdictions; they are expected to promote the repair of the national environmental fabric where it has been damaged. They are also expected to take joint international action with a view to the preservation of the global environment. It is the global spill-over of environmental pollution—as in the case of ozone depletion—which gives stateleaders' custodial responsibility for the planet its distinctive normative shape. It is defined by an image of the earth as a shared habitat for all living creatures and indeed for life as such. In short, the ethics of the global commons are separate and distinct from the ethics of realism, rationalism, and cosmopolitanism.

The discretionary sphere of conservationist responsibility is filled in by the virtue of stewardship, which is a moral conception that emphasizes the notion of holding something valuable in trust and passing it on to the next generation in at least as good a condition as it was received from the previous generation and, hopefully, in a better condition. That is an ethic that looks back to the past and forward to the future and goes against the notion that certain goods are to be enjoyed (or consumed) today without regard for future generations. It goes against the idea of absolute ownership rights to do whatever one wishes with one's property. As indicated, environment ethics is a new version of the traditional moral idea of trusteeship. It is a responsibility for the good condition of the global habitat and its upkeep; and it is a responsibility not only to other people but to all who share the planet and depend upon it for their life. Those others are of course other living creatures, besides humans, and the habitats on which they must depend in order to survive.

Stateleaders must be prepared to justify their plans and actions in these terms. They cannot arbitrarily rule out any of these normative considerations even if they try to vindicate themselves by appealing selectively only to one or two of them. We can readily discern all these responsibilities in world politics at the present time. They are operative standards which statespeople themselves acknowledge, as shall be evident from the analysis in later chapters. They are the principal normative references for responding to the question: 'how do you justify that?' It is primarily for that empirical reason that they should also be basic normative references for academic inquiry.

These different responsibilities have come into view, they are there to be scrutinized and reflected upon, but they do not carry equal weight. That is largely defined historically. In the past half century, as indicated, human rights have been assigned greater weight than previously and environmental ethics have for the first time come into clear view in international relations. They are both legitimate points of reference in asking the question: 'how can you justify that?' But under most circumstances—in so far as one can generalize—neither human rights nor environment ethics can yet pre-empt the national responsibilities of stateleaders to their own citizens or their international responsibilities to each other, should they come into sharp conflict with them. However, if any one of the above norms were acknowledged and followed in a dogmatic or single-minded way it would invite justified criticism nowadays. That pluralist normative reality should be the main focus of international ethics as an empirical inquiry. Something like that is perhaps what Martin Wight had in mind when he spoke of 'the moral quandary in which *all* statecraft operates'.[50]

A philosopher might say that it is all very well to appreciate that ethical decisions in international relations are normatively complicated and usually involve choosing between rival courses of action each one of which might have some justification. But how do we choose? What is the basis of choice? The philosopher is looking for some overruling consideration according to which the foregoing standards themselves can be judged and ranked: perhaps the principle of fairness or that of utility or those of natural law. That is what a coherent moral philosophy requires.

But this is not what empirical political science requires because, in practice, such questions can only be answered in the living context of historical events. Abstract or theoretical answers divorced from those events are all very well, but they are of limited assistance for understanding the practitioner's world. The weight assigned to any of the foregoing standards can only be that jointly designated in practice by statespeople themselves. The challenge for political scientists, as indicated, is to discern the extent to which statespeople are living up to their own standards of conduct. That does not rule out an assessment of the normative standards themselves: the global covenant is subjected to such an assessment in the final two chapters. But in that assessment, the standards of the practitioners and not those of the philosophers must have the final word and cannot be set aside if we wish to be worldly in our approach to international ethics

Normative Pluralism in World Politics

The *societas* of states is a pluralist arrangement of world politics in two important and distinctive respects. First, it is an association of multiple political authorities based on the values of equal sovereignty, territorial integrity, and non-intervention of member states. If we lived in a world of one state or even a world of many states which were not independent but were subordinate to one political community—in an empire—that would indicate a solidarist world and not a pluralist world: a global *universitas*. But we live in a world of many independent states. We could refer to that condition as jurisdictional pluralism, which is the constitutional basis of Westphalian international relations. That is

---

[50] Wight, *International Theory*, 258 (emphasis added).

what classical international society scholars, such as Hedley Bull, are usually referring to when they use the term 'pluralism'. Second, it is an arrangement in which the domestic affairs of states are their own affair, which means that statespeople and citizens are free to compose their own domestic values and orchestrate them in their own way. State sovereignty should be expected to accommodate a diversity of such values. We could refer to that second form of pluralism, the pluralism of domestic values, as value pluralism. That is the deeper pluralism of world politics that the *societas* of states exists to uphold.

A word of caution on the use of the term 'pluralism' is necessary. The foregoing classical political science meaning of the term should not be confused with the contemporary social science meaning. The latter meaning expresses the sociological idea that other organized groups besides states—including international organizations and non-governmental organizations—are significant actors in world politics. That sociological fact is seen to diminish the weight of state sovereignty in world politics.[51] That is not what the classical international society scholars mean by 'pluralism'. They use the term in its original meaning in legal and political theory. They refer to the territorial-jurisdictional pluralism of the society of states and the value-diversity that such a *societas* accommodates. Pluralism is thus an expression of the constitutional freedom of sovereign states and the wide variety of domestic values accommodated by those same states. Pluralism in that classical meaning is meant to be contrasted with the opposite ideas of monism and solidarism: the singular notion of one commanding authority (source of law) that everybody must obey and one directing doctrine (religion or ideology) that everybody must follow, in other words, *universitas*.

Isaiah Berlin wrote several essays on the following theme (which is a quotation from Kant): 'Out of the crooked timber of humanity no straight thing was ever made.'[52] Berlin expresses the same idea with another metaphor: 'In the house of human history there are many mansions.'[53] These metaphors refer of course to the obvious diversity of human ways of life around the world, which is disclosed by the proclivity of people to come together in particular territorial groups and live their lives more or less according to the values of their group. There are many groups in world politics, each with different values, or different versions of the same value, which are distinctive to themselves.

Men congregate in groups because they are conscious of what unites them—bonds of common descent, language, soil, collective experience; these bonds are unique, impalpable and ultimate. Cultural frontiers are natural to men, spring from the interplay of their inner essence and environment and historical experience. Greek culture is uniquely

[51] P. Willetts, 'Transnational Actors and International Organizations in Global Politics,' in J. Baylis and S. Smith (eds.), *The Globalization of World Politics* (Oxford: Oxford University Press, 1997), p. 289.

[52] I. Berlin, *The Crooked Timber of Humanity* (New York: Vintage Books, 1992).

[53] Ibid. 80.

and inexhaustibly Greek; India, Persia, France are what they are, not something else. Our culture is our own; cultures are incommensurable.[54]

Berlin's intention is clearly to affirm value pluralism and to reject the solid-arist ethics of a global *universitas* on moral grounds of human freedom. It might seem surprising that Berlin quotes Kant to make his pluralist point. But even Kant, who had a more powerful political imagination than any other philo-sopher and could imagine states as servants of humanity, could not foresee a world without states[55] He saw world community arising out of the inclination of liberal-constitutional states ('republics') to recognize each other and respect each other. But he did not see world community as going completely beyond the society of sovereign states. Kant's global *universitas* was qualified by multi-ple statehood based on separate local social contracts, which make possible inter-national covenants between states: Kant the international rationalist.[56] That reality of the global diversity of ways of life is an age-old feature of the human condition that presents itself to and indeed weighs heavily on anyone who seeks to inquire into the normative architecture of world politics. It is a reality that cannot be ignored or sidestepped by any normative inquiry that hopes to be real-istic and down to earth.

It might be supposed that 'the right to be oneself, to live in the light of one's own ideal values' is suggestive of a contrary doctrine, that of value relativism: the incommensurability of the values of separate civilizations. Berlin also rejects that claim.

The fact that the values of one culture may be incompatible with those of another . . . does not entail relativism of values, only the notion of a plurality of values not struc-tured hierarchically; which, of course, entails the permanent possibility of inescapable conflict between values, as well as incompatibility between the outlooks of different civ-ilizations or of stages of the same civilization.[57]

Berlin's response to the political and moral predicament presented by the incommensurability of the values of separate civilizations is to notice two ways by which it is attenuated.[58] The first is the way of natural law separated from its Christian theological baggage: the necessity of living in a world with other human beings whose civilizations are different and distant from our own does not overcome our ability to recognize those others as fellow human beings like ourselves, to claim recognition from them in return, and thus to respect each other's dignity and freedom. 'We cannot help accepting these basic principles

---

[54] I. Berlin, *The Crooked Timber of Humanity* (New York: Vintage Books, 1992) 38.

[55] See the discussion of this point in W. B. Gallie, *Philosophers of Peace and War* (Cambridge: Cambridge University Press, 1978), 9–10.

[56] Kant, 'Introduction to the Science of Right,' 452–6.   [57] Berlin, *Crooked Timber*, 80.

[58] For a sociological study of that problem see S. P. Huntington, *The Clash of Civilizations and the Remaking of World Order* (New York: Simon & Schuster, 1996), part iv. I review and criticize Huntington's argument in Ch. 14.

because we are human.'[59] That recalls the Grotian notion of 'the great society of all humankind', the moral voice of rationalism in world affairs. The second is the way of utilitarianism: to avert the human suffering that value conflicts can so easily produce we have become aware of the dangers of treating values as absolute. 'The best that can be done, as a general rule, is to maintain a precarious equilibrium that will prevent the occurrence of desperate situations, of intolerable choices.'[60] That is the morality of enlightened self-interest in which it is recognized that, unless statespeople adhere to the ethics of responsibility, they will risk contributing to international situations that get out of hand. That is the moral voice of realism in world affairs.

The argument advanced in this book is that the way to alleviate the tyranny of relativism and the clash of civilizations is not limited to the paths of a secularized natural law or a utilitarian foreign policy. While it presupposes these paths, the global covenant arranges a more articulate mode of human intercommunication and political accommodation across the planet: the dialogue and mutual give and take of sovereign states expressed via diplomatic practice, international law, and the political virtues embodied by the ethics of statecraft. State sovereignty does not liberate people from their destiny of living in a world alongside other people who are similarly organized. On the contrary, it recognizes it: the world of states is a social world based on explicit norms of mutual recognition and respect. It recognizes that we in our country must share the planet with many other people and their countries. We have little choice about that—unless we are determined to exterminate them, subordinate them (enslave them or colonize them), or remake them in our own self-image (convert them to our ways and values). At different times and places in the past Europe and later the West tried these policies but they failed, and rightly so, because they were trespassing on human freedom and the entailed right of people everywhere to live their own domestic lives, in their own way, according to their own values.

The modern international *societas* which gives expression to the doctrine of normative pluralism is the most basic and at the same time the most articulate institutional arrangement that humans have yet come up with in response to their common recognition that they must find a settled and predictable way to live side by side on a finite planetary space without falling into mutual hostility, conflict, war, oppression, subjugation, slavery, etc. Jurisdictional pluralism is an accommodation of human diversity via the institution of state sovereignty. That makes possible value pluralism by placing political responsibility for creating and safeguarding particular values in the hands of local people who enjoy and exercise political independence. Those people are the only legitimate judges of the following questions. Which values are best for us? How shall we jointly live our lives? In short, sovereignty is conducive to value pluralism because it

[59] Berlin, *Crooked Timber*, 204.   [60] Ibid. 17–18.

provides a constitutionally safeguarded territorial space, free from outside interference, in which such choices can be made.

The historical project of the global covenant, in this regard, is to forestall hostilities and collisions between different political groups over issues of values. The *societas* of states is arranged in such a way as to reduce unnecessary political confrontation based on value conflict. 'Unnecessary' in this context signifies values which are internal to states: values that properly belong to domestic jurisdiction, self-regarding values. Religious values have been assigned to that category since 1648. Westphalia represents the taming and domestication of religion. In the twentieth century political ideology was shoe-horned, with great difficulty, into the same category. Political religion and political ideology—both our religion and your religion, our ideology and your ideology—are considered to be internal values that have no place in international society, in the sense that they cannot be used to judge the legitimacy and legality of other countries and much less to justify intervention in those countries. Such values cannot justifiably be imposed on independent countries who do not wish to have them. Such values would of course include the core self-regarding belief systems of the major civilizations. That would thus exclude from international relations the Western political ideology of democracy, just as it would exclude the Muslim religious belief system of *jihad* and the revolutionary ideologies of communism or fascism or imperialism, as well as any other religious or political belief system that repudiates the *societas* of states.

The taming and domestication of religion and ideology is one of the most significant and consequential historical achievements associated with modern international *societas*. It is a practical achievement that gives expression to our common human capacity to recognize and respect each other without assimilating each other's values and becoming all alike. It makes it possible for us to turn a blind eye to each other's domestic values when we disagree with them and reject them for ourselves. The global covenant embodies and asserts the norm of neutrality regarding the domestic values of other countries. It teaches the virtues of toleration and self-restraint with regard to those countries and their domestic values. The importance of that normative achievement is not always recognized by international relations scholars.

II

Practices and Problems of
Contemporary International Society

8

Security in a Pluralist World

The normative aspects of security are often ignored by positivist international relations scholars who preoccupy themselves with instrumental questions, such as deterrence strategy, defence policy, coercive diplomacy, and the like.[1] They are often confused by post-positivists who have difficulty distinguishing ethics from ideology. Security is not only or even primarily an instrumental question. Nor is it an ideological question. It is a moral question. Security is a foundation value of human relations. It is a core subject of political theory as well as international theory. This chapter renovates the classical approach which strives to arrive at a clear understanding of what security in international human relations involves. What is the character and *modus operandi* of security as a value? What is the role of the state and what are the responsibilities of statespeople when it comes to the provision of security? Who are the main clients of security? Individuals? States? The society of states? What is the role of the great powers? Is there a discernible cosmopolitan right of human security? The chapter presents preliminary answers to these questions that clear a path to the interrogation of several closely related questions in subsequent chapters.

The Value of Security

Thomas Hobbes is the foremost political theorist of security and anyone who wishes to understand the subject would be well-advised to start with some of his insights. Without security, according to Hobbes, 'there is no place for industry . . . no arts, no letters, no society; and which is worst of all, continual fear, and danger of violent death; and the life of man, solitary, poor, nasty, brutish, and short'.[2] That might seem like an overstatement but it will only seem that way to people who are fortunate enough to live in successful states that enable them to take security more or less for granted. But that is not the case for many people today. And it was not the case for Hobbes in seventeenth-century

---

[1] A noteworthy and important exception is Barry Buzan, *People, States and Fear* (Chapel Hill, NC: University of North Carolina Press, 1983).

[2] Thomas Hobbes, *Leviathan*, ed. Michael Oakeshott (Oxford: Basil Blackwell, 1946), esp. ch. 13.

England which was in a condition of civil war when he wrote these words. That adverse condition of insecurity is particularly evident in circumstances of war where the activities and resources of people are devoted if not indeed sacrificed to their own immediate safety and survival. Insecurity is associated with war and its threat, as Hobbes makes plain. Security, by contrast, is associated with peace and the good 'life and is indeed a fundamental good in itself, both a personal good and a political good. For Hobbes security is the most basic of all human values. It is the bedrock upon which we build our individual and collective lives.

The state was originally a security arrangement and that is what it still is at base. The personnel, finances, organization, equipment committed to police forces and armed forces in most states is substantial to say the least. A concern for the personal security of citizens and their property is a preoccupation of the criminal law in states that are worthy of the name. National security is a norm that often pre-empts other fundamental norms. In most states if somebody is deemed to be a national security threat he or she may be subject to laws and regulations that override normal legal protections or constitutional rights. That pre-emptive character of the security norm is widely understood and accepted; it is indicative of Hobbes's claim that security is the foundation of a flourishing human society.

But when we speak of 'security' what are we referring to? What sort of human relations do we have in mind? We can begin by saying that the quest for security is our defensive posture and self-protecting response to what we believe is a world that contains menacing people who must somehow be kept at bay. If there were no threatening or dangerous people the value of security would disappear and the problem of obtaining it would evaporate. (Only natural dangers would remain.) But human history unfortunately furnishes ample evidence for the belief that there are always some people who pose a threat to other people within their reach. That being so the problem of security continues to present itself—to the theorist as well as the practitioner.

We should distinguish between personal security and national security. Personal security is a basic value because it is an essential requirement, or condition, of a successful and fulfilling human existence: it liberates people (both physically and mentally) to get on with the business of building their lives without undue fear of those around them. Personal security is our individual insulation from threat, danger, or harm, the source of which is always *other people*. Security is also peace of mind: liberation from the anxiety and apprehension associated with fear of those who are in a position to harm us. The means of personal security are analogous to the locks, bolts, and alarms that we install in our house to deter or thwart intruders. It is the peace of mind we experience in the safety of our protected dwelling. But personal security is never absolute. Somebody could still break in if he or she were clever enough and determined enough to do so. Personal security is always relative because it depends on the intentions and actions of other people who are in a position to protect us or menace us. The main point of security policy is to deter any such menace, and to thwart it or defeat it if it cannot be deterred.

The logic of national security is the same as that of personal security but applied to the populations of countries: national security is a political good as well as a personal good. National security involves our country's insulation from foreign dangers and menaces from threats, intervention, blockade, invasion, destruction, occupation, or some other harmful interference by a hostile foreign power—or terrorist group. The means of national security are analogous to the great walls of the city and its object or condition is akin to the peace of mind we experience living under the protection of such ramparts. National security also is relative because it depends on the intentions and actions of other states (or comparable organizations) who are in a position to menace us. The main point of national security policy is to deter any such menace, and to thwart it or defeat it if it cannot be deterred.

Hobbes's solution to the problem of personal security is the construction of a sovereign state to protect people. The state for Hobbes is basically a security arrangement. But as he famously indicates, that statist solution to the problem of personal security simultaneously creates a novel 'state of nature' between independent states: 'kings, and persons of sovereign authority, because of their independency, are in continual jealousies, and in the state and posture of gladiators; having their weapons pointing, and their eyes fixed on one another . . . and continual spies upon their neighbors; which is a posture of war'.[3] So the statist solution to the problem of personal security leads to a consequential problem of national insecurity by bringing into existence an international anarchy of armed states which are exposed to each other and are thus mutually insecure at least to some degree. That security dilemma has long been a conspicuous feature of international relations based on sovereign states. It is important to emphasize that this condition of international anarchy and the insecurity that stems from it is not 'natural' in any meaningful sense of the word. Rather, it is social and indeed political: it is arrived at, somewhat inadvertently, as a consequence of separate state-building projects which result in a number of armed independent states within striking distance of each other.

In trying to grasp the notion of security it is fundamentally important not to collapse the distinction between personal security and national security. Without that distinction we would fail to notice that national security by no means translates readily into personal security. One might perhaps think that these two values come down to the same thing in the end. But they are not the same thing. Hobbes recognized that citizens of states could enjoy personal security under the protection of a state while their national security was at risk, at least potentially, owing to the international anarchy of armed states. He believed that people

---

[3] Thomas Hobbes, *Leviathan*, ed. Michael Oakeshott (Oxford: Basil Blackwell, 1946), 83.

would still be wise to constitute themselves into states because the gains in personal security would more than compensate for the consequent risks of national insecurity. That is so if the state delivers personal security to its population. Hobbes did not seem to recognize a reverse distinction: a state could enjoy national security in relations with other states if some kind of international security guarantee could be arranged. A post-1945 arrangement of that sort is the rule of non-intervention and the prohibition against aggression. But even with such a guarantee a state's population or segments of it could still experience personal insecurity in their relations with fellow citizens. The source of that adverse condition could be the government's failure or refusal to enforce law and order and other domestic civil conditions which are conducive to personal safety and survival. States that pose a security threat to their own people unfortunately are not an uncommon occurrence historically and at the present time.[4]

Hobbes equated security with the state, and he equated insecurity with its non-existence: what he referred to as 'the state of nature'. He seemed to assume that a state which failed to furnish the general condition of personal security would collapse and cease to exist. In that event there would be a state of nature and no longer a state. But the complete collapse of a state would not quite happen if the society of states could guarantee its external sovereignty—its bordered juridical statehood—whether or not its government provided personal security for the people. Hobbes was a seventeenth-century realist who could not foresee a *societas* of states such as the one in which we now live. Today that guarantee of external sovereignty is embodied in the UN charter and other international covenants which unintentionally foster the conditions of personal insecurity in more than a few UN member countries by underwriting the continued independence of failed states and abusive states.[5] That post-1945 and post-colonial international guarantee gave the ethics of security a novel twist in the second half of the twentieth century. I shall return to this issue later in the chapter.

Security in Political Theory

This is a convenient place to emphasize again that security is entirely a social condition and not a mechanical or functional arrangement: we are dealing exclusively with human relations and all that that implies. Security is a problem of living within reach of other people, or other states, at least some of whom cannot be counted on to respect our independence and leave us alone. Security is a normative idea that can be unpacked by addressing the following questions: security in (or of) what, from what, for what, and by what means?

---

[4] See I. W. Zartman (ed.), *Collapsed States* (Boulder, Colo.: Lynne Rienner, 1995).
[5] For further exploration of this situation see Robert H. Jackson, *Quasi-States: Sovereignty, International Relations and the Third World* (Cambridge: Cambridge University Press, 1990).

A classical political theorist who can help us unpack the concept of security is R. N. Berki, who focuses primarily on personal security although his analysis also has application to national security.[6] He begins with the negative concept of 'insecurity' which, like other negatives such as disorder or injustice, is usually easier to clarify than the positive concept.[7] As indicated, insecurity is a potential or actual threat, danger, or menace presented by other people, whether individuals or groups, internal or external to one's state.[8] A hermit confronts natural dangers and hazards but he or she can avoid the problem of insecurity which only comes with the presence of other people. Robinson Crusoe had the opportunity of greater welfare through human co-operation when Friday made his appearance. But Crusoe also now faced the risk of insecurity: Friday might have turned out to be his foe rather than his friend. 'It happened one day, about noon, going towards my boat, I was exceedingly surprised with the print of a man's naked foot on the shore, which was very plain to be seen in the sand. I stood like one thunderstruck, or as if I had seen an apparition.'[9] Insecurity is thus a *social* problem of living among other individuals or groups (including states) whose inclinations or actions could present or do pose a danger to us. Social life has many advantages but one of its big liabilities is the threat presented by other people who might not only let us down but also do us in.

Insecurity is the fear we experience living among capable and wilful others who are imperfectly civilized and might harm us. The very basis of civilized life is the conduct of refraining as far as possible from the threat or use of force in the resolution of human conflict and always subjecting it to procedural and prudential disciplines if it must be resorted to.[10] In a nutshell, that is the political theory of the just war, which has great respect for the possibilities of evil. If human life were completely civilized the problem of security would not arise because civilized people would find peaceful and non-threatening ways to resolve their disputes if the opportunity were available. Everybody would love peace and hate war. If international relations were like that, chapter VI of the UN charter—which lays out articles for the 'pacific settlement of disputes'—would prevail in international conflict resolution. A more restricted version of that pacific thesis has been made in connection with democracies which, it is claimed, do not wage war with each other owing to the civilized character of their domestic political life.[11] Such 'pluralistic security communities' have

---

[6] R. N. Berki, *Security and Society* (London: Dent, 1986).

[7] Arnold Wolfers remarks that 'security after all is nothing but the absence of the evil of insecurity, a negative value so to speak'. *Discord and Collaboration: Essays on International Politics* (Baltimore: The Johns Hopkins University Press, 1965), 153.

[8] Berki, *Security and Society*, 3.

[9] Daniel Defoe, *Selected Writings of Daniel Defoe* (Oxford: Blackwells, 1927).

[10] R. G. Collingwood, *The New Leviathan: Man, Society, Civilization and Barbarism* (New York: Crowell, 1971), 292.

[11] Michael Doyle, 'Kant, Liberal Legacies, and Foreign Affairs', *Philosophy and Public Affairs*, 12 (1983), 205–35, 323–53.

existed for a long time between Britain and the USA, and for a lesser time between a larger circle of democratic states.[12] In that historical experience there is room for the hope that the 'pacific settlement of disputes' may eventually prevail in international relations, provided that democracy spreads around the world. Democracy and security would go hand in hand.

However, the states system is still very far from consisting only of peace-loving democracies—even if the pacific thesis about democracies is true, which is open to question. We know from experience that human life is never completely civilized: the civil condition is imperfect because the people who must be relied upon for civility are almost always intellectually and morally flawed to some degree. International society is also imperfect. We know from past and present experience that some statespeople will trespass on the rights and legitimate interests of other states if the opportunity arises and there is some advantage in doing that. There always will be some predatory people who escape socialization and live at the margins of international society. Adolf Hitler is only the most infamous twentieth-century example of an international predator. Chapter VII of the UN charter recognizes that reality by laying down articles which address problems of 'threats to the peace, breaches of the peace, and acts of aggression'. The Security Council was instituted to deter such threats, and to defeat any that cannot be deterred. That sober view of security is characteristic of both classical realism and classical rationalism.

1. Security in (or of) What?

The answer to this question is rooted in the vulnerability of all humans: they can be deprived of life, limb, liberty, and property, not to mention family, friends, neighbours, and much else, by the malevolent acts of other people, either fellow citizens or foreigners. To be insecure is to be wanting in these basic necessities of human well-being. In security our lives might flourish, but in its absence human life would be extremely difficult, which is exactly how Hobbes conceives of human existence in the 'state of nature' where there is no security but only a war 'of every man against every man'.[13] For Hobbes human life is intrinsically valuable. Life is to be enjoyed. Living is enjoyable or is at least preferable to not living. Death is worthless and useless. But the world is a dangerous place. That is why we strive to make our lives safe and secure.

2. Security from What?

I have so far mentioned several sources of threat (which can, of course, also be sources of security): other individuals, groups, states. In Hobbes's 'state of

---

[12] Karl. W. Deutsch, *Political Communities in the North Atlantic Area* (Princeton: Princeton University Press, 1957).

[13] Hobbes, *Leviathan*, 83.

nature' all people are at least a potential threat because they are all wilful and more or less equally capable rivals in circumstances of scarcity. And they are all intellectually and morally flawed at least to some degree. We can trust or have confidence in others but it could never be absolute: human life is contingent and conditional; it brings with it an unavoidable element of risk because we are inevitably exposed—at least to some degree—to unreliable or hostile others. Perfect security does not exist in any human society. Some measure of insecurity, however large or small, is always present or possible. People who live in some of the safest countries still put burglar alarms on their houses and take other measures to secure their persons and property. Even those fortunate people who live in comparatively civil states under relatively capable and responsible governments are aware of real situations where something resembling Hobbes's 'state of nature' can and does exist—the most obvious example is dangerous districts of big cities, usually at night, where there is a definite possibility of being mugged or even murdered. It is thus clear, as indicated, that one could enjoy national security to the full without enjoying personal security, as residents of certain American cities are only too well aware.

3. Security by Means of What?

As indicated, personal and national security are associated with the protections and guarantees of the sovereign state which has been the prevailing security organization in world politics since at least the seventeenth century. For Hobbes, the sovereign state resolves the problem of security by concentrating a monopoly of force (the sword) in the office of a sovereign ruler who henceforth is responsible for defending citizens (subjects) from both internal and external threats. The ruler is 'judge of what is necessary for the peace and defense of his subjects'. And among the 'rights of sovereigns' is 'the right of making war and peace with other nations'.[14] Here, then, is the classical political theory of the state as a security arrangement under the control of statespeople among whose primary responsibilities is the safety of their citizens.

The principal means by which the state provides personal and national security is of course the apparatus of force at the disposal of rulers: primarily police and military power, but also the financial, industrial, organizational, technological, scientific, educational, and other instrumental means that underwrite it. Just as important and indeed probably more important is the deterrent effect of the security apparatus of the state: the state as a psychological agent. By that I mean the cautioning effect—on the perceptions of people both inside the country and outside who otherwise would be a threat—of stateleaders' capability and willingness to employ police powers and military force in defence of their citizens.[15]

[14] Ibid. pp. 117–18.
[15] See T. Schelling, 'The Diplomacy of Violence', in *Arms and Influence* (New Haven, Conn.: Yale University Press, 1996), 1–34.

There are, then, two important aspects of the security relationship both of which should be noted: there is the credibility of the deterring agent, and there is the diffidence of the deterred. Some theories of security tend to place the emphasis on the credibility of the means of deterrence, which is often viewed as a basic method of obtaining security. That was the prevailing approach of the USA to national security during the cold war.[16] Hobbes, however, places the emphasis on the other side of the relationship: on diffidence, which is a mental condition that disables people who otherwise would be a threat.[17] Machiavelli takes a similar view: better to be feared than loved.[18] Producing that apprehensive mental state in one's adversary is the object of deterrence. Providing security is thus the same as fostering—in the mind of an actual or potential threatening agent—fear and therefore caution, hesitation, reconsideration, and hopefully an aversion to even contemplate, let alone engage in, assaults or other aggressive or belligerent actions.

4. Security for What?

The answer to this question should now be clear: so that people can enjoy the advantages of living together while limiting the risks. Security is a desirable and necessary condition for developing and enjoying the fruits of our own endeavours and also of our joint enterprises with those who are travelling through life with us. In short, security is a foundation value of human relations. The necessity of security arises from the fact that people must live together and are thus exposed to each other, and from the fact that some people present a threat which cannot and should not be tolerated. These are people who live outside the self-restraints of civilized life and who cannot refrain from the arbitrary threat or use of force if the opportunity arises. The correct term to describe such people is 'barbarians'.[19] Barbarians do not live in foreign countries. They live in every country. Providing security is coming to grips with that human reality. Security makes possible what otherwise probably would not be possible or perhaps even conceivable: a flourishing human existence in the company of our fellow men and women and relatively safe from predators. Of course, one can never be absolutely safe. That is the point of being vigilant in the defence of people. Being vigilant usually involves instituting and maintaining in good working order a standing police and military apparatus consisting of men and women who are prepared and equipped to perform that essential role for the public good.

---

[16] Ibid. Also see T. Schelling, *The Strategy of Conflict* (Cambridge, Mass.: Harvard University Press, 1980).
[17] Hobbes, *Leviathan*, 81.
[18] Niccolo Machiavelli, *The Prince* (Harmondsworth: Penguin Books, 1961), 96.
[19] Collingwood, *New Leviathan*.

Confusing and Deconfusing Security

There is confusion in international studies nowadays concerning the notion of security, and related concepts, which are being stretched and twisted to refer to many different human activities and conditions that lie well outside and some-times far away from those captured by the family of ordinary English words and expressions commonly used to speak and write of such matters. Some of the most important are 'safety', 'protection', 'guard', 'shield', 'safeguard', 'defence', 'keep vigil', 'keep watch over', 'sentinel', 'sentry', 'under the protection of', 'out of harm's reach', 'out of danger', among others. These terms of common language are also necessary to capture the meaning of security in academic study—as indicated in the previous sections. The English language, and any other vernacular language, has an armoury of terminology for understanding the human world of security. Any scholar who wishes to say something coherent and precise about the character and *modus operandi* of security in world politics should start by employing that linguistic equipment which is the usual way that classical international society scholars embark on their enquiries.

Ordinary language is not the starting-point for many positivist and post-positivist social science approaches to the study of security. That is somewhat surprising because the vocabulary of security contains many subtle distinctions for thinking and writing about security in a precise way. But these social scien-tists are inclined to make up their own definitions for their own purposes in the evident belief that they can thereby achieve a clearer and deeper knowledge of the subject. But if the results of their studies to date are anything to go by, the opposite is more likely. Closing a classical text on security and opening almost any volume on the subject by a contemporary post-positivist commentator is something like leaving an alpine lake—whose waters may be cold but they are also clear—and sliding into a swamp which may be warm but is infested with obscure jargon, muddy syntax, and precarious reasoning. There has unfortun-ately been a proliferation of confusing notions of security in international stud-ies since the end of the cold war as international relations scholars desperately try to say something new.

Many contemporary studies of security seek to enlarge our knowledge by showing how security is multifaceted.[20] In making that important point they are moving away from the narrow and one-dimensional analyses of positivist theor-ists of national security. They are surely correct in trying to do that: national security is a larger and fuller idea than nuclear strategy, coercive diplomacy, defence policy, etc. In addition to national security, international security and personal security are part and parcel of our subject. And when personal

---

[20] See e.g. B. Buzan, O. Waever, and J. de Wilde, *Security: A New Framework for Analysis* (London: Lynne Rienner, 1998) and E. Adler and M. Barnett (eds.), *Security Communities* (Cambridge: Cambridge University Press, 1998).

security is viewed from a cosmopolitan perspective it discloses itself as human security. A pluralist or multi-dimensional approach is necessary to respond to the diverse existential world of security.

The problem with many post-positivist studies of security, however, is their twisting and stretching of the idea far beyond these rational bounds. Some constructivist scholars speak of 'economic security', 'societal security', 'environmental security'.[21] Economic insecurity is said to involve threats to firms or national economies: e.g., threats of bankruptcy, threats to the means of providing for the material needs of the population. Societal insecurity is held to involve threats to collective identities: for example, 'immigration threats' to national identity. Environmental security is seen to involve threats to the survival of species, threats to habitat, threats to the biosphere. These topics clearly are very important. They ought to be studied and they are being studied. There is a language for dealing with each one of them *in their own terms*. We speak of bankruptcy in terms of 'debt', 'solvency', 'liabilities', and we speak of the material needs of populations in terms of 'national wealth and welfare','national income', 'national deficit and debt', 'national productivity and income', that is, in the language of business and economics. We speak of national identity and immigration in the language of social relations and social policy. We speak of the survival of species, the preservation of habitats, and the protection of the biosphere in the language of ecology and the environment. In short, there are established appropriate vocabularies for discussing almost any subject under the sun. That clearly applies to the age-old subject of security.

But to talk and write about security in terms of bankruptcy or immigration or the biosphere is a steep slide into confusion. One half of the confusion stems from stretching and twisting the notion of 'threat'. The other half derives from misconstruing a contingent or causal relationship for a conceptual relationship. The problem is rooted in the unwillingness to abide by the ordinary meaning of words and the desire to stipulate new meanings. Social science positivism and post-positivism, in that regard, is like Humpty Dumpty:

'There's glory for you!' 'I don't know what you mean by "glory",' Alice said. 'I meant "there's a nice knock-down argument for you".' 'But "glory" doesn't mean "a nice knock-down argument",' Alice objected. 'When *I* use a word,' Humpty Dumpty said in a rather scornful tone, 'it means just what I choose it to mean—neither more nor less.'[22]

Consider the first half of the problem: many threats encountered in everyday living are not security threats, including the above-noted threats. We can be threatened by many things, either as individuals or as members of collectivities including states, and still be fundamentally secure in the ordinary meaning of

[21] Thomas Homer-Dixon, 'Environmental Scarcities and Violent Conflict: Evidence from Cases', *International Security*, 19 (Fall 1994), 5–40.

[22] Lewis Carroll, *Through the Looking Glass*, ch. 7: see *The Oxford Dictionary of Quotations*, 2nd edn. (London: OUP, 1955), 131.

the term. My health can be threatened by my bad eating habits or by a doctor's strike or by a public policy that cuts back on funding health services. My investments can be threatened by a stock market crash. My job can be threatened by technological innovation. Threat clearly is a generic feature of human relations. But these threats, as important as they may be, are very different from the danger presented by somebody who is prepared and equipped to break into my house or invade my country. The latter threats clearly are security threats in the ordinary meaning of the term, threats to safety. Most of the above-noted threats are not security threats. An economic depression might threaten my personal welfare as well as the national welfare, but it is no threat to my safety or my country's security. Immigration into historic countries that are based on a culturally or linguistically distinctive nationality may indeed threaten the collective identity of the native-born population, in the sense that it may disrupt it and change it in the longer term; but immigration will not threaten the country's security and survival in the ordinary meaning of those terms. The pollution of the air I breath and the water I drink threatens my health, but it is no threat to my security. Unfortunately, the elastic use of the notion of 'security' or 'threat' is all too common among international relations scholars nowadays. The predictable result is a loss of clarity and the spread of mist and fog in studies of security.

That brings us to the second half of the problem: the confusion that stems from the conflation or fusion of different concepts and ideas. That is evident in some of the above-noted conceptions of security. This requires immediate qualification. The use of military force to cut the economic lifeline of a country (a blockade) is a security concern and indeed an act of war which is recognized as such by international law. People may also be placed in jeopardy by pollution of their supplies of drinking water. A scorched-earth strategy is a security issue. Attacks on the environment such as those instigated by Saddam Hussein during the Gulf War when he commanded Iraqi forces to torch the oilfields of Kuwait are recognizable as instances of warfare. The use of the economy or the environment as weapons to threaten people or countries is unambiguously an issue of security. All of that and much else like it falls entirely within the classical purview of the subject. There are many different ways and means of threatening or invading the safety of people. But to include the economy or the environment *within* the notion of security *as such*—by conceptually marrying welfare and security, or ecology and security—only serves to obscure these distinctive notions, the different core values at stake, and their relation, which is a contingent relation and not a conceptual relation. Strictly speaking, the expressions 'economic security' or 'environmental security' are instances of category mistakes: they conflate two different ideas and thereby foster academic confusion and disorganization. Unfortunately, this malpractice is widespread in positivist social science and in some branches of post-positivism, for example, constructivism.

The crux of security for our purposes is captured by Hedley Bull: 'Security in international politics means no more than safety: either objective safety, safety which actually exists, or subjective safety, that which is felt or experienced.'[23] Safety is a condition of human relations. Safety is shelter and assurance in our relations with other people. Our safety is provided by creating shields, bulwarks, ramparts, police forces, armed forces, which are geared to our protection. They stand guard, they give us shelter, they keep us out of harm's way. The opposite of safety is the condition of being vulnerable, exposed to danger, in peril, at risk. Safety is something that anyone can enjoy: poor and rich, young and old, male and female. To realize that valued human condition, to experience security, requires only that everybody respect everybody else's freedom and leave them alone. That is not a question of poverty: poor people can respect each other and live in safety. Nor is it a question of ecology: polluted cities can be safe places in which to live. It is a question of human restraint. It is a question of civilization. Security is obtained when people either as individuals or as groups forbear from threatening and harming each other. Anybody can hold to that self-discipline. But the fact is that not everybody will hold to it. There are barbarians out there. We put locks on our doors, we create police forces and armed forces, to handle that contingency. Insecurity is created when some people will not hold themselves in check and cannot be deterred or blocked by others.

As indicated, security is a social problem created by the presence of such people in our lives. Security policy is an attempt to address that problem—whether the object of security is an individual citizen or a nation-state or the society of states or people everywhere. The world of insecurity is thus a world of threat which carries the notion of harm or injury or damage to our persons or possessions or our family or friends or fellow citizens or fellow human beings. Security policy recognizes that in human relations there almost always will be some individuals or groups or countries who will menace us, intimidate us, utter threats against us, terrorize us, and thus give us a reason to be apprehensive, anxious, alarmed, frightened, or terrified. A secure world is thus a world of protection against such possibilities. It is our rational and effective response to the dangers and menaces presented by other people or groups or countries among whom we must live. The usual way of arranging such protection beyond what we can arrange ourselves is to provide police forces and armed forces. That is the heart of security policy in modern states.

Security in Classical International Theory

There are two predominant classical approaches to the ethics of security: the realist approach, which lays the emphasis on national security, and the rational-

---

[23] Hedley Bull, *The Anarchical Society*, 2nd edn. (London: Macmillan, 1995), 18.

ist approach, which emphasizes international security. National security reveals the perspective of Hobbesian realism; international security discloses that of Grotian rationalism. Both approaches are pluralist: they focus on either the system of states or the society of states as the principal security arrangements in world politics. Both approaches also express a communitarian conception of international ethics: what goes on inside independent states by and large is not an international concern providing it does not trespass on the prudential or procedural precepts of international relations. There is a third classical approach to the ethics of security: the cosmopolitan approach. It places the emphasis on human beings and the community of humankind and views personal security as an international problem and not merely an issue of domestic jurisdiction. It is concerned with the safety of people everywhere in the world, regardless of the country in which they happen to live or happen to be at that time: human security. This latter approach reveals the perspective of Kantian universalism.

1. National Security

Classical realists generally assume, following Hobbes, that we live in a world in which states are at one and the same time both the primary sources of security and the main security threats. The problem of national security arises out of the political-legal fact of international anarchy: a pluralistic world of independent and armed states which are in proximity to each other and are thus in a position to affect each other's security, either positively or negatively. Responsible statecraft involves not only ensuring that the means exist to provide for national security but also making sure that the credibility of those means is never in doubt in anyone's mind, particularly that of a potential enemy. Providing national security is an activity of building and deploying armed forces for national defence and for the deterrence of any conceivable foreign threats. It is also an activity of abetting one's own state's capacity in that regard by entering into alliances with other states. That is disclosed by the central contracting norm of the North Atlantic Treaty Organization (Article 5) which reads as follows:

The Parties agree that an armed attack against one or more of them in Europe or North America shall be considered an attack against them all; and consequently they agree that, if such an armed attack occurs, each of them, in exercise of the right of individual or collective self-defense recognized by Article 51 of the Charter of the United Nations, will assist the Party or Parties so attacked by taking forthwith, individually and in concert with the other Parties, such action as it deems necessary, including the use of armed force, to restore and maintain the security of the North Atlantic area.

Classical realists also believe, again following Hobbes, that an effective state is one that can deal with any internal threats to security: criminals, rebels, terrorists, etc. Otherwise the state would not exist. Its existence is proof of its capability. Existential states are effective by definition. So there is an assumption on the part of classical realists that national security is not only security for the state; it is also security for its citizens in whatever corner of the state they happen to live. But that is not always a safe assumption. The Soviet Union is a well-known case in point: the Soviet state was defended effectively during the cold war but many Soviet citizens were at risk—not from the USA or NATO but from their own government. A secure totalitarian state may be the most profound source of personal insecurity. That security predicament is not handled at all well by classical realists.

2. International Security

Classical rationalists generally believe that the responsibility for providing security rests not only with individual states and alliances but also with international society at large. But international security is a less straightforward and more confusing idea than that of national security or that of personal security. The latter ideas presuppose a threatened self and a counterpart threatening other: we/they. For national insecurity that threatening other is usually other states, often neighbouring states. For personal insecurity that threatening other is usually other people within one's own country, especially people in the local neighbourhood. But there is no counterpart threatening other for international security: the threat does not come from outside international society. There no longer is an outside: contemporary international society is global. The threat comes from within, usually from other member states; sometimes it comes from terrorist groups which may or may not be backed by a state. There could be other sources of threat but these are the main ones. In the UN charter there is an assumption of an international security community to which all states belong and whose norms they are all bound to respect. International society is a constitutional sphere of citizenship in which statespeople are the citizens. States that fail to respect international norms are outlaws. Terrorists are also outlaws.

That kind of reasoning about security became prominent during the twentieth century as the idea of a global society of states gained ground. It was already evident in the covenant of the League of Nations (1919): 'Any war or threat of war, whether immediately affecting any of the Members of the League or not, is hereby declared a matter of concern to the whole League, and the League shall take any action that may be deemed wise and effectual to safeguard the peace of nations' (Article 11). Here the League is assuming procedural and prudential responsibility for the security of international society as a whole. It is evident in the charter of the United Nations whose primary purpose is stated as follows: 'To maintain international peace and security, and to that end: to take effective collective measures for the prevention and removal of threats to the peace, and for the suppression of acts of aggression or other breaches of the peace . . .' (Article 1). Here the UN refers explicitly to 'international peace and security' and 'suppression' of international lawlessness.

International security is thus an *internal* problem for international society as a whole. In a well-ordered international society war takes on the character of an internal and indeed almost a domestic conflict which must be stamped out. Aggressors are rebels against international law and order. Military actions to beat down such rebellions are acts of international law enforcement: they are akin to police actions within states. The best example and also one of the very few examples of international security in operation since the society of states was reconstituted in 1945 is the Gulf War. Iraq's invasion of Kuwait was viewed by the vast majority of UN member states and by the Security Council—including all permanent members—as a violation of international law and a threat to international peace and security.

International security is another name for a general condition of peace, order, and lawfulness within the society of states. It is the rule of law internationally. It is the collective good of the whole society and not merely the individual good of particular member states or alliances. National security may on occasion be subordinated to international security and may even be sacrificed to it. According to Hedley Bull, 'international society has in fact treated preservation of the independence of particular states as a goal that is subordinate to preservation of the society of states itself'.[24] Bull is referring to independence, but the same thing could be said of security: the security of particular states is subordinate to the security of the society of states. That is at the heart of the doctrine of international security. At that point Hobbes is shaking hands with Grotius.

3. Human Security

As indicated, there is a third classical approach to the ethics of security: the cosmopolitan approach which places the emphasis on human beings and the community of humankind, and views personal security as an international problem and not merely an issue of domestic jurisdiction. In this context, personal security is more aptly referred to as human security: the safety of people everywhere in the world regardless of the state in which they happen to live or happen to be at the time. Human security is becoming fashionable among politicians and academics but it is not a completely new way of thinking about security. Kant understood all individual humans as having a natural right to free action and thus a duty of limiting his or her action out of regard for the freedom of other people.[25] That duty was universal: it applied to everybody without exception.

That normative reasoning can apply to security. Everybody has a natural right to be safe and secure and everybody therefore has a duty not to threaten anybody or do anything else that would jeopardize their security. The use of coercion, force, etc., would only be justified for enforcing conditions that are

[24] Ibid. 17.
[25] I. Kant, 'The Science of Right', in R. M. Hutchins (ed.), *Great Books of the Western World*, xlii *Kant* (Chicago: Encyclopedia Britannica, 1952), 398.

conducive to the security of people: civil conditions, the rule of law, juridical security. Juridical security is not identical with personal security. Rather, it is the civil condition created and upheld by the state which keeps barbarians at bay and personal insecurity to a minimum. That is the role of the constitutional state: *civitas* or *Rechtstaat*. State authorities have a duty to uphold the civil conditions that make the enjoyment of juridical security possible for their citizens.

This reasoning extends to international relations. Both states and the relations of states are a juridical domain of 'public right'. The state is a 'juridical union' which exists to defend its citizens and thus to uphold 'national right'. That implies the notion of national security. International relations involves an 'international right' of states to exist and to coexist with each other: *jus gentium*. That implies the notion of international security. Lastly, and crucially for our purposes, Kant makes reference to the idea of a 'universal right of mankind', by which he means the legitimate claim of all men and women to recognition and protection by public authorities as individual human beings: *cosmopolitical right. jus cosmopoliticum*.[26] That implies the notion of human security. Kant sees national right and international right as 'necessarily culminat[ing]' in this final form of public right: human rights are no longer only natural rights but are now also positive legal rights upheld by states and by international society. He makes a point of emphasizing the 'interconnectedness' of these juridical arrangements, such that the failure of any one of them to embody and express the fundamental principles of rightful human conduct will undermine the others 'and the whole system would at last fall to pieces'.[27] This is Kant in his revolutionist persona. It is that latter kind of reasoning that is involved in the ethical notion of human security in world politics.

According to that reasoning, the interconnectedness of these three basic constituents of security is such that national security and international security could not be completely safeguarded if human security was not safeguarded. If anyone in the world is juridically unsafe, nobody is safe. If human insecurity were tolerated in some states it would threaten the entire edifice of security because of the interconnectedness of the parts that form the whole. In other words, the human security doctrine cannot accommodate failed states or abusive states because any state that tolerated juridical insecurity would undermine the rule of law not only in that state but everywhere. The juridical elements of international society cannot be justified in isolation. Public right cannot exist in parts. It can only exist as a whole. Personal security, national security, and international security are all part of the same overall juridical arrangement. That is of course a normative statement, a conceptual relation, and not a causal statement or relation. If anybody in the world is juridically unsafe, nobody is juridically safe because the world of states is tolerating barbarians in its midst. It

[26] I. Kant, 'The Science of Right', in R. M. Hutchins (ed.), *Great Books of the Western World*, xlii *Kant* (Chicago: Encyclopedia Britannica, 1952), 434.
[27] Ibid. 435.

therefore is not possible, in Kantian terms, to separate national security and human security, or international security and human security. The spread of republican government is supposed to institute *jus cosmopoliticum* in practice. Kant of course recognizes that what can be achieved in that regard can only be 'an approximation' to the ideal.[28]

The objection of contemporary Kantians to the post-1945 arrangement of security in world politics becomes clearer: the national security of some states and the international security of the society of states cannot be fully and finally justified if people in certain parts of the world are suffering from juridical insecurity. If that is the case, the UN charter cannot be justified on the above-noted Kantian grounds. Such suffering cannot be tolerated by civilized men and women, or by civilized governments, who are duty bound to uphold the *jus cosmopoliticum*. Human rights violations, genocide, torture, judicial killings, domestic lawlessness, civil war, terrorism, and any other barbarian activities within states or between states, perpetrated by state authorities or by non-state agents, cannot be condoned if security in that fuller human meaning is to prevail on earth, if the entire population of the world is to be juridically safe. Sovereign governments are not exempt from that judgement. That humanitarian doctrine is gaining ground in world politics at the present time even though it is still very far from being generally accepted.

International Security as a Great Power Responsibility

The primary responsibility for providing international security obviously rests with the great powers: they are among the small number of states in a position to threaten that political value, and they are the only states in a position to deter such threats or take effective military actions against them. There is a special ethics of responsibility which has to do with international security and applies exclusively to the great powers. The big historical problem of international security is that of ensuring that all of the great powers remain good citizens and always choose to act as international law enforcers rather than as international rebels and outlaws. Whenever a great power fails to do that, international security is put at risk and catastrophic warfare could result. The great powers were tolerably united for most of the nineteenth century following the end of the Napoleonic Wars in 1815—although not without occasional lapses such as the Crimean War between Britain and Russia (1853–56) and the Franco-Prussian War (1870–1).[29] But for most of the twentieth century, beginning in 1914 and ending in 1989, the great powers were divided. On two occasions (1914–18,

---

[28] Ibid. 455.

[29] See the analysis in K. J. Holsti, *Peace and War* (Cambridge: Cambridge University Press, 1991), 165–9.

1939–45) they were involved in the most devastating wars in history. They were also divided during the cold war which persisted for more than four decades following the end of the Second World War, during which time many people lived in dread of a nuclear Armageddon.

International security presupposes two linked institutions which failed to operate for long periods during the twentieth century: the balance of power and the concert of great powers. The balance of power is an institutional and not a mechanical concept, as indicated in a famous definition by Vattel: 'a state of affairs such that no one power is in a position where it is preponderant and can lay down the law to others'.[30] The balance of power underwrites the values of pluralism and the society of states as against those of a hegemonic state or a world empire or world government. A concert of great powers is a closely connected idea: namely that great powers shall co-operate in upholding international peace and security. Because of their paramountcy they alone among all states possess joint responsibility for safeguarding international society and its core values—especially the value of international security—and for jointly laying down the law in that regard for themselves and all other states.

These ideas and institutions have been around for a long time: there are intimations of them as far back as the Peace of Westphalia (1648) and they are clearly discernible in the Concert of Europe following the Congress of Vienna (1815).[31] They have been evident since the founding of the United Nations in 1945 and they are explicit in the institution of the Security Council.

The UN charter can be read as the 'law' of international security enacted by the victorious Allied powers under the leadership of the USA and with the support, or at least the acquiescence, of all sovereign states. The founding fathers of the UN were acting in the manner of a constitutional convention of international society. The responsibilities to provide international security are set out in chapter VII of the UN charter: 'The Security Council shall determine the existence of any threat to the peace, breach of the peace, or act of aggression and shall . . . decide what measures shall be taken . . . to maintain or restore international peace and security.' Packed into that small text are the pivotal ideas of the normative doctrine of international security. First, there is the postulated existence of a concert of great powers: the five permanent members of the Security Council. Second, there is the assumption of international peace and security as a basic value which it is the special responsibility of the Security Council to protect and preserve. Third, there is the implication that any action by a state or states which threatens or violates that norm is a grave matter of concern to international society as a whole. Fourth, there is the responsibility of the Security Council to actively find a way to 'restore international peace and security' when it has been disrupted. Finally, under Articles 41 and 42 the

---

[30] Quoted in Bull, *Anarchical Society*, 97.
[31] See the balanced discussion in Holsti, *Peace and War*, ch. 6.

Security Council may decide what measures to take to enforce the norm, including the use of military force.

Here, then, is a clear expression of international peace and security as a general value to be enjoyed not just by some states or many states but, rather, by all states: it is a common good of the international society as a whole. It is a responsibility of all states to respect that fundamental value, but it is the special joint responsibility of the great powers to ensure that the conditions of international peace and security are upheld. The Security Council exists primarily to underwrite that basic norm, and come to its rescue when it has been violated by outlaw states. All of that unequivocally presupposes the existence of both a great power concert and an international security community.

How significant is this notion of international security? Is there any evidence to suggest that it is more than merely a noble idea? Has it entered into the practice of states in any noteworthy ways? Looking back on the cold war during the second half of the twentieth century it is easy to conclude that it was not very significant and was perhaps insignificant most of that time. That is not to suggest that there was a complete breakdown of international society during that time, because clearly there was not. The USA and the Soviet Union conducted diplomatic dialogue during the cold war. They agreed treaties between themselves on matters of pressing mutual concern: the Nuclear Test Ban Treaty (1963), the Strategic Arms Limitation Treaties (1972, 1979). They also took a leading role in concluding multilateral treaties and agreements: the Nuclear Non-Proliferation Treaty (1968), the Helsinki Accords (1975). Yet, in spite of those dialogues and agreements, there certainly was no great power concert, in the above meaning, either at the UN or anywhere else during the cold war.

A big part of the bankruptcy of international society between the great powers during the cold war was abuse of the veto power by permanent members of the Security Council. That constitutional abuse reflected the underlying division and rivalry that existed between the West and the communist bloc at that time. The cold war was not only a fundamental conflict of national interests; it was also a deep and unyielding ideological and quasi-religious conflict between the Western democracies and the communist countries, particularly the Soviet Union. That may have led many scholars who were hypnotized by the cold war to assume there can be no concert among the current great powers. However, the resuscitation of the Council since 1990 suggests that the concert institution may not be obsolete. That is evident in an unprecedented series of Security Council resolutions made in connection with international crises in different places around the world. These pronouncements and the actions they launched were only possible because the permanent members of the Council refrained from abusing their veto power during that period.

That was evident in the Gulf War (1990–1) which can easily be read as a military action by a coalition of powers undertaken in the name of the United Nations and with the express authority of the Security Council to defeat an international outlaw, namely Iraq, and restore international peace and security. The first Security Council resolution on the crisis (resolution 660) declared 'that there exists a breach of international peace and security as regards the Iraqi invasion of Kuwait', demanded that Iraq withdraw all its forces 'immediately and unconditionally', and called on Iraq and Kuwait to resolve their differences by negotiations. All subsequent actions by the UN to uphold and implement resolution 660—including the authorization of armed force (resolution 678) and its deployment by a coalition of states under American leadership to drive the Iraqi army out of Kuwait—received near-universal support from the society of states. In short, the Gulf War was a rather unambiguous instance of international security in practice.

But it was also evident in the international response to the 1992–5 conflict in Bosnia-Herzegovina which became a subject of widespread international concern and was brought to an end by a concert of major powers under the leadership of the USA and with the important and indeed crucial participation of Russia. The terms of the 1995 Dayton Peace Accords were laid down for the warring parties—Yugoslavia (Serbia), Croatia and Bosnia-Herzegovina—by a group of major powers—including Russia, Britain, France, and Germany—under the leadership of the USA. Article 1 encapsulates the basic norms of international society on the issue of international security:

The Parties shall conduct their relations in accordance with the principles set forth in the United Nations Charter, as well as the Helsinki Final Act and other documents of the Organization for Security and Cooperation in Europe. In particular, the Parties shall fully respect the sovereign equality of one another, shall settle disputes by peaceful means, and shall refrain from any action, by threat or use of force or otherwise, against the territorial integrity or political independence of Bosnia and Herzegovina or any other State.

Article 10 reiterates the injunction against territorial revisionism: 'The Federal Republic of Yugoslavia and the Republic of Bosnia and Herzegovina recognize each other as sovereign independent States within their international borders.' The agreement was enforced by NATO with Russian troops included among the peace enforcers.

Even though the historical period since the end of the cold war is still far too brief to sustain any firm conclusions about a more permanent shift from national security to international security among the major powers, there is ample evidence that international security is something more than merely a noble idea that appeals to rationalist philosophers. The decade of the 1990s saw many instances of international security in action. However, the fact remains that, in moving toward international security, states have certainly not been giving up on national security. None of the foregoing developments call upon major powers or minor powers to surrender their right of self-defence and their capacity to enforce that right independently. Nobody is questioning the ethics of Article 51 of the UN charter. The great powers, including not only the USA and Russia but also China, France, and Britain, continue to possess very substantial military force (including nuclear weapons) under their own independent control. Nuclear weapons have been developed by other important powers including India, Pakistan, and probably Israel. In that fundamental respect, the world of security is still a realist world.

Protected Jurisdictions and Insecure Populations

The commentary so far is suggestive of a familiar historical world of national security and international security. However, it is also possible to discern a novel form of international security that gives categorical legal protection to what for lack of a better term can be called quasi-states: states that enjoy full sovereignty in international law but disclose limited substance and capability in domestic reality. They are not very effective security arrangements. These protected jurisdictions are characteristic of post-colonial international society and also—but to a lesser extent—of post-Soviet Union international society.[32] Their existence reflects the doctrine of non-intervention and the abolition of rights of conquest and colonization which became central normative features of world politics in the latter half of the twentieth century. This development turned upside down Hobbes's classical realist theory of the state as a protectorate of its population. For what are protected by these norms are state jurisdictions and not necessarily their populations.

As indicated earlier, the sovereign state, and even more so the nation-state, has long been understood as a protectorate of its people: a bulwark against both internal and external security threats. The normative vindication of the state's police and military power traditionally has to do with the basic value of security. That is captured by the Latin expression *ubi bene, ibi patria* (where it is well with me, there is my country). Of course that is the political theory, but in many instances it is also the historical reality, particularly in that part of the world where modern sovereign statehood was first instituted: Western Europe and North America. But it may not be the reality in some other regions of the world where the institution is a historically late arrival on the scene. Today that includes not only sub-Saharan Africa and some other parts of the Third World, but also parts of the former Soviet Union and former Yugoslavia.

In the usual normative theory of the sovereign state, it bears repeating, statespeople are responsible for providing both national security and personal security

---

[32] The argument in this section is an abridgement of a more extensive analysis contained in Jackson, *Quasi-States*. Also see R. Jackson, 'The Security Dilemma in Africa', in B. Job (ed.), *The Insecurity Dilemma: National Security of Third World States* (Boulder, Colo.: Lynne Rienner, 1992), 81–94.

and they can be held to account for neglecting or failing to fulfil their security mandate. Citizens can be condemned for ignoring or dodging or refusing to comply with any reasonable security demands that statespeople place upon them. That reciprocal security obligation between stateleaders and citizens is the normative bargain upon which the state as protectorate rests. What such a bargain entails and how it might be instituted are among the central questions of political theory. So in theory there is not a divorce between rulers and ruled: the state is a united political community that consists of both parties who have mutual responsibilities.

A well-organized and well-managed nation-state can be a formidable security organization. The ramparts (physical and psychological) embodied by the well-defended and well-policed state are standard means by which security is still pursued today. The only security arrangements that measure up to states in that regard are alliances and international organizations composed of states. Alternative conceivable security organizations, such as families, cities, trading companies, NGOs, companies of mercenaries, religious organizations, political factions, and almost any others that one can think of, are usually at a definite competitive disadvantage to the state in that regard. The state historically supplanted clans, tribal societies, fiefdoms, free cities, medieval guilds, duchies, small principalities, trading companies with land charters (for example, the East India Company and the Hudson's Bay Company), among others, by proving to be a superior security arrangement. One of the most striking differences between the medieval era and the modern era is the extent to which the state emerged as an unrivalled security organization.

Private security arrangements are of course necessary in modern states and they are still resorted to. We install alarms on our houses and cars. In the USA private security firms are a growth industry which make money by assisting people to deal with the residual security problem in that country—the residual state of nature—that is fed by the widespread and easy availability of guns. The Lockean constitution of the United States gives citizens the right to bear arms. Every other Western democracy prefers Hobbes's strictly policed state monopoly of the means of force. But in every advanced country—including the USA—the majority of people remain wedded to the state as a provider of security.

We might even say that the history of Western countries bears out Hobbes' argument that a secure state is a foundation for pursuing human well-being. That is not to deny that there are other important sources of human flourishing. It is only to claim that national security and personal security afforded by the state are among them. People who live in comparatively secure states—such as we find nowadays in Western Europe, North America, and Japan—have achieved the highest standards of living in human history. Those states have provided a protected sphere that has enabled their citizens to build their lives at a cost in national defence, domestic policing, and other security measures that is not prohibitive or self-defeating. Perhaps for that reason most citizens of such states have accepted, at least grudgingly, the tax and other burdens that an effective system of public security lays upon them.

The traditional mark of a sovereign state is its ability to enforce domestic law and order and to safeguard national defence, either alone or in alliance with other states. State security and survival are the ultimate proof of state sovereignty. In classical international law that proven ability was a precondition for recognition as a sovereign state and membership in the society of states.[33] Protectorates and protected states that lacked that ability were colonies in all but name.[34] In contemporary international law that is of course no longer the case. Since the end of colonialism international society has underwritten the external security and survival of many weak states, particularly those in the Third World, which for all intents and purposes are protected states of the United Nations. Nowadays all states possess a virtual guarantee of non-aggression and non-intervention—including states which are internally chaotic and even those (for example, Somalia, Chad, Liberia, Sierra Leone, Cambodia, Afghanistan, among others) which scarcely exist as organized political systems. The possibility of international legal existence as a sovereign entity (juridical statehood) in the absence of internal socio-political existence as an effective state (empirical statehood) became a noteworthy feature of international society in the second half of the twentieth century. As indicated, that unusual condition is a direct consequence of changes in norms of state recognition connected with the right of self-determination and the abolition of colonialism. It is unprecedented and has no clear parallel with any previous period of modern international history.

Post-1945 and post-colonial international society encompassed many protected jurisdictions that were not directly involved in the cold war. Some parts of Asia and most parts of sub-Saharan Africa, the Caribbean, Latin America, and Oceania were not participants in that conflict. They were spectators. Yet they generally did not rely on their own military means, either alone or in alliance, for external protection. These states rely upon the general prohibition against aggression and armed intervention underwritten by the UN charter and supplemented by parallel regional security communities, such as the Organization for African Unity (OAU) whose key Article 3 reiterates leading principles of the UN charter: the 'sovereign equality of Member States', 'non-interference in the internal affairs of States', and respect for the 'sovereignty and territorial integrity of each State'.[35] In many of these states the military faces inward at the population rather than outward at other states, and often it tends to operate more like an army of occupation than an organization of national defence. That is made possible not least by their UN security guarantee.

---

[33] Jackson, *Quasi-States*, chs. 2 and 3.

[34] See the discussion in Martin Wight, *British Colonial Constitutions: 1947* (Oxford: Clarendon Press, 1952), 7–11.

[35] See I. Brownlie (ed.), *Basic Documents on African Afffairs* (Oxford: Clarendon Press, 1971), 3.

Here, then, is a procedural expression of international security which is almost completely lacking in means of enforcement and depends more or less entirely on the willingness of all states and particularly the great powers to respect international law. It is perhaps comparable to a world-wide extension of the rule of neutrality. Throughout the cold war most of the non-aligned states of the Third World were treated in effect as neutrals by both the Soviet Union and the United States.

This purely normative arrangement of international security did not hold up very well where the superpowers were determined to conduct their rivalry at the expense of the security of states that were useful to one party or the other or were in the way, as happened in connection with certain Third World countries during the cold war: Vietnam, Laos, Ethiopia, Angola, Chile, Nicaragua, among others. There were compelling reasons—strategic location, communist revolutions—which helped to decide which Third World states would be drawn into the cold war and which ones would be left alone. Most were not drawn in. They lay outside the calculations of each superpower; they did not figure in the contest. That is the usual explanation and it is important. But it is only half the story. The superpowers were generally loath to trespass on the norms of the UN charter and other covenants of the society of states. Such action would be in clear violation of international law and would invite general and vocal condemnation. In the Third World region with which I am most familiar, sub-Saharan Africa, the superpowers generally respected the intervention prohibitions of the UN and the OAU. The principal exceptions concerned Ethiopia and Angola, which became entangled in the East–West conflict in the 1970s. Yet during the cold war most of that region could be accurately characterized as a Pax Africana: its international relations generally conformed with Article 3 of the OAU charter.[36]

Before 1945 there was still a discernible norm that weak states would have to arrange their own security by entering into alliances with major powers. The biggest problems faced by the many new and weak states of East and Central Europe formed at the end of the First World War was the problem of security: who will protect us if we cannot protect ourselves? Many could not protect themselves either alone or in alliances with other powers and they were easy prey for Nazi Germany. The difference between the pre-1939 era and the post-1945 era in that regard is one of sharp contrast. The norm of equal state sovereignty and the rights of weak states were not only generally affirmed but were also by and large upheld after 1945, outside the sphere of cold war confrontation. The underlying ethos of international security for protected states was not repudiated during the cold war—even by the superpowers. The United Nations never received the contempt that was heaped upon the League of Nations. It is important to be clear about this point. I am not saying that the rationalist doc-

---

[36] See Robert H. Jackson and Carl G. Rosberg, 'Pax Africana and its Problems', in R. E. Bissell and M. S. Radu (eds.), *Africa in the Post-Decolonization Era* (New Brunswick, NJ: Transaction Books, 1984), 157–82.

trine of international security has enjoyed universal respect since 1945. Nor am I saying that states have given up on the realist doctrine of national security. I am only saying that the rationalist doctrine has proved difficult for statespeople to repudiate publicly. It has become a normative pillar of international diplomatic culture.

The effects of these international moral and legal changes have generally been to accommodate the existence and survival of quasi-states and failed states, some of which might very well have lost their sovereignty if the old positivist norms of international law were still in effect. These states disclose two fundamental deficiencies as political systems. First, their territorial jurisdiction is deeply divided and is often marked by internal conflict and in some cases even by civil war. Second, their governments are generally illegitimate and relatively incapable, and ruling élites are usually dedicated to their own political survival and personal enrichment and little else.[37] The first characteristic is strikingly revealed by some prevalent facts about war since 1945. Until the post-cold-war conflicts broke out in some parts of the former Yugoslavia and the former Soviet Union, almost all wars that occurred since 1945 took place in the Third World. Most of those wars were internal to states, civil wars. They concerned domestic problems of national liberation, social revolution, and state-building.[38] But in virtually none of those cases has war disrupted the juridical statehood of the countries involved, or produced changes to the political map.[39] In virtually every case external state security and survival has been effectively guaranteed by international society.

As indicated, those guarantees are not without important unintended political consequences. They arguably have the effect of tolerating and perhaps even inviting domestic insecurity by preserving jurisdictions which are conflict-ridden and may be dangerous to live in. Two tragic examples from the 1990s were Liberia and Sierra Leone, which lacked even the rudiments of empirical statehood and were two of the most dangerous countries in which to live at that time. Yet there was no question about their right to exist as sovereign jurisdictions, and there was no doubt that they both would continue to occupy their allotted places on the political map of Africa.

There clearly are countries which are states in international law but are still far from being states in domestic reality: they possess juridical statehood but

---

[37] An extensive argument to that effect can be found in Robert H. Jackson and Carl G. Rosberg, *Personal Rule in Black Africa* (Berkeley, Calif.: University of California Press, 1982).

[38] 'The whole Clausewitzian conception of war—a conception reflecting a high degree of institutionalization—begins to break down in many Third World contexts.' K. J. Holsti, 'International Theory and War in the Third World', in Job, *The Insecurity Dilemma*, 49. Also see K. J. Holsti, *The State, War, and the State of War* (Cambridge: Cambridge University Press, 1996).

[39] For a detailed survey see Robert H. Jackson and Mark W. Zacher, *The Territorial Covenant: International Society and the Legitimization of Boundaries* (Occasional Paper; Institute of International Relations, University of British Columbia, 1997).

they are severely deficient in empirical statehood. The state as a legal entity is secure. The men with guns may be relatively secure in the domestic state of nature they have created. But the common people of such states—the ordinary men, women, and children who cannot arrange alternative means of security— are insecure. In some cases their lives and limbs are in immediate danger. The biggest security threat in many protected states is the government and particularly the so-called security forces, which often consist of freelancing soldiers who cannot or will not be controlled by their political superiors. If the soldiers are under political control they may be in a conspiracy with the politicians against the citizens. Other domestic menaces in such countries are local warlords, terrorist gangs, militant revolutionaries, political separatists, guerrilla movements, drug barons and their private armies, and various armed bands who flourish in a vacuum of domestic anarchy and behave in such a way as to give effect to a Hobbesian state of nature rather than a state. Citizens may have to fall back upon other organizations for whatever security they can obtain: for example, kinship groups, clan or ethnic groups, religious communities.

These protected states obviously are not protectorates of their populations. They are legal shells of limited substance that have fragmented into subnational organizations of one kind or another which either threaten the security of people or try to protect them. That has ironically reversed the usual historical tendency since the medieval era for states to supersede and displace all other organizations as the main source of security. Many such states are tolerated by international society. That provides moral ammunition for the Kantian argument that juridical insecurity inside certain member states of international society must be stamped out if security in the fuller human meaning is to prevail on earth.

Human Security in a World of States

The international guarantee of juridical statehood thus raises some perplexing and ironical issues for the realist and the rationalist ethics of security which usually presuppose that a fundamental justification of states is their ability to provide domestic security for their populations. The issues are perplexing because the normative practices of post-1945 international society seem to condone the insecure domestic conditions associated with some and perhaps many internationally protected jurisdictions. The issues are ironical because the pluralist doctrines of self-determination and state sovereignty which normatively ground that international insurance arrangement presuppose the value of those states to their populations. The international experience of the past fifty years clearly indicates that these presuppositions are problematical.

Perhaps with such states in mind it was recently asserted that 'All people, no less than all states, have a right to a secure existence, and all states have an obligation to protect those rights.'[40] Is there a cosmopolitan right of human security? Should such a right be instituted by international society? These are the most difficult normative questions addressed in this study and we shall come back to them in different guises in later chapters. They are not merely academic questions. They are practical questions of foreign policy. At the start of the twenty-first century some Western countries were adopting foreign policies that actively promoted the goal of human security.[41]

As indicated in a previous chapter, the post-1945 society of states instituted an elaborate regime of international humanitarian law, beginning with the Universal Declaration of Human Rights (1948). An example is the convention on genocide which authorizes contracting parties to call upon the UN to take 'appropriate' actions 'for the prevention and suppression' of 'acts committed with intent to destroy, in whole or in part, a national, ethnical, racial or religious group'.[42] The term 'appropriate' recognizes that any such actions are a matter of judgement, of prudential ethics. So the convention on genocide is not the radical humanitarian charter that it might seem to be at first glance. But it is significant. Human rights are a recurring normative concern in international dialogue, especially involving Western states. According to John Vincent, such developments are testimony to the spread of a 'global cosmopolitan culture' in which the boundaries between domestic society and international society 'become fuzzier with the accumulation of more conventions in the international law of human rights'.[43]

A doctrine of human security that echoes Kant was enunciated in the mid-1990s by the Commission on Global Governance:

global security extends beyond the protection of borders, ruling elites, and exclusive state interests to include the protection of people . . . To confine the concept of security exclusively to the protection of states is to ignore the interests of people who form the citizens of a state and in whose name sovereignty is exercised. It can produce situations in which regimes in power feel they have the unfettered freedom to abuse the right to security of their people . . . All people, no less than all states, have a right to a secure existence, and all states have an obligation to protect those rights.[44]

Despite that claim—which suggests that human security is an established right in current international practice—the Commission is constrained to point out that state sovereignty is 'the cornerstone of the modern interstates system'.[45] It is compelled to do that because non-intervention is still a pre-emptive norm of

---

[40] *Our Global Neighbourhood: The Report of the Commission on Global Governance* (Oxford: OUP, 1995), 84.

[41] The Canadian Foreign Minister was a vigorous and active advocate of the doctrine in the late 1990s and he was attempting to secure resolutions from the UN Security Council which would endorse it.

[42] The Convention on the Prevention and Punishment of the Crime of Genocide, Article VIII.

[43] John Vincent, 'Grotius, Human Rights and Intervention', in H. Bull, B. Kingsbury, and A. Roberts (eds.), *Hugo Grotius and International Relations* (Oxford: Clarendon Press, 1990), 255.

[44] *Our Global Neighbourhood*, 81–4.   [45] Ibid. 68.

international relations. Human rights are, of course, recognized by international law but international society usually has not seen fit to trespass on the territorial jurisdictions of states when the personal security of their citizens is put in jeopardy either by fellow citizens or by the government. Human rights generally have not trumped sovereign rights in state practice. That has only happened on rare occasions and even then it is hedged and qualified in various statist ways—as later chapters indicate.

The Commission nevertheless seeks to justify its claim by noting that certain threats to the security of people warrant international concern, and action, owing to their severity—as measured for instance by the number of people under threat and by the immediacy of the threat. They suggest that Article 2 of the UN charter should be respected except for 'cases that constitute a violation of the security of people so gross and extreme that it requires an international response on humanitarian grounds' and they argue for a Kantian revision of the charter to that effect. They claim that 'would both strengthen the worldwide acceptance of the concept of the security of people and keep the evolution of humanitarian response to its violation within strictly observable limits'.[46] The Commission does not seem to recognize the full implications of the proposal. To 'require' an action is far more binding than merely to invite an action or even to permit an action: a requirement for action is a demand for action—in this case a demand based on what amounts to a pre-emptive norm of human rights. That goes well beyond the discretionary and prudential limits recognized by the convention on genocide, and by other universal covenants of international society, including the UN charter.

If such an amendment were made to the charter it would be nothing less than a normative revolution in world politics: away from national and international security and toward human security. It would be revolutionary because it would place human rights and the positive international responsibility to promote human security above state sovereignty and the negative international responsibility to respect the rule of non-intervention. It would destroy the pluralism of international society. Kant in his most revolutionist persona would take over and Grotius and Hobbes would have to retire. International society, in that important connection, would become a *universitas*. The UN would be converted into a latter-day secular equivalent of the medieval *respublica Christiana*; the universal duty to protect human rights would take the place of Christian duties—the enforcement of which also was a universal commandment which applied to Christian rulers and their subjects. The doctrine of human security also has some parallels with the historic practice of Western states of enforcing capitulations and imposing unequal treaties on non-Western states to protect Western traders, missionaries, etc., who were resident in those states, by exempting them from local jurisdiction. The doctrine of human security would, so to speak,

[46] *Our Global Neighbourhood*, 90.

extend that doctrine to all people regardless of their citizenship or their residency if their safety were at stake. Politicians and academics who are advocating the doctrine of human security do not seem to be aware of these historical parallels.

The prospect of justifying the use of armed force to protect civilians in foreign countries raises fundamental normative issues which human security advocates and activists often fail to consider. Since the Peace of Westphalia the society of states has viewed intervention on religious or ideological grounds as an extremely dangerous doctrine that is a standing invitation to abuses by righteous powers who might be prepared to use armed force to promote their beliefs and convictions. It has recurrently endeavoured to come up with rules and practices that foreclose on that possibility. Historically, the society of states has accepted that war is sometimes necessary, but over time it has limited the *jus ad bellum* to national security and international security, which is the restricted definition instituted by the statespeople who met in San Francisco in 1945. International society has consistently endeavoured to abolish holy wars and limit the justifications for going to war. The classical norm of *cujus regio, ejus religio* forbids intervention on religious grounds. The latest version of that norm is Article 2 of the UN charter which forbids coercive or forcible intervention in a sovereign state on any grounds except those of national self-defence and international peace and security.

As indicated, revolutionist Kant argues that national security and international security could not be completely safeguarded if human security was not juridically safeguarded. His only qualification is practical: what can be achieved in practice can only be 'an approximation' to the juridical ideal. In making these connections the way he does, by implying an overriding duty of all states and of international society as a whole to defend human security, Kant discounts the normative standing of state sovereignty. Contemporary Kantian activists and advocates of human security do much the same. But anyone who takes up Kant's theory in order to promote the doctrine of human security would be led astray by it. Since 1945 sovereignty has been an international assurance that states shall enjoy freedom from foreign intervention. That international right is only fenced in juridically by the requirements that sovereign governments respect the constitutional independence of other sovereign states, and that they support international society as a whole. If Kant's doctrine of human security were instituted it would reverse the historic trend to limit the right of war. That would be nothing less than a revolutionary change of international society.

Kant acknowledges that his normative argument is subject to practical limits, but the practical obstacles facing the attempt to make the doctrine of human security a reality in contemporary international society are daunting. Setting aside the wisdom of human security as a goal of international society, present-day Kantians pay insufficient attention to political realities which would frustrate and probably defeat any attempt to institute it as a *Grundnorm* of international society. Could statespeople turn around after half a century of upholding the juridical statehood of all peace-loving UN member states and make sovereignty universally conditional on respect for human rights? That such a change would be construed by many Asian and African leaders as merely another form of Western imperialism is very likely, in so far as human rights are strongly associated historically with Western civilization. Their fathers and grandfathers rebelled against Western imperialism. Would they not be inclined to condemn it and resist it? And would they not have some compelling normative arguments to make their case? I have in mind arguments that draw upon the illegitimacy and unlawfulness of colonialism, the right of self-determination, equal sovereignty, the doctrine of non-intervention. Any attempt to make human rights mandatory around the world would come into conflict with the politics of accommodation and the ethics of toleration upon which the pluralistic society of states is based.

But a bigger immediate political obstacle is the difficult position of the major powers who would most likely be called upon to enforce a *Grundnorm* of human security. That is not merely a question of approximating a valid ideal, of falling short but still striving to reach the ideal. It is a question of conflicting standards of conduct. Would the USA be prepared to take on that heavy responsibility if it was a 'requirement' rather than merely a discretionary right? Among other things, that would place the constitution of international society above the US constitution. Would Britain or France or Germany or any other responsible member of international society be prepared to do that? Would they be prepared to comply with an international obligation to put the lives of their soldiers at risk to protect the lives of people in foreign countries—particularly countries outside the West? Would they be prepared to do that without first taking other important considerations and responsibilities into account? If they were not prepared to do that, where would that leave human security as an international standard of conduct?

The post-cold-war experience of these weighty normative questions is neither uncomplicated nor straightforward, as the discussion in several later chapters indicates. But one elementary thing is clear: the consistent enforcement of human security around the world is impossible. The world may be shrinking in some respects, but it is still far too big to make enforcement a realistic possibility. The most qualified enforcers—including the USA—lack the military ability and the political will to be the world's policemen. More significant for our purposes, the world is normatively more complicated and more contradictory than revolutionist Kantians seem to recognize. American and other leading statespeople are responsible for defending their own national interests and that responsibility will come before their responsibility to save people in foreign countries who are suffering at the hands of the government or other political-military segments of the population. On this fundamental issue there is a clear penchant for international practice to follow Hobbes and Grotius rather than Kant.

The contemporary world of security could be portrayed as comprising three concentric circles of independent states. There is an outer circle of quasi-states on the periphery of global international society, where security is limited to protection of territorial jurisdictions; that security is generally guaranteed by international society and can be obtained by the willingness of states to respect the foundation norms of the UN charter. There is an intermediate circle of substantial and mostly non-Western states where security is national and international and is based on the capacity of states or alliances to defend themselves and to promote regional international order. There is an inner circle, almost an inner sanctum, of democratic and mostly Western or Western-gravitating states where security is not only national and international but also human and personal. Only in this inner sphere is human security an enforcible international norm—however imperfectly it is enforced in practice even here. In short, the present-day world of security is made up of different normative spheres: for all states it is still a pluralist world, but for the states of the West in their own relations it is, in addition, a solidarist world. Respect for human security in the West has little or nothing to do with international society or international law or international ethics. It has almost everything to do with the geographical proximity, the shared historical experiences, the general legacy of secularized Christian ethics, and the common civic culture of most of these countries—which sharply differentiates their moral life from that of the two outer circles.

9

Justifying Conventional War

A summary diagnosis of the 1990–1 war in the Persian Gulf indicates that an international discourse of justification and condemnation was intrinsic to the conduct of the belligerents involved in that conflict—not at the periphery but at the centre. This chapter explores that discourse with the aim of understanding the normative character and *modus operandi* of conventional war in contemporary international society. The classical rationalist distinction between *jus ad bellum* (justification of resorting to war) and *jus in bello* (justification in waging war) is employed to structure the argument. Among the selected normative issues addressed are: the justifications of the UN and Iraq for resorting to war, the responsibilities of citizens during wartime, the responsibilities of soldiers in waging war, the normative reality of unlevel battlefields, distributive and corrective justice in war, and the constitutional aspects of conventional war between member states of contemporary international society. The Gulf War was as near to a legitimate and lawful war as any war of the twentieth century. But that may have been owing to the special international circumstances of the 1990s which are briefly discussed at the end of the chapter.

Eight Thoughts on War as a Human Activity

Iraq's invasion and occupation of Kuwait can of course be analysed wholly from an instrumental perspective, such as the contribution it made, temporarily, to Saddam Hussein's power and prestige in the Arab world, or the threat it presented to Western investments. Many foreign-policy analysts looked at the event in exactly these terms. The actors certainly made reference to costs and benefits, risks and opportunities, advantages and disadvantages, and other instrumental considerations. But that was by no means all they did. On every major issue they justified their demands and actions and condemned those of their adversary. At every turn plans and acts involving military force and other instruments of war were interrogated by normative expectations and considerations. Even something as ostensibly instrumental as oil figured prominently in the normative discourse of the Gulf War. That should not be surprising: to interrupt the provision of an essential commodity upon which many countries and hundreds of millions of people are heavily dependent would be to deal arbitrarily with the welfare of nations and individuals. Such an action must be justified or else it must be condemned. Oil is thus not only a strategic asset or capitalist commodity; it is a national and international good.

In sum, the actors construed the episode not only in terms of power and narrow self-interest but also in terms of justice and injustice: normative as well as instrumental discourse was involved from beginning to end. All war, even high-tech warfare, is a fundamentally normative activity. That is a reality we cannot ignore if we hope to understand the Gulf War in more comprehensive terms. The important questions concerned whose claims and conduct could be vindicated legally and morally, and whose could not. As leader of a member state of contemporary international society Saddam Hussein could not escape from these questions—any more than the UN Security Council, the USA, the anti-Iraq coalition states, or the very few states that sided with Iraq. There are standards of conduct for assessing the Gulf War that can be applied to all the states and statespeople involved. Any attempt to understand the Gulf War exclusively as an instrumental activity would not only pass by an important dimension of that war but it would end up by misunderstanding it because it would not see that that war, too, was a normative activity from start to finish. The following eight reflections expand on this line of reasoning with the aim of setting the stage for the normative inquiry that follows.

First, to repeat an important thesis of Hedley Bull, 'war is unimaginable apart from the rules by which human beings recognize what behavior is appropriate to it and define their attitudes toward it'.[1] When they are at war stateleaders may be severely constrained but they make choices none the less which are often onerous in the extreme; and we hold them accountable for the choices they make. War is certainly about interests. But it is also about interests which are considered to be legitimate, it is about rights, it is about responsibilities, it is about claims, grievances, violations, injuries, damages, and the rest. Those who cannot agree probably see moral claims in international relations as a smoke screen on calculated narrow self-interest—again the 'window-dressing' critique. In previous chapters I have tried to show that that argument is a shaky foundation for the empirical study of world politics. It overlooks the fact that in public life, including international relations, normative claims are subject to scrutiny. Much international discourse consequently involves strenuous efforts at justification and condemnation which, in turn, necessitate appealing to standards of conduct which most people recognize. That applies to war—if anything it applies even more so to war.

Second, the familiar realist distinction in international relations—between on the one hand an international anarchy restricted to instrumental relationships

---

[1] Hedley Bull, 'Recapturing the Just War for Political Theory', *World Politics*, 31 (1979), 595.

and on the other hand domestic civil societies based on morality and law—is deeply misleading. International relations, even during times of war, as this chapter will indicate, offer ample evidence that statespeople have practical need of normative as well as instrumental discourse to justify their own foreign policies and actions and assess those of other states.[2] They seek to justify their international activities not only to themselves or even to their citizens but also to other statespeople and their citizens. As indicated throughout this study, there are established international standards which serve that human requirement.

Third, we should recognize that human beings at war cannot operate with normative standards which are out of line with human moral capacities and the terrible circumstances that war involves. The laws and ethics of war are only realistic to the extent that they are within the moral reach of average people in their concrete circumstances. Standards of conduct fit only for heroes or saints have no place in war or in any other human sphere; but standards must not be set too low, either, or else the temptation of 'anything goes' will threaten to take over. That is a slippery slope from civilization to barbarism. The procedural requirements and prudential maxims of contemporary international society, including the laws of war, are constructed with a view to avoiding both extremes: that is the rationalist middle way of the ethics and laws of war.

Fourth, the normative study of war must likewise be a discipline of interrogating the conduct of actors in terms of appropriate standards—appropriateness defined as those which properly belong (are internal) to the subject. The practices and procedures of the global covenant are examples of such reference points: the UN charter, the Geneva Conventions, etc. International relations scholars do not have a licence to stipulate their own preferred (external) standards to assess the conduct of politicians and soldiers at war. That is the way of ivory-tower philosophy or political ideology rather than classical political science. Sound normative inquiry does not exclude honest disagreement: that is inevitable. What is questionable is the easy condemnation of war based on stipulated standards of evaluation which the commentator derives from scholastic philosophy or his or her own political beliefs. Unfortunately, as will become evident, more than a few commentators on the Gulf War resort to that malpractice.

Fifth, the Gulf crisis suggests that there are fundamental standards of international conduct about which the vast majority of states, if not yet every last one, can agree. One such standard is Article 2 and related articles of the UN charter. That world-wide norm is testimony against the claim that relativism holds sway in international ethics.[3] The world is still a very plural place, of course, and many different conceptions of right and wrong, justice and injus-

---

[2] For some probing reflections on these vocabularies see M. Oakeshott, 'The Vocabulary of the Modern European State', *Political Studies*, 23 (1975), 319–41.

[3] See T. Nardin, 'The Problem of Relativism in International Ethics', *Millennium*, 18 (Summer 1989), 149–62.

tice, undoubtedly exist. But on this point there is evidence of near universal-agreement.

Sixth, a central feature of world politics is international law, which for too long has been marginalized in political science. This does not mean that political scientists must become international lawyers. It only means that they should be sufficiently familiar with the framework of international law to interrogate the conduct of stateleaders and other international actors in these terms. International law must in other words be understood less as a textbook or series of legal cases (that is the business of lawyers) and more as the evolving constitution of international society.[4]

Seventh, war is of course a human relation and is in that regard no different from any other international relations: it is between people, especially the political representatives and military agents of states. The ethics of war apply to all the parties involved and not just to one side. In the case of the Gulf War, we must accordingly assess the conduct of the UN Security Council as well as that of the Iraqi government on the question of *jus ad bellum*; and we must appraise the conduct of the coalition armed forces as well as that of the Iraqi armed forces on the question of *jus in bello*.

Finally, the inquiry suggests that a fruitful way to study international ethics is by reference to the moral and legal discourse of statespeople.[5] They are the principal actors involved in shaping events and their discourse consequently is the most important discourse to scrutinize if we hope to get to the normative heart of our subject. That clearly applies to the statespeople involved in the Gulf War. A main point here, to repeat it once again, is that the language of instrumental calculation cannot be divorced from that of normative appraisal. Both discourses were clearly evident in the Gulf crisis. We may analyse such an episode exclusively from an instrumental perspective and undoubtedly we will learn something from that. If my argument is valid, however, such an approach will overlook important normative issues which not only contribute to the meaning and shaping of events but largely define the human activity involved in them—in this case the activity of conventional war in a military era of high technology.

Resorting to War

The Gulf War properly understood began with the Iraqi invasion of Kuwait on 2 August 1990. A normative inquiry must accordingly take its departure from

---

[4] An excellent example is Alan James, *Sovereign Statehood: The Basis of International Society* (London: Allen & Unwin, 1986).

[5] For elaboration on this point see M. Oakeshott, 'Political Discourse', in *Rationalism in Politics and Other Essays*, new and expanded edn. (Indianapolis: Liberty Press, 1991), 70–95.

no later than that time—and certainly not from mid-January 1991 when coalition air attacks on Iraq began. The international response to the invasion is consistent with this claim. On the day of the invasion the UN Security Council invoked chapter VII of the charter which deals with acts of aggression. The Council passed resolution 660 which condemned Iraq's action as 'a breach of international peace and security' and called upon Iraq to withdraw its forces and settle its differences with Kuwait by negotiations. That response by the Council was an authoritative signal that an act of war had taken place in violation of the UN charter. Aggression is an act of war. When there was no positive response from Iraq, the Council on 6 August imposed a total world-wide trade and financial embargo against Iraq and occupied Kuwait (resolution 661). In a third resolution (662) three days later the Council declared Iraq's annexation of Kuwait to have no legal basis and called upon member states 'to refrain from any action or dealing that might be interpreted as an indirect recognition of the annexation'. On 25 August the Council in resolution 665 made an appeal to member states with navies to enforce the sanctions by establishing a blockade, which is an act of war. Resolution 665 was an authoritative signal that international society had joined the conflict in an act of war on the side of the victim of aggression: Kuwait.

These resolutions culminated in the most difficult decision made by the Council in the entire Gulf crisis: whether or not to authorize the use of military force against Iraq. On 29 November the Council passed resolution 678 which contained such an authorization which would come into effect after 15 January 1991—unless the Iraqi government gave a clear indication that it was complying with the previous UN demands. When Operation Desert Storm was launched by the coalition states, just after the expiry of that period of grace, to drive the Iraqi armed forces from occupied Kuwait, it carried UN sanction. All subsequent actions of importance by the coalition powers were also taken by reference to the UN charter and other bodies of international law. The decisions of international society to resort to war in their conflict with Iraq conformed as well as could reasonably be expected to the current norms of *jus ad bellum*.

If Iraq's aggression 'could not be allowed to stand', as President George Bush declared, it would require the mobilization of an alliance of military powers behind the leadership of the USA. Realism required a military coalition. But to have full international legitimacy and legality the operation had to possess a warrant which could only be obtained at the UN Security Council. With the end of the cold war such an authorization stood a good chance of receiving the necessary votes and not being vetoed for ideological reasons. The Council could therefore operate as originally planned with great powers and supreme authority constitutionally harnessed together.[6] Without UN authority any war against

---

[6] M. Wight, *International Theory: The Three Traditions* (Leicester: Leicester University Press, 1991), 33–4.

Iraq could easily be construed as Western imperialism, which is exactly how Saddam Hussein sought to portray it. But with such a warrant it could be justified as a legitimate and lawful action of international society in defence of peace and the security of all nations, large and small.

The Security Council was criticized for ratifying decisions which were determined in back rooms under the influence of the USA.[7] It was implied that the Council was merely the puppet of the USA. It is important to emphasize, however, that constitutionally it does not matter how or where co-operation among members of the Council is obtained or what the motivation of each member happens to be. All that matters is that members observe the procedures of the charter in their deliberations, decisions, and actions—such as Article 27 which prescribes the voting procedure.

In the Gulf crisis the Council conformed to chapter VII of the charter as well as one can reasonably expect in regard to standards of conduct which inevitably must leave room for interpretation and judgement. For example, Article 41 gives the Council latitude to 'decide what measures not involving the use of armed force are to be employed to give effect to its decisions', and Article 42 likewise leaves it to the Council to determine when such measures 'would be inadequate or have proved to be inadequate' at which time it can resort to armed force.[8] On the occasion of the Gulf War, members of the Council made the political judgement that, after several months in use without effecting a climbdown by Iraq, the sanctions had proved inadequate. They overwhelmingly decided—in accordance with Article 42—to support resolution 678 which authorized the use of military force to restore the independent government of Kuwait. The fact that a large majority vote was obtained and the veto was not resorted to by any of the permanent members tells us something important about the international legitimacy of the episode.[9]

That was not the case with Saddam Hussein's international behaviour. His invasion of Kuwait immediately presented his foreign policy with a big moral and legal deficit: the widespread and strong impression that he had committed an unambiguous act of aggression and therefore a breach of the UN charter. He recognized this and endeavoured to justify his action in various ways. At the first meeting of the Security Council on the crisis (2 August 1990) Iraq's UN ambassador justified the invasion in the following terms: it was solicited by the 'Free Provisional Government of Kuwait' and Iraqi forces would 'withdraw as soon

[7] See P. Taylor and A. J. R. Groom, 'The United Nations and the Gulf War 1990–91: Back to the Future?' (work in preparation for the Royal Institute of International Affairs, Dec. 1991), 40.

[8] For a careful legal analysis of the relationship of resolution 678 to the UN charter see D. J. Scheffer, 'Commentary on Collective Security', in L. F. Damrosch and D. J. Scheffer (ed.), *Law and Force in the New International Order* (Boulder, Colo.: Westview, 1991), 101–10.

[9] It is a not only a considerable overstatement but also a misunderstanding to claim the Security Council in this episode was 'manipulated' and the authority of the UN was 'usurped' by the USA. See Richard Falk, 'How the West Mobilized for War', in John Gittings (ed.), *Beyond the Gulf War* (London: Catholic Institute for International Relations, 1991), 13–15.

as order has been restored'. Because solicited interventions are entirely consistent with international law, that raised the question as to whether such a government could be said to exist, and, if so, was it the lawful government of Kuwait. The overwhelming international response to these questions was in the negative.

Later Iraq offered several additional justifications for their invasion which relied heavily on historic claims.[10] First, they claimed that Kuwait was part of Iraq historically but was cut off from the main body by the British during the era of European imperialism. It was this earlier action of colonial divide and rule which was unlawful and was standing in the way of the unity of not only Iraq but the Arab nation as a whole. That claim was refuted by Kuwait in an alternative historical argument that was judged to be valid.[11] Second, Iraq alleged that the government of Kuwait was pumping too much oil and thereby depressing the price which was undermining the ability of Iraq to recover economically from its war with Iran (1980–8). Saddam Hussein spoke of this action by Kuwait as 'a kind of war against Iraq'.[12] Finally, they said Kuwait was unwilling to resolve a long-standing border dispute between the two countries by negotiating a transfer to Iraq of territory under which lay a huge pool of oil that Kuwait was stealing. These were unwarranted provocations which compelled Iraq to invade Kuwait. Saddam Hussein's normative problem was the flimsiness of these justifications: they were seen by the vast majority of states as amounting to little more than excuses fashioned for the moment. On the other hand, Kuwait claimed that 'the regime of Saddam Hussein does not honor any international rules or norms'.[13] That came to be a very widely held view among the members of international society.

The nearly universal condemnation of Iraq's action could not be brushed aside without disregarding the immediate concern the action provoked and the gravity with which nearly the entire political world undertook to denounce it. The Security Council and the coalition at every stage of their response to the Iraqi invasion and occupation of Kuwait had recourse to standards of conduct embodied in international law. Their response was explicitly based on the UN charter which prohibits unprovoked armed conflict as a legitimate instrument of national policy and defines the restricted legal grounds for launching war. To repeat an important point made in previous chapters, Article 2(4) declares that 'All members shall refrain from the threat or use of force against the territorial integrity or political independence of any state'. There is no right of conquest in contemporary international law. About the only use of armed force that carries categorical legal sanction nowadays is a war against an aggressor who has (by definition) violated the *Grundnorm* of the charter. Aggression is the great

---

[10] E. Lauterpacht (ed.), *The Kuwait Crisis, Basic Documents* (Cambridge: Grotius Publications, 1991), 73–7.

[11] Ibid. 78–82. [12] Quoted by *The New York Times* (12 Aug. 1990).

[13] Lauterpacht, *Kuwait Crisis*, 82.

crime of the contemporary *jus ad bellum*. The right to embark on war nowadays is confined to the determination by the Security Council of 'the existence of any threat to the peace, breach of the peace, or act of aggression' (Article 39), its right and duty to take 'action by air, sea, or land forces as may be necessary to maintain or restore international peace and security' (Article 42), and, of course, by 'the inherent right of individual or collective self-defense' (Article 51).[14]

By invading Kuwait without any legal warrant, Iraq clearly committed the great crime of contemporary international society. There was no antecedent recognized international injury done by Kuwait to Iraq; Kuwait and not Iraq was the victim of injustice. This normative reasoning was not incidental to the international response to the Iraqi invasion; it was central to it. Such reasoning was also central to a host of other important issues and controversies which arose during the course of the Gulf War. Some of them are addressed below. Taken together they strongly bear out Hedley Bull's contention that war 'is as a matter of fact an inherently normative phenomenon'.[15]

Attacking the Social Base

We now turn to some of the most important issues of *jus in bello* that were raised by the Gulf War. The first issue is that of the status of civilians during times of war. The ethics and laws of war have generally maintained that there is a significant moral distinction between civilians and soldiers. In the just-war tradition armed force must be used with discrimination (only soldiers should be targeted) and with restraint (excessive force should not be employed) so that both deliberate and accidental killing is minimized. But the distinction between combatants and non-combatants is not straightforward. That is especially so for wars between nation-states in which national interests are at stake and national populations are involved. The responsibilities of citizens do not cease during times of war. If anything, they become greater.

Warfare has rarely been confined to combatants. Civilians have usually been among the casualties or suffered in other ways: as displaced persons or refugees, for example. Siege warfare is an ancient practice of applying military pressure directly on non-combatants. Economic sanctions and blockades enforced by military power are legitimate and lawful means of putting pressure on an aggressor state at the present time: as indicated, a naval blockade was deployed against Iraq during the Gulf War. Modern warfare (air war especially) has a double social effect: it inflicts great indiscriminate suffering and damage on civilians and

[14] There is controversy surrounding the issue of whether the violation of human rights within the domestic jurisdictions of sovereign states constitutes an added justification of the contemporary *jus ad bellum*. See Ch. 10.

[15] Bull, 'Recapturing the Just War', 595.

their necessities of life. Yet the waging of modern war is ultimately made possible only by a social base which sustains the warring nations and supplies the soldiers with materiel and weapons of war. Modern wars between nation-states frequently are 'total wars'. Communications, roads, railways, bridges, harbours, airports, electric generation and transmission, petroleum and chemical industries, and other infrastructures of nation-states are essential for waging modern war. They are therefore necessary targets of war. Military success might necessitate the crippling or even the destruction of such facilities, which means that civilians will be at risk. Although that has long been a temptation and a feature of war, it became a major normative conundrum of warfare, especially aerial bombardment, in the twentieth century.

Officials at the Pentagon claimed that in the first twelve hours of the air war more bombs were dropped on Iraq and Kuwait than during one of the most intensive campaigns in Vietnam which lasted seventeen days. The exact quantity of explosives dropped by coalition forces during the six-week battle is a subject of debate. Some estimates put the figure as high as 90,000 tons, although other estimates are far lower. Regardless of the discrepancies, one thing seems clear: the intensity of bombing during Operation Desert Storm was very great indeed. Even though many bombs were targeted against Iraqi troop concentrations dug into the desert sands of Kuwait and southern Iraq, which were well away from civilian population centres, many other bombs were directed at military targets in Baghdad, Basra, and other Iraqi cities and towns.

The coalition evidently engaged exclusively in 'precision' bombing whenever they attacked targets of military value located in or nearby urban areas. Hence, they entirely avoided 'area' bombing which indiscriminately aims at breaking the will of civilian populations—such as the Allied bombing of German cities during the Second World War. This policy of discriminating urban bombardment sets the air campaign apart from most other air campaigns of the twentieth century. Yet, in so far as the bombing adversely affected the lives of civilians and in so far as this effect was anticipated in advance and was accepted by coalition military planners, the air campaign was consistent with air campaigns of other major wars.[16]

Various reports made at the time or shortly afterwards indicate that destruction, both intentional and accidental, was extensive. A UN report quotes an Iraqi estimate of 9,000 homes destroyed, leaving some 72,000 people homeless.[17] Yet reports also indicate that—compared to the intensity of the bombing—civilian casualties were surprisingly low. Foreign journalists who remained in Iraq believed that civilian casualties during the war were 'under 10,000 dead'.[18] Greenpeace estimated that between 5,000 and 15,000 Iraqi civilians died during

---

[16] See the incisive account of aerial bombardment in Geoffrey Best, *Humanity in Warfare* (London: Methuen, 1983), 262–85.

[17] Quoted by *The New York Times* (24 Mar. 1991).

[18] J. Ridgeway (ed.), *The March to War* (New York: Four Walls, Eight Windows, 1991), 229.

the war.[19] John Simpson, a journalist who covered the war for BBC television, writes that the Iraqis 'suggested a figure of 2,000' civilian deaths and he comments: 'This was a new kind of war. Perhaps for the first time since 1918, a major conflict was fought by concentrating on the destruction of the opposing army, not on civilian morale.'[20] This is somewhat misleading because cities were heavily attacked and civilians suffered both physically and emotionally. But the coalition aim was not to break the will of the civilian population, as British night bombing of Germany tried to do during the Second World War.[21] The purported aim was exclusively to destroy Iraq's war-related facilities. This evidently was (more or less) achieved at a cost in civilian casualties that was probably far lower, at least proportionately if not absolutely, than any previous major bombing campaign. This was indeed a new kind of aerial warfare and that should be kept in mind in any normative appraisal of the campaign.

Aerial warfare and particularly air bombardment, because it is so crucial to instrumental success and so difficult to use with moral discrimination, has eluded international legal regulation to date: the 1923 Hague Draft Rules concerning this branch of warfare were never adopted in legally binding form.[22] Yet no other form of modern warfare more profoundly affects the lives of civilian populations: as indicated, it is in many respects the modern equivalent of siege warfare. However, even if no specific legal rules of aerial warfare have been adopted to date, other parts of international humanitarian law—such as Geneva Convention IV Relative to the Protection of Civilian Persons in Time of War (1949) and Geneva Protocol I Additional to the Geneva Conventions Relating to the Protection of Victims of International Armed Conflicts (1977)[23]—still proclaim the fundamental distinction between combatants and non-combatants upon which, as Geoffrey Best puts it, 'the whole idea of a law of war absolutely depends'.[24] Common morality judges aerial bombardment in exactly these terms. Such judgements were frequently made during the coalition bombing campaign in January–February 1991.

Operation Desert Storm evidently was a war in which civilians could be distinguished and separated from air attack to a greater extent than was possible in the Vietnam War, the Korean War, and the Second World War, all of which involved indiscriminate aerial bombardment. Coalition pilots were expected to take risks to avoid civilian casualties: they were under orders not to attack unassigned targets, not to drop their bombs if they could not hit their targets, and to return with their ordinance in such circumstances. If that was indeed the bombing policy, and if it was carried out to the best of those pilots' abilities

---

[19] See *The New York Times* (24 Mar. 1991).

[20] John Simpson, *From the House of War* (London: Arrow Books, 1991), xv.

[21] See Best, *Humanity in Warfare*, 278.

[22] A. Roberts and R. Guelff (eds.), *Documents on the Laws of War*, 2nd edn. (Oxford: Clarendon Press, 1989), 122–3.

[23] Both documents are reprinted ibid. 271–338, 387–446.

[24] Best, *Humanity in Warfare*, 265.

subject to the technical limits of their equipment, it conforms tolerably well with normative standards in waging modern war. 'Smart' bombs and missiles were employed in significant numbers for the first time during the Gulf War. There is reason to believe that this technology killed or injured fewer people and thus saved more lives than would have been spared with older bombing methods.

A recurring normative argument against air bombardment is the contention that bombing technologies are too devastating and too blunt to be able to separate combatants from non-combatants and therefore to make possible right conduct in warfare in accordance with traditional standards. It must therefore be banned. Yet the instrumental advantage of air power is far too great for this to be a realistic possibility. So we continue to be saddled with air warfare, including the bombing of cities. If in the future aerial bombardment is brought more definitely within the compass of *jus in bello* it will probably be owing primarily to developments in technology, particularly precision-guided bombs and missiles. It is fairly obvious that we are dealing here with a knotted moral issue that is difficult to untie.

General Norman Schwarzkopf, the American commander of Operation Desert Storm, writes that a strategic aim of the coalition was to 'cripple Iraq's military system while leaving its agriculture and commerce intact and its civilian population largely unharmed'.[25] The repeatedly declared bombing policy was to minimize civilian casualties and also to avoid hitting cultural targets, such as Muslim holy sites and historic monuments. In other words, the declared intention was to hit military targets only and to keep to a bare minimum any 'collateral damage'—that is, accidental destruction especially to civilian residential areas. That declared strategy generally conforms to *jus in bello* as we understand that normative standard of conduct nowadays. To the extent that it was followed it would go a long way to justifying the coalition air campaign.

Collateral damage is unintentional damage to non-military targets caused by military action, typically by aerial bombardment of cities and towns. The operative normative idea is 'unintentional': if the damage done to non-military targets were intentional, it would not be collateral damage. Hence, the Iraqi targeting and firing of Scud Missiles at Saudi Arabian and Israeli cities during the Gulf War could not be construed as collateral damage. These are indiscriminate weapons which lack the precision guidance systems to accurately hit small distant targets. The intention of employing such weapons in that way could only be to terrorize civilian populations or gain prestige in certain quarters or widen the conflict, for example, by drawing in Israel. If these were the Iraqi intentions in firing the Scuds they are entirely instrumental and, as such, are in violation of the laws of war.

Many thousands of coalition bombing sorties were flown during the Gulf War, and many of them were directed at targets nearby or inside populated areas. It

---

[25] N. Schwarzkopf, *It doesn't Take a Hero* (New York: Bantam, 1992), 421.

is likely that substantial collateral damage resulted, even if highly trained pilots and missile controllers employing the latest technology operated with the best of intentions to limit it. Pentagon officials told congressional leaders that although 80 per cent of coalition missions on the first day of the air war managed to reach their target areas and drop their bombs, only 50 per cent hit the targets and many repeat bombing raids had to be carried out.[26] One must conclude from this that the other 50 per cent either landed harmlessly or hit civilian areas adjacent to the planned targets. Referring to the initial air attacks, General Schwarzkopf writes that 'flight crew's accuracy had been initially less than predicted—F-117s in the first wave had dropped just fifty-five percent of their bombs on target, and F-111s about seventy percent . . . [although] their accuracy had been steadily improving throughout the day'.[27] Later US Air Force figures indicated, according to *The New York Times*, that 70 per cent of bombs missed their targets, although the figure presumably refers to old-fashioned bombs targeted mainly if not entirely at Iraqi troop concentrations. But even precision-guided bombs evidently went astray 10 per cent of the time.[28]

The following headline appeared in a leading American newspaper: 'Carnage in Baghdad Erases Image of an Antiseptic War'. It went on to describe 'the smoking ruins' of a Baghdad building 'where allied bombing apparently killed hundreds of civilians'.[29] British and American television showed graphic scenes of the destruction, with foreign correspondents saying that many civilians had been killed and that none of what they saw had been staged for them by the Iraqi authorities. The shelter, in the middle-class Amiriyah district of Baghdad, contained about 400 people, according to one of the survivors quoted by Middle East Watch, an American human rights organization.[30] Two laser-guided bunker penetration bombs hit the shelter, according to US military authorities: the second exploded inside, burning people to death, most of them beyond recognition. Iraqi authorities initially said hundreds of civilians died in the bombing. The official Iraqi death toll was later put at 310, of whom 130 were children, according to Middle East Watch.[31]

Was this building a command and control centre as coalition spokesmen argued or was it a civilian bomb shelter as the Iraqis claimed? Were coalition commanders genuinely unaware that civilians were present? Did Saddam Hussein cunningly place the shelter near one of his command and control facilities, thereby using civilians as military shields? Was this an instance of collateral damage in which the bombs hit the wrong target by mistake? Or was the bunker incorrectly identified as a military target? Was it a negligent military action? Or was it a deliberate act of putting civilians at risk or perhaps even targeting them?

---

[26] Reported in *The Sunday Times* (20 Jan. 1991).
[27] Schwarzkopf, *It doesn't Take a Hero*, 415.   [28] *The New York Times* (24 Mar. 1991).
[29] *The New York Times* (14 Feb. 1991).
[30] As reported in *The Globe and Mail* (14 Mar. 1991).   [31] Ibid.

I was not able to answer these questions. I shall leave them to historians to answer when the facts become clearer. But they are the sort of questions that one would have to ask if one hoped to sort out the responsibility of the people involved on both sides. They thus provide an occasion for reflection on responsibility in warfare. If the bombing of the Baghdad shelter was truly a case of collateral damage then it cannot be condemned by existing standards of military conduct. If it was a deliberate action, against what was sincerely believed to be a military target, which went very wrong, it cannot be condemned for such regrettable incidents are to be expected in war. If the coalition attack was a case of mistaken identity—in which a military target was incorrectly identified and bombed—then admitting to the mistake would seem to be the compassionate thing to do. Such an admission would be an acknowledgement of tragic accidents in war: a sphere which is beyond human responsibility but within human sympathy. But if coalition planners knew that it was an air-raid shelter and attacked anyway, the attack must be condemned in the strongest terms. Even if the coalition merely suspected this might be the case but made no attempt to check it out—within their ability to do so—before going ahead, they would still be guilty of something akin to criminal negligence. If Saddam Hussein intentionally placed the shelter beside a military facility for protection then his action and not the coalition's would be a clear violation of the laws of war.

These are only some of the normative questions which give an indication of the ethics involved in such an event. They can easily enough be raised in theory but they are exceedingly difficult to deal with in operational reality—and it is with that reality that scholars who seek empirical knowledge of the ethics of warfare must be concerned. Yet that does not mean that rules of conduct in aerial warfare are impossible or unreasonable; it only means that they are difficult to operate with even in the best of circumstances. Many practical difficulties, uncertainties, and indeed hazards confront air commanders, air controllers, and airmen who are required to operate with a bombing policy which seeks to limit collateral damage. Some operational problems are conceptual and informational. What, for example, is a 'military target'? How can anyone be confident that the target selected is a military target and not something else? The honest answer is that one probably can never be entirely sure; but this does not release anybody from the duty of being as sure as he or she can be in the circumstances.

Some operational problems are technical. If we deem a technology legitimate in waging war then we must apply standards of conduct appropriate to it. Thus, if we accept that air bombardment is a justified method of warfare we cannot condemn the airmen for not achieving levels of precision that are beyond the capability of their bombsights and bombs. But we can still ask whether technology adequate to hit the designated military target and curtail collateral damage is available and is being used. And we can ask whether technology adequate to certify that a designated military target is in fact a military target is also available and used. Reflecting on a related issue after the Gulf War General

Schwarzkopf wrote: 'our problem was that our technological ability to engage targets exceeded our ability to identify targets clearly'.[32] He was referring to tragic incidents of 'friendly fire' (attacks carried out by mistake against one's own forces) but his observation also applies to precision bombing against military targets in populated areas.

The policy of limiting collateral damage—no matter how sincere the combatant's commitment to it, or how precise the available bombing technology—will always come into contact and perhaps conflict with the primary responsibility of all humane commanders: protecting their own people. We arrive at one of the troubling moral choices that warfare forever presents to those involved. The first moral responsibility of any commander who has committed his troops to battle is their survival. Thus, where limiting collateral damage is an operational policy, air commanders have a dual responsibility which may conflict at certain points: minimizing the military risks their airmen must take while at the same time minimizing civilian casualties and destruction. The airmen themselves confront the daunting task of carrying out their mission and endeavouring to hit their assigned target, while coping with the extreme demands of high-speed flight and the danger and terror of enemy fire. The latter point is a reminder that, unless total air superiority has been achieved and anti-aircraft fire silenced, air bombardment is usually carried out in difficult conditions of warfare in which the lives of air crews are at risk and perhaps in extreme peril. Those circumstances must be taken into account in any judgements we make about the conduct of the people involved.

Citizens as Combatants Once Removed

The morality of limiting collateral damage is prima-facie clear if we assume that a basic normative distinction must be drawn between combatants and non-combatants. In which case civilians must not be attacked. But that raises a deeply troubling question that is fundamental to a normative understanding of modern warfare: can citizens of modern nation-states which are at war reasonably expect to be protected from the hostilities as far as that is possible? Can they be given immunity? Are civilians entirely free from responsibility in wars between modern nation-states?

The just-war tradition which derives from natural law postulates categorical protection for non-combatants. Here we come into contact with not only an awkwardness but a real difficulty with the just-war tradition: it does not come to grips with the ethics of citizenship; it is cosmopolitan in its ethical outlook. The notion that citizens have responsibilities during both peace and war is based

---

[32] Schwarzkopf, *It doesn't Take a Hero*, 500.

on communitarian reasoning: the notion of a *societas* of nation-states; the pluralist ethics of war. When nation-states are at war, their citizens are also at war, for they are part and parcel of what modern nation-statehood involves. They are involved in the war but they are not involved as combatants: their responsibility is accordingly different than that of combatants.

I am inclined to think that citizens must bear some responsibility during wartime. They cannot be beneficiaries of their state's security without contributing in some way to its collective defence. This has long been recognized by both the theory and the practice of political obligation. Nor, as citizens, can they entirely opt out of any responsibility for their government's policies or actions, even though they obviously cannot be held as responsible as public officials who make the decisions and must bear immediate responsibility for them. In short, citizens are morally and legally bound to their nation's foreign policy—and that remains so whether we justify the state and the citizen's place in it in terms of nationalist, conservative, liberal democratic, social democratic, communist, or any other notion of collective responsibility. George Walden, a former British diplomat and Member of Parliament, addresses a version of this question: do citizens share responsibility for foreign policy?

Carlyle's judgment that the shoeblack and the sovereign were equally to blame for the French Revolution may seem hard on those who had no vote at the time. But in the case of the conduct of the foreign policy of a modern democratic state, the message is surely irrefutable: Namely that whether they like it or not, whole peoples are directly or indirectly responsible, together with their representatives, for misdemeanors against the legitimate interests of other peoples. If the people cannot be held to blame, who can?[33]

But Carlyle, a famous nineteenth-century British historian of war and revolution, has a point: citizen responsibility is not confined to democracy. Rulers and subjects in non-democratic states are also bound in a relation of political obligation which is a larger and deeper idea than that of democracy. Michael Howard has pointed out that from the time of John Seldon's seventeenth-century legal commentaries, 'British jurists argued that the economic activities of civilians, in so far as they made possible the belligerent acts of governments, were a perfectly legitimate target for military activity.'[34] If that can be said of civilians 300 years ago when many state activities were carried on far over the heads of most ordinary people, then it can be said far more readily of citizens of modern socially mobilized nation-states, whether they are democracies or not. Twentieth-century warfare greatly reduced the distance between the state and the citizen and launched a movement toward the creation of huge mechanized citizen armies which, in turn, were dependent upon the resources and support

---

[33] *Ethics and Foreign Policy* (London: Weidenfeld & Nicolson, 1988), 85. Also see P. French, 'Morally Blaming Whole Populations', *Philosophy, Morality and International Affairs* (Oxford: OUP, 1974).

[34] M. Howard, '*Temperamenta Belli*: Can War be Controlled?', in J. B. Elshtain (ed.), *Just War Theory* (Oxford: Blackwell, 1992), 30.

of an even larger army of citizens. This reality of modern war was captured in a paper presented by the British Naval Staff to the Committee of Imperial Defense in 1921:

Nothing can be clearer than the fact that modern war resolves itself into an attempt to throttle the national life. Waged by the whole power of the nation, its ultimate object is to bring pressure on the mass of the enemy people, distressing them by every possible means, so as to compel the enemy's government to submit to terms.[35]

The responsibility of the citizenry may be less in countries like Iraq where citizens do not have the vote and are in other ways denied representation and participation in their government. However this cannot eliminate the remaining fact that Iraq is where they make their homes and subject themselves to the state. During the Gulf War they were members of a state at war: a state which in its war effort depended on them, for example through industrial and agricultural work, taxation, and conscription. If citizens or subjects of authoritarian states are contributing to the war effort they are combatants once removed.

On this reasoning precision bombing which aims at reducing the war-making capacity of a nation-state by attacking, for example, its weapons factories and other war-related facilities arguably would be a legitimate attack, even if the managers and workers were on the site when the attack occurred. One can reasonably assume that they must have taken defensive measures for such contingencies. As far as I am aware, such air attacks were carried out by the coalition air forces during Operation Desert Storm. There is often uncertainty about whether such actions can be justified. I think they can be, on the above-noted grounds that citizens have residual responsibilities for the foreign policies and military actions of their governments.

The issue gets more clouded if we extend the target to include, say, power grids which are essential to war-making but are also essential to civilized existence. Michael Walzer has argued, in this connection, that such attacks (which were carried out against Iraq during the Gulf War) cannot be justified: 'power and water, water most clearly, are very much like food: they are necessary to the survival and everyday activity of soldiers, but they are equally necessary to everyone else. An attack here is an attack on civilian society.'[36] I think he is half-right: water unambiguously is a human necessity and to destroy water purification or distribution facilities will very soon result in illness and even death on a large scale, especially in an arid country like Iraq. I am not convinced, however, that the same can be said of electricity: human beings survived for a very long time before the age of electrical power and presumably they could do so again if they had to. Attacking the electrical grid is far more akin to attacking communications facilities, oil storage facilities, and oil pipelines, which are fundamental economic means upon which modern war-making depends. Yet wherever

---

[35] Quoted ibid. 31.

[36] Michael Walzer, *Just and Unjust Wars*, 2nd edn. (New York: Basic Books, 1992), xx.

we draw the line there is no denying that this is a difficult and deeply troubling area of military ethics and I have the greatest sympathy for anyone who must decide such questions during the actual conduct of military operations.

I am aware that this line of argument will be hard for many to accept. Yet if one believes that warfare between nation-states can be justified in appropriate circumstances—such as wars of self-defence or wars against aggressors—some such conclusion cannot be avoided if one also recognizes that civilian populations do not merely reside in sovereign states but are members of them and bear some responsibility for their common affairs. This is an inevitable consequence, it seems to me, of living in a world of independent states in which each state is seen not merely as a utilitarian arrangement but also as a political community in its own right. In other words, the population of any state are not only resident human beings; they are also citizens or subjects of a state. During times of war as human beings they are protected by the humanitarian laws of war pertaining to non-combatants. But as citizens or subjects of a state they have certain war-related responsibilities. The citizenry of modern nation-states at war thus seem to constitute an uneasy intermediate normative category between strict combatants, who can be a legitimate target of attack and are subjects of the laws of war which apply to combat, and strict non-combatants, who cannot be a legitimate target and are subjects of the laws of war which apply to non-combatants. Perhaps that ambiguous position can be captured by the expression: combatants once removed.

On this normative reasoning, citizens bear some of the burden of responsibility for war, although obviously little or no answerability as compared to government officials who must be held directly and immediately accountable for political decisions, including the decision to go to war and decisions relating to the conduct of warfare. Thus, if at the end of a war an aggressor nation-state is defeated and occupied, only its most responsible officials are legitimate subjects of prosecution and punishment. The general citizenry can perhaps legitimately be punished in less severe ways, for example by reparations if they have not already been punished enough by the war. Something like this normative reasoning seems implicit in the way war between modern nation-states is justified in practice.

Restraint in Battle

We now turn to the second important issue of *jus in bello* that was raised by the Gulf War: moral restraint in armed combat. The ethics and laws of war have always maintained that, although killing is justified in waging war as a means to victory, it is not an end in itself. Human lives are precious and they cannot be gratuitously or wantonly or casually destroyed during war or at any other time.

Although there is a significant moral distinction between soldiers and civilians, soldiers are still human beings. That morally limits what can be tolerated during battle.

The conduct of warfare is aimed at winning battles or not losing them, at an acceptable sacrifice in people and treasure. For a commander that means, among other things, destroying the will and capacity of the enemy to carry on with the war, which, in turn, means inflicting the maximum battle casualties on enemy forces and putting enemy assets out of the war while minimizing losses to his or her own forces. Causing battle casualties, which is to say deliberate killing and maiming of combatants, is thus part and parcel of the conduct of warfare. Within certain limits it is normatively acceptable. That makes the legal and moral environment of war different, indeed very different, from that of peace. Not only is it legitimate and legal, it is rewarded and honoured. Military glory and many specific honours bestowed upon commanders and ordinary soldiers in wartime are determined by success on the battlefield. To be sure, select honours may pay homage to exceptional acts of courage and personal sacrifice: war is an occasion for heroes. But heroism is not necessary for success at war, as the title of General Schwarzkopf's autobiography—*It doesn't Take a Hero*—clearly suggests. What is necessary, other things being equal, is an effective military force consisting of well-led, well-trained, and well-equipped soldiers who disclose by their conduct the ordinary military virtues, particularly discipline.

Yet military success can never be an absolute doctrine if war is also to be conducted with respect for humanitarian principles. Success at any price in which the ends justify the means is intolerable to the laws of war. Scorched-earth policies are generally regarded as reprehensible military conduct. There are limits on what is acceptable conduct: states at war and their armed forces do not have an unlimited choice of methods and means of warfare; those which cause unnecessary losses or excessive suffering are prohibited by the laws of war. Thus, for a humanitarian commander, waging war involves deliberately inflicting casualties and other losses on the enemy while at the same time trying to protect his own forces and observe the laws of war which, as indicated, forbid actions which cause losses or suffering beyond what would be required to win or avoid defeat on the battlefield. 'Necessity' largely depends on circumstance: having one's back against the wall and contemplating the possibility of conquest by a ruthless enemy who threatens to enslave one's fellow citizens is categorically different from enjoying military superiority and having great liberty in choosing the means and methods of winning. Britain's position in the Second World War was closer to the former pole, whereas the coalition position in the Gulf War was closer to the latter pole. That is an important normative consideration in any judgement about the military conduct of coalition forces in the Gulf War.

Probably 'wanton' killing and 'gratuitous' destruction better convey the appropriate normative limits in the conduct of warfare. Thus, although killing and wounding and destroying is clearly lawful in war, doing this to no legitimate military purpose or doing it for its own sake is a serious breach of the ethics and laws of war. We arrive at a major normative boundary which separates the civilized conduct of warfare from the barbarous waging of war.

The strategy of coalition commanders during the Gulf War clearly was to protect their own forces while at the same time inflicting disabling losses on the Iraqi side. The latter was indeed the means by which the former was pursued. Protecting their own troops was uppermost in the minds of American officials. President George Bush, Defense Secretary Richard Cheney, and American commanders repeatedly declared that their first priority was limiting allied battle casualties. British officials and commanders expressed the same concern. Worry about coalition casualties recurs over and over again in the autobiographical accounts of General Norman Schwarzkopf and the British commander, General Sir Peter de la Billière. Asked at the start of the air campaign how long Operation Desert Storm might take, General Schwarzkopf said: 'We're going to do it as rapidly as we possibly can. But we're also going to do it in such a way that we try and minimize [our] casualties. We don't want to have to pay a terrible price just to get it over with quickly.'[37]

Thus, at the start of Operation Desert Storm in mid-January 1991, coalition commanders emphasized that the air campaign could last well into February and even longer and would not give way to a land battle until all of Iraq's offensive capability had been destroyed or degraded very significantly.[38] In practice this was a strategic and tactical consideration consistent with the instrumental art of war. But it also meant reducing Iraqi morale and capability to a level where coalition commanders could be confident of military success without asking for needless sacrifice from their troops and thus without risking the loss of any more of their lives than the absolute minimal required for winning. Thus the air-bombing campaign methodically worked its way through a long list of preselected Iraqi targets, day after day, consistent with this aim. Air force commanders checked reconnaissance assessments of damage to a target and ordered repeated attacks until they were fully satisfied it had been rendered ineffective. All of this could be justified in terms of minimizing casualties to their own soldiers.

Undoubtedly the worry about coalition casualties was a political concern. It reflected full awareness of the sensitivity and fickleness of public opinion, particularly in the USA. With the Vietnam experience uppermost in their minds American politicians and commanders obviously feared that the US public would turn against the war if large numbers of dead soldiers began arriving home in 'body bags'. The desire to limit casualties to their own troops also probably disclosed the great military advantage—in weapons technology and airpower—enjoyed by the coalition, who were not in anything even remotely resembling a desperate fight for survival and who therefore enjoyed unusual

---

[37] Quoted in *The Financial Times* (19/20 Jan. 1991).
[38] Quoted in *The Sunday Times* (20 Jan. 1991).

freedom to maximize the protection of their own forces without giving up any military advantage to their Iraqi adversary. But it also disclosed a moral concern: not to waste the lives of any coalition soldiers. This strongly felt moral duty comes through clearly in the autobiographical accounts of General Schwarzkopf and General de la Billière.

Minimizing coalition battle casualties led to very heavy emphasis on the 'preparation' of the battlefield by massive and continuous coalition bombing strikes against Iraqi troops which aimed at gradually wearing down their will and capacity to fight. B-52 strategic bombers carried out attrition bombing against conscript troops dug in along the Kuwait–Saudi border and against élite Republican Guard armoured units positioned in southern Iraq. The attrition bombing evidently was deliberately timed to disrupt the sleep and in other ways undermine the morale of Iraqi troops who were not killed or maimed. The bombing campaign also involved a major component of psychological warfare, including broadcasts and leaflet-dropping, to urge desertion.[39] According to General de la Billière, it 'proved very effective'.[40]

Reporters at coalition air bases said that Iraq's élite Republican Guards deployed near Basra, in southern Iraq, were bombarded with cluster bombs.[41] American officials also reportedly said they were 'experimenting on the enemy' with massive 15,000 lb conventional high explosive bombs known as Daisy Cutters. These weapons evidently were used to demolish physical obstacles and clear paths through an estimated 500,000 landmines laid by the Iraqis along the Kuwait–Saudi border. They were also reportedly used on groups of Iraqi vehicles. Some reports intimated that 'fuel air weapons', which cause enormous destruction far in excess of conventional high explosives of the same tonnage, were employed. Even personnel on the fringes of such explosions would suffer severe internal injuries owing to their high blast power.[42]

The laws of war require, as indicated, that the weapons employed are of a nature not to cause unnecessary or excessive human suffering. Thus parties to a conflict and members of their armed forces do not have 'an unlimited choice of methods and means of warfare'.[43] If the foregoing reports are true, they raise some troubling questions about coalition conduct. Using the above weapons exclusively with the intention of demolishing physical obstacles is not a moral offence if one can be confident that non-combatant casualties are not likely to result. It is a less clear-cut question and something of a grey area if combatant casualties are a side-effect and thus a moral risk. The question might be decided by determining whether there is concern about this or indifference on the part of the attackers. But if such devastating weapons are intentionally targeted at combatants the line between civilized and barbaric warfare would be crossed:

---

[39] *The Globe and Mail* (9 Feb. 1991).
[40] P. de la Billière, *Storm Command* (London: HarperCollins, 1992), 218.
[41] *The Financial Times* (19/20 Jan. 1991).   [42] *The Financial Times* (16/17 Feb. 1991).
[43] Roberts and Guelff, *Documents on the Laws of War*, 470.

such action would trespass on the fundamental norm of restraint of war. This is the same moral failure as would occur if other grossly non-discriminatory weapons were used on the battlefield, such as chemical weapons or tactical nuclear weapons. If the foregoing weapons were in fact used in that intentional way, it is a black mark on the coalition record.

Perhaps the most horrendous image of the Gulf War was the cremated debris of a destroyed Iraqi column chaotically scattered for several miles along both sides of a highway running north from Kuwait City to Basra in southern Iraq. Although television showed the devastation only on this road, Iraqis columns retreating along other roads were also attacked by coalition forces. The Iraqis were hit from the air by aircraft and helicopter gunships while ground forces blocked off escape routes. The 'highway of death' became the most vivid scene of military devastation in the six-week air and land war, bringing home to millions of television viewers around the world the ferocity of high-tech warfare. The image stuck even though it later turned out to be something of a misnomer. Many more Iraqis evidently escaped into the desert or were taken prisoner than were killed. Western reporters who visited the scene at Matla Ridge shortly afterwards estimated that a total of 200 to 300 Iraqis had been killed. John Simpson later thought 'there were probably no more than 400 deaths there—a massacre, certainly, but not the bloodbath on the scale many people in the West assumed'.[44]

When it became evident about twenty-four hours after the start of the ground war, which was launched on 24 February 1991, that the Iraqi forces were disintegrating, Baghdad radio made the following announcement: 'orders have been issued to our armed forces to withdraw in an organized manner to the positions they held prior to 1 August . . . as practical compliance with resolution 660'.[45] Presumably this instruction was made in a desperate attempt to save as much of the Iraqi army in Kuwait as possible, in the undoubtedly correct anticipation that otherwise it would be destroyed. However, this command was not accompanied by any official Iraqi statement of surrender or any other authoritative indication that Iraq would meet all UN demands and conditions. The orders were evidently obeyed by all Iraqi personnel in a position to do so and resulted in a headlong stampede north to safety. US military authorities said their main purpose in attacking the columns was to protect allied forces on a dangerous battlefield by cutting off potential reinforcements for Iraqi Republican Guard divisions north and west of Kuwait. They conceded in retrospect that the Iraqis crowded on the highway north of Kuwait City probably wanted to go home and were giving up the fight, but there was no way for coalition forces to know this with certainty in the heat of battle.[46]

The highway episodes provoked commentary on tactical rules of engagement by coalition spokesmen as to whether the Iraqi columns were a withdrawal, a

[44] Simpson, *From the House of War*, 350.
[45] As quoted in the *Guardian Weekly* (17 Mar. 1991).   [46] Ibid.

retreat, or a surrender. US military officials emphasized that if Iraqi forces really were surrendering and leaving Kuwait on that basis they had to voluntarily abandon their weapons and armour to avoid allied firepower. In other words, any responsible military commander knows that to modify his plans on the basis of ambiguous intentions on the part of the enemy is to place his or her own troops at risk. Hence, no commander could accept anything less than a completely unambiguous signal that the enemy is in fact surrendering and not engaging in a tactical deception or playing some kind of quasi-political game. Since neither Baghdad nor the Iraqi field commanders issued any such sign, their movement to the rear still fell within the normative sphere of continuing armed combat. And, according to the laws of war, retreating armies are fair game precisely because they may later regroup and attack. Retreat is thus a continuation and not a suspension of armed hostilities.

It is hardly surprising, therefore, that the Iraqi move was characterized by coalition field commanders as a tactical manœuvre to regroup and to fight from a better position at a more favourable time. It would have been a failure of duty if coalition commanders had allowed the Iraqis to escape. This reasoning was clearly in the minds of coalition commanders. In an interview at the time US Brigadier General Richard Neal said:

By definition, a withdrawal is when you pull your forces back, not under pressure by the attacking forces. Retreat is when you're required to pull your forces back . . . by the action of the attacking forces. The Iraqi army is in full retreat . . . Until we're notified by higher authorities, we're going to continue to execute our mission as it has been handed to us by the initiators of the plan.[47]

What normative conclusions about modern armed combat can we derive from the Matla Ridge episode? In considering this question we must keep in mind that warfare rarely accommodates categorical evaluations. We should also remember that the second responsibility of military commanders, whatever side they are on, is the safety and welfare of their own troops. (Their first responsibility is to achieve a military victory.) There are rules of warfare, however, and also a sense of proportion which involve obligations toward enemy troops as well as non-combatants. The highway episodes specifically invoke that part of *jus in bello* which concerns the welfare of enemy combatants and, in particular, the humanitarian restraint that must be exercised during combat. One fundamental rule is that which forbids killing or wounding an enemy 'who surrenders or who is *hors de combat*'.[48] Another rule is that, if the pace and fog of battle allows, the enemy must be given quarter—that is, given the opportunity to surrender. The fact that military advantage was on the coalition side has no bearing at all;

[47] As quoted ibid.
[48] See '1978 Red Cross Fundamental Rules of International Humanitarian Law Applicable in Armed Conflicts', reprinted in Roberts and Guelff, *Documents on the Laws of War*, 470. This document is not strictly part of the laws of war but it does embody in abridged form fundamental principles of international humanitarian law concerning warfare.

warfare is not an activity in which adversaries are given a sporting chance to win—although enemy troops should be given quarter when it becomes evident that they are clearly beaten. Continuing to press the attack in such circumstances would amount to wanton killing and maiming in violation of the laws of war.

But giving quarter is perhaps easier said than done, largely because of the fog of war and the rapid pace of events in high-tech combat such as occurred in the brief land phase of the Gulf War which lasted for less than 100 hours (from 24 to 28 February 1991). The personal accounts of the American commander and his British counterpart convey something of the blitzkrieg character of the battle.[49] Not only does the chaos and confusion of combat limit and distort the information available to commanders and soldiers in the field, but it severely compresses the available time to make fully considered moral choices. In short, we should empathize with soldiers in the heat of battle and take fully on board their combat circumstances and turbulent mental states—their difficulty in grasping the pace of events, their excitement, their fear, their fatigue, and their instinctive reactions. Any normative analysis which ignores such circumstances will be not only unrealistic but also unjust to the people involved.

Any judgement concerning the conduct of warfare in a particular engagement is of course conditional on the evidence. What the commanders knew or believed about the military condition and intentions of the enemy is a particularly important consideration. These beliefs would enter into their tactical decisions and actions and this would affect our evaluation of them. In the case of Matla Ridge we would need to know what the time frame of the engagement was (seconds? minutes? hours? days?), what the attacking commanders honestly believed about the future military intentions of the enemy commander, and what they knew about the potential and existing combat readiness and military capabilities of the defending troops. If the attacking commanders knew at some point during the attack that the enemy was clearly defeated, did they give the enemy a chance to surrender? Did they have sufficient time to do so or was the engagement over before defeat was apparent? If it were possible, would a break in the engagement provide such an opportunity for the enemy or would it merely defeat the coalition's element of surprise and thus endanger coalition troops? Did they believe that a break in the engagement would provide an opportunity for the enemy to regroup and thereby defeat the coalition's military advantage and perhaps threaten the lives of coalition troops? Did the attacking commanders engage in combat when the enemy was already down or did they exploit an opportunity to destroy the enemy with the least casualties to their own forces? The first action is contemptible but the second is a fundamental rule of military tactics.

Warfare always involves at least two responsible parties. Thus we also need to know what the beliefs and decisions of the defending commanders were.

---

[49] Schwarzkopf, *It doesn't Take A Hero*, ch. 23, and Billière, *Storm Command*, ch. 12.

What orders did they give to their troops in Kuwait: if they ordered them to withdraw or retreat (rather than surrender) they surely risked leaving them fatally exposed to attack by what they must have known was deadly air power. Perhaps they were under orders from Saddam Hussein, as seems very likely, and would suffer severe punishment (imprisonment or even execution, possibly to their family members as well as themselves) if they failed to carry them out. In other words, the first responsibility for the lives and welfare of the Iraqi troops in the highway columns rested with the Iraqi commanders and probably with Saddam Hussein if, as is likely, the order to withdraw originated with him. Perhaps military discipline had broken down and nobody was really in control of the columns: it is possible that it was every soldier for himself. Perhaps the fleeing Iraqis failed to realize that by trying to get back to Iraq in this undisciplined way they were placing themselves in enormous danger. In coming to any balanced normative judgement about the Matla Ridge episode these are questions that must be answered.

In armed combat it is not the duty of a commander to give the enemy a sporting chance because this would place his own forces at risk. A commander does have a responsibility whenever possible to give his own troops such a chance. However, the fact that the columns were attacked over and over again by wave upon wave of coalition aircraft after those columns had evidently been disabled and no longer posed any present or future military threat suggests that the engagement might very well have been pressed beyond the humanitarian point. There is reason to doubt that the fog of war was an extenuating circumstance, at least after the early part of the engagement—reference to a 'turkey shoot' or a 'duck shoot' by the coalition pilots involved suggests a contrary condition of calm, cool, and deliberate military action.

On the other hand, the reportedly small number of dead Iraqi soldiers found in the wreckage strongly suggests that the vehicles had probably been abandoned after the first attacks as the soldiers scattered into the desert. General Schwarzkopf in his biography says: 'Though many Iraqis in the convoy had died, most had jumped out of their vehicles and run away.'[50] It would be important to know if coalition commanders and pilots realized after the first wave of attacks that the targets consisted of abandoned hardware, which would eliminate any moral censure of the repeat strikes. General Schwarzkopf indicates they did know that: 'We bombed the hell out of every convoy we could find—but between air strikes we flew over the battlefield with Black Hawk helicopters equipped with loudspeakers . . . telling the Iraqis in Arabic, "Get out of your vehicles, leave them behind, and you will not die. We will let you go home." '[51] If this was indeed the case—and whether or not it truly was the case is an important question for historical research—it discloses humanitarian respect for the enemy broadly consistent with *jus in bello*. Thus, although I do not know for

---

[50] Schwarzkopf, *It doesn't Take A Hero*, 468.   [51] Ibid. 466.

certain whether the highway engagements were pressed beyond the humanitarian point, thereby violating the general norm of restraint in warfare, there is at least some evidence of an awareness of this point by coalition commanders and a desire not to trespass.

In any war killing is a means to an end: namely victory. But for warfare to be morally and legally tolerable, killing is not the object; victory is the object. Killing is a means that must conform to the prudential considerations and procedural restraints of the ethics of war. That gives armed combat its special moral character. There is evidence of restraint on the part of the coalition forces in the Gulf War: victory was the object: the eviction of Iraqi forces from Kuwait. That can be contrasted with Vietnam where killing became an object: success for the USA came to be defined by a 'body count'. Hans Morgenthau, who opposed the Vietnam war, commented on the moral stain that produced: no civilized country, he argues, 'can wage such a war without suffering incalculable moral damage'.[52] There is no doubt but that the United States was morally damaged by its conduct in Vietnam. The 'damage' was produced by expectations on the part of American citizens, traditional allies of the USA, and others that war, if it is to be permissible as a foreign policy, must tolerably conform to civilized standards of conduct. The USA's stature as a civilized nation was tarnished by some of its policies and operations in the Vietnam War.

We can begin to draw out some of the normative implications of the foregoing inquiry. One cannot evaluate war strictly in terms of either procedural or prudential ethics. *Jus ad bellum* involves both types of ethics: we need valid procedural grounds to embark on a policy of war, but we also need to prudently weigh the (anticipated) consequences of any decision to go to war. Such a decision could be considered wrong if it had no legal or moral justification recognized by international society; it would also be wrong if it was reasonably clear in advance that stateleaders were needlessly placing their citizens in jeopardy. Saddam Hussein can be condemned on both grounds. By invading Kuwait and refusing to withdraw peacefully when called upon by the UN Security Council to do so, Iraq's actions were disclosed as blatantly contemptuous of international law. By risking war with the US-led coalition which presented great military danger, Saddam Hussein showed contempt for the lives of Iraqi soldiers and civilians, some of whom would be needlessly sacrificed if armed conflict did result; and in contemplating and later taking such a gamble he also demonstrated his indifference to the national security interest of Iraq.

Jus in bello also centrally involves both types of ethics: armed combat is an activity governed by rules of restraint, the laws and ethics of waging war. It also involves prudential considerations: a commander could be condemned for launching or continuing an operation when it is clear that his troops will be sac-

---

[52] Hans Morgenthau, *A New Foreign Policy for the United States* (New York: Praeger, 1969), 138. I am grateful to Will Bain for bringing this to my attention.

rificed with little or no chance of military gain. Military commanders in the First World War (1914–18) were frequently blamed for doing that. But there will always be uncertainty, risk, and danger in war and thus the possibility of bad consequences; even when the greatest care is taken something can go terribly wrong. Tragedy is an inherent feature of war and is perhaps more inherent in that sphere than any other sphere of human relations. But there do not have to be evil intentions: that is a matter exclusively of human decision and is thus entirely avoidable; war can be conducted in a way that intends to limit needless harm, needless pain and suffering, needless damage and destruction, so far as it is humanly and technically possible in the circumstances. If war is not conducted in that way, it is deserving of blame and censure. The ethics of war are fundamentally about disciplining intentions and the actions which stem from them: at least condemning, if not eliminating, acts which disclose evil intent or indifference to the likely harmful effects of one's military plans, strategies, and tactics. Such issues of conduct and misconduct in warfare can fittingly be understood in terms of the (military) virtues which centrally include discipline, both organizational discipline and personal self-discipline.

Unlevel Battlefields

During the air war General Schwarzkopf was reported as saying that the number of Iraqi dead, particularly along the Kuwait–Saudi front where the bombing was heaviest, was 'very, very large'.[53] Other allied officials at that time said tens of thousands of Iraqi soldiers had died in battle, and that a final death toll might never be known. Estimates of Iraqi battlefield deaths have subsequently ranged from a high of 100,000–150,000 shortly after the end of the battle to lower numbers later on.[54] John Simpson thought the true figure was probably far lower: 'maybe thirty thousand killed, and fifty thousand wounded, though this can only be a guess'.[55] If the latter figures are accurate, they suggest that enemy soldiers who are dug in are rather well protected from even the heaviest aerial bombing. The psychological damage to the Iraqi army may have been far greater than the actual casualties inflicted by this method of warfare.

By comparison to Iraqi casualties, only 139 coalition soldiers were reportedly killed in action; indeed, the number of coalition casualties inflicted by Iraqi fire was lower than those caused by friendly fire.[56] The contingent of US Marines consisted of two large divisions: 30,000 combat troops. They lost only three killed in their ground offensive against coastal Iraqi forces—six fewer than were killed by their own aircraft in a friendly fire 'blue-on-blue' accident during an

---

[53] Quoted in *The New York Times* (28 Feb. 1991).
[54] See Ridgeway (ed.), *March to War*, 229.
[55] Simpson, *From the House of War*, p. xv.   [56] Ridgeway, *March to War*, 229.

Iraqi attack on the Saudi border town of Khafji. A significant proportion of coalition battle deaths resulted from friendly fire incidents: twenty American soldiers and nine British soldiers evidently died in that way. The latter tragedy, in which American ground attack aircraft were involved, was the largest loss of coalition life in any one incident on the battlefield.[57]

The one-sided carnage of the Gulf War was very controversial among many Western intellectuals and politicians. What should our normative response be? Is this imbalance irrefutable evidence that the coalition did not restrain itself by humanitarian considerations? Many people were inclined to believe so.

Before addressing this question it is important to review circumstantial considerations. First, the size and firepower of Iraqi ground forces deployed in Kuwait or southern Iraq, even if they were not as great as the coalition originally believed or claimed, were very substantial by any estimate. Second, responsible military commanders quite rightly make every effort to limit risks to their soldiers after they commit them to battle. That means giving them as near to a decisive military advantage as possible. John Simpson claims that the coalition enjoyed a battlefield advantage in troops 'of between two and two-and-a-half to one, depending on how large the Iraqi rate of desertion was'.[58] Third, a responsible commander cannot in good conscience initiate warfare without a reasonable chance of victory—unless there are valid extenuating circumstances, such as putting some units at risk to save other units or to prevent a larger military disaster. Fourth, superior air power and early achievement of air supremacy gave an enormous military advantage to the coalition. Fifth, extremely low casualties in the land battle on the coalition side reflected superior leadership, strategy, tactics, operations, training, organization, weaponry, communications, logistics—virtually every element necessary to the successful waging of modern warfare. In short, there are compelling military and moral reasons on the coalition side for the profoundly unequal casualties.

What about the Iraqi side? Here reverse conditions contributed to the uneven slaughter. From Saddam Hussein on down, the first concern of leaders evidently was not the survival of their troops or citizens. Saddam and his commanders were prepared to sacrifice Iraqi soldiers for a political cause: the soldiers manning the defensive barriers in Kuwait were literally used as cannon fodder. Officers were inclined to abandon their soldiers in the face of adversity. Many soldiers were poorly trained and ill-equipped conscripts. They wanted above all to survive, regardless of the outcome, and they knew everybody was trying to do that even if nobody could say so openly. Military duty and combat discipline, including self-discipline, evidently had little hold on most Iraqi soldiers. Here was the fatal military vulnerability of Saddam Hussein and his dictatorial regime, which was designed to be successful as a police state against its own

---

[57] See the discussion by Billière, *Storm Command*, 292–7, and Simpson, *From the House of War*, 347.

[58] Simpson, *From the House of War*, 333.

people. His only loyal troops were the Republican Guards, who benefited materially from his regime and constituted its praetorian component for keeping him in power. The rest were frightened and ready to seize upon any opportunity to survive. So when the ground fighting began—and in some cases even before— Iraqi troops surrendered or ran away in droves.

If one applies the ethics of responsibility to the question of Iraqi battle casualties it is clear where primary responsibility lies. Saddam Hussein sacrificed the lives of thousands of his soldiers in a lost cause. In so doing he failed to act either intelligently or humanely in the face of a military adversary of awesome power. The coalition actually gave greater survival opportunities to Iraqi troops than their own leaders gave them. Thus, to suggest, as some commentators did suggest, that the profoundly unequal casualties of the Gulf War incriminate the victor (and presumably exonerate the vanquished) is to surrender to a confused way of thinking which has no place on the field of battle and should have no place in the ethics of war. If anyone embarks on war he or she should not expect a level battlefield.

As the above figures also indicate, from the viewpoint of minimizing coalition battle casualties, Operation Desert Storm was hugely successful. Until that time probably no other military commanders in the history of modern warfare returned home after victory with so many of their troops—indeed nearly all of them—completely unscathed. (By that standard only the NATO air war against Yugoslavia in 1999 was a greater triumph: there were no casualties to NATO airmen. But no NATO ground troops were involved.) On the other hand, coalition casualties almost certainly would have been far higher if the battle had been prolonged by a decision to take Baghdad and occupy Iraq. General de la Billière believes that Iraqi casualties, both military and civilian, also would have been far higher had the battle been prolonged and he was thankful the war ended when it did.[59] Yet there are surely few precedents in modern war when, at the moment of its greatest advantage, the victorious army pulls up short and refuses to inflict a total military defeat on the enemy.

The termination of the battle by the coalition at that point was politically expedient because a continuation of the battle would have invited widespread international criticism and the coalition almost certainly would have collapsed. But it also disclosed the moral concern of coalition political leaders and military commanders not to sacrifice needlessly the lives of soldiers under their command or the lives of Iraqi civilians. The decision also fastidiously respected the UN mandate which authorized the expulsion of Iraqi forces from Kuwait but not a coalition occupation of Iraq. That underlying preoccupation with legality tells us something fundamental about the Gulf War: at base it was a war against an aggressive military dictatorship that had violated the constitution of international society.

---

[59] Billière, *Storm Command*, 319.

Distributive and Corrective Justice

There are some normative aspects of the Gulf War that fit the traditional categories of *jus ad bellum* and *jus in bello* rather awkwardly at best. Two closely
related aspects are of particular interest because they featured prominently:
issues of distributive and corrective justice between states. The first may be
defined as that of sharing the burdens and benefits of the war among member
states of international society on an equitable basis. The second may be defined
as compensation for unintended and undeserved losses, injuries, and damages.
This is a normative sphere into which the ethics and laws of war are at the present time expanding. Arguably that is owing to the political and economic integration of international society that occurred in the twentieth century. This
process of global integration raises some important normative questions which
may give intimations of the international society into which we are moving at
the start of the twenty-first century.

A prominent normative controversy during the Gulf War was the profoundly
unequal adverse consequences on third parties resulting from UN sanctions
against Iraq. As indicated, UN Security Council resolutions 661 and 665 respect-
ively imposed economic sanctions and a naval blockade on Iraq and Iraqi-
occupied Kuwait under the authority of chapter VII of the charter. Article 50
recognizes that such action can impose economic hardship on innocent third
parties and gives any state 'which finds itself confronted with special economic
problems arising from' such measures 'the right to consult the Security Council
with regard to a solution to those problems'. Prior to the Gulf War, legal practice on this issue was 'relatively undeveloped'—as one important study put it—
which was perhaps understandable 'given the few previous incidents of this
kind'.[60] But the Gulf War broke new ground in that regard. A great deal of discussion at the UN during the crisis was taken up with the question of corrective justice between states.

A number of countries experienced substantial hardship as a result of the
blockade against Iraq and occupied Kuwait, owing to the interruption of oil
imports, the loss of economic trade, the loss of remittances from their nationals
working in Iraq or Kuwait, and so forth. Security Council resolution 669
addressed the adverse economic consequences on third-party states and undertook to examine requests for assistance from states under the provisions of
Article 50 of the UN charter. Nineteen countries eventually made hardship
applications to the UN. The Council Sanctions Committee carried out investigations and made recommendations for compensation to the most adversely
affected states. The Council called upon agencies of the United Nations and

---

[60] D. L. Bethlehem (ed.), *The Kuwait Crisis: Sanctions and their Consequences*, part I (Cambridge:
Grotius Publications, 1991), xliv.

member states to respond to the petitions of the adversely affected states for some compensation and, in particular, 'to the pressing needs of Jordan' which was most severely affected by the UN sanctions regime.[61] The USA and other industrialized powers, including notably Japan and Germany, became involved in making provision through the World Bank and the IMF to offset at least some of the damages.

In traditional international ethics such damages probably would have been construed as a misfortune of war thereby raising no claim to justice. In other words, it was bad luck for Jordan to be located right next to Iraq and thus to suffer disproportionately from the sanctions; but it was nobody's fault. That is a classical realist view. If evidence from the Gulf War is any indication, that older view is falling away: the integration of international society and the interdependence of states is taking its place. The background moral issue at stake is a novel ethic which has been evident only since decolonization: the assumption that some countries (the strongest and most developed) have a duty to assist other countries (the weakest and least developed) which are unduly exposed to international economic disruptions. That is especially so when the disruption is unintentionally brought about by the deliberate actions of international society— as happened in this case. If we express this emerging norm in terms of rights, certain underdeveloped or vulnerable states are entitled to positive assistance from international organizations and developed states to deal with the unduly severe effects of such international crises on them. They are in effect claiming subsistence rights and the normative issue at stake is a version of international distributive justice.

Another issue in the Gulf crisis which also invoked distributive justice, but in a very different context, was that of burden sharing among participating members of the coalition against Iraq. This might seem to be little more than an instrumental problem but in fact it is far more than that; it is a question of justice among co-operators. There was a normative dialogue among the coalition states concerning the question of sharing the military and financial burden involved. That clearly implies that free riders cannot be tolerated which, in turn, postulates some principle of distributive equity.

Perhaps burden sharing ought to be based on ability. According to that normative reasoning, America, as the preponderant military power in the coalition, would be bound to contribute the bulk of the armed forces. Japan, as the second most important capitalist state but not a comparable military power, would be expected to make a commensurate financial contribution to help defray the heavy costs of the military operation. Germany, at that time constitutionally and politically unable to contribute armed forces to the coalition but a large and wealthy country, could be expected to make a similar financial contribution for

---

[61] The UN decisions and actions on compensation of adversely affected states are collected ibid., part II.

the same reason. Or perhaps burden sharing should be determined by a country's stake in a successful outcome. According to that normative reasoning, Saudi Arabia and other vulnerable oil-exporting states in the Gulf might be expected to make the greatest contributions in relation to national wealth because they were among the most important stakeholders. Kuwait clearly was the most important stakeholder: it would have the most to gain from a successful war to evict Iraq from its territory and so it should be expected to contribute proportionately the most. If stake were defined economically in terms of assured future access to Middle East petroleum supplies, it would require a major contribution from the USA, Japan, Germany, France, Italy, and other members of the coalition who were heavily dependent on those supplies. In this connection the substantial military contribution of Britain, which is not dependent on foreign oil, appears to have exceeded what morality requires. But Britain's contribution probably was commensurate with its responsibilities as a permanent member of the Security Council.

Since by far the greatest contributions and sacrifices among the developed countries aligned against Iraq were made by the USA that country should derive proportional benefits from the coalition's defeat of Iraq. This could take the form of having the greatest say among coalition members in shaping the post-crisis Middle East or being the main beneficiary in the rebuilding of Kuwait—both of which proved to be the case. Because of America's world-wide interests and global military reach this was likely to happen anyway and it could of course be explained in instrumental terms. This inquiry merely identifies an important normative justification of such an outcome.

A Constitutional War?

Saddam Hussein's armed forces invaded Kuwait without any justification recognized by international law. His armed forces deliberately inflicted suffering on the people of Kuwait and other people as well, as a result of their invasion. He was given repeated opportunities to withdraw from Kuwait and settle his dispute by peaceful means. He spurned all of them and chose battle instead. In waging war he targeted non-combatants. He sacrificed thousands of Iraqi soldiers and civilians in a lost cause. In his struggle to stay in power after his defeat he drove into exile substantial numbers of his own population. This might approximate a summary of the indictment against Saddam Hussein if he could be brought before an international tribunal for war crimes and crimes against humanity. On the other hand, the war to liberate Kuwait was to stop a breach of international peace and restore the independence of Kuwait. Furthermore, it had the express legal sanction of the UN Security Council. The international response to Iraq's action—including the imposition of a trade embargo, the resort to war, the conduct of war, and the enforced disarmament of Iraq after the hostilities—probably was as consistent with international law as one could reasonably and realistically expect.

Although Saddam Hussein offered normative reasons for his invasion of Kuwait, they cannot fulfil the basic conditions set down by *jus ad bellum*: defence against injury, recovery of what is rightfully one's own, or infliction of punishment for wrongdoing. Before the invasion, Iraq was suffering from the consequences of its previous war with Iran and not from any recognizable injuries or damages inflicted by Kuwait. The disputed Kuwaiti oil fields and territory could be considered Iraq's and not Kuwait's only by a huge act of imagination which denied the legitimacy and legality of existing international boundaries. The invasion of Kuwait could be construed as punishment—rather than aggression—only if one ignored the normative facts of the case. In short, the Iraqi action was undertaken without authority, its goal was not peace, and it was not a last resort.

The justice of launching Operation Desert Storm to liberate Kuwait is not as straightforward. That the war aimed at defeating a criminal action by Iraq and restoring the sovereignty of Kuwait and peace in the Gulf is not in doubt. The main points of uncertainty concern whether the war was a last resort and whether it could reasonably be expected to result in greater good than evil. Critics—including many members of the US Congress—wanted more time for diplomacy and for the pains of the embargo to be felt by Iraq. Since nobody can ever know what will happen in the future the question boiled down to a political judgement concerning the most likely future behaviour of Saddam Hussein: would he eventually respond to the embargo and diplomatic entreaties to withdraw or only to military force? What course would involve the least human suffering: the former or the latter? In the end the military option prevailed in the UN Security Council and the US Congress—by a very narrow margin in the latter. The Senate granted President Bush the authority to launch war by a vote of 52 to 47.

Everything considered, I believe the war to liberate Kuwait was warranted by the values it preserved and the way it was prosecuted. It upheld the fundamental norm of non-intervention and the right to resist aggression by force. It restored a measure of international peace and security to the strategic oil-producing region of the Middle East. It exercised restraint and obeyed international law at its moment of triumph by holding back from invading and occupying Iraq. Coalition commanders and soldiers conducted their military campaign with what could be termed imperfect justice: they endeavoured to operate in a civilized way and, although there are some stains on their record, they by and large succeeded in doing that. The determination to compensate third parties, particularly Jordan, for damages caused by the embargo against Iraq is indicative of the UN's lively sense of justice in its conduct of the war— especially since Jordan was one of very few states which did not condemn Iraq's action and therefore seemed to condone it.

In war even more than in other human relations, what we can reasonably hope for is not the best but only the best in the circumstances. Operation Desert Storm was about as close to a lawful and legitimate war as one could realistically expect in the circumstances. Imperfection and inadequacy should always be distinguished from misconduct, however, and it is in that regard that the regime of Saddam Hussein stands condemned before the world.

But all of this must be qualified in an important way if we want to avoid drawing misleading lessons from the Gulf War, which was an unusual conflict. The circumstances were auspicious for the United Nations and the coalition powers. After the cold war the threat of great power war receded as the USA, Russia, and China set aside the issues that had divided them for more than forty years. That enabled them to come together and establish a new concert of the great powers: something that had not been possible for most of the twentieth century. The Gulf War was unusual because the great powers were not divided over it: while most of them were involved in it they were not involved as adversaries. That was different from most of the wars of the twentieth century in which the great powers were involved; it was different from the First World War, the Second World War, the Korean War, the Vietnam War, and the cold war more generally. In the Gulf War the great powers either were military allies (USA, Britain, France, Japan, Germany) or they were non-obstructive (Russia, China). The Gulf War and some other armed conflicts of the 1990s were more like colonial wars in which the great powers acted as international law enforcers. Only in the war in Kosovo in 1999 did that great power concert come close to falling apart as both Russia and China registered strenuous vocal opposition to NATO's bombing campaign against Yugoslavia. But they did not become involved militarily on the side of Yugoslavia.

The laws and ethics of war, including both the *jus ad bellum* and the *jus in bello*, arguably stand a far better chance of being invoked and respected in a military campaign against an outlaw state, in which the great powers are united and hold most of the political, economic, and military cards. If that is indeed so, then one of the important lessons of the Gulf War is one of the oldest lessons in the book of war: that the great powers should avoid engaging in foreign policies and military actions that threaten to divide them and to provoke war between them. Instead, if they hang together, and act in concert, belligerent governments can be marginalized and international peace and security safeguarded. It was by this means that the founding fathers of the United Nations hoped to avoid any repetition of the mistakes and the horrors of the first half of the twentieth century.

10

Armed Intervention for Humanity

This chapter begins by canvassing some basic normative considerations that would have to be taken into account in justifying armed intervention in contemporary world politics. It goes on to glance at the cold war experience with intervention. Then, against that background, it reviews four cases of international intervention after the cold war: Iraq, Somalia, Bosnia, and Kosovo (Yugoslavia). Should international society intervene with armed force in an independent country where there are gross violations of human rights or other grave humanitarian problems but where no obvious threats to peace and security are involved? Should they do that without the consent of the government? These questions cannot be answered categorically because any answer will depend on the circumstances of the case and the normative practices at the time. The chapter approaches the issue of humanitarian intervention with that contextual reality in mind. In the course of the twentieth century, the grounds of legitimate and lawful intervention in sovereign states by armed force, *jus ad bellum*, were restricted by international society.[1] Several interventions at the end of the century prompt the question whether they are now being expanded and, if so, can that be justified in a pluralist world? The chapter concludes with some reflections on that larger question.

The *Jus ad Bellum* of Intervention

Intervention in world politics 'raises questions of the utmost moral complexity: adherents of every political belief will regard intervention as justified under certain circumstances'.[2] That observation of Martin Wight is as applicable today as ever. Any scholar who seeks to shed light on post-cold war interventions in

---

[1] 'Intervention' in the technical legal meaning is 'interference with matters within the exclusive jurisdiction of a subject of international law and, unless justified by a specific rule to the opposite effect, constitutes an illegal act'. G. Schwarzenberger and E. Brown, *A Manual of International Law*, 6th edn. (London: Professional Books, 1976), 228. The current legal seat of that doctrine is Article 2(7) of the UN charter. This chapter is limited to intervention by threat or use of armed force, which is the ambiguous borderland between intervention and war. Hence the discussion in terms of *jus ad bellum*.

[2] M. Wight, *Power Politics* (Harmondsworth: Penguin Books, 1979), 191.

Bosnia or Kosovo will quickly come up against some of the most knotted moral questions of international relations. There is, however, a classical conception of intervention that can be used to clarify the subject: interference by a sovereign state, group of such states, or international organization, involving the threat or use of force or some other means of duress, in the domestic jurisdiction of an independent state against the will or wishes of its government.[3] That concept should be the starting-point in any endeavour to understand the theory and practice of intervention in world politics.

There are three noteworthy academic misadventures in the study of intervention which should be avoided by anyone interested in the subject. The first misadventure is that of abstract philosophical inquiry. Stanley Hoffmann indicates the right approach: the study of international ethics 'is not the province of the ethical philosopher'; it is the province of the international relations scholar.[4] It is doubtful that there could be an 'ethics of intervention' in the purely abstract sense as a study in moral philosophy. What the most responsible choice would be in any particular case is not something that can be determined in principle or in advance. If the normative predicaments of statespeople are to be properly grasped, the analysis must be empirical in orientation: it must be located in the historical situation. As indicated in previous chapters, international ethics is situational and most international situations are difficult to evaluate. The ethics of intervention—like that of statecraft generally—is subject to the norms of the international society in existence at the time and the circumstances of the case in question.

The second misadventure is that of instrumental policy analysis. Some scholars are inclined to approach intervention as largely if not exclusively an instrumental question.[5] But that would be to ignore the fundamental issue facing statespeople: whether in any particular case they ought to violate the sovereignty of a state, even if they are in a position to do so, could very likely pull it off, and could derive important advantages from it. Whether any state should intervene in the domestic jurisdiction of another state certainly depends on whether it is instrumentally feasible. But merely being in a position to intervene, or having a good chance to succeed, or knowing how to pull off an intervention, or even having solid reasons to suppose that the benefits will far outweigh the costs of intervention, is not yet having any moral or legal warrant to do so. Intervention inescapably involves normative questions as well as instrumental

---

[3] This definition is a slightly modified version of those used by Hedley Bull and John Vincent. See Hedley Bull (ed.), *Intervention in World Politics* (Oxford: Clarendon Press, 1984), 1, and John Vincent, *Non-Intervention and International Order* (Princeton: Princeton University Press, 1974), 13.

[4] Stanley Hoffmann, *Duties Beyond Borders* (Syracuse, NY: Syracuse University Press, 1981), 189.

[5] For a typical instrumental analysis see Richard Connaughton, *Military Intervention in the 1990s* (London and New York: Routledge, 1992).

questions: the former questions are the most important and also the most knotted. If we pass them by in our quest for a policy science of intervention we shall never get to the heart of the subject.

The third misadventure is that of political economy analysis which creates conceptual confusion by equating state sovereignty and state autonomy. The classical concept of intervention is external armed encroachment on the sovereign jurisdiction of a state: a political and legal concept. A contemporary concept of intervention is the international socio-economic constraint on state autonomy: a sociological and economic concept. Autonomy and sovereignty are not the same. Very few sovereign states, if any, are socio-economically autonomous. But all sovereign states are constitutionally independent. Intervention is an intentional political and military action; it is not a consequence of socio-economic transactions. States nowadays are enmeshed in a complex global network of transnational socio-economic relations which raises important questions about state autonomy.[6] But it is threats and acts of military intervention in state sovereignty in violation of the norm of non-intervention that is of fundamental concern to international society. It is thus confusing and misleading to conceive of socio-economic transactions as a form of intervention. As a normative issue, intervention can only be coherently understood as coercive or forcible interference with the legal independence of states.

I shall therefore be sticking to the classical definition of intervention. The existence of constitutionally independent countries (sovereign states) in external relationships that can be characterized as an international *societas* sets the stage for the normative problem of intervention, including intervention on humanitarian grounds. The classical ethics of intervention is a negative ethics premissed on a sovereign state's constitutional immunity and therefore its fundamental right of non-intervention. If priority is to be given to human rights in any particular case there must be compelling and indeed overwhelming reasons to interfere with the sovereign rights of states and their citizens. That is the burden of proof concerning humanitarian intervention at the present time.[7] The doctrine of humanitarian intervention is a positive ethics in which human rights displace state sovereignty as the primary normative consideration in deciding questions of intervention. If world politics operated with a doctrine of humanitarian intervention it would mean that states were no longer protected (normatively speaking) by their sovereignty and would not enjoy any pre-emptory right of non-intervention—apart from the limitations placed on that right by the UN charter (see below). International society would be a *universitas* in that regard. Does experience since the end of the cold war offer any solid evidence for the claim that in certain circumstances humanitarian considerations

---

[6] See M. Zacher, *Governing Global Networks* (Cambridge: Cambridge University Press, 1996).

[7] For an important discussion of this issue see Andrew Linklater, *Men and Citizens in the Theory of International Relations*, 2nd edn. (London: Macmillan, 1990).

come before sovereign rights in the justification of military intervention?[8] Is there evidence of a normative sea change on this issue, from a *societas* of sovereign states to a global *universitas* of some kind?

As I indicated, in classical negative international ethics, intervention is prima-facie wrong and must therefore be justified or else it must be condemned. Non-intervention is the pre-emptive norm of a pluralistic international society. The current legal site of that norm is Article 2 of the UN charter, the pertinent sections of which read as follows: 'All members shall refrain in their international relations from the threat or use of force against the territorial integrity or political independence of any state . . . Nothing contained in the present Charter shall authorize the United Nations to intervene in matters which are essentially within the domestic jurisdiction of any state.' Because sovereign states have a right to have their jurisdictions respected by all other states, and by international society, they also have a corresponding duty to respect that right unless there are valid reasons to make an exception to the rule. Non-intervention is the norm and acts of intervention are what must be justified. Intervention is therefore an exceptional international action, and normative reasons must weight heavily to warrant such an action.

The current justifications for overriding that norm can be boiled down to three: (1) international order: the intervention is taken for valid reasons of international peace and security or national security. (2) consent: the intervention is at the request of the legal government of the target state—perhaps to assist that government to counter a prior intervention or to defend itself against an armed rebellion. (3) humanitarianism: the intervention is to protect the population of the target state (or segments of it) from grave abuses at the hands of their own government or anti-government rebels or as a result of domestic anarchy. The first two justifications are, for all intents and purposes, universally accepted among statespeople; the third is controversial.[9]

Conventional practice identifies chapter VII and Article 51 as the only valid grounds for overriding Article 2 of the UN charter. As indicated in previous chapters, key articles authorize the Security Council to identify 'any threat to the peace, breach of the peace or act of aggression' (Article 39) and, if such a threat is determined by the Council, 'it may take such action by air, sea, or land forces as may be necessary to maintain or restore international peace and security' (Article 42).[10] Article 51 reads as follows: 'Nothing in the present Charter

---

[8] For a qualified answer in the affirmative see Christopher Greenwood, 'Is there a Right of Humanitarian Intervention?', *The World Today*, 49 (Feb. 1993), 40. Also see the discussion of this point in Adam Roberts, 'Humanitarian War: Military Intervention and Human Rights,' *International Affairs*, 69 (July 1993), 444.

[9] The international case law of these and other justifications is unsettled. See Michael Akehurst, *A Modern Introduction to International Law*, 6th edn. (London: Allen & Unwin, 1987), 281–90. Also see the essays in L. F. Damrosch and D. J. Scheffer (eds.), *Law and Force in the New International Order* (Boulder, Colo.: Westview, 1991).

[10] Anthony Arend and Robert Beck, *International Law and the Use of Force* (London and New York: Routledge, 1993), 31–2.

shall impair the inherent right of individual or collective self-defense.' That is the only justification of military intervention that remains wholly in the hands of individual sovereign states. Since 1945, as one commentator puts it, 'the state's right to use violence otherwise than in self-defense has been transferred to the security council of the United Nations'.[11] These norms express the *jus ad bellum* of post-1945 international society as defined by the UN charter.

The justification that came to the fore in the twentieth century was that of consent. We should understand this norm in the historical context of the colonial era when many Asian and African countries were ruled by European governments without their consent. Consent is the pre-emptive norm *par excellence* of weak ex-colonial states. A solicited intervention, strictly speaking, is not an intervention at all because it is not an interference in state sovereignty. On the contrary, it is a response to a request by the government of a target state which logically cannot violate its own sovereignty. The norm of consent is a clear bow toward the sovereignty of that government. It is an act in defence of state sovereignty. But, because external armed force is involved, solicited intervention is conventionally understood as a form of intervention.[12]

The third justification for intervention (humanitarianism) is controversial because it does not require consent by the target state and it seems to go beyond UN charter rules regarding international peace and security and legitimate self-defence. The charter proclaims human rights as a goal of the UN but it does not include human rights as a specific ground for international intervention in state sovereignty. Humanitarian intervention thus seems to repudiate the foundational norm of state sovereignty. It is very controversial among non-democratic and authoritarian governments who, as the most likely targets of humanitarian intervention, are jealous about their sovereignty and normally claim the absolute priority of the right of consent. Some legal scholars deny that there is any such justification in international law.[13]

An important caveat about these justifications deserves emphasis: none of them is without problems in its practical application to particular cases. All of them are ambiguous to some degree. That is so even for consent, which arguably is the least equivocal of the three. For example, if consent is to be valid in law it must emanate from the legal government of a sovereign state and be freely given. The basic normative concern is to ensure that an invitation is not spurious, which is a question of fact and judgement in any particular case. Similar questions also arise in connection with self-defence (is there a bona-fide threat to the state involved?) and in connection with humanitarian justifications (is the human suffering of sufficient magnitude to warrant a violation of state

---

[11] P. Calvocoressi, 'A Problem and its Dimensions', in N. S. Rodley (ed.), *To Loose the Bands of Wickedness* (London: Brassey's, 1992), 2.

[12] Martin Wight includes both 'solicited' and 'imposed' forms of intervention in his definition. See his *Power Politics*, ch. 11.

[13] See M. Akehurst, 'Humanitarian Intervention', in Bull, *Intervention in World Politics*, 95–118.

sovereignty?). Like most questions of international ethics, intervention is a question of judgement. But that should not deter us from studying it since it surely also is one of the most important normative questions of contemporary international relations.

To sum up thus far: since the adoption of the UN charter in 1945 and even more so since the termination of colonialism, which notionally can be said to have occurred in 1960, international society has been not only cool but hostile to the practice of intervention. This negative posture is nowhere better captured than by the UN General Assembly's 1970 'Declaration on Principles of International Law concerning Friendly Relations and Cooperation among States', which asserts that 'the practice of any form of intervention . . . violates the spirit and letter of the Charter'.[14] That is the restrictive doctrine of intervention which is undoubtedly subscribed to by a large majority of states at the present time.

Intervention during the Cold War

There were many interventions during the cold war by the USA and the Soviet Union (and their allies or clients) and by other states as well, although perhaps not as many as one might have expected given the pervasiveness and relentlessness of their rivalry. Some interventions trespassed on the norms of post-1945 international society. That usually happened in zones of confrontation between the superpowers. Limitations of space only permit a summary analysis of some noteworthy instances of intervention during that time.

Because they were driven by considerations of political and military advantage, one might have thought—following a narrowly realist line of reasoning—that superpower interventions would not be accompanied by normative justifications. An instrumental analysis would be sufficient for understanding them. But that was not the case. Both the USA and the Soviet Union justified their interventions. That undoubtedly served their propaganda purposes and could thus be construed as window-dressing. But it also indicates that, even though they might have gotten away with it, the superpowers could not operate in an exclusively instrumental fashion—at least not if they wished to enjoy high approval ratings in international society. They usually felt a need to justify their actions to other states, and to international society at large, by reference to the standards of conduct in existence at the time. The cold-war protagonists could not arbitrarily cast the conventional morality of international society aside. When they did occasionally do that they typically furnished normative justifications for doing so.

---

[14] See M. Akehurst, 'Humanitarian Intervention', in Bull, *Intervention in World Politics*, 108.

By far the most important, most extensive, and most sustained intervention during the cold war was the post-1945 Soviet intervention in Eastern Europe. Indeed, that action was responsible for creating the cold war. Unlike the US armed forces, which were largely withdrawn from Europe after the defeat of Germany in 1945, the armed forces of the Soviet Union were kept in their positions of military occupation. Stalin subsequently succeeded in installing communist regimes across Eastern Europe that were politically subservient to the Soviet Union. Henceforth Moscow would dictate the foreign and military policies of these states on issues that were deemed to affect the Soviet Union's vital concerns. If any of them gave a sign of steering a course that was independent of Moscow, they would risk Russian military intervention. That happened, notoriously, on two major occasions: the Soviet army intervened in Hungary in 1956 and in Czechoslovakia in 1968. Thus, instead of constituting a *societas* of states which respected each other's sovereignty and the rule of non-intervention, the states of Eastern Europe were subordinate to Moscow during the cold war. Their relationship was that of a communist quasi-empire or *universitas*: the only truly independent country among them was the Soviet Union.

That hierarchical relation between the Soviet Union and the states of Eastern Europe was difficult to justify by reference to the pluralist norms of international society as newly defined by the UN charter in 1945, at the heart of which was Article 2. The USSR operated in a fashion that could only be justified, if justified at all, by a concept of legitimate spheres of influence. That harkened back to an older doctrine of the right of intervention of powerful states in their declared neighbourhoods. A well known historical example is the Monroe doctrine (1823) by which the USA declared that Europe and the Americas constituted two separate spheres, and that states in one sphere should not interfere in the other sphere. The most famous Soviet example was the Brezhnev doctrine, which stipulated that Moscow had the right to intervene in the states of Eastern Europe to defend the communist revolution. That meant that no East European state was free to abandon communism or enter into normal relations with West European neighbours. Eastern Europe was in the Soviet sphere. The fledgling USSR was itself the target of that neighbourhood doctrine in 1918 when Britain, France, Italy, Japan, Canada, and the USA intervened, unsuccessfully, after Lenin had taken Russia out of the First World War and made a separate peace with Germany that threatened the Allies on the western front. The Allied intervention continued for some time after the end of the war and expressed Western concern that communist Russia was a revolutionary threat to the new international society centred on the League of Nations.[15] The validity of spheres of influence was confirmed by the League covenant (Article 21). Both the USA and the Soviet Union proclaimed the doctrine in their neighbourhoods during the cold war, but it had no clearly legitimate place in international society after 1945.

---

[15] G. Smith, *Woodrow Wilson's Fourteen Points after 75 Years* (New York: Carnegie Council, 1993), 12–13.

In attempting to understand the quasi-imperial relations between the Soviet Union and the states of Eastern Europe after 1945 we should of course be mindful of the historical context, which is captured by Louis Halle in a brilliant early study of the cold war:

It is really not conceivable that the rulers of Moscow, with a thousand years of desperate struggle for survival behind them, would have abjured power-politics after the war and cooperated in the organization of a postwar world that represented the ideals of Anglo-Saxon political philosophy. This would have been for them to commit a kind of suicide, for it would have implied the dissolution of the secret and tyrannical regime on which they depended, inside Russia, for their own survival.[16]

That is what eventually happened to Gorbachev and his reform communists after they signalled in 1989 that East Germany and by implication all of the states of Eastern Europe were henceforth free to go their own way and no longer had to toe Moscow's line. That came to be known as the Sinatra doctrine: 'I did it my way'. The Brezhnev doctrine was formally repudiated by Gorbachev in a 1989 speech to the Council of Europe which acknowledged the pluralist norms of international society: 'Any interference in domestic affairs and any attempts to restrict the sovereignty of states—friends, allies or any others—are inadmissible . . . it is time to deposit in the archives the postulates of the cold war period when Europe was . . . divided into "spheres of influence".'[17] The 1975 Helsinki Accords had launched this reconciliation of Russia with the non-interventionist norms of international society and it was completed by the 1990 Charter of Paris—signed by twenty-two states of Europe, both east and west, and by Canada and the USA, which declared the end of the 'era of confrontation and division of Europe' and acknowledged their obligations 'to refrain from the threat or use of force against the territorial integrity or political independence of any state'. That affirmation of the *Grundnorm* of post-1945 world politics marked the return of Russia and the political systems of Eastern Europe to the *societas* of sovereign states.

Apart from Soviet-controlled Eastern Europe, undoubtedly the area of the most pervasive intervention during the cold war was the Middle East.[18] The immediate source of that conflict was the UN partition of Palestine, which launched an independent Jewish state in 1948 which the Arabs refused to accept. Recurrent war and intervention between Israel and Arab states was the consequence, with major episodes occurring in 1948, 1956, 1967, 1973, and 1982. As if re-enacting the experience of inter-war Europe, the international boundaries of 1948 were repeatedly violated and altered by armed force. The UN became deeply involved in attempting to manage the Arab–Israeli conflict, the modern institution of peacekeeping was invented in connection with the con-

---

[16] L. J. Halle, *The Cold War as History* (New York: Harper, 1967), 76.
[17] Quoted by H. Kissinger, *Diplomacy* (New York: Simon & Schuster, 1994), 794.
[18] A. Parsons, *From Cold War to Hot Peace* (London: Penguin Books, 1995), 3–43.

flict, troops under the UN flag were assigned to monitor ceasefire lines, recurrent UN resolutions were passed, repeated rounds of negotiations were held, the superpowers became deeply entangled, and in short the conflict—which involved comparatively small if not tiny territories and populations—demanded and received the attention of the world for half a century.

During that entire period, however, the UN and the vast majority of its member states consistently denied the legitimacy of territory acquired by military intervention and occupation, most of which consisted of Arab lands seized by Israel (Gaza Strip, Golan Heights, West Bank, East Jerusalem, etc.). UN Security Council resolution 242 which was adopted after the 1967 war expressed the norm by calling for military withdrawal from conquered territory and the restoration of the pre-war boundaries. That same norm was reiterated in principle if not in every detail in a formal peace agreement signed between Israel and Egypt in 1979 and between Israel and the Palestinian leadership in 1993. Even in such a zone of protracted and embittered conflict, a zone fractured by history, by religion, by ideology, and divided further by the cold war, the sanctity of borders and the ethics of non-intervention have been a recurrent refrain of international discourse. They provide the only generally recognized normative foundation for regional peace and security.

The history of the cold war could leave the impression that international politics is mostly an activity of intervention rather than respect for a norm of non-intervention. But the opposite is closer to the reality. Outside their zones of confrontation both the Soviet Union and the USA generally respected the norm of non-intervention. In Africa, for example, each superpower was conscious of the importance of the principle of respect for ex-colonial boundaries which was the basis of international order in that continent. To be sure, the USA was criticized by African states for intervening in the Angolan civil war in 1975 in support of anti-government and ostensibly anti-communist rebels and without the consent of the quasi-Marxist Angolan government of the day. Neither Cuba nor the Soviet Union could be censured for coming to the military aid of that same government whose claim to sovereignty was generally recognized by that time. In the 1977 war between Somalia and Ethiopia in which the Ogaden region of Ethiopia was invaded and occupied by Somalian armed forces, the USA responded by indicating that they would not provide Somalia with any military arms or equipment until their forces withdrew behind the ex-colonial international borders. Soviet military assistance later helped Ethiopia to drive the Somalian forces back across the border into Somalia. But Moscow was not prepared to support an Ethiopian invasion of Somalia or any violation of the existing international boundary between the two countries.[19] That was consistent with the fundamental non-interventionist norm of both the UN charter and the charter of the Organization of African Unity.

[19] R. Jackson and C. Rosberg, 'Pax Africana and its Problems', in R. Bissell and M. Radu (eds.), *Africa in the Post-Decolonization* Era (New Brunswick, NJ: Transaction Books, 1984), 157–82.

The typical normative ground for Third World interventions during the cold war was solicitation by the target state. The Soviet Union intervened in Ethiopia and Angola and the USA intervened in Lebanon, the Dominican Republic, and South Vietnam on that basis. France intervened repeatedly in Francophone African states at the request of sovereign governments and under provisions contained in treaties with many of her former African colonies. Occasionally the principal of consent was stretched beyond credibility. In addition to claiming a right of self-defence, the Soviet Union claimed they were invited by the pro-Moscow government in Kabul to intervene in Afghanistan in 1979. But the international status of that recently installed government, whether it was the legal government of Afghanistan or a puppet of the Soviet Union, and thus whether it had a right to issue such an invitation, were the important questions.

International involvement by the UN in regional conflicts during the cold war was carefully adjusted to the principle of consent. UN peacekeeping operated with the consent of the quarrelling parties, which was the only basis on which the permanent members of the Security Council could agree to sanction such operations.[20] Furthermore, once the blue berets were on the ground in the Sinai, the Golan Heights, Cyprus, and other places, they were effective in keeping the peace only because the quarrelling parties were prepared to co-operate with them. Consent was also at the forefront of humanitarian activities during the cold war: when humanitarian NGOs attempted to help starving Ethiopians in the mid-1980s they first had to secure the agreement of Mengistu Haile Mariam, the military dictator of Ethiopia, who had his price which had to be paid before the food could be delivered to those in need.

Non-intervention (negative freedom) and in particular the principle of consent are norms favoured by weak states who only have international law and public opinion to safeguard their independence. Powerful states can defend themselves (positive freedom) and thus have no need of such a norm because nobody except other powerful states could even contemplate intervening in their jurisdictions. By bringing numerous weak states into existence, decolonization created a vastly enlarged operational scope for the norm of non-intervention. The Third World itself is in some fundamental respects an expression of that norm. Leaders of weak states were not against intervention: they knew that they might have to call on other states from time to time for military assistance. They were against intervention without their consent, which means that they wanted to retain the right to solicit interventions and thus to have their sovereignty respected if interventions were to take place. Above all, they did not want to have the cold war waged at their expense.[21]

[20] S. Morphet, 'UN Peacekeeping and Election-Monitoring', in A. Roberts and B. Kingsbury (eds), *United Nations, Divided World*, 2nd edn. (Oxford: Clarendon Press, 1993), 184.

[21] I discuss this issue at length in *Quasi-States: Sovereignty, International Relations and the Third World* (Cambridge: Cambridge University Press, 1990).

During the cold war there were three interventions which some legal scholars have construed as instances of humanitarian intervention: the Indian intervention in East Pakistan (Bangladesh) in 1971, the Tanzanian intervention in Uganda in 1978, and the Vietnamese intervention in Cambodia in 1979. These interventions were controversial at the time: even Tanzania's intervention in Uganda, which resulted in the overthrow of Idi Amin's tyrannical regime, was widely criticized by African states and by the Organization of African Unity. The opinions of legal scholars on intervention and other international questions are of some importance. But the most important opinions by far are those of the statespeople involved. Although they bowed in the direction of humanitarianism, the interventionist leaders involved in these episodes justified their actions on conventional grounds of self-defence.[22]

The absence of humanitarian interventions during the cold war was not owing to any lack of human suffering in countries around the world at that time. Nor was it because of indifference to the plight of people in those countries. It was rather that the political opportunity was not available to make armed humanitarianism a course of action for international society and particularly the UN Security Council to contemplate or pursue. The reason is to be found in the organization of the cold war itself: there was no singular organized will and capacity for international armed intervention during that period; instead there were conflicting superpower wills that checkmated each other and thereby blocked armed internationalism for humanitarian or any other purposes. Thus the Security Council, which requires great power co-operation to be effective, was incapacitated: the most that could be agreed was UN peacekeeping, which could do little more than police the lines of silenced conflict between previously warring parties in conflict zones. Upholding a provisional ceasefire between the Greeks and the Turks in Cyprus, which lasted for several decades without achieving a permanent peace settlement, is the classic case in point.

Intervention by international society became politically feasible after 1989. The ending of the cold war changed the prevalent relationship of the USA and Russia into one of co-operation or at least non-competition on many issues where previously such action had been thwarted by their incessant political and military rivalry. China also proved to be co-operative—or at least non-obstructive. That was one of the most significant consequences of the end of the cold war. On certain crucial issues it was now possible to generate a single international will between the great powers which disclosed a concert that was manifested in the collaboration and joint action of the permanent members of the Security Council. The Council could now perform the international security role which the founders of the UN had originally envisaged. How enduring that relationship will prove to be only time can tell.

---

[22] See the discussion of state practice on intervention since 1945 in Akehurst, 'Humanitarian Intervention', 95–104.

Intervention in Iraq

A conspicuous feature of world politics after the end of the cold war was the sharp increase in international involvement in armed conflicts. Among other indications, that was evident from a proliferation of Security Council resolutions and deployments of UN peacekeepers around the world. Immediately following Iraq's invasion of Kuwait there was an acceleration of UN resolutions and actions on a wide front. Between August 1990 and October 1991 twenty-four resolutions were passed on the Iraq–Kuwait conflict alone.[23] In 1992 there was an almost fivefold increase in the deployment of UN peacekeepers, from 11,000 at the start of the year to 52,000 at the end.[24] Blue berets were deployed to Iraq and Kuwait, El Salvador, Haiti, Angola, Western Sahara, Somalia, Rwanda, Mozambique, Cambodia, Macedonia, Croatia, and Bosnia.

As indicated, one of the most telling signs of a changed international situation after 1989 was the rebirth of the UN Security Council, which had been unable to perform its security role throughout most of the cold war era. The role of the Council as set out in the UN charter is one of safeguarding international peace and security, defending the principle of non-intervention, and responding to aggression and illegal acts of intervention. All permanent members of the Council generally supported that role after the cold war—the clearest example being the Council's response to the 1990 Iraqi invasion of Kuwait. One can never be certain of underlying motives for diplomatic decisions, and no doubt there were various and conflicting foreign-policy considerations by the states involved in that episode, especially the great powers. For our purposes of normative inquiry, however, the motives are less important than the actions themselves and their justifications. If the five permanent members did not vote in unison on every significant issue brought before them after 1989, the veto nevertheless became almost dormant. As a result of that unprecedented co-operation among the major military powers, the Council was more actively involved in more conflicts around the world than at any time in its history. The Kosovo crisis of 1999, in which NATO bombed Yugoslavia without express authorization from the Council, was the first major indication that such co-operation might not be as regularly forthcoming in the future as it was in the 1990s.

The rebirth of the Security Council can conveniently be dated as occurring on 2 August 1990, when it passed resolution 660 which condemned Iraq's invasion of Kuwait and demanded that Iraq withdraw all its forces immediately and unconditionally. That launched the Council on a course of unprecedented activism which left in its wake a large number of resolutions on a variety of

---

[23] See E. Lauterpacht *et al.* (eds.), *The Kuwait Crisis: Basic Documents* (Cambridge: Grotius Publications, 1991).

[24] Marrack Goulding, 'The Evolution of United Nations Peacekeeping', *International Affairs*, 69 (July 1993), 451.

international conflicts. Most of them disclosed the Council's conventional role in promoting international peace and security. But some of them indicated the evolution of the Council as an international decision-making body concerned with humanitarianism and human rights. It is inconceivable that such a battery of UN resolutions and actions could have been taken at the time of the cold war with respect to a region that was a major zone of East–West conflict. We can only speculate about what the international response would have been if Iraq had invaded Kuwait during that time but I think we can rule out the possibility that the Council would have played the role it did play in 1990–1.

The main Security Council resolutions directed at Iraq (660, 678, 687, and 688) are a confirmation of the post-1945 norm that, except for self-defence, the sovereign state's right to use armed force is now exercised by international society. The most significant international involvement in Iraq after its defeat by the coalition powers was authorized by resolution 687. This broke new ground by mandating a UN supervised destruction or disabling of all biological, chemical, and nuclear weapons or facilities in Iraq. In particular, it provided a mechanism of international inspection to enforce Iraq's obligations under the Geneva Protocol for the prohibition of poisonous gases, the convention on the prohibition of biological weapons, and the treaty on the non-proliferation of nuclear weapons.[25] All five permanent members and seven non-permanent members of the Council supported the resolution. The inspection persisted for several years after the end of the battle and was intended to last until the destruction of all offending military capabilities had been carried out to the UN's satisfaction.

Resolution 687 has been characterized as 'unquestionably the most intrusive and wide-ranging array of demands made on a sovereign state since the creation of the UN in October 1945'.[26] But it was hardly surprising that the Security Council passed such a resolution. Although Iraq was defeated on the field of battle, the coalition had not invaded and occupied its territory. Not all of Iraq's offensive military capabilities were destroyed. The post-war opportunity to take control of the country, demilitarize it, and prepare it for readmission to international society as a respected member—the way the victorious Allied powers took control of Germany and Japan following their defeat in the Second World War—was not available. An alternative means of ensuring that Saddam Hussein would not present a threat to international peace and security in the future had to be created. Resolution 687 and the post-war interventionist activities carried out by UN inspectors under its authority and under the umbrella protection of coalition air power constituted those novel international means.

The UN intervention in Iraq also had humanitarian elements. Some resolutions registered little departure from traditional international practice in that regard. Resolutions 664, 666 and 674 demanded, among other things, that Iraq stop holding foreign citizens hostage and stop mistreating and oppressing

[25] P. Towle, *Enforced Disarmament* (Oxford: Clarendon Press, 1997), ch. 10.
[26] Parsons, *From Cold War to Hot Peace*, 68–9.

Kuwaiti nationals. In dealing with a state's responsibilities to citizens of foreign countries, these resolutions were consistent with customary international law regarding humanitarian issues. In that regard they did not break any new ground.

However, one resolution seemed to signal a break with past practice. In resolution 688 (also adopted after the end of the ground war) the Security Council expressed grave concern about 'the repression of the Iraqi civilian population in many parts of Iraq', demanded that Iraq 'immediately end' the repression, insisted that 'Iraq allow immediate access by international humanitarian organizations to all those in need of assistance in all parts of Iraq', and demanded, further, that Iraq cooperate with the UN Secretary-General to that end. Resolution 688 received less support than resolution 687: ten affirmative votes, with one permanent member abstaining (China). The resolution was followed by the establishment of 'safe-havens' in northern Iraq to allow hundreds of thousands of Kurds to return to Iraq and resume residence there under international protection. (Whether or not such action was authorized by resolution 688 was a matter of debate.) The Kurds had unsuccessfully revolted against Saddam Hussein at the end of the ground war, had come under attack by remnants of the Iraqi army, and had then fled into neighbouring states. That led to Operation Provide Comfort by which the USA, Britain, and France enforced 'no-fly zones' within Iraq to which Iraqi aircraft were denied access. The government of Iraq thereby lost control of a substantial segment of its territorial jurisdiction at least for the time being. Nine years after the start of the Gulf War American and British warplanes were still patrolling the skies over Iraq and periodically attacking Iraqi anti-aircraft radar and missile sites.

How should we interpret the post-war international interventions in Iraq as justified by resolutions 687 and 688? It is the normative basis of these interventions and the circumstances under which they occurred that must be investigated in seeking an answer. The main question is whether these UN resolutions and the actions carried out under their authority signal a normative change in the direction of humanitarian intervention. The role of the Security Council has not conventionally been understood as one of defending human rights. The Council's role of safeguarding international peace and security is unambiguously evident in these resolutions. Resolution 687 is preoccupied with the question of Iraq's remaining offensive weaponry in the area of chemical, biological, and nuclear warfare and it justifies post-war intervention to eliminate that remaining threat. The preamble of resolution 688 is 'mindful' of the Council's 'duties and responsibilities under the Charter of the United Nations for the maintenance of international peace and security'.

The fundamental circumstance of the intervention in Iraq was that of war: the UN and the coalition of member states that carried out its will had recently been at war with a state designated as an aggressor and thus a violator of the fundamental norm of the UN charter. By committing the crime of aggression, and thereby becoming an international outlaw, Iraq forfeited its right of non-intervention. Both the air campaign and the ground battle conducted by the coalition were waged to drive the armed forces of Iraq from Kuwait and without regard for the territorial sovereignty of Iraq if it was necessary to carry out operations in Iraqi territory in order to accomplish the UN's military objective. We should also interpret resolutions 687 and 688 as necessary and innovative interventions in lieu of the impossibility of occupying Iraq after the end of the ground war. That circumstance, which really constituted a quandary for international society, is the key for interpreting resolutions 687 and 688. If Iraq had been occupied the necessity to intervene after the battle to destroy or disable surviving Iraqi warfare capabilities and facilities would not have occurred. By the same token, if Iraq had been occupied, the humanitarian problem of protecting the Kurds would not have arisen. There consequently would have been no need for that armed humanitarian intervention. If this interpretation is valid, the international intervention in Iraq after the ceasefire was not as fundamental a departure from conventional practice as it might otherwise appear to be. It was an innovative response to the problem created by not invading and occupying Iraq.

The argument to this point can be summarized. The ending of the cold war made possible unprecedented international collaboration within the Security Council. The Gulf conflict is undoubtedly the issue on which the greatest international collaboration has occurred to date. But it fitted well with the conventional peace and security role of the Council. The international intervention in Iraq both during the armed conflict and after the ceasefire was basically an instance of responding to an act of aggression by Iraq against Kuwait, and to the threat that that posed to international peace and security. Humanitarian intervention developed within the framework of that role. It would therefore be misleading to claim that the coalition intervention in Iraq to protect the Kurds signals a fundamental normative change in international relations. That would ignore the circumstances of the case. It would also ignore the wording of resolution 688 which makes the international peace and security concern abundantly clear. There is no telling evidence from the Iraqi case to conclude that the norm of non-intervention is losing its peremptory standing in international relations or that a norm of humanitarian intervention is gaining ground at its expense.

Intervention in Somalia

In 1990–1, following the collapse of a military dictatorship, the African state of Somalia fell apart and ceased to exist in any recognizable configuration. There was no national government. Power had fallen, in several pieces, into the hands of rival warlords who held political sway over different clans and territories into which the country was divided. The clans in north-east Somalia established their own state of Somaliland, in the area of a former British Protectorate of the same name. However, it failed to secure international recognition. The rest of the country was in a condition of anarchy. That turmoil was particularly evident in the capital city, Mogadishu, where armed gangs patrolled in different districts. Somalia was also in the grip of a severe drought. Thousands of Somalis were dying and many thousands more were suffering from starvation or malnutrition and would perhaps also die if political anarchy and clan warfare continued. Although the humanitarian crisis was exacerbated by acts of nature it was primarily a consequence of political chaos. NGOs called for international intervention to prevent a famine.[27]

In December 1992 the UN Security Council authorized a military operation (resolution 794) to stop Somali warlords and armed gangs from plundering emergency food supplies and menacing NGO personnel who were attempting to distribute food to starving Somalis. It followed upon the heels of five previous resolutions passed during 1992 which failed to come to grips with the crisis. That action by the Council was in response to an offer made by President George Bush: namely that the USA would be ready, if the Security Council called upon them, to organize and command a military operation to safeguard the delivery of relief supplies in Somalia. Resolution 794 spoke of 'the magnitude of the human tragedy caused by the conflict in Somalia', noted that the international humanitarian effort was being obstructed by Somali warlords, and that there were reports of 'widespread violations of international humanitarian law', including 'violence and threats of violence against personnel participating lawfully in impartial humanitarian relief activities'. The resolution declared that the magnitude of the human crisis and the obstacles to the international relief effort constituted 'a threat to international peace and security'. The Council endorsed the Secretary-General's recommendation, in positive response to the American offer of military assistance, that action be taken under chapter VII of the UN charter 'to establish a secure environment for humanitarian relief operations in Somalia as soon as possible'.

The USA provided the largest contingent of troops for a UN intervention in Somalia that was conducted under the code-name of Operation Restore Hope; other countries contributed smaller military contingents. The intervention initially made it possible to bring an end to starvation in most parts of the country at the cost of very few deaths or injuries—either to Somalis or to UN or NGO personnel. In that important respect the intervention was a success: many thousands of Somalis were saved from starvation.

In spring 1993, however, the intervention took a more worrying turn. Fighting broke out between UN forces and armed supporters of Somali factions,

---

[27] See J. Mayall (ed.), *The New Interventionism 1991–1994* (Cambridge: Cambridge University Press, 1996), 94–124.

and in one skirmish a number of UN soldiers were killed. In response, the Security Council passed a further resolution (837) which condemned the 'unprovoked attack' and called for the arrest and punishment of those responsible. At this point the UN was taking on the difficult and questionable role of a sheriff's *posse comitatus*. American soldiers subsequently attempted to arrest the clan leader, General Aideed, who was alleged to be responsible for the attacks on UN personnel. Gun battles erupted between UN forces and armed Somalis on several different occasions. A number of non-combatant Somalis, including women and children, were killed or wounded during some of these skirmishes. A US helicopter was shot down. American and Italian soldiers were killed, and foreign journalists were attacked and lynched by a mob. These battles changed the image of Operation Restore Hope from that of a humanitarian success story to one of political and military blunder.[28] What had been achieved in forestalling the famine was in danger of being lost by this turn of events which gave the UN intervention in Somalia the more dubious character of a manhunt for General Aideed.

The international intervention in Somalia seemed to have stumbled on to a slippery slope. Questions were raised about the UN's mandate and particularly whether it extended to the business of getting directly involved in Somalia's civil wars. American politicians voiced concerns about the US national interest. Some members of Congress demanded that President Clinton—who succeeded President Bush in January 1993—withdraw US military personnel from the country. A decision to that effect was taken in October 1993. The Security Council subsequently revoked its order to arrest Somali warlords who were obstructing the UN mission. By the spring of 1994 the last American troops had gone home and the UN had reverted to its more traditional role of peacekeeping, relying on a smaller and more lightly armed multinational force to exercise its mandate.

How, then, should we interpret this international action in Somalia? Does it signal a departure from conventional practice and a movement in the direction of armed humanitarianism under UN auspices? As in the Iraq case, this is the subject of a lengthy debate which it is impossible to review here. But it is possible to look at the main normative considerations and circumstances that would have to be taken into account in order to come up with a satisfactory answer.

The intervention in Somalia conforms very awkwardly to the conventional norms stated above. Article 51 was not invoked, which indicates that no states considered themselves to be under external threat. The intervention was not solicited by anyone who could credibly claim to be the sovereign government of Somalia. No such government existed at the time. Indeed, the crisis was rooted in the absence of any effective state authority in Somalia. UN Secretary-General Boutros Boutros-Ghali justified the intervention as an international response to

---

[28] See the pointed analysis in Mayall, *New Interventionism 1991–1994*, 121–4.

a 'threat to peace' whose 'repercussions' affected the security of 'the entire region'.[29] But it is difficult, indeed it is impossible, to identify any threat to international peace and security emanating either from within Somalia or from other states in the region. There were no credible peace and security reasons for intervening in Somalia. The crisis was internal and not international. The Secretary-General's justification is thus problematic, in so far as it represents a definite stretching and twisting of the conventional norm of international security. His choice of wording and that of the Security Council in resolution 794 must presumably be understood as necessary, given the conventional international peace and security language of chapter VII of the charter. It could of course also be understood as rhetoric in all likelihood designed to mollify African states who might be alarmed at what could easily be seen by them as a new form of colonialism under UN auspices.

US President George Bush characterized Operation Restore Hope as an affirmative response by the USA and other countries to appeals by humanitarian agencies 'for outside troops to provide security so they could feed people'. He also made a point of saying to Somalis: 'We respect your sovereignty and independence.'[30] That statement could be interpreted as a commitment not to remain in the country any longer than was necessary to carry out the aims sanctioned by resolution 794, namely to establish internal security in order to bring an assured end to the famine. The security norm that was invoked by the Security Council, by President Bush, and by others, was not the conventional pluralist notion of national security or international peace and security. It was a solidarist notion of human security. US Defense Secretary Dick Cheney portrayed the intervention as 'a humanitarian mission'. The humanitarian justification is plausible and accords with the public perception of the action at the time of the intervention in December 1992, at least in Western Europe and North America. But there are no clear grounds in chapter VII of the UN charter to warrant intervention to establish internal security in a state for the purposes of alleviating a humanitarian crisis. The question therefore arises: did the Security Council set a precedent of humanitarian intervention in the Somalia case?

Some commentators emphasized the unique circumstances of the intervention, namely the fact that no Somali state existed at the time. After the cold war the UN performed what might be called a quasi-trusteeship role of rehabilitating states. That happened in regards to Namibia, Cambodia, Angola, El Salvador, Bosnia, and Kosovo. The UN established a 'Development Office for Somalia' whose mandate was the 'rehabilitation and reconstruction' of the country. At one time an international authority temporarily filled the political vacuum in Somalia: it consisted of the UN commander, a UN envoy, a US envoy, and an advisory committee of Western humanitarian NGOs. Thus not only did the UN intervene militarily in Somalia but, in effect, international society temporarily took over the

²⁹ As quoted by Roberts, 'Humanitarian War', 440.   ³⁰ As quoted ibid. 439, 441.

responsibility of governing the country until such time as the Somali state was restored. That is the fundamental circumstance in which to interrogate the intervention in Somalia. Adam Roberts points out that the chaotic conditions of Somalia are long-standing grounds for military intervention in international law if there are good prospects that order will be restored and that the state will be brought back to existence as a result of such action.[31]

The Somalia case certainly discloses more than a hint of international trustee-ship, which marks a departure from the post-colonial norm of non-intervention except with the consent of the target state. The Somali state had ceased to exist in anything but name, and international society tried to fill the vacuum. Yet no formal trusteeship was declared, or could be declared, owing not only to the political opposition that would provoke from among ex-colonial states but also owing to the legal contradiction that posed for the UN charter. Trusteeship under the UN is restricted to a transitional phase of political development from colonial status to independence (Article 77). It does not provide for trusteeships in the case of already independent countries. Indeed, it expressly forbids them (Article 78). That restricted practice is surely why the trusteeship argument was not made and could not be made to justify international intervention in Somalia. This issue is explored at greater length in Chapter 11.

There are two fundamentally conflicting views as to what the Somali case intimates about international intervention after the cold war. On the one hand, it can be argued that no clear doctrine of humanitarian intervention was invoked, that the majority of states are opposed to any such international norm, and that international society remains committed to the principle of non-intervention. A version of that view arrives at a restrictive conclusion: 'What has occurred is a subtly developing practice in special circumstances, and in which some degree of authority from the Security Council has a significant part.'[32] That implies a change of practice, but an incremental change rather than a revolutionary change. On the other hand, it can be argued that by invoking chapter VII of the charter in speaking of the necessity of 'a secure environment for humanitarian relief operations', resolution 794 established an explicit link between a human-itarian crisis and the norm of international security as a justification for inter-national intervention. As indicated, the Security Council justified the action by reference to a norm of human security and in doing that it set a precedent. A version of that view arrives at a more expansive conclusion: 'Compared to the much more restrictive interpretation of the Charter during the cold war, this is in itself a remarkable change of the norms of international society.'[33]

Clearly the language of human security is on record in the UN Security Council and that constitutes a precedent of some kind. But in view of the hasty

[31] Ibid. 440.   [32] Roberts and Kingsbury, *United Nations, Divided World*, 36.
[33] T. Knudsen, 'Humanitarian Intervention Revisited', *International Peacekeeping*, 3 (1996). Also see by the same author 'Humanitarian Intervention and International Society', Ph.D. dissertation, University of Aarhus, 1999.

exit by the USA when their troops were on the verge of falling into the snares and traps of the domestic anarchy in Somalia, it is difficult to see that experience as setting an operational precedent of humanitarian intervention that states, especially the great powers, will wish to follow. The US government clearly revealed their unwillingness to risk the lives of their soldiers exclusively for the sake of alleviating human suffering in Somalia. With only a humanitarian justification and without any clear national interest, the Americans were not prepared to take casualties, and at the first sign of resistance by armed Somalis, they withdrew. That may indicate the practical inadequacy of humanitarian justifications for military interventions that cannot also be justified by conventional norms of national security and international security. Somalia might very well be a precedent, but one that statespeople may wish to avoid in the future.

Intervention in Bosnia

Probably the most knotted, frequently the most dispiriting, but also the most instructive post-cold-war lesson of international intervention is that of Bosnia, one of the successor states of the former Yugoslavia.[34] Between 1992 and 1995 it was the site of a bitter and brutal war, in which civilians were military targets in gross violation of international humanitarian law. War had returned to Europe for the first time since 1945 and along with it a major humanitarian crisis. Thousands of people were killed, 1 million were displaced internally, and more than 1 million fled the country. The Bosnian economy declined to a third of its pre-war level. External financing for reconstruction in Bosnia was estimated at about $5 billion, which included housing reconstruction, repatriating refugees, rebuilding utilities, schools, transport, and telecommunications. What were the responsibilities of outside powers who were in a position to intervene in Bosnia and possibly alter the situation for the better—the USA, the major states of the European Community, and Russia? What light does the Bosnia experience shed on the contemporary ethics of war and intervention?

In 1991 communist Yugoslavia began to come apart when the internal republics of Slovenia and Croatia took steps towards greater political freedom from Belgrade, the logical end of which was complete separation. An EU committee, chaired by Robert Badinter, President of the French Constitutional Council, was convened to judge the validity of various claims for self-determination in Yugoslavia. It ruled that Macedonia and Slovenia fulfilled all the conditions for independence but that the recognition of Croatia and Bosnia was premature.[35] Their inquiry and recommendations were overtaken by events. In June 1991

---

[34] The correct name is Bosnia-Herzegovina, but for sake of brevity I use the shorter form.
[35] See A. Pellet, 'The Opinions of the Badinter Arbitration Committee', *European Journal of International Law*, 3 (1992), 178–85.

Croatia and Slovenia declared independence. By summer of that year ethnically homogeneous and geographically peripheral Slovenia, which borders on Austria and Italy, had broken away after a very brief war of independence. Ethnically divided and more centrally located Croatia, which borders on Serbia and Bosnia, became the scene of a far more destructive war for territory in its Slavonia and Krajina regions, where secessionist Serb minorities took up arms against the emergent Croatian state. They were evidently armed by Serbia—still known as Yugoslavia—which inherited the bulk of former Yugoslavia's large military arsenal. About a third of Croatia was taken over by Serb militias. Ethnically mixed Bosnia, whose social landscape is a complicated quilt of interwoven Muslim, Serbian (Orthodox Christian), and Croatian (Roman Catholic) areas, became the scene of a fratricidal war that was even more devastating than that in neighbouring Croatia.[36] By spring 1992 Slovenia, Croatia, Macedonia, and Bosnia had been recognized and admitted to the UN.

These post-cold-war conflicts in the Balkans provoked international involvement which quickly became extensive and resulted in a concerted attempt to come to grips with a humanitarian crisis brought on by the wars of secession in Croatia and Bosnia. In July 1991 the EU imposed a freeze on arms and aid for the former Yugoslavia. In September the UN Security Council passed resolution 713, which proclaimed a complete arms embargo and called for an immediate end to hostilities and a peaceful and negotiated settlement of the conflict. In the same month an EU peace conference declared that the borders of the successor states cannot be changed by force and that the rights of minorities must be guaranteed. Those two related issues were the heart of these conflicts. In February 1992 the Security Council authorized a UN Protection Force for Croatia to police ceasefire lines.[37] The UN, the EU, and the OSCE called for the protection of minorities in the new states. But that was not heeded by the newly independent governments of Croatia and Bosnia. And the new international boundaries were not accepted by all the ethnonations of Yugoslavia.

In August 1992 a London conference on the former Yugoslavia proclaimed that Bosnia's borders must be respected and that its territory could not be conquered or divided by force. All parties publicly subscribed to that principle but the Bosnian Serbs in particular soon disregarded it. A war for territory was launched in various regions of Bosnia by local Serbian militias who had no intention of settling down within an independent multi-ethnic Bosnian state. Croatian militias also got involved in what eventually became a three-way fight, the implication of which was the forcible partition of the country along religious-national

[36] In former Yugoslavia 'ethnicity' is based on religious differences that have become secularized and politicized: the three 'ethnic groups' are Muslims, Croats (Catholics), and Serbs (Orthodox). Bosnia is a multi-ethnic state in this meaning. All of the people speak the same Slavic language, Serbo-Croat.

[37] See Alan James, 'The UN in Croatia: An Exercise in Futility?', *The World Today* (May 1993), 93–6.

lines. Each side employed armed force to evict members of other ethnic groups from certain sought-after territories by a notorious practice of ethnic cleansing which had the aim of creating homogeneous ethnic states in the former Yugoslavia but had the effect of fostering massive human rights violations and a refugee crisis of major proportions. The Bosnian Serbs were the big winners in this anti-humanitarian campaign and grabbed the lion's share of territory; the Bosnian government and local Croat militias ended up with smaller shares. The government-controlled area was an awkward archipelago of small territories bounded by and sometimes surrounded by Serb or (in a few cases) Croat areas.

A second UN protection force was authorized by the Security Council but in Bosnia, unlike Croatia, there was no ceasefire and hence no peace to monitor. Peacekeepers instead became involved in a humanitarian relief operation to aid the civilian population whose daily lives were severely disrupted by the war, to the point of near-starvation in some cases. A major UN humanitarian force was on the ground in war zones around the country and NATO provided fighter aircraft to patrol air exclusion zones. The Security Council responded to the humanitarian crisis by enacting various resolutions, including resolution 824 which declared that certain towns and cities constituted 'safe areas', and resolution 827, which established an international war crimes tribunal to prosecute persons responsible for grave breaches of humanitarian law in former Yugoslavia. By 1994 there were some indications that the war was winding down. But there was as yet no peace. Although armed combat was in some places being conducted at lower levels of intensity the slaughter of civilians was continuing.

Various plans were proposed by the UN and the EU to end the Bosnian war and provide an enduring constitutional basis for the survival of Bosnia as an independent state. In early 1993 a complex plan provided for the reorganization of Bosnia-Herzegovina into ten semi-independent provinces with a decentralized constitution. It failed to secure agreement from the warring parties. In June of that year, agreement was reached on a plan that divided the country into three separate territories legally joined within a loose federal framework. But the fighting continued and it came to nothing. In summer 1994 the Bosnian Serbs rejected a proposed plan to divide Bosnia-Herzegovina on a basis of 51–49 per cent between a joint Muslim–Croat territory and a Serb territory. As time went on it appeared increasingly likely that the conflict would only be ended when the belligerents came to an agreement that involved the partition of Bosnia. The time would presumably come, whether sooner or later it was impossible to say, when all the warring parties would calculate that they had achieved about all that they were likely to achieve by military means. When that happened they would presumably be prepared to make a lasting deal at the conference table. That was the standard scenario of realist analysis at the time.

However, events took a different course and were increasingly determined by international society and its major powers, particularly the USA. In 1995 a transformation from UN peacekeeping to NATO peace enforcement in Bosnia became evident. NATO indicated they were prepared to use air power to enforce a 20 kilometre artillery exclusion zone around Sarajevo. International determination to employ force was provoked by a Serb mortar shell deliberately fired into a crowded Sarajevo market, which resulted in many civilian deaths. Bosnian Serbs threatened UN personnel and at one point several peacekeepers were held hostage and humiliated. In effect, the Serbian warlords were treating the UN Security Council with contempt. France and Britain secured UN authorization to deploy a Rapid Reaction Force, consisting of their own infantry, to protect peacekeeping troops in Bosnia. It was not part of UN peacekeeping operations. That turn of events seemed to indicate that those who had been calling for military intervention to deter the armed secessionists were right all along. Determination to move in that direction was rekindled in the summer of 1995 when UN-designated 'safe areas' were attacked with impunity by Bosnian Serb militias and the male Muslim populations were rounded up and murdered. That severely challenged the authority of the UN, which had guaranteed the safety of civilians in those zones. It also underlined the military infirmity of UN peacekeepers in Bosnia, who were incapable of enforcing Security Council resolutions. Finally, in August the Croatian army liberated the Serb-occupied Krajina region of Croatia in a dramatic military move which had the effect of eroding Serb military credibility. It also involved massive ethnic cleansing of ethnic Serbs by the Croatian army, to which NATO turned a blind eye. That would later be pointed out by NATO's critics when it was justifying its military intervention in Kosovo on the grounds that it was trying to prevent the Yugoslav army from cleansing the province of its Albanian majority population.

The final transformation of the Bosnian quandary from UN peacekeeping to NATO peace-enforcement was signalled when the USA, after several years of vacillation, began to employ its prestige and power to get the belligerents to enter serious negotiations for peace. The US government made it clear that any settlement had to be based on the non-intervention *Grundnorm* of international society: there could be no partition of the Bosnian state; minorities would have to be protected, and the Muslims, Serbs, and Croats in Bosnia would have to commit themselves to a constitutional settlement which accepted those conditions. The American involvement proved persuasive when the US government indicated its willingness to contribute the main contingents of a major NATO ground force that would be sent to Bosnia to enforce a peace agreement. That altered the situation by changing the political and military calculations of the warring parties about how much they stood to gain or lose by continuing the war. Not only the Serb militias and the Bosnian government but also the governments of Croatia and Serbia were persuaded to commit themselves to an American-brokered negotiated settlement.

The General Framework Agreement for Peace in Bosnia and Herzegovina (Dayton Agreement) was signed in December 1995 by the presidents of the

Republic of Bosnia and Herzegovina, the Republic of Croatia, and the Federal Republic of Yugoslavia (Serbia). It bound the parties to 'conduct their relations in accordance with the principles set forth in the United Nations Charter, as well as the Helsinki Final Act and other documents of the Organization for Security and Cooperation in Europe'. It committed the signatories to 'fully respect the sovereign equality' of each other, to 'settle disputes by peaceful means', and to 'refrain from any action, by threat or use of force or otherwise, against the territorial integrity or political independence of Bosnia and Herzegovina or any other State'. It also committed them to 'comply fully' with provisions concerning human rights and particularly 'the protection of refugees and displaced persons'. It bound the Federal Republic of Yugoslavia and the Republic of Bosnia and Herzegovina to 'recognize each other as sovereign independent States within their international borders'. The agreement provided a novel framework for the maintenance of a unified and independent Bosnia awkwardly consisting of two 'entities' which were separately administered: the Muslim–Croat Federation of Bosnia and Herzegovina with 51 per cent of the territory, and the Republika Srpska with 49 per cent. They clearly are not sovereign states, but what they are was not made clear. The Dayton Accords also set out international responsibilities to ensure that the peace would succeed, including a most important provision that NATO would back the agreement by providing an Implementation Force (IFOR) initially composed of some 60,000 troops under a US commander, including an all-important US contingent of some 20,000 troops and also Russian troops. This unprecedented peace enforcement by NATO brought the conflict in Bosnia to an end at least for the time being.

How should we interpret the international response to the crisis in Bosnia? Does it signal a break with existing practice? The international intervention in Bosnia reflected a concern for international order and disclosed the prudential ethics of statecraft. The major powers were prepared to intervene in Bosnia's right of self-defence by imposing an arms embargo if that was necessary to preserve international peace and security. The principle of consent was also evident, although less important in so far as Bosnia had little choice but to accept the UN intervention even if that curtailed or compromised their freedom to defend themselves against the Serb secessionists and their backers in Belgrade. The international involvement in Bosnia did not indicate moral indifference or a lack of humanitarian concern on the part of the statespeople who were in a position to do something. Nor did it indicate the easiest choice in the circumstances, which would have been to stand aside and do nothing at all. It indicated anguish and frustration concerning what, if anything, could be done about the human suffering the conflict was producing. It initially reflected an absence of confidence that armed intervention could successfully deal with the problem; indeed, the principal Western military powers feared that intervention would cause an even greater loss of life to the civilian population of Bosnia as well as their own forces. But it later revealed an altered assessment of the risks disclosed by a shift from UN peacekeeping to NATO peace enforcement. That development in international intervention has no clear precedent. It would, however, be a compelling precedent for NATO policy in Kosovo.

Prior to the Dayton Agreement two opposed arguments took shape in the course of a protracted debate over the question of military intervention in Bosnia. That debate can only be summarized briefly. From one side, arguing against intervention, it was claimed that the conflict was essentially a civil war and that there were no grounds in international law for armed intervention in such conflicts. Bosnia was a quagmire: if military intervention were launched it would get bogged down with no prospects of succeeding, it would involve heavy casualties to civilians as well as soldiers, and it would be difficult to withdraw. The consequences of military intervention were incalculable. The UN Secretariat, no doubt reflecting the concerns of the countries contributing the peacekeeping troops, feared that their military and civilian personnel would become targets of the warring factions the moment armed intervention was launched. It might even lead to a general war in the Balkans, which was something that everybody wanted to avoid. International involvement must be confined to humanitarian assistance.

This can be recognized as a classical realist argument, which expresses the primacy of prudential ethics modified by a secondary and definitely circumscribed humanitarian concern. Non-combatants in Bosnia were an object of genuine moral concern, but the foremost normative consideration was the traditional responsibility of stateleaders for the well-being of their own people, including, in this case, their soldiers and civilians serving in Bosnia under the UN flag. Those leaders could not responsibly protect Bosnian non-combatants and thus prevent suffering if they unduly put their own people in harm's way; the most those leaders could responsibly do was provide humanitarian assistance and try to persuade the warring parties to settle their disagreements around the peace table. The Bosnian government was sovereign and bore the responsibility of protecting its people; it could not expect other countries to take moral risks with their own peoples' lives to guarantee its independence. But the Bosnian government could legitimately be denied access to military arms and equipment if there was good reason to believe that would discourage the intensification of the conflict and its extension to other parts of the Balkans, some parts of which—Kosovo, for example—were tinder dry and waiting to explode. If it came down to a hard choice between Bosnia's right of self-defence and the risk of a wider and more dangerous war, the responsible choice was clear: keep that risk to a minimum even if it necessitated interference with Bosnia's inherent right of self-defence.

From the other side, arguing for military intervention, it was noted that Bosnia was an independent state recognized as such by the United Nations. There was a government in Sarajevo which attempted to speak for a multiethnic Bosnia against both Serbian and Croatian secessionists. The conflict was not a civil war at all. The former Yugoslavia no longer existed. Bosnia was a victim of aggression by Serbian militias and, to a lesser extent, Croatian militias, who were bent on partitioning the country and transferring the conquered and ethnically cleansed territory to their parent states, either Serbia or Croatia, who were instigating and materially supporting the enforced partition of the country. Furthermore, the international community had already intervened massively by imposing an arms embargo which put the Bosnian government at an enormous military disadvantage since Serbian militias were supplied with weapons from the well-stocked armouries of the Yugoslav national army and Croatian militias were able to get arms from Croatia. The embargo was an obvious denial of Bosnia's fundamental right of self-defence and only helped the Serbs and, to a lesser extent the Croats, to seize territory by force—which itself violated one of the most fundamental principles that international society was trying to uphold in Bosnia. It was a profound injustice to the Bosnian government for the UN to assume a position of neutrality in relation to the warring parties: the Bosnians were the victims and the other parties, particularly the Serbs, were the aggressors. If the safety of UN personnel was an overriding concern it could be addressed simply by evacuating them from the country. The Bosnian government should then be supplied with arms so that it could defend itself, which it had every right to do under international law.

The second argument expressed an international ethic in which the UN and the major powers were being called to task for their injustice against the government of Bosnia, which was a victim of armed intervention by Serbia and Croatia in violation of the UN charter. Bosnia's right of self-defence was being interfered with unlawfully. Bosnian civilians were victims of horrible crimes in violation of international humanitarian law. One experienced commentator noted the unfortunate contrast between 'the square jawed firmness of the rhetoric of Security Council resolutions' and 'the unwillingness to translate this torrent of words into action on the ground'.[38] In condemning the severe military handicaps imposed on Bosnia and underlining the faint-heartedness of the Council in failing to back its words with action, this argument invoked a more expansive conception of international responsibility.

Stateleaders who were in a position to affect the course of events in Bosnia—the leaders of the USA, Britain, France, and (more ambiguously) Russia—were presented with what boiled down to three possible courses of action. Two are normatively straightforward even if still highly controversial: absolute non-intervention in which responsibility for events would be in the hands of Bosnian, Serbian, and Croatian parties to the conflict; or full-scale military intervention in which the international community and particularly its major powers would assume a heavy responsibility for events. To follow the first course would be to abandon international responsibility for events in the Balkans, but to follow the second course would be to disregard prudential considerations.

[38] Parsons, *From Cold War to Hot Peace*, 242.

The path that was taken from 1992 until NATO was authorized to intervene in late 1995, under the terms of the Dayton Agreement, was a normatively equivocal third way which sought to respond to the humanitarian crisis and to bring the war to a negotiated settlement, yet which also deprived the state of Bosnia of many of its rights of sovereignty, particularly the right of self-defence, but stopped short of taking on responsibility for the adverse consequences of those interventionist actions. The normative difficulty of this middle course derived from the fact that it had unintended consequences adverse to its humanitarian goals which the intervening parties could not come to grips with because of the circumscribed nature of their intervention. In effect the United Nations, and the major powers in particular, seemed to be rewarding the aggressors and punishing the victims.

The following are a few instances of this predicament. The creation of safe-areas provided temporary sanctuaries for some Bosnian Muslim civilians but it also played into the hands of Serb policies of 'ethnic cleansing' and disarming Bosnian forces—the latter being a Serbian condition for allowing safe-areas to be set up by the UN. In many safe-areas not only the civilians but also the UN troops protecting them were in effect hostages to surrounding Serb forces. The pursuit of a negotiated settlement by the international community without an effective threat of military action made it possible for the Serbs to play for time in the negotiations while continuing to conquer territory and commit human rights violations with impunity. By treating the Bosnian government as equally responsible for the war along with the Serbian and Croatian militias it obscured the distinction between the aggressors and the victims. By calling upon all parties to negotiate, it in effect asked the victims to capitulate to the political dismemberment of their state. By showing no resolve to intervene with force until very late in the day, international society deprived their negotiators of the most effective tool to secure negotiations in good faith by the stronger party and their best chance to achieve if not a just peace then at least a settlement that would be tolerable to the weaker party. By threatening military intervention but failing to be credible in their threats, until very late in the day after many casualties and much damage had already been inflicted, international society seemed only to discredit itself and embolden the war-makers. The UN claimed to be neutral in Bosnia, but unfortunately the consequences of their actions were not and arguably could not be neutral at all.

Yet if we take on board the discipline of imagining ourselves in the shoes of the stateleaders who were confronted with the problem of Bosnia, it is not difficult to understand why the ambiguous middle course was selected, perhaps backed into, and stayed with for three years in spite of these criticisms: it is the response that one would expect from any responsible stateleader who had a genuine desire to do something of moral value but solid prudential reasons to stay out. Non-intervention would involve disregarding the human rights and humanitarian needs of the Bosnian people, but full military intervention would involve taking risks that might conceivably result in even greater human suffering all round. British, French, and American leaders who were in the best position to intervene militarily were the least inclined to do so. Other leaders who were more inclined to call for military intervention were not in the same position of responsibility. That included leaders of countries whose own troops would not be called upon to intervene; it also included opposition politicians of countries that had supplied civilian and military personnel but who would not have to accept responsibility if things went badly wrong. German leaders were more inclined than their British or French counterparts to support military intervention; presidential candidate Clinton was more inclined to do the same than President Clinton; members of opposition parties in the British Parliament were more favourably disposed to such action than members of the governing party.

That suggests that the ethics of statecraft on such a difficult issue must be determined by those wearing the shoes. It is not that stateleaders have deeper moral insight into such issues: they are no better equipped than most other people in that regard. It is rather that they are the ones who are saddled with the responsibility for taking the decisions and being in that position they are likely to err on the side of caution and to avoid taking unnecessary risks. Not being in the same moral position, leaders of minor powers without personnel on the ground, opposition leaders, and members of the general public are at liberty to have a more expansive or a more restricted conception of international responsibility, as the case may be. In the Bosnian case they were the ones who were more likely to urge upon governments either massive military intervention or strict non-involvement, the first two courses of action identified above. These are the policies that people without any responsibility for events might be expected to urge on those with the responsibility. But the leaders of the major powers involved in the episode enjoyed no such liberty. They had to take the moral risks involved: to make the decision, whatever it was, and live with the consequences.

With the advantage of hindsight it is easy to place the responsibility for a great deal of human suffering in Bosnia at the feet of the major Western governments and especially the President of the United States and the foreign-policy leadership in the US Congress. They recognized the new successor states of the former Yugoslavia and thus took some responsibility for their independence. Yet they failed to defend the sovereign rights of Croatia and Bosnia and the human rights of the people who lived there. For three years they hesitated to act decisively. 'If there is a lesson of the past five years, it is that half-hearted, or timorous, Western intervention in Bosnia achieved little.'[39] Another version of the same critique is the following: 'The international community had a choice between shutting up or putting up. It tried to do both and achieved neither.'[40]

---

[39] *The Economist* (19–25 July 1997), 16.   [40] Parsons, *From Cold War to Hot Peace*, 243.

There is more than a grain of validity in these criticisms, because there is no question that, in regard to Bosnia, the major Western powers talked tough but for three years displayed anxiety, apprehension, and indecisiveness. During that time by far the worse humanitarian crisis in Europe since 1945 was produced, mostly by the human rights violations of the Serbs.

But if we read the situation that way, historically backwards as it were, we would be ignoring the moral force of the arguments against armed humanitarianism, summarized above, which undoubtedly weighed heavily on the key decision-makers at the time. In effect, we would be ignoring the circumstances, which seemed extremely difficult to the statespeople who were in a position to act. The fact that circumstances later proved to be less difficult than originally feared, and the Serbs were discovered not to be the danger they pretended to be, is a comment on the perceptions and judgements of the statespeople who were responsible at the time. With the advantages of hindsight it is clear they misread and misjudged the situation. However the question still remains: if we were in their situation, knowing what they knew at the time and believing what most responsible statespeople then believed, would we have acted differently?

Humanitarian War: Kosovo

A humanitarian crisis in Kosovo that had long been anticipated by many Balkan political observers accelerated in 1998 and exploded in March 1999 when NATO attacked Yugoslavia with air power. Operation Allied Force was a milestone: the first time in NATO's fifty-year history that it had gone to war, and primarily for a humanitarian cause rather than a defensive or security reason. NATO's intervention began several months earlier at a peace conference at Rambouillet, outside Paris, where it dictated terms affecting Yugoslavia's sovereignty which the government in Belgrade was obliged to accept, or suffer the military consequences.

International intervention in Bosnia had the consent of the newly independent Bosnian government, whose sovereignty was challenged by armed Serb and Croat secessionists. But international intervention in Kosovo was denied consent by the sovereign government of Yugoslavia, which was similarly challenged by armed Albanian secessionists. NATO's eventual intervention in Bosnia, after several years of vacillation, was to enforce an international agreement between the belligerent parties designed to preserve the Bosnian state, and protect human rights. NATO's intervention in Kosovo was to save the Kosovo Albanians, at the risk of partitioning the Yugoslav state. The Kosovo intervention trespassed on basic norms of the UN charter and took place without a mandate from the UN Security Council. The primary justification for NATO's intervention— in the crisp language of the British Foreign Office—was 'overwhelming humanitarian necessity'.[41] NATO is described as having had a 'sense of shame' stemming from their four years of anxiety, indecisiveness, and inaction in Bosnia.[42] NATO states were concerned about the organization's credibility. Moreover, NATO's intervention in Kosovo was targeted against the government: the USA, Britain, and some other NATO countries clearly wanted to get rid of the government of Slobodan Milosevic.[43] They explicitly said they were not attacking the Serbian people.

Kosovo had long been part of the Ottoman Empire when it was conquered by Serbia in 1912. That right of conquest was confirmed by the League of Nations at the end of the First World War by the inclusion of Kosovo in the new state of Yugoslavia. Kosovo was never a self-governing republic within the Yugoslav Federation—unlike Slovenia, Croatia, Macedonia, and Bosnia. Instead, it remained part of the Serbian republic. Kosovo acquired a measure of self-administration within Serbia under the 1974 Yugoslav Federal Constitution which defined it as 'a composite part of the Socialist Republic of Serbia'. Kosovo's limited political devolution within Serbia was taken away by Yugoslav President Milosevic in 1989 and direct rule from Belgrade was imposed. Kosovo was recognized as an integral part of the Federal Republic of Yugoslavia (that is, Serbia) by the European Union after the former and larger Yugoslavia fell apart in 1991–2. The 1995 Dayton Accords upheld the sovereignty and territorial integrity not only of Croatia and Bosnia but also that of Serbia.

The province became a cockpit of Albanian secessionism, government repression, and increasing civil war in the late 1990s, accompanied by a growing exodus of ethnic Albanian refugees from Kosovo. In 1998 the Kosovo Liberation Army (KLA) mounted an offensive against the Yugoslav army and police. It was met with a military response and reprisals against Kosovo Albanians suspected of supporting the KLA. Serbian paramilitaries got involved to defend Serb villages from the KLA, and to terrorize Kosovo Albanian villagers. Fearing that the civil war might spread into neighbouring states and that the refugee crisis might develop into a major humanitarian disaster, the UN Security Council and NATO became involved. During the course of the conflict, thousands of Kosovo Albanians were killed or maimed by Yugoslav regular or paramilitary forces. Villages were destroyed. Serb villagers, although fewer, suffered the same fate at the hands of the KLA. At the height of the crisis perhaps as many as 1.5 million Kosovo Albanians fled into the mountains or sought exile in neighbouring countries.

During 1998 the Security Council passed several resolutions on the Kosovo conflict, acting under chapter VII of the UN charter. They called upon

[41] As quoted by A. Roberts, 'NATO's "Humanitarian War" over Kosovo', *Survival*, 41 (Autumn 1999), 106.

[42] Ibid. 104.

[43] Roberts has noted that this intention is in conflict with an underlying principle of the laws of war, namely 'that the only legitimate object which States should endeavor to accomplish during war is to weaken the military forces of the enemy' (ibid. 116).

Yugoslavia to 'achieve a political solution to the issue of Kosovo through dialogue'; they also called upon Kosovo Albanian leaders 'to condemn all terrorist action' and to pursue their political goals by peaceful means. Both parties were urged to enter into 'meaningful dialogue' and 'without preconditions'. The settlement was to be based on the fundamental principle of territorial integrity of Yugoslavia and on the humanitarian standards of the OSCE and was to include a substantial 'degree of autonomy and self-administration' for Kosovo. Resolution 1199 expressed concern about 'the flow of refugees' into neighbouring countries and called upon the Yugoslav authorities and the Kosovo Albanian leaders 'to improve the humanitarian situation and to avert the impending humanitarian catastrophe'. It reiterated the requirement for a negotiated resolution of the conflict. More emphatically, it demanded that the Yugoslav authorities refrain from using their security forces for civilian repression in Kosovo. It firmly declared that the Kosovo Albanian leadership should condemn all terrorist action. It called upon the Yugoslav government to facilitate the safe return of refugees. Resolution 1203 demanded that the government of Yugoslavia 'comply fully and swiftly' with the above Security Council resolutions.

These UN demands upon the government of Yugoslavia and the Kosovo Albanian leadership were not met with a positive response. Instead, the political situation in Kosovo deteriorated throughout 1998 and into 1999. In October 1998 an agreement was reached between NATO and Yugoslavia which committed the latter to curb its use of military and police force in Kosovo and to end repression of the Albanian population. The commitment was not honoured by President Milosevic. Nor did the KLA restrict its use of violence. The civil war continued unabated. By early 1999 there was a massive forced expulsion and flight of Kosovo Albanians into neighbouring Albania, Macedonia, and Montenegro (a separately governed part of Yugoslavia).

NATO's member states became deeply concerned about the deteriorating humanitarian situation in Kosovo. In January the Yugoslav government and the Kosovo Albanian leadership were issued with a 'summons' by NATO to attend the Rambouillet peace conference which involved Russia as well as the leading NATO powers. In February a basis for a settlement of the conflict was laid down at Rambouillet which contained the following terms. First, that Kosovo should enjoy 'substantial autonomy' without violating the 'national sovereignty and territorial integrity' of Yugoslavia. Second, it should be based on democratic institutions and should ensure the protection of human rights and the rights of national minorities (that is, of Serbs) in Kosovo. Third, all Yugoslav armed forces were required to withdraw from Kosovo. Fourth, security was to be guaranteed by 30,000 international troops, including a core component of NATO forces, deployed on the ground in Kosovo. Lastly, an international conference was to be convened three years after the agreement went into effect to determine a basis for a final settlement of the conflict which would reflect 'the will of the people' of Kosovo (not Yugoslavia). If the parties failed to reach agreement on these terms NATO declared itself 'ready to take whatever measures are necessary' to secure 'compliance with the demands of the international community and the achievement of a political settlement'.[44] That clearly was an ultimatum.

The Rambouillet dictate was accepted by the Kosovo Albanian leaders most of whom were seeking political independence. However, President Milosevic refused to comply arguing that it infringed Yugoslavia's sovereignty by demanding that Yugoslav forces vacate Kosovo and be replaced by an international force run by NATO. The Yugoslav government also pointed out that the requirement that the final settlement should reflect the will of the Kosovo people was not only in conflict with the rival principle of territorial integrity of Yugoslavia but it also seemed to prejudge the political resolution of the dispute in favour of Kosovo independence. Richard Holbrooke, the American diplomat who brokered the Dayton Agreement, made a final attempt to arrange a diplomatic settlement but he failed to move Milosevic from his position.

NATO made good on their threat by launching an air war against Yugoslavia on 24 March 1999. The NATO political and military leadership believed that the 'degrading' of Yugoslavia's armed forces and infrastructure would oblige President Milosevic to accept NATO's terms. They clearly expected the Yugoslav dictator to capitulate quickly in the face of NATO bombing. That proved to be unrealistically optimistic. President Milosevic kept waiting for NATO to fall apart, but that did not happen either. He only came to terms in early June after weeks of increasingly heavy air bombardment that eventually involved over 900 warplanes, over 14,000 strike missions, and resulted, according to NATO's estimates, in the death of 5,000 Yugoslav combatants and 1,200 civilians. It also reportedly caused 'enormous damage' to the roads, bridges, and industry of Yugoslavia.[45] The EU estimated the cost for reconstructing Kosovo at between $2 billion and $3.5 billion.

The general terms of the peace were based on principles agreed by members of the G-7 leading industrial nations plus Russia. The agreement was confirmed and sanctioned by UN Security Council resolution 1244 (1999) which was passed by a vote of 14 to 0, with 1 abstention (China). The terms were substantially the same as those of Rambouillet which the Yugoslav government had previously rejected: an immediate end of violence and repression in Kosovo, verified withdrawal of all Serb military forces from Kosovo, deployment in Kosovo of an international security presence under the authority of chapter VII of the UN charter, safe and free (that is, uncoerced) return of all refugees and displaced persons, establishment of an interim UN civil administration that would lead to a form of Kosovo provincial government within a federal Yugoslavia, and demilitarization of the KLA. Resolution 1244 authorized deployment into Kosovo of a heavily armed international security force (KFOR) of some 50,000

---

[44] *NATO Press Release* (30 Jan. 1999).
[45] S. Myers, as quoted by Roberts, 'NATO's "Humanitarian War" over Kosovo', 119.

troops who were allowed to defend themselves and to use 'all the necessary means'—including military force—to carry out their responsibilities. NATO was the main component and a NATO general was in command. Russia provided a troop contingent and it was expected that their military relationship to NATO would be based on a co-operative model similar to the one used in Bosnia. The UN Security Council also 'demanded full cooperation by all concerned, including the international security presence, with the International Criminal Tribunal for the Former Yugoslavia'. Finally, it reaffirmed 'commitment of all member States to the sovereignty and territorial integrity of the Federal Republic of Yugoslavia and the other States of the region, as set out in the Helsinki Final Act'.

The NATO powers clearly saw these terms as a vindication of their intervention by guaranteeing the safe return of the refugees and restoring Kosovo autonomy within Yugoslavia. The Yugoslav government and the Russians saw them in a rather different light: as confirming the sovereignty and territorial integrity of Yugoslavia and the superior and supervisory role of the UN.

The unleashing of armed force is the most perilous international activity that states or alliances or international society as a whole can engage in. It is obviously dangerous: there is always a very real possibility that it can make things worse. It is highly provocative and thus calls for justifications of a fundamental kind. That was manifestly the case with NATO's bombing of Yugoslavia.[46] President Clinton declared: 'We are upholding our values, protecting our interests, and advancing the cause of peace.' He also said the Kosovo crisis was a 'genocide in the heart of Europe' that was 'testing our humanity'. People are being 'slaughtered at NATO's doorstep'; we are 'preventing another holocaust'. He remarked that 'in Bosnia we failed to act in time, we left it too late' and that mistake was not going to be repeated in Kosovo: there are 'great dangers of not acting now'; 'inaction invites brutality' but 'firmness saves lives'. Finally, he said, 'we need a Europe that shares our values'; the USA was defending 'a peaceful, united, democratic Europe'. The implication is clear: dictatorships and abusive governments had no place in Europe and were to be stamped out. Europe was defined as a region of democracies which respected human rights.

Other major Western leaders echoed and amplified President Clinton's comments.[47] NATO Secretary-General Javier Solano said 'NATO is not waging war against the Yugoslav people' but against the brutal regime of President Milosevic. The Yugoslav government was portrayed as an outlaw regime, but the Yugoslav people were seen as tools and victims of Milosevic. The German Chancellor Gerhard Schröder declared the air strikes were 'not aimed at the Serbian people' and the NATO allies 'will do all they can to avoid loss of civilian lives'. The German Foreign Minister Joschka Fischer said, 'This is about preventing a human catastrophe.' French President Jacques Chirac claimed the

---

[46] *BBC News Online Network* (27 Mar. 1999).   [47] Ibid.

air attacks were launched to defend 'peace on our soil, peace in Europe'. British Prime Minister Tony Blair asserted: 'Barbarity cannot be allowed to defeat justice.' The NATO action was necessary 'to curb Milosevic's ability to wage war on an innocent population'. The British Defense Secretary said, 'the international community is not prepared to stand idly by and witness a human crime perpetrated by Milosevic'. The British Foreign Secretary, Robin Cook, noted that 'we have tried repeatedly—right up to the last minute—to find a way to halt the repression of Kosovo Albanians through negotiation . . . We were left with no other way of preventing the present humanitarian crisis from becoming a catastrophe, than by taking military action to limit the capacity of Milosevic's army to repress the Kosovo Albanians.' Japanese Foreign Minister Masahiko Komura was careful to point out that 'Japan understands NATO's use of force as measures that had to be taken to prevent humanitarian catastrophe.' The humanitarian tenor of most of these remarks is clear.

That was not so with the condemnations of the action not only by Yugoslavia but also by Russia and China, whose opposition indicated the Security Council was deeply divided on the issue of Kosovo. That was a worrying departure from the post-cold-war cases discussed above, all of which rested on great power unity at the most crucial moments. The Yugoslav government repeatedly condemned NATO for committing an act of aggression against its sovereign territory and the Yugoslav people. It was NATO and not Yugoslavia that was violating the most fundamental norms of international society. Russian President Boris Yeltsin expressed the same concerns: 'Russia is deeply upset by NATO's military action against sovereign Yugoslavia, which is nothing less than open aggression.' Russia's UN Ambassador said it was a 'dangerous precedent' for NATO to assume the role of a 'world gendarme' and to disrespect the basic norms of the UN charter. Russia's Ambassador to London pointed out 'that breaking international law leads to catastrophes . . . Nothing in the UN charter or the North Atlantic treaty can justify taking military action against the sovereign state of Yugoslavia.' He said that NATO attacks were a dangerous precedent because they were 'a signal to the nationalistic elements all around Europe that they can have their way and destroy the existing state'. Chinese President Jiang Zemin called 'for an immediate halt to the air strikes and a return to the search for a political solution to the Kosovo problem through peace negotiations'. The Chinese criticisms became more pointed and severe after NATO bombed their embassy in Belgrade by mistake. The tenor of most of these remarks are clearly concerned with traditional international law and the most fundamental values of the UN charter: national sovereignty, territorial integrity, and international peace and security.

Perhaps the most penetrating critique of NATO was that of former Russian Prime Minister Victor Chernomyrdin. He became involved as one of three principal envoys who were charged with attempting to broker an agreement between NATO and Yugoslavia and he participated in the final settlement of the conflict. But in a major newspaper essay while the bombing was still taking place he complained that NATO's aim was to secure 'Milosevic's capitulation' and 'the establishment of a *de facto* NATO protectorate over Kosovo.' He said 'these NATO goals run counter to Russia's stance, which calls for the introduction of United Nations forces into Kosovo with Yugoslavia's sovereignty and territorial integrity intact.'

The new NATO strategy, the first practical instance of which we are witnessing in Yugoslavia, has led to a serious deterioration in Russian–US contacts . . . because a sovereign country is being bombed . . . This approach clashes with international law, the Helsinki agreements and the world order that took shape after world war II.

He ended his remarks by warning that NATO was 'headed for a Pyrrhic victory, whether the conflict ends with the Serbs capitulating or in an invasion of Yugoslavia'.[48]

The Russians and the Chinese were concerned that NATO was setting a precedent of intervention that would make states with national minorities vulnerable to secession movements. Yugoslavia was fighting a civil war against an armed insurgency. But NATO's action was increasing the likelihood that Kosovo would be carved out of Yugoslavia, thereby setting a terrible precedent of sanctioning ethnic secessionism in multi-ethnic states, which was a standing danger to the states system. Russia saw NATO's action as a threat to its own domestic stability. Foreign Minister Ivanov said NATO's attempt to 'tear Kosovo out of Yugoslavia' jeopardized Russia's relations with its own Islamic minorities in the Caucasus region and elsewhere. China was also vulnerable to secessionism in Taiwan and Tibet. That anti-secessionist view is undoubtedly very widely held among UN member states many of which have at least potential minority problems.

Critics of NATO's intervention, including among them former leading Western statesmen, invoked the closely connected language of prudence and international order. Henry Kissinger echoed the remarks of Victor Chernomyrdin by pointing out to the readership of a popular American weekly newsmagazine that NATO's intervention was gambling with international order by provoking 'an outraged sense of humiliation' among Russians that 'threatened to blight US–Russian relations for years to come'.[49] It was also damaging American–Chinese relations. Dennis Healey, a former British Defence Secretary, expressed the same concern: 'We risk our relations with Russia and China and this could produce consequences for the whole of the world far worse than what is happening in Kosovo.' The implications of these remarks are clear. Russia and China are of much greater importance to NATO and the West than the domestic politics of a small Balkan state. Dividing the great powers, or even risking that division, is always the most dangerous policy. There is a basic

---

[48] *International Herald Tribune* (28 May 1999).
[49] Henry A. Kissinger, 'New World Disorder', *Newsweek* (31 May 1999).

responsibility not to split the great powers into antagonistic camps if it can be avoided. Even actions that risk dividing them require compelling justification.

Some of these critics also said it was a terrible mistake to launch military action without first securing a mandate from the Security Council. The veto is a 'reserve power' of the permanent members of the Security Council which rests on the principle of prudence and exists exclusively to preserve international order.[50] To bypass the Council in order to avoid a veto would be to trample upon the constitution of international society at its most important point. The veto is a legal recognition that armed intervention by international society must rest on a great power consensus. Otherwise it undermines international order and could prove to be dangerous. According to this way of thinking, diplomacy is always preferable to force if there is a choice of means and methods. Former American President Jimmy Carter criticized the Clinton government for committing a major blunder in its Kosovo policy which had led to a quagmire:

Washington has become increasingly inclined to side-step the time-tested premises of negotiation, which in most cases prevent deterioration of a bad situation and at least offer the prospect of a bloodless solution . . . the [NATO] decision to attack the entire nation has been counterproductive, and the destruction of civilian life has now become senseless and excessively brutal . . . Washington has . . . short-circuited the long-established principles of patient negotiation . . . by-passing the Security Council . . . Even for the world's only superpower, the ends don't always justify the means.

Another concern of those who opposed the NATO intervention, or were sceptical about its wisdom and worried about its consequences, was the fear that it would result in the creation of a second NATO protectorate in the Balkans.[51] Kosovo would join Bosnia as two protected territories where final responsibility for security, and probably also for local administration and policing, physical reconstruction, and future state-building, would ultimately rest with the USA and its major European allies. And since the Kosovo protectorate would have been imposed by NATO's military power it would be difficult to distinguish from colonial protectorates of an earlier era installed by gun-boat diplomacy. That would be the view of many states in Asia and Africa which had previously been Western colonies. Was NATO's military actions in the Balkans signalling a return to an era when Western values were imposed on obstinate governments by force?

According to the UN charter, as indicated previously, the only valid grounds for the use of armed force (*jus ad bellum*) are self-defence and military actions taken to maintain or restore international peace and security. Although the Security Council characterized the crisis in Kosovo as a threat to international peace and security, it did not authorize the use of force against Serbia prior to

---

[50] Schwarzenberger and Brown, *A Manual of International Law*, 230.
[51] *CNN interview* (26 Mar. 1999).

NATO's military action. NATO members of the Security Council did not try to obtain such a resolution because it would have been vetoed by China and Russia. Thus, NATO's bombing appeared to be in clear violation of the UN charter. It also seemed to go directly against NATO's own pact, the 1949 North Atlantic Treaty, which was defensive in character and portrayed aggression as the supreme international crime. Articles 1 and 7 of the Treaty bind NATO states to act within the rules of the UN charter, Articles 5 and 6 limit the use of force by NATO to defence of any member of the alliance from attack. In strict legal terms, therefore, NATO's action in bombing Serbia seemed to be in violation of the UN charter and its own treaty. That provokes the following questions. Did not NATO commit an act of aggression against the sovereign state of Yugoslavia? Does that not clarify why NATO studiously avoided describing its air campaign against Yugoslavia as a 'war'?

NATO justified its military intervention in Yugoslavia by claiming, among other things, that it was permitted under international law. The repression of the civilian Albanian population by the Serb army and police forces in Kosovo was contrary to international humanitarian law; their ethnic cleansing could also be in violation of the UN Genocide Convention. The Milosevic government defied several resolutions by the UN Security Council taken under chapter VII provisions of international peace and security which all UN member states are duty bound to obey. Yugoslavia also failed to honour an October 1998 agreement with NATO to end its repressive use of armed force against Albanian civilians in Kosovo and to scale down Yugoslav forces in the province to a level consistent with civil policing activities. Quite clearly the Milosevic regime was in breach of some of its international agreements and undertakings and was treating them with contempt. The American UN Ambassador was undoubtedly justified in arguing that the Yugoslav government was a repeat international lawbreaker: they had violated 'international humanitarian law', engaged in 'unlawful repression of Kosovars', created 'half a million refugees', put 'pressure on neighboring countries', and broken their 'international commitments'. Moreover, a draft resolution placed before the Security Council on 26 March 1999 by the Russian Federation and supported by India and Belarus, which demanded an immediate halt to NATO's bombing and called for resumption of negotiations, was defeated by 12 votes to 3.

However, that was not the same as a positive UN Security Council resolution, under chapter VII of the charter, authorizing the use of armed force against Yugoslavia. A positive resolution was not obtained. Without such a mandate it is impossible to avoid the conclusion that NATO's action in bombing Serbia was not in full conformity with established international law. Perhaps it would be more accurate to say it skirted the edge of international law without securing a full mandate. As one legal scholar put it, NATO's bombing 'flouts the traditional interpretation of the charter . . . but it is compatible with the emerging international humanitarian law that recognizes the rights of individuals to be protected from genocidal practices, torture and other gross human rights abuses'.[52]

Thus, although it can be argued that the intervention in Kosovo by NATO was justified on humanitarian grounds and also on grounds that the action was consistent with several prior UN Security Council resolutions, it is more difficult to argue that such legitimacy and legality is sufficient to override the fundamental non-intervention norm of international law without a clear and uncontested indication that the action was fully consistent with the *jus ad bellum* rules of the UN charter. Uncontestability would be indicated by a positive resolution of the Council that expressly authorized the action and escaped veto by any of the permanent members. That the NATO states later recognized and agreed to the principle that the Council should sanction the terms of the peace agreement with Yugoslavia was dictated by the Russians who were a crucial player in making any agreement with Milosevic possible at all. NATO needed the Russians to broker an agreement with Yugoslavia if they were to escape the military logic of having to conquer the country in the event that Milosevic refused to capitulate to their air power. Perhaps the Russians saw some urgency in the task of arranging a *modus vivendi*—not least for the sake of their own national economic interests. Important members of NATO, particularly Germany and France, also wanted the sanction of the Security Council. The NATO states belatedly seemed to recognize the problems and dangers of dividing the great powers and they evidently wanted to repair the damage by getting Russia back on side, even if it required, as in fact it did require, some compromise with the peace terms of the Yugoslav government. But they did not recognize that from the start. Or perhaps they recognized it but chose to ignore it. Either way their conduct raises serious concerns.

According to that way of thinking, while the Yugoslav government and President Milosevic in particular were guilty of presiding over massive human rights violations against Kosovo Albanians, Yugoslavia was still a victim of unwarranted military action in violation of its national sovereignty and territorial integrity. That, it seems to me, is an inescapable conclusion if we accept that the traditional norms of international society, particularly the fundamental norm of non-intervention and related restrictions on the use of armed force, are still the basic references for making such judgements. Whether the *jus ad bellum* is being expanded to include humanitarian and other justifications is discussed in the final section.

Even if Yugoslavia had procedural international legality on their side, President Milosevic could still be condemned for political recklessness and callousness of the worst kind. He gambled with the security and welfare of his own Serbian people, knowing full well that he could not defend them in a military conflict with a far superior adversary whose air power could penetrate every cor-

---

[52] Allan Gerson and T. G. Carpenter as quoted by *The New York Times* (27 Mar. 1999).

ner of Yugoslavia virtually at will. The people of Yugoslavia and not merely the soldiers would undoubtedly suffer if it came to an armed conflict with NATO. In other words Milosevic disregarded his fundamental national responsibility. Instead, he played a game of brinkmanship with his own people's safety and welfare. He gambled that the alliance would lose its nerve in the face of the prospect of actually having to go to war if its coercive diplomacy failed. He lost the gamble. So, in addition to inflicting terrible suffering on more than a million Kosovo civilians, Milosevic also brought down a calamity on the Serbian people.

Expanding *Jus ad Bellum*?

Does experience since the end of the cold war offer any solid evidence for the claim that in certain circumstances humanitarian considerations pre-empt sovereign rights in the justification of military intervention? As indicated at the beginning of the chapter, during most of the twentieth century the grounds of legitimate and lawful intervention in sovereign states by armed force, *jus ad bellum*, were curtailed by international society. The right of conquest was abolished. Unequal treaties and capitulations were relegated to the scrap heap of Western imperial history. Colonialism was outlawed. Protectorates and trusteeships became things of the past. All of that restriction reflected the classical liberal doctrine of international *societas*, namely, that states which mind their own business have a right to be left alone: *laissez-faire*.

But in light of some of these cases, particularly that of Kosovo, it might be argued that the normative grounds for armed international intervention are becoming less restrictive once again. Is there an emerging doctrine of justified armed intervention in world politics that moves beyond the prudential and procedural ethics of the 1945 UN settlement? Is there a new 'standard of civilization', according to which armed intervention can be justified on the grounds of defending human rights?[53] Is there a return to an era of geographical morality in which certain civilizations, such as Europe, define their own pre-emptive international norms, such as democracy, for the employment of armed force in their region? Are legitimate spheres of influence creeping back into world politics? Are internationally mandated protectorates coming back into vogue? If so, should we welcome such a change or worry about it? These issues are addressed at greater length in the next chapter. But some preliminary comments in the light of these post-cold-war interventions are necessary at this point.

[53] '. . . crimes against humanity, violations of the 1948 Genocide convention, and violations of the 1949 Geneva Conventions may all constitute grounds for intervention . . . In this perspective, it cannot be right to tolerate acts which violate widely supported legal norms just because the Charter does not explicitly provide for military action in such circumstances, or because a veto on the Security Council makes UN-authorized action impossible.' Roberts, 'NATO's "Humanitarian War" over Kosovo', 106–7.

Pluralist ethics of state sovereignty were clearly evident in all these cases. The intervention in Iraq was provoked by an act of aggression against a member state of the United Nations and the threat that posed to international peace and security. Humanitarian intervention developed within that normative context. It would therefore be misleading to claim that the coalition intervention to protect the Kurds signals a fundamental normative change in the direction of Kantian ethics. In Somalia international peace and security concerns were substantially absent. The relevant context of that intervention was the collapse of an independent state. The norm that was invoked by President Bush and by others was not the conventional pluralist notion of international peace and security. It was a cosmopolitan notion of human security. But traditional pluralist values were invoked by both the Secretary-General and the Security Council of the United Nations.

Concerns about international order were far from absent in the cases of Bosnia and Kosovo. Interference with Bosnia's right of self-defence was justified on the grounds of preserving international peace and security in the Balkans. The debate between those who gave priority to international order and those who defended Bosnia's right of self-defence was conducted within the pluralist framework of international ethics. The NATO intervention in Kosovo also involved pluralist and prudential concerns. President Clinton, Prime Minister Blair, and other NATO leaders expressed their fear that a massive exodus of Kosovo refugees might upset the social and political stability of neighbouring countries, which, in turn, could destabilize the entire Balkan region. On the other side, concern was expressed about the dangers of dividing the great powers. Critics of NATO said it was a terrible mistake to launch military action without first securing a mandate from the Security Council. There was no consensus in the Council for humanitarian intervention in Kosovo. That justification was largely confined to NATO member states who seemed to be selectively applying humanitarian values in justifying their military action. They were alarmed at ethnic cleansing by the Serbs in Kosovo but they had turned a blind eye to Croatia's ethnic cleansing of Serbs from the Krajina region of Croatia in 1995.

Pluralist norms also were strongly indicated by the unwillingness of intervening powers to take risks with the lives of their soldiers. Indeed, their interventionist policy was virtually dictated by the mandate that casualties to their own troops must be minimal or possibly must not be tolerated at all. That was an important consideration in the refusal of the leading coalition powers and particularly the USA to invade and occupy Iraq at the end of the Gulf War. The US government also refused to risk the lives of their soldiers for the sake of alleviating human suffering in Somalia. Humanitarian intervention in Somalia came to an end when the circumstances changed and the military risk increased. That case suggests that norms of humanitarian intervention can be operative internationally but only in circumstances defined as presenting low military risk.

With only a humanitarian justification and without any clear national interest in Somalia the Americans were not prepared to take casualties, and at the first sign of resistance by armed Somalis and the first loss of life to their own troops, they went home. In Bosnia armed humanitarianism became possible when it became evident that the military risks were lower than had previously been thought.

The same reluctance to take risks for humanitarian values was evident in the refusal by most of the leading NATO powers, including the USA, to invade Kosovo with ground troops. In Kosovo the safety of NATO's troops dictated an air campaign to compel the Yugoslav government to come to terms. The exclusive use of air power led to the morally questionable decision to deliberately put civilians on the ground at risk to reduce the risk to pilots in the air. As it turned out, civilians were in far greater danger than the air crews who carried out the bombing from high altitude which sacrificed precision for air-crew safety. No NATO fliers were killed but an estimated 1,200 civilians died as a result of collateral damage or mistaken targeting. All the cases disclosed a humanitarian concern on the part of international society, but military risk and particularly the danger of casualties to intervention soldiers were the crucial consideration. That suggests the practical inadequacy of humanitarian justifications for military interventions that cannot also be justified by conventional norms of national security and international order. Countries that champion humanitarian values, such as the USA, are unwilling to risk the lives of their soldiers to defend human rights.

This is not to imply that humanitarianism and human rights were empty rhetoric or hollow values in any of these episodes. They were significant normative considerations for the principal players involved. But it would be a mistake to conclude from these cases that solidarism is pre-empting pluralism in international ethics. Rather, they indicate that humanitarianism can be pursued within the pluralist framework of international society at least up to a point. The ethics of human rights have to be fitted into the pluralist framework of international society and cannot sidestep that framework. That is the only operational context within which human beings can be defended in contemporary world politics. Human rights and humanitarian action have no actuality outside that pluralist framework. Solidarism is clearly subordinate to pluralism.

In attacking Yugoslavia NATO side stepped the Security Council and the UN doctrine of non-intervention and justified its action primarily on humanitarian grounds. But the Kosovo conflict was also portrayed by Western leaders as a conflict between democracy and dictatorship. In a BBC television interview NATO Secretary-General Javier Solano pointedly said that 'dictators have no place in the Europe of the twenty-first Century'. As indicated, President Clinton called for a Europe that shared America's values and he justified NATO's bombing of Yugoslavia as being 'for the sake of our values'. The United States was defending 'a peaceful, united, democratic Europe'. French President Jacques Chirac claimed the air attacks were launched to defend 'peace on our soil, peace in Europe'. The implication is clear: dictatorships and abusive governments had no place in Europe and were to be stamped out. The leading states of Western Europe were defining the terms of legitimacy and legality of states everywhere in Europe—up to but not including the border countries of Russia. The terms were different and more demanding than those of the United Nations. Territory anywhere in this Europe was characterized as the common property of all Europeans and not the exclusive property of particular sovereign states. Sovereignty in Europe was conditional on democracy and human rights. No longer would a dictator in Europe be allowed to flout these values by hiding behind state sovereignty and the doctrine of non-intervention. The war in Kosovo was a war of democracy against one of the last remaining dictatorships in Europe. All of that is strongly suggestive of a geographical sphere of influence where Western norms and values shall prevail.

In condemning the 'barbaric' domestic policies of Milosevic and attempting to impose 'civilized' policies by force, the NATO states invoked a standard of conduct that also brings to mind the old European 'standard of civilization'.[54] In attacking the sovereign state of Yugoslavia NATO repudiated the traditional Westphalian doctrine of *cujus regio, ejus religio* and instead adopted a secular version of the older interventionist doctrine of *respublica Christiana*. Historically Europe and later the West operated with their own 'standard of civilization', originally defined by the Christian religion and later by secular Western values. The NATO attack on Yugoslavia was justified by the norms of democracy, human rights, rule of law, which are set out in NATO's post-cold-war doctrines of regional security. NATO demanded capitulation from Yugoslavia and obtained an unequal treaty—the Rambouillet dictate—which impaired the sovereignty and territorial integrity of Yugoslavia. The terms of Yugoslavia's capitulation resulted in Kosovo taking a place alongside Bosnia as two protected territories in the Balkans where final responsibility for domestic security, local administration, physical reconstruction, and future state-building rested with the United Nations and various European international organizations, including NATO, the EU, and the OSCE. And since the Kosovo protectorate was imposed by NATO's military power it had some parallels with European protectorates and trusteeships of an earlier era.[55]

Was NATO's military actions in the Balkans signalling a bold move into a new millennium? Or was it indicating an unwitting and unrecognized return to an earlier era when Western values were imposed on obstinate governments and populations by armed force? Are we witnessing a retrogression to an era of geographical morality in which certain regions of the world determine their own pre-emptive international norms for the employment of armed force in their

---

[54] See G. W. Gong, *The Standard of "Civilization" in International Society* (Oxford: Clarendon Press, 1984).

[55] See the discussion of British protectorates in M. Wight, *British Colonial Constitutions: 1947* (Oxford: Clarendon Press, 1952), 7–11.

region? Do regional states, in this case the NATO states, have a right to use armed force unilaterally within their region without the authorization of the UN Security Council? Does NATO now have the role of a regional police force that serves summons to non-NATO European states that defy the regional norms of democracy and human rights, even if they have not clearly violated the UN charter? Does NATO have a freelancing right to impose their values in Europe by military means when diplomatic means prove unsuccessful? That also recollects the doctrine of the right of intervention of powerful states in their own neighbourhoods which, as indicated, was asserted by the USSR in its control of Eastern Europe following the Second World War and by the USA in its so-called backyard: the Caribbean and Central America. The above-noted evidence suggests an affirmative answer. If that is the correct inference, it suggests that the future of international relations may be more like the past than we may care to admit.

The debate on humanitarian intervention is not a debate between those who are concerned about human rights and those who are indifferent or callous about human suffering. Every decent person has these concerns. It is not even a debate about how to best go about preventing human suffering. That is an important question. But it is of secondary importance. It is a debate about the basic values of international society. Issues of justifiable armed intervention and justifiable warfare are being raised that are at the very foundations of international society. The states who are in a position to pursue and preserve international justice have a responsibility to do that whenever and wherever possible. But they have a fundamental responsibility not to sacrifice or even jeopardize other fundamental values in the attempt. International order and stability, international peace and security, are such values. In my view, the stability of international society, especially the unity of the great powers, is more important, indeed far more important, than minority rights and humanitarian protections in Yugoslavia or any other country—if we have to choose between those two sets of values.

It is not only that peace and security are values that are important in themselves, which is obvious. It is also that humanitarian values are never under greater threat than when states get involved in wars and international peace and security are placed in jeopardy. War is the biggest threat to human rights. War between the great powers is the biggest humanitarian threat of all. Nothing else comes close. The facts and reasons are incisively stated in the following comment by Adam Roberts: 'All major cases of genocide and ethnic cleansing in the twentieth century have occurred during or immediately after major wars: the chaos and hatred unleashed in war, and the secrecy that wartime conditions engender, can provide the necessary conditions for such mass cruelty.'[56] A pressing question at the time of writing was whether the ethnic cleansing of

---

[56] Roberts, 'NATO's "Humanitarian War" over Kosovo', 114.

Kosovo Albanians, and the human suffering and destruction associated with it, would have reached the same epidemic proportions if NATO had not dropped bombs on Yugoslavia. That is, of course, a counterfactual question that can never be answered. But it must be asked. And there is historical evidence and reasoning to believe that it probably would not have reached such disastrous levels if NATO had not attacked. That is the larger humanitarian value at stake. Responsible leaders of major powers, whose compassion inclines them to consider using armed force in the defence of humanity, should never lose sight of that larger moral consideration.

But that issue seems to be lost on at least some of the NATO politicians who came to power in Western countries during the 1990s: the generation of American and European leaders born after the end of the Second World War. What seems to be absent from their political minds is a heightened awareness of the extreme dangers of war. If that is so, it is surely surprising because such insight can easily be derived even from a casual acquaintance with the violent history of much of the twentieth century. Have the leading NATO statespeople of our time forgotten a fundamental lesson of international relations that their immediate predecessors always had at the front of their minds?

That is not to forget even for one moment that Kosovo was a humanitarian disaster for the people of Kosovo and of Yugoslavia more generally. But it was a disaster of their own making. It was their domestic crisis. Kosovo was significantly different from Croatia and Bosnia in that crucial respect. President Milosevic played political roulette by arbitrarily taking away Kosovo's rights of local autonomy within the state of Yugoslavia. The majority population of Yugoslavia, the Serbs, supported him, probably overwhelmingly. In that regard, the Serbian leader could be accused of acting as a demagogue rather than a statesman. The minority Kosovo Albanian population overwhelmingly opposed him. Kosovo Albanian militants, later known as the Kosovo Liberation Army (KLA), threw their own political caution to the wind by engaging in armed rebellion against the Yugoslav state with the aim of carving Kosovo out of Yugoslavia. In doing that they split with the peaceful party of Kosovo Albanians who sought a *rapprochement* with Belgrade that would restore their constitutional rights. But many Kosovo Albanians supported the secessionist KLA. The Kosovo disaster was thus created by President Milosevic with the popular support of the Serbs; it was enlarged by certain Kosovar Albanian warlords who enjoyed substantial popular support from among the Kosovo Albanian people.

The Kosovo disaster was a tragedy for everybody, Serbs and Albanians alike, who was caught in it and victimized by it. That it was a humanitarian disaster there can be no doubt—although of far lower magnitude than originally estimated by NATO.[57] But the claim that it was an international crisis that required

---

[57] NATO originally estimated 100,000 civilian killings but six months after the conflict UN investigators reported finding approximately 2,000 victims and expected the number to increase to 10,000. *The Globe and Mail* (11 Nov. 1999).

military intervention was unfounded. It did not present a serious threat to international peace and security either in the Balkans or beyond. It became a major international crisis only when NATO decided to intervene on its own initiative and without a full international mandate. NATO got involved for humanitarian reasons that no civilized person could question. But the leading NATO powers, and in particular the USA, could be criticized for losing sight of the bigger picture. There is some basis for believing that, by intervening, NATO may have made the humanitarian disaster worse rather than better. What it made definitely better were the secessionist prospects of the Kosovo Albanians.

11

Failed States and International Trusteeship

This chapter addresses the question whether international society has or should have any responsibility concerning the domestic civil conditions of independent countries. Some states clearly are a calamitous reality for their populations. But do they constitute a normative problem for international relations? Who is responsible for the uncivil and often unsafe domestic conditions of what are usually termed failed states? Are the government and citizens of those countries responsible? Is the society of states responsible? Is there any place for international trusteeships or protectorates in contemporary international society?

Sovereignty can be Dangerous

Anybody who pays attention to world politics will be aware of independent countries which fail to safeguard basic civil conditions domestically and which consequently contradict the usual normative justifications for sovereign statehood.[1] Some states could accurately and legitimately be advertised by the following public notice posted on large signs at all border entrances: 'Warning: this country can be dangerous to your health.' Foreign governments are well aware of unsafe countries and they make it their policy to advise their citizens to avoid them. Some countries are only unsafe for foreigners. They fail to fulfil Kant's third article of perpetual peace: universal hospitality.[2] But some countries present a hazard to their own populations as well. Some countries are safer for foreigners than they are for their citizens: that is, they are more civilized internationally than they are domestically. Afghanistan, Albania, Algeria, Armenia, Azerbaijan, Burundi, Cambodia, Chad, Colombia, Congo (Zaire), Georgia, Haiti, Indonesia, Iraq, Liberia, Rwanda, Sierra Leone, Somalia, Sri Lanka,

[1] See, among others, Christopher Clapham, *Africa and the International System: The Politics of State Survival* (Cambridge: Cambridge University Press, 1996), I. William Zartman (ed.), *Collapsed States* (Boulder, Colo.: Lynne Rienner, 1995), K. J. Holsti, *The State, War, and the State of War* (Cambridge: Cambridge University Press, 1996), and R. Jackson, *Quasi-States: Sovereignty, International Relations and the Third World* (Cambridge: Cambridge University Press, 1990)

[2] I. Kant, 'Perpetual Peace', repr. in H. Reiss (ed.), *Kant's Political Writings* (Cambridge: Cambridge University Press, 1977), 105.

Sudan, and former Yugoslavia (Bosnia-Herzegovina, Croatia, and the province of Kosovo in Serbia) were some of the most dangerous countries in the 1990s. Their existence raises important questions about the responsibilities of states and the *societas* of states.

As indicated in Chapter 8, sovereign states are classically understood and justified as places of refuge and not places of danger. Thomas Hobbes thought that sovereign statehood was a necessary political arrangement for safeguarding social peace.[3] There was no point in having states if they could not make a decisive contribution to domestic civil conditions: 'such things as are necessary to commodious living'.[4] He noted the security dilemma of a world of independent political leviathans which created conditions of domestic peace but simultaneously provoked conditions of war internationally.[5] The existence of failed states is a curious inversion of Hobbes's security dilemma: in regard to such states peace usually exists internationally while war exists domestically. Failed states turn Hobbes's political theory on its head. A failed 'state' would be indistinguishable from the 'state of nature' in which armed anarchy is a way of life and death. Today we know that countries just like that are a reality in some parts of the world. Anarchy and even chaos is a domestic condition.

By 'failed states' I shall not be referring to the social disruptions produced within countries by natural disasters—earthquakes, floods, droughts, etc. They are usually a temporary circumstance, an emergency, that can be addressed by domestic and international relief to help repair the damage and restore pre-existing conditions. Nor shall I consider the question of economic assistance to poor countries. A failed state is not necessarily underdeveloped economically. There are relatively underdeveloped states that are tolerably civil (for example, Botswana) and relatively developed states that are comparatively uncivil (for example, some successor states of former Yugoslavia). Civility is not a responsibility only of the rich. Poverty is not an excuse for barbarity. Africans are no more exempt than Americans or Europeans or anyone else from basic standards of human conduct. Nor do I refer to states destroyed by international war. Failed states have not collapsed under external military pressure—as Germany and Japan collapsed in 1945 but soon recovered. They have self-destructed by armed anarchy from within. Their adverse condition is self-inflicted. They are political failures: the government has failed the citizens and maybe the citizens have failed the government too. Even to speak of 'government' and 'citizens' in connection with such countries is misleading because these roles scarcely exist in any meaningful sense. Nor do I refer to countries that are undemocratic. Most

---

[3] T. Hobbes, *Leviathan* (Oxford: Blackwell, 1946), ch. 13.   [4] Ibid. 84.

[5] Ibid., ch. 13. In the same vein but with a different purpose Kant remarks: 'The same unsociability which forced men to do so gives rise in turn to a situation whereby each commonwealth, in its external relations (i.e., as a state in relation to other states), is in a position of unrestricted freedom. Each must accordingly expect from any other precisely the same evils which formerly oppressed individual men and forced them into a law-governed civil state.' 'Idea for a Universal History with a Cosmopolitan Purpose', repr. in Reiss, *Kant's Political Writings*, 41.

countries, both historical and contemporary, are not democracies. A country can be a safe place to live without being a democracy.

Failed states are a more limited category than undemocratic states or even authoritarian states. By 'failed states' I shall be referring exclusively to states which cannot or will not safeguard minimal *civil* conditions for their populations: domestic peace, law and order, and good governance. The expression 'failed state' is something of a misnomer. Hobbes would not understand a failed state as a state at all. Failed states are juridical shells that shroud an insecure and even a dangerous condition domestically, a state of nature. Such states have an international legal existence but very little domestic political existence. Some failed states clearly are a consequence of the end of the cold war, such as Albania and some states of former Yugoslavia. But Chad was a failure almost from the time of independence in 1960.[6] Sudan has been a failure since the British departed in 1956. Haiti has been more or less a failure since it broke free from the French Empire in the early nineteenth century. Most failed states are successor states of defunct colonial empires or communist federations. They failed to consolidate themselves internally after they became independent. They exist because the outside world recognizes them and respects their sovereignty regardless of their domestic conditions. They have a juridical existence but little if any empirical existence.[7]

That external guarantee of legal independence is primarily owing to the emergence of a post-colonial international society that is highly tolerant of different degrees of statehood across the world. Tolerance is high because self-determination and international recognition is not conditional on the substantive domestic conditions of states. People living in former Western colonies or former 'republics' of the now defunct USSR or Yugoslavia have an unhindered right to independence within the territorial framework of their inherited borders, whether or not they are prepared or equipped for it. They possess juridical statehood unconditionally. Recognition of governments is *de jure* and not *de facto*; it is not conditional on empirical statehood: 'a government as being in active control of a territory'.[8] That international guarantee of juridical statehood has brought into existence a number of insubstantial or marginal or even nominal states: what for lack of a better term might be called 'quasi-states', of which some have clearly failed and cease to be 'states' in any significant empirical meaning of the term.[9]

We can begin to understand the seeming paradox of juridical statehood in the absence of empirical statehood in the light of a political sleight of hand in the

---

[6] 'In Chad, the "modern" state inherited from the colonial period no longer exists.' *Le Monde* (30 Dec. 1980).

[7] See R. Jackson and C. Rosberg, 'Why Africa's Weak States Persist: The Empirical and the Juridical in Statehood', *World Politics*, 35/1 (Oct. 1982), 1–24.

[8] G. Schwarzenberger and E. Brown, *A Manual of International Law*, 6th edn. (London: Professional Books, 1976), 554.

[9] See Jackson, *Quasi-States*.

application of the rules of the UN charter regarding the admission of new states.[10] That is especially so for ex-colonial states, but it is also a feature of some new states of the former Soviet Union and former Yugoslavia. The charter contains a substantive requirement for membership expressed by Article 4 which declares that member states 'are able and willing to carry out' their charter obligations. Failed states are an international reality because that requirement of empirical statehood was winked at by international society in the admission of new states at the same time that the procedural norms of equal sovereignty and non-intervention were generally observed, in accordance with Article 2.[11] If Article 2 were not generally respected and Article 4 were not generally disregarded failed states would probably not exist. Instead, colonies, protectorates, trust territories, and other kinds of dependent states would still be in existence. In the light of international episodes and developments of the 1990s, particularly in Bosnia and Kosovo, the question arises: are we perhaps witnessing a return to an era of international trusteeship?

International Society as a Benevolent Association

The ethics that have underwritten international society since 1945 have been basically pluralist: that is, they are concerned primarily to uphold international order and the sovereignty of independent states. During that same period, as we have seen, norms have also been instituted by international society which endorse human rights. There is now an extensive body of international humanitarian law. Since the end of the cold war there has been a rapidly growing number of Security Council resolutions directed at massive human rights abuses in certain states. As indicated in Chapter 10, the domestic jurisdiction of a few states was encroached upon by UN Security Council resolutions: for example, 688 on Iraq, 794 on Somalia, 713 on Bosnia, 1244 on Yugoslavia (Kosovo).

Those developments prompt the following question: are the ethics of international society becoming more Kantian, i.e. solidarist?[12] Is it now possible to argue that the sovereignty of UN member states is protected not only for the sake of international order and political independence but also to secure domestic civil conditions? Did Yugoslav President Milosevic forfeit Yugoslavia's sovereignty over the region of Kosovo when he instituted a policy of political repression and ethnic cleansing directed against its majority Albanian population in the 1990s? A former US Undersecretary of State for African Affairs argues that failed states present a challenge to the post-1945 international order:

---

[10] I am indebted to Will Bain for drawing this to my attention.

[11] See M. J. Peterson, *Recognition of Governments* (London: Macmillan, 1997), 68–71.

[12] Hedley Bull raised that question in *Justice in International Society: The Hagey Lectures* (Waterloo, Ont.: University of Waterloo Press, 1985).

Not since the Napoleonic upheavals (if not the Peace of Westphalia in 1648) have the rights of states, people and governments been so unclear . . . What 'sovereign' rights, if any, do governments have to prevent outsiders from telling them how to treat their people . . . And what about the rights of outsiders to come to the aid of peoples victimized by the actions or inactions of local governments—or to create the functional equivalent of government where, as in Somalia, none exists?[13]

That raises further questions concerning the responsibilities of state sovereignty which shall occupy centre stage in this chapter. Do the uncivil domestic conditions of certain countries constitute valid grounds for setting aside pluralist norms of equal sovereignty and non-intervention? Do they establish the case for making independence conditional on agreed minimal standards of domestic peace, law and order, and good governance as determined by international society? Should the 'successful' members of international society be responsible for failed states—beyond the duty to respect their external sovereignty and thereby allow them to sort out their domestic affairs by themselves and free from foreign interference? Should international society have any responsibility for states that clearly are a calamity for their population but only a nuisance for their neighbours and other outsiders? The qualification is crucial: if failed states pose a threat to international order there is no normative predicament because the great powers are charged specifically with defending international peace and security under the UN charter. They have a right and even a duty of intervention in carrying out that responsibility. If the answers to these questions are in the affirmative there would have to be space in international society for trusteeships or protectorates or comparable benevolent arrangements that would put failed states into political receivership or political care until their domestic civil conditions were restored to minimally acceptable standards.

Implying affirmative answers, R. J. Vincent compares international society to an egg-carton.[14] The sovereign states are the eggs, the carton is international society, and the point of that arrangement obviously is to separate and cushion the eggs. Egg-cartons are necessary because eggshells are fragile and their contents are valuable. The container reduces the chances of cracking or smashing the eggs and decreasing or destroying their valuable contents. By analogy, international society serves an important value beyond that of international order (the fundamental value) and that of political independence of member states (the value next in importance). It also serves the good life *within* member states. That, according to the logic of Vincent's argument, is its further and more fundamental justification.

That justification of international society is challenged by the existence of failed states. Egg-cartons would be pointless for rotten eggs. All that one can do with rotten eggs is throw them away and replace them with fresh eggs. Vincent's

---

[13] Chester Crocker, Assistant Secretary of State for African Affairs, US State Department, 1992.

[14] R. J. Vincent, *Human Rights and International Relations* (Cambridge: Cambridge University Press, 1986), 123–5.

analogy carries solidarist implications that failed states should lose their sovereign rights and privileges and be made wards of international society until such time as domestic civil conditions are restored. According to this reasoning, the non-intervention principle only makes sense if states are at least benign if not beneficial places in which to live. What is the point of protecting and upholding the independence of states where large numbers of people gain no protection from the state authorities and many people if not most live in fear of the government or their fellow citizens or both?

'What ought to be done about the condition of states?' Mervyn Frost raises that question in an important essay.[15] He argues that sovereign states in an international society 'reciprocally constitute one another', by mutual recognition and by subjecting themselves to a common norm of state sovereignty and non-intervention.[16] According to this way of thinking, recognition is *de facto* and not merely *de jure*. The society of sovereign states is a club of civilized statesmen and stateswomen. There is no room for barbarians. 'In order to be recognized as an autonomous state, the state must meet certain specific requirements . . . An autonomous state is one in which the citizens experience the well-being of the state as fundamental to their own well-being.'[17] Any truly sovereign state, for Frost, is a state whose citizens are substantially free as individual human beings and are not merely inhabitants of a juridically independent country. Every member state of international society should thus be able to claim the recognition of every other member state on that substantive basis: *de facto* recognition. Every state should be both a contributor to and a beneficiary of the society of states. That would be international reciprocity in the full meaning of the word. The ultimate justification and indeed the only final justification of international society is the good domestic life of the citizens of all independent states who would recognize and enfranchise each other via the legitimate activity of international relations. Truly sovereign states are those which convert political independence into personal freedom.

But failed states cannot or will not manage that conversion: their statehood in that regard is malformed and incomplete. Their governments tolerate and may even promote adverse domestic conditions that foster barbarism and servitude rather than civility and freedom. That must be a matter of concern to the society of states as a whole: a legitimate international society must rest on the premiss that its member states are sanctuaries and homes rather than gulags or jungles. They uphold Kantian conditions of juridical security domestically (see Chapter 8). The adverse civil conditions of failed states must also be a specific

[15] M. Frost, 'What ought to be Done about the Condition of States?' in C. Navari (ed.), *The Condition of States* (Buckingham: Open University Press, 1991), 183–96. Also see by the same author *Ethics in International Relations: A Constitutive Theory* (Cambridge: Cambridge University Press, 1996), 153–5.

[16] Frost, 'What ought to be Done about the Condition of States?', 183–96.

[17] M. Frost, *Towards a Normative Theory of International Relations* (Cambridge: Cambridge University Press, 1986), 179.

matter of concern to successful states because 'the recognition of slaves cannot establish the freedom of the master'.[18] If failed states are tolerated by successful states—if their independence is respected but nothing is done to correct their uncivil domestic conditions—neither failed states nor successful states will be truly free. Instead, their status and relation will be more akin to that of slaves and slave-masters, which is a condition that is outside the sphere of human freedom for both parties.

What action should international society take to correct the uncivil domestic conditions of failed states? Successful states ought to establish the condition of true or substantive freedom in their interactions with failed states. Creating the conditions of substantive freedom in states where they do not presently exist, according to Frost, requires international education and counselling similar to that of social workers who have the authority to take children away from their parents.[19] By that sort of reasoning failed states would have to be taken into care and reformed by international society. Truly free states would have to take on that responsibility on behalf of international society; representatives of the USA or Japan or Germany or other capable and publicly spirited states would have to become social workers in their relations with failed states.

Just as social workers attempt to educate inadequate parents to the responsibilities of parenthood . . . states and citizens ought to be educated about the ways in which freedom is constituted in the relations between sovereign states . . . A self-respecting free state is one that is recognized as such by other states. Subservient states, frail states and enslaved states cannot confer on strong states the recognition constitutive of freedom.[20]

The end point of such an arrangement would be to create an international society from which failed states—that is, servitude and barbarism in domestic political life—had been permanently abolished. International society would do that by taking over responsibility for governance of failed states with the sole aim of creating or restoring basic domestic conditions of security and freedom so that sovereignty could be returned to the local people in full confidence that they would henceforth be able to make good use of it. That would complete the project that decolonization only began: the project of bringing genuine freedom to all the people of the world.

There are four important assumptions and implications worth noticing about a conjectured reformation of international society of this sort. First, it assumes that a state's will and capacity to establish and enforce domestic civil conditions and to carry out international obligations should be a requirement for political independence. Second, it implies that states which fail to meet that standard should forfeit their independence until they can be prepared and equipped to re-enter international society on a basis of substantive freedom, equality, and reciprocity. Third, it justifies foreign intervention and governance of independ-

---

[18] Frost, 'What ought to be Done about the Condition of States?', 195.
[19] Ibid. (original italics).   [20] Ibid.

ent states with or without the consent of their government. Finally, it presupposes that successful states would take on the heavy responsibility of reforming failed states by taking them over for a period of time. All of this points toward an international change comparable to decolonization, but operating in reverse gear, a counter-reformation of international trusteeship.

That line of reasoning is indistinguishable from the colonial practice of *de facto* recognition based on the Western 'standard of civilization' that was in effect before 1960. It discloses a conception of international society as an association of civilized governments and not merely one of juridically independent states. Should some new version of the standard of civilization be adopted by international society to address the problems of failed states? Or should international society continue to be based on a less demanding pluralist norm of freedom from external political and military interference, the almost certain result of which will be the toleration of failed states and the human suffering caused from within such states by some members of their population, usually the government?[21] These questions can be put in terms of the operative concepts of this study: to what extent should international society continue to be a *societas* of independent states and to what extent should it revert to a *universitas* which presupposes the existence of both independent states and dependent states based on a principle of competence or merit in providing domestic peace, law and order, and good governance? These obviously are fundamental questions that go to the normative heart of contemporary international relations.

Reverting to International Trusteeship?

The defunct international society of Western political empires embodied institutions of trusteeship. That normative doctrine was famously expressed in 1783 by Edmund Burke in a debate in parliament on British rule in India: 'all political power which is set over men . . . ought to be some way or other exercised ultimately for their benefit . . . every species of political dominion . . . are all in the strictest sense *a trust*; and it is of the essence of every trust to be rendered *accountable*'.[22] In other words, Britain was responsible for the civil conditions of British India, then under the administration of the East India Company which was accountable to the British government. Britain would have to exercise that tutelary responsibility until such time as India could stand on her own feet and become a full and equal member of the family of nations. That is what trusteeship calls for. If political power is not exercised by the trustees for the benefit

---

[21] On positive and negative freedom see I. Berlin, *Four Essays on Liberty* (London: Oxford, 1969), 118–72.

[22] 'Speech on Mr. Fox's East India Bill', in *The Works of the Right Honourable Edmund Burke*, iii (London: OUP, 1935), 60, original emphasis.

of their subjects, if it is used to exploit them or oppress them, or if it cannot protect them and make it possible for them to get on with their lives free of fear, then the trustees have broken the trust placed in them. That was the charge Burke laid against Warren Hastings who was governor of the East India Company at the time.

The British gave the theory and practice of trusteeship to international society. Not so very long ago the political world included UN trust territories (there may still be one or two left), League of Nations mandates, condominia (such as the Anglo-Egyptian Sudan), colonies, protectorates, protected states, among others.[23] Sovereign statehood was conditional on more than a right of self-determination. Self-determination was not a categorical right. It also had to be justified by reference to norms that specified minimal domestic conditions to qualify for political independence.[24] For those countries that could not meet the conditions some form of trusteeship was necessary. The discourse of trusteeship was a prominent feature of British colonial administration in Africa. Lord F. D. Lugard, the most famous imperial proconsul in Africa, laid down rules for a 'dual mandate': 'The British Empire . . . has only one mission—for liberty and self-development . . . [which] can be best secured to the native population by leaving them free to manage their own affairs through their own rulers, proportionately to their degree of advancement, under the guidance of the British staff, and subject to the law and policy of the administration.'[25] The Nigeria Protectorate Order in Council (1922), enacted under the authority of the British Foreign Jurisdiction Act (1890), gave the colonial governor responsibility 'to take care to protect . . . [the native inhabitants] in their persons and in the free enjoyment of their possessions, and by all lawful means to prevent and restrain all violence and injustice which may in any manner be practiced or attempted against them.' (Article 11) The same responsibility expressed in virtually identical language, was written into the 1946 Constitution of Colonial Nigeria and the 1934 instructions to the Governor of Kenya.[26] That language was scattered across the length and breadth of the British Empire.

Trusteeship was for a long time an important practice of Western-centred international society, which was involved in the domestic affairs of many non-Western territories whose populations were deemed to be not yet fit for political independence or, in most cases, even for internal self-government.

---

[23] See M. Wight, *British Colonial Constitutions 1947* (Oxford: Clarendon Press, 1952), 5–14. For a recent inquiry into the revival of trusteeship see P. Lyon, 'The Rise and Fall and Possible Revival of International Trusteeship', in M. Twaddle (ed.), *Decolonisation and the International Community: Essays in Honour of Kenneth Robinson, Journal of Commonwealth and Commonwealth Politics* 31 (Mar. 1993), 96–110.

[24] G. W. Gong, *The Standard of 'Civilization' in International Society* (Oxford: Clarendon Press, 1984).

[25] F. D. Lugard, *The Dual Mandate in British Tropical Africa* (Edinburgh: Blackwood, 1922), 94.

[26] See Wight, *British Colonial Constitutions: 1947*, 197, 231, and 293.

International law embodied norms of trusteeship. Article 6 of the General Act of the Berlin Conference (1885) bound all colonial powers involved in the partition of Africa 'to *watch over* the preservation of the native tribes and to *care* for the improvement of the conditions of their moral and material well-being'.[27] Article 22 of the League of Nations covenant declared that 'those colonies and territories . . . which are inhabited by peoples not yet able to stand by themselves under the strenuous conditions of the modern world . . . form a sacred trust of civilization'. 'Tutelage' of such peoples was 'entrusted' to certain 'advanced nations' and 'exercised by them as Mandatories on behalf of the League'. The League mandate system thus involved international governance by a designated foreign power of certain territories and populations deemed to be not yet prepared and equipped for self-government. The language of both the General Act and the League mandate system clearly is written with a British pen.

Article 73 of the UN charter acknowledged, in exactly the same idiom, the 'responsibilities' of certain UN member states 'for the administration of territories whose peoples have not yet attained a full measure of self-government', for recognizing 'the principle that the interests of the inhabitants of these territories are paramount', and for accepting 'as a sacred trust the obligation to promote to the utmost . . . the well-being of the inhabitants of these territories'. Articles 75 to 91 laid out the principles and procedures of the UN's international trusteeship system which involved the solidarist goal of promoting 'the political, economic, social, and educational advancement of the inhabitants of the trust territories, and their progressive development towards self-government or independence as may be appropriate to the particular circumstances of each territory and its peoples'. Expressions such as 'just treatment' of the inhabitants of trust territories and 'their protection against abuses' were prominent in the language of UN trusteeship.

Even though trusteeship was an international institution of the League of Nations and the United Nations, it was strongly identified with Western colonialism. In abolishing colonialism, international society, in effect, abolished trusteeship along with it. Political independence could no longer be made conditional on the capacity for self-government as defined by Western states. It was now a categorical right of all dependencies. The watershed of change was marked by UN General Assembly resolution 1514 (1960) which declared categorically that 'all peoples have the right to self-determination' and 'inadequacy of political, economic, social or educational preparedness should never serve as a pretext for delaying independence'. That language cannot coexist with the language of international trusteeship cited above; the two discourses are in contradiction. That Declaration on the Granting of Independence to Colonial Countries and Peoples is considered by Asian and African states and by many

---

[27] Emphasis added.

other states as a 'second charter' of the UN promulgated to liberate all remaining dependent peoples from foreign rule. From that time empirical statehood as a valid ground for determining the right to sovereignty went into eclipse and self-determination became the basic criterion: that is, the right of inhabitants of colonial territories to be independent if they so desire. *De jure* recognition displaced *de facto* recognition of governments. An equivalent change occurred in the breakup of the Soviet Union and former Yugoslavia.

But from the start of the post-colonial era there was a problem that did not pass unnoticed. In the early 1960s a leading British scholar of decolonization observed that political independence of developing countries did not by itself eliminate the problem for which trusteeship was originally instituted: the world was still fundamentally divided between the strong and the weak, the capable and the infirm, the organized and the disorganized, the experienced and the inexperienced:

The problems of trusteeship were the problems of power, of the *responsibilities* of the strong towards the weak. The unequal distribution of political and economic power in the world, which was the fundamental basis of colonialism, has not been suddenly abolished by the accession of most colonies to political independence . . . the rich and powerful countries of the world are not thereby absolved from any further *responsibility* toward those countries.[28]

Some statespeople made the same point. In the late colonial era following the Second World War it was still publicly argued that colonial tutelage would be necessary until a level of competence sufficient to manage an independent country had been achieved by colonial peoples. That point was put more dramatically by an outspoken leader of a British Labour government: transferring power without providing instruction would be 'like giving a child of ten a latch-key, a bank account and a shot-gun'.[29] After 1960 reservations on this point were still registered, in more diplomatic language, by prominent Western statespeople. In a message communicated to his British counterpart regarding the admission of states to the Commonwealth, Prime Minister Lester Pearson of Canada suggested that a different basis of membership for 'smaller dependent territories' might be necessary.[30] Prime Minister Robert Menzies of Australia warned against interpreting UN resolution 1514 too literally—otherwise many states might gain independence which would not be able to handle it.[31] In 1963 the US Ambassador to the United Nations argued that 'classical independence' might not be suitable for every country. Perhaps there ought to be a class of associate states.[32] It seemed that trusteeship was still necessary, at least in the minds of some Western leaders.

---

[28] Kenneth Robinson as quoted by Lyon, 'Revival of International Trusteeship', 105–6 (emphasis added).

[29] Labour deputy leader Herbert Morrison, as quoted by C. Cross, *The Fall of the British Empire, 1918–1968* (London: Macmillan, 1968), 262.

[30] D. J. Morgan, *Guidance Towards Self-Government* (London: Macmillan, 1980), 215.

[31] Ibid. 184.   [32] Ibid. 204.

Those observations and recommendations went largely unheeded at a time when international society was engaged in a global reformation of political independence that was justified and indeed driven by the moral imperative of self-determination. Colonialism was abolished. Recognition of governments was *de jure*. Article 2 of the UN charter prevailed over Article 4. The cold war made it politically inexpedient for the West to argue that some colonies were not yet fit for self-government—if they did not want to see anti-colonialism turn into pro-communism. From 1945 until the end of the cold war, legitimate and lawful international trusteeship was confined to UN supervised transition of a small number of territories from quasi-colonial status to independence. The UN Trusteeship Council was expected to go out of business when all trust territories became independent, which was not supposed to take forever. UN trusteeship was not intended to reverse the process and transfer already independent states back to a quasi-colonial status. As indicated previously, the UN charter does not provide for trusteeship for sovereign states: independence is a one-way street with no return to dependency status (Article 78). A basic norm of post-1945 world politics forbids the institution of trusteeship, colonial status, or any other form of international dependency where independence previously existed. Political independence was intended to be final and irreversible. Article 78 should be read as a confirmation and reinforcement of the *Grundnorm* of non-intervention.

But in the contemporary era of numerous civil wars and internal conflicts, of domestic anarchy and chaotic states, it is easy to see the need for some kind of international trusteeship which might take over responsibility for pacifying and governing what clearly are failed states until such time as domestic conditions can be restored to some minimal standards of security and civility and those countries can be returned to a government of their own people. According to Peter Lyon:

It is in the desperate situations of state collapse or near-collapse that the United Nations, or some other international body, is invoked to act as a surrogate sovereign and support system in the face of anarchy and human misery—and the signs are that such situations are currently on the increase . . . UN trusteeship would almost certainly be an improvement on the anarchical conditions of the several quasi-states the world has now.[33]

Lyon acknowledges the practical difficulties that would confront international trusteeship: 'Sustaining collapsing states, quasi-states, and merely nominal states becomes the main challenge and task for would-be trustees in the 1990s . . . [but] . . . it would be politically and psychologically unwise to saddle what would, in practice, be a freshly thought out system with the old name. Perhaps guardianship . . . would be appropriate.'[34] But whatever we decide to call the arrangement, sovereignty would be withdrawn from such states and vested in international society, at least temporarily.

[33] Lyon, 'Revival of International Trusteeship', 106.   [34] Ibid. 107–8.

Clearly the issue of international trusteeship is not merely a philosophical or historical question. Some of the cases of humanitarian intervention discussed in Chapter 10 have changed that. It is now an issue of foreign policy and diplomacy. The Dayton Agreement's provisions for the international military occupation and rebuilding of Bosnia give some evidence of that change. But the clearest evidence is provided by the case of Kosovo, which became an international protectorate in everything but name under the terms of UN Security Council resolution 1244 (1999). It provided for a military presence—in effect, an international army of occupation—and a civil administration with responsibilities not only to make possible the safe return home of a million or more Kosovo Albanian refugees and displaced persons but also to provide for the political reconstruction of Kosovo. It would of course be misleading to speak of Kosovo as a failed state, for it is not a state; rather, it is a region of Yugoslavia. And it was treated by NATO and later the UN as an international military protectorate. Armed force was used, successfully, to remove Kosovo, an integral part of the sovereign state of Yugoslavia (Serbia), from the control of the Yugoslav government in Belgrade. International society took full responsibility for governing Kosovo until its domestic security and stability could be restored and its people could safely and freely decide whether to remain as part of Yugoslavia or to secede from it.

Resolution 1244 made no mention of the temporary transfer of sovereignty over Kosovo from Yugoslavia to the United Nations. The word 'trusteeship' or its synonyms were not used. That is because the UN has no authority under the charter to transfer states, either in whole or in part, from a status of legal independence to a lesser status of trust territory or protectorate. As indicated, the charter expressly forbids such moves. Resolution 1244 reaffirmed the 'commitment of all [UN] member States to the sovereignty and territorial integrity of the Federal Republic of Yugoslavia'. But it clearly did interfere with the sovereignty of Yugoslavia. It repeated 'the call in previous resolutions for substantial autonomy and meaningful self-administration for Kosovo'. It demanded that Yugoslavia withdraw all its 'military, police and paramilitary forces' from the province, to be replaced by 'an international security presence'—that is, a force under the command of NATO. It provided for the deployment of a 'civil presence' directed by a UN 'special representative'. The civil presence was responsible for providing a 'transitional administration while establishing and overseeing the development of provisional democratic self-governing institutions to ensure conditions for a peaceful and normal life for all inhabitants of Kosovo'. It was also charged with 'overseeing the transfer of authority from Kosovo's provisional institutions to institutions established under a political settlement'. At that point political responsibility for Kosovo would revert to a local sovereign, either Yugoslavia or another authority if Kosovo seceded—perhaps an independent Kosovo or a greater Albania.[35] Clearly authority over Kosovo was removed from Yugoslavia and placed temporarily in the hands of certain representatives of the UN and NATO.

The military and political takeover of Kosovo was an international trusteeship in everything but name. The goal is to place part of a country under international control in order to reorganize it and re-equip it for self-government prior to restoring local sovereignty. The role and responsibilities of the 'security presence' are indistinguishable from that of an international military protectorate. The role and responsibilities of the 'civil presence' are identical to that of a colonial administration, a League of Nations mandate administration, or a UN trusteeship administration. That the language of international 'trusteeship' was never mentioned in connection with the creation of the Kosovo military protectorate may be an indication of just how controversial such a policy is bound to be in a post-colonial *societas* of states.

Kosovo indicates more clearly than any other case to date that the reformation of decolonization may not have been as final and irreversible as it previously appeared to be. For it is now clear that, in certain circumstances, international society can be persuaded that sovereign authority over populated territories can legitimately be taken away from an independent state even though it has not committed aggression against any of its neighbours or threatened international peace and security. What it has perpetrated or has allowed to happen is the massive violation of the human rights of the population within its domestic jurisdiction. The institution of trusteeship seems to have a place in international relations after all. If that is indeed a correct conclusion to be drawn from the Kosovo experience, it raises a fundamental normative issue for a post-colonial society of states.

At the end of the 1990s that issue had not yet been faced squarely by leading members of international society, including the USA, who were most actively responsible for the international occupation and administration of Kosovo. The humanitarian motives of those statespeople cannot be questioned. What can be questioned is their seeming unawareness—or if they were aware, their evident lack of concern—that their actions put in question some basic norms and values of pluralist international society. The Western statespeople most deeply involved in shaping the response of international society to the Kosovo crisis disclosed no public awareness that their action in taking over Kosovo by armed force had many parallels with the era of Western imperialism and colonialism. The military commanders of NATO seemed not to be aware that they were turning their armies into quasi-colonial forces of occupation and pacification. Even the British and French government gave no outward indication of realizing that they were engaging in foreign political and military activities that echoed their imperial and colonial past.

---

[35] If sovereignty over Kosovo were transferred to Albania that would be ironical and problematical in so far as Albania itself qualifies in many respects as a failed state. It would also be provocative of future conflict and possibly armed hostilities between Albania and Yugoslavia.

The Responsibility of Sovereignty

The inclination of most concerned and compassionate observers was to support if not indeed demand intervention in Kosovo. How else could its population be protected except by entering the country with military force and creating some sort of international protectorate? But the burden of argument for adopting trusteeship for dealing with domestic political failures is on those who propose such a change. That is because it challenges the most fundamental norm of a *societas* of states: that independent governments and their citizens are the ones who bear responsibility for their domestic affairs. That fundamental responsibility of political independence does not terminate when domestic conditions become difficult or even dangerous. Sovereignty is not a political arrangement only for fair weather and good times. It is an arrangement for all political seasons and for all kinds of political weather. It cannot be withdrawn whenever a ship of state's crew and passengers run into domestic difficulties. Sovereignty is no guarantee of domestic well-being; it is merely the framework of independence within which the good life can be pursued and hopefully realized. The domestic good life is not something that can be guaranteed—and certainly not by international society. It can only be pursued, strived for, and hopefully realized to some degree by the independent people involved in building any particular political community.

In this final section I shall address some normative questions about the responsibility of political independence raised by the existence of failed states and by demands for international trusteeship to deal with them. These questions concern issues of procedural responsibility, issues of prudential responsibility, and issues of moral responsibility.[36]

There are questions of a procedural nature. First, there is the issue of procedural criteria and their application. By what generally accepted legal criteria would international trusteeship for failed states be defined and determined, keeping in mind that the UN charter provides no express authority for such action and indeed forbids it? Who would determine the criteria? The UN Security Council? The General Assembly? Could specific international organizations lay down procedures for their own members? NATO? The OSCE? How high should the standards of peace, order, and good governance be? If they are set too high most states of the world would have to be placed in international care. If they are set too low it would not make much difference. How could we tell if a country had passed the threshold of political failure and was now subject to international trusteeship? What would be the measure of that? The truth is that it would be difficult in particular cases to decide exactly when a country or province had become so disrupted, anarchical, and chaotic internally as to forfeit its right of non-intervention.

---

[36] I am indebted to Jennifer Jackson Preece for clarification of these points.

Second, there is the question of exercising the responsibility of trusteeship. The League mandate system and the UN trusteeship system relied upon member states to act as trustees. Those organizations had no capacity of their own to carry out such demanding international responsibilities. Who would be called upon to bear the possibly heavy and thankless burden of serving as international trustee for failed states? Would that responsibility be voluntary or would it be obligatory? It is inconceivable that it could be obligatory in a world of sovereign states. If it is voluntary would it be carried out? Suppose it turned out to be far more costly, difficult, or dangerous than originally anticipated and the volunteer trustee decided to withdraw. How would that be overcome? Would any volunteer be acceptable? Would it have to fall upon designated capable and public-spirited states—for example, the USA, Britain, France, Japan, Germany, or coalitions of smaller countries such as Spain, Australia, the Netherlands? If so, would not such international arrangements bear remarkable similarities to the colonial era?

However, let us assume these problems could be sorted out. Suppose, then, that a trusteeship system were instituted to rehabilitate particular failed states that had been taken into international care. When would we know that they were restored to the point of being ready for independence once again? How could we tell if a country had passed the threshold of political development? What would be the measure of that? The difficulty of answering such questions with real confidence is an important reason why the doctrine of *de facto* recognition was abandoned in the late colonial period: it proved to be impossible to operate with a standard of domestic peace, order, and good governance to determine the question of independence. The ambiguity of the evidence was too great and the temptation of the political considerations were too strong. That is why UN General Assembly resolution 1514 declared so confidently against 'pretexts' for 'delaying independence' to argue their case for granting all colonies independence without further delay.

How can social workers be certain that the individuals in their care are now ready to assume the responsibilities of parenting and can have their children back? The truth is that we would only know if the trustees were successful in their project of political rehabilitation after their trusteeship was withdrawn and independence was restored to the local people. The proof of the pudding is in the eating. We might discover that the problem was still there. Should the country then be placed in international care again? Should there be provision for more or less permanent wards of international society for incorrigibly delinquent countries: Albania? Afghanistan? Cambodia? Haiti? Sudan? The problem of that scenario is obvious. That seems to suggest that the governance of countries—good, bad, or indifferent—is a domestic affair and should remain so.

This brings us to questions of a prudential kind. International trusteeship for failed states clearly would lay additional responsibilities on the great powers, particularly the USA, that would be difficult to carry out even in favourable circumstances and would, as indicated, provoke enormous controversy. If the great powers were divided on the question it could undermine the most fundamental international good that they are singularly responsible for upholding and defending: international order. The great powers were divided over Kosovo. For a time those divisions threatened the post-cold-war concert that was built in the 1990s. They were only papered over after it became clear that Moscow was not prepared to support Belgrade to the point of provoking a permanent split with the Western powers—which would have been disastrous for Russia's economic interests—and after it became known that Belgrade was willing to submit to the terms laid down by the Western powers in order to bring NATO's bombing campaign against Yugoslavia to an end. Suppose the great powers could not agree on a proposed case of trusteeship because their national interests were in conflict? In that event trusteeship would be provocative of international instability.

Even if agreement could be achieved, would any major power or any other power be willing to accept what could be a very long commitment involving years or possibly even decades? (I have in mind the decades-long unresolved conflict in Cyprus in which UN peacekeepers have been involved with no end in sight.) If responsible powers hesitate, would irresponsible powers exploit the situation by intervening in the name of trusteeship? Then there is the question of the wisdom of getting involved in other peoples' civil wars, which is what happened in Kosovo. The problems that result are well-known. Impartiality of a foreign authority in a deeply divided country is difficult even at the best of times, if it is possible at all. Convincing the warring factions and their supporters that the occupation is evenhanded is likely to be a thankless and fruitless assignment. They may be incapable of recognizing impartiality, even if it exists. And then there is the huge problem of actually being and remaining impartial—especially if the warring factions continue their quarrel and resort to guerrilla warfare to get their way. Impartiality is just as difficult if one side has the upper hand and tries to use its power to engage in reprisals against the other side. In such typical circumstances, impartiality usually goes out the window. Undiplomatic force comes to the fore. Trusteeship becomes martial law. These are the situations in which goodwilled outsiders are likely to find themselves in attempting to occupy, pacify, and rebuild a country that has experienced chaos and barbarism from within.

The lessons of history counsel against getting involved in somebody else's civil wars by attempting to play a pacifying and moderating role between the warring parties without the full consent of everybody. The dangers are considerable. The chances of achieving a permanent solution are not great. The occupying power is most likely to get sucked into a quagmire from which exit is difficult. But if the occupying powers run for the exits they morally undercut their noble mission. Although the cases are not entirely comparable, the dark experiences of the British in Kenya, Southern Rhodesia, and Palestine, of the

French in Algeria and Vietnam, and of the Americans in Vietnam come quickly to mind. Have these lessons already been forgotten by the countries that were involved in them and were morally as well as politically damaged by them?

Finally, then, there are questions of a strictly moral kind. The fundamental question that should be asked of those who advocate a social work relationship between successful states and failed states is: are they prepared to accept the moral implications of their argument which may be indistinguishable from paternalism? What does paternalism come down to in foreign affairs? It is taking on, at our own initiative, responsibilities that lie outside our sphere of jurisdiction, in the desire to do some good or to reduce some evil in a foreign country by placing the people who live there under our control and care without the consent of the sovereign government. Kant believed that a paternal government was 'the greatest conceivable despotism' because it treated adult and sane human beings 'as immature children' who cannot be entrusted with responsibility for their own lives. It thereby 'suspends' their freedom and obliges them 'to behave purely passively'.[37] The same moral criticism can be made against international trusteeship to rehabilitate failed states.

The post-colonial states system is based on the opposite norms of pluralism and anti-paternalism. When countries cease to be colonies and become independent the legal and political responsibility of state sovereignty passes from the imperial power to the government of the newly or once again independent state. The local government is from that moment responsible for the conduct of the domestic and foreign affairs of the state. The imperial government is no longer responsible. Authority has passed from a government run by outsiders, and responsible to a foreign authority, to a locally sovereign government run by members of the indigenous population. The imperial government is legally and politically now out of the picture. Their international duty is to stay out and henceforward to refrain from intervening in what is now the domestic jurisdiction of a foreign state. The newly independent government is henceforth answerable *for* both the domestic policy and the foreign policy of the ex-colonial state. It is answerable *to* its own people and *to* other sovereign members of international society. That is the doctrine of state sovereignty expressed in terms of responsibility. The same reasoning applies to successor states that emerged from the political disintegration of the Soviet Union and former Yugoslavia. The British used to refer to that shift of sovereign authority and power as the acquisition of 'responsible government'. I believe that is a useful term which precisely captures recent and current international practice in the post-colonial *societas* of states.

---

[37] I. Kant, 'On the Relationship of Theory to Practice in Political Right', repr. in Reiss, *Kant's Political Writings*, 74. Also see in the same vein J. S. Mill, 'A Few Words on Non-Intervention', in *J. S. Mill, Essays on Politics and Culture*, ed. G. Himmelfarb (New York: Anchor Books, 1963) and M. Walzer, *Just and Unjust Wars*, 2nd edn. (New York: Basic Books, 1992), ch. 6. See the interesting commentary in Samuel LaSelva, 'Selling Oneself into Slavery: Mill on Paternalism', *Political Studies*, 35 (1987), 211–23.

What, then, ought to be done about failed states? There are various international options available to members of international society for that purpose. The sovereignty of failed states cannot rule out the perfectly legitimate and legal questions: Should we continue to trade with such countries? Should we cut them off from foreign investment? Should we isolate their governments?[38] Should they be exiled from international society? It is up to members of international society to decide whether they wish to see failed states continue to participate in their exclusive club. Failed states could be banished to the outer fringes of diplomacy or beyond. They could be expelled from international organizations. At the time of writing the British Commonwealth was considering proposals for tough new membership criteria based on democracy and respect for human rights which could result in the expulsion of Kenya, Pakistan, Sri Lanka, Zambia, and Zimbabwe.[39] Members of international society are fully entitled to use their financial aid or technical assistance to reward or punish foreign governments. They are perfectly within their rights to lay down domestic conditions—such as the protection of human rights or respect for the rule of law or the holding of democratic elections—in exchange for their international aid. If the government of the target country cannot accept those conditions they are free to refuse them. International society can get involved in the pacification or reconstruction or development of any country with the consent of its government. Peacekeeping is widely practised. International aid is widely practised. Many other military and diplomatic stratagems for dealing with failed states without violating their sovereignty are also available.

By positing the equal domestic value of member states of international society—their substantial equality rather than merely their formal equality—the egg-carton analogy is misleading. The society of sovereign states is not analogous to an egg-carton. The equality of states in international law is a formal equality only. It can only be formal because if it were substantive it would interfere with the sovereignty of countries. International society is fundamentally concerned with maintaining the peaceful coexistence of states but it is not concerned with ensuring the internal value of states according to some general standard comparable to that of 'fresh eggs'. Contemporary international society does not operate generally (that is, universally) with mandatory standards which exclusively concern the domestic civil conditions of states. It only operates that way voluntarily in certain world regions, such as contemporary Europe, where, for example, member states of the Council of Europe, the EU, and NATO's Partnership for Peace consent to intrusive international standards—such as human rights, the rule of law, protection of minorities, liberal democracy.

---

[38] I have elaborated on this point in R. Jackson, 'International Community Beyond the Cold War', in G. Lyons and M. Mastanduno (eds.), *Beyond Westphalia?* (Baltimore: Johns Hopkins, 1995), 59–83.

[39] *Weekly Telegraph* (10 Nov. 1999).

It might be argued that human rights norms justify international trusteeship for failed states. In general, human rights norms do not pre-empt the *Grundnorm* of non-intervention.[40] If human rights were a pre-emptive norm that was generally observed as such—the way that non-intervention is observed—we would be living in a very different world in which the *Grundnorm* would effectively be intervention rather than non-intervention. World politics would no longer presuppose states as independent communities framed by an international ethic of pluralism. There would be no fundamental right of self-defence for states. Instead, there would be a singular world community with a solidarist ethic. International peace and security would be subordinate to global human security. The basic normative framework of international relations would be a *universitas* rather than a *societas*. But the fact is that such a radically different world does not exist nor is it looming on the horizon. There is no compelling indication in state practice of which I am aware that solidarist ethics are pre-empting pluralist ethics in world politics.

European governments and peoples may be entering an era in which flagrant human rights violations can no longer be tolerated in any state in Europe—defined as Western, Central, and Eastern Europe, up to but not including the western border countries of Russia, or Russia itself. The distinction between the domestic sphere and the international sphere is becoming blurred in Europe and in the West more generally. Beyond the West, however, a sharp division between the domestic sphere and the foreign sphere continues to be the norm and that seems destined to continue for the foreseeable future. Perhaps the West is reinstating a new version of the normative distinction it used to draw between its own civilization and the rest of the world, but this time the West is only enforcing its standards in its own neighbourhood. Failed states in the rest of the world are of no pressing concern, but failed states in Europe are a matter of the greatest concern because Europe is now defined politically by the rule of law, by civil rights, by democracy, by minority rights, etc. Yugoslavia is part of Europe. For that reason the Yugoslavian government's oppression of the Kosovo Albanians cannot be tolerated.

Beyond North America and Western Europe it is a different story. The Turkish government's oppression of its Kurdish minority can be tolerated: Turkey is not understood to be European, at least not entirely so, and Turkey is essential to the West as a borderland outpost on turbulent and strategically important Central Asia. Russia's heavy-handed military action against armed secessionists in Chechnya must also be tolerated: Russia ambiguously straddles Europe and Asia; it is far too important politically and militarily and could never be treated like Yugoslavia; and its post-Soviet domestic anarchy and turmoil leaves no other reasonable choice. Both Turkey and Russia are members of the

---

[40] That is not to doubt that the concept and doctrine of humanitarian intervention is presently undergoing revision. See O. Ramsbotham, 'Humanitarian Intervention 1990–95: A Need to Reconceptualize?', *Review of International Studies*, 23 (1997).

OSCE but the OSCE cannot operate with the same humanitarian standards in Ankara or Vladivostok as it does in Amsterdam or Vancouver.[41]

Should we be concerned that the stronger states of Europe and North America are prepared to impose their values by armed force on a weaker European state that spurns their values, even if we agree with those values? I think we should be concerned because that imposition of armed force, even in the name of democracy and human rights, is a repudiation of a more fundamental value that was hard won after a long period of struggle around the world: international freedom expressed as self-determination, equal sovereignty, and non-intervention. In principle there is no difference between the basic standards of conduct of international society in the West and beyond the West. The West cannot place itself above international society. It can only create its own regional standards defined by treaties to which Western states can voluntarily accede and adhere.

This raises a further question that should not escape notice. Pluralist international society rests on a basic norm of restraint and non-activism. Behind that norm is a doctrine of international *laissez-faire*: on balance, the more desirable arrangement of international society is deemed to be one in which people across the world can experience political independence and should be left alone to make the best of it. The doctrine can also be expressed as the morality of 'tending your own patch': if every country is responsible for their own affairs the world will be a better place than if certain powerful countries are deemed to be responsible not only for their own political affairs but also for the governance of people in other countries—even if that responsibility is exercised as an international trust.

Again it is worth remembering that, for several centuries prior to the middle of the twentieth century, an activist doctrine of military intervention and foreign rule was a norm that was imposed by the West on most of the world. By 1960 that old doctrine had been completely repudiated by international society. That was not because trusteeship could not produce peace, order, and good governance in some places. It was because it was generally held to be wrong for people from some countries to appoint themselves and install themselves as rulers of people in other countries—and to apply foreign standards locally. Self-government was seen to be morally superior to foreign government, even if self-government was less effective and less civil and foreign government was more benevolent. Political *laissez-faire* was adopted as the universal norm of international society. Whatever we may prefer to call it, trusteeship is sharply at odds with the doctrine of international freedom based on self-determination and self-government. That pluralist arrangement of international society became the basic normative framework, in my view quite rightly, during the era of decolonization.

---

[41] The OSCE recognizes that and attempts to arrange 'institutions' and 'mechanisms' to deal with the reality. See *OSCE Handbook*, 3rd edn. (Vienna: OSCE, 1999).

Western leaders have no right to place themselves above international society, even in their relations with another European state, as long as respect for state sovereignty continues to be the universal standard of international conduct. Having a good cause, in this case the cause of democracy and human rights, which are now generally accepted standards of domestic governance in the West, and having the power to impose those standards by armed force relatively free of military risk on any remaining failed states or abusive states in Europe, is not a justification for trespassing on state sovereignty in that region or anywhere else.

12

International Boundaries as a Planetary Institution

A conventional starting-point of international relations scholarship is the division of the world's populated territory into independent political communities, or states, and the distinctive issues that involves: national security, war, intervention, alliances, trade, aid, refugees, and so forth. We could not get very far in trying to make sense of such issues without an underlying assumption about territorial limits of specified normative significance which mark the divisions between independent states: international boundaries. For the past several centuries such divisions have characterized an originally European and now a global international society. It is thus remarkable that state borders are usually taken for granted by international relations scholars.[1] They are a point of departure but they are not a subject of inquiry. My aim in this chapter is to sketch a classical approach to the study of international boundaries. I shall confine myself to three questions. What is the character and *modus operandi* of international boundaries? How are they determined and changed? Can the current practice of endorsing inherited and existing borders be justified?

What are International Boundaries?

The familiar lines on the political map of the world readily imprint themselves on our minds and give rise to a fixed mental image of world politics. They can easily be regarded as natural or inherent divisions of some kind. Yet it is obvious that neither borders nor the states defined by them are given in the nature of things: the political map could be different and in the past it has been different. International boundaries are political constructs. They remain political constructs even where they follow physical landforms or where they accompany ethnic or religious or linguistic or cultural divisions. They may be aligned with

[1] For a brief survey of the theory and practice of international boundaries see Robert H. Jackson and Mark W. Zacher, *The Territorial Covenant: International Society and the Stabilization of Boundaries* (Occasional Paper; Vancouver: Institute of International Relations, University of British Columbia, 1997). Also see Robert H. Jackson, 'Boundaries and International Society', in B. A. Roberson (ed.), *International Society in International Relations Theory* (London: Pinter, 1998).

these things but they should never be confused with them because they are categorically different. On this point it may be worth quoting Karl Popper whose acute understanding of the subject discloses his Central European background which provides a rich storehouse of experience in such matters:

There are no natural boundaries to a state. The boundaries of a state change, and can be defined only by applying the principle of a *status quo*; and since every *status quo* must refer to an arbitrarily chosen date, the determination of the boundaries of a state is purely conventional . . . Here, if anywhere, we should learn from history; for since the dawn of history, men have been continually mixed, unified, broken up, and mixed again.[2]

All that exists 'naturally' are individual men and women with the inclination and aptitude to associate and dissociate in various, often complicated, and even paradoxical ways, in accordance with whatever ideas about their collective selves they have at hand at the time.

One such idea is international boundaries which currently divide the human population of the planet into about 190 independent states. A world without independent states would be a world without international boundaries, although obviously not without borders of some kind. And just like the states themselves, the boundaries between them are political arrangements: they can be set up, they can be defended, they can be violated, they can be disregarded, they can be moved, they can be dismantled, and their status and uses can be changed. The history of world politics is in significant part a story of such episodes. Boundaries are part and parcel of the historical institution of sovereign statehood.

We should distinguish territories and populations. International boundaries are territorial: geographical lines represented on political maps that divide the human population of the world into different residential territories. International boundaries are not, strictly speaking, sociological or anthropological. Particular human populations live in particular state territories but it is the territories that are marked by international boundaries and not the human populations that live in them. We should also therefore distinguish two fundamental kinds of political borders: those which disclose juridical differentiation in terms of state sovereignty, colonial status, provincial and municipal jurisdiction, and those which disclose sociological distinctiveness. International boundaries belong entirely to the juridical category, even where they follow the contours of culture, language, religion, etc.

State jurisdiction and sociological identity are two categorically different markers of human groups: the one may shed light on the other, the one may be in dialogue with the other, the one may add normative grounding to the other, the legality of one may conflict with the legitimacy of the other. But they should never be confused with each other or conflated even where they coincide. To do that is to make a category mistake, to muddle categorically different subjects.[3]

---

[2] Karl Popper, *The Open Society and its Enemies*, i (Princeton: Princeton University Press, 1971), 288 n. 7 (original emphasis).

[3] Gilbert Ryle, *The Concept of Mind* (Harmondsworth: Penguin Books, 1963), esp. ch. 2.

For, as Onora O'Neill points out, 'if the social conceptions of nation, tribe, community or people are to do the work of justifying the territorial boundaries between political units, they must not be redefined in terms that presuppose these boundaries. Such definitional strategies undercut the aim of vindicating territorial boundaries or changes in boundaries by appeals to national and other identities.'[4] Any inquiry that seeks to capture the *modus operandi* of international boundaries must take their juridical character fully on board.

There is nothing in the logic of international boundaries, *as such*, which presupposes something called the 'nation' or the 'nation-state'. That is a distinctive and fundamental justification of boundaries that was characteristic of the nineteenth and twentieth centuries and is likely to persist well into the twenty-first century. There have of course been other justifications in earlier centuries, the most common of which is that of dynastic title to territory: the usual normative claim of kingdoms. During the Middle Ages quasi-independent territory was held by bishops and other clerical authorities of the Christian Church: Europe was divided territorially into bishoprics as well as kingdoms; some bishops were quasi-independent and some were under the jurisdiction of the pope in Rome.[5] That created ambiguity regarding territorial jurisdiction which was an awkward feature of political life and a source of political conflict.

The key to international boundaries is not the nation or the tribe or the linguistic or religious community or any other sociologically distinctive group. Rather, it is the desire or determination or right or obligation or tradition or resignation or some other joint inclination of certain people—who may or may not be alike in important sociological respects—to reside territorially apart as a group on a basis of independence from all other such groups. The particular people residing in those territories may share sociological characteristics (language, religion, culture, etc.) and they may very well understand their common social identity as the underlying vindication of their claim to an independent state jurisdiction. But social identity is not the same as state jurisdiction, which may, and usually does, assemble within the same bordered territory groups of people who are different in sociological terms. Most states today are multiethnic in social composition.

International boundaries are artificial geographical lines which mark the furthest extent of the territorial jurisdictions of sovereign states. Beyond that limit a particular state has no jurisdiction—although its power, wealth, influence, or prestige may still be strongly felt. For beyond that line is the jurisdiction of another sovereign state or the absence of state jurisdiction—for example, the high seas beyond the maritime limits of particular states. Furthermore, even though states are separated by international boundaries they nevertheless share

---

[4] Onora O'Neill, 'Justice and boundaries', in Chris Brown (ed.), *Political Restructuring in Europe* (London: Routledge, 1994), 77.

[5] H. C. Darby and H. Fullard (ed.), *The New Cambridge Modern History Atlas* (Cambridge: Cambridge University Press, 1970), 66–7.

them: they hold in common that which divides them. An international border is, by definition and by geometry, always held by two sovereign states. The forty-ninth parallel belongs, so to say, to both the USA and Canada: it is the survey line that the USA and Great Britain came to accept historically (1818, 1846) as marking the border between their two international jurisdictions in the western half of the North American continent.[6] International boundaries signify not only the territorial jurisdictions of states but also the association of states: they are a constitutive element of international society.

Speaking metaphorically, the boundary is a fence or wall or moat around our place or home or sanctuary: a particular geographical space where we can enjoy or suffer our own independent political life without external interference. At one time, not very long ago, international boundaries delimited not only locally independent states but also colonial territories. Great Britain and British dependencies in North and South America, Asia, Africa, and Oceania composed one vast multi-territorial and transglobal state: the British Empire. But today there are no significant colonial territories; empires are a thing of the past. International boundaries nowadays delimit territorial spheres of local political independence: a place of government by ourselves rather than by somebody else. International boundaries are closely connected with the value of political freedom in the negative, non-interference meaning of the term.[7] Article 2 of the UN charter forbids 'the threat or use of force against the territorial integrity' of states. That rule applies to all sovereign states without exception. The UN charter does not forbid transnational activities across boundaries: that would be absurd. Nor does it forbid changes of borders that are consented to by the governments of all affected state jurisdictions. Nor does it forbid changes in their uses and significance. It only forbids intervention and other arbitrary and intrusive international activities that trespass on international boundaries and involve the threat or use of force. In other words it upholds the value of state sovereignty.

Boundaries frame the numerous territorial spheres of pluralist world politics with regard to which non-intervention and other sovereign rights and duties are defined. They also delimit the territorial sphere of the national interest and national security, although being formal arrangements they cannot of course by themselves provide the substance of national security. They do not delimit the non-territorial sphere of the national interest, which in the case of great powers can extend far beyond their national borders. To enjoy permanently secure borders, however, is not to live behind a maginot line. Rather, it is to live in an international society in which state borders are generally regarded as legitimate and lawful. Even though international boundaries are 'purely conventional' they nevertheless disclose remarkable stability and continuity over historical time.

---

[6] Ibid. 202.

[7] See Isaiah Berlin, *Four Essays on Liberty* (Oxford: Oxford University Press, 1969), ch. 3, and R. Jackson, *Quasi-States* (Cambridge: Cambridge University Press, 1990), ch. 2.

Expediency or inertia or habit or indifference can play an important role in preserving particular international boundaries in their existing locations. But they are sustained at a more fundamental level by their mutual acceptance, or at least their toleration, by the countries delimited by them and by any other countries with an interest or stake in them—especially major powers in a position to trespass on them.

That is a major international change from earlier periods when borders were more narrowly utilitarian, more instrumental and expedient. The alteration of international frontiers by force, usually as a result of war, was an accepted and not uncommon practice historically. Armed intervention and conquest of foreign territory used to be a right of sovereign states that was acknowledged as such by international law. In the twentieth century, however, borders have acquired heightened legitimacy, a degree of sanctity, and increased immunity to forced and unconsented change. That discloses the doctrine of *uti possidetis juris*, discussed below, according to which existing boundaries are the pre-emptive basis for determining territorial jurisdictions in the absence of mutual agreement to do otherwise. That conservative doctrine has increasingly taken hold in post-1945 and post-colonial international society. It was strongly evident in determining the international borders of the new states of Asia, Africa, and the Middle East, and of the emergent or re-emergent states of the former Soviet Union and the former Yugoslavia.

None of the foregoing is meant to deny the obvious fact that resident populations of independent states are subject to endless influences which originate beyond the borders of their state and profoundly affect their daily lives. Not only commerce or mass travel or global communications or environmental pollution or the internet but also many other influences, social and natural, regularly intersect international boundaries. That is only to be expected. I am not referring to physical separateness or political isolation or economic autarky or any other international quarantine or seclusion or solitude. Complete insularity is historically unusual and increasingly rare in a contemporary world that is globalizing and shrinking rapidly. I am referring to a fundamentally important kind of bordered territorial jurisdiction.

These remarks also are in no way intended to suggest that the uses and significance of international boundaries are immune to change. On the contrary, like states themselves, borders are an evolving institution. They have been put to different uses at different times and places. That is particularly so when it comes to the movements of people, money, and goods across them.[8] Some borders are higher in that respect. Some are lower. Some borders are policed more effectively than others. As indicated, they generally define a territorial space within which particular groups of people can live their collective lives free from

---

[8] See Brian Barry and Robert E. Goodin (eds.), 'Symposium on Duties Beyond Borders', *Ethics*, 98 (1988), 647–756 and by the same editors *Free Movement* (London: Harvester Wheatsheaf, 1992).

external interference. They can in that connection quite legitimately be used to bar foreigners from gaining access to the political, economic, and social goods associated with particular independent states. Immigration laws and refugee laws serve that legitimate purpose. But international borders can also occasionally be used to imprison people and to bar them from escaping a totalitarian state: the Berlin Wall and the rest of the East–West frontier was employed for that purpose by the Soviet bloc states during the cold war. They have been put to many other uses as well.

Yet, despite their changing uses, international boundaries disclose a more or less consistent normative logic as markers of independent state jurisdictions of a pluralistic international society. It is that constitutional aspect of international boundaries, what they are *in themselves* and the norms they embody rather than their instrumental or policy uses, that is the main concern of this chapter. Whatever we can learn about their normative logic should assist us to understand more fully the international society of which they are a constituent part.

Juridical Insiders and Sociological Outsiders

'Which peoples have the right to draw a line around themselves and constitute a sovereign state?'[9] This deceptively simple question was raised in a discussion of nationhood and nationalism. The question is misleading because it suggests that political groups can determine their borders by themselves. That overlooks the fact that borders are a social relation: they always involve the people on the other side with whom the border is shared. We are also dealing with a question that involves not only the right of self-determination but other international norms as well, among the most important of which are: respect for pre-existing territorial jurisdictions and the consent of independent states that partake of the same border.

In investigating the *modus operandi* of international boundaries, as a first approximation we can say that they disclose an obvious normative distinction between insider groups and outsider groups in international relations. That differentiation has a dual aspect. It can refer to the conspicuous territorial divisions between the different groups of people around the world who form contiguous sovereign states: the ordinary we/they of international relations: the USA, Canada, Mexico, etc. In that regard it is a dimension of state sovereignty. But it can also refer to the underlying constitutional division between, on the one hand, those residential groups who are members of international society and thus enjoy legal standing as sovereign states, and, on the other hand, those residential groups who do not possess sovereignty but who may harbour a desire

[9] 'The Warmth of Nationhood', *Times Literary Supplement* (19 Feb. 1993), 14.

to be full-fledged members of international society: for example, Canada versus Quebec. In that regard it is a dimension of self-determination.

Boundaries are a constitutive element of state sovereignty: they reveal the spatial aspect of the *societas* of states; they are an integral institution of international pluralism which today exists on a global scale. That is the common-sense understanding of boundaries as lines on the political map that mark the ordinary we/they of international relations. It is that practical reality of international boundaries that we experience when we travel outside our own country: our transborder movements can be subject to surveillance, regulation, and control of greater or lesser intrusiveness and effectiveness by border officials and other state authorities. Much the same can be said of the movement of money and goods around the world. That is notwithstanding the fact that nowadays some global transactions, especially the movement of money via computers, can escape from state monitoring and regulation. What international boundaries signify in terms of a check on the movement of people, money, and goods is something that varies from time to time and from place to place.[10] But whatever boundaries may signify operationally at any moment, it is clear that they constitute a barrier which is under the legal control of the states whose borders they happen to be.

Boundaries are also but perhaps less obviously an aspect of self-determination. In light of the doctrine of national self-determination which came to the fore in the twentieth century, it is perhaps ironic that most territory-based sociological groups from which people derive important identities (religious, ethnic, cultural, etc.) are international outsiders: they are not independent. To be sure, almost every last individual human being on earth is today an international insider in being a member of an independent state. That admission of virtually everybody to indirect membership of the *societas* of states is one of the great international changes of the twentieth century. It is an achievement, specifically, of decolonization: the dismantling of the obstacle which for so long barred so many people around the world from internationally recognized citizenship in a locally sovereign state. It is noteworthy and significant that that international enfranchisement was usually carried out only with regard to pre-existing juridical entities that were already on the map, although they were not independent: Nigeria, Sudan, Iraq, Philippines, etc. Colonial jurisdictions became independent states. But, as a rule, indigenous residential groups that never possessed a prior juridical existence did not become independent states: for example, the Ibo nation of eastern Nigeria, the African people of the southern Sudan, the Kurds of Iraq, the people of the Philippine island of Mindinao. They remain subordinated within independent state jurisdictions and often divided by international boundaries. That has resulted in the multi-ethnic statehood of the ex-colonial world.

The insiders of contemporary international society are those groups which exist on the juridical plane of political independence almost all of which are

---

[10] Barry and Goodin, *Free Movement.*

members of the United Nations. As indicated, at the start of the twenty-first century the number of such entities was about 190 and rising; prior to the Second World War it was much lower, owing to the existence of far-flung imperial states. At its founding in 1945 the UN had fifty-one members. The remarkable expansion of UN membership in the second half of the twentieth century was mostly a result of European decolonization and the breakup of the quasi-imperial Soviet Union and former Yugoslavia. Yet, in spite of that profound expansion of membership of the society of states, the number of independent countries in existence is still limited. Independence is a scarce commodity which has never been available to every residential group that might conceivably be a candidate for it. Most such groups are not themselves sovereign members of international society; they are segments of the population of sovereign jurisdictions. Independence has always been rationed and regulated by those who currently enjoy it. Hence its high value historically. Another way of putting that is to say that international society is an exclusive club that is not easy to join.

The outsiders of contemporary international society are those residential groups which enjoy no legal existence as independent states—no matter how profoundly significant they may be sociologically: for example, the Welsh, the Basques, the Kurds, the Chechyns, the Maoris, among many others. There are numerous groups of that kind around the world. But their prospects of gaining independence if they want it are not very good. That is because all the earth's territory has been parcelled into locally sovereign jurisdictions. Independence for particular religious, linguistic, or cultural groups in the present arrangement of world politics would involve a loss of territory for one or more independent states. That would be certain to provoke acute international controversy and determined opposition by negatively affected state parties.

State sovereignty is not something that is handed out on demand; nor is it readily partitioned and reapportioned. States are a positional good because they are based on territory which is finite: there is a limited supply of such goods and the market for them is zero-sum.[11] The reallocation of state sovereignty is dislocational and disruptive not only to the particular state involved, and its population, but also to neighbouring states and populations and to the states system at large. If Quebec becomes a sovereign state Canada must relinquish sovereignty over that territory and its population, the USA must accept a new state on its borders, and the international organizations to which both states belong must deal with that reality. Any change of status from outsider to insider would have to be justified to all affected parties. There is thus a rather strong and persistent conservatism in the drawing and enforcing of boundaries which favours existing states over potential new states, even if the prospective new states would very likely be a more rational political construct (Quebec) than the existing state

[11] For further discussion of the notion of 'positional goods' see F. Hirsch, *The Social Limits to Growth* (Cambridge, Mass.: Harvard University Press, 1976) and A. H. Halsey, *Change in British Society*, 2nd edn. (Oxford: Oxford University Press, 1981), 15.

jurisdiction (Canada). That conservatism is extremely difficult to overcome. As indicated, it has only happened in exceptional international circumstances, such as the end of major wars or the breakup of empires.

In the practice of twentieth-century world politics, the 'self' in self-determination is juridical and not sociological. Even though the Wilsonian doctrine of self-determination gave a strong ideological and political boost to new state formation in Central and Eastern Europe following the First World War, based on national identity, most of the entities that were internationally enfranchised had a previous juridical existence as subsidiary units of various kinds (provinces, administrative areas, military districts, etc.) within one or the other of the former German, Austro-Hungarian, Turkish, or Russian empires. As indicated, virtually all of the new states of the Third World previously were colonies or other jurisdictions created by Western colonialism. Not only in Africa but also in South America, and Asia, most existing borders are virtually identical to those of the colonial era. Even in North Africa and the Middle East the old colonial frontiers which divided the Arab 'nation' into many territorial jurisdictions have been not only accepted but declared as legitimate and legal by the vast majority of Arab states and their regional organizations: a juridical ethic which in Arab eyes not only condemned the 1948 borders of Israel, which were in conflict with the pre-existing borders of Palestine, but also Iraq's invasion of Kuwait in 1990.

The world's ethnonationalities usually have not been able to draw an international line around themselves. Virtually all the new states that were created or resurrected (Poland) in the aftermath of the First World War were multi-ethnic in social composition. Ethnonationalities which could not secure independent statehood for themselves were recognized and protected as national minorities under the League of Nations.[12] The new state jurisdictions of Asia and Africa were also multi-ethnic and usually contained significant minority communities, but they were not recognized internationally either by the UN or by regional international organizations. Minority rights have been confined largely to Europe. Most of the world's numerous ethnonational communities have no international status, either as independent states or recognized national minorities. They remain submerged within or between existing state jurisdictions.

It might be thought that the new states that emerged after the cold war in the former Soviet Union and former Yugoslavia contradict the practice of juridical self-determination. But the successor states that were established by the dismantling of the USSR had previously been federal administrative jurisdictions: the so-called national 'republics' which included Russia, Ukraine, Belorus, Georgia, Armenia, Azerbaijan, Tajikistan, among others. Many of these territo-

---

[12] Jennifer Jackson Preece, *National Minorities and the European Nation-States System* (Oxford: Clarendon Press, 1998). Also see her 'Minority Rights in Europe: From Westphalia to Helsinki', *Review of International Studies*, 23 (Jan. 1997), 75–92.

rial jurisdictions were originally framed in the eighteenth and nineteenth century by the Tsarist empire which the communists inherited in 1917 and perpetuated in the form of the USSR. The internal borders of former Yugoslavia which were later used to define the independent states of Slovenia, Croatia, Bosnia, etc. originally were administrative boundaries inherited from the late Habsburg and Ottoman periods that were reconsolidated by communist Yugoslavia after the Second World War.[13] The internal juridical borders of the Austro-Hungarian and Turkish Empires, rather than the ethnonational divisions of the resident populations, usually defined the boundaries of the new Balkan states. The border between the Czech Republic and Slovakia also originates in the Habsburg Empire.

To sum up thus far: the twentieth-century normative practice of upholding a universal right of self-determination effected a major expansion of international society which more than trebled the number of independent countries in the second half of the century alone. But the previously outsider groups who became sovereign insiders have in almost every case had an immediate prior existence as a juridical entity. Independence has almost always involved an elevation of the legal status of a territory. Most of these elevated territories formerly were either colonies of overseas empires or internal administrative units of federal states. In the practice of national self-determination the focus is thus on 'nations' defined in a juridical sense: the population residing within the boundaries of a particular territory. The focus is not on the sociological (ethnonational) characteristics of particular populations. In international politics during this period the juridical has clearly and decisively trumped the sociological. In short, ethnonational identity alone is not sufficient to give a group the right to draw an international boundary around itself. At a minimum what seems to be required is a prior existence as a juridical unit of some kind, already in possession of territorial borders which in the right circumstances can be elevated into international boundaries and recognized as such. International boundaries are almost always likely to be political borders that are historically inherited rather than drawn from scratch in accordance with ethnographic information.

The Principle of *Uti Possidetis Juris*

Historically in Europe, before the era of self-determination, international boundaries and the territories they defined were regulated by rules of inheritance, marriage, purchase, conquest, and so forth. Territory was exchangeable property. But above all borders were determined by war.[14] Territory was the spoils of military victory. There was an international right of conquest. Boundaries

---

[13] N. Malcolm, *Bosnia: A Short History* (London: Macmillan, 1994), p. xxii.
[14] See Jackson and Zacher, *Territorial Covenant*.

determined by armed force defined independent jurisdictions until such time as territorial conflicts again arose and a new *status quo* was established. At the start of wars, borders were crossed and jurisdictions invaded by military powers; at the end of wars, borders were redrawn to satisfy the victors. Thus in 1815 the borders of defeated France and in 1918 those of defeated Germany were altered to the advantage of the victorious powers. The Napoleonic Wars and the First World War reshaped the political map, as did other wars before and since. The last major realignment of international boundaries by force was of course wrought by the Allied powers in the Second World War and agreed, specifically, between the USA, the Soviet Union, and Great Britain at the Tehran conference (1943) and the Potsdam conference (1945).[15]

Today, however, we are living in a different political world, in which frontiers determined by force in violation of the UN charter cannot be recognized.[16] Since 1945 international society has been prepared to sanction the use of force only to defend, preserve, or restore existing borders. That is the obstacle that the Serbs were unable to overcome in their attempt at armed secession from Croatia and Bosnia-Herzegovina. It is the barrier that stood in the way of international recognition of borders imposed by the Israeli army in the Gaza Strip, the Golan Heights, the West Bank, and East Jerusalem. It prevented international recognition of Turkish occupied Cyprus and Indonesian occupied East Timor. That is a fundamental change in the *modus operandi* of international society, with many important and far-reaching consequences.

In the second half of the twentieth century, the political map of the world became frozen in its current juridical pattern. There was an entrenchment of the *status quo*: existing borders became sacrosanct and lawful border change correspondingly difficult. In post-1945 Europe and post-colonial Africa, juridical borders have been preserved almost without exception, even in the face of armed challenges to them. In Africa that is all the more surprising in light of the profound weakness of the existing states, most of which are seriously deficient in domestic legitimacy, stability, unity, and capability.[17] In Europe the major apparent exception is the unification of East and West Germany. It should be noted, however, that the external post-1945 borders of former East and West Germany were not altered in the slightest degree.

In Europe the preservation of existing borders is a central principle of the Organization for Security and Cooperation in Europe and the Council of Europe. The 1975 Helsinki Final Act expressed the principle that 'frontiers can [only] be changed, in accordance with international law, by peaceful means and by agreement'. The 1990 Charter of Paris for a New Europe reiterated the same principle. In Africa respect for borders is a sacred norm of the Organization of

---

[15] G. Weinberg, *A World at Arms* (Cambridge: Cambridge University Press, 1994), 630, 838.

[16] See Jackson and Zacher, *Territorial Covenant*.

[17] Robert H. Jackson and Carl G. Rosberg, 'Why Africa's Weak States Persist', *World Politics*, 35 (1982), 1–24.

African Unity. Everywhere it is a fundamental article of the UN charter: it is part and parcel of the *Grundnorm* of non-intervention. It seems nowadays that boundaries cannot be modified even to punish an aggressor state: Iraq retained its borders despite having committed the crime of aggression and having suffered an overwhelming military defeat in the Gulf War. We are living at a time when existing international boundaries are vested with exceptional and, indeed, almost absolute value: they are an expression of legitimacy as well as legality.

The principle involved is that of *uti possidetis, ita possideatis*: 'as you possess, so you may possess'. Translated into the normative discourse of contemporary international society the principle can be rendered as follows: respect current borders unless all of the states who share them consent to change them. That is the accepted norm for determining international boundaries in ex-colonial situations and in the context of the breakup of states if consent to redraw borders is not forthcoming from all affected states. Thus, if Quebec were to secede from Canada, its current provincial borders would serve as international boundaries in the absence of any agreement, between Ottawa and Quebec City and possibly also Washington, to change them.

That principle originated in nineteenth-century Latin America.[18] Colonial administrative boundaries were largely followed in drawing international frontiers in the absence of any alternative territorial norm that could secure general acceptance. Thus Peru, Chile, Ecuador (Quito), Columbia (Caracas), etc., became independent states. As Fred Parkinson remarks, 'The principle of *uti possidetis juris* was a great help in enabling the region to weather the storm of state succession.'[19] The new states of Latin America converged on that norm and they have kept with it. Since 1930 it has been not only a generally recognized practice but also an explicit principle of international law in treaties between Latin American states. The Latin American precedent was followed in Africa at the time of decolonization in the 1960s: colonial borders were the only generally acceptable basis for determining the new international frontiers of the continent. The Organization of African Unity is based on that principle, which is expressed in Article 3 of its charter. In both Latin America and Africa *uti possidetis juris* was closely connected to the search for a viable normative foundation for regional peace, order, and security after decolonization.

The latest stage in the evolution of *uti possidetis juris* was the disintegration of the USSR and former Yugoslavia at the end of the cold war. As regards the breakup of the USSR, the internal (federal) administrative borders became the international boundaries of the successor Commonwealth of Independent States

---

[18] For the origins and development of this practice in the emergence of independent states in the new world see Fred Parkinson, 'Latin America', in Robert H. Jackson and Alan James (eds.), *States in a Changing World* (Oxford: Clarendon Press, 1993), 240–61. For a comparison of the practice in Latin America and Africa see A. Kacowicz, *Zones of Peace in the Third World* (New York: SUNY Press, 1998), chs. 3 and 4.

[19] Parkinson, 'Latin America', 241.

(CIS). As regards former Yugoslavia, whose disintegration was more violent and more dangerous, the internal administrative borders were used to define the successor states. As indicated in Chapter 10, in 1991 the EU created an Arbitral Commission chaired by Robert Badinter, President of the French Constitutional Council, to rule on the validity of various claims for self-determination in former Yugoslavia. They underlined the crucial importance of *uti possidetis juris*: 'The territorial integrity of States, this great principle of peace, indispensable to international stability . . . has today acquired the character of a universal and preemptory norm. The people of former colonial countries were wise to apply it; Europeans must not commit the folly of dispensing with it.'[20] That same norm was the basis of the Dayton Agreement arranged by American diplomacy and signed between Bosnia-Herzegovina, Serbia, and Croatia.

The current international norm of *uti possidetis juris* can be summarized as follows: (i) existing interstate borders are legitimate, legal, and inviolable; (ii) change of borders by force is illegitimate and illegal; (iii) if borders are to be changed, all states affected by the change must give their consent; (iv) in the absence of general consent to change borders, if secession is to occur international boundaries of seceding states should follow the internal administrative boundaries of the state from which they seceded; (v) ethnonations have no inherent right of self-determination, and the only recognized nation-state is the population group residing within borders defined by juridical boundaries, that is, the political or civic nationality.[21] In short, ethnonationality or any other exclusively sociological definition of the collective self is not, by itself, a valid basis for a claim of self-determination.

Redrawing International Boundaries by Force

In order to assess the significance of the foregoing norm it may be instructive to glance back at some important territorial conflicts that occurred in the twentieth century after the end of colonialism to see what international precedents have been set.

Other episodes could be mentioned but the following ones can perhaps suffice to indicate the geographical scope of the issue: Israeli conquest and occupation of the West Bank and East Jerusalem, the Golan Heights, and the Gaza Strip; North Korea's unsuccessful invasion of South Korea; North Vietnam's invasion, conquest, and annexation of South Vietnam; a war of conquest and subjugation waged by Morocco to prevent the emergence of Western Sahara (former Spanish Sahara) as an independent state; a successful war of independ-

---

[20] A. Pellet, 'The Opinions of the Badinter Arbitration Committee', *European Journal of International Law*, 3 (1992), 178–85.

[21] This formulation draws on Jackson and Zacher, *Territorial Covenant*.

ence by Eritrean secessionists against the government of Ethiopia; the military partition of Cyprus as a result of a Turkish invasion and occupation of the northern part of the island; the forcible takeover of Goa (a contiguous Portuguese territory) by India; a civil war in Pakistan that involved the intervention of India and resulted in the partition of the country and the independence of Bangladesh (formerly East Pakistan); the invasion, occupation and attempted annexation of East Timor (a former Portuguese colony) by Indonesia; the invasion and takeover of Tibet by China; the unsuccessful invasion, occupation, and attempted annexation of Kuwait by Iraq; the secession of northern Somalia as the self-styled Republic of Somaliland.

The 1947 partition of British India which produced two successor states—mainly Hindu India and Muslim Pakistan, the latter state consisting of two non-contiguous territories a subcontinent apart (East and West Pakistan)—is an exception to the practice of *uti possidetis juris*. When Pakistan later was forcibly divided into two successor states, the boundaries of Bangladesh were identical to those of former East Pakistan. The 1948 partition of Palestine is another exception. But the subsequent Israeli occupation of neighbouring Arab territories by means of war was never recognized and the vast majority of states support UN Security Council Resolution 242 which recognizes the 1948 borders and calls upon Israel to return the Arab lands it has conquered. The Korean War resulted in a stalemate along a demilitarized zone close to the thirty-eighth parallel that originally separated the two Koreas. The armed annexation of Portuguese Goa by India is best understood as an act of anti-colonial liberation. The communist victory in the Vietnam War restored the unity of Vietnam that existed prior to the 1954 Paris peace accord which partitioned French Indochina into two independent states. The forcible integration of Portuguese East Timor into Indonesia was highly controversial within international society for more than two decades, was never recognized, and Indonesia vacated the territory in 1999 in response to a UN Security Council resolution to that effect. An apparent exception is the Chinese takeover of Tibet. But the legal independence of the latter before the takeover was in doubt: China's historic relationship to Tibet was one of suzerainty and not one of equal sovereignty; Tibet was a 'vassal state' of China.[22] The Turkish occupation and partition of Cyprus was never recognized.

Eritrea and Somaliland appear at first glance to confound existing practice, yet on closer examination they both disclose unmistakable features of *uti possidetis juris*. Eritrea is a former Italian colony which was incorporated into Ethiopia in 1952 after the UN General Assembly recommended that it become an autonomous province of Ethiopia.[23] Following a long civil war it became independent in 1993 with the consent of Addis Ababa. It should be noted that

---

[22] G. Schwarzenberger and E. Brown, *A Manual of International Law*, 6th edn. (London: Professional Books, 1976), 568.
[23] See Martin Shaw, *Title to Territory in Africa* (Oxford: Clarendon Press, 1984), 118–19.

other rebellious regions of Ethiopia which previously had not been separate colonies have not followed Eritrea into independence. The Republic of Somaliland is broadly similar, in so far as it was the 'British Protectorate of Somaliland' before being integrated into Somalia in 1960 through union with the former Italian Somaliland. At the time of writing, its prospects of gaining international recognition were slim, despite the virtual disappearance of Somalia as an organized state. Somalia would have to consent to any such change, which is unlikely. But even if Somaliland became a member of international society it would be as consistent with juridical practice as the case of Eritrea, since pre-existing colonial boundaries would define its territorial jurisdiction.

Recent armed conflicts in the ex-USSR and former Yugoslavia pose a more serious challenge to the practice of juridical self-determination and might appear to violate the norm of *uti possidetis juris*. The breakup of the Soviet Union was followed by several ethnonational discords with a potential for disrupting inter-national borders including, for example, the Armenia–Azerbaijan War over the disputed territory of Nagorno-Karabakh, and the war in the Russian Federation involving Chechnya. Even in these cases, however, demands for independence were registered in terms of existing juridical borders: Nagorno-Karabakh is a region on the map of the Caucasus and Chechnya is an autonomous republic of the Russian Federation. These conflicts primarily concerned the status of those borders: the main issue at stake was whether their current status would be changed or not.

Probably the most serious challenge to the practice of respecting existing jurid-ical borders was registered in the former Yugoslavia. In 1992, following the inde-pendence of Croatia and Bosnia-Herzegovina, armed conflicts broke out (in Croatia) over territory populated in significant part by ethnic Serbs and (in Bosnia-Herzegovina) over territories populated substantially by ethnic Serbs or by ethnic Croats. In Croatia, about a third of the country was seized by Serb militias during an intense war for control of two regions (the Krajina and Slavonia), both of which were heavily populated by Serbs. Serb militias took control of an arc of Serb-populated territory with the evident aim of forming a close association, and perhaps uniting, with neighbouring Serbia. Croat militias did the same in south-ern Herzegovina, aiming, presumably, at a political linkage with the contiguous coastal territories of Croatia. The greater part of Bosnia-Herzegovina was carved up by military force. However, the international community responded to these events by absolutely refusing to recognize any further redrawing of the political map of the Balkans by force. That categorical refusal was underwritten by the OSCE, upheld by the UN and the EU, affirmed at a 1992 conference in London, and enshrined in the Dayton Agreement. The successor states of the former Yugoslavia, Slovenia, Croatia, Bosnia-Herzegovina, Macedonia, and the residual Yugoslav rump state of Serbia-Montenegro, remained intact. The remaining test cases in the Balkans are Kosovo and Montenegro both of whom were in rebellion against rump Yugoslavia at the time of writing.

In short, even though there have been significant territorial wars since 1945, many of them rooted in ethnonational conflicts, they have not dented the norm of *uti possidetis juris*—at least not to date. If anything, they are the exceptions that prove the rule. In the determination of international boundaries it is juridical considerations and not sociological criteria that count. International society does not look kindly on territorial partition: no doubt with the troublesome partitions of Ireland, Palestine, and India in mind.

Justifying Juridical Statehood

The deeply troubled experience of Bosnia and Kosovo in the 1990s raises a fundamental question about the wisdom and compassion of the current juridical practice regarding international boundaries. Lord Carrington, a former EU emissary to Bosnia, remarked in a 1994 interview:

You could make out a very good argument—though it would be considered probably very callous—that by intervening [in Bosnia] we [the UN and the EU] have actually caused more casualties, more ethnic cleansing, more misery than if we'd never intervened at all. Because if we had not intervened this thing would have been settled two years ago. There would have been some very unhappy people, but at the end of all this there are going to be very unhappy people whatever happens.[24]

That is the argument of classical realism and the right of conquest: providing they pose no international threat, it is better to allow territorial wars to take their course than to try to bottle them up, because they are a cleaner and quicker method of resolving ethnic conflicts than trying to pacify them by foreign intervention. Suppressing them is likely to produce more rather than less human suffering.

Yet that is not the prevailing sentiment among international policy-makers nowadays. No responsible statesman or stateswoman wants to restore the right of conquest and forced population transfer.[25] That idea was killed and buried after the Second World War. Apart from recent ambiguous events in the Balkans, there is little sign that it will soon be resurrected. If historical experience is anything to go by, there is a profound international reluctance to include non-juridical considerations such as ethnicity, language, religion, or culture in determining international boundaries. Given the numerous places around the world where the status or the location of boundaries is in dispute, it seems highly unlikely that international society and the vast majority of its members

---

[24] *The Financial Times* (31 Dec. 1994).

[25] See J. Jackson Preece, 'Ethnic Cleansing as an Instrument of Nation-State Creation', *Human Rights Quarterly*, 20 (1998), 817–43. Also see J. Schechtman, *European Population Transfers 1939–1945* (New York: OUP, 1946).

would wish to see any return to the traditional practice of territorial revision by armed force. The 1995 Dayton Agreement and the subsequent NATO occupation of Bosnia should be understood as the use of armed force to defend the principle of *uti possidetis juris* and not to reinstate the classical realism of an earlier era of world politics. Even the NATO occupation of Kosovo, which had the effect of strengthening demands for its secession from Yugoslavia, held back from supporting any secession that was not based on consent. The Rambouillet statement, which became the basis of the military and political settlement of the Kosovo crisis, registered respect for the territorial *status quo*. That is in keeping with established international practice, as affirmed by the UN, the OSCE, the EU, and other international organizations. There was a note of ambiguity, however, because Rambouillet also provided for an international conference to determine 'a final settlement for Kosovo' on the basis of 'the will of the people'. Since 'the people' evidently referred to the population of Kosovo, and not that of Yugoslavia, this introduced an element of sociological self-determination for Kosovo Albanians—who constitute a large majority of the population—which is difficult to reconcile with the principle of *uti possidetis juris*.

Kosovo brings clearly into view a big practical problem involved in the recognition of ethnonational borders which was initially encountered in Central and Eastern Europe at the end of the First World War but is now evident in many places around the world. It is the demographic-territorial fact that ethnonational populations are not located at fixed and consolidated positions on the ground, with clearly defined geographical borders that can readily be turned into international boundaries.[26] The fact is that ethnonational groups are residentially intermingled in most territories and it is impossible to draw geographical borders which neatly separate them. Ethnonational self-determination is not possible to achieve on the ground without engaging in forced population transfer, ethnic cleansing. That is a lesson of the breakup of the Austro-Hungarian Empire in 1918. It is also a lesson of the partitions of British India (1947) and Palestine (1948). It is the lesson of the redrawing of borders in Eastern Europe at the end of the Second World War. That same point has been made recently by Vernon Bogdanor in connection with Northern Ireland:

There is no way of drawing a boundary . . . which would not leave a large Nationalist minority in Northern Ireland. Were one or more counties to secede from the province the effect would be merely to create another dissident minority, of Unionists, in the republic . . . Thus the principle of self-determination . . . is of little help in a situation in which majorities and minorities are so inextricably bound together. The truth is that the problems of Northern Ireland cannot be solved by drawing lines on a map but only by developing relationships of consent inside and outside the province.[27]

In addition, there is a prudential concern that any broadening of the grounds of self-determination to include ethnonational considerations would spark

---

[26] See Jackson Preece, 'Minority Rights in Europe'.
[27] Letter to *The Times* (20 Apr. 1994).

demands for separatism or irredentism in many multi-ethnic states around the world. Since most states are multi-ethnic that could potentially result in a redrawing of international boundaries and the displacement of people on a global scale. That obviously would play havoc with international order. It would trespass upon what has become a well-established covenant of post-1945 international society: that states have a right to exist undisturbed in their current bordered territorial locations as long as they mind their own business. It is therefore out of the question. The vast majority of states seem to regard inherited boundaries as, on balance, both advantageous and legitimate and thus as a basis of both order and justice in world politics.

The sanctity and stability of inherited boundaries is a fundamental building block of international society and a principle behind which the vast majority of sovereign states can rally. A majority of the members of international society, probably the vast majority, would be adversely affected if the current practice were abandoned or even called into serious question out of preference for a sociological doctrine of national self-determination. If that were allowed to happen in Croatia or Bosnia-Herzegovina or Kosovo, for example, it could trigger demands for independence and possibly armed challenges to the sovereignty of other multi-ethnic states in the Balkan neighbourhood and beyond. There is thus a compelling common international interest in supporting the current juridical norm. Existing borders express a rare international consensus that gets beyond culture, religion, language, and most other sociological divisions between people. It even bridges the so-called clash of civilizations.[28] Of course, that does not mean that every state is likely to be satisfied with its current borders; many states may be dissatisfied. It means something more fundamental: that however awkward or unsatisfactory those borders may be in any particular case, they—and the juridical practice which underwrites them—can be a stable and generally accepted point of reference for everyone. In short, they can serve as a constitutive norm of international politics.

International boundaries provide the same fundamental service that constitutional rules provide for states domestically: a universally recognizable standard to live by. It may not be fair. It may not be just. It may not be equitable. But it has the enormous practical advantage of being determinate and predictable. Boundaries are a nexus between the interests of states and the norms of the society of states, in rather a parallel way to constitutional rules within states which are a nexus between the interests of political incumbents and the authority of the political offices they occupy. In a famous essay James Madison spoke of the necessity of balancing ambition and interests in a well-ordered constitution: 'Ambition must be made to counteract ambition. The interest of the man must be connected with the constitutional rights of the place.'[29] In successfully

---

[28] Samuel P. Huntington, *The Clash of Civilizations* (New York: Simon & Schuster, 1996). I expand on this point in Ch. 14.

[29] James Madison, *The Federalist*, No. 51, repr. in *American State Papers* (Chicago: Encyclopaedia Britannica, 1952), 163.

institutionalized domestic politics that connection is provided by an enlightened and effective constitution. In successfully institutionalized international politics, it is provided, in part, by stable, legitimate, and permanent boundaries which clearly delineate every independent country and mark its recognized and safe-guarded place on the map of the world.

Yet the current practice of sanctioning inherited and existing juridical bor-ders produces a significant normative problem of contemporary world politics. If ethnonational groups have no right to draw international boundaries around themselves and form independent states without first receiving the consent of all affected states—which is unlikely to be forthcoming in most cases—the ques-tion then becomes their political identity, security, and constitutional status in whatever existing state they find themselves. The sharply felt insecurity of Serbian minorities and their desire to remain in Yugoslavia without having to pack up and move away from where they were living were of course the vexing issues that provoked the armed conflicts in Croatia and Bosnia-Herzegovina. International society told them in no uncertain terms that they did not have any right to secede by force. Yet the Croatian and Bosnian Serbs did have a legit-imate claim to recognition and respect as a national minority. The Kosovo Albanians can make the same claim. European international society has estab-lished a precedent of recognizing the rights of national minorities within the framework of existing sovereign states.[30]

If *uti possidetis juris* is to be justified it would seem to call for the recognition of minority rights, or multiculturalism, on a much wider basis than exists at pre-sent. Otherwise it is exposed to the charge that it is unjust. It may also provoke rebellion by ethnonational groups against those states of international society in which they are resident, thereby undermining international order. The project of instituting some general norm of international legitimacy for national minor-ities would seem to be an important one to undertake if international society wishes to come to grips with conflicts that are provoked by the tendency in many places for juridical borders and sociological borders to diverge. That is all the more necessary if international society is no longer prepared to sanction the tra-ditional practices of determining boundaries by armed force and allowing forced population transfers. A gap in state practice was opened in the twentieth cen-tury by the abandonment of rights of conquest and forced population transfer, on the one hand, and the failure to promote minority rights, on the other hand. That is where this profoundly important issue stood at the start of the twenty-first century.

Of course there is an important quid pro quo: in such arrangements eth-nonational groups would have a reciprocal obligation to the state in which they enjoy minority rights. Such a constitutional bargain could be conceived as

---

[30] I am indebted to Jennifer Jackson Preece for the following discussion. See her *National Minorities and the European Nation-States System*.

involving, on the part of the former, loyalty to the state in which they reside and, on the part of the latter, political accommodation and legal recognition of resident minority groups. The Kosovo Albanian minority in rump Yugoslavia would accordingly be obliged to accept the authority of the Serb-dominated state and to respect resident Kosovo Serbs; the government in Belgrade would be bound to provide a safeguarded place for the Albanian minority within the state of Yugoslavia. That may not be possible owing to the profound mutual hostility between Albanians and Serbs generated by the violent conflicts between those groups in the 1990s. But some such political arrangement might prove applicable in many other places. That is the direction that international society ought to take if *uti possidetis juris* is to be justified in a world of multi-ethnic states.[31]

---

[31] A prescription to that effect has been made by the Badinter commission. See Pellet, 'Badinter Arbitration Committee'.

13

Democracy and International Community

This chapter addresses some questions that arise in connection with democracy as a basis of international community. It opens with a brief inquiry into the idea of community in world politics, and several of its manifestations. It proceeds to examine a debate on the European Union as a political community and goes on to look at the international community of the West, focusing particularly on NATO. It reviews a noteworthy speech by the leader of a major Western power who advocates a 'doctrine of international community', which would involve making democracy and human rights a global standard of conduct. These different strands are brought together by joining the debate whether democracy ought to be the foundation of a global *universitas*, in place of the existing *societas* of states.

Community in World Politics

'Community' usually signifies a form of human relations in which fundamental goals and values are affirmed by those involved as their guiding light; communities are about unity in the pursuit of a joint purpose: a *universitas*.[1] Communities have a teleology which societies lack. A society is like an electoral system, but a community is like a political movement or party. A political community expresses a belief system or ideology that affirms a self-styled superior way of life; it captures the identities and loyalties of its members and mobilizes them into ideologically correct action. Political communities define members as adherents to their values and supporters of their aims. They require conformity on the part of their members. They are politically and ideologically exclusive. Many different kinds of political community have existed historically. But undoubtedly the most important in recent centuries are nation–states. They are the primary political communities of the modern world. There is not one political *universitas*; there are many of them at the present time.[2]

[1] This definition of 'community' is influenced by M. Oakeshott, *On Human Conduct* (Oxford: Clarendon Press, 1975), part III. Also see R. G. Collingwood, *The New Leviathan* (New York: Crowell, 1971), 138.

[2] Michael Oakeshott views the modern European state as a combination of *universitas* and *societas* in its domestic life. See *On Human Conduct*, part III.

The contemporary world-wide association of independent states does not have earmarks of a political community.[3] There are few goals and values that are held in common by the world's population around which they can rally. People around the 'world do not share a common identity. They do not follow the same ideology. There is no world political authority to mobilize the world's population into ideologically correct action. The people of the world have no allegiance to the world and they are not politically mobilizable as such. They are only available for mobilization by nation-states or comparable political communities. For most people the international community is a vague abstraction, if they have heard of it at all. The global guardians who serve under the pale blue and white banner of the United Nations are still few and far between, as compared to the numerous patriots who hold high the colourful flags of the world's independent nations. Identity, loyalty, patriotism, nationalism, political and ideological partisanship, and related political dispositions and sentiments of importance in world politics are orchestrated by nation-states—or similar political groups.

The world political order is geared to national communities: it is prudential and rational-legal in character; it calls for mutual recognition and self-restraint rather than joint commitment and action; it is conducted mainly by agents and representatives of states who are charged with responsibilities for framing foreign policies and carrying on relations with foreign governments. What are universally shared by statespeople are a few general norms which specify equal immunities and rights of a negative rather than a positive kind (such as Article 2 of the UN charter) which underwrite the pluralism of the world's diverse and far-flung member states. Statespeople also share diplomatic practices and discourse built around those basic norms. Throughout this study that normative arrangement of world politics has been characterized as an international *societas*.

Certain states that are mostly located in the same world region, whose population are involved in the same civilization, may nevertheless share far more than that. In spite of their obvious national personalities, such states may all be more or less the same in their domestic ways of political life. Their leaders and peoples may hold political beliefs and convictions which, at base, are little different from one country to the next. Such convergent countries may arrange a political community between themselves consisting of joint international organizations which are dedicated to the pursuit of their shared political goals and values. That is the situation of the states of North America and Europe who collectively form the international community known as 'the West' to which a few states outside that geographical area also belong. Western leaders and peoples hold more or less the same political beliefs and convictions based on democracy. Of course they have their political differences and disagreements on many important issues. But on the fundamental issue of democracy they can all agree.

[3] See the debates in James Mayall (ed.), *The Community of States* (London: Allen & Unwin, 1982).

In short, some states—usually congregated in particular geographical regions—may form a deeper international community defined by a common way of political life. The states of the West are increasingly interlocked via overlapping and reinforcing international organizations and multilateral diplomacy: NATO, EU, OECD, etc.[4] Those organizations and activities capture and express not only the individual interests of member states but also the political goals and values that they share and, indeed, their common political way of life which is based on democracy. We can speak of the West as a political community of democratic states: a democratic *universitas*.

World Political Community

World politics, whatever else it may also be, is still fundamentally a world of sovereign states. The centrality of state sovereignty in international relations is frequently questioned but it is impossible to ignore.[5] Even its severest critics take it as a starting-point.[6] If world politics is on a course of fundamental normative change, which is debatable, it can only be a change from sovereignty to some other set of basic norms. That is the relevant context of any discussion of world political community.

As indicated elsewhere in this volume, by 'sovereignty' I refer to the word's conventional meaning in diplomatic practice and international law: the constitutional independence of states which are recognized as such by international society.[7] That defining feature of sovereignty was captured in 1826 by James Kent, an American Federalist: 'When the United States ceased to be a part of the British empire, and assumed the character of an independent nation, they became subject to the system of rules which reason, morality, and custom had established among the civilized nations of Europe, as their public law.'[8] That route to political independence has been followed time and again ever since the American colonists seceded from the British Empire in the late eighteenth century. I employ this definition of state sovereignty not only because it is the

---

[4] See *NATO Handbook* (Brussels: NATO Office of Information and Press, 1995), part I. See Michael Walzer, *Thick and Thin: Moral Argument at Home and Abroad* (London: University of Notre Dame Press, 1994).

[5] See Robert Jackson (ed.), *Sovereignty at the Millennium*, *Political Studies* (special issue), 47 (July 1999).

[6] Richard Falk, 'A New Paradigm for International Legal Studies: Prospects and Proposals,' in Falk, F. Kratochwil, and S. H. Mendlovitz (eds.), *International Law: A Contemporary Perspective* (Boulder, Colo.: Westview, 1985), 651–702.

[7] Alan James, *Sovereign Statehood: The Basis of International Society* (London: Allen & Unwin, 1986), 25.

[8] Quoted by D. P. Moynihan, *On the Law of Nations* (Cambridge, Mass.: Harvard University Press, 1990), 15. Prior to the American Civil War (1861–5) reference to the USA was made in the plural.

historical and still current international practice but also because it is the most fitting point of departure and point of reference for an inquiry into political community in contemporary international relations.

1. A Community of States

The year 1945 marks not only the end of a devastating world war but also the founding of a new universal organization of states defined by an explicit set of rules. That international organization is of course the United Nations. In its foundation articles the UN charter discloses a negative and non-activist doctrine of coexistence and non-intervention. It also contains some important articles that reveal a positivist and activist conception of international community: the most noteworthy are those pertaining to the interventionist role of the Security Council as the UN's law enforcement agency: chapter VII. These latter provisions, however, are in defence of an international order based on negative norms of state sovereignty. The UN charter and other important bodies of international law also prescribe cosmopolitan norms of human rights that may conflict with the pluralist norms of state sovereignty and may, at least in principle, justify positive actions that may override the norm of non-intervention. But it is clear from practice that humanitarian norms are subordinate to sovereignty norms: that has been borne out historically since 1945. As indicated in previous chapters, it is also borne out by important events and episodes which have agitated international society since the end of the cold war.

One can of course point to an international *societas* more fundamental than the UN: the one identified by James Kent which existed for three centuries prior to the UN and still exists. That underlying international society is called into being by the presence of independent governments on their own territories, which must, of necessity, live and deal with each other. It is that fundamental social arrangement of sovereign states—the necessity of international society— that the term Westphalia signifies in international relations. Among its long-standing norms and practices are mutual recognition, equal sovereign immunities, reciprocity, adherence to treaties, safe conduct of ambassadors, and so forth.[9] The UN is the most universal current organizational expression of that basic relationship of sovereign states. In 1945 it took the place of the defunct League of Nations, just as in 1919 that latter body took the place of the discredited Concert of Europe. This is merely to repeat a basic point of this study: namely, that the underlying *societas* of states is more fundamental than the particular international organizations that such states arrange between themselves from time to time. We probe those international organizations to penetrate the deeper normative logic of international society.

When states and other international actors justify their political activities by universal standards of conduct it is primarily by making reference to norms

[9] M. Wight, *System of States* (London: Leicester University Press, 1977).

sanctioned by the UN charter. Although sovereign states are not obliged to join the UN, virtually all of them do belong to it; new states continue to join; and its rules can be applied to non-members. For these reasons I believe the UN nowadays best represents global international society in formal organizational terms, even\though that society would of course exist in the absence of the UN or any other international organization, providing the world was still divided into sovereign states. The UN should thus be seen as currently the principal universal organization of the *societas* of states whose basic norms are reiterated and reaffirmed by regional arrangements, such as the Organization of American States, the Organization of African Unity, and so forth.

However, the universality of its membership and its pluralist ethic renders the UN a thin international community as compared, for example, to a regional security organization such as NATO, which has some important characteristics of a *universitas*. That is because the UN must accommodate, and it does accommodate, the entire compass of states in the contemporary world—north, south, east, and west—whose individual cultures, histories, constitutions, belief systems, and so forth, are enormously varied. The UN can exist as a universal organization because it can be acknowledged by sovereign states around the world. It is open to diversity. That is only possible because it is so thin: it only demands respect for a few basic and mostly negative rules which acknowledge the equal sovereignty of a diverse assortment of particular states from every corner of the world; it is tolerant of their domestic ways of political life.[10] By respecting and safeguarding their sovereignty and not interfering with their domestic life-ways it can secure their association and endorsement.

Post-cold-war NATO stands in marked contrast to the UN in that regard. NATO takes its meaning not only from its geographical area of operation, or from the combined national interests of its member states and associated states, but also from the convergent political ideologies and political institutions of those states, which affirm and express the same basic goals and values of democracy. National leaders must register their unwavering commitment to democracy and the political life of their states must rest on democratic institutions to qualify for membership in NATO and even to qualify for close association with the alliance. NATO is only open to states which are prepared to conform to its democratic goals and values as well as its military doctrines. Conformity to the same goals and values is also a requirement for membership in the EU, the Council of Europe, and many other Western-centred international organizations. Democracy has become the political orthodoxy, and one is tempted to say the political religion, of the West. Democracy is an international movement largely of the twentieth century, for the success of which Americans can take most of the credit.

In short, the UN is open to all sovereign states, regardless of their domestic goals and values, whereas NATO and many other Western organizations are

---

[10] See Walzer, *Thick and Thin*.

based on a political and ideological selection principle. The NATO states are all aligned in the same way, with the same goals and values in view, like a political party or movement. That emergent Western community is reminiscent of an older European community of states that rallied around the shared goals and values of Christian civilization.

2. A Community of Humankind

One can point to another international community that some theorists consider to be more fundamental: the cosmopolitan community of humankind. According to that Kantian view, the community of states, morally speaking, is always secondary and subservient to the community of humankind which is primary. Humans are prior to states historically: all states, even the oldest states, are merely political arrangements fashioned and sustained by particular people at particular times and places. People were trying to make the best of their political situation long before states were invented and they will still be trying to do that long after states have been consigned to the scrap heap of history. People are also prior to states ontologically: the community of humankind exists 'naturally' in virtue of rational human nature which is universal, as natural law theorists argue.

In international law, according to Antonio Cassese, human beings were considered to be 'under the exclusive control of States' from as far back as 1648. In the twentieth century, however, and particularly since the end of the Second World War human rights have acquired unprecedented international legality. Individuals have been released from the exclusive jurisdiction of states.[11] As indicated in earlier chapters, that is disclosed by the Nuremberg war crimes tribunal (1946), the Universal Declaration of Human Rights (1948), the Geneva Conventions (1949), the European Convention for the Protection of Human Rights and Fundamental Freedoms (1950), the UN Covenants on Human Rights (1966), the American Convention on Human Rights (1969), and the Helsinki Final Act (1975)—among others. These international covenants posit a community of humankind whose members are bound to respect each other as fellow human beings even if they are separated from each other by national citizenship—or by race, language, religion, political ideology, etc.

But that cosmopolitan argument should be qualified. The community of humankind exists in operational fact only because international and domestic humanitarian law recognize human rights. If people have been released from the exclusive jurisdiction of states it is statespeople who liberated them. Whatever normative standing the community of humankind enjoys in practice nowadays depends on the willingness and ability of statespeople to recognize and respect human rights. All the lawful rights of humankind that presently exist, global,

[11] Antonio Cassese, *International Law in a Divided World* (Oxford: Clarendon Press, 1986), 99–103.

regional, and specialized, have been created by international society. Humanitarian norms in international relations are a specific construct of the *societas* of states. Human rights have no positive international standing outside that arrangement.

3. A Community of National Citizenries

There is third way in which contemporary international society discloses itself as a community: it is based on popular legitimacy; it is a community of national citizenries, although it is not yet anything even approaching a community of democracies. The doctrine of self-determination is indicative of that: sovereignty is understood as vested in the populations of states. The sanctity of international boundaries is indicative of it too: existing borders cannot be arbitrarily interfered with or relocated because they are assumed to delimit the territorial jurisdictions not merely of sovereign governments but also of sovereign peoples. The state nowadays is legitimated as the home of a certain group of people conceived as a national citizenry. In that respect, all the states of the world are nation-states, even if most of them are nation-states only in that respect. That has important implications for the conduct of international relations.

An international community of national citizenries would be minimalist in its legitimate grounds for intervention, owing to the fact that constitutional independence would be more deeply rooted among the population of a state. The national citizenry would enjoy the rights and shoulder the duties of state sovereignty. That is the case even more so for democratic states. In a bona-fide democracy, we cannot separate the state and the citizens and ultimately hold only the former responsible—not if citizenship involves what it surely must involve in a democracy: self-determination and self-government. In a workable democracy, the rulers are installed by the people who are the final source of authority in the state: this is popular sovereignty. Because it rests on the sanctity and inviolability of national populations, a world of democracies would be a world of general non-intervention and non-aggression. If democracy became an international norm as well as a domestic norm, that would raise even higher the barrier to external intervention *in democracies*. That is a basic premiss of the democratic peace thesis.[12]

But an international norm of democracy would lower the normative barrier to external intervention *in non-democracies*. If international community posited some kind of basic democratic norm, sovereign states whose citizens were not democratically enfranchised could not claim equality with democracies in that regard. The international party of democracy would have difficulty recognizing

---

[12] Immanuel Kant, 'Perpetual Peace: A Philosophical Sketch', in Hans Reiss (ed.), *Kant's Political Writings* (Cambridge: Cambridge University Press, 1977), 93–130. Also see, in particular, Michael Doyle, 'Kant, Liberal Legacies and Foreign Affairs I and II', *Philosophy and Public Affairs*, 12 (1983), 205–36, 325–53.

and tolerating, as equals, non-democratic states. Non-democracies could be construed as illegitimate and perhaps unlawful in the eyes of democratic statespeople and their citizens. Dictatorships, racial or ethnic oligarchies, even dynastic monarchies and other authoritarian states could be seen as having fewer rights and immunities. Democratic states might justify foreign intervention to enfranchise the populations of non-democratic states; they might intervene to install democratic governments via internationally supervised elections. They might justify that as necessary to bring such states into the international community of democracies: the expanding democratic *universitas*. They might also justify that by claiming thereby to promote world peace, the claim being that democracies do not wage war against each other; so the more democracies there are, the more peace there will be. A significant and very likely a provocative normative divide would thus be opened in world politics between democratic states and non-democratic states. It could not be finally closed until all states became democracies.

Religious and ideological divisions between states, and groups of states in particular, have unsafe implications for universal international society and its basic norms of equal sovereignty, territorial integrity, and non-intervention. Such divisions are not conducive to international toleration and coexistence. We cannot easily tolerate what we judge to be fundamentally wrong or bad. Organized groupings of states based on a religious or ideological membership principle is conducive to international divisions, aversions, antagonisms, enmities. The statespeople on one side are inclined to stand in judgement of those on the other side whose domestic policies are standing acts of contempt against their own most cherished values and beliefs. They may be tempted to make those judgements part of their foreign policy. They may even be inclined to take some kind of positive action directed at the other side. Activist leaders of democracies may see themselves as missionaries who seek converts to democracy by bringing the good news of its superior ways to the rest of the world. They may strive to promote democracy around the world. More worrying, they may see themselves as having a responsibility to employ whatever influence and power they have, including in extreme cases military power, to take action against statespeople who refuse to convert their regimes to democracy. That kind of normative reasoning has revolutionary implications for the existing *societas* of states, and the possibility of some such revolution has too be taken seriously owing to the fact that the international party of democracy is by far the strongest political movement in world politics today.

Positive international action based on that sort of ideological conviction has a name: it is called crusading. Drawing a normative division between democratic states and non-democratic states, by regarding the latter as illegitimate, invites the opposite conduct from that which is required to sustain a *societas* of states. It invites righteous condemnation of non-democracies. But an international society calls for toleration and coexistence. It opposes crusading—for democracy or any other belief system—on the solid historical grounds that that is conducive to discord, disorder, conflict, turmoil, and in the end war. Crusading in international relations is associated historically with just wars and holy wars brought on by the assertion of religion or ideology by states and especially by groups of states which adhere to the same religious or political values. In the sixteenth and seventeenth centuries crusading was evident in the religious wars between Protestant states and Catholic states. It was obvious throughout most of the history of relations between the West and the non-Western world. In the twentieth century crusading was discernible in the USA's belated involvement in the First World War, the Allied crusade against fascism in the Second World War, and the American crusade against communism during the cold war. The communists and the fascists also embarked on their own crusades against each other and against the West. Fundamentalist conflicts in world politics over religion or ideology are anything but new. They constitute the most enduring and the most dangerous threat to international society.

To sum up the discussion thus far: there is a discernible universal *societas* of states which since 1945 has been centered on the UN and is defined by operative standards of conduct specified by the charter. That world-wide political and legal arrangement is a noticeably thin community, based on negative norms, that is open to a diverse assortment of member states. NATO, by comparison, is a far more substantial international community, based on agreement among its members concerning the fundamental goals and values of democracy: a discernible regional *universitas* that is open only to those who conform with its democratic norms. Individual human beings have acquired normative standing in international law regardless of their citizenship—however circumscribed their human rights may as yet be in practice. We can thus also speak of a community of humankind, even if that expression must immediately be qualified by noting that it is contingent on the prior existence of sovereign states that agree to recognize human rights. Finally, the citizens of states are surfacing as members of the international community once removed: international relations is becoming in certain respects a community of national citizenries, although it still is very far from being a community of democracies.

However, if democracy in domestic political life were actively promoted as a basic norm of international community—that is, as the ruling orthodoxy—that would have revolutionary implications for the conduct of international relations. Global pluralism would no longer be tolerated and much less would it be celebrated by the most important group of states in the world: the Western democracies. Conformity to democratic goals and values would be actively promoted by them as the valid global norm of domestic governance. Countries which did not conform would be candidates for democratic conversion. They might also be candidates for intervention and political reconstruction to bring them into line with that norm. If we replaced the word 'democratic' with the word 'Christian' we would be characterizing relations of the European world and the non-European world over several centuries before the establishment of the global covenant.

Regional Political Community: Europe

Given the universal desire for sovereign statehood, as indicated by Western decolonization and the breakup of the Soviet Union and former Yugoslavia, and given the premium conservative value placed on the existing distribution of territorial sovereignty, it would seem rather surprising if any states were prepared to surrender their sovereignty either in whole or in part. It has happened in the past. The political unifications of Italy and Germany in the mid-nineteenth century are instances of smaller states and statelets transferring their sovereignty, either voluntarily or under military duress, to a government of one larger resultant national state. Nationalism was a powerful impetus in each case, however.

An earlier example is that of the American colonists who, after liberating themselves from the British Empire in their war of independence (1776–83), were determined to form a larger sovereign state, the United States of America, and thus to constitute and exercise their newly acquired sovereignty jointly instead of each colony becoming independent on its own territory—as usually happened in twentieth century decolonization. Americans were determined to avoid what they understood were the lessons of European history, namely that states systems foster incessant conflict and warfare. According to Alexander Hamilton, 'to look for a continuation of harmony between a number of independent, unconnected sovereignties in the same neighbourhood, would be to disregard the uniform course of human events, and to set at defiance the accumulated experience of ages'.[13] Hamilton was a federalist rather than an internationalist. Americans were determined to build a single nation-state for themselves which rested on a common citizenship. So, to avoid the errors and follies of Europe and to affirm and defend their independence, the American ex-colonies formed a federation, a national *universitas* rather than a *societas* of states, among themselves.[14]

That constitutional arrangement has had a few predecessors and imitators: Switzerland, Canada, Australia. North America is noteworthy for its two transcontinental federations, its paucity of sovereign states, and its consequently limited international political life. But most of the world's states have been

---

[13] Alexander Hamilton, *The Federalist*, 6, repr. in R. M. Hutchins (ed.), *Great Books of the Western World*, xliii. *American State Papers* (Chicago: Encyclopaedia Britannica, 1952), 39.

[14] That is not to suggest that the Americans turned away from war in their continent. They obviously did not. They fought the British Empire in the north and the Mexican republic in the south. But the most important wars for them were their wars of territorial conquest as they moved the frontier westward and, of course, the American Civil War.

determined to hold sovereignty exclusively rather than hold it jointly with somebody else. Other geographical regions stand in sharp contrast to North America in that regard. Of the post-colonial federations in Asia, Africa, and the Caribbean that were constructed before independence, virtually all of them collapsed into their constituent ex-colonial parts not long afterward. *Societas* Europe and not federalist America was the wave of the future almost everywhere in the world after 1945.

Sovereignty clearly is not a political status that is lightly surrendered or easily foregone. The most noteworthy instances of the widespread transfer of sovereignty are those in which imperial states gave up sovereign title over what had been their colonial territories. They relinquished jurisdiction over their foreign territories.[15] But those same states retained jurisdiction over their home territories. Territorially speaking, their sovereignty shrank, in most cases enormously. It is all the more interesting, therefore, that in Western Europe since the 1950s steps have been taken by a growing number of sovereign states, including several former imperial states, to establish a European Union, in which the question 'Who is sovereign here?' has increasingly come to be asked. One implication drawn from the integration of Europe via the EU is that the sovereignty of the member states is diminishing and that of the EU is expanding. Another implication is that state sovereignty is merely being held jointly while remaining fully refundable. The two implications obviously collide.

This is a question of political community. Is the political community in Western Europe limited by the borders of existing sovereign states, of Britain, France, Greece, etc.? Or is the political community in that area defined by the borders of the EU which in 1999 consisted of fifteen member states? Where does the political *universitas* in Europe reside? There is a continuing debate on this question which cannot be investigated in any detail. But the main arguments can perhaps be reduced to the following two opposing views. (1) There is something that is fundamentally new in the EU: its member states have come together to form a European political and legal authority which is constitutionally distinct from those states and with regard to which the states have limited their sovereign rights and prerogatives in certain important areas of jurisdiction. Europe is becoming more like the USA; that is, the logic of European unification is pointing in the direction of a federation or a comparable constitutional arrangement, a *universitas* of some kind. (2) There is nothing new in the EU: the member states of the European Union remain sovereign; political community is confined within their borders. They have merely formed an international organization devoted to improving their socio-economic conditions by means of co-operation, which does not involve any permanent and irrevocable transfer of sovereignty. The EU is a 'union of sovereign states' and nothing more, a *societas* of states.

---

[15] British imperial jurisdiction over foreign territories was vested in the prerogative of the crown, the Foreign Jurisdiction Act, the British Settlements Act, and other bodies of domestic law. See M. Wight, *British Colonial Constitutions: 1947* (Oxford: Clarendon Press, 1952), 8.

The EU, according to the first argument, is not merely an international organization. Rather, it is a polity of a novel kind whose member states have relinquished some of their independent jurisdiction with the effect that EU Europe is in certain important respects moving beyond the *societas* of states in its common political life. The European Court of Justice can rule on the validity of national legislation in certain areas of common policy, such as social and economic policy, some aspects of which have been placed under the jurisdiction of the Treaty of Rome and subsequent EU treaties.[16] The Court has ruled that the various EU treaties, as well as the norms set up under their authority, have established 'a legal order of a new and unique kind to which the member states have freely transferred certain of their sovereign rights'.[17]

The EU is a new kind of polity in the following ways. On the one hand, the member states are no longer fully independent; they have endowed the EU with some of their sovereign authority, especially as regards the making and conducting of social and economic policy. Common obligations under EU law remove from member states some of their previous freedom of action in these policy areas. On the other hand, the EU does not constitute a fully sovereign entity either. It is still far from being a federation, even if the drift of constitutional change points in that direction. The relations between the EU and its member states have been characterized as 'co-ordinately valid legal systems', in that each side of the relationship 'for certain purposes presupposes the validity of the other'. At least to that extent, it is argued, the EU is an important instance of Europe going 'beyond the sovereign state'.[18]

In the same vein, the EU is seen to be fostering a 'supra-national citizenship'. That argument has been made in connection with a celebrated case of the European Court of Justice (the Van Gend en Loos case) which ruled that the EU 'constitutes a new legal order' with regard to which member states 'have limited their sovereign rights'. According to that judgment, EU law imposes direct obligations and confers direct rights on individual Europeans regardless of the member states of which they are citizens. Here the EU is seen to constitute a new political order whose subjects are not only the member states but also their nationals, who are becoming, in a somewhat awkward arrangement, citizens of Europe while still remaining citizens of their own country.[19] Some legal scholars argue that the EU should therefore be understood as not merely 'an agreement among States' but also 'a "social contract" among the nationals of those States'.[20] One such analysis concludes: 'It is not inevitable, but it is

---

[16] K. J. Alter, 'Who are the "Masters of the Treaty"?: European Governments and the European Court of Justice', *International Organization*, 52 (Winter 1998), 121–47.

[17] N. MacCormick, 'Liberalism, Nationalism and the Post-Sovereign State', *Political Studies*, 44 (1996), 555.

[18] Ibid. 561–7.

[19] Quoted by J. H. H. Weiler, 'European Neo-constitutionalism: In Search of Foundations for the European Constitutional Order', *Political Studies*, 44 (1996), 520–1.

[20] Ibid. 526–8.

possible, that what we are now embarked on in Western Europe is a thorough-going transcendence of the sovereign state as the essential model for legal security and political order.'[21]

This image of the EU as an emerging polity that is more than the sum of its partner states is reminiscent, somewhat, of the old European *universitas*—with the Christian religion replaced by a secular European identity based on democracy and with EU citizens, like their medieval Christian ancestors, retaining a significant attachment to their individual homelands. Here, too, is an intimation that Europe has finally seen the light and is now belatedly following in the footsteps of Alexander Hamilton's federalist America.

The EU, according to the second answer, is still basically an international organization, a 'union of sovereign states'. According to that way of thinking, the member states have authorized all of the European Union's basic rules, institutions, and organizations. If we probe the constitutional basis of the EU, to discern the justification for the authority of EU law, what we find is a familiar and traditional norm of a society of states, namely *pacta sunt servanda*: the principle of reciprocity between equally sovereign member states who remain fully in charge of the EU. On that view, the international agreements upon which the EU is built are entirely consistent with international law, which rests squarely on the institution of sovereignty.[22] The EU is the child and not the parent or even the sibling of its member states. That subordinate status of the EU as an international organization rather than a supranational organization is particularly evident in those areas of international activity that traditionally indicate the presence of sovereign statehood externally, namely foreign policy and military policy. Far from the EU taking over responsibility for security and order in Europe, some of its member states as well as some other states continue to bear that responsibility on an individual basis or in alliance with each other. The security of Europe remains firmly in the hands of the USA, supported by Britain, France, and Germany—in other words, NATO. In short, there is nothing new about the EU.[23] Europe continues to be a *societas* of states rather than an embryonic political *universitas*.

But let us suppose that the first argument is more accurate. An important element of that argument is the claim that territory in Europe is being redefined and reconstituted, away from the states and towards the EU.[24] At the same time that internal borders within the EU come down, to foster easier movement of people and goods—thereby making European citizenship more of a reality—the external EU border goes up, to prevent illegal migrants, smugglers, drug dealers, etc., from coming into the EU and taking advantage of the situation. That is a line of security to protect the citizens of the EU not so much from attack

---

[21] MacCormick, 'Liberalism, Nationalism and the Post-Sovereign State,' 555.

[22] This argument is presented and rejected by Weiler.

[23] Weiler, 'European Neo-constitutionalism', 518.

[24] U. Preuss, 'Two Challenges to European Citizenship', *Political Studies*, 44 (1996), 543–4.

as from infiltration and exploitation of the civic liberties and socio-economic opportunities they now enjoy on a wider European scale.

In whatever ways it might make sense to conceive of the European Union as 'going beyond sovereignty', there would still be a sharply defined external border around the EU which is increasing in height at the same moment that the internal EU borders between member states are coming down. That there is a border that separates Europe from the rest of the world is nothing new. In the past Europe had its own identity based on the goals and values of Christian civilization. Today that identity is based on the goals and values of democracy. What is new is that the rest of the world today is a world of sovereign states, whereas the rest of the world in the past was mostly a world of European empires and, before that, it was a world of separate civilizations based in different regions. If the EU were to become an independent polity there would then be fifteen fewer states in the world and one new superpower. The continent of Europe would look more like North America. That would be a revolutionary change for Europe. It would also be an important international development of more general consequence because it would realign the balance of power in world politics. The balance of power would have a major new balancer. But it would not alter the *societas* of states on a global scale in any fundamental way. In that regard it would not be a revolution or even a reformation of the sovereign states system. It would recollect comparable changes in the past which significantly reduced the number of sovereign states: for example, during the era of European empires. A politically united Europe would still be part of a world of sovereign states.

But more interesting for our purposes is the question: how might the emergent European political community conduct itself in relation to states in its neighbourhood which are not members and which might not share its political goals and values? It should be kept in mind that the EU defines itself politically in terms of democracy. Would the EU respect the basic norms of the UN charter and thus operate in accordance with the *laissez-faire* conduct requirements of the global *societas* of states? Would the EU be defensive or would it be assertive in its relations with neighbouring states which are not democracies? Would the EU demand conformity to its own political norms by neighbouring states? In other words, would a politically united Europe place itself above the global covenant when approaching and dealing with non-democratic European states? If the EU is a *societas* of states we should expect a negative answer. But if the EU is a *universitas* we should anticipate an affirmative answer because it would then be a political movement that would affirm its own goals and values and would seek adherents in the pursuit of its teleology. The question becomes heavier if the democratic community of Europe is defined not only by the EU but also by NATO, whose memberships largely overlap. What norm shall be supreme in Europe if they come into conflict: the basic universal norm of sovereignty and non-intervention or the basic regional norm of democracy, human rights, and the rule of law in domestic governance?

Expanding Western Political Community

The march towards democracy is not only a domestic affair: it is also an international movement. International democracy arguably began with the arrival of the USA in 1917 as the only leading power capable of determining the outcome of the First World War. The historical significance of that somewhat delayed appearance of America at centre stage of world politics can hardly be overstated. It had a direct and immediate impact on international society, as indicated by the defeat of the Central Powers, the breakup of the empires of Eastern Europe and the installation of an assortment of new nation-states in their place, and the founding of the League of Nations. America was not going to all the trouble of sorting out Europe's sorry affairs without having a political vision of a better world. President Woodrow Wilson expressed that vision as America's willingness to sacrifice its soldiers and treasure in its determination to make the world 'safe for every peace-loving nation', which could only be a world of democracies.[25] Throughout most of the twentieth century the democratic movement in world politics moved backward and sideways as well as forward. But the Americans never wavered in their devotion to the democratic cause and it gathered renewed momentum after the Berlin Wall was demolished in 1989.

The revolutionary moment of the twentieth century proved to be 1917, when two progressive political-ideological movements, democracy and communism, each projecting its own vision of a future *universitas*, collided almost head-on. Russian communism could not tolerate states whose domestic political life was not aligned with the Soviet interpretation of Marxism. Moscow was ideologically and for a time also politically committed to liberate the working class of capitalist states. In short, communism was a revolutionary international movement that did not respect the sovereignty of capitalist states and justified foreign intervention on ideological grounds. That attitude was reciprocated, at least to some extent, by the West, which militarily intervened in the Soviet Union at the end of the First World War. That opened a great rift in twentieth-century international society which lasted until 1989, apart from a brief interregnum during the Second World War, and came to be known as the cold war. Democracy emerged triumphant from that struggle.

The Western democratic community of states was for a long time centred on the Anglo-American relationship (the Western alliance) that was constructed by Roosevelt and Churchill during the Second World War, which confirmed the USA as the world's foremost military and economic power. That democratic *universitas* did not extend very far into Central, Southern, and Eastern Europe in the early post-war years. In the east it was blocked by the Soviet army. In

---

[25] See Gaddis Smith, *Woodrow Wilson's Fourteen Points after 75 Years*, 12th Morgenthau Memorial Lecture on Ethics and Foreign Policy (New York: Carnegie Council, 1993). Also see the sceptical discussion in Kissinger, *Diplomacy*, 218–45.

the south it was hindered by the legacy of fascism. There used to be a division in Europe between the democratic north and west, and the authoritarian south and east. It still exists in some places. The democratic community of states expanded south-eastwards historically but successful and unequivocal democratization east of the Rhine and south of the Elbe was a late occurrence. Most of the new states that emerged in Central and Eastern Europe at the end of the First World War did not succeed in becoming democracies; some scarcely made any attempt to do so. President Wilson's doctrine of self-determination ironically resulted in the spread of authoritarianism. Clearly self-determination and democracy are not the same thing. West Germany and Italy only became solid members of the democratic West in the 1950s. Spain, Portugal and Greece arrived in the 1980s, following a post-war era of fascist or military dictatorship.

But there were more converts to democracy after the cold war. Some states returned to the Western fold after almost half a century of exile imposed by the Soviet Union from 1945 until 1989. Austria and Finland achieved a democratic political life after the Second World War but they were kept in purgatory between the West and the East by the Soviet Union. They did not completely enter the West until the cold war was over. East Germany arrived via German reunification in 1990. Most states of Central and Eastern Europe were marching towards the West, with widely varying determination and progress, in the 1990s: the Czech Republic, Poland, Hungary, Estonia, Latvia, Lithuania, Slovakia, Bulgaria, Rumania, Albania, and the former Yugoslav republics of Slovenia, Croatia, Bosnia, and Macedonia. Even Russia is a convert to democracy, albeit still wavering in its democratic commitments, uncertain in its democratic capabilities, and giving no clear signal that it will successfully complete its perilous political journey any time soon.

The international organizations of the West are based on the premiss, usually understood as a requirement, that the domestic political goals and values of member states shall be democratic. Most of the above-noted states, including Russia, signed the 1990 OSCE Charter of Paris, which affirmed the fundamental value of democracy and reaffirmed the 1975 Helsinki Accords. Many joined the Council of Europe, and thereby subjected themselves to its Convention on Human Rights which gives citizens of signatory states the right of appeal to the European Court of Human Rights against rulings by national courts of law. Some East European states applied for full membership in NATO. At the time of writing, the Czech Republic, Poland, and Hungary had been admitted. The Baltic States were knocking on the door. Many states entered into a special security arrangement with NATO that stops short of full membership: the 'partnership for peace'. One of the most important conditions laid down by the OSCE, the Council of Europe, and NATO is democratic self-government.

The Charter of Paris, which marked the end of the cold war at least procedurally, proclaimed a new era of democracy, peace, and unity. Its signatory states bound themselves to conduct their domestic political affairs according to declared principles of democratic government. It recognized individual rights and liberties, including freedom of religion, freedom of association and peaceful assembly, freedom of movement, the right to participate in free and fair elections, the right to a fair and public trial, and the right to own property, among others. The signatories pledged themselves to strengthen democratic institutions and promote the rule of law, to protect the ethnic, cultural, linguistic, and religious identity of national minorities, to combat all forms of racial and ethnic hatred and discrimination, and to undertake other actions of a similar kind.[26] These are the norms of the political way of life of the West. This is not to say that the signatories did not also commit themselves to uphold conventional international norms of the Helsinki Final Act and the UN charter: they were required to refrain from the threat or use of force against the territorial integrity or political independence of any state and to settle disputes by peaceful means.

But notwithstanding these traditional international obligations, the OSCE states that signed the Charter of Paris committed to govern themselves according to the requirement that their domestic political life should be fully aligned with norms of democracy. They could not be part of the West without converting to democracy. After 1990 there was a discernible ideological progression of NATO from a narrower security community preoccupied with the Soviet military threat to a broader security community concerned to uphold and advance the democratic peace of an expanding area of Europe.

When NATO was originally founded in 1949 it was conceived to be an alliance of 'free' and 'independent' countries which shared 'a common interest in maintaining peace and defending their freedom through political solidarity and adequate military defense to deter and, if necessary, repel all possible forms of aggression against them.'[27] Its ethic was defensive, in conformity with Article 51 of the UN charter which recognizes 'the inherent right of individual or collective self-defense'. It was formed to defend the freedom and independence of its member states against the threat of expansive Soviet communism in Europe projected by the Red Army. The solidarity of NATO was defined by the common enemy of its member states. The original twelve members were all democracies, except for Portugal which was a fascist dictatorship at the time. In 1952, during the height of the Korean War, Greece and Turkey became members. Neither of these countries could at that time be regarded as having a democratic way of life. They were admitted on realist grounds. Turkey is still in a quasi-

---

[26] *Charter of Paris for a New Europe* (Paris: OSCE, 1990). The charter was signed by Belgium, Bulgaria, Canada, the Czech and Slovak Federal Republic, Denmark, France, Germany, Greece, Hungary, Iceland, Italy, Luxembourg, the Netherlands, Norway, Poland, Portugal, Romania, Spain, Turkey, the USSR, the UK, and the USA. Also see Stockholm International Peace Research Institute, *SIPRI Yearbook 1991* (Oxford: OUP, 1991), 603–10, A. Venema and H. Romijn (eds.), 'Charter of Paris for a New Europe: A New Era of Democracy, Peace and Unity', in *Documents on International Security Policy May 1989–December 1991* (The Hague: Netherlands Atlantic Commission, 1992), 26–35.

[27] *NATO Handbook*, 17.

democratic condition. Even though an overwhelming majority of NATO member states were and are democracies, it is clear that during the cold war 'freedom' and 'independence' meant national security and international security from the military threat of expansive Soviet communism. It did not yet mean making Europe safe for democracy. Western Europe was not completely democratic for much of that time. In its defence of freedom NATO was prepared to include members that were not bona-fide democracies and turn a blind eye to their domestic politics. That changed after the cold war was over.

Member states and associate states of NATO were required not only to ally themselves with each other militarily but also to align themselves with each other politically. The discourse of NATO emphasized not only freedom but also, increasingly, democracy. The alliance made more explicit what was originally taken for granted with regard to its large majority of democratic member states and conveniently ignored with regard to its small minority of authoritarian or quasi-democratic states, namely that it is an alliance of democracies *as such*. Democracy here signifies not merely formal political structures but a domestic way of life and an international outlook which are at the heart of contemporary Western civilization. Democracy is the *weltanschauung* or political world-view of the West.

That is clearly evident in NATO's Partnership for Peace, which gives states the opportunity to be associated with the alliance without being a full member. The main political condition is 'commitment to democratic principles that underpin the Alliance'.[28] Article 2 of the 'Framework Document' declares that 'the member States of the North Atlantic Alliance and the other States subscribing to this Document . . . are committed to the preservation of democratic societies, their freedom from coercion and intimidation and the maintenance of the principles of international law'. The Partnership for Peace cannot contribute substantially to the security of NATO. But NATO states can draw a further perimeter around their partner states within which a democratic way of life can be actively promoted. Here, then, is a condition for international affiliation with by far the most important security alliance in the world, and a definition of its political goals and values, that goes well beyond the sort of international arrangements that we associate with a *societas* of states or a traditional military alliance.

In 1997 NATO expanded eastward by admitting Poland, the Czech Republic and Hungary to full membership. That moved the border of NATO closer to the border of Russia and provoked the perplexing and deeply controversial issue of the relations that ought to obtain between that Slavic great power and NATO.[29] Russia is an ambiguous country with a split personality: traditionally Christian, but Orthodox; geographically both European and Asian; internally divided between internationalist and pro-Western elements on the one hand,

---

[28] Ibid. 265.
[29] See the debate between M. McGwire, 'NATO Expansion', and C. Ball, 'Nattering NATO Negativism', in *Review of International Studies*, 24 (Jan. 1998), 23–68.

and nationalist and Slavophile elements on the other hand. It probably is easier to deal with Moscow via conventional international relations than to include Russia as a part of the West. To include Russia would open the West to a serious internal problem of unity. At the time of writing, an alternative arrangement was agreed with Russia: Moscow would remain outside the Partnership for Peace but would be involved in a special security relationship with Brussels. That arrangement was put to the test and to some extent confirmed by the involvement of Russian troops in the Bosnian and Kosovo protectorates discussed in Chapter 11. That co-operation is a reminder that Russia belonged historically to Europe, and withdrew from the European society of states not in 1946 or 1947 but, rather, in 1917, under the revolutionary communist dictatorship of Lenin.

That raises the issue of NATO's relationship, as a regional security community of democracies, to the universal international society of the UN. As already indicated, according to the pluralist logic of the UN charter, all sovereign states have a fundamental obligation to respect the universal *Grundnorm* of equal state sovereignty, territorial integrity, and non-intervention. The Security Council is responsible for upholding international peace and security. In NATO, however, there is an exclusive additional obligation of its member states to each other. The basic norm, as expressed by Article 5 of the North Atlantic Treaty, is the security of its member states jointly and exclusively: international solidarity, all for one and one for all. The crucial line of division on the map is the line around the security community of NATO. Does that obligation supplement and augment the obligations of those same states under the UN charter, as NATO officially declares? Or does it conflict with and perhaps even subordinate those latter obligations? Is the main effect of NATO expansion a strengthening of universal international society, by enlarging the security community of a world region historically known for its recurrent turmoil and warfare? Or is it a weakening of universal international society by undercutting the UN Security Council? When the chips are down, where do NATO's primary obligations reside: with the universal international community or with its own members? That brings us to an issue that will be pursued in the remainder of this chapter, namely the relations between the democratic states of the West and the existing international *societas*.

These questions give rise to contradictory historical answers. During the cold war the answer clearly was: with its members. During the Gulf War the answer was: with the UN Security Council. During the war in Kosovo the answer was equivocal; initially NATO skirted the UN Security Council but belatedly, and expediently, NATO went back to the Council for a resolution that vindicated its military action against Yugoslavia. NATO presupposes that its member states, both full members and associate members, are democratic political communities. That is the doctrine, even if it is not yet entirely the reality. NATO states hold to the view that they have every right not only to defend their sovereignty but also to advance their democratic goals and values. They undoubtedly have a right to do that by peaceful means. But is there a right to do that by military means that is recognized by international society? The scope of that right (*jus ad bellum*) was at the normative heart of the controversy surrounding NATO's military actions against Yugoslavia in 1999. During the war in Kosovo the political and military leaders of NATO—including the American President, the British Prime Minister, and the American commander—repeatedly claimed they were fighting for 'values' and not merely for interests: that is, for democracy, human rights, minority protections. They evidently saw 'values' as a more noble justification of war. They clearly conceived of their war against Yugoslavia as 'a just war'.

The NATO states declare their determination 'to safeguard the freedom, common heritage and civilization of their peoples, founded on the principles of democracy, individual liberty and the rule of law'.[30] Without too much stretching, that could be interpreted as a responsibility not only to defend democracy but also to promote a more democratic world, at least on the borders of the West. It could be understood as a requirement that all states in that geographic region conform to the political norms of the West. Many Western political leaders nowadays, by no means exclusively Americans, hold that view or something like that. Would that commitment justify international crusading to make the borderlands of Europe safer for democracy? Would it justify military activity by Western powers to intervene in authoritarian states in Europe, or nearby, or perhaps even further away, to convert their political systems to democracy? Are we witnessing a new doctrine of international community enunciated and implemented by NATO? Evidence from the NATO military activities in the Balkans indicates that this is not an academic question.[31]

'The Doctrine of International Community'

Perhaps the most noteworthy attempt by any national leader to frame a positive answer was made by British Prime Minister Tony Blair in a speech delivered in Chicago on the eve of NATO's fiftieth anniversary in April 1999. He called it 'the doctrine of international community'.[32] Blair referred to NATO's action in Kosovo as 'a just war, based not on any territorial ambitions but on values'. A war for 'values' became the mantra for NATO's justification of its air campaign against Yugoslavia and its occupation of Kosovo. Blair said the new doctrine contained 'the explicit recognition' that states nowadays were 'mutually dependent' and that 'the national interest' of states was 'to a significant extent governed by international collaboration'.

---

[30] *NATO Handbook*, 231.

[31] See P. Rutland, 'NATO Old and New', *Prospect* (July 1998), 58.

[32] 'Speech to the Economic Club of Chicago' (United Kingdom, Foreign and Commonwealth Office, 22 Apr. 1999).

No longer is our existence as states under threat. Now our actions are guided by a more subtle blend of mutual self interest and moral purpose in defending the values we cherish. In the end values and interests merge. If we can establish and spread the values of liberty, the rule of law, human rights and an open society then that is in our national interests too. The spread of our values makes us safer.

Prime Minister Blair acknowledged that NATO military actions taken in places like Bosnia and Kosovo would not have taken place 'twenty years ago'. At that time, 'we would have turned our backs'. But fundamental changes, especially the end of the cold war, now made possible the use of armed force to spread Western values. Those changed realities not only made such actions possible, they made them necessary, and they facilitated the co-operative international relations required to undertake them and sustain them. 'We are all internationalists now, whether we like it or not.' The 1999 idea of security was a larger and more complete idea than the 1945 notion of security; it was also less tidy. No longer was it restricted to national security and international peace and security. It was now a more fully developed idea of human security: the universal goal was the safety of every man, woman, and child everywhere on earth, regardless of their citizenship. Blair repeated a Kantian declaration of President Kennedy: 'Freedom is indivisible and when one man is enslaved who is free?' But human beings could only be safeguarded in an international community of democratic states which instituted human rights protections in their domestic political life.

In Blair's political mind the old distinction between the international sphere and the domestic sphere was becoming blurred.[33] 'Just as within domestic politics, the notion of community—the belief that partnership and co-operation are essential to advance self-interest—is coming into its own; so it needs to find its international echo.' That was the clearest refrain in his speech. The doctrine of international community was, for the British Prime Minister, a doctrine of overcoming and breaking down the separation and isolation of states from each other. It was a doctrine of recognizing their mutual dependence on each other and promoting their co-operation in common endeavours. 'By necessity we have to co-operate with each other across nations.' No longer can states turn their backs on international economics and prosper. Nor can they turn their backs on international politics and flourish. International relations was a co-operative enterprise defined by the pursuit of shared goals and values: a *universitas*. States must come together and participate jointly in an international community based on 'our values'—that is, the values of the West, which should generously make them available to the people of the world, as far as that is possible. Democracy and human rights were core goals and values, the teleology, of the emerging international community.

---

[33] For the same view held by a leading scholar see John Vincent, 'Grotius, Human Rights and Intervention', in H. Bull, B. Kingsbury, and A. Roberts (eds.), *Hugo Grotius and International Relations* (Oxford: Clarendon Press, 1990), 255.

That meant, among other things, that dictatorships could no longer be tolerated. They are a standing act of contempt for democratic and humanitarian values. They stand in the way of progress towards democracy and human rights in world politics. They must therefore be removed. Dictators, such as Yugoslavia's Slobodan Milosevic or Iraq's Saddam Hussein, must be put on notice that their 'minority rule', 'ethnic cleansing', and other 'dangerous' and 'barbarous acts' cannot and will not be tolerated. 'We must not rest until it is reversed.' In Blair's mind, and no doubt in the minds of most other Western leaders, dictatorship was an internationally illegitimate form of government that should be stamped out. In Kosovo that demanded military intervention. 'If NATO fails in Kosovo, the next dictator to be threatened with military force may well not believe our resolve to carry the threat through.' Military success meant winning the war against Yugoslavia. But it also meant more than that. If NATO's military actions in Kosovo were to be vindicated it meant bringing the blessings of democracy to the people. That required taking over the government of Kosovo for a temporary period until the political system could be reformed along democratic lines. The ultimate war aim of NATO in Kosovo was to integrate the people who lived there into the democratic community of the West.

A further intention of Prime Minister Blair's speech was to make it clear that the 'doctrine of international community' was not confined to Europe or even the West; it was meant to apply around the world. To date, however, the steps taken to institute this new international community had been 'ad hoc'. It was now time 'to establish a new framework'. Blair said it was necessary to focus in a sustained way on the principles of the emerging international community and on the institutions that embody and express them. 'If we want a world ruled by law and by international co-operation then we have to support the UN as its central pillar.' But the UN would have to be reformed. That called for a re-examination 'of the role, workings and decision-making process of the UN, and in particular the UN Security Council'. Blair allowed that non-intervention 'has long been considered an important principle of international order'. He added: 'it is not one we would want to jettison too readily'. Now, however, that principle had to be 'qualified'. The qualifications he had in mind were fundamentally humanitarian: 'Acts of genocide can never be a purely internal matter.' Humanitarian abuses within sovereign states that produce 'massive flows of refugees' which 'unsettle neighboring countries' could 'properly be described as "threats to international peace and security"'. In short, the UN charter should be amended to include humanitarian grounds as part of the *jus ad bellum* of international law.

The British Prime Minister was well aware of arguments about double standards in humanitarian intervention: that Western states were prepared to intervene to save refugees in the Balkans but they were not prepared to do the same thing in other parts of the world, such as Rwanda, Liberia, or Sierra Leone. He said that 'the most pressing foreign policy problem we face is to identify the

circumstances in which we should get actively involved in other people's conflicts'. He noted that around the world there were still 'many regimes' that were
'undemocratic and engaged in barbarous acts' but he added: 'If we wanted to
right every wrong that we see in the modern world then we would do little else
than intervene in the affairs of other countries.' He said it was important to be
able to make the right decision when and where to intervene and he proposed
five major considerations. First, the international community has to be sure that
armed force is the correct means to deal with the problem. 'War is an imperfect instrument for righting humanitarian distress, but armed force is sometimes
the only means of dealing with dictators.' Second, have all diplomatic options
been exhausted? 'We should always give peace every chance'. Third, 'on the
basis of a practical assessment of the situation, are there military operations we
can sensibly and prudently undertake?' Fourth, 'are we prepared for the long
term?' Lastly, 'do we have national interests involved?' He hastened to add that
he was not suggesting that these are 'absolute tests'. But he said they were the
most important considerations when contemplating a decision to intervene with
armed force.

Blair's observation that the UN charter would have to be amended was an
indication that the doctrine of international community is not yet part of international law. The current doctrine of *jus ad bellum* enshrined in the UN charter is a doctrine of non-intervention. Blair's doctrine of international community
is an interventionist doctrine which connects national security and international
security to human security in foreign countries: 'we cannot turn our backs on
the violation of human rights in other countries if we want to be secure'. That
places an important Kantian qualification on the principle of non-intervention
that seems to suggest that if human rights are threatened anywhere, including
inside foreign countries, then people everywhere are threatened and their countries are threatened too. Not only that, it envisions the policy of intervention as
leading to domestic political reform along democratic lines: the expansion of the
international community of democracies. Democratic reform is required to
ensure that human rights shall be safeguarded in the future and the people shall
never have to endure politically imposed suffering again. If circumstances permit international actions, including armed intervention, that stand a reasonable
chance of preventing or stopping atrocities and building democracies which in
the future will be free of such horrors, then such actions ought to be taken. The
prospect of future international peace would require elimination of dictatorship
and abusive rule within sovereign states and installation of democracy in its
place. 'The spread of our values makes us safer.'

At the time of writing, this was the clearest and most forceful statement of
the normative requirements of a new international order made by any leading
statesman since the end of the cold war. Prime Minister Blair's doctrine of
international community calls for a significant expansion of the post-1945
grounds for the legitimate use of armed force in world politics. When he was

propounding his doctrine the UN charter had not been revised along the lines he was urging. That the five permanent members of the Security Council would agree to such an amendment of the charter seemed unlikely—if the negative response of China and Russia to NATO's 1999 air war against Yugoslavia is indicative of their views on such a fundamental change. But my concern is to reflect on what such a change would portend for international society.

Although Blair understood his doctrine as innovative and progressive, what he was expressing was in significant ways a revision of an old doctrine and not the invention of a new one: the just-war doctrine that expresses a conception of international society as a *universitas* based on Christian values. As indicated, he repeatedly and emphatically spoke of 'values' as NATO's justification for using force against Yugoslavia. Other Western political and military leaders did the same. They were of course referring principally to human rights and democracy. Just wars are wars for values of a certain kind. Human rights are secularized Christian values. Democracy is the latest stage in the political evolution of the West. These values are close relations: democratic states institute the protection of human rights as part of their constitutional and political life.

What the British Prime Minister was advocating is sometimes referred to as international liberalism. But that is an unfortunate and misleading use of the term because liberalism as classically understood is associated with pluralism of values and negative liberty. The post-1945 *societas* of states is liberal in the classical meaning of the term. Blair's doctrine is pre-liberal more than liberal and in some ways it is pre-modern. It is really a doctrine of Western international community and it is clearly recognizable as the descendant of the old European 'standard of civilization'. It is a conception of international community defined by values which in origin are Christian and are still largely although no longer exclusively confined to the Western world.

The British leader, in that important respect, was expressing a *weltanschauung* held by many Americans. Henry Kissinger portrays it as a universalist conviction that, once 'the peoples of the world had tasted of the blessings of peace and democracy . . . [they] would no longer have reason to go to war to oppress others'.[34] In calling for UN reforms Prime Minister Blair's doctrine clearly was intended to be a universal doctrine and not merely a Western doctrine. He spoke enthusiastically and confidently about 'the spread of our values'. He questioned the *Grundnorm* of non-intervention and hinted at its obsolescence. His recommendations and urgings implied an international reformation coming from one direction (the West) in which the basic UN doctrine of equal sovereignty, territorial integrity, and non-intervention would be subject to qualification and

---

[34] H. Kissinger, *Diplomacy* (New York: Simon & Schuster, 1994), 221–2. That world-view is already evident in American opinion in the late eighteenth century. Alexander Hamiltan argued strenuously against the belief held by many Americans of his day that a world of independent republics would be a world of peace. Hamiltan said that belief defied history and experience. See Alexander Hamilton, *The Federalist*, 6, repr. in Hutchins, *Great Books*, xliii. 38–41.

perhaps revision. The normative restrictions on intervention would be lowered for dictatorships that trample on the human rights of their population or abuse them in other ways. Eliminating an abusive dictatorship by armed force would call for a period of military occupation to set up a democracy in its place. The only restraint on foreign intervention in abusive dictatorships would be prudential considerations and the national interests of those states who would carry out such military activities on behalf of the international community.

If we follow through on the normative implications of Prime Minister Blair's 'doctrine of international community' there would evidently be two categories of states: a first-class category of democracies which would enjoy complete sovereignty and all the immunities that entails, and a second class category of non-democracies which would not be unequivocally sovereign and would be candidates for foreign military intervention. The international movement of democracies would presumably aim at the eventual elimination of the latter. If that inference is correct, such a political goal would involve a transformation of the *societas* of states into an international community (*universitas*) based on democracy and human rights.

Making Converts to Democracy World-Wide

Democracy is a belief system whose adherents in the West are often moved by the generous desire to give it to the rest of the world or even to install it as the exclusive form of universal polity.[35] Many Americans are prone to that political sentiment. But it should be kept in mind that democracy, although of fundamental importance to Americans and Europeans, is not among the core values to be found in world politics at the present time. There is a constellation of such values: peace, order, political independence, state equality, religious and cultural freedom, coexistence, self-determination, reciprocity, to name some of the most important ones.

These values have far more to do with liberty than democracy. They are the international values of classical liberalism espoused, for instance, by John Stuart Mill.[36] It was those liberal international values that in the twentieth century came to be taken up voluntarily, and usually enthusiastically, by the entire world. In many places, of course, they were not adopted as domestic values. That is one of the paradoxes of the expansion of international society: the international political world is liberal, but many domestic political worlds are illiberal and some are anti-liberal. Yet it is not really a paradox, for it is only to be expected that if states are free to govern themselves they will exercise that free-

---

[35] See Francis Fukuyama, *The End of History and the Last Man* (New York: Avon Books, 1992).
[36] J. S. Mill, *On Liberty*, in J. Robson (ed.), *John Stuart Mill: A Selection of his Works* (New York: Odyssey Press, 1966), 1–147.

dom in their own way. International liberalism makes domestic dictatorship possible in exactly the same way that it makes domestic democracy possible: by safeguarding independent states from foreign intervention and thus opening a space for their governments and peoples to pursue their own domestic enlightenment or unenlightenment, as the case may be.

Liberal democracy emerged historically out of the womb of liberalism; but it is not the same as liberalism. Even self-determination, a value that is often equated with democracy and is affirmed by liberal international society, may be in conflict with democracy if people are determined to live under some other form of government—revolutionary Islam, for example. Democracy must take its place within the constellation of important international values, particularly freedom and order, and cannot override them, if freedom and order are to remain the basic values of world politics.[37] And in so far as those latter values create the opportunity for local people to build domestic democracy without fear of foreign intervention then those values are fundamental to self-chosen and self-determined democracy. That is probably the only kind of democracy that has a good chance of being successful in the long run. That means that democracy must remain secondary to international freedom and order.

The democratic way of life has many obvious benefits, and no doubt that goes far to explain the popularity and expansion of democracy. It clearly is worth defending by armed force if necessary. Democracy is also a value that is worth exporting so that as many people as possible around the world can enjoy its obvious benefits. But defending democracy and selling democracy is not the same as treating democracy as the highest value of world politics and trying to impose it on the non-democratic part of the world. Despite the dissemination of democracy in Eastern Europe and Latin America that has occurred since the end of the cold war, there are still numerous authoritarian states around the world, as Prime Minister Blair recognized. As long as such states exist we should expect the indignation and even the anger of democracies to be sometimes aroused.

But can we go further—as Prime Minister Blair clearly believes we can and should? Should the Western democracies be prepared to use armed force to spread their values: presumably, to make the whole world, someday, safe for democracy? Would it be justified for democracies to pursue the abolition of authoritarian governments and press actively and resolutely for the institution of democracy in their place, believing, sincerely, that that would not only be right in itself but would also have good consequences, that it would enhance world peace? President Woodrow Wilson clearly thought so. Would the militant spread of democracy make the world safer, or would it make it a more dangerous place? It is surprising that that question is not addressed by Prime Minister Blair's speech. It is surprising because international peace and security has been

---

[37] See Georg Sørensen, *Democracy and Democratization* (Boulder, Colo., and London: Westview, 1993).

identified by the UN charter, by the North Atlantic Treaty Organization, by the Helsinki Final Act, and by most Western statespeople since at least 1945 as a core value to be upheld and defended by armed force if necessary. It has not been understood as a value that is subordinate to or conditional on democracy and human rights.

John Stuart Mill argues that it is wrong for outsiders to intervene benevolently to establish 'civilized government' in foreign countries unless there are well-founded justifications for doing that—such as a threat to national security or international peace and security if one failed to intervene.[38] What is 'civilized government' for Mill is democracy and human rights for contemporary Americans and Europeans. Mill's argument can be expressed in terms of the global covenant. Once countries are members of international society (recognized as enjoying constitutional independence) they have a fundamental right to be treated equally and without discrimination. That is a classical liberal norm. At the present time, democracies do not possess special rights to disregard the non-interventionist provisions of the UN charter. Non-democratic states are not second-class citizens. Democracies and non-democracies possess equal rights. Making the world safe for democracy by force of arms is contrary to established international norms. If that were to be the foreign policy of the USA or NATO it would divide the world more deeply and would probably make the world less safe rather than more safe.

Mill also argues that international efforts to provide people in other countries with foreign institutions are likely to be futile. Outsiders cannot readily give people in other countries democracy: that usually is not in their power. If Yugoslavia is going to be a democracy that respects the human rights of all its citizens, it will be up to the Yugoslavs and not the American government or the British army or any other foreign political or military agency. The Yugoslav government can of course call on outsiders for help. Outsiders are free to lend them support and assistance. Hopefully outsiders would be generous if called upon. Everybody has the right to be generous. But nobody has any right to become involved without being invited if there is no threat to somebody's national security or international peace and security. What the Americans, the British, and everybody else are duty bound to do is refrain from obstructing the attempt of the Yugoslavs to carry on with whatever domestic political life they have and to change it in whatever way they will. The Yugoslavs would be wise to democratize their political system, if they are up to it, because that would probably give them a better life than they presently have. But foreign governments are not responsible for the domestic political affairs of Yugoslavia. The Yugoslavs are responsible.

---

[38] John Stuart Mill, 'A Few Words on Non-Intervention', in *Essays on Politics and Culture by John Stuart Mill*, ed. G. Himmelfarb (New York: Anchor Books, 1963), 368–84. Also see Michael Walzer, *Just and Unjust Wars*, 2nd edn. (New York: Basic Books, 1992), ch. 6.

Mill is arguing from the perspective of classical liberalism as it applies to international relations: he is affirming the principle 'let other nations alone'.[39] Outsiders cannot take it upon themselves to get involved in the domestic affairs of independent countries, even if their motives are entirely benevolent, which is not usually the case. For outsiders to get involved on their own initiative and with the best of intentions would be a form of paternalism, as indicated in Chapter 11. Pluralism is sharply at odds with ideological crusading in world politics, and that must include crusades for democracy. Pluralism and paternalism are contradictory values. Pluralism is tolerant of difference and intolerant of imposition, even if it is an act carried out by decent people with good intentions. If universal international community is still organized fundamentally on the basis of pluralism—and the burden of argument clearly is on those who would deny it—there cannot be any room for democratic crusading in world affairs at the present time.

There is ample historical evidence to support the scepticism of Mill concerning the folly of trying to establish democracy in foreign countries from outside. Democracy has been brought into existence in a country by the efforts and resources of outsiders only in the most unusual circumstances—such as the successful democratization of West Germany after the Second World War at the dictation of the occupying Western powers, particularly the USA. Even in that case, influential German leaders of democratic convictions who had opposed the Nazis—such as Konrad Adenauer and Willy Brandt—were energetic collaborators in post-war democratic reconstruction. Historically and culturally Germany is part of the West and the West German public not only accepted democracy but welcomed it. The far more typical historical experience we ought to keep in mind is the sobering experience of Britain and France in seeking to endow their colonial subjects in Asia and Africa with democratic institutions before they decolonized. One also cannot overlook the frustrated American attempt to build democracies in South Vietnam and Central America. With very few exceptions— probably India, perhaps Malaysia, maybe a few other places—these efforts were total failures: once the foreigners packed up and went home, the struggle for power got under way in earnest. Instead of democracies, what usually emerged were regimes of authoritarian rule.[40]

That post-colonial enlargement of the authoritarian world was of course underwritten by the cold war which made it very unwise strategically for Western powers to insist on democratic government before entering into political, economic, and military relations with ex-colonial states. The Third World was a construction, at least to some extent, of the cold war. The end of the cold war was a loss of influence, position, and prestige for the Third World generally and for smaller and weaker authoritarian states in particular. They now

---

[39] Mill, 'Few Words on Non-Intervention', 368.

[40] R. Jackson and C. Rosberg, *Personal Rule in Black Africa* (Berkeley, Calif.: University of California Press, 1982).

confront a new situation in which it is no longer possible for them to play the democratic West off against the communist East in an ironical inverted system of divide and rule, as they regularly used to do. The southern tail can no longer wag the northern dog. Third World states have lost the privileged bargaining position in international relations that the cold war gave them and today they are more exposed to the West than at any time since decolonization.

Are Western democracies now in a stronger international position to shape the domestic political life of authoritarian countries with a view to promoting democracy within them? That is a complicated question and thus a difficult one to reply to briefly. One way to simplify the question is by drawing a distinction between large and important authoritarian states and small and unimportant ones. There are not many of the former, because most of the significant and weighty states in the world nowadays are democracies; there are many of the latter, however.

Presumably Western democracies will be very circumspect in their pro-democratic campaigning when it comes to major authoritarian powers. Consider China as a case in point. Such a country is too strong militarily and too important economically to be moved against its political will by Western demands for democratization or the protection of human rights. No foreign power can threaten China militarily on its own territory. The most the United States can do is confine China's military within its borders and offshore waters—that is, check an expansionist China. Few if any Western nations would want to risk being shut out of what promises to be the biggest economic boom in world history. They are usually prepared to temper their criticism of China's authoritarianism if that is necessary to gain access to her economy. That is Beijing's trump card. If Western nations want to participate in what is, potentially, a market of a billion producers and consumers, then the export of democracy—and by implication human rights—to China will probably have to take a back seat to commercial interests if that is what Beijing is determined to insist upon. Neither Prime Minister Blair nor any other responsible leader of a Western democracy would be prepared to demand that China sign up for 'the doctrine of international community'. That would go against the fundamental commercial interests of such countries. It would be an irresponsible and unrealistic foreign policy. If China ever sets course to become a democracy that will be the determination and decision of the Chinese government, and if it is successful that will be the achievement of the Chinese people.

That puts the values of democracy and human rights in perspective: it may be desirable to see the democratic world enlarged—I believe it would be desirable—but it must be subject to more fundamental considerations and values embodied by the global covenant. Democracy and human rights cannot be pursued in disregard of those values. They can and should be pursued within the framework of international *societas*. The end of the cold war might be an auspicious moment for democratic proselytizing by Western states and the international organizations they control. We see evidence of that in the policy of making international finance (by the World Bank, the IMF, and most Western governments) conditional on certain domestic reforms, not only economic reforms such as free-market economies or transparent banking regulations but also political reforms, including the protection of human rights, the rule of law, and free and fair elections. Although conditionality in the form of 'structural adjustment' predates 1989 and indeed goes back to the 1970s, it has been a striking feature of North–South relations, particularly involving sub-Saharan Africa, since the end of the cold war.[41]

Would conditionality be a justifiable method of promoting democracy in weak authoritarian states? The answer clearly is yes. As long as no military threats are involved and recipient states can decide to accept conditionality of their own free will, there is nothing wrong with the practice. It is entirely consistent with the global covenant.

Profound material inequality between developed and underdeveloped countries does not alter that legality and morality. If a poor country decided to take out an IMF loan which carried conditions, then that would be their choice even if it is a hard choice. To argue that poor countries have little choice but to accept conditionality because of their abject poverty is undoubtedly true. Poverty has always limited the choices that individuals can make and the lives they can lead and the same material constraint applies to states. Economic backwardness used to be grounds for denying membership in the international community and for justifying Western imperialism and colonialism. That changed with decolonization: poverty then became the basis of a moral claim for foreign aid from rich countries.[42] But rich countries have no generally recognized international obligation to provide financial or other material means to improve the living conditions of poor countries. They are at liberty to be generous or selfish; most rich democratic states are far more selfish than generous and that surely tells us something about their commitment to humanity. Foreign aid does not alter the ethical practice of the states system which rests on a liberal ethic and not a socialist ethic; foreign aid is voluntary and not obligatory. Rich countries can choose to give international aid and to tie their aid in whatever way they like. Poor countries are at liberty to refuse structural adjustment loans from rich countries, and the economic and political strings attached to them.

Making democratization a condition of external financial aid in the present international community would not be democratic crusading because it would not trespass on the basic norm of state sovereignty and non-intervention. What it would be is democratic proselytizing and there is nothing wrong with that in current international practice. Western governments can be missionaries for democracy. What they cannot be are soldiers for democracy. A proselyte is a convert: somebody who has been persuaded to change his or her beliefs and has

[41] G. Sørensen (ed.), *Political Conditionality* (London: Macmillan, 1993).
[42] R. Jackson, *Quasi-States* (Cambridge: Cambridge University Press, 1990), ch. 5.

thus converted to a new belief system. Conversion is not compulsion. If democratic states take it upon themselves to win converts to their political ideology from among weak authoritarian states that is not something that anybody could object to on currently existing international legal and moral grounds.

The Hubris of the West?

The global covenant, however inadequate it may be, is still the one political-legal framework that can transcend all the manifold differences between the countries of the world, can accommodate their various belief systems and domestic ways of life, and can serve as a normative basis for their coexistence and co-operation. That is not something that devotees of democracy can take it upon themselves to ignore simply because it is inconsistent with their own most cherished values and beliefs, even if they genuinely do believe that their values and beliefs are truer than any others currently on offer and would be good for the rest of the world. Reforms of the kind that Prime Minister Blair was calling for in 1999, if they are to possess international legality and legitimacy, could only proceed with the consent of all important sectors of international society; they could not proceed arbitrarily from only one quarter of the world (the West) even if that quarter is by far the most important militarily and economically.

As indicated, there is a greater international good than democracy, and that good is pluralism or international freedom, which itself makes democracy possible by giving people a choice and a space to build democracy in their own country—if that is what they desire and if they have the political virtues to do it. We democrats deem democracy to be good because it rests on the freedom and responsibility of the citizen. But there is a freedom and a responsibility that is more fundamental than that of democratic citizenship. It is a freedom and a responsibility that is prior to the constitution of any democracy. That is the freedom and responsibility of obtaining democracy for oneself if one desires to have it: the freedom to create citizens and build a constitutional democracy. That is what the Americans, the British, and the French demonstrated in their political histories. It is basically the same for all well-founded and long-lasting democracies. International pluralism is the fundamental condition for the flourishing of democracy—or any other valued and preferred national way of life. The history of successful democratic self-determination is a history of self-reliance more than anything else.

Historically many Americans have seen themselves as a chosen people who have been placed on earth to give hope to men and women everywhere and do good in the world. It is not that Americans are an aggressive nation, for they clearly are not. It is, rather, that Americans are an activist nation, convinced beyond doubt of the superiority of their own values. When Americans have gone

to war, usually with the greatest reluctance, they have fought with overwhelming determination and courage for their values: they have been crusaders for
democracy. We should not underestimate the force of that political sentiment in
American culture. In the past many Europeans held a similar world-view of the
superiority of European civilization. They saw their international responsibility
as that of using their power and wealth to spread their civilization around the
world. Western imperialism and colonialism was based on that attitude. At the
end of a century of American ascendance in world politics, after the defeat of
fascism by America and its allies in the Second World War, and now after the
disintegration of the Soviet Union and the end of the long cold war, self-
confidence and conviction in their international responsibilities to spread their
values around the world may again be widely shared by governments and citizens throughout the West—especially among a younger generation of American
and European politicians who came to power in the 1990s.

But if international history is anything to go by, that is a dangerous attitude
because it could provoke conflicts over belief systems which, seen from the angle
of their believers, may be equally valuable and equally deeply held. It bears
repeating that democracy is a belief system. For its most devoted adherents, the
Americans, it is something very close to a political religion. The history of the
relations of major religions is very largely a history of intolerance, of persecution,
of a struggle to assert values that are deemed to be morally superior by those who
hold them. That is a world that invites just wars and holy wars. That defined
the relations between the Christian world and the Muslim world for many centuries. It defined the relations between European Protestants and European
Catholics for two centuries. It doggedly defines the relations between many different political-religious communities even today, and not least those between
Irish Catholic republicans and Ulster Protestant unionists or between Arab
Muslims and Israeli Jews or between Turkish Cypriots who are Muslims and
Greek Cypriots who are Orthodox Christians. That is what peace must struggle
against in Ireland, the Middle East, and other such places. If there is a lesson to
derive from the historical role of religion and ideology in world politics it may
be the following one: all fundamentalism is to be avoided and shunned in the
conduct of foreign policy, and that must include democratic fundamentalism.

The basic inclination of an international *societas* is a negative inclination in
favour of restraint on the part of its member states. That also applies to the great
powers. They are only released from that restraint when they are called upon to
defend the global covenant. They are not released from it merely by declaring
their desire to spread their own most cherished values beyond their own jurisdiction. They are not released from it merely because, as Prime Minister Blair
put it, their 'existence as states' is no longer 'under threat'. On the contrary,
in that circumstance of greater freedom they are called upon to be even more
careful. Is there not a danger when one great power or alliance of states, in this
case NATO, enjoys international pre-eminence and no longer has to face a

disciplining balance of power? That kind of tempting situation is difficult for statespeople to handle. It is a temptation that should be resisted; that would be a test of political virtue in the exercise of great power. Even a historically peace-loving power like the USA may surrender to hubris. That is the arrogance of power feared by classical liberals, as captured by Lord Acton in a famous phrase: 'power corrupts, and absolute power tends to corrupt absolutely'.[43] The English poet John Dryden wrote in the seventeenth century,

> But when the chosen people grew more strong
> The rightful cause at length became the wrong.[44]

If modern international society was instituted for anything, it was to prevent unnecessary confrontations and collisions between different states that are inspired and driven by the assertion of their own preferred values. It was originally a response to the persistence of religious warfare in Europe. 'Unnecessary' in this context signifies values which are internal to states and define the way of life of their people: values that properly belong to domestic jurisdiction. These are values which have no place in international relations in the sense that they cannot be imposed on others who do not wish to have them. Such values would of course encompass the core self-regarding values of the major civilizations, including Western civilization. That would thus exclude from international relations the Western political value of democracy, just as it would exclude the Muslim religious value of *jihad* or the revolutionary ideologies of communism or fascism or imperialism or any other assertive belief system whose adherents are prepared to repudiate the *societas* of states for the sake of their own values.

A fundamental concern of modern international society for the past 350 years, perhaps the most fundamental, has been the concern to confine religious and ideological *weltanschauungen* within the territorial cages of national borders. The domestication of religion and ideology arguably is the most significant historical achievement associated with that society: *cujus regio, ejus religio*. At first that norm of toleration was only applied in Europe. Only much later was it applied around the world, thus making possible a global political covenant that gives expression to our common human capacity to recognize each other as formal equals and tolerate each other's beliefs and convictions even though we disagree with them and may even find them repugnant. The profound significance of that historical achievement has not always been appreciated by international relations scholars. It should be firmly grasped by all statespeople. The failure of academics to understand it can only be a matter of regret; the failure of the world's foremost leaders of the current era to be fully aware and very mindful of it should be a matter of the greatest concern.

[43] Also see Lord Acton, 'Beginning of the Modern State', repr. in W. H. McNeill (ed.), *Lord Acton: Essays in the Liberal Interpretation of History* (Chicago: University of Chicago Press, 1967), 400–19.

[44] John Dryden, 'Absalom and Achitophel: A Poem', in M. H. Abrams (ed.), *The Norton Anthology of English Literature*, 4th edn., i (New York: Norton, 1962), 1753.

III

Value and Future of International Society

14

Alternatives to International *Societas?*

In previous chapters I argued that the normative foundation of international relations is pluralistic and that it must be so to accommodate the assorted civilizations and cultures of the globe whose values may be inconsistent, divergent, incompatible, or even mutually antagonistic. This chapter contemplates some important alternative images of present and future world politics which take issue, either explicitly or by implication, with the morality of the sovereign state and the ethics of statecraft. They portray world politics as embarked on a course of fundamental transformation that renders the post-1945 international *societas* increasingly out of date and even obsolete. They see the emergence of a global *universitas* based on a hierarchy of values, at the top of which is their own preferred values, usually democracy or human rights. Or they detect a retreat into a fractured and fragmented world characterized by relativism. This chapter assesses these arguments with a view to clearing the ground for a defence of the global covenant which shall be presented in the final chapter.

Beyond Non-Intervention?

One revisionist school argues that it is necessary to adopt an activist international morality for our rapidly changing world. At the heart of this argument is the claim that non-intervention produces, or at least it tolerates, needless human suffering in many countries around the world. It does that by preserving states which have failed their own people, and by protecting governments which allow or commit serious human rights violations. These critics thus argue from a normative perspective in which the sovereign state is no longer privileged and the taboo against intervention is relaxed, usually on humanitarian grounds.

This critique of the global covenant draws our attention to the commission of 'human wrongs' in numerous countries around the world.[1] Humanitarian monitoring organizations report widespread and recurrent human rights abuses,

---

[1] K. Booth, 'Human Wrongs and International Relations', *International Affairs*, 71 (1995), 103–26.

many of which are condoned or even perpetrated by member states of inter-national society. Such abuses include genocide, ethnic cleansing, arbitrary arrest, political imprisonment without trial, racial discrimination, torture, rape, depri-vation of livelihood, child labour, among others. The legitimacy of contempor-ary international society is confronted by the following evidence: 'a world [where] . . . 123 states practice torture or ill-treatment of prisoners; where geno-cide occurs and goes unpunished; where 40,000 children die daily of preventable diseases; and where millions—especially women—live hopeless and wretched lives'.[2] Even if some of this is inflated, the point still remains. This critique identifies what seems to be a glaring moral failure of contemporary international society. Many states around the world, including many offending states, are signatories of the International Covenant on Civil and Political Rights, the Convention on the Prevention and Punishment of the Crime of Genocide, the Convention against Torture and Other Cruel, Inhuman and Degrading Treatment or Punishment, and other human rights conventions. It is not diffi-cult to sustain the claim that massive violations of human rights are occurring regularly in many of the states which participated in establishing international human rights laws.

Some critics argue for an ethic of 'global responsibility' which would not only authorize but would oblige Western governments to employ their military power to intervene in states which fail to abide by international standards of human rights.[3] Here international society is held responsible for solving the problem of abusive states and failed states. The proposed solution implies a fundamental change in the moral outlook of the major Western powers and particularly the USA. Other critics argue that an ideology of 'statism' is at the root of the prob-lem and is obstructing the 'world order values' of an emergent global civil soci-ety in which, it is assumed, 'human wrongs' would no longer be committed.[4] In other words, the society of states as it presently exists is the source of the prob-lem. The solution implies a root and branch reorganization of international soci-ety. If the legitimacy of international society depends on the premiss that all states must actually be safe places where human rights actually are protected, then the foregoing evidence of 'human wrongs' is a massive indictment of the global covenant. Scholars, such as myself, who defend the international ethics of pluralism are thus exposing themselves to charges of complacency and per-haps even moral neglect. Yet this critique is wide of the mark, as I argue at greater length below. Here a brief preliminary response must suffice.

Far from being morally defective, the existing normative foundations of inter-national society can be justified in the present conditions of world politics. As indicated, upholding the *Grundnorm* of non-intervention only makes normative

---

[2] Nicholas J. Wheeler, 'Guardian Angel or Global Gangster: A Review of the Ethical Claims of International Society', *Political Studies*, 44 (1996), 131, 134.

[3] M. Shaw, *Global Society and International Relations* (Cambridge: Polity, 1994), 132–5.

[4] Booth, 'Human Wrongs', 103–26.

sense if the states being defended give, or can at least plausibly be assumed to give, the opportunity for their citizens to pursue the 'good life', however differently that domestic political condition may be understood from one time or place to the next. Non-intervention is a prohibition and thus a negative liberty: freedom from outside interference.[5] It is an international guarantee that makes the pursuit of the 'good life' possible within independent countries without worrying about foreign intervention. But it is not any assurance that the good life will actually be forthcoming: it is not an enabling condition or positive liberty.[6] Whether the citizens of particular states actually manage to build and enjoy their own 'good life', or not, is up to themselves; it is not a responsibility of international society. It probably is not within the power of international society either.

Contemporary international society does not operate universally with enforceable standards which exclusively concern the domestic conditions of states. It only operates that way in particular world regions—such as Europe and North America—where, for example, member states of the Council of Europe, the EU, and NATO's Partnership for Peace consent to intrusive international standards, such as human rights, the rule of law, liberal democracy, market economy. The operative word is 'consent'. The regional agreements of Western states to observe certain domestic standards of conduct do not conflict with their obligations to respect the global covenant in their international relations generally. There is also nothing to prevent voluntary international action by rich countries to assist poor countries to improve their living conditions. International aid is widely practised. But it is deferential to state sovereignty. It is not conducted independently of international borders. Nor could it be that way if the political independence of existing states, including both those states which supply aid and those states which receive aid, is to be preserved.

In general, human rights norms do not pre-empt the *Grundnorm* of non-intervention. If human rights were a pre-emptive norm, we would be living in a different world. It would be a world in which the fundamental norm would effectively be intervention rather than non-intervention. If intervention became the basic norm, state boundaries would no longer be a significant normative barrier against the international use of armed force. There would be intrusive norms that could justify intervention, perhaps something along the lines of the old 'standard of civilization' which was employed by Western states in the nineteenth century to justify their colonization of Africa and some other parts of the non-Western world. Gerrit Gong suggests that such a standard exists in the form of 'human rights' and 'development'.[7] Since the end of colonialism,

---

[5] See I. Berlin, *Four Essays on Liberty* (London: OUP, 1969), 118–72.

[6] I have explored the distinction between negative sovereignty and positive sovereignty in *Quasi-States: Sovereignty, International Relations and the Third World* (Cambridge: Cambridge University Press, 1990).

[7] G. W. Gong, *The Standard of 'Civilization' in International Society* (Oxford: Clarendon Press, 1984), 90–2.

however, such norms have respected the *Grundnorm* of non-intervention. They are non-intrusive. If they were an intrusive standard that could be used to justify intervention it would provoke some disturbing historical memories for many people outside the West. And if the USA and its major Western allies were truly obligated to engage generally in humanitarian rescue operations we could probably expect their governments to find many reasons and ways to avoid such action if unacceptable risks and sacrifices to themselves were likely to be involved. An instance of that was NATO's unwillingness to allow its air crews to fly below an altitude of 15,000 feet while waging humanitarian war against Yugoslavia in 1999 out of a concern for their safety, knowing that those rules of engagement definitely increased the dangers to civilians on the ground.

But, as indicated previously, the fact is that such an interventionist world does not exist nor is it looming on the horizon. Apart from the ambiguous case of Kosovo, there is no compelling indication in state practice of which I am aware that solidarist ethics are pre-empting pluralist ethics in world politics. It is only happening voluntarily and to a limited extent within the Western international community among states who share the same political values. Informed critics of state sovereignty usually acknowledge that. They want that activist humanitarian posture to be applied on a world-wide basis. They do not want it confined to the West. They are providing a prescriptive theory and not a descriptive theory of human conduct in world affairs. Two questions they have to confront are: first, what realistic basis is there in the existential world of international practice for their prescriptive arguments? If there is no basis, are they not exposed to the criticism that their analyses are flights of intellectual fancy divorced from political reality? And, secondly, what solid reasons are there for supposing that an activist international ethics of reduced sovereignty and expanded humanitarian intervention would be morally superior to the non-activist practices and principles of the global covenant? More specifically, what are the conceivable dangers and hazards of an interventionist world? These questions would have to be addressed by anyone who seriously advocated an activist ethics of humanitarian intervention.

Beyond the Ethics of Statecraft?

Another critique portrays the society of states as the support structure of an exclusive club of ruling élites under the managerial control of the rich and powerful countries of the West.[8] The target of this neo-Marxist argument is the ethos of an international society in which the great powers play the leading managerial role. Statecraft is criticized as an exploitative political activity stage-

---

[8] Wheeler, 'Guardian Angel', 123–35.

managed by the leading Western powers, especially the USA. It is seen as a wholly instrumental activity which upholds the existing states system with all its material inequalities. It thereby perpetuates social injustice on a global scale and blocks progressive international change. If that portrait is accurate the ethics of statecraft obviously cannot have any valid moral basis. To place this critique in its proper context it may be useful to reiterate briefly what one such critic has called the 'guardian angel' role prescribed for the great powers by theorists of international society.[9] The foremost theorist in that regard is undoubtedly Hedley Bull and he is clearly the main target of these criticisms.

In the current practice of world politics, according to Bull, great powers perform a managerial role and for that purpose they enjoy special rights and duties which are generally recognized and acknowledged by international society.[10] Great powers are responsible for 'determining issues that affect the peace and security of the international system as a whole'. That means they have a duty to shape and adjust their own foreign policies with those desirable international conditions firmly in view. It also means that they can legitimately be criticized for failing in that responsibility. 'Great powers can fulfill their managerial functions in international society only if these functions are accepted clearly enough by a large enough proportion of the society of states to command legitimacy.' According to Bull, that is usually the case: 'the great powers enjoy a wide measure of support throughout international society'.[11] How far that support extends at any time obviously is an empirical question. Today the USA, Russia, China, Britain, and France are generally acknowledged as being in that category—along with Japan and Germany who are not permanent members of the Security Council. These are the powers who count at the present time, with the USA clearly first among equals: they are usually included in the international circles whose decisions and judgements on important international issues must be taken into account by everybody else. But Bull's point is not about particular powers. It is about the institution of great powers as such and the expectations involved, regardless of which states happen to be the great powers at that time.

The validity and credibility of Bull's claims about great power responsibility have come in for strenuous criticism which often expresses doubt that borders on disbelief. The critics argue that the notion of great power responsibility merely presents a respectable face which masks the true reality of a hegemonial world order that is founded on coercion and maintained by the pervasive background threat of the military might of the great powers.[12] In other words, the great powers create international order not by carrying out their heavy responsibilities to defend that value but, rather, by imposing their strong and

[9] Ibid.

[10] Hedley Bull, *The Anarchical Society*, 2nd edn. (London: Macmillan, 1995), 194–222.

[11] Ibid. 221.

[12] F. Halliday, *Rethinking International Relations* (London: Macmillan, 1994), 102.

irresistible political wills on everybody else and using their coercion to derive maximum advantages and benefits from that situation. The greatest offender is the capitalist USA, viewed as the world's hegemon.

The ethics of statecraft is thus a masquerade. The reality behind the mask of great power responsibility is a hegemonial world order orchestrated by the great powers for their own benefit and particularly for that of the hegemon. Statecraft is a wholly instrumental and self-serving political activity. The main beneficiaries are the state élites and the class interests they serve. The virtue of prudence is actually the vice of élite and class selfishness. The real intentions of statespeople are to exploit and oppress those who are less powerful than themselves. The great powers dominate lesser powers and minor powers with that end in view. Equal state sovereignty is an illusion. The sovereignty of the weak is merely a concession from the strong which serves their interests. The ruling élites of weak states use their token sovereignty to keep their countries subservient to the Western powers and to exploit them for their own profit. In that regard one critic argues that 'a society of states run by Western governments and a variety of local strongmen . . . bears an uncomfortable resemblance to a global protection racket'.[13]

This critique also has important moral implications concerning the responsibilities of international relations scholarship. Scholars who take an ethics of statecraft approach expose themselves to charges of complacency and moral indifference. They are too readily disposed to rationalize foreign-policy decisions as the best moral choices that could be expected under the circumstances.[14] There is no doubt that political science scholarship can become corrupted by surrendering to the charms of official sanction and approval. Herbert Butterfield warned against the temptations of 'official history', which was the threat that 'officially-favored' historians presented to freedom of thought in the writing of diplomatic history.[15] Diplomatic historians, if they surrender to the seductions of writing official histories, often end up as captives of foreign offices and rationalizers of their foreign policies. That is the temptation faced by academic consultants and advisers to governments. But that is a question of personal academic integrity. Trying in a detached way to make scholarly sense of the political activity of international statecraft is not placing one's academic independence at risk. Nor is it being complacent or demonstrating moral indifference. There is nothing inherently corrupt in trying to give a scholarly account of the foreign policies and actions of statespeople by making reference to the norms and values of international society which they have instituted.

Half the critique that the ethics of statecraft is a sham would itself be placed in doubt if one accepted that the national interest is a bona-fide moral category

[13] K. Booth, 'Duty and Prudence', in L. Freedman (ed.), *Military Intervention in European Conflicts* (Oxford: Blackwell, 1994), 57.
[14] Booth, 'Human Wrongs'.
[15] H. Butterfield, *History and Human Relations* (London: Collins, 1951), 182–3.

and that defending that interest is a legitimate action on the part of statespeople. Neo-Marxist critics cannot accept that. They conceive of states as instrumental agencies of power in the hands of puppet political élites but under the firm control of selfish economic interests that manipulate them. In so doing they take what can only be characterized as an exaggerated view of the abilities of such subterranean people to control events; it is out of proportion with political reality. The global hegemon is cast as a God-like agent: seeing everything, knowing everything, all-powerful. The model is largely deterministic and correspondingly unrealistic. There is no room for intelligence, stupidity, experience, judgement, misunderstanding, foresight, miscalculation, lack of foresight, knowledge, limited information, misinformation, folly, and other all too human strengths, weaknesses, and failings involved in political activity—the kind noted by Machiavelli's political science.[16]

Nor is there any room for moral ideas and discourse in this analysis, except the self-selected ideological prescriptions of the external critic which are held and applied uncritically.[17] But the practical discourse of politicians and diplomats is clearly normative and not merely instrumental. Its main basis of justification is the state and the society of states and not the social or economic class. It includes the moral notion of the responsibility of statespeople to defend the national interest and the moral idea of the responsibility of great powers to maintain the conditions of peace and security which make that possible. Statespeople cannot conduct international relations without that moral discourse because they have to justify their policies and actions to each other—often to their citizens as well—and these are the relevant terms for doing that. If statespeople operated according to the neo-Marxist view they would possess no practical moral discourse and would thus be deprived of any shared means of condemnation and justification. They would have no responsibilities. They would only have desires and power. The strong would be free to exploit their power to the full. The weak would be obliged to surrender in silence to the hegemon or else face the consequences. Is that how members of international society, great and small, conduct themselves in their relations? I believe the evidence indicates otherwise.

The other half of the critique would be undermined if the enormous power differentials and the reality of coercion in world politics—which no informed observer could deny—were understood against a more relevant normative background than the lofty ideals of global social justice which shape the cosmopolitan moral outlook of neo-Marxism. Anybody familiar with world history would

---

[16] N. Machiavelli, *The Prince*, tr. and ed. George Bull (Harmondsworth: Penguin Books, 1961).

[17] 'It is one of the great alibis, pleaded by those who cannot or do not wish to face the fact of human responsibility, the existence of a limited but nevertheless real area of human freedom, either because they have been too deeply wounded or frightened to wish to return to the traffic of normal life, or because they are filled with moral indignation against the false values and . . . repellent moral codes of their own society . . .': Berlin, *Four Essays on Liberty*, 116.

have difficulty disagreeing with David Hume's sardonic eighteenth-century observation—arguing to deflate the social contract theory of state formation—that 'almost all the governments which exist at present, or of which there remains any record in history, have been founded originally either on usurpation or conquest or both'.[18] Even though many of these despotisms have now been tamed, and some have been democratized, that is a significant reality of world politics. International order and justice obviously have to be built on that reality. Defending the less than ideal but still valuable international society that presently exists and seeking where possible to improve upon it could be seen as legitimate responsibilities of the great powers. By and large those responsibilities are carried on, imperfectly, by those same powers.

There is a clear implication in the foregoing critique that Hedley Bull's claims about great power responsibilities are not only morally compromised but are also politically naïve. Behind the critique is the window-dressing argument discussed in previous chapters, which is popular with commentators on world affairs who adopt the privileged standpoint of an external critic unencumbered by the limits of choice and the circumstances of action placed upon practitioners. But who is more naïve: the international society scholar who probes with detachment but not without vicarious emotion the situated choices of statespeople in seeking to give a well-founded and balanced interpretation of their foreign relations, or the critical theorist who soars above international politics and portrays those same choices from the perspective of his or her lofty ideals and convictions? C. P. Snow argued in one of the wisest political novels of the twentieth century that the peculiar handicap of intellectuals is to misconstrue statecraft as the predictable supremacy of powerful and sinister interests, rather than as the uncertain interactions of intellectually and morally flawed human beings. That latter image strikes me as being far nearer to reality.[19]

Another Grotian Moment?

That the contemporary world may be entering another 'Grotian moment' is a thought provoking idea associated with the work of Richard Falk.[20] Reduced to fundamentals it is the claim that a transformative change in the organization and *modus operandi* of international life is presently occurring that is reminiscent of

[18] See C. W. Hendel (ed.), *David Hume's Political Essays* (Indianapolis: Bobbs-Merrill, 1953), 43–61.

[19] C. P. Snow, *Corridors of Power* (New York: Scribner's, 1964).

[20] The 'Grotian moment' argument is made in various writings by Richard Falk. However, I shall confine my references to the succinct statement of the argument in his essay 'A New Paradigm for International Legal Studies: Prospects and Proposals', in R. Falk, F. Kratochwil, and S. H. Mendlovitz (eds.), *International Law: A Contemporary Perspective* (Boulder, Colo. and London: Westview, 1985), 651–702. All subsequent quotations from Falk are taken from this essay.

a revolutionary change three or four centuries ago that was captured by the jurisprudence of Hugo Grotius. Richard Falk is an advocate of a solidarist conception of international society in which the global community of humankind has normative priority and the society of states is in conflict with it. By contrast, classical international society scholars view the states system as the only practical institution presently at hand by which the values and interests of humankind can be defended and advanced. According to that approach, Hugo Grotius is the theorist *par excellence* of international society.[21]

What, then, can the word 'Grotian' signify for our purposes? Although Grotius's celebrated work on the law of nations was published some 375 years ago, it is possible to retrieve two fundamental ideas about international conduct from that famous study.[22] The first idea is the notion that all humans are subject to natural law which is revealed to them by their rational faculties and is independent of their religious beliefs. The second idea is the notion that all sovereigns are subjects of the customs and practices of international positive law, what he referred to as 'human volitional law'.[23] In Grotius's thought the former norm has normative priority, but the latter norm is a political reality. The problem for Grotius is reconciling these seemingly contradictory norms when they come into conflict, as they are bound to do from time to time.

Grotius saw clearly that medieval Christendom was breaking up and the states of Europe were not only asserting their independence but in many cases they were demonstrating it. There no longer was an overarching religious-political hierarchy throughout Western Europe as there had been, at least in theory if not always in practice, in the Middle Ages. Christian unity had been shattered by the Protestant Reformation and there was a growing international anarchy of independent or semi-independent governments. An alternative foundation was required upon which a modicum of order and justice between those governments could be established. Even though the sovereign rulers of the emerging anarchical society of Europe were independent of each other, they were still subjects of the law of nature and were duty bound to obey it just like everyone else. That is the heart of natural law doctrine in the Grotian law of nations. Yet sovereign rulers were also authors and subjects of positive law. The second main normative element of Grotius's conception of international law is the accepted customs and practices of states and sovereigns in their relations with each other. Those customs and practices, in virtue of their acceptance and use, have the authority of law. That is Hugo Grotius's positive law of nations: the *jus gentium inter se.*

There is an obvious problem here that Grotius grappled with: sovereign rulers are in a double bind; what shall take precedence when pluralist norms of

---

[21] H. Lauterpact, 'The Grotian Tradition in International Law', *British Yearbook of International Law* (1946), 1–53; Martin Wight, *International Theory: The Three Traditions* (Leicester: Leicester University Press, 1992); Bull, *Anarchical Society.*

[22] Hugo Grotius, *De Jure Belli ac Pacis Libri Tres*, tr. Francis Kelsey (Oxford: OUP, 1925).

[23] Grotius also distinguished 'divine volitional law' or the law of God.

state sovereignty come into conflict with solidarist norms of human rights? Grotius gives no clear and unequivocal answer to that fundamentally important question. That is because there cannot be a principled answer in the pluralistic international society in which Grotius lived and we continue to live, which (at a minimum) is a world of *both* sovereign states and their citizens, on the one hand, and common humanity regardless of citizenship, on the other hand. As Richard Falk comments:

the tension between domestic jurisdiction and human rights is as old as the persecutions of the Huguenots or Puritans and as contemporary as the persecution of Soviet Jewry. The question as to whether deference to state sovereignty should take precedence over efforts to rescue victims of governmental abuse remains necessarily ambiguous and controversial in each context.

Sovereign rights coexist with human rights, and the long history of international relations suggests that there is no absolutely principled way of determining which takes priority when they come into conflict. People involved in world affairs are bound to be confronted by situations that present normative dilemmas in which the right course of action is not certain. It is obvious that the problems that Hugo Grotius addressed in his international jurisprudence are still very much with us, and there is a clear sense in which his Grotian moment is also our Grotian moment because the international world that he discerned before almost anybody else is still very much in evidence today.

In addition to that original Grotian moment, is there another Grotian moment of international change that in some sense parallels, but this time in reverse gear, the change from medieval to modern? Is there an emerging transformation from modern to postmodern, from a pluralist society of states to a solidarist community of humankind? Richard Falk argues that international life is undergoing a transformative reorganization that will result in 'drastic modifications of the world order system that has prevailed since the Peace of Westphalia'. However, the currently unfolding world order is a 'reversal' of the earlier transformation. The first Grotian moment was the culmination and completion of a gradual historical change that had been under-way for several centuries before Westphalia: from 'nonterritorial central guidance' (based on the medieval papacy and feudal loyalties) to 'territorial decentralization' (based on the system of sovereign states). The second Grotian moment involves a change from the anarchical society to a new world order of increasing 'central guidance' and expanding roles for 'nonterritorial actors', thus reinstating two organizational principles of the medieval era. The national 'loyalty and legitimacy' upon which the state, and also the society of states, could previously depend is 'relocating' away from the state: upward to the centre of the globe, or the world as a whole, and downward to the local community. The role of the individual and also that of 'subnational movements for self-determination' are expanding. Religious and political movements with 'cosmopolitan identifications' are growing rapidly and it is now possible to speak intelligibly of a 'planetary community'. In short, individuals, groups, and the world as a whole are breaking free of the states system. Falk speaks of this world-historical change as a 'juridical revolution'.

The correct intellectual grasp of this second world order transformation in international jurisprudence is the task that Richard Falk sets for himself: 'Today, as in the seventeenth century, the time is ripe for preliminary efforts to give juridical shape to a new paradigm of global relations, one that corresponds more closely than statist thinking to the needs, trends, and values of the present state of global politics.' Falk seeks to provide a world juridical 'paradigm' that can not only comprehend the transformation but can also provide the basis for guiding it in a benevolent direction: away from power élites, whether those of statist international politics or those of capitalist global economics, and toward populist human goals. To give such direction is, according to Falk, an important role that international scholars can perform.

Falk identities four alternative models that set out different historical paths that the second Grotian moment could take: (1) 'utopian legalism' that envisages and pursues 'world government', (2) the 'concert of great powers', presumably under USA direction, (3) the 'concert of multinational corporate elites', in which transnational global capitalism is predominant around the world, and (4) 'global populism' or a cosmopolitan world order based on 'human solidarity' in which ordinary men and women take precedence over both great power statism and global capitalism. Falk gives an assessment of each model. The problem with the first model, as he rightly notes, is its naïveté: it fails to grasp the nature and significance of power in world politics and, particularly, the relationship of power to 'benevolent ends'. The problem with the second model is its tendency to foster destructive wars which can be seen to derive from international anarchy based on state sovereignty. The problem with the third model is that it is driven by the ideology of a powerful 'multinational corporate elite' who seek 'to subordinate territorial politics' to their transnational economic goals 'just as the papacy . . . sought to place the spiritual sword of the Church above the secular sword of national kings'.

Richard Falk sees the fourth model as the only one that should be encouraged by progressive world jurisprudence. That is how he conceives of his own role. For he is not content merely to analyse legal change as a detached scholar. He seeks to become politically engaged with the process by trying to provide intellectual guidance. 'The central feature of the normative challenge that I would propose . . . rests upon an acceptance of human solidarity and all of its implications, especially a shared responsibility to seek equity and dignity for every person on the planet without regard to matters of national identity, territorial boundary, or ideological affiliation.' Falk emphasizes that the fourth model thus aims at 'the well-being of the species as a whole' and in that regard it is responsive 'to the objective realities of the misery that afflicts most of the human race'. The fourth model, unlike any of the other three, is the only one that can respond to 'populist claims for peace, economic equity, social and political dignity, and ecological balance'. It is in connection with the possibility of this fourth model that Falk speaks of another Grotian moment.

It is difficult to disagree with Falk's assessment of the first model as politically naïve and there is little that can be added to that point. However, problems arise in his estimate of the other three models. Nobody who is even slightly aware of the history of world politics could dispute the fact that the states system has been a cockpit of warfare that has produced enormous human suffering. But war is not the uncomplicated and unmitigated political evil that Falk implies. War is a producer of both good and evil, and some wars can be justified more readily than others. Very few countries have ever been prepared to give up their right to wage war and hardly any countries have ever existed that did not possess armed forces. War is an institution of the states system. Some scholars also suggest that there is a positive and reinforcing historical connection between war and prosperity in the modern states system.[24] Those states that have produced the highest standards of living in human history have been militarily proficient: the historically unprecedented material progress of European countries occurred alongside the most devastating wars in human history in which those states fought mainly against each other.

What can be said of the institution of war can also be said of modern nation-states and the system of states: they are sources of both good and evil, prosperity as well as misery. At a minimum, states are justified as a necessary evil to provide basic security and safety. That is Hobbes's seventeenth-century sovereign state. At a maximum, they are seen as an essential institution for achieving and enjoying the good life for the greatest number of people. That is the political ideal of Bentham's and Mill's nineteenth-century public utilitarian state and of most socially conscious thinkers' twentieth-century welfare state. The fact is that people who live under the ramparts of some modern nation-states, regardless of the ideologies of the political parties in power, have enjoyed standards of living which are the highest in all of human history. Citizens of the developed OECD countries on average live longer, healthier, more comfortable, more varied, and more enriched lives than any large population groups in history. It is nevertheless also a fact that the contemporary states system contains many other states whose populations suffer from extremely low living standards: the material circumstances of the large majority of people in Africa are wretched by comparison with the living conditions of most people of Western Europe, North America, and Japan. Which sort of state should we take as a baseline for evaluating the contemporary states system: those of the North, or those of the South? The only reasonable answer is of course both. Richard Falk resists such a balanced view of the sovereign state and the states system. He sees the dark side

---

[24] See E. L. Jones, *The European Miracle: Environments, Economics and Geopolitics in the History of Europe and Asia* (Cambridge: Cambridge University Press, 1981), esp. chs. 6–7.

but he is blind to the advantages and benefits of the modern state and the society of states.

Anybody who is aware of global capitalism can recognize elements of truth in Richard Falk's portrait of the third model. However, it seems to postulate a disjuncture between the states system, on the one hand, and global capitalism, on the other hand, which cannot be sustained. There have been times when the state has sought to manage the economy and has gained the upper hand in that regard—as in the mercantilist era of the seventeenth and eighteenth centuries and again in the neo-mercantilist era of the mid-twentieth century. Adam Smith argued against state-dominated economies. However, there have been other times when the relationship was reversed: in the early nineteenth century, markets broke free of states and transformed national governments into advocates and even auxiliaries of global capitalism. Karl Marx argued against market-dominated economies.

We are living in an era when global capitalism, now based on post-industrial technology, is again reducing the autonomy of independent governments in the sphere of economics. Richard Falk compares our era of global markets to the medieval era in Europe when the Christian Church stood above kings and other secular rulers. But the medieval Church was a clerical-political bureaucracy, whereas the global market consists of numerous rival business firms, from large corporations to small entrepreneurs. A more apt comparison is the early modern era of merchant capitalism, when Dutch and English commercial adventurers, investors as well as traders, were building the first world economic system, still relatively free of the dictates and demands of nation-states.[25] That is the world that Grotius was living in. Merchant capitalism and, later, industrial capitalism led to the expansion of European sovereign states via imperialism and colonialism to the four corners of the world. And while states are clearly working in the service of markets today, that reflects a recognition of the reality of globalization and the electronic technology upon which it is based. It also reflects a cold calculation that that is in the best interests of states and their citizens. Richard Falk makes no allowance for the possibility of a new *modus vivendi* between states and markets.

However, it is toward the fourth model that Richard Falk directs his intellectual energies and ideological concerns as an international legal scholar working in the tradition of prescriptive jurisprudence.[26] In that 'world order perspective', the separation of academic study and political action is abolished and the legal scholar takes on the role of the politically engaged activist. This is not the place to discuss that school of international jurisprudence, but their

---

[25] See Immanuel Wallerstein, *The Modern World-System* (New York: Academic Press, 1974). Also see some of the essays in H. Bull and A. Watson (eds.), *The Expansion of International Society* (Oxford: Clarendon Press, 1984).

[26] See Myers S. McDougal *et al.*, *Studies in World Public Order* (New Haven, Conn.: Yale University Press, 1960).

ideological support of progressive causes in world affairs is an essential background for understanding Falk's argument. What, then, are the merits of this fourth model as a goal worthy of a politically progressive world jurisprudence? As indicated, the model rests on the desire to direct international legal studies towards a global condition in which every man, woman, and child on earth can live in peace and harmony, can be confident of social and political dignity, can enjoy economic equity, and can live in a balanced natural environment. No enlightened person would disagree with any of these goals. Problems only arise in attempting to know how best to pursue them. Should they be pursued within the framework of the states system? Can they be pursued outside that framework?

Richard Falk argues that the states system is an obstacle to global human solidarity which must be populist and not statist. He poses a fundamental conflict between populism and statism. He believes that world-wide human solidarity can only be achieved outside the framework of the states system. But is there really a fundamental conflict? Even if there is, which is debatable, is it reasonable to suppose that populism would triumph in the struggle? These are questions which should be asked of Falk's world order thesis.

Richard Falk believes that to overcome the statist barrier to human progress it is necessary to distinguish between 'the well-being of governments and the well-being of peoples or their countries'. There is certainly no question but that governments can abuse their sovereignty and large numbers of people can suffer as a result. What is questionable is Falk's clear implication that that state-produced suffering is a defining feature of the states system rather than a contingent feature of many states, as I have argued in this book. The fact is that the contemporary states system is composed of member states whose domestic living conditions vary enormously, from the affluence of a Switzerland at one extreme to the destitution of an Ethiopia at the other. The states system based on international anarchy is associated with both affluence and destitution, and not just with one of them.

Even if we take Richard Falk's negative view of the modern state, the fact remains that the contemporary states system is dominated and controlled by the developed OECD states and it is highly unlikely that their governments or citizens are going to do anything out of regard for global human solidarity that would place their high national living standards at risk. It is equally implausible that stateless global humanity could oblige them to do that. The fact is that the only political organization available to humankind on a global scale is the states system and probably the only way to effectively promote human well-being world-wide is via that same states system. The possibility of a non-state political organization of humankind that could rival and somehow displace the states system is far-fetched to say the least. Richard Falk's argument about 'global populism' belongs to the same quixotic genre as arguments about 'world government' which he rightly debunks.

Richard Falk has misconstrued the Grotian moment in world politics. Grotius is not a premodern theorist of the European Middle Ages. Nor is he a post-modern theorist of a 'global populism'. Grotius is the legal theorist *par excellence* of international society, which means that he is a theorist of the state-centric and human-focused world that has been evolving for the past three or four centuries and continues to evolve. If there is a Grotian moment, it is measured by that entire span of time. It would be generally accurate to say that the twentieth century, especially the post-1945 era, is a neo-Grotian era in so far as solidarist principles have been reinvigorated. At the same time, however, pluralist practices have not been abandoned or even downgraded. On the contrary: they continue to be fundamental to international politics and international law. I think it is reasonable to conclude from the historical evolution of international society that state sovereignty and humanitarianism belong together and cannot permanently be kept apart. That is arguably one of the most important conclusions of Grotius's international jurisprudence, even though he never anticipated a global society of states.

A Global Civic Ethic?

Although the foregoing academic critiques give some general outlines of alternative world orders which are sought after by certain progressive thinkers, they provide few specific guidelines, if any, for getting beyond the global covenant. However, the 1995 Report of the Commission on Global Governance prescribes a 'global civic ethic' which, if it were instituted, would fundamentally alter the normative framework of world politics.[27] That alternative ethic is called for by 'the changes of the last half-century' which, in the Commission's view, have begun to transform world politics into an 'incipient global neighborhood'. The global civic ethic is intended not only to fill the normative gap opened by a supposedly retreating society of states. It is also intended to balance the rapidly advancing system of global markets made possible by information technology.

The Commission correctly points out that the UN system was a further stage in the evolution of the Westphalian framework of international relations based on state sovereignty. The UN charter was fashioned for a society of independent states. It was not a revolutionary break with the past. The statespeople who assembled at San Francisco in 1945 were determined to draft a framework law for world politics that would make it possible to avoid the tragedy of world war that had occurred on two occasions in the first half of the twentieth century. They were looking back at the recent past. Their solution was embodied in

---

[27] The quotations in this section are derived from *Our Global Neighbourhood: The Report of the Commission on Global Governance* (Oxford: OUP, 1995), ch. 2.

universal norms of equal sovereignty and non-intervention, on the one hand, and special responsibilities for the great powers, on the other. None of the statespeople at San Francisco questioned the sovereign state as the foundation of world affairs.

UN norms are seen by the Commission to be outdated: they do not correspond with social and technological changes that have occurred since 1945 and are continuing to occur at an accelerating pace. The Commission points to growing interdependence in world politics which they believe is eroding basic statist norms such as territoriality, independence, and non-intervention. 'What happens far away matters much more now.' National boundaries are becoming far more 'permeable' under the impact of 'waves of intellectual and technological change'. Environmental degradation pays no respect to territorial sovereignty. Conventional notions of citizenship and self-determination are held to be losing their meaning as people around the world respond to these unprecedented changes. People nowadays are called upon to co-operate in many areas of life to deal with what have become transnational problems of security, welfare, inflation, recession, migration, refugees, pollution, climate change, pandemic diseases, the spread of weapons, desertification, terrorism, famine, drug trafficking, and much else. These problems can no longer be dealt with adequately within the bordered framework of the existing society of states. A global civil society is beginning to emerge as non-state groups are finding ways to cooperate with their counterparts around the world.

It is noted by the Commission that a world order tailored to the needs of the 'global neighbourhood' still has not been put in place. It is now time to do that by instituting new norms that are adapted to what are claimed to be contemporary non-state realities. The Commissiom calls for a global civic ethic that applies not merely to sovereign states but to all who are involved in world affairs. It speaks of rights and responsibilities that are shared by all actors, public and private, collective and individual, which would strengthen the sense of common obligation within the global neighbourhood. Is sees an urgent need to embody this new ethic in international law, where necessary by adapting existing norms of state sovereignty. It does not see the state as obsolete, but as in need of a major redesign and reconstruction. In certain policy areas, such as the environment and the global commons more generally, sovereignty must be exercised collectively—and not merely individually by states or in partnerships between states. It acknowledges that the efficacy of the global civic ethic 'will depend on the ability of people and governments to transcend narrow self-interests and to agree that the interests of humanity as a whole will be best served by acceptance of a set of common rights and responsibilities'. The Commission evidently believes that that is a definite possibility.

The members of the Commission seem to have in mind some kind of global *universitas* in which states are not abolished, but are downgraded and lose their primacy in world affairs. They note that the global civic ethic will depend on new institutions and laws of global governance based on democracy. Until now democracy has only extended to national, regional, and local governments *within* sovereign states. They question 'the double standards that demand democracy at the national level but uphold its curtailment at the international level'. They see the confinement of democracy to the nation-state as no longer adequate to the reality of an interdependent world and they recommend the democratization of international society. They specifically call for reform of the Security Council by making it more representative, and they see the great power veto as 'unacceptable' in a system of global governance based on democratic principles and practices. They go further: international democracy should give a voice to all interests and concerns that are involved in the emergent global neighbourhood. The time has come to conceive of self-determination within a context of global diversity in which many selves can be expressed and many voices heard. They call for the 'empowerment of people' by means of decentralization, for new forms of participation, and for greater involvement of people than has so far been possible in traditional representative democracy confined within separate nation-states.

The 'global civic ethic' recommended by the Commission also involves an expanded concept of human rights and human responsibilities. Its members see an urgent need to enlarge the existing body of international humanitarian law by recognizing that governments are not the only threat to human rights, and also by recognizing that government action alone will not be sufficient to protect human rights. They contend that all humanity should uphold 'the core values of respect for life, liberty, justice and equity, mutual respect, caring, and integrity'. They echo Kant in his more revolutionary persona by speaking of a 'universal moral community' that derives from the principle 'that people should treat others as they would themselves wish to be treated', according to which everybody is bound together morally, regardless of their distance from each other, their particular interests, or their distinctive cultures or identities. The Commission expresses the hope that these cosmopolitan norms eventually will be embodied in a 'charter of civil society' which could be enforced and could thus provide a solid foundation upon which the 'global civic ethic' could be based.

The Commission is pointedly concerned about the world-wide problem of human security which exists at the present time. In situations where people are subjected to massive suffering, a state's right to independence must be weighed against its people's right to security. It draws our attention to extreme circumstances within countries when the security of people is 'so extensively imperiled that external collective action under international law becomes justified'. It declares that a threat to human security anywhere in the global neighbourhood must no longer be construed as solely an internal matter for particular independent states; rather, it must be seen as a threat to everybody everywhere. It consequently argues that 'in certain severe circumstances' the basic interests of common humanity 'must prevail over the ordinary rights of particular states'. Such action should be taken as far as possible with the consent of the authorities in the country but that 'will not always be possible'.

The Commission seems to believe that their proposals for overhauling the institutions of world politics are practical and realistic and stand a chance of being adopted in the present circumstances of world politics. But if the recommendations summarized above were instituted it would add up to very significant change indeed, which at many points would repudiate existing norms of state sovereignty and would in that regard be nothing less than revolutionary. The Commission does not seem to realize where their proposals ultimately lead. The following assessment is intended to give an indication of where that might be.

As indicated, the report explicitly notes that, where people are subjected to massive suffering a state's right to independence must be weighed against its people's right to security. International action to uphold human security should be taken with the consent of the authorities in the country, but that will not usually be possible because few sovereign governments would freely give such consent. That should not be a barrier to international humanitarianism. That would mean that the immunities afforded by Article 2 of the UN charter would be qualified by human rights. In a similar vein, the Commission sees the great power veto as 'unacceptable' in a system of global governance based on democratic principles and practices. Their logic cannot be faulted. Yet if the great powers are to continue to have great responsibilities and will still be called upon to uphold international peace and security, now with the important added responsibility of enforcing a new norm of human security world-wide, it is extremely unlikely that they would be prepared to do that without the protection that the veto affords to their national interests. To assume otherwise is to ignore political reality. If the great powers are not available to take on that crucially important role, then who is?

The conventional notions of citizenship and self-determination are said to be losing meaning as people around the world respond to globalization. But the fact is that people still claim their collective political rights in terms of sovereign nation-statehood. The breakup of the Soviet Union and the former Yugoslavia is instructive in that regard. However, suppose this analysis is correct and self-determination in the future must get beyond the confining context of a world of separate or separating nation-states. If that is meant to imply that various collective selves within the domestic jurisdiction of existing sovereign states— national minorities, ethnic associations, occupational groups, environmental groups, gender categories, age categories—are going to possess a recognized international status, then it is essential to know what it would be. Would those new self-determining political voices be under the jurisdiction of states or would they be somehow free of states? If they are to be equal at least in some respects to states, as the Commission seems to indicate, that would also have the effect of qualifying the existing principle of state sovereignty. If they are to be independent of states that would be a revolutionary change—and a very difficult one to conceptualize or conjecture.

As indicated, the Commission sees the confinement of democracy to the nation-state as no longer adequate to the reality of an interdependent world and they recommend the democratization of international society. On what basis would international society be democratized? One state, one vote? One person, one vote? If international society is a democracy in which states are equal on a basis of one state, one vote, then individuals will be profoundly unequal because states are profoundly unequal in population and almost every other way. If individuals are equal on a basis of one person, one vote, then states will be profoundly unequal and the world will be governed by the most populous states. Coalitions of such states would rule the world. China and India might jointly prevail against everybody else. States with small populations would be consigned to the distant margins of international society. There would be a problem of protecting international minorities, that is, small states. The democratization of international society would run up against basic normative questions of this kind. But perhaps these ones can suffice to expose the adventurous temper of such a proposal. And then there is the immediate practical question: what are the chances that any proposal for democratic reform would be accepted by international society as it currently exists?

The Commission calls for the 'empowerment of people' by means of decentralization, new forms of participation, and greater involvement of people than has so far been possible in traditional representative democracy based on the nation-state. What, exactly, that implies concerning practical institutional change is never made clear in the report. But if it is meant to be a reform in which the 'rights' and 'responsibilities' of international governance are widely shared not only among states but among all international actors then clearly that would be utopian. It would be the end of sovereign states as we know them. Other prescriptions of the Commission lead to the same destination of a brave new world beyond the sovereign state. Most of them are fanciful and unrealistic. They stand virtually no chance of getting beyond the stage of political advocacy within small and confined international circles of mostly Western intellectuals, academics, and NGO activists.

The source of the Commission's confused recommendations is the report's theoretical foundation which is fatally flawed in its assumptions and inferences. They are derived from the Commission's misunderstanding of the globalization thesis. That thesis is a useful sociological account of important international changes that obviously are occurring widely at the present time. The problem is the mistaken political inference drawn from those changes by the Commission, which has erroneously concluded that the socio-economic changes captured by the globalization thesis necessitate corresponding changes of a normative kind to alter state sovereignty. That socio-economic determinism is a misleading way to think about the society of states, as I shall indicate in the next chapter. At this point the kernel of that argument must suffice, namely that the most important norms of international society, including state sovereignty, are not rendered irrelevant or obsolete by the socio-economic changes involved in globalization. On the contrary, such norms are proving to be adaptable to those changes. That should come as no surprise to anybody who is aware of the history of state sovereignty, which has been adapting successfully to profound socio-economic changes for the past three or four hundred years.

After International Society: Universalism or Relativism?

There was much speculation after the cold war about the present and future directions of world politics. That speculation usually rests on the assumption, explicit or implicit, that post-1945 international society is in decline and is being displaced by an alternative political arrangement of some kind. Two contrasting images of the political future were circulating widely when this book was being written: Francis Fukuyama's neo-Hegelian image of the end of history brought about by the triumph of liberal democracy, and Samuel Huntington's modernization theory image of a breakdown of world order and a coming clash of civilizations.[28] Fukuyama's philosophical vision of world politics is optimistic, integrationist, and universalist. Huntington's sociological vision is pessimistic, disintegrationist, and relativist. Each vision is fundamentally at odds with that of a *societas* of states.

Before these images are discussed it might be useful to recollect some remarks of Hedley Bull about alternatives to the society of states which can set the stage for our inquiry.[29] Bull addresses the following conceivable possibilities: (1) a system but not a society, (2) states but not a system, (3) a unified world government, (4) a solidarist world political system, and (5) a new medievalism. Regarding the first possibility, he notes a deterioration of international society since the First World War owing to the communist revolution in Russia, the Third World revolt against Western imperialism, and the worldwide expansion of the states system beyond the West. According to Bull, the eventual disappearance of the societal element of world politics is 'entirely possible' but there is no reason to assume that it is inevitable. Regarding the second possibility, he suggests that that would be rather like a return to world politics before the nineteenth century, when there were states and 'regional political conglomerations' in different parts of the world but there was no

---

[28] Francis Fukuyama, *The End of History and the Last Man* (New York: Avon Books, 1992) and Samuel P. Huntington, *The Clash of Civilizations and the Remaking of World Order* (New York: Simon & Schuster, 1996). All subsequent quotations from Fukuyama and Huntington are from these books.

[29] Bull, *Anarchical Society*, ch. 11.

global system to which all states belonged. The world then was disjointed politically: there was no world politics as such; there were separate political worlds with little or no contact between them. Catastrophic changes, such as nuclear war, would be required for that global fracturing to occur again. Regarding the third possibility, Bull is deeply sceptical that world government could be founded either by consent or by a global imperialism of some kind. Even a brief glance at international history confirms his scepticism. Regarding the fourth possibility, he notes that there, indeed, is 'a wider world political system of which the states system is only a part' but he adds that that has always been so and that in any case the primacy of the states system 'is for the time being assured'.

Bull devotes most of his discussion to the possibility that international society might be yielding to 'a secular reincarnation of the system of overlapping or segmented authority that characterized medieval Christendom'. He notes that states in some parts of the world are coming together in projects of regional integration, that some states elsewhere are coming apart internally, that private international violence is on the increase, that transnational organizations are expanding, and that the technological unification of the world is well under way. But he concludes in the same sceptical vein that none of these developments, taken either individually or collectively, have the effect of rendering international society obsolete. On the contrary, Bull draws our attention to 'the continuing vitality of the states system' which has successfully adjusted to social change time and again over a period of several centuries. He attributes that historical flexibility not least to 'the tyranny of the concepts and normative principles associated with it', which he compares to an intellectual prison from which escape is difficult. That is because it is very hard to think about convincing alternative world images without employing the categories and concepts associated with the *societas* of states.

The cold war was still in effect in the 1970s when Hedley Bull made his analysis of alternatives to international society and it is reasonable to assume that that reinforced his scepticism about the likelihood of fundamental change in world politics. Since then, however, discussion and debate on this issue has been stimulated not only by the end of the cold war but also by the turning of a new century. Two alternative images that Bull might have examined had he lived beyond the cold war are the arguments of Fukuyama and Huntington. Although they do not conform exactly to any of Bull's alternative possibilities, they clearly do overlap with some of them. Fukuyama's proclamation of an emergent global *universitas* based on democracy accords rather well with Bull's fourth possibility of a solidarist world polity based on domestic standards, in this case those of liberal democracy. Huntington's warning of an impending collision of world civilizations is not far removed from Bull's second image of a politically fragmented world in which communication and co-operation across geo-cultural divides is problematic.

Fukuyama's thesis is an intellectual version of the triumphalism that circulated in some corners of the West at the end of the Gulf War in 1991.[30] He argues that a consensus on the legitimacy of liberal democracy has emerged in world politics following the failure of leading rival ideologies, particularly communism. That ideological triumph is not a temporary stopping-point along the road of human history. Rather, it is the 'end point of mankind's ideological evolution', the 'final form of human government', and thus the 'end of history' as an expression of humankind's political destiny. What has come to an end is not the flow of ordinary events which can be expected to continue indefinitely. Rather, what has ended is history with a capital H: world history, universal human history, history as progress, the historicist view of history as leading to a final destination. For Hegel that historical terminus is the liberal state. For Marx it is the society of communism. For Fukuyama it is liberal democracy. That is the end of history. There can be no further progress because at that point the great question of politics is finally answered. All remaining questions are residual or derivative.

Fukuyama argues that it makes sense at the end of the twentieth century once again to speak of a 'coherent and directional History of mankind' that will eventually carry humanity to liberal democracy. He offers two separate reasons for that prognosis. One reason is the achievement of economic progress via globalization: the free market has succeeded in generating unprecedented material prosperity on a world-wide basis and that is likely to continue indefinitely as all countries are drawn toward economic modernization and increasingly come to resemble each other. The other reason is the struggle for human recognition: the universal human desire for dignity, for self-esteem, to be recognized as a human being of equal worth with all other human beings. For Hegel, that spiritual struggle is the driving force of human history.[31] For Fukuyama, liberal democracy based on the principle of popular sovereignty and the guarantee of fundamental rights under the rule of law is the only political institution that can actualize on a world-wide basis that universal human desire to be recognized as a worthy equal.

Recognition is 'the central problem of politics' because the desire for recognition is common to all men and women without exception and is thus universal. But most solutions to the problem of recognition are biased in favour of particular individuals or groups. Recognition can include some while it excludes others. The dictator can be recognized to the detriment of everybody else. The colonial power can be recognized to the detriment of the indigenous people. The bourgeoisie can be recognized to the detriment of the proletariat. These political biases are at the source of tyranny, colonialism, and capitalism. According to Fukuyama, liberal democracy provides a solution whereby not one or a few

---

[30] The following abridged version of Fukuyama's argument is taken from the introduction to *The End of History and the Last Man*, xi–xxiii.

[31] A. V. Miller (tr.), *Hegel's Phenomenology of Spirit* (Oxford: OUP, 1977).

or even many are recognized; rather, everyone is recognized. Constitutional democracy and the rule of law based on universal rights is a political formula whereby all people without exception finally have their dignity respected on the basis of equal worth. Fukuyama argues that the greatest political struggle 'over the millennia of human history' has been the struggle to solve the problem of human recognition once and for all. The final solution to that fundamental and long-standing problem is the distinctive world-historical achievement of liberal democracy.

That has an important bearing on international relations. A world consisting of liberal democracies would have few good reasons to wage war because, being democracies, 'all nations would reciprocally recognize one another's legitimacy'. Today that proposition is well-known and widely accepted among international relations scholars, even if it is not universally accepted. But Fukuyama probes that thesis at a more fundamental level: he sees democratization around the world as bringing universal human recognition into historical existence on a per-manent institutionalized basis. Democracy is the only political formula that is truly universal in that fundamental way. At the end of his book Fukuyama employs the analogy of a long wagon train slowly winding its way westward across the prairie toward its final destination. Each wagon carries a separate fam-ily which is engaged in a particular human adventure consisting of many per-sonal experiences. Each family and indeed each family member is involved in a unique particular story. Yet every wagon is linked in a common destiny and when looking back at their journey after they arrived in California any reason-able person 'would be forced to agree that there had been only one journey and one destination'. Thus from many unique personal and family histories there still emerges one History that everybody involved in the wagon train was caught up in. And once they were settled down in California all further political ques-tions became residual or derivative. California was the end of history.

Samuel Huntington is deeply sceptical of any notion that world politics is marching down a road signposted 'liberal democracy'. He debunks the univer-salist premises of Western civilization. He pointedly criticizes the American belief in the universal superiority of their culture and claims that it suffers from three fatal weaknesses: 'it is false; it is immoral; and it is dangerous'. It is based on the mistake of failing to recognize that other civilizations have values and norms true to themselves. It expresses the arrogance of cultural imperialism. And it could lead to major inter-civilizational war: what he refers to as 'fault line wars'. He argues that his fellow Americans have to bury the idea of universal-ist, global civilization based on the Western model. He specifically disagrees with Fukuyama's thesis about the end of history as the triumph of liberal democracy.

According to Huntington, world politics is entering a new and perilous stage of history. Instead of bringing about a universalist civilization of Western origins, modernization generally and the end of the cold war specifically both unite people and divide people in different parts of the world along cultural or civilizational lines. General alignments of world politics defined by universal ideologies and superpower conflicts which were characteristic of the post-1945 era are giving way to post-cold-war alignments defined by particular cultures and civilizations. Cultural communities are replacing cold-war blocs, and the 'fault lines' between civilizations are becoming the points of conflict in world politics. Fault-line conflicts are 'communal conflicts' between groups from different civilizations. Political boundaries, he claims, are being redrawn to coincide with communities based on ethnicity, religion, culture, and civilization. He contrasts the Bosnian war between Muslims, Orthodox Christians (Serbs), and Roman Catholics (Croats) with the Spanish Civil War which was a war fought over ideology, with fascists on one side and democrats, socialists, and communists on the other side. Ideological conflicts are universalist in character: they are struggles to impose a singular world-view on everybody. Fault-line conflicts are particularistic and relativist in character: they are struggles to divide the world into separate civilizational or cultural compartments with a high wall around each one.

The people of the world are not in historical motion at different stages along a highway to a final political destination called Westernization or democracy. In human history there are numerous roads and destinations defined by many cultures and civilizations. According to Huntington, that raises a post-cold-war problem of world peace that is different from the problem raised by the cold war. For the West and particularly the USA, the cold war was a problem of world order that could be addressed by countervailing alliances, by nuclear deterrence, and by determination to stay the course. The post-cold-war problem of world peace depends upon cultural insight and understanding by the leaders of the world's major civilizations, including not only their political leaders but also their spiritual and intellectual leaders. That responsibility is particularly heavy for Americans who have long been convinced not only of the superiority of their civilization but also of their responsibility to make it available to everyone on earth. That is the missionary impulse in American history. Failing such insight and understanding on the part of those leaders, civilizations will increasingly clash and world order will be imperilled.

Huntington has three prescriptions to avert major inter-civilizational wars in the future. First, core states at the centre of each civilization, such as the USA, must refrain from intervening in the 'internal' conflicts of other civilizations. Second, core states must seek each other out to engage in joint mediation 'to contain or to halt fault line wars between states from different civilizations'. Finally, in a multicultural and multicivilizational world, people in every culture and civilization 'should search for and attempt to expand the values, institutions, and practices they have in common with peoples of other civilizations'. Huntington quotes Lester Pearson, a former Prime Minister of Canada and holder of the Nobel Peace Prize: 'different civilizations will have to learn to live side by side in peaceful interchange, learning from each other, studying each other's history and ideas and art and culture, mutually enriching each others' lives. The alternative, in this overcrowded little world, is misunderstanding, tension, clash, and catastrophe.'[32]

Huntington's analysis leaves the reader with the definite impression that the author is not overly confident that such an enlightenment can be achieved in time to avert a disastrous clash of civilizations. He ends his book with a dire warning that draws on Benjamin Franklin's famous remark to John Hancock at the signing of the American Declaration of Independence:

Europe and America will hang together or hang separately. In the great clash, the global 'real clash', between Civilization and barbarism, the world's great civilizations . . . will hang together or hang separately. In the emerging era, clashes of civilizations are the greatest threat to world peace, and an international order based on civilizations is the surest safeguard against world war.

These two fundamentally contradictory but equally imaginative visions of future world politics can be contrasted with the post-1945 and post-1989 historical actuality of an evolving international society based on the global covenant. When we do that the misdirected optimism of Fukuyama's triumphant democracy and the equally misguided pessimism of Huntington's clash of civilizations should become apparent.

Fukuyama presents a choice between universalism and relativism, which he conceives as a choice between democracy and non-democracy, that must be made if human beings the world over are to achieve equal recognition. If liberal democracy is the only political organization of human freedom, and if it does not yet exist in some parts of the world, there would be a heavy obligation on the part of those who already enjoy democracy and believe in democracy to come to the assistance of those who are still denied democracy. Fukuyama's argument leads to the conclusion that armed intervention and war by democracies against non-democracies is necessary and justified to arrive at the final destination of human history. In order to reach California the American pioneers were obliged to fight the native Americans who tried to block the settlers' progress. Both Hegel and Marx saw warfare as a midwife that could speed up the birth of human freedom. The predictable result of such a crusade for democracy would be increased international conflict which very possibly would destroy the pluralist framework of coexistence. Huntington is right to condemn it.

It is not necessary to choose between universalism and relativism in world politics because there is a median possibility: what I have been referring to in this book as normative pluralism. That pluralist choice was made by the statespeople at San Francisco in 1945. That choice has been reiterated and reconfirmed ever day since then by the law-abiding actions of members of international society. It leaves open to everybody on earth the opportunity of

---

[32] S. P. Huntington, *The Clash of Civilizations and the Remaking of World Order* (New York: Simon & Schuster, 1996), 321.

instituting liberal democracy or any other form of enlightened self-government that captures and expresses their desire for recognition and respect as human beings. It places the responsibility for deciding whether or not to proceed down that path where it belongs: with the local people involved. It respects local state sovereignty. It seeks to confine revolutionary struggles for democracy within the domestic jurisdictions of states and thereby to diminish the dangers of provoking war by the internationalization of such struggles. In short, normative pluralism provides a locally determined path to democracy that insulates international political and economic life from the threat of instability, disorder, and war that political crusades no less than religious crusades usually present.

That brings me to Huntington's ominous vision of a future clash of civilizations. At the heart of his thesis is the argument that fault-line wars between civilizations are a new kind of warfare which threatens international order. But fault-line wars are not new at all. History is full of that kind of conflict. The medieval era and the early modern era were eras of fault-line wars: between different religious civilizations (Christians and Muslims), and between different sects of the same religious civilization (Catholics and Protestants). The era of European imperial expansion overseas was an era of fault-line wars in the Americas, the Middle East, Asia, and Africa between Western states and non-Western political systems. The fault-line wars of the early modern era in Europe were finally brought to an end by the institution of the *societas* of states and its foundation principle: *cujus regio, ejus religio*. The fault-line wars of European imperialism in other continents were finally brought to an end by decolonization and the admission of non-European peoples to international society on a basis of equal state sovereignty. The rules and institutions of international society exist precisely to discourage fault-line wars by banning their justification. Fault line conflicts within states have been increasingly commonplace since 1945. But they have been contained within states: they have been internal wars and international society has not been unduly threatened by them.[33]

In light of that fundamentally important historical experience Huntington's three normative prescriptions for resolving the supposed threat posed by the impending clash of civilizations appear overly simplified. Fortunately, as already indicated, there are norms that exist that are far more explicit and elaborate, that have been tested by the experience of world politics over several centuries, and that are universally recognized today around the world: the norms of the global covenant. Huntington's comparative sociological analysis of civilizations gives little indication, if any, that he is aware of that body of international rules, practices, and institutions. That evident lack of awareness severely handicaps his analysis and the normative prescriptions that flow from it.

Huntington's abstention norm already exists, but in regard to sovereign state jurisdictions and not to civilizations. If it applied to civilizations that would be

---

[33] See the insightful discussion in K. J. Holsti, *The State, War, and the State of War* (Cambridge: Cambridge University Press, 1996).

disruptive of international order because it would recognize civilizations in addition to recognizing states. It would therefore elevate the international legitimacy and legality of civilizations and, at least in certain respects, make them normative equals of sovereign states. It flies completely in the face of the international experience of the past three or four centuries which has involved major efforts to neutralize and domesticate civilizational norms by establishing bona fide transcivilizational (that is, international) norms that can be acceptable to states of different religions, cultures, and civilizations. The most historical and fundamental of those norms is *cujus regio, ejus religio*.

His remarks about 'cultural coexistence', 'the interests of civilizations', 'equality among civilizations', and—above all—his astonishing argument that 'each major civilization should have at least one permanent seat on the Security Council' clearly implies that civilizations would have an international legal status. They also imply that non-intervention would now refer to civilizations, perhaps even more than to sovereign states, and that intervention in sovereign states by other states from within the same civilization would be acceptable. That would undermine the *Grundnorm* of post-1945 international society. Huntington seems to imply that peoples who belong to the same civilization would be prepared to have their independence interfered with, or have it taken from them, as long as the imperialist is from within their own civilization. That would invite suzerain states systems such as existed outside the West before the colonial era: the ancient Chinese Empire in East Asia, the historic Mogul Empire in South Asia, and the Ottoman Empire in the Middle East, the Balkans, and North Africa. It is also reminiscent of various pre-modern empires in Europe that existed prior to the Westphalian era: the medieval Christian Empire, the Byzantine Empire, and of course the Roman Empire.

There is little historical evidence to support either of these implications. There is an abundance of historical evidence that contradicts both of them. Only a few highlights can be mentioned. The Muslim Ottoman Empire had to contend with rebellions from Arabs and other Muslim peoples. Muslim East Pakistan did not wish to be an integral part of Muslim Pakistan and seceded by force to become independent Muslim Bangladesh. Muslim Kurds do not wish to be a part of Muslim Turkey and Muslim Iraq. South Korea shares the Confucian civilization with China and used to be under Chinese suzerainty but the South Koreans give every indication that they do not wish to be under the imperial sway of China. Much the same could be said of Taiwan.

But the best evidence of a strong intra-civilizational desire for sovereignty and non-intervention is found within Christian civilization historically. On several occasions certain Christian nations defended themselves against the attempts by other Christian nations to impose or restore *respublica Christiana*—the most noteworthy occasion is of course the Thirty Years War (1618–48). On major occasions some Western states united to defeat bids for European or world empire from among their own ranks: the successful Anglo–German–Austrian–

Russian alliance against Napoleonic France in the early nineteenth century, and the successful Anglo-American alliance against Nazi Germany, in the mid-twentieth century. (Russia was involved in both alliances but is awkwardly classified by Huntington as a separate Christian civilization—Orthodox—which fails to recognize the deep historical involvement of Russia in European international society.) It is not clear whether Huntington is prepared to accept the consequences of intra-civilizational imperialism. However, it is clear that the vast majority of states would not be prepared to live with a norm that justified intervention, whether the interventionists come from within their own civilization or from without.

Huntington's second normative prescription of joint mediation by core states to contain or to halt fault-line wars seems to be a reiteration of an ancient diplomatic practice. One of the most important traditional responsibilities of diplomats is the duty to seek and hopefully find a negotiated basis of resolving conflicts between states. For centuries, diplomats have attempted to interpose themselves between conflicting state parties to promote reconciliation, to find a workable compromise, and to bring about a settlement of their dispute. Huntington's third prescriptive guideline that leaders in every culture and civilization should 'expand the values, institutions, and practices they have in common' is unnecessary in so far as they already have in common a workable arrangement of international norms that is far superior to Huntington's rudimentary prescriptions: the norms of the global covenant.

Huntington claims that 'most of the principal international institutions date from shortly after World War II and are shaped according to Western interests, values, and practices'. That is true, but it is also misleading. It is true that the norms of the global covenant have Western origins. It is true that the USA was the major architect of the post-1945 international society. But the basic norms of those institutions are deeply historical and have become truly global. It is misleading to imply that states from non-Western civilizations have difficulty living with those norms. On the contrary—and ironically in terms of Huntington's thesis—an overwhelming number of African, Islamic, Sinic, Hindu, Orthodox, and Buddhist states as well as Japan (which Huntington classifies as a separate civilization) have embraced those norms. Non-Western states are the most vocal advocates and the staunchest defenders of equal state sovereignty, territorial integrity, and non-intervention.

As indicated in previous chapters, one of the oldest lessons of international history is the lesson that religions are provocative of extremism and thus of instability, disorder, and war. They must therefore somehow be kept in harness. The fundamental rule of Westphalia, *cujus regio, ejus religio,* is such a restraint. That basic norm and the other key norms of the global covenant discussed in this book should be understood as an elaborate and sophisticated historical arrangement to hold religious norms in check and to modify their destabilizing effects by dividing religious civilizations into numerous independent states. The last thing that anybody should do who is concerned about international order is to elevate the status and standing of religious civilizations. Huntington's book gives little indication, if any, that he is aware of this important international history and its enormous significance for world politics.

In short, Huntington's sweeping analysis of an impending clash of the world's major civilizations and his simplistic prescriptions for turning such an imagined political disaster aside discloses an unawareness of international history and a blindness to international society and its *modus operandi*. Neither Fukuyama's universal democracy, nor Huntington's cultural and moral relativism, but, rather, international pluralism is probably the only way the far-flung and diverse world can hang together politically—in the future as in the past.

The various images discussed in this chapter suggest that the political imaginations of intellectuals and scholars who offer prognoses of the future of world politics are soaring high above experience and history. That is not in itself objectionable. Some of the greatest commentators on world politics are great because they could see further and more clearly into the future than anybody else. Machiavelli's foresight in discerning the emergent politics of the modern world is one case in point. Grotius's foresight in recognizing the emergent law of nations is another. Perhaps one of the foregoing visions of a new world will someday be recognized as displaying a similar sort of uncanny insight into the future: something equivalent to the Machiavellian moment or the Grotian moment in world politics.[34] However, there is no convincing evidence of which I am aware that people around the world are giving up on the *societas* of states in the various ways that these alternative images predict or prescribe.

[34] J. G. A. Pocock, *The Machiavellian Moment* (Princeton: Princeton University Press, 1975), R. Falk, 'The Grotian Moment', *International Insights*, 13 (Fall 1997), 3–34. For a criticism of Falk, see R. Jackson, 'The Grotian Moment in World Jurisprudence', *International Insights*, 13 (Fall 1997), 35–56.

15

Justifying the Global Covenant

This chapter stands back and assesses the *societas* of states from a broader perspective of human conduct. The first section recollects two limiting conditions of human relations with regard to which the global covenant should be understood as an institutional response: human diversity and human imperfection. Human diversity separates people into different personalities and collectivities. Human imperfection, on the other hand, unites people via their shared intellectual frailties and common moral deficiencies. Against that background, the chapter proceeds to defend the moral and legal foundations of the global covenant: normative pluralism, political anti-paternalism, international law, and political virtue. They are justified as serviceable international norms that come to grips with the unavoidable realities of human diversity and human imperfection.[1] They compose a workable ethics of international relations. The final section examines the evolutionary character of the *societas* of states and offers some concluding reflections on its historical staying power and future prospects as a normative framework of world politics.

Human Diversity and Human Imperfection

International ethics, just like any other practical morality, must deal with human beings not as we might wish them to be but rather as they are, 'warts and all', and as they disclose themselves by their actions in the circumstances in which they live. The diversity of human life-ways and living conditions to be found within the approximately 190 member states that make up contemporary global international society is huge and impossible to summarize even in the most general terms. That should be obvious to any informed observer of world politics. Anyone who has travelled abroad will be aware of that diversity; indeed, to witness it at first hand is one of the main reasons for travelling in foreign countries. If we could be travellers in time as well as space we would see far more human diversity: most of our ancestors would be remote and probably incompre-

---

[1] We should distinguish between the justification of policies/actions, and the justification of procedures/institutions/practices. Here I am interested in the latter type of justification. See Kurt Baier, 'Justification in Ethics', in J. Roland Pennock and J. W. Chapman (eds.), *Justification: Nomos XXVIII* (New York: New York University Press, 1986), 4.

hensible strangers. Perhaps the future will disclose less diversity than the present and the past, as the world shrinks in the face of accelerating globalization. But even then it will require extraordinary convergence to reduce significantly human diversity around the world. We have little choice but to accept that reality.

Human imperfection is not as self-evident as human diversity and some who believe in the perfectibility of human beings cannot accept the proposition. But my reading and research and also my personal experience tell me that men and women are less than perfect social beings. That is a practical reality that I have to come to terms with in my dealings with others. That is the same practical reality that my family, friends, colleagues, and acquaintances have to come to terms with in dealing with me and with everybody else in their circle of human relations. I think the evidence is overwhelming that it is the same for everybody. So while the human family discloses divisions into an almost endless number of different branches, it also reveals a curious but fundamental unity and—one might be tempted to say—solidarity. Our shortcomings unite us: we are all flawed both intellectually and morally. We also have little choice but to accept that reality. Of course that is not the kind of solidarity that international relations solidarists have in mind. They are propounding an opposite solidarity of human perfectibility and progress. The problem with that is obvious to any empiricist and sceptic: it soars above human history and experience, above reality.

These basic features of the human condition can be sketched in somewhat greater detail, starting with human diversity. Human beings are different in many significant ways: physical stature, strength, vitality, stamina; appearance, attractiveness; intelligence, aptitude, talent, skills, gifts; experience, knowledge, judgement; perseverance, resourcefulness; personality; wit and humour; sociability, responsibility, reliability—to mention only a few of them. Roget notes many different human attributes that are sufficiently important and enduring to be marked by ordinary English vocabulary.[2] The same is true of other vernacular languages. The characteristics that differentiate people in detail are virtually endless. That is a field day for novelists, who seek to dissect human relations, but it is a frustration for social scientists, who seek to generalize about those same relations. We need only pause to think of the people in our own social orbit: no two individuals are exactly alike. We have to deal with those people regardless of their personal idiosyncrasies—which may sometimes disclose unpredictable and even quirky personalities. We need at least a modest repertoire of human relations skills to adjust ourselves to the diverse human world in which we live and move. We should reflect on the fact that that proposition about human relations applies not just to ourselves or the people around us but to everybody on earth.

To the diversity of individual human beings must be added the further diversity of human societies. That is more significant for our purposes. That second

---

[2] *Roget's International Thesaurus*, 3rd edn. (New York: Thomas Crowell, 1962).

dimension of diversity reflects the group identities of people. Men and women everywhere are identified by their group affiliations which give their lives meaning on a larger social and political scale. That reduces or at least smoothes some of the differences between people who belong to the same group; at the same time it sharpens the distinctions and deepens the divisions that separate people whose lives are located on different sides of the lines that are drawn. Human traffic and communication across group divisions is usually more awkward and difficult than it is within the same group. That is strikingly evident in the case of linguistic groups. But it applies to most groups and certainly to those that are territory-based (nations, tribes, etc.). When we add it up globally we are presented with a mind-boggling assortment of humanity that must somehow be accommodated if the human world is to live together and hang together rather than fall apart and hang separately. It flies in the face of common sense, experience, and history to expect anything but that some such significant divisions between people are likely to persist indefinitely. It will therefore have to be accommodated, in some way, if there is to be one political world.

What does human diversity look like at the international level in a world of states? One way to approach that question is via noteworthy socio-economic differences between the member states of contemporary international society. The following countries represented about 13 per cent of the total membership of international society at the end of the twentieth century:

Switzerland, Spain, Brazil, Senegal, Ethiopia.
China, USA, South Africa, Jordan, Trinidad.
Canada, Egypt, Thailand, Hungary, Singapore.
Japan, Malaysia, Nicaragua, Pakistan, Sierra Leone.
Botswana, Norway, United Kingdom, Venezuela, Uganda.

This selection is not random. Each line is a ranking of independent countries by the World Bank from highest to lowest in terms of: gross domestic product per capita, population size, geographical size, life expectancy, and rate of economic growth.[3] Switzerland had a GNP per capita of $21,330 whereas Ethiopia registered only $130. China had a population of over one billion people but Trinidad (which is not the least populous state) had just over a million. Canada had an area of 9,976,000 square kilometres and Singapore had under 1,000. (Russia is larger than Canada but was not listed.) Japan had an average life expectancy at birth of seventy-eight years but Sierra Leone had scarcely more than half that figure, at forty-one years. Botswana had the highest annual rate of economic growth at 8.9 per cent, while Uganda had a negative rate of −2.7 per cent. Some of these *differentia* are more fluid and variable; some of them are more permanent and fixed. But socio-economic diversity of this sort can be found across the entire spectrum of independent countries. These measures will of course change over time, and some countries will relocate along a particular

    [3] *World Development Report 1989* (New York: OUP, 1989), 164–5.

scale, but the basic socio-economic disparities between countries should be expected to persist indefinitely.

States are different from each other, indeed hugely different, in many additional significant ways, including: their geographic location and shape, their topography, their weather and climate, the racial and ethnic makeup of their population, the place of religion and the character and consequences of its moral precepts, the work ethic of their population, the role of the family, the role of women, their class structure, their degree of urbanization, the quality and extent of their education system, their scientific and technological capability, the credibility and reliability of their armed forces, the probity and efficiency of their public administration, the entrepreneurship of their business people, the law-abiding propensities of their citizens, the legitimacy of their political institutions, the degree of their political stability, the extent of their political unity, and other significant ways too numerous to summarize in a few words. There is almost unlimited heterogeneity in the history, politics, ideology, religion, language, ethnicity, culture, customs, traditions, of the member states of global international society.

It would be unrealistic to expect those differences to be significantly reduced or marginalized or rendered irrelevant to world political life any time soon. Human diversity is a reality of world politics. Statespeople must somehow find a way to navigate across that differentiated human world. They cannot do that by overlooking it or disregarding it or by trying to escape from it or by endeavouring to impose their will upon it or erase it. That ignorance or indifference or naïveté or arrogance would also be impossible to justify. The only practicable and justifiable course is to take that reality fully on board and conduct foreign relations out of regard and respect for it. That would seem to be a matter of common sense and elementary justice. That is the justice of the *societas* of states.

The global covenant can be understood as an institutional answer to the diversity of humankind. It acknowledges and accommodates the fact that human beings are inclined to associate under different flags in different groups that occupy different territories on the planet. People want to do their own thing in their own way in their own place. At the start of the twenty-first century, international society recognized approximately 190 of those local places as independent territorial jurisdictions that are legally equal with each other and have a right to be left alone. Of course, it is a far from perfect accommodation of human diversity. Most territory-based diversity is not recognized at the international level of political life. Nor could it be recognized. There is just too much of it: it would be impossible to accommodate internationally all the territory-based identities around the world which number into the thousands. A thousand states—and probably far more than a thousand—would involve state partition on a global scale: a revolutionary prospect and one that is impossible to contemplate in any sober way. It makes far more sense to leave most of that accommodation to domestic politics.[4]

----

[4] Arendt Lijpardt, *The Politics of Accommodation* (New York: Prentice-Hall, 1967).

Even though the global covenant can only recognize important territorial groups and a small fraction of the unimportant ones, there is no realistic and workable alternative international arrangement on offer at the present time. Nor is anything like that looming on the political horizon. But the most important thing is to have a local sovereign jurisdiction within which different groups of people can endeavour to build their own political life according to their own enlightenment and free of foreign interference. A large part of that free political endeavour will involve learning to live together with each other within their own state. Domestic political accommodation is attainable and there are countries that attest to that fact: Britain, the USA, India, Canada, Australia, Malaysia, Belgium, Holland, Switzerland, among others. If there is to be peace and prosperity among such groups, that will have to be arranged domestically by enlightened and skilled political leaders. They are the only ones who can arrange it. It cannot be arranged by foreigners acting on behalf of international society. The experience of European colonialism is clear on that point. When the foreigners go home the true test of independent self-government must begin all over.

Human imperfection is perhaps not as self-evident as human diversity. By that I mean a hindrance or handicap of all human beings, although affecting individuals to different degrees, which impairs or limits their intellectual capability and their social responsibility. According to J. R. Lucas, there are three main areas in which people are limited in that regard.[5] These areas overlap to some degree.

First, people are handicapped by the imperfect information and knowledge with which they must operate. We rarely, if ever, have a complete picture of the social and political situations in which we find ourselves. That leaves us in doubt about what others will do and about what we ought to do. That leads to disagreements about the best course of action. We are Plato's people of the cave: our social and political lives must be carried on even though we cannot see things clearly when it comes to knowing what is required and how to arrange it.[6] There is no philosophy or religion or science or technique that can show us the way out of the cave of our imperfect grasp of ourselves and our situation. Even Plato could not show us the way. We have to spend our entire lives in the shadows of our limited understanding. That is no less true of statespeople. Adequate information for the practice of statecraft is difficult to obtain. Perfect information is out of the question. That means governments must operate in the dark at least some of the time—no matter how efficient their central intelligent agencies or their statistical units or their information technology manages to be.

Secondly, the judgement of people, including statespeople, is fallible: the insight any person or group of persons has into their human surroundings is

[5] J. R. Lucas, *The Principles of Politics* (Oxford: OUP, 1985), esp. 1–5, 372–8.
[6] F. R. Cornford (tr.), *The Republic of Plato* (London: OUP, 1945), ch. 25.

never completely reliable; people are prone to make mistakes even if they have all the information necessary to make a decision. Even if our information is relatively accurate and complete and we are knowledgeable, we still may not make the best use of it: our limited intelligence may get in the way. Human error is a fact of life and thus it is something that we must live with—when we are citizens of a state no less than when we are passengers on a Boeing 747. Good judgement is a virtue because bad judgement is not uncommon. When we enter into relations with other people it is always an adventure because something or somebody can fail. Things can go wrong. Somebody will make a mistake. There is 'Murphy's law' to contend with. If we are attuned to human relations we should not be surprised when it happens. Often it does not greatly matter: our mistakes or the mistakes of others have no great impact. But the greater our responsibilities, the greater the impact of our misunderstandings and oversights and miscalculations and other blunders. Murphy's law has the greatest impact in politics and war. That is why good judgement is so important to statecraft. More people are affected by mistakes in this sphere than in any other sphere of human relations. Human imperfection calls for an international morality in which prudence and related political virtues have a very important role. I elaborate on this point below.

Thirdly, human interaction is fostered by values that are held in common but it is limited by values that divide people. Without shared values, international relations would be confined to instrumental activities which respond only to perceived narrow self-interest. That would drastically restrict the possibilities of international communication and traffic. For human relations to be more than merely narrowly self-regarding and instrumental—that is, to exist on a plane of mutual respect, confidence, and reciprocity—some common standards for judging human conduct are necessary. Common standards of conduct obviously are more readily installed within states than between states. Yet although they are more difficult to establish in world politics they are attainable and evident in that sphere too. But the standards of conduct that can be held in common internationally are fewer and narrower owing to the basic features of human relations already noted.

On the other hand, as indicated, the intellectual frailties and moral deficiencies of people the world over unites them in a curious but also a fundamental way. Everybody everywhere expects the people they deal with to be flawed in these entirely commonplace ways. We do not expect people to be geniuses or morons. We do not expect people to be saints. Nor do we expect them to be criminals. We expect them to be average human beings like ourselves. That is the only practical basis upon which we can approach them and deal with them. That means that we hold common expectations about the conduct of others. Those common expectations do not change over distance or time: they remain the same everywhere and at all times. That establishes a fundamentally important platform upon which a global moral life can be constructed. And it is on that solid platform of human imperfection, and not the precarious stilts of human rights or political hopes, that international ethics has been built historically.

There are of course many intellectuals and academics, and even some politicians, who believe in the perfectability of men and women, which is supposed to be achieved in a future world society that is free from the defects and disabilities attributed to the state and the *societas* of states. Like Marx and Rousseau they place their hope in a rational political formula which is far superior to past and present political arrangements and will, somehow, someday, enable men and women to realize fully their potential and thus achieve perfection. The critical theorists will construct that political formula and give it to the world as their contribution to the progress of humankind. There are two important responses to those who believe in human perfection. The first was noted by Martin Wight, who pointed out that 'hope is not a political virtue; it is a theological virtue'.[7] The second is captured in a reflection of Alexander Hamilton at the constitutional moment of the United States in 1787 when he was moved to reply to those of his compatriots who thought Americans were exempt from ordinary human vices:

Have we not already seen enough of the fallacy and extravagance of those idle theories which have amused us with promises of an exemption from the imperfections, weaknesses, and evils incident to society in every shape? Is it not time to awake from the deceitful dream of a golden age, and to adopt as a practical maxim for the direction of our political conduct that we, as well as the other inhabitants of the globe, are yet remote from the happy empire of perfect wisdom and perfect virtue?[8]

Global Political Ethics

As indicated, the global covenant can be understood as an institutional adaptation to the world-wide realities of human diversity and human imperfection. Its standards of conduct are not set any higher than what the statespeople involved could reasonably be expected to acknowledge and abide by. That is how we should understand its main foundations: normative pluralism, political antipaternalism, international law, and political virtue.

1. Normative Pluralism

There is a fundamental tension in human relations that has been noted by commentators down through the ages. On one side is the common humanity of all

---

[7] As quoted by H. Bull, 'Martin Wight and the Theory of International Relations', *British Journal of International Studies*, 2 (1976), 108.

[8] Alexander Hamilton, *The Federalist*, 6, repr. in R. M. Hutchins (ed.), *Great Books of the Western World*, xliii. *American State Papers* (Chicago: Encyclopaedia Britannica, 1952), 41.

men and women. On the other side is their different and various experiences that produce remarkable human diversity. That tension between the general and the particular was captured by Hannah Arendt in one of the most magnificent sentences of twentieth-century political thought: 'Plurality is the condition of human action because we are all the same, that is, human, in such a way that nobody is ever the same as anyone else who ever lived, lives, or will live.'[9] We humans are all different and indeed unique individual personalities. Yet we are all the same creatures: we share a common human nature. Michael Oakeshott made the same point in reflecting on the political theory of Hobbes and drawing on the scepticism of Montaigne: 'The nature of man is the predicament of mankind. A knowledge of this nature is to be had from introspection, each man reading himself in order to discern in himself, mankind.'[10] We see others as different from ourselves. Yet we also see ourselves in others. We are all different and yet we are all the same. In earlier chapters of this book I argued that the global covenant is the most articulate and far-reaching institutional expression of the pluralist ethic so far registered in world history.

It is important to emphasize, at the risk of repetition, that pluralism does not embrace relativism of values. By relativism is meant the doctrine that standards of conduct are socially conditioned—by culture, by history, etc.—and consequently that non-instrumental communication and interaction between people of different cultures and civilizations is impossible. Relativism postulates moral silence between people of different cultures and civilizations: there is no greater world than those same cultures and civilizations. Relativism presents an image of hermetically sealed populations that excludes even the possibility of international ethics. If people endeavour to interact across cultural and civilizational divides, the best they could hope for would be to have instrumental relations, if they could have any relations at all. By that I mean they could only understand those other people as instruments or opportunities for their own benefit.

Pluralism, in marked contrast, is a doctrine of recognition and communication and traffic between different peoples, based on values and norms they have in common and regardless of the particular enlightenment they hold to in carrying on their distinctive domestic ways of life.[11] Writing of two pluralist thinkers of the eighteenth century, Giambattista Vico and Johann Gottfried Herder, Isaiah Berlin observes that for them every society has 'its own vision of reality . . . These visions differ . . . each must be understood in its own terms . . . there is a plurality of civilizations'. Pluralism, according to Berlin, is 'the conception that there are many different ends that men may seek and still be

---

[9] Hannah Arendt, *The Human Condition* (Chicago and London: University of Chicago Press, 1958), 8.

[10] Michael Oakeshott, *Hobbes on Civil Association* (Oxford: Blackwell, 1975), 29.

[11] See Isaiah Berlin, *The Crooked Timber of Humanity* (New York: Vintage Books, 1992), 72–90. On relativism see T. Nardin, 'The Problem of Relativism in International Ethics', *Millennium*, 18 (1989), 149–61, and R. D. Spegele, *Political Realism in International Theory* (Cambridge: Cambridge University Press, 1996), 212–29.

fully rational, fully men, capable of understanding each other'. That is what different civilizations express. Berlin adds that intercommunication and intercourse between civilizations is nevertheless possible 'because what makes men human is common to them, and acts as a bridge between them'.[12] Pluralism embraces the principle of common humanity while fully respecting the dignity of different cultures and civilizations.

Pluralism is an awkward and equivocal normative doctrine: on the one hand, pluralists resist the universalistic and hierarchical claim that there is one supreme morality against which all values can be judged—for example, the doctrine of human rights as a categorical imperative. On the other hand, however, they equally oppose the relativist claim that the values of different civilizations are incommensurate and that there cannot be any non-instrumental communication and traffic between different civilizations. Pluralism recognizes that there is a variety of moral universes framed by different civilizations and cultures. The normative standards of one civilization cannot be used to judge those of another. Pluralism repudiates cultural imperialism. However, pluralism equally denies that there are no standards of conduct that civilized men and women around the world can have in common. Pluralism repudiates the alleged moral anarchy of a multicivilizational world. It affirms the possibility of mutual intelligibility, recognition, communication, and interaction between people of different civilizations. There is thus a tension within pluralism between diversity and commonality, because there is a refusal to uphold one at the expense of the other: neither relativism nor universalism but instead pluralism.

That implies a minimalist international civilization. 'There are, if not universal values, at any rate a minimum without which societies could scarcely live. Few today would wish to defend slavery or ritual murder or Nazi gas chambers or the torture of human beings for the sake of pleasure or profit.'[13] 'Civilization' is not the best term to capture this international minimum. 'Civility' is a better term to avoid the erroneous conclusion that there is a global civilization that is comparable to Western civilization or Islamic civilization or Confucian civilization or any other particular human civilization but is superior to them. The international conduct prescribed by the global covenant is not a civilization in the sense that China or the Muslim world or the West are civilizations. It is no more a superior civilization than international politics is superior to domestic politics. It is simply the norms, practices, and institutions of civility that apply to human relations within the international sphere which often cut across civilizations. It consists of the minimal standards that people from different cultures and civilizations have managed to arrange between themselves to conduct their political business with each other.

Throughout this study I have argued that the global covenant ought to be understood as a constitutional arrangement that seeks to accommodate human

---

[12] Berlin, *Crooked Timber*, 8–11.   [13] Ibid. 18.

diversity while trying to uphold common humanity. It gives institutional expression and substance to pluralism. That pluralist ethic was already evident in Europe in the Westphalian accommodation of religious differences between Protestant rulers and Catholic rulers. The global expansion of international society from Europe to the rest of the world can be understood as the universalization of that same ethic of accommodation.[14] The cultural and religious diversity of contemporary global international society obviously is far more pronounced than that of seventeenth-century European international society or any other previous society of states. From that fact it might be thought that the global covenant is tilted in favour of human diversity and against common humanity. It may at times seem so, but it is not that way at all.

During the colonial era the recognition of non-Western political communities was contingent on not only the acceptance but also the demonstration of Western standards of conduct by non-Western peoples. Needless to say that very few non-Western political systems were recognized. The eventual international recognition of political communities that belong to civilizations other than the West involved an abandonment of that previously exclusive, excluding, and ethnocentric principle of recognition based on the standards of Western civilization. That is what decolonization involved and indeed required. In the absence of a single overarching global civilization that did not then exist and still does not exist, universal recognition required a realistic and workable standard of human conduct to substitute for the Western 'standard of civilization'. The norm of common humanity, expressed politically as a universal right of self-determination based on an existing territorial jurisdiction, typically a colonial territory, served that purpose.

Normative pluralism in world politics is thus not only an accommodation of human diversity but also an affirmation of common humanity via the principle of self-determination which is institutionalized after independence by the basic norms of equal sovereignty, territorial integrity, and non-intervention. Self-determination in international relations is the right to be politically independent, to be free from intervention by foreign governments: negative freedom. Understood in that way, the values of human diversity and common humanity are compatible and reconcilable rather than contradictory and conflictual. The normative framework of that reconciliation is the global covenant.

The pluralist ethic of the society of states, then, upholds the value of political independence and thereby acknowledges and accommodates the different and indeed diverse ways of life of normatively equal human beings around the world. Owing to that human diversity, those norms must be based on standards of conduct that statespeople everywhere can acknowledge regardless of their own cultural backgrounds.[15] If the global covenant is going to be generally supported,

---

[14] See Hedley Bull and Adam Watson (eds.), *The Expansion of International Society* (Oxford: Clarendon Press, 1984).

[15] For an exploration of 'thin' moralities see Michael Walzer, *Thick and Thin: Moral Argument at Home and Abroad* (London: University of Notre Dame Press, 1994).

that is likely to be forthcoming only if its core norms respond to the legitimate interests and concerns of the member states of contemporary international society. Its norms must be divorced or at least distanced from the norms of any particular civilization. That must include those of Western civilization.

It is necessary to repeat an important caveat at this point. The global covenant is not about democracy. It is about freedom; it is about political independence. Freedom is not the same as democracy.[16] Independent states could be democracies but they could also be non-democracies. Political independence based on state sovereignty is the most geographically extensive kind of liberalism: international liberalism. The foundation norm of international liberalism based on states, as of domestic liberalism based on individuals, is negative liberty.[17] The underlying ethos of the global covenant is fundamentally liberal in that negative sense: it is the ethos of coexistence, of live and let live, of tend to your own affairs. It assumes that the people on the spot, the local people, are in the best position to know what is best for them. They know the circumstances better than anybody else because they experience them and live with them on a daily basis. They are thus in a better position than anybody else to arrive at the best decision in the circumstances.

Normative pluralism is the morality of 'tending your own patch' and that means having a patch and being free to occupy it and cultivate it in your own way. A core human value of the global covenant is the opportunity it affords to people the world over to make of their local political independence whatever they can without having to be unduly concerned about unwarranted interference by neighbours or other outsiders. The global covenant provides a normative guarantee of political independence. However, it offers no guarantees, normative or otherwise, that international freedom will be used wisely or effectively. There can be no such guarantees in human affairs. Nor does it eliminate the ordinary circumstances of world politics or world economics in which people organized as states are entangled. Political independence does not liberate people from their destiny of living in a world alongside other independent people and often cheek by jowl with them. It does not provide any escape from the vast differences of power and wealth between sovereign states. It is not an insulation against global market forces. It would be a familiar category mistake to condemn the global covenant for not keeping globalization at bay: that would be mistaking independence for autonomy.

The morality of 'tending your own patch' does not save people from the encroachments of the global economy. Nor does it sacrifice human beings on the altar of state sovereignty. But it does locate political responsibility within their

---

[16] Contemporary international relations scholars who write about liberalism and perhaps consider themselves to be liberals not infrequently conflate liberalism with democracy. That is evident in the literature on democracy and war. See, e.g. M. W. Doyle, 'Kant, Liberal Legacies, and Foreign Affairs', *Philosophy and Public Affairs*, 12 (1983).

[17] See I. Berlin, *Four Essays on Liberty* (London: OUP, 1969), 122–31.

own hands. People who live in independent countries protected by a right of non-intervention are free from external intervention to succeed in their common endeavours as a political community. They are also free to fail. Whether they succeed or fail is up to them. People who live in independent countries, rather than colonies or other dependencies, possess what used to be called 'responsible government'. That useful expression was employed in previous chapters, but the idea bears repeating: it means that final political decision-making authority in a country has passed from the imperial power to local people who previously had been colonial subjects. They are now citizens of an independent state and are thus responsible for their own political affairs. Responsibility is the mark of freedom—in a society of states no less than a society of individuals. That is the normative outlook of classical liberalism, which can be defined as a willingness not only to accept or tolerate pluralism but to take it fully on board as a value.[18] We might even go so far as to say that the global covenant is the ultimate political liberalism because it conveys freedom to every corner of the globe.

This brief discussion of the normative pluralism of the *societas* of states can be summarized as follows. In the course of living their lives according to their own enlightenment, humans around the world affirm ends or values or claims that are 'equally absolute'. That means that no one value can justifiably be imposed on people who may not hold that value. Values, like countries, must be allowed to coexist. That course is dictated by the norm of prudence as well as that of toleration. It follows that humans must find a way of limiting value conflicts and avoiding the destruction that often results from such conflicts when neither side is prepared to recognize and respect the other side. As noted above, Berlin says that the best we can hope for is to engage in dialogue and try to maintain thereby 'a precarious equilibrium'. The argument made in this study does not disagree with that thesis, but it does go beyond it. Berlin was not a student of international society. If he had been he would have noticed how the normative arrangements of world politics work to mitigate value conflicts. The principal way that that is arranged is by domesticating the values of different cultures and civilizations. International law and diplomacy try to confine conflicting values to the domestic jurisdiction of states and keep them imprisoned there. It does that by upholding the pluralist doctrine of self-determination, equal sovereignty, and non-intervention. That does not mean that two or more states cannot pursue common values jointly or build their own regional or functional association on them. It only means that they cannot shove them down the throat of a third party, even if they believe, like our mothers believed as they forced cod liver oil down our throats, that it is good for them.

---

[18] See Berlin, *Crooked Timber*.

2. *Political Anti-Paternalism*

If political independence is withheld or withdrawn from certain territorial groups against their wishes and without their consent, and if there is no over-riding issue of international peace and security that would justify it, that repudiation of self-determination and self-government will have to rest on some kind of benevolent or paternalist principle—such as international trusteeship. That justification is deeply problematical in a world of sovereign states, because it considers the people for whom it is arranged as unfit and incompetent; it treats them as wards; it thereby deprives them of their adulthood and denies their freedom and responsibility. International trusteeships are expressions of paternalism in world politics.

Michael Walzer has written: 'As with individuals, so with sovereign states: there are things that we cannot do to them, even for their own ostensible good.' And in a follow-up comment he adds: 'the most obvious way of not qualifying for non-intervention is to be incompetent (childish, imbecilic, and so on)'.[19] Contemporary international society is based on anti-paternalism. Decolonization was a vigorous and consequential expression of anti-paternalism in world politics. Yet a paternalist attitude is not far beneath the surface of some current international humanitarianism. In their moral enthusiasm to rescue suffering people in foreign countries and rehabilitate their governments along democratic lines, some Western humanitarians are prepared to intervene in those countries with armed force, to assume the responsibilities of governance temporarily, and thus to repudiate their political freedom for their own ostensible good for the time being—without the consent of the government or any valid justification recognized by the UN charter.

What, then, is the normative shape of the paternalist doctrine? People could be said to be acting paternalistically with regard to somebody else when they are 'acting as a father acts with respect to his child or children'.[20] A defining characteristic of paternal action is that the agent taking the action—the 'father'—is acting on his or her own initiative with the intent of benefiting the subject of the action—the 'child'—who has no choice in the matter.[21] Paternalism is defined by Ronald Dworkin as 'interference with a person's liberty of action justified by reasons referring exclusively to the welfare, good, happiness, needs, interests or values of the person being coerced'.[22] Paternalism is a policy of protecting people from themselves by interfering with their actions in a benevolent way. It does not matter whether the agent taking the paternalist action and the subject who is the concern of that action is an individual or a country. If the action has these characteristics it is paternalist.

---

[19] Michael Walzer, *Just and Unjust Wars*, 2nd edn. (New York: Basic Books, 1992), 89.
[20] N. Fotion, 'Paternalism', *Ethics*, 89 (Jan. 1979), 191.   [21] Ibid. 197.
[22] Quoted ibid. 194 n.

Political paternalism is a self-assumed responsibility leading to a self-initiated action based on a self-righteous outlook: to direct or correct others for their own good. It is an activist and interventionist doctrine. It is not based on equality or reciprocity. It does not involve consultation and consent: children are not at the age of consent; they do not have to be consulted. Paternalism is based on an assumed hierarchical responsibility of some people (parents, teachers, Western democracies) to correct, guide, assist or protect other people (children, pupils, citizens of foreign countries or their governments), who are deemed to require it whether they want it or not. The paternalistic relationship is fundamentally one of inequality, although not permanent inequality. Paternalism implies that the parenting role will eventually no longer be necessary: it operates on the expectation that in the course of time the putative child will become an adult.[23] But until that maturation takes place, benevolent protection, correction, or guidance will be necessary. Political paternalism is a benevolent despotism, albeit a temporary one.

Paternalism is a necessary and highly desirable moral doctrine for a society that includes both children and adults—if it is directed at children by adults. In that social context it is readily justified and to be expected; indeed, for real parents, or guardians who are acting on behalf of parents, it arguably is the only justifiable policy to adopt with regard to dependent children for whom they are responsible. All countries of which I am aware operate with a fundamental normative distinction that divides their population into legally competent adults, who are considered to be full subjects of the law, and legally incompetent children, who have not yet reached the age of consent and do not yet possess all the rights and responsibilities of citizenship. It is difficult to imagine a country, or any other human group that contained people of all ages, that did not operate with such a fundamental distinction. Paternalism only becomes controversial when it is applied to adult human beings.

What, then, would characterize paternalism in world politics? A foreign state (or group of states or international society as a whole) would be acting paternalistically with respect to another state or states if it were acting as a responsible father acts in regard to his child or children. Paternalism in a society of states would basically involve (1) international interference with a country's sovereignty, (2) justified exclusively by reference to the good (domestic security, welfare, education, etc.) that it aims to impart to the country's people, (3) whose sovereign government is not asking for it or consenting to it—and may even be refusing it and resisting it—but the country is considered none the less to be in urgent need of it, and (4) with the assumption of a responsibility to take over the country, either in whole or in part, and run it until such time as its people, particularly its rulers, can be made fit for self-government. Paternalism in contemporary world politics would involve withholding or withdrawing political

---

[23] Ibid. 192–3.

independence from a country or part of its territory until it can be politically rehabilitated.

An international trusteeship or military protectorate based on paternalism postulates a temporary responsibility of foreigners to govern countries that currently are believed to be unable or unwilling to govern themselves and to continue governing them until they grow up politically. A paternalist norm would sanction armed international humanitarian action to rescue some people of an independent state from other people of the same state. It would sanction international trusteeship for failed states. It would justify an international military protectorate for people who had fallen into civil war. It would involve placing the state, either in whole or in part, in temporary receivership and transferring its authority and powers to international soldiers, administrators, etc., until such time as the country was deemed by international officials to be sufficiently rehabilitated to resume political independence.

It is important to emphasize that many forms of foreign or international involvement in an independent country are not paternalist. There is ample provision in world politics for outside humanitarian involvement based on consent: that is, when it is solicited by or receives the authorization of the target state that it seeks to assist. The protection of a state from external attack or from intervention which violated the UN charter would not be paternalism. The national security delivered to small member states of NATO by the USA is not paternalism. Both arrangements involve reciprocal rights and responsibilities of all member states of those international organizations. Pluralism does not preclude action to assist people in foreign countries without interfering with their sovereignty. It does not rule out peacekeeping or peace enforcement based on consent. It does not prohibit international economic assistance by developed countries or international organizations. It does not preclude private humanitarianism by NGOs. On the contrary, it makes it widely possible. During the past fifty years, humanitarian activities of that sort have expanded many times over and they are now a striking feature of international relations. Pluralism leaves open the possibility of assisting countries militarily, economically, technically, scientifically, and in many other ways, by both public action and private action.

Some countries, perhaps many countries, have incompetent and corrupt governments. Some have abusive and malevolent governments. Some have deeply divided populations. Some have large numbers of disaffected and even disloyal citizens. Some countries are in a condition of civil war. Some countries may be ungovernable. A few are 'basket cases'. All of that is a feature of contemporary international society. The global covenant does not prevent foreigners from addressing those problems but it does require that any international action to do so must be consistent with its basic norms. If we go beyond that and assume that the rulers or citizens of certain countries are incompetent or self-indulgent or negligent or abusive or divisive or turbulent to the extent of requiring an international rescue from themselves, we are operating with a radically different standard of international legitimacy and legality. It remains so if it is the intent to rescue people from their own governments. The point of responsible self-government is the responsibility of citizens to govern themselves and thus to form their own government and deal with their own government by themselves in their own way. Western governments or international organizations cannot take on that responsibility at their own initiative when sovereign rulers or citizens fail in that regard.

Paternalism was a basic international norm during the era of Western colonialism when the political systems of the world were divided into two categories: responsible and almost exclusively Western states that possessed sovereignty, and not yet responsible and almost exclusively non-Western dependencies of Western states. Colonialism was justified as an international project to bring Western civilization to non-Western peoples, whether they wanted it or not. Paternalism and colonialism went hand-in-hand. The paternalist doctrine was not abandoned until the advent of decolonization in the second half of the twentieth century. Paternalism in a post-colonial era is something of a contradiction. International trusteeship today would confront the same fundamental question that Western colonialism had to confront: why should foreigners be entrusted with the government of countries that belong to somebody else? What assurance would there be that foreigners would always act in the best interests of the people they were temporarily governing but who had no right to elect them or reject their policies or send them home?

The pluralist ethics of world politics holds that the citizens of independent states are responsible for their own affairs. They are the best judges of their circumstances. Not only that, pluralists believe they are the only ones who ought to be responsible. Pluralists reject the thesis that final responsibility for the domestic well-being of people in independent countries rests with anybody other than those same people. Perhaps more important, they repudiate the revolutionary idea that there is a global community, above the *societas* of states, that has final responsibility for the domestic conditions of its member states and thus for state governance. There is no such community and pluralists would be dead set against creating one even if it were feasible. Foreigners can assist countries in difficulty or in need in whatever way they can, and hopefully assistance will be generously provided by foreign governments, international organizations, NGOs, and private individuals. But it is not up to foreigners to take on the final responsibility of domestic governance at their own initiative. They have no right to do that. If they do it they are trespassing—even if their motives are pure. The main point of the global covenant is to guarantee the international conditions that make it possible for local people to try to build their own 'good life' according to their own enlightenment, without having to contend with unwarranted interference from meddlesome foreigners, including humanitarians who want to help them and are so strongly moved by this feeling of pity and compassion that they are prepared to go ahead on their own initiative and without proper international authority.

3. International Law and Political Virtue

A major controversy in international ethics is whether there are any moral injunctions that are authentically universal in character, that apply to people everywhere and at all times. Proponents of natural law believe there is a universal morality rooted in the rational faculties of human beings which are equally available to all people and enable them to recognize and abide by the same rightful standards of conduct. Immanuel Kant believed there is a categorical imperative to do to others what one would wish and expect others to do to oneself, in other words, to be treated fairly and impartially and without prejudice or bias or discrimination.[24] The problem with Kant's categorical imperative, however, is the difficulty of nailing it down in practice without taking other important moral considerations into account. A categorical imperative is just that: it is completely binding or deontological; it allows for no qualifications or exceptions based on circumstances or consequences; it is considered to be always and everywhere absolutely valid *in itself*. Natural law is likewise considered to be a universal moral truth. The limitation of all such standards of human conduct is well-known: at some place or time not only will it be necessary to disregard the moral imperative, but this will be justified in the circumstances. No responsible government could ever operate with a foreign policy of human rights as a categorical imperative. No responsible government could ever operate with any categorical imperative. That is because categorical imperatives ignore what is crucial: the circumstances in which human conduct must always take place.

But incorporated in the *societas* of states are two elements which disclose universal norms: international law and the political virtues, particularly the virtue of prudence. As indicated, the law of nations was for a long time merely a regional body of political norms which applied to the sovereign states of Europe and later the West. It was the legal framework of their exclusive international association. But international law is today a truly global body of norms that apply directly to every independent state around the world and indirectly to every human being on earth considered as a citizen of a particular state. International law has not only been tolerated by the non-European world; it has been demanded by them. Its universality is based on a quite remarkable degree of local affirmation and consent. In short, during the past century, and particularly since the end of colonialism, international law has become globalized. It embodies standards of conduct that are valid everywhere now that the entire world is within the *societas* of states. It is the only body of law that is truly

---

[24] I. Kant, 'Fundamental Principles of the Metaphysic of Morals', repr. in R. M. Hutchins (ed.), *Great Books of the Western World*, xlii *Kant* (Chicago: Encyclopedia Britannica, 1952), 283.

world-wide. No other legal norms even begin to have the scope of applicability of international law.

International law is universally recognized and accepted because its norms are minimal in what they demand of sovereign states. The norms of international law respond to the facts of diversity and imperfection discussed previously. They are non-controversial because they are mostly negative: they recognize and respect the independence of states; they call for self-restraint and forbearance in the relations of sovereign states; they draw upon the desirability and they promote the value of coexistence. They are significantly positive only when it comes to defending national security or defending international peace and security. They consequently fit the political facts of the world. They do not demand conduct beyond what most people and countries are prepared and equipped to deliver.

International law does not ask statespeople to take actions they are unwilling and perhaps unable to take. It is not based on positive norms. It is not an activist morality. Activism in world politics is voluntary rather than obligatory. International law is a sphere of moderation and restraint, mostly self-restraint. It calls upon statespeople to exercise forbearance in their relations. It requires that they refrain from taking actions that infringe upon the independence of other countries. It requires that they respect each other's sovereign rights and immunities. If statespeople are prepared and equipped to co-operate internationally in the pursuit of additional joint goals or purposes, they are free to do that—as long as they respect the norms of the *societas* of states.

That opens a space that leaves statespeople and countless other people free, within the limits set by the global covenant, to engage in international activities of hugely various kinds. Hobbes said that liberty is the silence of the law.[25] By the same reasoning, we could say that international liberty is the silence of the global covenant. The free international activities carried on by private organizations (for example, NGOs) could be understood as forming or at least giving evidence of a global civil society which fills in the space opened up by the global covenant. It is important to emphasize that that world-wide civil society is not something that happens independent of the *societas* of states. It is not an autonomous social process. On the contrary, it is made possible by and is underwritten by the global covenant. Global civil society is a child of the global society of states. The former could not exist without the latter. That fundamental point is sometimes lost upon international relations scholars.

The world of states generally is not prepared, at least not yet, to accept positive international norms that apply to internal affairs and domestic governance. Only some states are prepared to do that: mainly those of Western Europe and North America who have incorporated democracy and human rights into their domestic laws and politics. They are doing it on a free basis of reciprocity: they

[25] T. Hobbes, *Leviathan*, ed. M. Oakeshott (Oxford: Blackwells, 1946), 143.

agree to be democracies and to protect human rights in their domestic jurisdictions. But beyond the West that is not the case; most states of the world have not aligned their domestic politics according to the norms of democracy or human rights. At best they have only declared their intention to do that, for example, by being signatories to international human rights covenants. But, as indicated previously, that does not involve the surrender of state sovereignty, nor does it signal any abandonment of the doctrine of non-intervention.

That brings us to the political virtues and particularly the virtue of prudence. The political virtues are the moral skills necessary to engage in politics, especially statecraft, in a way that could be justified as being responsible in the circumstances. The political virtues are attuned to the intellectual frailties and moral shortcomings that all people disclose, including statespeople. One could not participate in political activity with any degree of success and for any length of time without possessing and exercising—at least in some degree—the virtues of judgement, moderation, patience, perseverance, circumspection, evenhandedness, and so forth. These virtues and others were discussed in Chapter 7. What is important here is the drift of that discussion: that the political virtues are attuned to both features of the human condition noted above by Hannah Arendt: they respond to varying human conditions and circumstances (human diversity) but they also disclose a basic element of common humanity.

The political virtues provide moral bearings for politicians somewhat in the same way that a compass provides directional bearings for navigators. They inform the moral choices that statespeople must make but they do not make the choices for them. Or to change the metaphor, the political virtues are like a toolkit with different tools for different tasks and situations: prudence, judgement, moderation, etc. Prudence is a moral tool for successful living everywhere and at all times. Prudence is for everybody and not merely for certain people in certain parts of the world at certain times. Any average person can be prudent. They can see the point in being prudent. And if they fail to be prudent their actions can be criticized and maybe condemned. The virtue of prudence can be a virtue across national, linguistic, class, cultural, civilizational, and gender frontiers. Men can be as prudent and realistic as women. What has been said of prudence can also be said of judgement, moderation, and all other political virtues. The virtues presuppose that people everywhere are the same in their basic desire to live and if possible to flourish. The political virtues are essential tools for building and maintaining a viable and valuable political life.

The political virtues are not divorced from circumstances or blind to consequences. On the contrary, they are attuned to actual human conditions: they call for conduct that statespeople are capable of in the circumstances in which they find themselves. They are not overly demanding. They are not undemanding. They are available and applicable to responsible statesmen and stateswomen everywhere. One of the most deservedly famous bodies of political and military wisdom places prudence at the core of its strategic doctrine by emphasizing the avoidance of defeat and the preservation of one's military force to be able to fight again in the future. That famous book is *The Art of War* by the ancient Chinese philosopher Sun Tzu.[26] The same idea is captured by the English aphorism: 'discretion is the better part of valour'.

That prudential doctrine can be grasped by anyone, ancient or modern, Chinese or European, because its importance for human flourishing is immediately and unambiguously recognizable. Any political or military leader can see the necessity of forethought, foresight, caution, and circumspection in carrying out his or her responsibilities. And if he or she cannot see it, we can justifiably criticize them or condemn them for their shortsightedness or blindness, because they should see it. Anyone with his or her eyes half-open would see it. Closing one's eyes to dangers and risks is a universal moral failing. Arrogance and blind overconfidence is an invitation to defeat and maybe disaster. It is a particularly serious failing of political and military leaders upon whose decisions and policies many others depend. Why can we say that? It is because the question of being prudent is not a scientific question or a technical question or an economic question or an educational question or a cultural question or a racial question or a question of time or place. It is a human question. It is a question of age and maturity and also experience. Statespeople do not require scientific or technical or academic experts to advise them how to be cautious and circumspect in their foreign relations. Everybody who has reached a certain stage of freedom and responsibility in his or her life—which is normally defined as maturity or adulthood—can see the point of being prudent in the circumstances and can act accordingly without anybody's assistance. I believe that that is as close to a universal proposition about human conduct as anyone can get.

Westphalia Evolving

The global covenant is not a static arrangement of norms. Any institution that has responded successfully to unprecedented changes in human relations during a lengthy and turbulent period of world history (the modern period) could not be static and still be in existence. The global covenant is an evolving institution. Hedley Bull draws our attention to 'the continuing vitality of the states system' which answered to recurrent social changes, in some periods social upheaval, since it was consolidated in the middle of the seventeenth century.[27] We should remember how parochial international society was at that time: a restrictive association of mostly dynastic states that emerged out of the ruins of medieval Latin Christendom in Western Europe. It was initially a European institution. It next

---

[26] *The Art of War*, tr. and with an introduction by Samuel Griffith (London: OUP, 1971).
[27] H. Bull, *The Anarchical Society*, 2nd edn. (London: Macmillan, 1995), ch. 11.

became a transatlantic institution following the American revolution of the late eighteenth century. Only in the second half of the twentieth century did it finally become an inclusive global association.

During that period of more than three centuries, the changes in human affairs have been profound and unprecedented in their scope and magnitude. Many of those changes were as disruptive and disorienting as the changes we are witnessing at the present time. They can only be summarized briefly. Westphalia originally was an institutional answer to a revolutionary transformation of European social and political life precipitated by the Renaissance and the Reformation, which eventually destroyed medieval society and ushered in the modern age at the centre of which was the sovereign state. It adapted to the scientific revolution of the seventeenth century, which set in motion changes that eventually transformed the way people understood the cosmos and their place in it. It adjusted to the Enlightenment and the political revolutions of the eighteenth century, which contributed enormously to the secularization of modern political life, provided rational criteria of public policy, and launched political ideas that led to the emergence of the modern nation-state. It accommodated the industrial revolution of the nineteenth century, which multiplied the power of modern technology, spread it throughout national populations, and fostered the modern mechanized society. It witnessed the mass movement of millions of people from the countryside to the cities and the explosion in the size of national populations that resulted from demographic and socio-economic change. It took on board the doctrine of nationalism and the national state by changing its basis of legitimacy and law. It did not require constitutional or ideological conformity on the part of member states. It could accommodate republics alongside monarchies and, at a later stage, democracies alongside authoritarian states. It adjusted to all that social change and more.

In the twentieth century alone, the versatility and vitality of the *societas* of states was remarkable. Its foundations withstood the two world wars of the first half of the century, whose destructiveness and revolutionary effects were unprecedented. It survived the Russian revolution of 1917 and an era of communist crusading in world affairs that continued for decades afterwards. It survived the great depression of the 1930s. It survived the Nazis and the fascists. It not only answered the demands for Third World decolonization in the middle decades of the century but it supplied the ideas and norms that inspired and guided that transformation.[28] It also responded to the nuclear age and the space age. It became blind to distinctions of race and culture and ideology, just as at an earlier time it had to be blind to religion. It is also blind to gender.

There are two reliable reasons for the successful adjustment of the *societas* of states to fundamental social changes. The first is its decentralization. Being

---

[28] R. Jackson, 'The Weight of Ideas in Decolonization', in Judith Goldstein and Robert O. Keohane (eds.), *Ideas and Foreign Policy* (Ithaca, NY: Cornell University Press, 1993), 111–38.

decentred and non-hierarchical it cannot be broken the way that the universal medieval empire was broken by the Renaissance and the Reformation or the way the Roman Empire was broken and destroyed by the 'barbarian' invasions of the Germanic 'tribes'. It would require an extraordinary change to overturn it. We should expect it eventually to wither away but probably not to fall. The second reason, mentioned previously, is given special emphasis by Hedley Bull: 'the tyranny of the concepts and normative principles associated with it' which constitute an intellectual prison from which escape is difficult.[29] That is because it is very hard to think about convincing alternative images of international life without employing the ideas and language associated with the society of states. They are too basic and too deeply ingrained in our thought.

Throughout the lengthy time from its inception, the pluralist framework of international society was periodically rearranged in response to new ideas and circumstances. The *societas* of states was initially little more than an exclusive club of a distinctive class of European rulers and dynasties who were deemed to be sovereign—they had no recognized superiors in their territories except their Christian God. That initial exclusivity did not prevent international society from responding to major reconceptions and reconstitutions of the state: from monarchy to republic to democracy; from mercantilist state to capitalist state to welfare state to mass media and consumer state. The basic norms of the global covenant have been revised in other ways too. At one time sovereign states had a right to initiate aggressive war in pursuit of their self-defined interests. That right was extinguished in the twentieth century. At one time sovereign states could control foreign populated territory as their colonial dependencies. That right was also extinguished. Sovereignty was changed from being a prerogative of rulers and dynasties to being a right of peoples and nations, to being in some cases little more than a putative collective right that attaches to particular bordered territories marked on political maps within which no real or empirical state could be said to exist. *Cujus regio, ejus religio* evolved into Article 2 of the UN charter. Independent governance has changed from an activity of presiding over the quasi-private affairs of a dynasty to one of addressing and managing shifting public opinion in electronically wired mass democracies. Many other examples could also be given, but hopefully these can suffice to make the basic point.

That the *societas* of states has proved over time to be a remarkably flexible institutional arrangement will come as no surprise to students of successful and long-lasting institutions. The American constitution has been able to accommodate extraordinary social changes since it was adopted in 1787. The USA has changed to such an extent that it is difficult to remember how modest the initial political experiment was: it has grown from a small European immigrant state of mostly British stock scattered along the western shore of the North Atlantic Ocean to become a continental superstate populated by immigrants

---

[29] Bull, *Anarchical Society*, ch. 11.

from all over the world, who continue to be attracted by its open and affluent society. At the start of the twenty-first century it was by far the wealthiest, most powerful, and most dynamic nation-state on earth—and it had been that way for most of the twentieth century. Apart from a few amendments, its constitution has remained basically the same: America continues to be a federal state whose constituent governments, including the federal government, is still based on a division of powers between the legislative, executive, and judicial branches. The British constitution is older than the American constitution and is far more evolutionary: it has responded to the transformation of England from a minor kingdom on the frontier of north-western Europe during the Middle Ages, to the greatest empire on earth of modern times, to the first advanced industrial state, to one of the first welfare states, and then to one of the major democracies of the European Union.

The evidence of remarkable institutional continuity is not by any means confined to the political sphere of human relations. Many European universities are older than most European states. The universities of Oxford and Cambridge have a continuous history that goes back to the thirteenth century: they reconstituted themselves during that time from medieval schools of theology to eighteenth-century schools for English gentlemen to twentieth-century world-class research universities. During that period Aristotelian cosmology was replaced by Copernican cosmology and Newtonian mechanics and they were succeeded by Einstein's relativity theory and Stephen Hawkings's cosmology. Similar changes occurred in many other fields of knowledge. But in all that time, through all that change, the organization of these universities into bodies of scholars grouped into halls, colleges, schools, and faculties has remained basically unchanged. The Catholic Church reaches much further back through the Middle Ages to the Roman Empire of late European antiquity: its liturgy and episcopal organization remains basically the same, in spite of upheavals in the surrounding society, including the Reformation, which dramatically reduced its scale and stature, and the more recent secularization of society, which has had earth-shaking effects on religious belief, at least in the West.[30]

There are many other examples of institutional longevity and adaptability in the face of massive and often completely unanticipated social change. They suggest, perhaps paradoxically, that continuity and change in human affairs often march hand-in-hand. But it is no paradox: people confronting change need something to hold on to. Human beings are creatures who construct their own social worlds and in the course of doing so they create social change, often surprising and far-reaching changes, intentionally and inadvertently. Evolving institutions provide important handholds and directions for people to hang on to and keep their bearings on the stormy seas that they set in motion by their own wave-making activities.

---

[30] J. McManners (ed.), *The Oxford History of Christianity* (Oxford: OUP, 1993).

Why are some human institutions so enduring? Why do humans hold to certain institutional arrangements for such a long time? I think it is because they are exceedingly well attuned to human requirements. They fit the needs and circumstances of the people involved in them. Indeed they fit so well that the people involved scarcely think about them. They are so taken for granted, so ingrained into habits and expectations that they become virtually invisible. They are used without hardly being noticed in their use.

It may be worthwhile to call attention to the enduring and seemingly permanent place in human life of such conventions and contrivances as numeric notation, alphabets, musical notation, parts of speech, calendars, clocks, maps, units of measure, denominations of currency, forms and signs of greeting, forms of courtesy, practices of etiquette, rites of passage, long-standing games such as chess and cards, and other standardized *modus operandi* of human life that are far too numerous even to mention in passing. Those arrangements of human affairs and activities endure for very extensive periods of time in spite of technological innovations or social changes which transform human life in others respects out of all recognition. They remain basically the same in the face of profound social changes. They emerge from political upheavals unscathed. And throughout turbulent periods of change they continue to provide the same predictable and confident service they always have provided to those who understand them and know how to make use of them. The Western alphabet, the Roman calendar (*Calends*), European numerals, the clock, and other conventions that are deeply ingrained in human relations, have been entirely unaffected by the computer revolution which has in fact made ample use of these long-established artefacts.

That is because they provide something elementary: a fundamental and stable standard of social expectation, communication, and interaction in the different areas of human life in which they are used. They are solid platforms upon which people can stand while confronting seeming inevitable and unceasing social sea changes. Those elementary human arrangements endure for generations, sometimes for centuries, and occasionally for millennia. In that regard they are very much like vernacular languages. Vocabulary and idiom may change to some extent, words and expressions may come and go, but the structure of the language—the grammar and syntax—remains basically the same. The *societas* of states is something like that. It is the grammar of international relations which has remained essentially the same since the seventeenth century, in spite of many changes of vocabulary and idiom during the intervening period between then and now.

People hold on to conventional ways of arranging and conducting human affairs in the various departments of life, each generation passes them on to the next generation, and the cycle repeats itself over and over. Institutions serve as steady frameworks with regard to which people can communicate and interact in the confident expectation of being recognized and understood. They supply practices or procedures or precedents or mutually recognized symbols or signs for carrying on the various social activities in which people are ordinarily and regularly involved. They provide stability and predictability. So we hang on to them and periodically renovate them. These examples of successful institutional adaptation, and many others we could think of, should make us sceptical about claims that international relations are getting beyond the *societas* of states. Many scholars, journalists, and politicians who make such claims pay close attention to short-term contemporary innovations without noticing long-term historical continuities in international relations.

There is nothing that is inevitable or sacrosanct about the *societas* of states. It could change fundamentally. It could disappear just as the Roman and British Empires disappeared. Such an event would of course mark a world-historical change.[31] It would be a global revolution. Maybe it is happening as we enter a new millennium. In light of the survivability demonstrated by the *societas* of states over the past three or four centuries, however, it seems far more likely that state sovereignty is evolving yet again. Of course it remains to be seen whether it will adapt as successfully to the scientific, technical, social, and economic revolution that we summarize by the term 'globalization' as it adapted to the revolutionary changes already noted. The global covenant could perhaps eventually die from marginalization brought on by globalization: it could bleed to death from a thousand small cuts. But there is a long and impressive history of successful adaptation to technological and economic change which suggests that Westphalia will continue to evolve in the foreseeable future as it has in the past.

If I had to place a bet on the shape of world politics at the start of the twenty-second century, my money would be on the prognosis that our great-great-grandchildren will live in a political world that would still be familiar to us, that would still be shaped politically by state sovereignty. Peoples around the world will still be organized and recognized as independent states. They will still coexist and communicate and interact and transact their political business to a significant extent via the *societas* of states. The current political map will still be more or less in place. Even if it changes noticeably as a result of the partition or amalgamation of existing territorial jurisdictions, I would expect that there will still be a political map that delineates independent territorial jurisdictions, most of which would be recognizable to us and would still have the same names. There will still be the USA, Russia, Germany, Egypt, Iran, India, China, Japan. Even in Europe, after more than a century of economic and political integration via the EU, it will still be possible to distinguish, not only by language and culture but also by a significant form of national citizenship, Frenchmen, Germans, Danes, Spaniards, Italians, Greeks, and the rest. And even if Europe is by then

---

[31] On the revolutionary state in international society see David Armstrong, *Revolution and World Order* (Oxford: Clarendon Press, 1993).

a great political federation, it will still be very easy to distinguish the European Union from the USA in terms of state sovereignty.

But I would not bet that sovereign states a century from now will be exactly the same institutions that they are today. By that time they might have evolved beyond the nation-state, just as they previously evolved beyond the dynastic state. Maybe they will be multinational or multicultural. Maybe citizenship will become more open and less restrictive than it is today. Maybe there will be post-modern states by then.[32] But even though the adjective changed I would expect the noun still to be the same: our great-great-grandchildren will still be citizens of states which will still be vital components of their lives: there will be a familiar world of states whose relations will be defined by basic norms not unlike equal sovereignty, territorial integrity, and non-intervention.

The global covenant is the most encompassing normative framework that humans have fashioned thus far, to deal with each other politically by recognizing each other as fellow human beings but without demanding of each other that they must sacrifice their local group existences, their distinctive ways of life, and their sovereignty over their own affairs. The historical fact that the global covenant is able to serve as a normative bridge not only between all the territorial populations organized as separate states, but also between the cultures and civilizations that infiltrate and shape the domestic life-ways of those same states, tells me that it is not likely to be abandoned or even changed fundamentally very soon.

The *societas* of sovereign states accommodates the phenomenal diversity of human social organization around the world that must be taken into account if the world political system is to have some general basis of validity. Without some such accommodation no international institution could acquire general legitimacy across the world. Montaigne famously put the point as follows: 'Let every foot have its own shoe.'[33] That could mean a different law for different states, which is what happens domestically.[34] It could also mean a law sufficiently general to embrace human diversity. That is what Montaigne was driving at: 'the most desirable laws are those that are rarest, simplest, and most general'.[35] That is what the foundation rules of the global covenant are. Notwithstanding its very real limitations and imperfections, to date the *societas* of sovereign states has proved to be the only generally acceptable and practical normative basis of world politics. At present there is no other world-wide political institution that can perform that service for humankind. Another way of

---

[32] Georg Sørensen, 'An Analysis of Contemporary Statehood: Consequences for Conflict and Cooperation', *Review of International Studies*, 23 (July 1997), 253–69.

[33] D. M. Frame (tr.), *The Complete Essays of Montaigne* (Stanford, Calif.: Stanford University Press, 1958), book 3, ch. 13, p. 816. This translation is from P. Burke, *Montaigne* (Oxford: OUP, 1981), 33.

[34] See M. Oakeshott, *On History and Other Essays* (Oxford: Blackwells, 1983), 145n.

[35] Frame, *Complete Essays of Montaigne*, book 3, ch. 13, p. 816.

putting that is to say that the above-noted norms are among those very few values around which the world can unite politically. In making that argument I have in mind a famous claim about democracy attributed to Winston Churchill: it is the worst form of government except for all the rest.

Bibliography

The references are intended to provide a comprehensive collection of the most important studies in the classical approach to international relations. They include citations from the text as well as further references from the main body of literature on international society, both traditional and contemporary. Important references from closely related literatures are also included.

Acton, Lord, 'Beginning of the Modern State', in W. H. McNeill (ed.), *Lord Acton: Essays in the Liberal Interpretation of History* (Chicago: University of Chicago Press, 1967).

Adler, E., and M. Barnett (eds.), *Security Communities* (Cambridge: Cambridge University Press, 1998).

Alderson, Kai, and Andrew Hurrell (eds.), *Hedley Bull on International Society* (London: Macmillan, 2000).

Alter, K. J., 'Who are the "Masters of the Treaty"?: European Governments and the European Court of Justice', *International Organization*, 52 (1998).

Akehurst, M., 'Humanitarian Intervention', in H. Bull (ed.), *Intervention in World Politics* (Oxford: Clarendon Press, 1984).

—— *A Modern Introduction to International Law*, 6th edn. (London: Allen & Unwin, 1987).

Anderson, M. S., *The Rise of Modern Diplomacy* (London: Longmans, 1993).

Arend, A., and Robert Beck, *International Law and the Use of Force* (London and New York: Routledge, 1993).

Arendt, H., *The Human Condition* (Chicago: University of Chicago Press, 1958).

Aristotle, *The Politics*, tr. T. A. Sinclair (Harmondsworth: Penguin Books, 1962).

Armstrong, David, 'Law, Justice and the Idea of a World Society', *International Affairs* 75/3 (1999), 547–61.

—— and E. Goldstein (eds.), *The End of the Cold War* (London: Frank Cass, 1990).

—— *Revolution and World Order* (Oxford: Clarendon Press, 1993).

—— 'Law, Justice and the Idea of a World Society', *International Affairs* 73/3 (1999).

Aron, R., *Peace and War: A Theory of International Relations* (London: Weidenfeld & Nicolson, 1966).

Aron, R., *Clausewitz: Philosopher of War*, tr. C. Booker and N. Stone (Englewood Cliffs, NJ: Prentice-Hall, 1985).

Ashley, R., 'The Achievements of Post-Structuralism', in S. Smith, K. Booth, and M. Zalewski (eds.), *International Theory: Positivism and Beyond* (Cambridge: Cambridge University Press, 1996), 240–53.

Ayer, A. J., *Language, Truth and Logic* (London: Penguin, 1960).

Baechler, Jean, 'Virtue: Its Nature, Exigency and Acquisition', in J. W. Chapman and W. A. Galston (eds.), *Virtue: Nomos XXXIV* (New York: New York University Press, 1992).

Baier, K., 'Justification in Ethics', in J. Roland Pennock and J. W. Chapman (eds.), *Justification: Nomos XXVIII* (New York: New York University Press, 1986).

Ball, C. 'Nattering NATO Negativism: Reasons Why Expansion may be a Good Thing', *Review of International Studies*, 24 (1998).

Barry, B., and Robert E. Goodin (eds.), 'Symposium on Duties Beyond Borders', *Ethics*, 98 (1988).

—— and Robert E. Goodin (eds.), *Free Movement* (London: Harvester Wheatsheaf, 1992).

Bartelson, J., *A Genealogy of Sovereignty* (Cambridge: Cambridge University Press, 1995).

Baun, Michael J., *An Imperfect Union: The Maastricht Treaty and the New Politics of European Integration* (Boulder, Colo.: Westview, 1996).

Baylis, J., and N. J. Rengger (eds.), *Dilemmas of World Politics* (Oxford: Clarendon Press, 1992).

——and S. Smith (eds.), *The Globalization of World Politics* (Oxford: Clarendon Press, 1997).

Beck, Robert J., Anthony Clark Arend, and Robert D. Vander Lugt (eds.), *International Rules: Approaches from International Law and International Relations* (Oxford: Oxford University Press, 1996).

Beiner, R., 'The Moral Vocabulary of Liberalism', in J. W. Chapman and W. A. Galston (eds.), *Virtue: Nomos XXXIV* (New York: New York University Press, 1992).

Beitz, C., *Political Theory and International Relations* (Princeton: Princeton University Press, 1979).

Berki, R. N., *Security and Society* (London: Dent, 1986).

Berlin, I., *The Hedgehog and the Fox: An Essay on Tolstoy's View of History* (London: Weidenfeld and Nicolson, 1953).

—— 'Realism in Politics', *Spectator*, 193 (1954).

—— *Four Essays on Liberty* (London: OUP, 1969).

—— *Vico and Herder* (New York: Viking Press, 1976).

—— *Against the Current: Essays on the History of Ideas* (New York: Viking Press, 1980).

—— *Concepts and Categories: Philosophical Essays* (Harmondsworth: Penguin Books, 1981).

—— *The Crooked Timber of Humanity* (New York: Vintage Books, 1992).

Berridge, G., 'The Political Theory and Institutional History of States-Systems', *British Journal of International Studies*, 6 (1980).

—— *Diplomacy: Theory and Practice* (Hemel Hempstead: Harvester Wheatsheaf, 1995).

Best, G., *Honour among Men and Nations* (Toronto: University of Toronto Press, 1982).

—— *Humanity in Warfare* (London: Methuen, 1983).

—— *War and Law since 1945* (Oxford: Clarendon Press, 1993).

—— 'Justice, International Relations and Human Rights', *International Affairs*, 71/4 (1995), 775–99.

Bethlehem, D. L. (ed.), *The Kuwait Crisis: Sanctions and their Consequences* (Cambridge: Grotius Publications, 1991).

Biersteker, Thomas J., and Cynthia Weber (eds.), *State Sovereignty as a Social Construct* (Cambridge: Cambridge University Press, 1996).

Bonanate, L., *Ethics and International Politics* (Cambridge: Polity Press, 1995).

Booth, K., 'Security and Emancipation', *Review of International Studies*, 17 (1991).

—— 'Security in Anarchy: Utopian Realism in Theory and Practice', *International Affairs*, 67 (1991).

—— 'Duty and Prudence', in L. Freeman (ed.), *Military Intervention in European Conflicts* (Oxford: Blackwell, 1994).

—— 'Human Wrongs and International Relations', *International Affairs*, 71 (1995).

—— (ed.), *Statecraft and Security* (Cambridge: Cambridge University Press, 1998).

—— and N. J. Wheeler, *The Security Dilemma* (London: Macmillan, 1998).

Boyle, J. 'Natural Law and International Ethics', in T. Nardin and D. Mapel, *Traditions of International Ethics* (Cambridge: Cambridge University Press, 1992).

Bozeman, Adda, *Politics and Culture in International History* (Princeton: Princeton University Press, 1960).

Bredvold, L. I., and R. G. Ross (eds.), *The Philosophy of Edmund Burke* (Ann Arbor: University of Michigan Press, 1967).

Brierly, J. L., *The Law of Nations*, 2nd edn. (London: OUP, 1938).

Brown, C., *International Relations Theory: New Normative Approaches* (New York: Harvester, 1992).

—— (ed.), *Political Restructuring in Europe* (London: Routledge, 1994).

—— 'International Theory and International Society: The Viability of the Middle Way', *Review of International Studies*, 21/2 (1995).

—— 'Cultural Pluralism, Universal Principles and International Relations Theory', in S. Caney, D. George, and P. Jones (eds.), *National Rights, International Obligations* (Boulder, Colo.: Westview, 1996).

—— 'Contractarian Thought and the Constitution of International Society Perspective', in David R. Mapel and Terry Nardin (eds.), *International Society: Diverse Ethical Perspectives* (Princeton: Princeton University Press, 1998).

Brownlie, I. (ed.), *Basic Documents on African Affairs* (Oxford: Clarendon Press, 1971).

—— *Principles of Public International Law*, 3rd edn. (Oxford: Clarendon Press, 1979).

Buell, R., *International Relations*, revised edn. (New York: Henry Holt & Co., 1925).

Bull, H., *The Control of the Arms Race: Disarmament and Arms Control in the Nuclear Age* (London: Weidenfeld & Nicolson, 1961).

—— 'Society and Anarchy in International Relations', in H. Butterfield and M. Wight (eds.), *Diplomatic Investigations* (London: Allen & Unwin, 1966).

—— 'The Grotian Conception of International Society', in H. Butterfield and M. Wight (eds.), *Diplomatic Investigations* (London: Allen & Unwin, 1966).

—— 'International Theory: The Case for a Classical Approach', in K. Knorr and J. N. Rosenau (eds.), *Contending Approaches to International Politics* (Princeton: Princeton University Press, 1969).

—— 'Order vs. Justice in International Society', *Political Studies*, 19/3 (1971)

—— 'The New Balance of Power in Asia and the Pacific', *Foreign Affairs*, 49/4 (1971).

—— 'World Order and the Super Powers', in Carsten Holbraad (ed.), *Super Powers and World Order* (Canberra: Australian National University Press, 1971).

—— 'International Law and International Order', *International Organization*, 26/3 (1972).

—— 'International Relations as an Academic Pursuit', *Australian Outlook*, 26 (1972).

—— 'The Theory of International Politics, 1919–1969', in B. Porter (ed.), *The Aberystwyth Papers: International Politics 1919–1969* (London: OUP, 1972).

Bull, H., 'War and International Order', in A. James (ed.), *The Bases of International Order: Essays in Honour of C. A. W. Manning*, (Oxford: OUP, 1973).

—— 'New Directions in the Theory of International Relations', *International Studies*, 14 (1975).

—— 'Martin Wight and the Theory of International Relations', *British Journal of International Studies*, 2 (1976).

—— 'The Third World and International Society', *The Year Book of World Affairs*, 33 (London: Institute of World Affairs, 1976).

—— 'Natural Law and International Relations', *British Journal of International Studies*, 5/2 (1979).

—— 'Recapturing the Just War for Political Theory', *World Politics*, 31 (1979).

—— 'The State's Positive Role in World Affairs', *Daedalus*, 108/4 (1979).

—— 'The Universality of Human Rights', *Millennium*, 8/2 (1979).

—— 'Kissinger: The Primacy of Geopolitics', *International Affairs*, 56 (1980).

—— 'The Great Irresponsibles? The United States, the Soviet Union and World Order', *International Journal*, 35 (1980).

—— 'Force in International Relations', in R. O'Neill and D. Horner (eds.), *New Directions in Strategic Thinking* (London: George Allen & Unwin, 1981).

—— 'Hobbes and the International Anarchy', *Social Research*, 48/4 (1981).

—— 'Of Means and Ends', in R. O'Neill and D. Horner (eds.), *New Directions in Strategic Thinking* (London: George Allen & Unwin, 1981).

—— 'The Revolt against the West', in M. S. Rajan and S. Ganguly (eds.), *Great Power Relations, World Order and the Third World* (New Delhi: Vikas Publishing, 1981).

—— 'The West and South Africa', *Daedalus*, 111/2 (1982).

—— 'Intervention in the Third World', *The Non-Aligned World*, 1/3 (1983).

—— (ed.), *Intervention in World Politics* (Oxford: Clarendon Press, 1984).

—— *Justice in International Relations*, the 1983–4 Hagey Lectures (Waterloo, Ontario: University of Waterloo Press, 1984).

—— (ed.), *Intervention in World Politics* (Oxford: Clarendon Press, 1984).

—— 'Hans Kelsen and International Law', in R. Tur and W. Trining (eds.), *Essays on Kelsen* (Oxford: Clarendon Press, 1986).

—— *The Challenge of the Third Reich*, the Adam von Trott Memorial Lectures (Oxford: Clarendon Press, 1986).

—— *The Anarchical Society: A Study of Order in World Politics*, 2nd edn. (London: Macmillan, 1995).

—— *Hedley Bull on International Society*, ed. Kai Alderson and Andrew Hurrell (London: Macmillan, 1999).

—— and Wm. Roger Louis (eds.), *The Special Relationship: Anglo-American Relations since 1945* (Oxford: Clarendon Press, 1986).

—— and Adam Watson (eds.), *The Expansion of International Society* (Oxford: Clarendon Press, 1984).

—— K. Kingsbury, and A. Roberts (eds.), *Hugo Grotius and International Relations* (Oxford: Clarendon Press, 1990).

Burckhardt, J., *The Civilization of the Renaissance in Italy*, 2 vols. (New York: Harper & Row, 1958).

Burke, Edmund, *Reflections on the Revolution in France*, ed. J. G. A. Pocock (Indianapolis: Liberty Press, 1987).

—— 'Letters on a Regicide Peace', in F. W. Raffety (ed.), *The Works of Edmund Burke*, vi (Oxford: Oxford University Press, 1928).

Burke, P., *Montaigne* (Oxford, OUP, 1981).

Burton, John, *World Society* (Cambridge: Cambridge University Press, 1972).

Bussmann, K., and H. Schilling (eds.), *1648: War and Peace in Europe*, 2 vols. (Munich: Bruckmann, 1998).

Butler, Peter F., 'The Individual and International Relations', in J. Mayall (ed.), *The Community of States* (London: George Allen & Unwin, 1982).

Butterfield, J., *Statecraft of Machiavelli* (London: Macmillan, 1940).

—— *Christianity and History* (London: George Bell, 1949).

—— *The Whig Interpretation of History* (London: George Bell, 1949).

—— *History and Human Relations* (London: Collins, 1951).

—— 'The Scientific versus the Moralistic Approach in International Affairs', *International Affairs*, 27 (1951).

—— *Christianity, Diplomacy and War* (London: Epworth, 1953).

—— *International Conflict in the Twentieth Century: A Christian View* (New York: Harper & Row, 1960).

—— 'The Balance of Power', in H. Butterfield and M. Wight (eds.), *Diplomatic Investigations* (London: Allen & Unwin, 1966).

—— 'The New Diplomacy and Historical Diplomacy', in H. Butterfield and M. Wight (eds.), *Diplomatic Investigations* (London: Allen & Unwin, 1966).

—— 'Morality and an International Order', in B. Porter (ed.), *The Aberystwyth Papers: International Politics, 1919–1969* (London, OUP, 1972).

—— 'Global Good and Evil', in K. W. Thompson and R. J. Myers (eds.), *A Tribute to Hans Morgenthau* (Washington: The New Republic Book Co., 1977).

—— and Martin Wight (eds.), *Diplomatic Investigations: Essays in the Theory of International Politics* (London: Allen & Unwin, 1966).

Buzan, B., *Peoople, States and Fear* (Chapel Hill, NC: University of North Carolina Press, 1983).

—— 'From International System to International Society: Structural Realism and Regime Theory Meet the English School', *International Organization*, 47/3 (1993).

—— 'International Theory and International Society', in R. Fawn and J. Larkin (eds.), *International Society after the Cold War* (London: Macmillan, 1996).

—— O. Waever, and J. de Wilde, *Security: A New Framework for Analysis* (London: Lynne Rienner, 1998).

Byers, Michael, *Custom, Power and the Power of Rules: International Relations and Customary International Law* (Cambridge: Cambridge University Press, 1999).

Caney, S., D. George, and P. Jones (eds.), *National Rights, International Obligations* (Boulder, Colo.: Westview, 1996).

Canning, J., *A History of Medieval Political Thought, 300–1450* (London; Routledge, 1996).

Carr, E. H., *The Twenty Years' Crisis* (New York: Harper & Row, 1964).

—— *What is History?*, 2nd edn., ed. R. W. Davies (London: Penguin, 1987).

Cassese, Antonio, *International Law in a Divided World* (Oxford: Clarendon Press, 1986).

Chapman, J. W., and W. A. Galston (eds.), *Virtue: Nomos XXXIV* (New York: New York University Press, 1992).

Charvet, John, 'What is Nationality, and is there a Moral Right to National Self-Determination?', in S. Caney, D. George, and P. Jones (eds.), *National Rights, International Obligations* (Boulder, Colo.: Westview, 1996).

—— 'International Society from a Contractarian Perspective', in David R. Mapel and Terry Nardin (eds.), *International Society: Diverse Ethical Perspectives* (Princeton: Princeton University Press, 1998).

Chadwick, H., 'The Early Christian Community', in J. McManners (ed.), *The Oxford History of Christianity* (Oxford: Oxford University Press, 1993).

Churchill, Winston S., *Closing the Ring: The Second World War* (Boston, Mass.: Houghton Mifflin, 1951).

Clapham, C., *Africa and the International System: The Politics of State Survival* (Cambridge: Cambridge University Press, 1996).

—— 'Sovereignty and the Third World State', in R. Jackson (ed.), *Sovereignty at the Millennium, Political Studies*, 47/3 (special issue, 1999).

Clark, George, *Early Modern Europe: From about 1450 to about 1720* (London: OUP, 1960).

—— *The Seventeenth Century*, 2nd edn. (London: OUP, 1960).

Clark, I., *Waging War* (Oxford: Clarendon Press, 1990).

—— 'Traditions of Thought and Classical Theories of International Relations', in I. Clark and I. B. Neumann (eds.), *Classical Theories of International Relations* (London: Macmillan, 1996).

—— and Iver B. Neumann (eds.), *Classical Theories of International Relations* (London: Macmillan, 1996).

Claude, Inis, *Swords into Plowshares*, 4th edn. (New York: Random House, 1971).

Coates, A. J., *The Ethics of War* (Manchester: University of Manchester Press, 1997).

Cobban, A., *The Nation State and National Self-Determination* (New York: Crowell, 1969).

Coll, A., *The Wisdom of Statecraft: Sir Herbert Butterfield and the Philosophy of International Politics* (Durham, NC: Duke University Press, 1985).

—— 'Normative Prudence as a Tradition of Statecraft', *Ethics and International Affairs*, 5 (1991).

Collingwood, R. G., *An Autobiography* (London: OUP, 1939).

—— *The New Leviathan: Man, Society, Civilization and Barbarism* (New York: Crowell, 1971).

—— *The Idea of History* (London: OUP, 1975).

—— *Essays in Political Philosophy*, ed. David Boucher (Oxford: Clarendon Press, 1989).

Connaughton, R., *Military Intervention in the 1990s* (London and New York: Routledge, 1992).

Cornford, F. R. (tr.), *The Republic of Plato* (London: OUP, 1945).

Cox, R., 'Social Forces, States and World Orders', *Millennium*, 10 (1981).

—— *Approaches to World Order*, with Timothy J. Sinclair (Cambridge: Cambridge University Press, 1996).

Crawford, J. (ed.), *The Rights of Peoples* (Oxford: Clarendon Press, 1988).

Cutler, Claire A., 'The "Grotian Tradition" in International Relations', *Review of International Studies*, 17/1 (1991).

Czempiel, Ernst-Otto, and James N. Rosenau (eds.), *Global Changes and Theoretical Challenges* (New York: Lexington Books, 1992).

Damrosch, L. F., and D. J. Scheffer (eds.), *Law and Force in the New International Order* (Boulder, Colo.: Westview, 1991).

Davis, N., *Europe: A History* (London: Pimlico, 1997).

De la Billiere, P., *Storm Command* (London: HarperCollins, 1992).

D'Entreves, A. P., *Natural Law* (London: Hutchinson, 1970).

Der Derian, James, 'Introducing Philosophical Traditions in International Relations', *Millennium*, 17/2 (1988).

—— (ed.), *International Theory: Critical Investigations* (London: Macmillan, 1995).

—— 'Hedley Bull and the Idea of Diplomatic Culture', in R. Fawn and J. Larkin (eds.), *International Society after the Cold War* (London: Macmillan, 1996).

Donelan, Michael (ed.), *The Reason of States: A Study in International Political Theory* (London: Allen & Unwin, 1978).

—— 'Spain and the Indies', in H. Bull and A. Watson (eds.), *The Expansion of International Society* (Oxford: Clarendon Press, 1984).

—— *Elements of International Political Theory* (Oxford: Clarendon Press, 1990).

Donnelly, J., 'Twentieth-Century Realism', in Terry Nardin and David Mapel (eds.), *Traditions of International Ethics* (Cambridge: Cambridge University Press, 1992).

—— 'Human Rights: A New Standard of Civilization?', *International Affairs*, 74/1 (1998), 1–23.

—— *International Human Rights Dilemmas in World Politics* (Boulder, Colo.: Westview, 1998).

Doyle, Michael, 'Kant, Liberal Legacies and Foreign Affairs', *Philosophy and Public Affairs*, 12 (1983).

—— 'Liberalism and World Politics', *American Political Science Review*, 80 (1986).

Dunne, Tim, 'The Social Construction of International Society', *European Journal of International Relations*, 1/3 (1995).

—— *Inventing International Society: A History of the English School* London: Macmillan, 1998).

—— and Nicholas Wheeler, 'Hedley Bull's Pluralism of the Intellect and Solidarism of the Will', *International Affairs*, 72/1 (1996).

—— —— *Human Rights in Global Politics* (Cambridge: Cambridge University Press, 1999).

—— M. Cox, and K. Booth (eds.), *The Eighty Years Crisis: International Relations 1919–1999* (Cambridge: Cambridge University Press, 1999).

Dworkin, R., 'Is Law a System of Rules?', in Ronald Dworkin (ed.), *The Philosophy of Law* (Oxford: OUP, 1979).

Ehlstain, Jean Bethke, *Women and War* (New York: Basic Books, 1987).

—— (ed.), *Just War Theory* (Oxford: Blackwell, 1992).

Epp, Roger, 'The "Augustinian Moment" in International Politics: Niebuhr, Butterfield, Wight and the Reclaiming of a Tradition', *International Politics Research Occasional Paper*, 10 (Aberystwyth: Department of International Politics, 1991).

—— 'Martin Wight: International Relations as Realm of Persuasion', in F. A. Beer and R. Hariman (eds.), *Post-Realism: The Rhetorical Turn in International Relations* (East Lansing, Mich.: Michigan State University Press, 1996).

—— 'The English School on the Frontiers of International Relations', in Dunne, Cox and Booth (eds.), *The Eighty Years Crisis* (Cambridge: Cambridge University Press, 1999).

Evans, Tony, and Peter Wilson, 'Regime Theory and the English School of International Relations', *Millennium*, 21/3 (1992).

Falk, Richard, 'A New Paradigm for International Legal Studies', in Falk, F. Kratochwil, and S. H. Mendlovitz (eds.), *International Law: A Contemporary Perspective* (Boulder, Colo.: Westview, 1985).

—— 'The Grotian Moment', *International Insights*, 13 (1997).

—— F. Kratochwil, and S. H. Mendlovitz (eds.), *International Law: A Contemporary Perspective* (Boulder, Colo.: Westview, 1985).

Fawn, Rick, and Jeremy Larkin (eds.), *International Society after the Cold War* (London: Macmillan, 1996).

Figgis, J. N., *The Divine Right of Kings* (New York: Harper & Row, 1965).

Finnis, J., *Natural Law and Natural Rights* (Oxford: Clarendon Press, 1980).

Forbes, Ian, and Mark Hoffman (eds.), *Ethics and Intervention* (London: Macmillan, 1993).

Forsyth, Murray, 'The Classical Theory of International Relations', *Political Studies*, 26 (1978).

Fotion, N., 'Paternalism', *Ethics*, 89 (1979).

Fox, W., *Theoretical Aspects of International Relations* (Notre Dame, Ind.: University of Notre Dame Press, 1959).

Frame, D. M. (tr.), *The Complete Essays of Montaigne* (Stanford, Calif.: Stanford University Press, 1958).

Freedman, L. (ed.), *Military Intervention in European Conflicts* (Oxford: Blackwell, 1994).

French, P., 'Morally Blaming Whole Populations', *Philosophy, Morality and International Affairs* (Oxford: OUP, 1974).

Frost, M., *Towards a Normative Theory of International Relations* (Cambridge: Cambridge University Press, 1986).

—— 'What ought to be Done about the Condition of States?', in C. Navari (ed.), *The Condition of States* (Buckingham: Open University Press, 1991).

—— *Ethics in International Relations: A Constitutive Theory* (Cambridge: Cambridge University Press, 1996).

Fukuyama, Francis, 'The End of History?', *The National Interest*, 16 (1989).

—— *The End of History and the Last Man* (New York: Avon Books, 1992).

Gaddis, J., *The Long Peace: Inquiries into the History of the Cold War* (New York, OUP, 1987).

Gallie, W. B., *Philosophers of Peace and War: Kant, Clausewitz, Marx, Engels and Tolstoy* (Cambridge: Cambridge University Press, , 1978).

—— 'Wanted: A Philosophy of International Relations', *Political Studies*, 27 (1979).

George, S., 'The Reconciliation of the "Classical" and "Scientific" Approaches to International Relations', *Millennium*, 5 (1976).

Gierke, O., *Political Theories of the Middle Age*, tr. F. W. Maitland (Cambridge: Cambridge University Press, 1987).

Gilpin, Robert, *War and Change in World Politics* (Cambridge: Cambridge University Press, 1981).

—— 'The Richness of the Tradition of Political Realism', *International Organization*, 38/2 (1984).

Goldstein, J., and R. Keohane (eds.), *Ideas and Foreign Policy* (Ithaca, NY: Cornell University Press, 1992).

Gong, Gerritt W., *The Standard of 'Civilization' in International Society* (Oxford: Clarendon Press, 1884).

Goulding, M., 'The Evolution of United Nations Peacekeeping', *International Affairs*, 69 (1993).

Grader, Sheila, 'The English School of International Relations: Evidence and Evaluation', *Review of International Studies*, 14 (1988).

Greenwood, C., 'Is there a Right of Humanitarian Intervention?', *The World Today*, 49 (1993).

Griffiths, Martin, *Realism, Idealism and International Politics: A Reinterpretation* (London: Routledge, 1992).

Grotius, Hugo, *De Jure Belli ac Pacis Libri Tres*, tr. Francis Kelsey (Oxford: OUP, 1925).

Grube, G. M. A. (tr.), *Plato: Republic* (Indianapolis: Hackett, 1992).

Hale, J. R., *Renaissance Europe* (Berkeley, Calif.: University of California Press, 1971).

—— *The Civilization of Europe in the Renaissance* (New York: Simon & Schuster, 1995).

Halle, L., *The Nature of Power: Civilization and Foreign Policy* (London: Rupert Hart-Davis, 1955).

—— *The Society of Man* (London: Chatto & Windus, 1965).

—— *The Cold War as History* (New York: Harper, 1967).

Halliday, F., *Rethinking International Relations* (London: Macmillan, 1994).

—— and J. Rosenberg, 'Interview with Ken Waltz', *Review of International Studies*, 24 (1998).

Hamilton, Alexander, *The Federalist*, No. 6, repr. in R. M. Hutchins (ed.), *Great Books of the Western World*, xliii. *American State Papers* (Chicago: Encyclopaedia Britannica, 1952).

Hamilton, Keith, and Richard Langhorne, *The Practice of Diplomacy* (London and New York: Routledge, 1995).

Harris, Ian, 'Order and Justice in *The Anarchical Society*', *International Studies Quarterly*, 69/4 (1993).

Hayek, F. A., *Law, Legislation and Liberty*, i. *Rules and Order* (Chicago: University of Chicago Press, 1973).

Helman, Gerald B., and Steven R. Ratner, 'Saving Failed States', *Foreign Affairs*, 89 (1992).

Hendel, C. W. (ed.), *David Hume's Political Essays* (Indianapolis: Bobbs-Merrill, 1953).

Henkin, Louis (ed.), *Right v. Might: International Law and the Use of Force* (New York: Council on Foreign Relations Press, 1991).

Herz, J., *Political Realism and Political Idealism* (Chicago: University of Chicago Press, 1951).

Hill, C., 'The Study of International Relations in the United Kingdom', in H. C. Dyer and L. Mangasarian (eds.), *The Study of International Relations* (London: Macmillan, 1989).

—— and Pamela Beshoff (eds.), *Two Worlds of International Relations: Academics, Practitioners and the Trade in Ideas* (London: Routledge, 1994).

Hinsley, F. H., 'The Concept of Sovereignty and the Relations between States', in W. J. Stankiewicz (ed.), *In Defense of Sovereignty* (New York: The Free Press, 1964).

—— *Sovereignty* (London: Watts, 1966).

—— *Power and the Pursuit of Peace* (Cambridge: Cambridge University Press, 1967).

Hobbes, T., *Leviathan,*, ed. M. Oakeshott (Oxford: Blackwells, 1946).

—— *Man and Citizen (De Homine and De Cive)*, ed. B. Gert (Indianapolis: Hackett, 1991).

Hoffmann, S., *Duties Beyond Borders* (Syracuse, NY: Syracuse University Press, 1981).

—— *Janus and Minerva: Essays in the Theory and Practice of International Politics* (Boulder, Colo.: Westview, 1987).

—— 'International Society', in J. D. B. Miller and J. Vincent (eds.), *Order and Violence: Hedley Bull and International Relations* (Oxford: Clarendon Press, 1990).

—— 'Ethics and Rules of the Game between the Superpowers', in Louis Henkin, *Right V. Might: International Law and the Use of Force* (New York: Council on Foreign Relations Press, 1991).

—— and D. Fidler (eds.), *Rousseau on International Relations* (Oxford: Clarendon Press, 1991).

Holbraad, C., 'Hedley Bull and International Relations', in J. D. B. Miller and J. Vincent (eds.), *Order and Violence: Hedley Bull and International Relations* (Oxford: Clarendon Press, 1990).

Hollis, M., and S. Smith, *Explaining and Understanding International Relations* (Oxford: Clarendon Press, 1991).

Holm, Hans-Henrik, and Georg Sørensen (eds.), *Whose World Order? Uneven Globalization and the End of the Cold War* (Boulder, Colo.: Westview, 1995).

Holmes, R., *On War and Morality* (Princeton: Princeton University Press, 1989).

Holsti, K. J., *Peace and War: Armed Conflicts and International Order 1648–1989* (Cambridge: Cambridge University Press, 1991).

—— 'International Theory and War in the Third World', in B. Job (ed.), *The Insecurity Dilemma* (Boulder, Colo.: Lynne Rienner, 1992).

—— *The State, War and the State of War* (Cambridge: Cambridge University Press, 1996).

Howard, Michael, 'Problems of a Disarmed World', in H. Butterfield and M. Wight (eds.), *Diplomatic Investigations* (London: Allen & Unwin, 1966).

—— 'War as an Instrument of Policy', in H. Butterfield and M. Wight (eds.), *Diplomatic Investigations* (London: Allen & Unwin, 1966).

—— *War in European History* (Oxford: OUP, 1976).

—— *War and the Liberal Conscience* (Oxford: OUP, 1981).

—— 'Ethics and Power in International Policy', Martin Wight Memorial Lecture, reprinted in Howard, *The Causes of War and Other Essays* (Cambridge, Mass.: Harvard University Press, 1984).

—— *The Causes of War and Other Essays* (Cambridge, Mass.: Harvard University Press, 1984).

—— 'The Military Factor in European Expansion', in H. Bull and A. Watson (eds.), *The Expansion of International Society* (Oxford: Clarendon Press, 1984).

—— '*Temperamenta Belli*: Can War be Controlled', in J. B. Elshtain (ed.), *Just War Theory* (Oxford: Blackwell, 1992).

Huntington, S. P., 'Political Development and Political Decay', *World Politics*, 17 (1965).

—— *The Clash of Civilizations and the Remaking of World Order* (New York: Simon & Schuster, 1996).

Hurrell, Andrew, 'International Society and the Study of Regimes: A Reflective

Approach', in V. Rittberger (ed.), *Regime Theory and International Relations* (Oxford: Clarendon Press, 1993).

—— 'Vattel: Pluralism and its Limits', in I. Clark and I. B. Neumann (eds.), *Classical Theories of International Relations* (London: Macmillan, 1996).

—— 'Society and Anarchy in the 1990s', in B. A. Roberson (ed.), *International Society and the Development of International Relations Theory* (London: Pinter, 1998).

—— 'Power, Principles and Prudence: Protecting Human Rights in a Deeply Divided World', in T. Dunne and N. J. Wheeler (eds.), *Human Rights in Global Politics* (Cambridge: Cambridge University Press, 1999).

—— and B. Kingsbury (eds.), *The International Politics of the Environment* (Oxford: Clarendon Press, 1992).

Hutchins, R. M. (ed.), *Great Books of the Western World*, xlii. *Kant* (Chicago: Encyclopedia Britannica, 1952).

—— (ed.), *Great Books of the Western World*, xliii. *American State Papers* (Chicago: Encyclopedia Britannica, 1952).

Irwin, T. (tr.), *Aristotle: Nicomachean Ethics* (Indianapolis: Hackett, 1985).

Jackson, R., 'Quasi-States, Dual Regimes, and Neoclassical Theory: International Jurisprudence and the Third World', *International Organization*, 41/4 (1987).

—— 'Civil Science: Comparative Jurisprudence and Third World Governance', *Governance*, 1/4 (1988).

—— 'Martin Wight, International Theory and the Good Life', *Millennium* 19/2 (1990).

—— *Quasi-States: Sovereignty, International Relations and the Third World* (Cambridge: Cambridge University Press, 1990).

—— 'Pluralism in International Political Theory', *Review of International Studies*, 18 (1992).

—— 'The Security Dilemma in Africa', in B. Job (ed.), *The Insecurity Dilemma* (Boulder, Colo.: Lynne Rienner, 1992).

—— 'The Weight of Ideas in Decolonization', in J. Goldstein and R. Keohane (eds.), *Ideas and Foreign Policy* (Ithaca, NY: Cornell University Press, 1993).

—— 'The Political Theory of International Society', in K. Booth and S. Smith (eds.), *International Relations Theory Today* (Cambridge: Polity Press, 1995), 110–28.

—— 'International Community beyond the Cold War', in G. Lyons and M. Mastanduno (eds.), *Beyond Westphalia?* (Baltimore: Johns Hopkins University Press, 1995).

—— 'Can International Society be Green?', in R. Fawn and J. Larkin (eds.), *International Society after the Cold War* (London: Macmillan, 1996).

—— 'Is there a Classical International Theory?', in S. Smith, K. Booth, and M. Zalewski, *International Theory: Positivism and Beyond* (CUP 1996).

—— 'The Evolution of International Society', in J. Baylis and S. Smith (eds.), *The Globalization of World Politics* (Oxford: Clarendon Press, 1997).

—— 'The Grotian Moment in World Jurisprudence', *International Insights*, 13 (1997).

—— 'Boundaries and International Society', in B. A. Roberson (ed.), *International Society and the Development of International Relations Theory* (London: Pinter, 1998).

—— 'Introduction: Sovereignty at the Millennium', in Jackson (ed.), *Sovereignty at the Millennium*, *Political Studies* 47/3 (1999).

—— (ed.), *Sovereignty at the Millennium*, *Political Studies* 47/3 (special issue, 1999).

Jackson, R., 'Sovereignty in World Politics: A Glance at the Conceptual and Historical Landscape', in Jackson (ed.), *Sovereignty at the Millennium, Political Studies*, 47/3 (1999).

—— and A. James (eds.), *States in a Changing World* (Oxford: Clarendon Press, 1993).

—— and C. Rosberg, 'Why Africa's Weak States Persist: The Empirical and the Juridical in Statehood', *World Politics* 35/1 (1982).

—— and —— 'Pax Africana and its Problems', in R. Bissell and M. Radu (eds.), *Africa in the Post-Decolonization Era* (New Brunswick, NJ: Transaction Books, 1984).

Jackson Preece, J., 'Minority Rights in Europe from Westphalia to Helsinki', *Review of International Studies*, 23 (1997).

—— 'National Minorities versus State Sovereignty in Europe Today: Changing Norms in International Relations?', *Nations and Nationalism*, 3/3 (1997).

—— 'Ethnic Cleansing as an Instrument of Nation-State Creation: Changing State Practices and Evolving Legal Norms', *Human Rights Quarterly*, 20/4 (1998).

—— *National Minorities and the European Nation-States System* (Oxford: Clarendon Press, 1998).

James, A. (ed.), *The Bases of International Orders: Essays in Honour of C. A. W. Manning* (Oxford: OUP, 1973).

—— 'International Society', *British Journal of International Studies*, 4/2 (1978).

—— *Sovereign Statehood: The Basis of International Society* (London: Allen & Unwin, 1986).

—— 'The Equality of States: Contemporary Manifestations of an Ancient Doctrine', *Review of International Studies*, 18/4 (1992).

—— 'Diplomacy', *Review of International Studies*, 19/1 (1993).

—— 'System or Society', *Review of International Studies*, 19/3 (1993).

—— 'The Practice of Sovereign Statehood in Contemporary International Society', in R. Jackson (ed.), *Sovereignty at the Millennium, Political Studies*, 47/3 (1999).

Job, Brian (ed.), *The Insecurity Dilemma: National Security of Third World States* (Boulder, Colo.: Lynne Rienner, 1992).

Johnson, J. T., *Can Modern War be Just?* (New Haven, Conn.: Yale University Press, 1984).

—— *Just War and the Gulf War* (London: University Press of America, 1991).

Joll, James, 'Politicians and the Freedom to Choose: The Case of July 1914', in Alan Ryan (ed.), *The Idea of Freedom: Essays in Honour of Isaiah Berlin* (Oxford, OUP, 1979).

Jones, D. V., 'The Declaratory Tradition in Modern International Law', in Terry Nardin and David Mapel (eds.), *Traditions of International Ethics* (Cambridge: Cambridge University Press, 1992).

Jones, E. L., *The European Miracle: Environments, Economics and Geopolitics in the History of Europe and Asia* (Cambridge: Cambridge University Press, 1992).

Jones, P., 'International Human Rights: Philosophical or Political?', in S. Caney, D. George, and P. Jones. (eds.), *National Rights, International Obligations* (Boulder, Colo.: Westview, 1996).

Jones, R. J. Barry, 'The English School and the Political Construction of International Society', in B. A. Roberson (ed.), *International Society and the Development of International Relations Theory* (London: Pinter, 1998).

Jones, Roy E., 'The English School of International Relations: A Case for Closure', *Review of International Studies*, 7 (1981).

Jørgensen, Knud Erik (ed.), *European Approaches to Crisis Management* (The Hague: Kluwer Law International, 1997).

Kacowicz, A., *Zones of Peace in the Third World* (New York: SUNY Press, 1998).

Kant, I., 'The Science of Right', reprinted in R. M. Hutchins (ed.), *Great Books of the Western World*, xlii. *Kant* (Chicago: Encyclopaedia Britannica, 1952).

—— 'Fundamental Principles of the Metaphysic of Morals', in R. M. Hutchins (ed.), *Great Books of the Western World*, xlii. *Kant* (Chicago: Encyclopaedia Britannica, 1952).

—— 'Idea for a Universal History with a Cosmopolitan Purpose', in H. Reiss (ed.), *Kant's Political Writings* (Cambridge: Cambridge University Press, 1977), 41–53.

—— 'On the Relationship of Theory to Practice in Political Right', in H. Reiss (ed.), *Kant's Political Writings* (Cambridge: Cambridge University Press, 1977).

—— 'Perpetual Peace: A Philosophical Sketch', in H. Reiss (ed.), *Kant's Political Writings* (Cambridge: Cambridge University Press, 1977), 93–130.

Kantorowicz, E. H., *The King's Two Bodies* (Princeton: Princeton University Press, 1957).

Keen, M., *Medieval Europe* (Harmondsworth: Penguin Books, 1991).

Keens-Soper, Maurice, 'The Practice of a States-System', in M. Donelan (ed.), *The Reason of States* (London: Allen & Unwin, 1978).

Kelley, D. R., *The Human Measure: Social Thought in the Western Legal Tradition* (Cambridge, Mass.: Harvard, 1990).

Kennan, G., *Realities of American Foreign Policy* (Princeton: Princeton University Press, 1954).

—— *Around the Cragged Hill: A Personal and Political Philosophy* (New York: Norton, 1993).

Keohane, R. (ed.), *Neo-Realism and its Critics* (New York: Columbia University Press, 1986).

—— *International Institutions and State Power: Essays in International Relations Theory* (Boulder, Colo.: Westview, 1989).

—— 'Hobbes's Dilemma and Institutional Change in World Politics: Sovereignty in International Society', in H.-H. Holm and G. Sørensen (eds.), *Whose World Order?* (Boulder, Colo.: Westview, 1995).

—— and Stanley Hoffmann (eds.), *The New European Community: Decisionmaking and Institutional Change* (Boulder, Colo.: Westview, 1991).

—— Joseph S. Nye, and Stanley Hoffmann (eds.), *After the Cold War: International Institutions and State Strategies in Europe, 1989–1991* (Cambridge: Harvard University Press, 1993).

Kersch, T., 'The Idea of The National Interest: A Conceptual Analysis in the Context of the Gulf War', Ph.D thesis, University of British Columbia, 1995).

Keylor, W., *The Twentieth Century World: An International History* (New York: OUP, 1992).

King, C., 'Where the West went Wrong', *The Times Literary Supplement*, 5014 (7 May 1999), 3–4.

Kingsbury, Benedict, 'Grotius, Law and Moral Scepticism: Theory and Practice in the

Thought of Hedley Bull', in I. Clark and I. B. Neumann (eds.), *Classical Theories of International Relations* (London: Macmillan, 1996).

Kissinger, H., *Diplomacy* (New York: Simon & Schuster, 1994).

—— 'New World Disorder', *Newsweek* (31 May 1999).

Korman, Sharon, *The Right of Conquest: The Acquisition of Territory by Force in International Law and Practice* (Oxford: Clarendon Press, 1996).

Knudsen, T., 'Humanitarian Intervention Revisited: Post-Cold War Responses to Classical Problems', *International Peacekeeping*, 3/4 (1996).

—— 'European Approaches to Humanitarian Intervention: From Just War to Assistance—and Back Again?', in Knud Erik Jørgensen (ed.), *European Approaches to Crisis Management* (The Hague: Kluwer Law International, 1997).

—— 'Humanitarian Intervention and International Society', Ph.D. dissertation: University of Aarhus.

Kriegel, B., *The State and the Rule of Law* (Princeton: Princeton University Press, 1995).

Krasner, Stephen D. (ed.), *International Regimes* (Ithaca, NY: Cornell University Press, 1983).

—— 'Westphalia and All That', in J. Goldstein and R. Keohane (eds.), *Ideas and Foreign Policy* (Ithaca, NY: Cornell University Press, 1993).

—— *Sovereignty: Organized Hypocrisy* (Princeton: Princeton University Press, 1999).

Kratochwil, F., *Rules, Norms and Decisions* (Cambridge: Cambridge University Press, 1989).

—— and J. G. Ruggie, 'International Organization: The State of the Art on the Art of the State', *International Organization*, 40 (1986).

LaSelva, S., 'Selling Oneself into Slavery: Mill on Paternalism', *Political Studies*, 35 (1987).

Lauterpacht, E., C. J. Greenwood, M. Weller, and D. Bethlehem (eds.), *The Kuwait Crisis: Basic Documents* (Cambridge: Grotius Publications, 1991).

Lauterpact, H., 'The Grotian Tradition in International Law', *British Yearbook of International Law* (1946).

Layne, Cristopher, 'Kant or Cant: The Myth of the Democratic Peace', *International Security*, 19/2 (1994).

Lijpardt, A., *The Politics of Accommodation* (New York: Prentice-Hall, 1967).

Linklater, A., *Beyond Realism and Marxism: Critical Theory and International Relations* (London, Macmillan, 1990).

—— *Men and Citizens in the Theory of International Relations*, 2nd edn. (London: Macmillan, 1990).

—— 'The Achievements of Critical Theory', in S. Smith, K. Booth and M. Zalewski (eds.), *International Theory: Positivism and Beyond* (Cambridge: Cambridge University Press, 1996).

Lipschutz, Ronnie, 'Reconstructing World Politics: The Emergence of Global Civil Society', in *Millennium*, 21/3 (1992).

Little, Richard, 'International System, International Society and World Society: A Re-evaluation of the English School', in B. A. Roberson (ed.), *International Society and the Development of International Relations Theory* (London: Pinter, 1998).

Lodge, Juliet (ed.), *The European Community and the Challenge of the Future* (New York: St Martin's Press, 1993).

Lucas, J. R., *The Principles of Politics* (Oxford: OUP, 1985).

Lugo, L. (ed.), *Sovereignty at the Crossroads?* (New York: Rowman & Littlefield, 1996).

Lyon, P., 'The Rise and Fall and Possible Revival of International Trusteeship', in M. Twaddle (ed.), *Decolonisation and the International Community: Essays in Honour of Kenneth Robinson, Journal of Commonwealth and Commonwealth Politics*, 31 (1993).

Lyons, G. and M. Mastanduno (eds.), *Beyond Westphalia? State Sovereignty and International Intervention* (Baltimore: Johns Hopkins University Press, 1995).

MacCormick, N., 'Liberalism, Nationalism and the Post-Sovereign State', *Political Studies*, 44 (1996).

McDougal, Myers S., *et al.*, *Studies in World Public Order* (New Haven, Conn.: Yale University Press, 1960).

McGinn, C., 'The Hollow Man's Story', *The Times Literary Supplement* (25 June 1999).

McGwire, M., 'NATO Expansion: "A Policy Error of Historic Importance"', *Review of International Studies*, 24 (1998).

McIlwain, C. H., *The Growth of Political Thought in the West* (New York: Macmillan, 1932).

—— *Constitutionalism: Ancient and Modern* (New York: Cornell University Press, 1947).

McManners, J. (ed.), *The Oxford History of Christianity* (Oxford: Oxford University Press, 1993).

Machiavelli, N., *The Prince*, tr. and ed. George Bull (Harmondsworth: Penguin Books, 1961).

—— *The Discourses* (Harmondsworth: Penguin Books, 1970).

—— *The Art of War*, tr. and with an introduction by Samuel Griffith (London: Oxford University Press, 1971).

Madison, James, *The Federalist*, No. 10, in R. M. Hutchins (ed.), *Great Books of the Western World*, xliii (Chicago: Encyclopaedia Britannica, 1952).

—— *The Federalist*, No. 51, in R. M. Hutchins (ed.), *Great Books of the Western World*, xliii (Chicago: Encyclopaedia Britannica, 1952).

Manning, C. A. W., *The Nature of International Society* (London: Macmillan, 1962).

Malcolm, N., *Bosnia: A Short History* (London: Macmillan, 1994).

Mapel, David R., and Terry Nardin (eds.), *International Society: Diverse Ethical Perspectives* (Princeton: Princeton University Press, 1998).

Mattingly, G., *Renaissance Diplomacy* (New York: Dover, 1988).

Mayall, J. (ed.), *The Community of States: A Study in International Political Theory* (London: George Allen & Unwin, 1982).

—— '1789 and the Liberal Theory of International Society', *Review of International Studies*, 15 (1989).

—— *Nationalism and International Society* (Cambridge, Cambridge University Press, 1990).

—— (ed.), *The New Interventionism 1991–1994* (Cambridge: Cambridge University Press, 1996).

—— 'Intervention in International Society: Theory and Practice in Contemporary Perspective', in B. A. Roberson (ed.), *International Society and the Development of International Relations Theory* (London: Pinter, 1998).

—— 'Sovereignty, Nationalism and Self-Determination', in R. Jackson (ed.), *Sovereignty at the Millennium, Political Studies*, 47/3 (1999).

Mayr-Harting, H., 'The West: The Age of Conversion', in J. McManners (ed.), *The Oxford History of Christianity* (Oxford: Oxford University Press, 1993).

Mearsheimer, J., 'Back to the Future: Instability in Europe after the Cold War', in S. Lynn-Jones and S. Miller (eds.), *The Cold War and After: Prospects for Peace* (Cambridge, Mass.: MIT Press, 1993).

Meinecke, F., *Machiavellism: The Doctrine of Raison d'Etat and its Place in Modern History* (New Haven, Conn.: Yale University Press, 1957).

Midgley, E., 'Natural Law and the Anglo-Saxons', *British Journal of International Studies*, 5 (1979).

Mill, J. S., 'A Few Words on Non-Intervention', in *Essays on Politics and Culture: John Stuart Mill*, ed. G. Himmelfarb (New York: Anchor Books, 1963).

—— *On Liberty*, in J. Robson (ed.), *John Stuart Mill: A Selection of His Works* (New York: Odyssey Press, 1966).

Millennium: Journal of International Studies, 21/3 (1992), *Beyond International Society*.

Miller, A. V. (tr.), *Hegel's Phenomenology of Spirit* (Oxford: OUP, 1977).

Miller, J. D. B., and John Vincent (eds.), *Order and Violence: Hedley Bull and International Relations* (Oxford: Clarendon Press, 1990).

Monk, R., *Ludwig Wittgenstein: The Duty of Genius* (London: Vintage, 1991).

Morgenthau, Hans J., *Politics among Nations: The Struggle for Power and Peace*, 3rd edn. (New York: Knopf, 1960).

—— *Scientific Man versus Power Politics* (Chicago: Phoenix Books, 1965).

—— 'Human Rights and Foreign Policy', in K. W. Thompson (ed.), *Moral Dimensions of American Foreign Policy* (New Brunswick, NJ: Transaction Publishers, 1994).

Moynihan, D. P., *On the Law of Nations* (Cambridge, Mass.: Harvard University Press, 1990).

NATO Handbook (Brussels: NATO Office of Information and Press, 1995).

Nardin, Terry, *Law, Morality and the Relations of States* (Princeton: Princeton University Press, 1983).

—— 'The Problem of Relativism in International Ethics', *Millennium*, 18 (1989).

—— and David R. Mapel (eds.), *Traditions of International Ethics* (Cambridge: Cambridge University Press, 1992).

Navari, C., 'The Great Illusion Revisited: The International Theory of Norman Angell', *Review of International Studies*, 15 (1989).

—— (ed.), *The Condition of States* (Buckingham: Open University Press, 1991).

—— *Internationalism and the State in the Twentieth Century* (London: Routledge, 2000).

Newson, D. (ed.), *The Diplomacy of Human Rights* (New York: University Press of America, 1986).

Nicholls, David, *Three Varieties of Pluralism* (London: Macmillan, 1974).

Nicholson, M., *Causes and Consequences in International Relations* (London: Pinter, 1996).

—— 'The Continued Significance of Positivism?' in S. Smith, K. Booth, and M. Zalewski (eds.), *International Theory: Positivism and Beyond* (Cambridge: Cambridge University Press, 1996).

Nicolson, Harold, *The Evolution of Diplomatic Method* (London: Constable, 1954).

—— *The Congress of Vienna* (London: Cassell, 1989).

Nolan, C. J., *Ethics and Statecraft* (New York: Praeger, 1995).

—— *Power and Responsibility* (New York: Praeger, 2000).

Nye, Joseph S., Jr., *Bound to Lead: The Changing Nature of American Power* (New York: Basic Books, 1991).

Oakeshott, M., *Experience and its Modes* (Cambridge: Cambridge University Press, 1933).

—— (ed.), *Hobbes on Civil Association* (Oxford: Blackwell, 1975).

—— *On Human Conduct* (Oxford: Clarendon Press, 1975).

—— 'The Vocabulary of the Modern European State', *Political Studies*, 23 (1975).

—— *On History and Other Essays* (Oxford: Blackwell, 1983).

—— *Rationalism in Politics and Other Essays*, new and expanded edn., ed. Timothy Fuller (Indianapolis: Liberty Press, 1991).

—— *Religion, Politics and the Moral Life*, ed. Timothy Fuller (New Haven, Conn.: Yale University Press, 1993).

—— *Morality and Politics in Modern Europe: The Harvard Lectures*, ed. Shirley Robin Letwin (New Haven, Conn.: Yale University Press, 1993).

—— *The Politics of Faith and the Politics of Scepticism*, ed. Timothy Fuller (New Haven, Conn.: Yale University Press, 1996).

Ogley, R., 'International Relations: Poetry, Prescription or Science?', *Millennium*, 10 (1981).

O'Neill, O., 'Justice and Boundaries', in C. Brown (ed.), *Political Restructuring in Europe* (London: Routledge, 1994).

O'Neill, R., and D. Schwartz (eds.), *Hedley Bull on Arms Control* (London: Macmillan, 1987).

Onuf, N., *A World of Our Making* (Columbia, SC: University of South Carolina Press, 1989).

—— 'Intervention for the Common Good', in G. Lyons and M. Mastanduno (eds.), *Beyond Westphalia?* (Baltimore: Johns Hopkins University Press, 1995).

Our Global Neighbourhood: The Report of the Commission on Global Governance (Oxford: OUP, 1995).

Osiander, A., *The States System of Europe, 1640–1990* (Oxford: Clarendon Press, 1994).

Österud, Öyyvind, 'The Narrow Entry Gate: Entry to the Club of Sovereign States', *Review of International Studies*, 23/2 (1997).

Parekh, B., 'Beyond Humanitarian Intervention', in O. Ramsbotham and T. Woodhouse (eds.), *Humanitarian Intervention: A Reconceptualization* (London: Pinter, 1996).

—— 'Rethinking Humanitarian Intervention' *International Political Science Review*, 18/1 (1997).

Parkinson, F., 'Latin America', in R. Jackson and A. James (eds.), *States in a Changing World* (Oxford: Clarendon Press, 1993).

Parry, J. H., *Europe and a Wider World: 1415–1715*, 3rd edn. (London: Hutchinson, 1966).

Parsons, A., *From Cold War to Hot Peace* (London: Penguin Books, 1995).

Pellet, A., 'The Opinions of the Badinter Arbitration Committee', *European Journal of International Law*, 3 (1992).

Pennock, J. Roland, and J. W. Chapman (eds.), *Justification: Nomos XXVIII* (New York: New York University Press, 1986).

Peterson, M. J., 'Transnational Activity, International Society and World Politics', *Millennium*, 21 (1992).

—— *Recognition of Governments* (London: Macmillan, 1997).

Philpott, Daniel, 'Westphalia, Authority, and International Society', in R. Jackson (ed.), *Sovereignty at the Millennium, Political Studies,* 47/3 (1999).

Pocock, J. G. A., *The Machiavellian Moment* (Princeton: Princeton University Press, 1975).

Pompa, L., *Vico: Selected Writings* (Cambridge: Cambridge University Press, 1982).

Popper, K. R., *The Open Society and its Enemies,* i. *The Spell of Plato* (Princeton: Princeton University Press, 1971).

Porter, B. (ed.), *The Aberystwyth Papers: International Politics 1919–1969* (London: OUP, 1972).

—— 'Patterns of Thought and Practice: Martin Wight's "International Theory"', in M. Donelan (ed.) *The Reason of States* (London: Allen & Unwin, 1978).

—— 'Nationalism', in J. Mayall (ed.), *The Community of States* (London: George Allen & Unwin, 1982).

Prescott, J., *Political Frontiers and Boundaries* (London: Unwin Hyman, 1987).

Preuss, U., 'Two Challenges to European Citizenship', *Political Studies,* 44 (1996).

Raffety, F. W. (ed.), *The Works of the Right Honourable Edmund Burke* (Oxford: OUP, 1928).

Rajan, M. S., and S. Ganguly (eds.), *Great Power Relations, World Order and the Third World* (New Delhi: Vikas Publishing, 1981).

Ramsbotham, O., 'Humanitarian Intervention 1990–95: A Need to Reconceptualize?', *Review of International Studies,* 23 (1997).

—— and T. Woodhouse (eds.), *Humanitarian Intervention: A Reconceptualization* (London: Pinter, 1996).

Reiss, H. (ed.), *Kant's Political Writings* (Cambridge: Cambridge University Press, 1977).

Rengger, Nicholas, *Beyond International Relations Theory? International Relations, Political Theory and the Problem of Order* (London: Routledge, 1999).

Richardson, James L., 'The Academic Study of International Relations', in J. D. B. Miller and J. Vincent (eds.), *Order and Violence: Hedley Bull and International Relations* (Oxford: Clarendon Press, 1990).

Rittberger, Volker (ed.), *Regime Theory and International Relations* (Oxford: Clarendon Press, 1993).

Roberson, B. A. (ed.), *International Society and the Development of International Relations Theory* (London: Pinter, 1998).

Roberts, Adam, 'Humanitarian War: Military Intervention and Human Rights', *International Affairs,* 69/3 (1993).

—— *Humanitarian Action in War,* Adelphi Paper, 305 (Oxford: OUP, 1996).

—— 'NATO's "Humanitarian War" over Kosovo', *Survival,* 41 (1999).

—— and R. Guelff (eds.), *Documents on the Laws of War,* 2nd edn. (Oxford: Clarendon Press, 1989).

—— and B. Kingsbury (eds), *United Nations, Divided World: The UN's Roles in International Relations,* 2nd, revised edn. (Oxford: Clarendon Press, 1993).

Rodley, N. S. (ed.), *To Loose the Bands of Wickedness* (London: Brassey's, 1992).

Rorty, R., 'Sentimentality and Human Rights', in S. Shute and S. Hurley (eds.), *On Human Rights* (New York: Basic Books, 1993).

Rosenblum, N. L., *Bentham's Theory of the Modern State* (Cambridge, Mass.: Harvard University Press, 1978).

Rousseau, J.-J., *The Social Contract*, tr. Maurice Cranston (Harmondsworth: Penguin Books, 1968).

—— 'The State of War', in S. Hoffman and D. Fidler (eds.), *Rousseau on International Relations* (Oxford: Clarendon Press, 1991).

Ruggie, John, *Constructing the World Polity* (London: Routledge, 1998).

Ryan, Alan (ed.), *The Idea of Freedom: Essays in Honour of Isaiah Berlin* (Oxford: Oxford University Press, 1979).

Ryle, G., *The Concept of Mind* (Harmondsworth: Penguin, 1963).

Schechtman, J., *European Population Transfers 1939–1945* (New York: OUP, 1946).

Scheffer, D. J., 'Commentary on Collective Security', in L. F. Damrosch and D. J. Scheffer (ed.), *Law and Force in the New International Order* (Boulder, Colo.: Westview, 1991).

Schelling, T., *The Strategy of Conflict* (Cambridge, Mass.: Harvard University Press, 1980).

—— 'The Diplomacy of Violence', in R. Art and R. Jervis (eds.), *International Politics*, 4th edn. (New York: HarperCollins, 1996).

Schofield, M., 'Realism and Realpolitik', *The Times Literary Supplement*, 504 (7 May 1999), 34.

Schumpeter, J. A., 'The Sociology of the Intellectual', in J. Sklar (ed.), *Political Theory and Ideology* (New York: Macmillan, 1966).

Schwarzenberger, G., *Power Politics: A Study of International Society* (New York: Praeger, 1951).

—— 'The Grotius Factor in International Law and Relations', in H. Bull, B. Kingsbury, and A. Roberts (eds.), *Hugo Grotius and International Relations* (Oxford: Clarendon Press, 1990).

—— and E. Brown, *A Manual of International Law*, 6th edn. (London: Professional Books, 1976).

Schwarzkopf, N., *It doesn't Take a Hero* (New York: Bantam, 1992).

Shaw, Malcolm, *Title to Territory in Africa* (Oxford: Clarendon Press, 1984).

Shaw, Martin, 'Global Society and Global Responsibility: The Theoretical, Historical and Political Limits of "International Society"', *Millennium*, 21/3 (1992).

—— *Global Society and International Relations* (Cambridge: Polity, 1994).

Shue, H., *Basic Rights* (Princeton: Princeton University Press, 1980).

Shute, S., and S. Hurley (eds.), *On Human Rights* (New York: Basic Books, 1993).

Simpson, J., *From the House of War* (London: Arrow Books, 1991).

Smith, G., *Woodrow Wilson's Fourteen Points after 75 Years*, Twelfth Morgenthau Memorial Lecture on Ethics and Foreign Policy (New York: Carnegie Council, 1993).

Smith, M. J., *Realist Thought from Weber to Kissinger* (Baton Rouge, La.: Louisiana State University Press, 1986).

Smith, Steve, 'The Forty Years Detour: The Resurgence of Normative Theory in International Relations', *Millennium*, 21/3 (1992).

—— 'New Approaches to International Theory', in J. Baylis and S. Smith (eds.), *The Globalization of World Politics* (Oxford: Clarendon Press, 1997).

—— K. Booth, and M. Zalewski (eds.), *International Theory: Positivism and Beyond* (Cambridge: Cambridge University Press, 1996).

Sofer, S., *Zionism and the Foundations of Israeli Diplomacy* (Cambridge: Cambridge University Press, 1998).

Sørensen, G., *Democracy and Democratization: Processes and Prospects in a Changing World* (Boulder, Colo.. and London: Westview, 1993).

—— (ed.), *Political Conditionality* (London: Macmillan, 1993).

—— 'An Analysis of Contemporary Statehood: Consequences for Conflict and Cooperation', *Review of International Studies*, 23 (1997).

—— 'Sovereignty: Change and Continuity in a Fundamental Institution', in R. Jackson (ed.), *Sovereignty at the Millennium, Political Studies*, 47/3 (1999).

Spegele, R., *Political Realism in International Theory* (Cambridge: Cambridge University Press, 1996).

Stankiewicz, W. J. (ed.), *In Defense of Sovereignty* (New York: The Free Press, 1964).

Steiner, Hillel, 'Territorial Justice', in S. Caney, D. George, and P. Jones (eds.), *National Rights, International Obligations* (Boulder, Colo.: Westview, 1996).

Stern, Geoffrey, *The Structure of International Society: An Introduction to the Study of International Relations* (London: Pinter, 1995).

Stivachtis, Yannis A., *The Enlargement of International Society: Culture versus Anarchy and Greece's Entry into International Society* (London, Macmillan, 1998).

Suganami, Hidemi, 'A Normative Enquiry in International Relations: The Case of Pacta Sunt Servanda', *Review of International Studies*, 9/1 (1983).

—— 'The Structure of Institutionalism: An Anatomy of British Mainstream International Relations', *International Relations*, 7 (1983).

—— 'Reflection on the Domestic Analogy: The Case of Bull, Betz and Linklater', *Review of International Studies*, 12/2 (1986).

—— *The Domestic Analogy and World Order Proposals* (Cambridge: Cambridge University Press, 1989).

—— 'Grotius and International Equality', in H. Bull, B. Kingsbury, and A. Roberts (eds.), *Hugo Grotius and International Relations* (Oxford: Clarendon Press, 1990).

Taylor, Paul, 'The UN in the 1990s: Proactive Cosmopolitanism and the Issue of Sovereignty', in R. Jackson (ed.), *Sovereignty at the Millennium, Political Studies*, 47/3 (1999).

Thompson, K. W., 'Idealism and Realism: Beyond the Great Debate', *British Journal of International Studies*, 3 (1977).

—— *Masters of International Thought: Major Twentieth-Century Theorists and the World Crisis* (Baton Rouge, La.: Louisiana State University Press, 1980).

—— (ed.), *Herbert Butterfield: The Ethics of History and Politics* (Washington, DC: University Press of America, 1980).

—— (ed.), *Moral Dimensions of American Foreign Policy* (New Brunswick, NJ: Transaction Publishers, 1994).

—— and R. J. Myers (eds.), *A Tribute to Hans Morgenthau* (Washington, DC: The New Republic Book Co., 1977).

Tilly, C., *Coercion, Capital and European States* (Oxford: Blackwell, 1992).

Tooley, M. J. (tr.), *Bodin: Six Books of the Commonwealth* (Oxford: Blackwell, n.d.).

Towle, P., *Enforced Disarmament* (Oxford: Clarendon Press, 1997).

Tucker, R., *The Inequality of Nations* (New York: Basic Books, 1977).

Vasquez, John A., *Classics of International Relations* (Upper Saddle River, NJ: Prentice-Hall, 1996).

Venema A., and H. Romijn (eds.), 'Charter of Paris for a New Europe: A New Era of

Democracy, Peace and Unity', in *Documents on International Security Policy May 1989–December 1991* (The Hague: Netherlands Atlantic Commission, 1992).

Vincent, R. J., *Non-Intervention and International Order* (Princeton: Princeton University Press, 1974).

—— 'The Idea of Concert and International Order', *Yearbook of World Affairs*, 31 (London: Institute of World Affairs, 1975).

—— 'Western Conceptions of a Universal Moral Order', *British Journal of International Studies*, 4/1 (1978).

—— 'The Factor of Culture in the Global International Order', *The Yearbook of World Affairs*, 34 (London: Stevens & Sons, 1980).

—— 'The Hobbesian Tradition in Twentieth Century International Thought', *Millennium*, 10.2 (1981).

—— 'Race in International Relations', *International Affairs*, 58/4 (1982).

—— 'Realpolitik', in J. Mayall (ed.) *The Community of States* (London: George Allen & Unwin, 1982).

—— 'Change in International Relations', *Review of International Studies*, 9/1 (1983).

—— 'Edmund Burke and the Theory of International Relations', *Review of International Studies*, 10 (1984).

—— 'Racial Equality', in H. Bull and A. Watson (eds.), *The Expansion of International Society* (Oxford: OUP, 1984).

—— *Foreign Policy and Human Rights: Issues and Responses* (Cambridge: Cambridge University Press, 1986).

—— *Human Rights and International Relations* (Cambridge: Cambridge University Press, 1986).

—— 'The Response of Europe and the Third World to United States Human Rights Diplomacy', in D. Newson (ed), *The Diplomacy of Human Rights* (New York: University Press of America, 1986).

—— 'Grotius, Human Rights, and Intervention', in H. Bull, B. Kingsbury, and A. Roberts (eds.), *Hugo Grotius and International Relations* (Oxford: Clarendon Press, 1990).

—— 'Order in International Politics', in J. D. B. Miller and J. Vincent (eds.), *Order and Violence: Hedley Bull and International Relations* (Oxford: Clarendon Press, 1990).

—— 'The End of the Cold War and the International System', in D. Armstrong and E. Goldstein (eds.), *The End of the Cold War* (London: Frank Cass, 1990).

—— 'The Idea of Rights in International Ethics', in T. Nardin and D. Mapel (eds.), *Traditions of International Ethics* (Cambridge: Cambridge University Press, 1992).

—— 'Modernity and Universal Human Rights', in A. G. McGrew and P. G. Lewis, *et al.*, *Global Politics: Globalization and the Nation-State* (Cambridge: Cambridge University Press, 1992), 272–80.

—— and Robert O'Neill (eds.), *The West and the Third World: Essays in Honour of J. D. B. Miller* (Basingstoke: Macmillan, 1990).

—— and P. Wilson, 'Beyond Non-Intervention', in I. Forbes and M. Hoffman (eds.), *Ethics and Intervention* (London: Macmillan, 1993).

—— 'The Place of Theory in the Practice of Human Rights', in C. Hill and P. Beshoff (eds.), *Two Worlds of International Relations: Academics, Practitioners and the Trade in Ideas* (London: Routledge, 1994).

Walden, G., *Ethics and Foreign Policy* (London: Weidenfeld & Nicolson, 1988).

Wallace, W. (ed.), *The Dynamics of European Integration* (London: Pinter, 1990).

Waltz, Kenneth N., *Man, the State and War: A Theoretical Analysis* (New York: Columbia University Press, 1959).

—— *Theory of International Politics* (New York: McGraw-Hill, 1979).

—— 'The Emerging Structure of International Politics', *International Security*, 18/2 (1993).

Walzer, M., *Just and Unjust Wars*, 2nd edn. (New York: Basic Books, 1992).

—— *Thick and Thin: Moral Argument at Home and Abroad* (London: University of Notre Dame Press, 1994).

Ware, K., 'Eastern Christendom', in J. McManners (ed.), *The Oxford History of Christianity* (Oxford: OUP, 1993).

Warner, D., *An Ethic of Responsibility in International Relations* (Boulder, Colo.: Lynn Rienner, 1991).

Warner, Rex (tr.), *Thucydides: History of the Peloponnesian War* (London: Penguin Books, 1972).

Watson, A., *Diplomacy: The Dialogue between States* (London: Methuen, 1982).

—— 'Hedley Bull, States Systems and International Studies', *Review of International Studies*, 13/2 (1987).

—— 'Systems of States', *Review of International Studies*, 16/2 (1990).

—— *The Evolution of International Society* (London and New York: Routledge, 1992).

—— 'Diplomacy', in J. Bayliss and N. J. Rengger (eds.), *Dilemmas of World Politics* (Oxford: Clarendon Press, 1992).

—— *The Limits of Independence: Relations between States in the Modern World* (London: Routledge, 1997).

—— 'The Practice Outruns the Theory', in B. A. Roberson (ed.), *International Society and the Development of International Relations Theory* (London: Pinter, 1998).

Weber, M., 'Politics as a Vocation', in H. H. Gerth and C. Wright Mills (eds.), *From Max Weber: Essays in Sociology* (New York: OUP, 1958).

—— *The Theory of Social and Economic Organization*, ed. T. Parsons (New York: Free Press, 1964).

—— *Economy and Society: An Outline of Interpretive Sociology*, ed. G. Roth and C. Wittich (New York: Bedminster Press, 1968).

Wedgwood, C. V., *The Thirty Years War* (London: Pimlico, 1994).

Weiler, J. H. H., 'European Neo-constitutionalism: In Search of Foundations for the European Constitutional Order', *Political Studies*, 44 (1996).

Weinberg, G., *A World at Arms* (Cambridge: Cambridge University Press, 1994).

Weller, M. (ed.), *Iraq and Kuwait: The Hostilities and their Aftermath* (Cambridge: Grotius Publications, 1993).

Welsh, J. M., *Edmund Burke and International Relations* (London: Macmillan, 1995).

Wendt, A., 'Anarchy is what States Make of it', *International Organization*, 46 (1992).

—— 'On Constitution and Causation in International Relations', *Review of International Studies*, 24 (1998).

—— *Social Theory of International Politics* (New York: Cambridge University Press, 1998).

Wheeler, Nicholas J., 'Pluralist and Solidarist Conceptions of International Society: Bull and Vincent on Humanitarian Intervention', *Millennium*, 21/3 (1992).

—— 'Guardian Angel or Global Gangster: A Review of the Ethical Claims of International Society', *Political Studies*, 44 (1996).

—— and Justin Morris, 'Humanitarian Intervention and State Practice at the End of the Cold War', in R. Fawn and J. Larkin (eds.), *International Society After the Cold War* (London, Macmillan, 1996).

—— and Tim Dunne, 'Hedley Bull and the Idea of a Universal Moral Community: Fictional, Primordial or Imagined?', in B. A. Roberson (ed.), *International Society and the Development of International Relations Theory* (London: Pinter, 1998).

Wight, Martin, *Power Politics* (London: Royal Institute of International Affairs, 'Looking Forward' Pamphlet 8, 1946).

—— *The Development of the Legislative Council 1606–1945*, ed. M. Perham (London: Faber & Faber, 1946).

—— *The Gold Coast Legislative Council*, ed. M. Perham (London: Faber & Faber, 1947).

—— *British Colonial Constitutions: 1947* (Oxford, Clarendon, 1952).

—— 'The Balance of Power', in H. Butterfield and Wight (eds.), *Diplomatic Investigations* (London: Allen & Unwin, 1966).

—— 'Western Values in International Relations', in H. Butterfield and Wight (eds.), *Diplomatic Investigations* (London: Allen & Unwin, 1966).

—— 'Why is there No International Theory?', in H. Butterfield and Wight (eds.), *Diplomatic Investigations* (London: Allen & Unwin, 1966).

—— *Systems of States*, ed. Hedley Bull (Leicester: Leicester University Press, 1977).

—— *Power Politics*, ed. Hedley Bull and Carsten Holbraad (Harmondsworth: Penguin Books, 1979).

—— *Power Politics*, 2nd edn., ed. Hedley Bull and Carsten Holbraad (Harmondsworth: Penguin Books, 1986).

—— 'An Anatomy of International Thought', *Review of International Studies*, 13 (1987).

—— *International Theory: The Three Traditions*, ed. Brian Porter and Gabriele Wight (Leicester: Leicester University Press/Royal Institute of International Affairs, 1991).

Willetts, P., 'Transnational Actors and International Organizations in Global Politics', in J. Baylis and S. Smith (eds.), *The Globalization of World Politics* (Oxford: Clarendon Press, 1997).

Wilson, P., 'The English School of International Relations: A Reply to Sheila Grader', *Review of International Studies*, 15 (1989).

Wolfers, A., *Discord and Collaboration: Essays on International Politics* (Baltimore: The Johns Hopkins University Press, 1965).

Wolin, S., *Politics and Vision* (Boston, Mass.: Little, Brown, 1960).

Wright, Moorhead, 'An Ethic of Responsibility', in J. Mayall (ed.), *The Community of States* (London: George Allen & Unwin, 1982).

—— (ed.), *Morality and International Relations* (Aldershot: Avebury, 1996).

Zacher, M., 'The Decaying Pillars of the Westphalian Temple', in James N. Rosenau and Ernst-Otto Czempiel (eds.), *Governance without Government: Order and Change in World Politics* (Cambridge: Cambridge University Press, 1992).

—— *Governing Global Networks* (Cambridge: Cambridge University Press, 1996).

Zartman, I. W. (ed.), *Collapsed States: The Disintegration and Restoration of Legitimate Authority* (Boulder, Colo.: Lynne Rienner, 1995).

Zhang, Yongjin, 'China's Entry into International Society: Beyond the Standard of "Civilization"', *Review of International Studies*, 17/1 (1991).

—— *China in the International System, 1918–1920: The Middle Kingdom at the Periphery* (London, Macmillan, 1991).

—— *China in International Society since 1949* (Basingstoke, Macmillan, 1998).

Index

Lightning Source UK Ltd.
Milton Keynes UK

177057UK00001B/16/A